أهلاً وسهلاً

أهلاً وسهلاً

العربية الوظيفية الحديثة
للمستوى المتوسط
الطبعة الثانية

مهدي العش

منقحة مع ألن كلارك

دار جامعة ييل للنشر
نيو هيفن ولندن

Ahlan wa Sahlan

Functional Modern Standard Arabic
for Intermediate Learners

Second Edition

Mahdi Alosh

Revised with Allen Clark

Yale University Press
New Haven and London

First edition 2006. Second edition 2013.

Yale University Press books may be purchased in quantity for educational, business, or promotional use. For information, please e-mail sales.press@yale.edu (U.S. office) or sales@yaleup.co.uk (U.K. office).

Editor: Tim Shea

Publishing Assistant: Ashley E. Lago

Manuscript Editor: Noreen O'Connor-Abel

Production Editor: Ann-Marie Imbornoni

Production Controller: Katie Golden

Typesetter: Allen Clark

Printed in the United States of America.

ISBN: 978-0-300-17877-7

Library of Congress Control Number: 2012955362

A catalogue record for this book is available from the British Library.

This paper meets the requirements of ANSI /NISO Z39.48-1992 (Permanence of Paper).

10 9 8 7 6 5 4 3 2 1

To my wife

Ibtissam

and to the memory of my mother and father

Falak and Abulfaraj

To access the Online Interactive Exercise Program, go to

http: / /yalebooks.com /awsintermediate

Username: damascus

Password: aws2013

المحتويات

Introduction

Purpose and Approach

Picking up where *Ahlan wa Sahlan: Functional Modern Standard Arabic for Beginners* left off, *Ahlan wa Sahlan: Functional Modern Standard Arabic for Intermediate Learners* continues the development of overall proficiency in Modern Standard Arabic (MSA) through a functional approach to language learning. The authors remain dedicated to the idea that performing language functions and using them in contexts that simulate reality offers the language learner the most direct route possible to achieve their goals. This new volume embodies these concepts by offering no less than two communicative activities per lesson for dyad/triad and group work. Language is socially constructed and to improve our language skills we must, as learners, activate all four skills (e.g., speaking, reading, writing, and listening). To that end, we present engaging themes that range from Middle Eastern history to its cuisine, from poetry to award-winning literature that are in the service of language *use*.

AwS-II v.ii is specifically designed to take learners from the Intermediate to Advanced language proficiency. In terms of university-level instruction, this textbook is appropriate for the second year of language instruction providing approximately 150 contact hours, the equivalent of two semesters or three quarters of instruction.

The Learner

Research tells us that the human mind, regardless of how it acquires knowledge, assimilates, modifies, and reconstructs this knowledge and then applies it in ways specific for its use. But, because each one of us is different, we learn differently: there are those of us who benefit primarily from a functional presentation and practice while others find structural information useful. The aim of this book, therefore, is to synthesize learning styles into a comprehensive, holistic approach in an attempt to accommodate the needs and learning styles of most learners.

Lesson Format

Lessons in this book are structured similarly to one another. For instance, each lesson begins by stating its objectives to familiarize the learner with the content, topics, and grammatical points discussed. Objectives are followed by a short vocabulary list that includes those words and phrases that unlock the overall meaning of the main reading text. Matching and odd-word-out activities precede the main reading passage in order to engage the learner in actively using new key vocabulary words. The main reading passage is usually introduced by general discussion questions about the topic of the lesson to stimulate all related background knowledge in our minds. The main reading passage is followed by content questions that measure reading comprehension. Important grammatical features that occurred in the passage are brought to light in the grammar section. Listening passages grace the end of every lesson followed by a glossary of new vocabulary terms specific to the reading and listening passages of that lesson.

Learning Activities

Two major types of activities are included in each lesson: classroom and out-of-class. We designed the *classroom activities* to engage learners with one another in social interactions driven by communicative activities based on the theme of each lesson. As with the content of the lessons, the communicative activities progressively become more difficult and complex. We hope that the learners do not simply try to complete these activities, but rather be creative with them while incorporating new vocabulary items so that learning becomes permanent.

Out-of-class activities involve reading passages, audio passages, and written exercises. Research shows us that learners who reach the advanced-superior level of language learning tend to apply a listening technique that has come to be known as 'shadowing'. This involves repeating what is heard emulating intonation, pronunciation, and rhythm ***while*** listening to the reading/listening passage immediately following the speaker's voice. The authors hope that the learner applies this technique to train those muscles associated with oral communication to facilitate production.

Exercises: There are two types of exercises, those on the word level and those at discourse level. *Exercises on the word level* appear directly after the introduction of key vocabulary. These exercises are intended to reinforce the learning of new words through matching, and odd-word out. *Reading comprehension and writing exercises* follow each reading passage to encourage review and recall of the content covered in the main reading passage.

Reading passages: The reading material presented in this textbook is primarily expository prose, including personal journals written by the two main characters, Michael Brown and Adnan Martini, as well as authentic excerpts written by famous authors, poets, and historians. The reading passages are accompanied by illustrations, graphics, and maps designed to provide the necessary contexts for language functions represented by the objectives. Continuing with the approach that we used in *AwS v. i*, we use pictures (not words) to present vocabulary items whose meanings can be illustrated through graphic means. It is in this manner that the learner internalizes the word naturally without being encumbered with using another language.

Reading passages provide glimpses of the Middle Eastern culture promoting general knowledge through reading Arabic. This is the first step in a learner's journey toward content-based instruction paving the way for discipline based materials. It is at this stage that the learner becomes prepared to deal with source texts within a particular field of study.

Because this textbook is designed to help learners make the transition from reading controlled language to reading and understanding authentic texts, two types of passages are used, controlled (modified) and authentic. These two types of texts are intermixed in what we hope is a nonintrusive, seamless manner. We understand the debate that swirls around using modified texts and offer our interpretation of 'authenticity'. Authentic language is pragmatically used discourse, that is to say the language used by teacher and learner is considered authentic if it serves genuine functional or communicative purpose regardless of whether or not native speakers use the same forms orally to accomplish the same purpose. The selected passages can be considered both authentic in function and sociolinguistically appropriate, since they represent written communication (messages, postcards, letters), personal diaries, articles from the print media, and excerpts from modern Arabic literature, and poetry—discourse that places them in the realm of Modern Standard Arabic.

In order to make the reading passages more closely resemble what the learner might encounter in the print media, passages are not voweled. That being said, diacritical markers are provided on new vocabulary as well as any words that may be misconstrued as other words due to a lack of vowel markers. Also note that all grammatical examples as well as the vocabulary items in the glossaries are fully voweled.

Modern Standard Arabic (MSA) vs. Colloquial

We would like to take this opportunity to address the debate concerning the teaching of MSA vs. Colloquial in the American classroom environment. It is a given that no speaker of Arabic has MSA as their mother tongue; meaning that all native speakers of Arabic speak some local variety of Arabic. Advocates for teaching a variety of Arabic first followed by setting a foundation in MSA argue that this method of teaching more closely parallels the natural acquisition of language as experienced by native speakers of Arabic. The question then becomes more convoluted for authors of textbooks that have national and international markets. What variety of Arabic should be introduced in their approach? The native speaker of Arabic does not have a choice; they simply grow up using their local language. Yet, authors of textbooks do have a choice, which in turn leads to posing the quesion: do we introduce the most commonly understood and used varieties of Arabic? If we do, then every author would introduce Egyptian (i.e., Cairene specifically) and Syrian (i.e., Damascene) regardless of the author's mother tongue. As well, a textbook that is based on a variety of Arabic would necessitate that every teacher that uses it in their curriculum teach the variety introduced in the textbook, regardless of their local variety—a notion that is not very palatable to a number of instructors since language is part and parcel of identity.

Those of us who assert that MSA be taught first point to its universality and flexibility. If a learner is exposed to MSA first, the learner is then better prepared to acquire a local variety because الفُصحى acts as the foundation and base for all other Arabic varieties. Additionally, all of the phonemes in MSA are represented in its orthography, whereas not all of the phonemes in Arabic varieties find an equivalent graphic representation of their sound. This means that the words introduced in a textbook of an Arabic variety would have to be written using the Latin-based alphabet or the International Phonetic Alphabet. Moreover, MSA acts as a bridge between and among all Arabs, it is used in all major media outlets, it is the language of Qur'an, the language of liturgy, the language of scholarship, the language of literature and poetry—the language of prestige. We also point out that a learner with a solid base in MSA will be able to choose their local variety at a later point along their language journey that will, in all probability, involve residing in a city in the Arab world where they will naturally acquire its local variety. For these reasons, we present this textbook in which MSA sets the linguistic foundation for the learner's future development and growth.

Writing exercises: The authors encourage learners to share their written work with their classmates to promote friendly competition (always try to outdo what the best student in class has just done). We would also like to encourage those listening to take notes (in Arabic, of course) and ask questions about your peers' written work after it is read aloud. Writing exercises promote practice proceeding from highly controlled exercises (e.g., filling in the blanks) to free composition (e.g., journal, narrative, description). At the paragraph level and beyond, learners should attempt to make correct use of connectors and idioms whenever possible in order to enhance the quality of their writing and make it more cohesive.

Listening exercises: These audio exercises provide practice in recognition of speech delivered by a native speaker at natural speed. We encourage learners to read the content questions before listening to the passage in order to guide their ear to key information found in the passage. It is through this type of listening that we can train ourselves to listen attentively, intensively, and closely both inside and outside of class. We do ask learners to go beyond just labeling true and false questions with the word *true* or *false* and to push themselves to correct the false statements in order to reflect their understanding of the text.

Arab culture: The content of the reading passages offers insights into Middle Eastern culture. The authors hope that students of Arabic will be able to identify with the adventures and exploits of Michael Brown, the main character of *AwS v. i.* It is through his eyes that we witness Arab cultures—pluralized because we believe is important to realize that the Arab world is comprised of a multiplicity of cultures. Diversity, rather than homogeneity characterizes the cultures of the Arab world, and it is in this vein that we attempt to illustrate cultural variety through culture boxes that we titled تذوّق الثقافة العربية.

Grammatical explanations and exercises: The grammatical notes in this textbook are by no means comprehensive in nature, nor do they constitute a reference grammar for the student of Arabic. They do, however, provide the learner with a solid grammatical foundation, through a process of gradual (re)introduction. Like a blurry photograph upon which we place layers of clarification of each concept, with each visitation the grammatical aspect becomes clearer in the mind of the learner.

Grammar acquisition is not the goal of instruction, but rather a facilitating element to achieve the goal of linguistic proficiency. These grammatical explanations and clarifications provide the necessary knowledge about structures that occur in the reading passages and the practice needed to internalize this knowledge. The exercises, in turn, develop the ability to use MSA as native speakers would in formal and semiformal situations. The importance of the grammar section lies in its facilitating function. The ultimate test of its success is the learners' ability to perform functional tasks emulating the style and language usage of a native.

We strongly suggest that grammatical explanations and exercises be read and reviewed outside the classroom, preserving valuable class time for interactive activities between and among the classroom community of learners and their instructor. Instructors can, of course, provide brief feedback on their student's work on grammar exercises in class; but, we must bear in mind that grammatical explanations are information about the language that do not require social interaction.

Grammatical exercises are structured to proceed from simple to complex dealing with specific points. In the grammar section, example numbers restart with the beginning of each new section.

Glossaries: The authors have also included frequently occurring words and phrases in short vocabulary lists that precede the main reading passage. We hope that learners practice these vocabulary items in context (alone or with your teacher's guidance) prior to embarking on the lesson. Each lesson ends with an Arabic-English glossary of the new words presented in that particular lesson. At the end of this textbook the learner will find a cumulative glossary in which appear all the words compiled from the lesson glossaries marked with the lesson number of that lesson.

Idiomatic expressions: Most lessons include a section titled الأمثلة المتداولة على الألسن in which we introduce sayings and expressions that are frequently used by native speakers of Arabic in social situations. These expressions are accompanied by explanations about how and when to use the expressions in social contexts. The learner will find a cumulative list of these expressions that occurs after the main glossary section of this textbook.

Appendices: Appendix A of this book is an answer key to all the reading, writing, and listening exercises in this book. Appendix B presents verb conjugation charts that act as a representative sample of verb conjugation paradigms showing tense, mood, verbal nouns, and active and passive participles.

Audio Material

The audio program that accompanies *AwS-II v.ii* contains listening comprehension passages (signaled by an icon 🔊) recorded by a team of native speakers reading and interacting at a normal, natural speed. Three of these five speakers hail from Egypt while the other two come from Syria. The listening exercises aim at developing listening comprehension skills within the learner by gradually offering more extended passages of greater complexity. Thematically related to the main reading passages, the content of these audio exercises ranges from advertisements to the poetry of Adonis, from the kitchen of Om Walid to the singing of Fairuz—offering the learner a wide variety of audio samples from the Arab world.

Online Material

Our companion website houses video clips, exercises, and external links to learning resources that support *AwS-II v.ii*. The learner will find images taken from the lessons' opening illustrations on our home page that act as hyperlinks to the content of each lesson. By simply clicking on the image, the learner will move from the home page to a page that has a video that has been cut into manageable three to five minute segments. Content questions about the video excerpt flank these images.

Similar to the audio material, those materials online share themes with the main reading passages in the textbook. All of the video clips found on the *AwS-II v.ii* website were created by Arabs for an Arab listening audience—meaning that their speech flows at a natural speed. The online materials are offered as a supplement to the reading and listening passages in the textbook while adding a video dimension to the fold.

Proficiency Levels

The authors hope that *AwS-II v.ii* provides an enticing learning environment conducive to effective acquisition of the four language skills. Upon completing this course and performing the associated activities, the average learner should expect to achieve a proficiency level within the Intermediate High to Advanced range according to the scale used by the American Council on the Teaching of Foreign Languages (ACTFL). Naturally, some learners may achieve a higher or lower level.

Mahdi Alosh
Professor of Arabic and Applied Linguistics
Mahdi.Alosh@gmail.com

Allen Clark
Assistant Professor of Arabic
The University of Mississippi
University, MS 38677

Acknowledgments

I am indebted to so many individuals whose contributions improved the quality of this work, including students of Arabic at various institutions inside and outside of the United States as well as colleagues who used the first edition and took time out of their busy schedules to provide me with feedback. I am especially indebted to my wife, Ibtissam, for putting up with the endless hours I spent on developing the material that accompanied the first edition. I would like to acknowledge the extraordinary assistance and input by Allen Clark, who serves as a co-author of the second edition. He brings with him extensive experience in teaching from the first edition as well as the perspective of the learner and specialist. I also appreciate the expert assistance of Fayez Al-Ghalayini, whose meticulous editing of the Arabic portion of this textbook and assiduous input and profuse comments on the grammatical aspect improved the quality of this work and made it more accurate. The peripheral materials associated with the textbook have received much assistance from several individuals. I thank Ahmed Mansour and his team of experts for the many hours they devoted to the recording of the audio material.

Finally, I thank the outside reviewers, whose comments on the manuscript and suggestions for improvements are gratefully appreciated:

Mariam Babiker, Elmhurst College

Salem A. Salem, North Georgia College and State University

Lina Kholaki, University of Southern California

Nijmeh Zayed, George Mason University

Cliff Breedlove, Portland State University

Barbara Romaine, Villanova University

Yahya Kharrat, University of Western Ontario

David DiMeo, US Military Academy

الدَرْسُ الأوَّل

رمسيس
سطحى
Ramsis Sq.
علوى
برج القاهرة
Cairo Tower
ط.الأسكندرية الصحراوى
Alex Desert Rd.

الربـاط
RABAT
المدينة العتيقة
ANCIENNE MEDINA
الحي الإداري
QUARTIER ADMINISTRATIF
المـيـنـاء
PORT

Objectives

- Introduction to announcements and advertisements in Arabic
- Learning to identify meanings of Arabic signs and billboards
- **Grammar**: Introduction to conditional sentences with إذا, defective nouns الاسم المنقوص, and the noun structure اسم الفعل
- **Revisiting**: The imperative, verbal nouns, active and passive participles, multiple إضافة and the passive voice

رُكنُ المُفْرَداتِ الجَديدةِ

to head toward	اِتَّجَهَ / يَتَّجِهُ / اِتِّجاه
to benefit (from)	اِسْتَفاد / يَسْتَفيد / اِسْتِفادة (مِن)
sign; signal	إشارة ج إشارات
as of; effective from	اِعْتِباراً مِن
to announce	أعْلَن / يُعْلِن / إعْلان
to close	أغْلَق / يُغْلِق / إغْلاق
simple; no problem	بَسيط
to control	تَحَكَّم / يَتَحَكَّمُ / تَحَكُّم (في)
public; a crowd	جُمْهور ج جَماهير
service pl. services	خِدْمة ج خَدَمات
to allocate; designate	خَصَّص / يُخَصِّصُ / تَخْصيص
to pay; to push	دَفَع / يَدْفَعُ / دَفْع

المُفرداتُ الجَديدةُ في صُوَرٍ عَديدةٍ:

مُغْلَق

مَفْتوح

عِطْر ج عُطور

لافِتة ج لافِتات

مُكالَمة ج مُكالمات

مُشَجِّع ج مُشَجِّعون

دَخَّن / يُدَخِّن / تَدْخين

وَقَف / يَقِف / وُقوف

تمرين ١

وافق بين كلمة من العمود الأول وكلمة من العمود الثاني واكتبهما في العمود الأوسط:

١	مُرور		نَقّال
٢	سيلان (سْري لانكة)		مُغْلَق
٣	ماء		صَحيفة
٤	اِسْحَب		فَرْع
٥	مَفْتوح		حافِلة
٦	أحمر شفاه		اِدْفَع
٧	جَوّال		شاي
٨	مَصْرِف		شُرْب
			مَسحوق تَجْميل

تمرين ٢

اِختَرِ الكَلِمةَ الّتي لا تُناسِب باقي الكَلِماتِ في كُلِّ مَجْموعةٍ وبَيِّن السَبَب:

١- أسبوع　　　بضاعة　　　ملابس　　　أحذية

٢- دخول　　　خروج　　　ادفع　　　شاشة

٣- لافتة　　　جامع　　　دعاية　　　إعلان

٤- استمتع　　　استخدم　　　مسحوق　　　استفد

٥- إعلان　　　جمال　　　مجلة　　　دعاية

٦- مشجع　　　ملابس　　　مباراة　　　منتخب

تمرين ٣

أعد ترتيب الكلمات في كل مجموعة لتشكّل جملاً مُفيدة:

١- في　　　عنوان　　　دُبي　　　التجاري　　　المحل

٢- الأبواب　　　كلمة　　　على　　　اِسحب　　　تُكتَب

٣- إلى　　　الهاتف　　　مكان　　　مكان　　　الجوّال　　　يُحمل　　　مِن

٤- قبل　　　المسجد　　　إلى　　　المصلّون　　　الدخول　　　يخلع　　　أحذيتَهُم

لافتات وإعلانات ودعايات

توجد اللافتات والدعايات والإعلانات في كل مكان. إذا مشيتَ في الشارع فإنكَ ترى لافتات في الطريق وعلى المحلات التجارية وعلى الحافلات. وإذا جلستَ تشاهد التلفاز ترى إعلانات ودعايات مختلفة. وإذا نظرتَ إلى الصحيفة أو المجلة تقرأ دعايات وإعلانات.

تشمَل اللافتات إشارات المرور مثل إشارة الوقوف وإشـارة الاتِّجاه الواحد وغيرها وكذلك اللافتات الجدارية مثل «ممنوع التدخين» ولافتات الدخول والخروج وغيرها كما في اللافتات الآتية:

هذه الكلمات تراها مكتوبة على الأبواب العامة وأبواب المحلات التجارية:

اخلع حذاءك قبل الدخول
إلى المسجد من فضلك

في بعض المساجد هناك لافتات تطلب من المصلّين عادةً أن يخلعوا أحذيتَهُم قبل الدخول إلى المسجد، لأن المسلمين لا يدخلون المساجد بأحذيتِهِم.

تعلن اللافتة إلى اليسار أن الماء صالح للشرب، واللافتة الأخرى إلى الأسفل دعاية لشرب الشاي السيلاني، وهو الشاي المستورد من سيلان، الاسم القديم لسري لانكة.

إليك بعض الدعايات المأخوذة من الصحف العربية. هذه واحدة عن عطر نسائي يسمّى «عطر سيدتي». والدعاية الأخرى عن أحمر الشفاه ومساحيق التجميل.

مسحوق تجميل

أحمر شِفاه

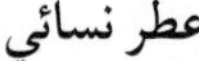
عطر نسائي

في ما يلي بعض الدعايات والإعلانات كما ظهرت في جرائد ومجلات عربية.

جديد في الأسواق

الهاتف الرقميّ الجوّال يحمي من التنصّت على المكالمات.

تصميم أنيق. استفد من أكبر شاشة عرض لهاتف نقّال* واستمتع بسهولة الاستخدام التحكُّم البسيط في الوظائف العديدة.

*(يسمّى الهاتف النقّال الهاتف الجوّال أو الهاتف الخَلَويّ أيضاً.)

وقت سيتيزن

ها قد حان وقت التجديد، وقت الجَمال، وقت الأناقة، وقت سيتيزن. صمّمت ساعات سيتيزن للسيّدات لتلائم شخصياتهن وتميزهن وجمالهن.

تمرين ٤

١- ما مناسبة التنزيلات بالأسعار؟ ________________

٢- ما اسم هذا المحل التجاري؟ ________________

٣- ما عنوانه وما رَقْم هاتفه؟ ________________

إعلان في صحيفة «الخليج»

أربعون حافلة خصصتها
((مؤسسة الإمارات))
لنقل المشجعين
إلى مدينة زايد

خصصت ((مؤسسة الإمارات)) العامة للنقل والخدمات أربعين حافلة لنقل جماهير مشجعي منتخبنا الوطني التي ستؤازر الفريق في مباراته اليوم أمام السعودية في نهائي أمم آسيا.

إليك أيضاً إعلاناً في جريدة لبنانية لفرع مصرف جديد في لبنان

مصرفكم أينما كنتم
فرنسبَنك يستقبلكم اعتباراً
من ١ تشرين الأول ٢٠١١ في فرعه الـ ٤٠

عين المريسة ــ بناية النورس ــ مقابل جامع عين المريسة
هاتف: ٧٤٠٤١٥ - ٧٤٠٤١٤ (٠٣)

تمرين ٥

أجب عن الأسئلة الآتية وفق نص القراءة:

١- ما اسم المصرِف في الإعلان؟ ________________

٢- ما عنوان الفرع الجديد لهذا المصرِف؟ ________________

٣- هل هناك مبنى هام قريب منه؟ ________________

٤- كَم خطاً هاتفياً لفرع المصرِف؟ ________________

٥- متى بدأ هذا الفرع أعماله؟ ________________

تمرين ٦

أكمل الجمل الآتية من نص القراءة:

١- تقول إحدى إشارات المرور ________________

٢- قد تقول لافتة في المسجد ________________

٣- الهاتف الرقْمي الجوّال له ________________

٤- لمصرِف «فرنسبنك» فَرْع في ________________

٥- يبيع محل «نيفين» ________________

تمرين ٧

نشاط المحادثة في الصف: الإعلانات الأمريكية والشرقية:

١- ما الفرق بين الإعلانات التي ظهرت على التلفاز في طفولتك والتي تُعرض في التلفاز الآن؟

٢- ما الفرق بين الإعلانات الأمريكية والعربية في رأيك؟

٣- ما أفضل إعلان شاهدته في حياتك ولماذا؟

٤- ما الإعلانات التي ظهرت على التلفاز أثناء بطولة كرة القدم الأمريكية النهائية التي أعجبتك أكثر؟ ولماذا؟

٥- هل أنت من النوع الذي يشاهد الإعلانات حتى نهايتها أم تغيّر القناة عند عَرْضها؟ ولماذا؟

القَواعِد

Remember: feminine plural nouns (i.e., plurals that end with ات like لافتات ومجلات) are diptotes. What's a diptote? That's a word, when declined, can only take two (= di-) of the three case markers. So, when the word is in حالة مرفوع, it takes a ضمة, when the word is in حالة منصوب or حالة مجرور, it takes كسرة. Did you happen to notice instances of this in our main reading passage?

1. Conditional Sentences Using إذا

إذا . . . فـ is a structure that parallels the English (if . . . then) conditional statement. The difficulty of this structure is twofold: first, we must remember that the verb following إذا is in الماضي, and second, learners seem to have a hard time figuring out where to place the فـ. Let's take a look at some examples and see if we can't come up with a rule for this second question.

If we go to Beirut, then we might swim in the	إذا سافَرْنا إلى بَيْروتَ فَقَدْ نَسْبَحُ في البَحْر.	١
If you arrive at the airport at night, then I will	إذا وَصَلتَ إلى المَطارِ لَيْلاً فَلَنْ أستَطيعَ أنْ أستَقبِلَك.	٢
If I listen to the six o'clock news, then I don't listen to the nine o'clock news.	إذا استَمَعْتُ إلى أخبارِ الساعةِ السادِسةِ فَلا أستَمِع إلى أخبارِ التاسعة.	٣
If you forget my name, then I'm not your	إذا نَسيتِ اسمي فَلَسْتُ صَديقَك.	٤
If you miss seeing the pyramids, then you	إذا فاتَتْكَ مُشاهَدةُ الأهراماتِ فَما زُرْتَ مَصر.	٥
If you live far from the university, then you	إذا كُنْتِ تَسكُنينَ بَعيداً عَنِ الجامعةِ فَستَركَبينَ الحافِلة.	٦
If you shop at this store once, then you will shop there every time.	إذا اشتَرَيْتَ مِن هذا المَحَلِّ مَرَّةً فَسَوْفَ تَشتَري مِنهُ كُلَّ مَرَّة.	٧

What rule did you come up with from these examples? The فـ, in fact, is used precisely where English speakers use the comma. We, then, would advise you to try and allow your pre-existing knowledge of comma placement to guide your فـ placement.

There is, however, an exception to using the ـفـ. The ـفـ cannot be directly attached to a verb; it has to have some sort of particle. Consider the following two examples:

٨	إذا كَتَبْتَ لي أكتُبُ لَك.	*If you write to me, I will/would write to you.*
٩	إذا كَتَبْتَ لي كَتَبْتُ لَك.	*If you wrote to me, I would write to you.*

SUMMARY

- ـفـ . . . إذا is very similar to the English (if . . . then) statement.
- إذا is followed by a past tense verb.
- The ـفـ falls where the English comma falls in (if . . . then) statements.
- The ـفـ is never attached to a verb in this conditional clause.

تمرين ٨

على ورقة مُنفصِلة تَرجِم هذه الجُمَل:

1. If I see the pyramids, then I will be happy.
2. If you study a lot, then you will succeed.
3. Hey Mom, if you buy me this book, then I will read it.

٤- إذا تخرجتَ من هذه الجامعة فستجد عملاً.

٥- إذا أخذتِ هذه المادة نجحتِ في برنامجكِ.

٦- إذا كانَ جو الصف مناسباً للتعلم والتعليم فستتعلّم الكثير.

تمرين ٩

للمحادثة: في مجموعات من اثنين، اسأل زميلك إذا:

١- سافر إلى بلدٍ عربيّ.

٢- عمل الرياضة اليوم صباحاً.

٣- ظنّ أن كرة قدم أمريكية عنيفة ولماذا.

٤- اِعتقد أن الأمريكيين يتفرّجون على التِلفاز أكثر من اللازم ولماذا.

٥- اِعتقد أن شُرْبَ فِنجان قهوة يومياً مفيد ولماذا.

2. Defective Nouns الاسم المنقوص

Nouns that end with a ي as their final root letter pose a bit of a problem, in particular when they are indefinite in the اسم الفاعل form. The final ي effectively disappears from the word when indefinite, but when definite, the ي reappears:

	نكرة	معرفة
١	رامٍ	الرامي
٢	قاضٍ	القاضي
٣	راضٍ	الراضي
٤	داعٍ	الداعي

أمثلة	نكرة	وصل قاضٍ إلى المحكمة.
	معرفة	وصل القاضي إلى المحكمة.
	نكرة	الرجل راضٍ بما عنده من المال.
	معرفة	الراضي بحاله في الحياة أسعدُ عائلته.

تمرين ١٠

Using the description of defective nouns above, try to write two short sentences (one definite; one indefinite) for each of the following verbs in their اسم الفاعل form as in the examples:

١- صلّى ______________________

____

٢- مضى ______________________

____

٣- رعى ______________________

____

٤- بقي ______________________

____

3. Nouns with a Verbal Force اسم الفعل

Imagine a noun that indicates some sort of action—that is exactly what we have here. There are two types of these nouns: a) those that occur in a prepositional phrase; and b) those that occur as independent words.

a. Examples of Nouns with Verbal Force in Prepositional Phrases

Take the book!	إِلَيْكَ الكِتابَ.	١
Ladies and gentlemen, I present to you the six o'clock news.	سيِّداتي وسادَتي إِلَيْكُم أخبارَ الساعةِ السادِسة.	٢
Exercise! (I advise you to exercise.)	عَلَيْكَ بالرياضَةِ.	٣

As you can see, the first two examples put the direct object in حالة المنصوب just as a verb would have. Example three, however, is a bit different as it entails advice, as in "you should do such-and-such"—a rhetorical device that can be very effective in both oral and written communication. Notice that example three takes the preposition بـ that you want to remember to add in the associated exercises.

تمرين ١١

Translate the following sentences into English:

١- عليكَ بالأكل الصحيّ. ________________________________

٢- شتان ما بين اللغة العربية والإنكليزية! ________________________________

٣- عليَّ الذهابَ إلى السوق. ________________________________

٤- هل عليكِ كِتابةَ الواجبات البيتية؟ ________________________________

٥- إليكِ الدفترَ يا أستاذة. ________________________________

b. Examples of Independent Nouns with Verbal Force

A common use of an independent noun with verbal force is شَتّانَ which has the meaning of بَعُدَ and can be translated as: what a difference between s.th. and s.th. else; how different blank and blank are! Another noun in this category is أفٍّ, an exclamation denoting vexation, distress of mind, or disgust. Note, though, that this word takes the preposition مِن to introduce what is vexing the person.

What a difference between the two cities!	شَتّانَ ما بَينَ المدينتين!	٤
Ugh, this heat!	أفٍّ مِن هذا الحَرّ!	٥

تمرين ١٢

Following the explanations of اسم الفعل, correctly translate these sentences into Arabic:

1. You should drink water.
2. What a difference between هالة and her sister!
3. Here's your pen!
4. Ugh, this weather!
5. Ladies and gentlemen, I give you Mr. ناجي الحلبي.
6. All the students must write a page on their favorite sport.

تمرين ١٣

Find out who in class:

1. has a much older brother or sister (شَتّانَ) ____________________
2. has lived in a foreign country (شَتّانَ) ____________________
3. thinks it is hot today (أفّ) ____________________
4. thinks Arabic is way difficult (أفّ) ____________________
5. has a lot of homework to do this week (على) ____________________

4. Revisited Structures مراجعة القواعد

a. Negating the Imperative النَهي

If you ever want to tell someone not to do something in Arabic, you will have to learn this structure; luckily it is fairly simple. Just place a verb in مضارع مجزوم after using لا. Consider the following table:

الضمير	الأمر	النَهي والمضارع المجزوم
أنْتَ	اُكْتُبْ	لا تكْتُبْ
أنْتِ	اُكْتُبي	لا تكْتُبي
أنْتُما	اُكْتُبا	لا تكْتُبا
أنْتُم	اُكْتُبوا	لا تكْتُبوا
أنْتُنَّ	اُكْتُبْنَ	لا تكْتُبْنَ

b. Active Participle Revisited اسمُ الفاعِل:

Form one verbs take the pattern فاعل such as كاتِب وخادِم ودافِع وطارِق. Forms II-X follow the pattern:

مُـ + _ + _ِ + _

That is to say that all you have to do to create the 'doer' of the action (i.e., writer, swimmer, walker) in Arabic, is to take a present tense verb, add a مُـ to the beginning, and then place a كسرة on the second to last letter of the word.

الفعل	التحويل	اسمُ الفاعِل	المعنى
يُخَصِّص	مُـ + خَصِّص	مُخَصِّص	*designator*
يُعْلِن	مُـ + عْلِن	مُعْلِن	*announcer*
يَسْتَفيد	مُـ + سْتَفيد	مُسْتَفيد	*benefiter*

c. Passive Participle Revisited اسمُ المَفعول

The meaning of the passive participle is 'that which is done to' (i.e., that which was 'add verb here' like 'written' or 'read' or 'announced'). Form one verbs take the pattern مَفْعول like مَكْتوب ومَعروف ومَسكون ومَربوط. Forms II-X take the pattern:

مُـ + _ + _َ + _

You may think to yourself, wait a minute, what's the difference between this form and the active participle? Well, the only difference is the فتحة that graces the next-to-last letter of the noun instead of a كسرة. So, follow the same directions as you would if you were creating an active participle, but place a فتحة in the place of the كسرة.

المعنى	اسمُ المَفْعول	التحويل	الفعل
designated	مُخَصَّص	مُـ + خَصَّص	يُخَصِّص
announced	مُعْلَن	مُـ + عْلَن	يُعْلِن
benefited	مُسْتَفاد	مُـ + سْتَفاد	يَسْتَفيد

Please refer to pages ٣١٧-٣١٥ of volume one of this series for additional help.
Now, let's try our hand at making these verb forms work for us:

تمرين ١٤

Using the new vocabulary words introduced in this lesson on page ١٧ try to express the following:

1. Nominator / Nominated ____________________ / ____________________
2. Smoker / Smoked ____________________ / ____________________
3. Supporter / Supported ____________________ / ____________________
4. Designer / Designed ____________________ / ____________________
5. Browser / Browsed ____________________ / ____________________

d. The Passive Voice المبني لِلمَجهول

This verb is what we call the 'blameless verb'. It comes in very handy when you do not want to tell someone who or what did something. An example of that is when your mom asks you, "who broke the window?!?" This is exactly the time in which this becomes very useful: "it broke".

To create this in Arabic, simply take the subject out of the sentence and make the following internal changes:

i. **In the Perfect Tense** الماضي

The verb takes a **ضمة** after the first consonant and a **كسرة** after the second:

	(was written)	كُتِبَ	كَتَبَ	١
When the middle letter is ا it changes to ي	*(was said)*	قِيلَ	قال	٢
When the last letter is ى it changes to ي	*(was named)*	سُمِّيَ	سَمَّى	٣

> REMEMBER
>
> - Arabic loves patterns, so you can apply these rules for all present tense verbs that fit into the above categories.
> - The weak middle and final radical turns into ي in passive voice.

ii. **In the Imperfect Tense** المُضارِع

The verb takes a **ضمة** after the prefix and a **فتحة** after the middle consonant:

	(is written)	يُكْتَب	يَكْتُب	٤
When the middle letter is و it changes to ا	*(it is said)*	يُقال	يَقولُ	٥
When the last letter is ي it changes to ى	*(is named)*	يُسَمَّى	يُسَمِّي	٦

تمرين ١٥

On a separate sheet of paper, express the following statements in Arabic:

1. Arabic is written from right to left.
2. It is said that Damascus is the oldest continually inhabited city in the world.
3. Aleppo is famous for its great food.
4. The pyramids were built thousands of years ago.
5. Gamal Abdel Nasser was born near Alexandria, Egypt.

تمرين ١٦

From the reading passages and ads, identify and list four instances of each of the following grammatical categories:

إضافة وإضافة مركبة	اسم فاعِل	اسم مَفعول	فِعْل أمْر	مَصدَر

تمرين ١٧

1. a. List three features that make the cellular telephone attractive in the ad.
   b. How many different words did you notice meant 'mobile' and what were they?
2. What words do you think would make the watch appealing to women?
3. In your own words in Arabic, summarize the article from **صحيفة الخليج**.

تمرين ١٨

آ- **أجب عن الأسئلة الآتية وفق نص الاستماع:**

١- في أي عام فتحت المدرسةُ فَرْعَها الجديد؟

٢- هل المدرسة للبنين أو للبنات؟

٣- ما اسمُ المدرسة؟

٤- في أي شارع تقع المدرسة؟

ب- **أكمل الجمل الآتية وفق نص الاستماع:**

١- مخبر المدرسة مجهّز لـ ________________.

٢- في المدرسة مسبح ________________.

٣- تقع المدرسة في حي ________________.

٤- هناك ملاعب لـ ________________.

ج- **أكمل الجمل الآتية بالاختيار المناسب وفق نص الاستماع:**

١- هذه المدرسة ________________ .

☐ ابتدائية ☐ متوسطة ☐ ثانوية ☐ كل ما سبق

٢- يبدأ التسجيل في ________________ .

☐ الساعة الرابعة ☐ شهر آب ☐ المخبر ☐ الألف الثالثة

٣- رقم هاتف المدرسة ________________ .

☐ ٧٧٢-٤٥٦١ ☐ ٢٧٧-٦١٥٤ ☐ ٢٩٧-٥٤٦١ ☐ ٧٧٢-٥٤١٦

د- **اكتب «خطأ» أو «صواب» بجانب كل جملة وصحّح الجمل الخطأ:**

١- لهذه المدرسة أكثر من فرع.

٢- لا يمكن للطلاب أن يسبحوا في المدرسة.

٣- لا يوجد في المكتبة عدد كبير من الكتب.

٤- مدرسوا ومدرسات المدرسة مُتَخَصِّصون في موادهم.

المـُفْرَدات

Listen to the vocabulary items on the audio program and practice their pronunciation.

اِتَّجَهَ	(يَتَّجِه)	اتِّجاه	(v.)	to head toward
آزَرَ	(يُؤازِر)	مؤازَرة	(v.)	to support; to cheer
اِسْتَفادَ	(يَسْتَفيد)	اِسْتِفادة (مِن)	(v.)	to benefit, make use of
إشارة	ج	إشارات	(n., f.)	sign, signal
اِعتِباراً (مِن)			(adv.)	beginning, as of, effective from
أعْلَنَ	(يُعْلِن)	إعْلان	(v.)	to announce
أغْلَقَ	(يُغْلِق)	إغلاق	(v.)	to close
إلَيْكَ			(prep.)	take! here you go
أمَّة	ج	أمَم	(n., f.)	nation
أيْنَما				wherever
بَسيط			(adj.)	simple, easy, plain, modest
بُطولة	ج	بُطولات	(n., f.)	championship
تَحَكَّمَ	(يَتَحَكَّم)	تَحَكُّم (في)	(v.)	to control
تَنَصَّتَ	(يَتَنَصَّت)	تَنَصُّت	(v.)	to eavesdrop, listen secretly
جَمَّلَ	(يُجَمِّل)	تَجْميل	(v.)	to beautify
جُمْهور	ج	جَماهير	(n., m.)	public
جَوّال			(n., m.)	mobile
حانَ	(يَحين)	حَين	(v.)	(for time) to come, approach, draw near

to protect	(v.)	حِماية	(يَحْمي)	حَمى
cellular	(adj.)			خَلَويّ
service	(n., f.)	خَدَمات	ج	خِدمة
to specify, allocate, designate	(v.)	تَخْصيص	(يُخَصِّص)	خَصَّصَ
penmanship, calligraphy, handwriting, line	(n., m.)	خُطوط	ج	خَطّ
to smoke	(v.)	تَدْخين	(يُدَخِّن)	دَخَّن
advertisement	(n., f.)	دِعايات	ج	دِعاية
to push	(v.)	دَفْع	(يَدْفَع)	دَفَعَ
clothing, apparel, uniform	(n., m.)	أزْياء	ج	زِيّ
to pull	(v.)	سَحْب	(يَسْحَب)	سَحَبَ
price	(n., m.)	أسْعار	ج	سِعْر
easy, plain	(n., m.)			سَهْل
easiness, facility	(n., f.)			سُهولة
old name for Sri Lanka	(name)			سيلان
screen	(n., f.)	شاشات	ج	شاشَة
to support, cheer	(v.)	تَشْجيع	(يُشَجِّع)	شَجَّعَ
lip	(n., f.)	شِفاه	ج	شَفَة
to contain, comprise	(v.)	شَمْل	(يَشْمَل)	شَمِلَ
to contain, comprise	(v.)	شُمول	(يَشْمُل)	شَمَلَ

suitable, fit, appropriate	(act. p.)			صالِح
newspaper	(n., f.)	صُحُف	ج	صَحيفة
to design, decide, be determined	(v.)	تَصْميم	(يُصَمِّم)	صَمَّمَ
to read, browse	(v.)	مُطالَعة	(يُطالِع)	طالَعَ
way, road	(n., m.)	طُرُق أو طُرُقات	ج	طَريق
period, era	(n., m.)	عُصور	ج	عَصْر
modern	(adj.)			عَصْريّ
perfume, fragrance	(n., m.)	عُطور	ج	عِطْر
spring (of water)	(n., m.)	عُيون	ج	عَيْن
to open	(v.)	فَتْح	(يَفْتَح)	فَتَحَ
large room, hall	(n., f.)	قاعات	ج	قاعة
sign, billboard	(n., f.)	لافِتات	ج	لافِتة
to be suitable, appropriate	(v.)	مُلاءَمة	(يُلائِم)	لاءَمَ
to pass through/by, go run	(v.)	مُرور	(يَمُرُّ)	مَرَّ
powder	(pass. p.)	مَساحيق	ج	مَسْحوق
fan	(act. p.)	مُشَجِّعون	ج	مُشَجِّع
worshiper	(act. p.)	مُصَلّون	ج	مُصَلٍّ
closed	(pass. p.)			مُغْلَق
open	(pass. p.)			مَفتوح
(telephone) call, conversation, talk	(n., f.)	مُكالَمات	ج	مُكالَمة

team	(pass. p.)	مُنْتَخَبات	ج	مُنْتَخَب
to prohibit, prevent	(v.)	مَنْع – مَمْنوع	(يَمْنَع)	مَنَعَ
to lower, to download	(v.)	تَنْزيل	(يُنَزِّل)	نَزَّلَ
to look at, regard, see, observe	(v.)	نَظَر	(يَنْظُر)	نَظَرَ
final	(adj.)			نِهائيّ
function, task, duty	(n., f.)	وَظائِف	ج	وَظيفة
to stop, halt	(v.)	وُقوف	(يَقِف)	وَقَفَ
there it is, there you are, here!	(voc. part.)			ها
to be quiet, be calm	(v.)	هُدوء	(يَهْدَأ)	هَدَأَ

الدَرْسُ الثاني

Objectives

- Learning how to describe yourself and others expressing your hobbies, pastimes, likes, and dislikes
- Familiarization with essential elements of letter writing
- **Grammar**: Expressing wishes with لو, describing hobbies and professions, using المصدر, verb-agent agreement, uses of لدى, redundant ما, the set of كان
- **Culture**: Introduction to Arabic musical instruments and pastimes

رُكنُ المُفْرَداتِ الجَديدةِ

to need (to)	اِحْتاجَ (يَحْتاجُ) اِحْتياج (إلى)
to receive	اِسْتَلَمَ (يَسْتَلِمُ) اِسْتِلام
help; aid	مُساعَدة ج مُساعَدات
to spread	اِنْتَشَرَ (يَنْتَشِرُ) اِنْتِشار
a problem; trouble	مُشْكِلة ج مَشاكِل
to endure; to bear	تَحَمَّلَ (يَتَحَمَّلُ) تَحَمُّل
to specialize (in)	تَخَصَّصَ (يَتَخَصَّصُ) تَخَصُّص (في)
to wish	تَمَنّى (يَتَمَنّى) تَمَنّي
to realize (a hope or dream)	حَقَّقَ (يُحَقِّقُ) تَحْقيق
desire (to)	رَغْبة ج رَغَبات (في)
to entertain s.o. or s.th.	سَلّى (يُسَلّي) تَسْلية
to play (an instrument)	عَزَفَ (يَعْزِفُ) عَزْف (على)

باب التعارف

التخصُّصات والهِوايات والتَسْلية

في بعض المجلات العربية هناك ما يُسَمّى «باب التعارف». تُنشَر في ذلك الباب معلومات يبعثها القُرّاء إلى المُحَرِّر عن أنفسهم مع صورهم. تَشمل هذه المعلومات الاسم والعنوان والدراسة والرياضة المُفضَّلة والهوايات وغير ذلك يُعلِن القُرّاء عن أنفسهم بهذه الطريقة لأنهم يرغبون بالتَراسُل مع القُرّاء الآخرين.

اسمي: جُمانة الدّجاني

سني: ٢١ سنة

دراستي: اللغة الإنكليزية

عنواني: القُدس، فلسطين

هواياتي: المطالَعة ونظم الشِعر العربيّ

آمالي: الحصول على شَهادة الماجستير باللغة الإنكليزية

لَوْني المُفضَّل: الأزرق

اسمي: زياد نِعمة

سني: ٢٠ عاماً

دراستي: علم الأحياء

عنواني: عمّان، الأردن

هِواياتي: المُراسَلة والرِحَلات وكرة القدم

آمالي: مُتابَعة دراستي بالوِلايات المُتَّحِدة الأمريكية

لَوْني المُفَضَّل: البُنيّ

اسمي: لانا خُضَري.

سني: ٢٠ عاما.

دراستي: أنظمة الحاسوب وبرمجته.

عنواني: دمشق، سورية.

آمالي: تأسيس شركة لتعليم الفتيات استعمال الحاسوب.

هواياتي: العَزف على العود والاستماع لأغاني فيروز ولعب الورق.

لوني المُفضَّل: الأحمر والبَنَفْسَجي

اسمي: فادي عبد الله.

سني: ٢٢ عاماً.

دراستي: العلاج الطبيعي.

عنواني: بيروت، لبنان

هِواياتي: النِجارة والإصلاحات المَنزلية ومشاهدة الأفلام.

آمالي: أن يكون لي عائلة من عشرة أطفال على الأقل.

لوني المُفضَّل: الأبيض

استلم فادي هذه الرسالة من اليمن:

أخي فادي،

سلام عليك من الله وأطيب التحية من اليمن.

يُسعِدني أن نَتكاتَب يا أخي فهناك أشياء مشترَكة كثيرة بيننا. أولاً أنا من أسرة كبيرة، إذ لي خمس أخوات وستة إخوة (من أم واحدة) أنا رابعهم. وأنت تريد أن يكون لك أسرة كبيرة. ثُمَّ إني أحبّ الأعمال اليدوية مثلك كالتَصليحات المنزلية بما فيها النِجارة وتصليح الكهرباء والدهان. والشيء الثالث المشترك بيننا هو رغبتي في مساعدة الناس. أتمنى لو درست الطب لكن علاماتي في امتحان المدرسة الثانوية لم تساعدني.

أدرس علم الأحياء في جامعة اليمن وأريد أن أتخصّص بالتحاليل الطبية. ولو تمكّنت من دراسة الطب وأصبحت طبيباً لخصصت يوماً من كل أسبوع لعلاج الفقراء مجّاناً.

أنا من قرية في شمال اليمن وليس عندنا دار سينما أو مسرح أو أي شيء من هذا. حين لا يكون لديَّ دراسة أو عمل أخرج إلى الجِبال وأقرأ الشعر العربي القديم. لدينا كلب لحراسة الأغنام يحبّ أن يمشي معي حين أمشي في الجبال.

أرجو أن نتراسل ونصبح صديقين وأتمنى أن نلتقي يوماً في مكان ما من هذا الوطن العربي.

أخوك عبد الله الصَرّاف

يستلم الذين يعلنون أسماءهم في «باب التعارف» عادة رسائل من قراء المجلة. إليك نص الرسالة التي استلمتها جمانة من تونس.

بسم الله الرحمن الرحيم

عزيزتي جُمانة   تونس في ٢٥ تشرين الأوّل ٢٠١٢

تحية طيبة من مدينة تونس. أنا مثلك أتخصص باللغة الإنكليزية وأدبها في جامعة تونس، وأتمنى مثلك أيضا لو أتابع دراستي في بريطانيا أو أمريكا. لكن مشكلتي أن أسرتي كبيرة ووالدي لا يستطيع أن يتحمّل تكاليف الدراسة في الخارج. لذلك أنوي أن أعمل إما في التدريس أو في وزارة الخارجية. كِلا العملين يعجباني.

في أية سنة دراسية أنت؟ أنا الآن في السنة الثالثة وأستمتع بقراءة الروايات والمسرحيات الإنكليزية. لقد قرأت مسرحية «مدرسة الفضائح» لشريدن ورواية «مرتفعات وذرينغ» لإميلي برونتي وأعجبتاني جداً. هل قرأتهما؟

لديَّ قطّة سمّيتها شامة. هي زيتونية اللون وأحبّها من كلّ قلبي. حين أكون في الدار لا تتركني أبداً. هل تحبّين الحيوانات الأليفة؟ إليك صورتها، تجدينها مع هذه الرسالة. أرجو يا جُمانة أن نتراسل دائماً. أتمنى لك النجاح في دراستك وأن تحقّقي آمالك. إلى اللقاء في رسالة مقبلة.

أختك المُخلِصة

زينب عَزّوز

صورة شامة قطة زينب

تمرين ١

اسأل زميلك في غرفة الصف هذه الأسئلة واكتب الأجوبة في الفراغات:

الاسم والشُهرة: ____________________

العُمر: ____________________

الجنسية: ____________________

العمل أو الدراسة: ____________________

الحالة الاجتماعية: ____________________

هِوايتك المُفضَّلة: ____________________

أجمل مرحلة في حياتك: ____________________

أفضل أيام الأسبوع عندك: ____________________

أفضل شهور السنة: ____________________

أفضل فصول السنة: ____________________

ماذا تتمنى في حياتك: ____________________

هل حققت هدفك أو لا: ____________________

موقف مُضحِك أو طريف حصل معك: ____________________

من هو مُطرِبك المُفضَّل: ____________________

ما هي الأغنية المُفضَّلة لديك: ____________________

والآن اكتب قصة قصيرة عنه مستخدماً المعلومات أعلاه:

____

____

____

____

____

____

الموسيقا العربية وآلاتها

الموسيقا العربية قديمة جداً وقد أخذها عرب الجزيرة العربية عن إخوتهم في بلاد ما بين النَهرين (العراق) وحافظوا عليها. بعد ظهور الإسلام انتشرت الموسيقا العربية في جميعِ بِلاد البَحر المتوِّسط.

من أهم الآلات الموسيقية العربية العود (أُخِذَت الكلمة الإنكليزية lute من كلمة «العود»). العود مصنوع من خَشَب الورد وله عشرة أوتار أو إثنا عشر وتراً ويُعزَف على الأوتار بالريشة.

من الآلات الأخرى الناي الذي يعود تاريخه إلى مصر القديمة، وهو أُنبوب مصنوع من قَصَب السكّر له ستة أو سبعة ثقوب يضع العازف أصابعه عليها حين ينفُخ فيه. ويُسمّى الناي أيضاً «الشبّابة».

الطبلة من الفخّار عادةً وتُسمّى أيضاً الدِرْبَكّة، وتُصنَع أحياناً من المَعدِن ويُشدّ على أحد طرفيها جلد الماعِز أو السَمَك.

والدَفّ من الخشب وجلد الماعِز وله صُنوج نحاسية.

والمِجوِز (أي المُزْدَوج) يُشبِه الناي، وهو مستعمل في بِلاد الشام.

النجارة وأدواتها

النِجارة هي العملِ بالخشب ونحتاج من أجل ذلك إلى أدوات كالمِطرَقة والمِنْشار والكَمّاشة والمِفَكّ. والنِجارة مِهْنة لكنها هِواية أيضاً.

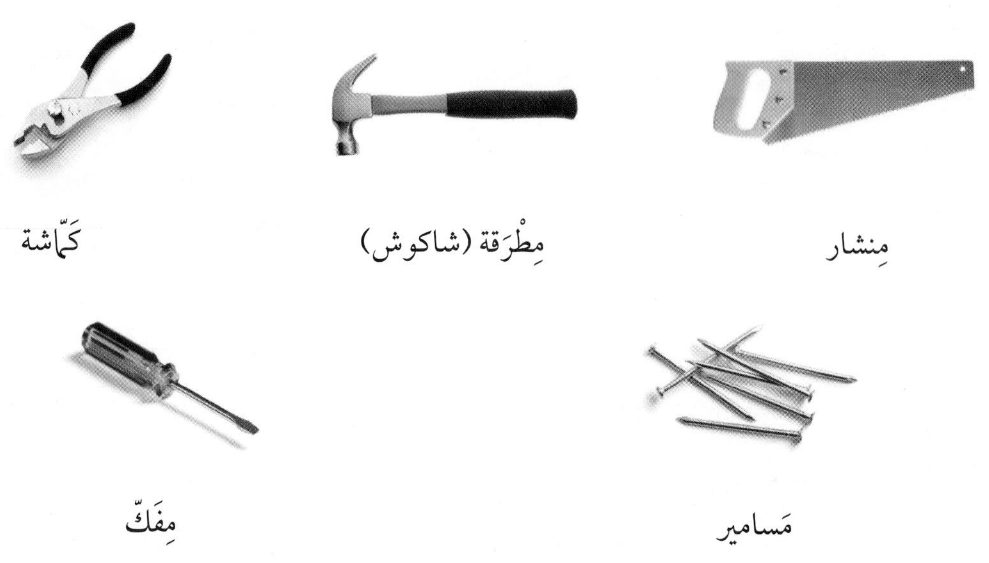

كَمّاشة

مِطْرَقة (شاكوش)

مِنشار

مِفَكّ

مَسامير

التَسلية

من أجل التَسلية يذهب الناس إلى دار السينما أو المَسرَح أو يذهبون إلى الحدائق أو يلعبون الوَرَق. ولَعِبُ الوَرَق هِواية لبعض الناس، مثل مُشاهدة الأفلام أو المُراسَلة وغير ذلك. يُمكن أن نلعب الوَرَق في كلِّ مكان تقريباً.

يُسَمّى وَرَق اللعب «الشَدّة» في بِلاد الشام و«كوتْشينة» في مصر. هناك ألعاب عديدة مثل «الكونكان» و«أبو الفول» و«البريبة» و«الباصرة» وغيرها كثير.

تمرين ٢

وافِق بين كُلِّ كَلِمة واكتُب الكَلِمَتين في الوسط:

١	جريدة		شِعر
٢	تَخصُّص		بَنَفسَجي
٣	رياضة		مِنشار
٤	ناي		صَحيفة
٥	اِستَلَم		بَرمَجة
٦	حاسوب		آلة موسيقية
٧	نَظَم		رِسالة
٨	خَشَب		كرة القدم
			طب

تمرين ٣

اِختَر الكَلِمةَ الّتي لا تُناسِب باقي الكَلِماتِ في كُلِّ مَجْموعةٍ وبَيِّن السَبَب:

١- مِسمار	كمّاشة	طَبلة	مِطرقة
٢- تَكْلِفة	تَسْلية	مَسرح	سينما
٣- كونكان	بَريبة	باصِرة	وَتَر
٤- عِلم الأحياء	أعمال يدوية	بَرمَجة الحاسوب	العِلاج الطبيعي
٥- مَسرَحيّة	رِواية	شِعر	لون
٦- قِطّة	شَركة	كَلْب	غَنَمة

تمرين ٤

أعد ترتيب الكلمات في كلّ مجموعة لتشكّل جملاً مُفيدةً:

١- مِن طالبٍ أوستراليا مع تَراسَلتُ

٢- الخارِج سامِر في الطبّ دراسة سيتابِع

٣- هل؟ رِوايةَ قرأتَ لنَجيب حفوظ «اللص والكِلاب»

٤- حَصَلَتْ في رشا الامتِحان جيّدةٍ على علامةٍ

تمرين ٥

اكتب إلى يسار كلّ صورة الكلمة التي تدلّ عليها. جميع الكلمات من هذا الدرس:

تمرين ٦

اكتب رقم الصورة في الفراغ إلى جانب الوصف المناسب لها:

١ 

___ يحمل الرجل لوحاً طويلاً من الخشب.

٢ 

___ يصنع الرجل أوانيَ فخّارية تُستعمَل لِزِراعة النَباتات.

٣ 

___ يُحاوِل الطَبيب البَيطريّ أن يُعالَج الكلب المَريض. هو يسمع نَبَضات قلبه.

٤ 

___ يَدُقّ الرجل المِسمارَ بالمِطرقة.

تمرين ٧

استخدم رسالتي زينب وعبد الله نموذجين لكتابة رسالة إمّا إلى زياد نعمة أو إلى لانا خُضَري.

Write a letter in Arabic to either Ziad or Lana, using the same style as those letters found in this lesson.

تمرين ٨

أكمل الجمل الآتية من نص القراءة:

١- يكتُب القرّاء في باب التَعارُف مَعلومات عن أنْفُسِهم تَشمَل ________________.

٢- مِن هِوايات زياد نِعمة ________________.

٣- لن تَدرس زَيْنب في الخارج ________________.

٤- لو صار عَبد الله الصَرّاف طَبيباً ________________.

٥- وُلِدَت الموسيقا العربية في ________________.

٦- يَستَعمِل النَجّار ________________.

تمرين ٩

أجب عن الأسئلة الآتية وفق نص القِراءة:

١- لماذا يُقَدِّم بعض القرّاء للمَجلّة معلومات عن أنْفُسِهِم؟

٢- مَن مِنَ القُرّاء يُحب العَزف على العود؟

٣- ماذا ستعمل زينب ولماذا؟

٤- اذكر بعض الأعمال اليدوية.

٥- صِف العود.

٦- ماذا تُسَمّى أوراق اللعب في بِلاد الشام وما اسم بعض الألعاب؟

تمرين ١٠

أعد ترتيب الجمل لتُشكِّل فقرة كاملة. الجملة الأولى في مكانها المُناسِب:

١- درس حازم الهندسة في جامعة القاهرة.

بعد سبع سنوات عاد إلى مصر حيث قابل زوجته.

عمل بعد تخرّجه في شركة لإنشاء الطرقات في شيكاغو.

حيث حصل على شهادة الماجستير في الهندسة.

عادا معاً إلى الولايات المتحدة ليعملا ويسكنا هناك.

ثم تابع دراسته في ولاية أيوا في الولايات المتحدة.

القواعد

1. Expressing Wish with لَوْ

Different from إذا, this particle is used in certain circumstances such as: a) to form the hypothetical 'if'; b) for wishes; c) extend an invitation; and d) rebuking someone mildly. While إذا and لَوْ both mean 'if', إذا is used for *possible* and *probable* conditions while لَوْ is used for *hypothetical* situations.

a. Hypothetical لَوْ

Consider example 1 where إذا is used and compare it to the examples of لَوْ that follow.

If you go to the bookstore today, you will get a book for free.	إذا ذَهَبْتَ إلى المكتبةِ اليومَ حَصلتَ على كِتابٍ مجّاناً.	١
If I were President, I would provide free [medical] care to all people.	لَوْ كُنتُ الرَّئيس لَقَدَّمتُ العِلاجَ مجّاناً لِكُلِّ الناسِ.	٢

This structure also has the ability to accept negating the first verb (i.e., example 3), the second verb (i.e., ex. 4) or both verbs (i.e., ex. 5).

If you had not called me, I would have forgotten our appointment.	لَوْ لَمْ تَتَّصِلْ بي لَنَسيتُ مَوعِدَنا.	٣
If you had come by car, you would not have been late.	لَوْ حَضَرْتَ بالسيّارةِ لَما تأخَّرت.	٤
If I had not lived in Cairo, I would not have seen the pyramids.	لَوْ لَمْ أسكُنْ في القاهِرةِ لَما شاهَدْتُ الأهراماتِ.	٥

As with إذا, there are two parts to this clause, the conditional phrase الشرط and the answer clause جواب الشرط. As you can see in examples 2-6 the way to express 'would' in Arabic is by inserting a لَـ before a *past tense* verb. You may have noticed that both verbs in الشرط and جواب الشرط are in past tense, so when you attempt to use this structure try to remember to put both verbs in the past.

Interestingly, you don't have to use a verb at all after لَوْ, consider example 6:

If the man were an American, he would have spoken English.	لَوْ أنَّ الرجُلَ أمريكيٌّ لَتَكَلَّمَ الإنكليزيّة.	٦

لَوْ can be combined directly to لا to form a negative clause:

Had it not been for the rain, the plants would have died.	لَولا المَطَرُ لَماتَ الزَرْعُ.	٧
Had it not been for them, we would have forgotten our tickets.	لَولاهُم لَنَسينا تَذاكِرَنا.	٨

b. Expressing a Wish using لَوْ

Unlike the other examples, when expressing a wish either a past (i.e., example 9) or present tense (i.e., example 10) verb may be used.

If only you had delayed your trip.	لَوْ أخَّرْتِ سَفَرَكِ.	٩
If only you would write me more.	لَوْ تكتُبينَ لي أكثر.	١٠

c. Extending an Invitation using لَوْ

Generally speaking, when extending an invitation using لَوْ a present tense verb is used:

If you stay with us, you will be immensely pleased.	لَوْ تَنزِلُ عِندَنا فتُسَرُّ كَثيراً.	١١

d. Expressing '*even if*' using وَلَوْ

This structure can be used in the same way *even if* is in English. The word that follows وَلَوْ can be a verb (i.e., example 12), an adverb (i.e., example 13), or a prepositional phrase (i.e., example 14).

He won't be happy here even if he gets a great deal of money.	لن يَكونَ سَعيداً هُنا وَلَوْ حَصَلَ على مالٍ كَثير.	١٢
I'll exercise every day even at night.	سألعَبُ الرياضَةَ كُلَّ يوم وَلَوْ ليلاً.	١٣
He tells the truth even about himself.	يَقولُ الحَقَّ وَلَوْ على نَفْسِه.	١٤

e. Expressing Wishes using لَوْ

Use this structure as an indirect way of speaking your mind concerning unpleasant or unacceptable behavior.

If someone else was late, Salma [it would be understandable].	لَوْ غَيرُكِ تأخَّرَ يا سَلمى.	١٥
If a child did that [it would be acceptable].	لَوْ طِفْلٌ فَعَلَ ذلِكَ.	١٦

SUMMARY

- لَوْ . . . لَـ is similar to the English *hypothetical* (if . . . would).
- لَوْ is followed by a *past tense* verb.
- In addition to expressing hypothetical statements, لَوْ can be used to 1) express a wish, 2) extend an invitation, 3) express 'even if', or 4) to rebuke someone mildly.

تمرين ١١

للمحادثة: اطرح الأسئلة الآتية على زملائك مستخدماً لَوْ:

ماذا تفعل لَوْ . . .

١- كان لديك ثلاث أمنيات؟

٢- كنت رئيس الولايات المتحدة الأمريكية؟

٣- كنت مَشهوراً؟

٤- كنت غنياً جداً؟

تمرين ١٢

Using لَوْ, express the following sentences in Arabic:

1. If I were rich, I would buy a new house.
2. If not for the rain, I would have gone to the party.
3. I wish my sister would call me more often.
4. If I had traveled by plane, I would not have seen those nice towns.
5. Had it not been for water, there would have been no life on Earth.
6. If only I had more time!

2. Describing Hobbies and Professions Using المَصدَر

When talking about hobbies you can use المَصدَر, but keep in mind that المَصدَر must be definite. For example, the verb رَسَم *to draw* yields the verbal noun رَسْم *drawing, painting*. So, you could say, هوايتي الرَّسْم. Study the following list of verbs and their derived hobbies/professions and commit those that are important to you to memory.

الترجمة	المَصدَر	الفِعل
running, jogging	جَرْي	جَرى
riding (bicycles, horses)	رُكوب (الدرّاجات، الخَيل)	رَكِبَ
dancing	رَقْص	رَقَصَ
driving (fast cars)	سِياقة (السيارات السريعة)	ساقَ
swimming	سِباحَة	سَبَحَ
watching (movies)	مُشاهَدة (الأفلام)	شاهَدَ
manufacturing (candies)	صُنْع/ صِناعة (الحَلوى)	صَنَعَ
photography	تَصْوير	صَوَّرَ
reading	قِراءَة	قَرَأَ
playing (cards)	لَعِبُ/ لُعْبُ (الوَرَق)	لَعِبَ
walking	مَشْي	مَشى
sculpture	نَحْت	نَحَتَ
repairing (old furniture)	تَصْليح (الأثاث القَديم)	صَلَّحَ

3. Verb-Agent Agreement مُطابقة الفِعل لِلفاعِل

When a verb precedes its modified noun, it agrees in *gender* only, not in *number*. When applied, this very important rule allows us to avoid difficult conjugations.

١	يُعلِنُ القارئُ عَن نفسِهِ.	المفرد
٢	يُعلِنُ القارِئانِ عَن نفسَيهِما.	المثنى
٣	يُعلِنُ القُرّاءُ عَن أنفسِهِم.	الجمع

Notice, if you will, that the verb, which preceded the subject, is in its *singular* form in all three examples.

Let's take a look at a similar set of examples with a feminine subject:

٤	تُعلِنُ القارئةُ عَن نفسِها.	المفرد
٥	تُعلِنُ القارِئتانِ عَن نَفسَيهِما.	المثنى
٦	تُعلِنُ القارِئاتُ عَن أنفُسِهِن.	الجمع

As you can see, the rule remains true—when the verb precedes the subject, the verb only has to agree in gender, not in number. Let's now take a look at the same set of examples, but with the subject *preceding* the verb:

٧	القارئُ يُعلِنُ عَن نَفسِهِ.	المفرد	المُذَكَّر
٨	القارِئانِ يُعلِنانِ عَن نَفسَيهِما.	المثنى	
٩	القُرّاءُ يُعلِنونَ عَن أنفُسِهِم.	الجمع	
١٠	القارِئةُ تُعلِنُ عَن نَفسِها.	المفرد	المُؤَنَّث
١١	القارِئتانِ تُعلِنانِ عَن نَفسَيهِما.	المثنى	
١٢	القارِئاتُ تُعلِنَّ عَن أنفُسِهِن.	الجمع	

The verb conjugation in examples 7 and 10 remains the same because the subject is in the singular; whereas the verb shows variation in the remaining examples because the subject has preceded the verb.

MEMORIZE

If the verb precedes its modified noun, it only has to agree in gender and not in number.

If the verb follows its modified noun, it agrees in both gender and number.

تمرين ١٣

Write the correct form of the verb in the blanks as in the example:

اكتب الشكل الصحيح للفعل كما في المِثال:

مِثال: الأولادُ (قَدَّمَ) قَدَّموا الطَعام للكَلبِ.

١- في درس أمس (قَرَأ) ______________ الطُلاّبُ الشِعرَ و(استَمَعَ) ______________ إلى الأغنية.

٢- الصَديقان (تَراسَلَ) ______________ لِمُدّةِ عام.

٣- (ظَهَرَ) ______________ المُغَنيَّةُ على شاشَةِ التِلفاز سعيدة في الليلة الماضية.

٤- (يَكتُبُ) ______________ أَخَواتي القِصَّةَ و(يَنظِمُ) ______________ الشِعر.

4. Redundant ما (ما الزائدة)

When integrated into your vocabulary, **ما الزائدة** will enable you to say 'some' as in 'some time', 'somewhere', 'someone', or 'ever' as in 'wherever', 'whenever', and the like.

This is an extremely useful rhetorical tool to add to your language toolbox. Take a look at **ما الزائدة** in action with past tense verbs:

١	أينَ + ما	= أينَما	*whenever*	أينَما ذَهَبتَ في إندونسيبيا تَرى الأزهارَ.
٢	كُلَّ + ما	= كُلَّما	*whenever*	قَدَّمَت لَنا الشايَ كُلَّما زُرناها.
٣	حينَ + ما	= حينَما	*when/whenever*	كُنّا في المَطارِ حينَما وَصَلَتِ الطائرة.

When followed by a present tense verb, they function as conditionals and put the verb in المَضارِعِ المَجزوم:

Wherever you live in the city, you will find a multitude of people.	أينما تَسكُنوا في المَدينةِ تجدوا ناساً كثيرين.	٤
Wherever you write to him, convey my greetings.	أينما تكتبي له فانقلي تحِيّاتي.	٥

The next type of ما is known as ما الإبهامية and is highly functional in terms of turning 'thing' into 'something', 'time' into 'sometime'; or any other 'some' that you wish.

I hope we meet someday somewhere.	أرجو أنْ نَلتَقِيَ يوماً ما في مَكانٍ ما.	٦
I spoke with someone about something.	تَكَلَّمتُ مع شَخْصٍ ما عن شيءٍ ما.	٧

5. Expressing Possession and Describing Place and Time with لَدى

This particle equals عِنْدَ in every way. Its primary function is to show possession (i.e., لَدَيْكَ = عِنْدَكَ).

Ahmed has a 1934 car.	لَدى أحمَدَ سيّارةٌ من طِراز سَنةِ ١٩٣٤.	١
I have an appointment.	لَدَيَّ مَوعِدٌ مَعَ أستاذي في الساعةِ العاشِرة.	٢

تَذَكَّروا

One thing to remember is when you add أنا to a final ى the result is يَّ as in example 2

لدى + أنا = لَديَّ

Similar to عِند, this particle can be used to describe the time of an action:

I'll meet Salma upon her return from Lebanon.	سَوْفَ أُقابِلُ سَلمى لَدى عَودَتِها مِن لُبنان.	٣
I'll see you at sunrise.	سَأراكَ لَدى ظُهورِ الشَمس.	٤

This particle can be used to describe the place of an occurrence:

The book is in Khalid's possession.	الكِتاب لدى خالِد.	٥

تمرين ١٤

Express the following sentences in Arabic using لَدى:

1. We met them as they were going to the movies.
2. هِشام has two sisters.
3. The keys are with the manager.
4. Do you have a pen?
5. I have a new address now.

6. The Set of كانَ Revisited

The set of words that means 'to become' in Arabic was derived from the times of day and signifies transformation at different stages of a process:

to become . . .		كان وأخواتها	
early in the process	أَصْبَحَ	*morning*	صَباح
a little later	أَضحى	*mid-morning*	ضُحى
in the twilight of the process	أَمْسى	*evening*	مَساء
late in the process	بات	*spending the night*	مَبيت

The lone word that does not fit neatly into this concept of 'stage of the process' is صار, which pertains to the process of transformation without denoting at what point the transformation is taking place.

It should be noted that in contemporary Arabic, these words are relatively interchangeable.

His brother became a doctor.	أصبَحَ أخوه طبيباً.	١
	صار أخوه طبيباً.	٢

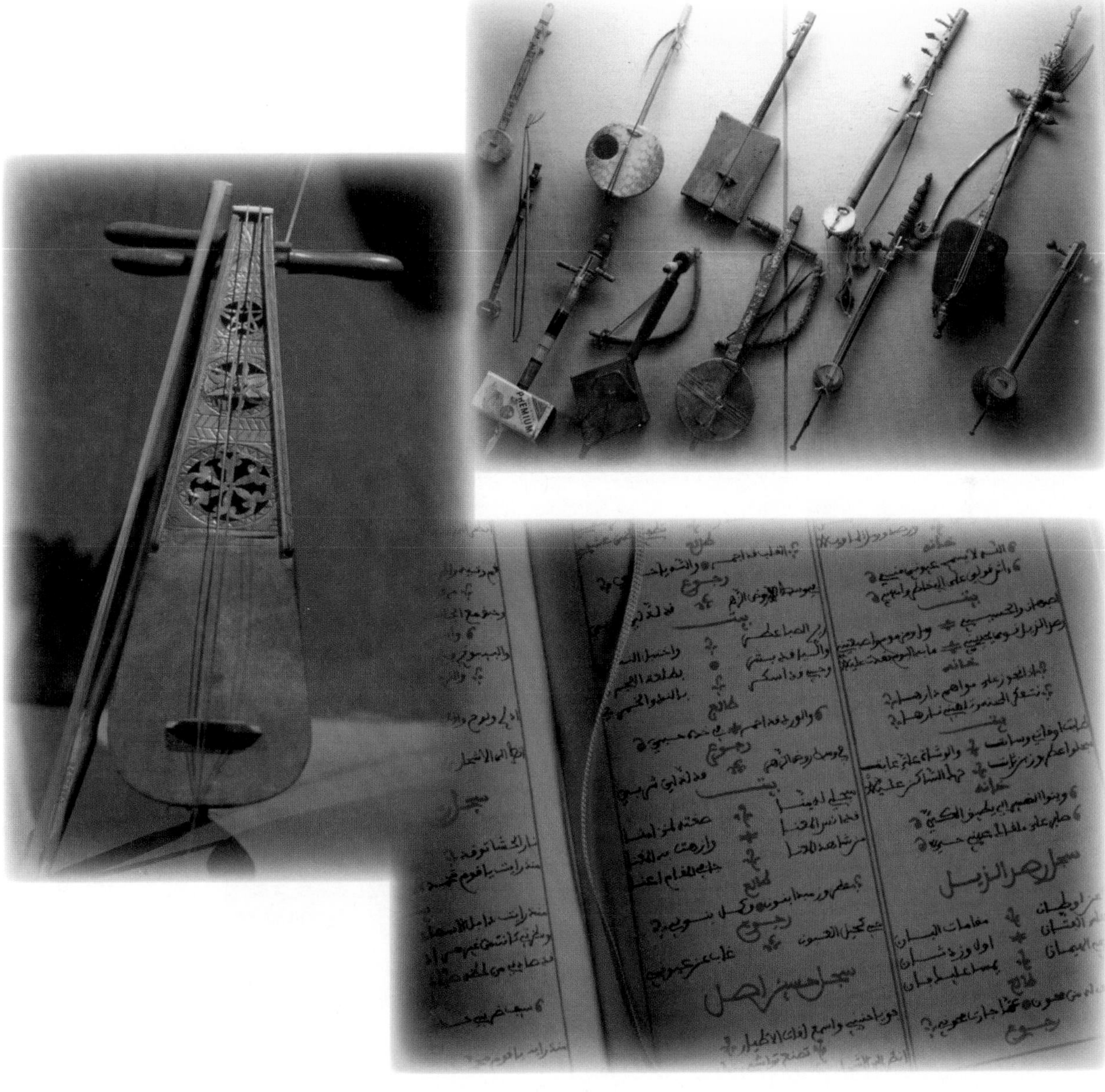

تمرين ١٥

آ- حدِّد الفِكرة الرئيسة في النص.

ب- اذكر بعض الأفكار الثانوية.

ج- Write a biographical sketch of the person described, similar to those found in the main passages of this lesson.

د- اكتب «خطأ» أو «صواب» بجانب كل جملة وصحِّح الجمل الخطأ:

١- تدرسُ سَلمى الأدَبَ العَرَبيّ.

٢- تُحِبُّ سَلمى السَفَر والطعامَ العَرَبيّ.

٣- لَدَيها آلَةُ تَصويرٍ جديدةٌ.

هـ أكمل الجمل الآتية بالاختيار المناسب وفق نص الاستماع:

١- تُصوِّر سَلمى ________________.

☐ أسرتها وأصدقاءها ☐ جامعتها ☐ البلاد العربية

٢- تُحِبّ سَلمى ________________.

☐ آلة تَصويرِها ☐ السَفَر ☐ اللون الأزرَق

٣- يُذكِّرها لونُها المُفَضَّل بـ________________.

☐ بَلَدِها ☐ الأشجار ☐ قِطَّتِها

المُفْرَدات

to need, to have to	(v.)	اِحْتِياج إلى	(يَحْتاج)	اِحْتاجَ
tool, implement, instrument	(n., f.)	أدَوات	ج	أداة
since, because	(part.)			إذْ
to receive	(v.)	اِسْتِلام	(يَسْتَلِم)	اِسْتَلَمَ
to please, to make happy	(v.)	إسْعاد	(يُسْعِد)	أسْعَدَ
blond	(color)	شُقْر	ج	أشْقر / شَقراء
finger	(n., f.)	أصابِع	ج	إصْبَع (أو أصْبُع)
to become	(v.)		(يُصْبِح)	أصْبَحَ
tame, domesticated, friendly	(adj.)			أليف
to examine, to test	(v.)	اِمْتِحان	(يَمْتَحِنُ)	اِمْتَحَنَ
hope	(n., m.)	آمال	ج	أمَل
to spread	(v.)	اِنْتِشار	(يَنْتَشِر)	اِنْتَشَرَ
chapter, column (in a newspaper)	(n., m.)	أبواب	ج	باب
to program	(v.)	بَرْمَجة	(يُبَرْمِج)	بَرْمَجَ
brown	(adj.)			بُنّيّ
to pursue	(v.)	مُتابَعة	(يُتابِع)	تابَعَ
to bear, to endure, to assume responsibility	(v.)	تَحَمُّل	(يَتَحَمَّل)	تَحَمَّلَ
greeting—to say 'greetings from __'	(n., f.)	تَحِيّات	ج	تَحِيَّة

to specialize	(v.)	تَخَصُّص	(يَتَخَصَّص)	تَخَصَّص
to correspond (with)	(v.)	تَراسُل (مع)	(يَتَراسَل)	تَراسَلَ
to leave, to abandon	(v.)	تَرْك	(يَتْرُك)	تَرَكَ
entertainment	(n., f.)	تَسالٍ	ج تَسْلِيات/	تَسْلِيَة
to be acquainted	(v.)	تَعارُف	(يَتَعارَف)	تَعارَفَ
cost, expense	(n., f.)	تَكْلِفات	ج	تَكْلِفة
to wish, to desire	(v.)	تَمَنٍّ	(يَتَمَنّى)	تَمَنّى
hole, perforation	(n., m.)	ثُقوب	ج	ثُقْب
skin	(n., m.)	جُلود	ج	جِلْد
to preserve, to protect	(v.)	مُحافَظة	(يُحافِظ)	حافَظَ
guarding, watching	(n., f.)			حِراسة
to realize, to fulfill, to make something come true	(v.)	تَحْقيق	(يُحَقِّق)	حَقَّق
wood	(n., m.)	أَخْشاب	ج	خَشَب
to teach	(v.)	تَدْريس	(يُدَرِّس)	دَرَّس
tambourine	(n., m.)	دُفوف	ج	دَفّ
paint	(n., m.)			دِهان
to correspond	(v.)	مُراسَلة	(يُراسِل)	راسَل
desire	(n,, f.)	رَغَبات	ج	رَغْبة
novel	(n., f.)	رِوايات	ج	رِوايّة

playing cards (colloquial, Syria)	(n., f.)	شَدّات	ج	شَدَّة
poetry	(n., m.)	أشْعار	ج	شِعْر
to repair	(v.)	تَصْليح	(يُصَلِّح)	صَلَّح
brass disc, cymbals	(n., f.)	صُنوج	ج	صَنْج
to play an instrument	(v.)	عَزْف (على)	(يَعْزِف)	عَزَف
treatment, therapy	(n., m.)	عِلاجات	ج	عِلاج
grade, mark	(n., f.)	عَلامات	ج	عَلامة
lute	(n., m.)	أعْواد	ج	عود
earthenware, clay	(n., m.)			فَخّار
scandal	(n., f.)	فَضائح	ج	فَضيحَة
film, movie	(n., m.)	أفْلام	ج	فِلم
reader	(act. p.)	قُرّاء	ج	قارِئ
cat	(n., f.)	قِطَط	ج	قِطّة
heart	(n., m.)	قُلوب	ج	قَلْب
to correspond with	(v.)	مُكاتَبة	(يُكاتِب)	كاتَب
dog	(n., m.)	كِلاب	ج	كَلْب
pliers	(n., f.)	كَمّاشات	ج	كَمّاشة
playing cards (colloquial, Egypt)	(n., f.)			كوتشينة
at, by (= عِندَ)	(prep.)			لَدى

master's degree	(n., m.)			ماجِسْتير
goat	(act. p.)	مَواعِز	ج	ماعِز
height (e.g., the Golan Heights), hill	(pass. p.)	مُرْتَفَعات	ج	مُرْتَفَع
double, dual	(act. p.)			مُزْدَوِج
help, assistance, aid	(n., f.)	مُساعَدات	ج	مُساعَدَة
a play (theatrical)	(n., f.)	مَسْرَحِيّات	ج	مَسْرَحِيَّة
common, mutual	(pass. p.)			مُشْتَرَك
problem	(act. p.)	مَشاكِل	ج مُشْكِلات /	مُشْكِلة
hammer	(n., f.)	مَطارِق	ج	مِطْرَقة
bit of information	(pass. p.)	مَعْلومات	ج	مَعْلومة
screwdriver	(n., m.)	مِفَكّات	ج	مِفَكّ
saw	(n., m.)	مَناشير	ج	مِنْشار
music	(n., f.)			موسيقا
flute	(n., m.)	نايات	ج	ناي
carpentry	(n., f.)			نِجارة
brass	(n., m.)			نُحاس
passage, text	(n., m.)	نُصوص	ج	نَصّ
to write or compose poetry	(v.)	نَظْم	(يَنْظِم)	نَظَم
to blow, to inflate	(v.)	نَفْخ	(يَنْفُخ)	نَفَخ

to intend, to determine	(v.)	نِيَّة	(يَنْوي)	نَوى
string	(n., m.)	أوْتار	ج	وَتَر
playing cards	(n.)			وَرَق اللَعِب
(foreign) ministry; state department (US)	(n., f.)	وِزارات	ج	وِزارة (الخارجية)
hobby	(n., f.)	هِوايات	ج	هِواية
manual, done by hand	(adj.)			يَدَويّ

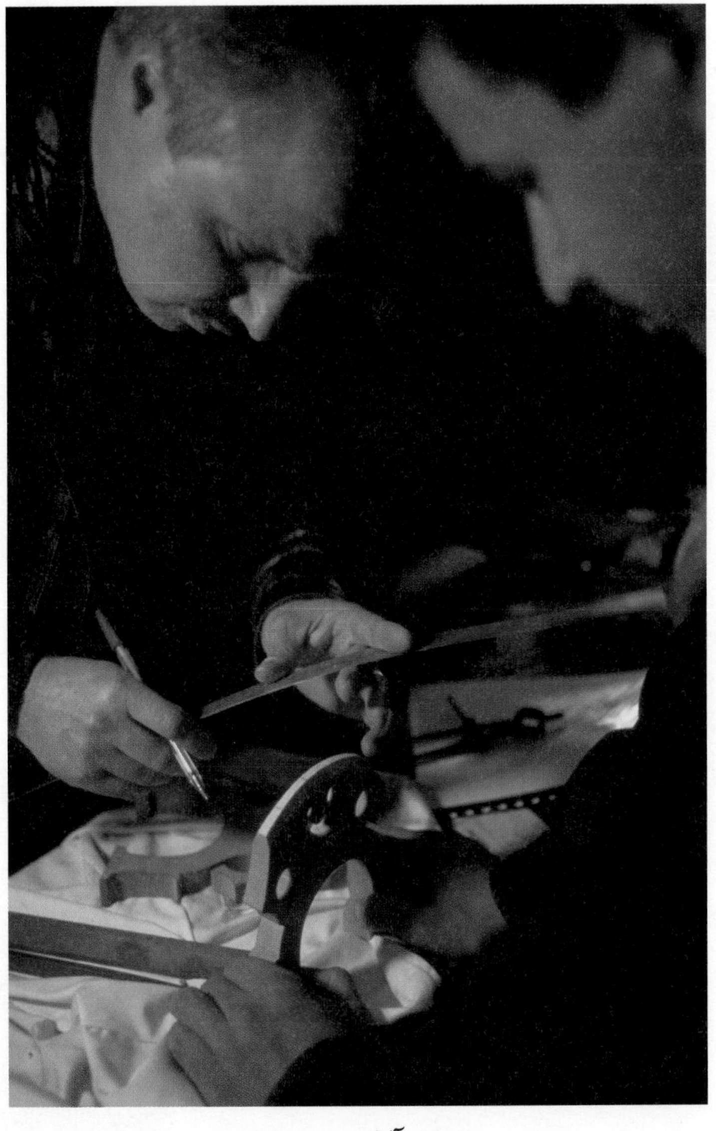

صانع آلات موسيقية

الدَرْسُ الثالث

Objectives

- Learning how to follow written recipes and how to describe food
- Introduction to giving and receiving instructions
- **Grammar**: Expressing obligation with يَجِب, explaining uses of the preposition بِـ, adverbial use of ordinal numbers
- **Revisiting**: The imperative, descriptive إضافة, and the particle ها

رُكنُ المُفْرَداتِ الجَديدةِ

during	أثْناء
to add	أضافَ (يُضيفُ) إضافة
to mix	خَلَطَ (يَخْلِطُ) خَلْط
to ask	سأل (يسألُ) سُؤال
speed; velocity	سُرْعة ج سُرْعات
to pour	صَبَّ (يَصُبُّ) صَبٌّ
difficulty	صُعوبة ج صُعوبات
to cook	طَبَخَ (يَطْبُخُ) طَبْخ
method, way, manner	طَريقة ج طَرائق
to be sufficient, enough	كَفَى (يَكْفي) كِفاية
suitable; appropriate	مُناسِب
employee, civil servant	مُوَظَّف ج مُوَظَّفون

مع أم وليد

برنامج تلفزيوني عن المطبخ الشامي

هريسة اللوز

تُقدّم أمُّ وليد برنامجاً تلفزيونياً في الساعة الثامنة من مساء كل ثُلاثاء تَشرح فيه طريقة طبخ أطباق شامية مختلفة. ها هي اليوم تشرح طريقة صُنع حلوى هريسة اللوز. أمّ وليد ربّة بيت وأمٌّ لثلاثة أطفال. كثيرات من ربّات البيوت والموظَّفات ينتظرْنَ هذا البرنامج.

أم وليد

أم وليد

سيداتي العزيزات، أسعد الله مساءكن. سأقدِّم لكن اليوم طريقةَ صُنع حلوى لَذيذة يمكن تحضيرها بسرعة وسهولة، لذلك هي مُناسِبة للسيّدات اللاتي يعملن. أولاً: يجب أن تُحضرن ورقةً وقلماً لكتابة الموادّ والمقادير، وهي تكفي لصينيّة دائريّة متوسّطة الحجم. نحتاج إلى كأسَين من السميد وكأس من جوز الهند المطحون وكأس سكّر وكأس لَبَن ونصف مِلعَقة شاي من الخميرة ونصف مِلعَقة من قِشر الليمون.

زُبْدة

صينية دائرية

والآن إليك الطريقةَ يا سيّدتي. أولاً: اخلطي السميد وجَوْز الهند والسكّر. في وعاء آخر اخلطي اللَبَن مع الخميرة إلى أن تفور الخَلْطة، ثمّ أضيفي قِشر اللّيْمون إلى خَلْطة اللَبَن والخميرة. أضيفي هذه الخَلْطة إلى السميد والسكّر وجوز الهند.

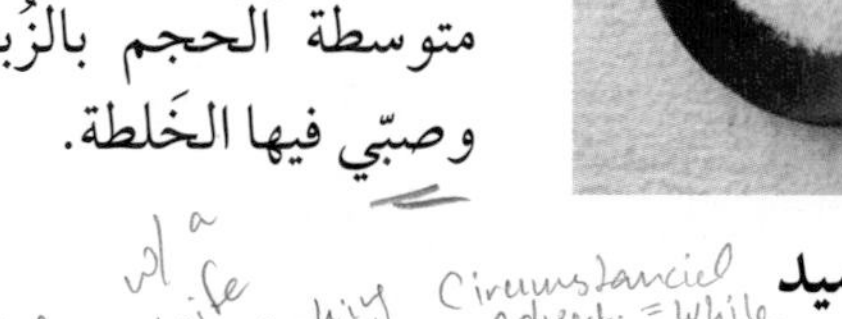

ثانياً: ادهُني صينيّة دائريّة متوسطّة الحجم بالزُبدة وصبّي فيها الخَلطة.

سميد

شجرة جوز الهند

ثالثاً: قطّعي الهريسة وهي في الصينيّة بالسكّين على شكل مُعَيَّنات، ثمّ ضَعي على وَجه كلّ مُعَيَّن لَوْزة. انتظري ساعة. بعد ساعة ضَعي الصينيّة في المَوقِد (الفُرن) لمدّة عشرين دقيقةً على حرارة ٤٠٠ إلى ٤٥٠ فرنهايت، أو إلى أن يَحْمَرَّ وجه الخَلطة.

أثناء وجود الصينيّة في المَوقِد حضِّري القَطْر وهذا تحضيره سهل، ليس فيه أية صعوبة. أحضري وعاءً عميقاً وصُبّي فيه كأس ماء ثمّ ضَعيه على نار قويّة إلى أن يغليَ الماء. أضيفي كأسين من السكّر على الماء مع مِلعَقتين من عصير الليمون. حرِّكي السكّر والماء إلى أن يختُر.

كأس

في هذا الوقت تكون الهريسة قد نَضِجت. أخرجي الصينيّة من المَوقِد وصُبّي القَطر عليها. قدِّمي الهريسة حين تبرد. بالهَناء والشِفاء. إذا كان عندكن أسئلة فاسألوني بالهاتف.

وعاء عميق

أدوات المائدة

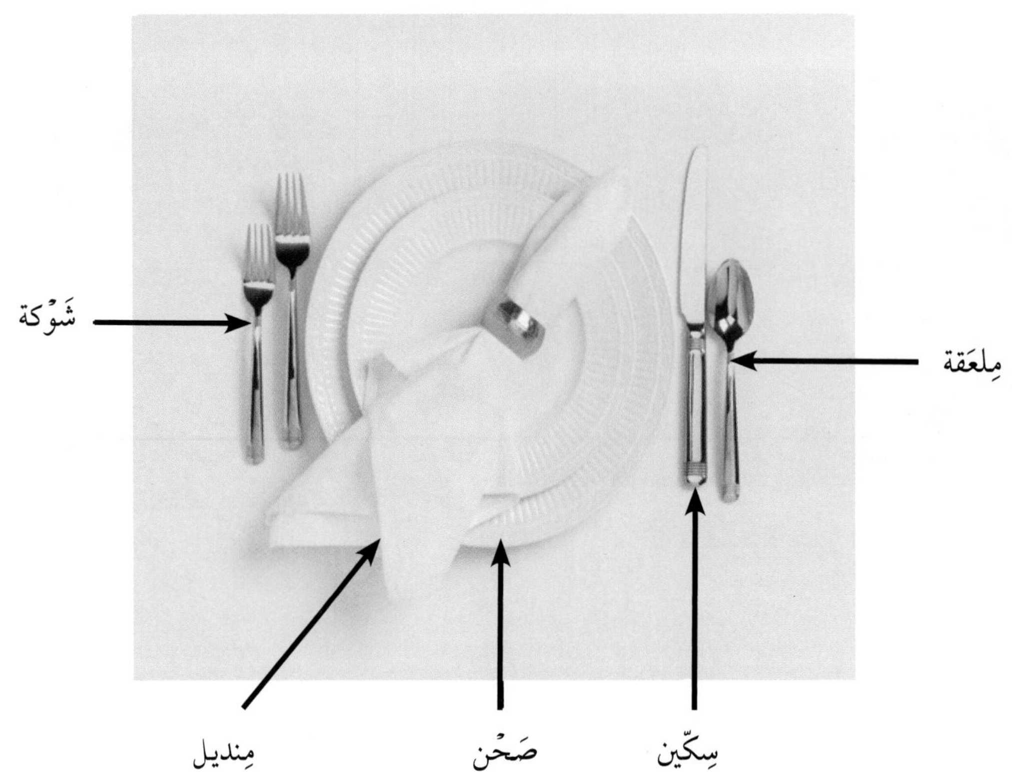

أشكال هندسية

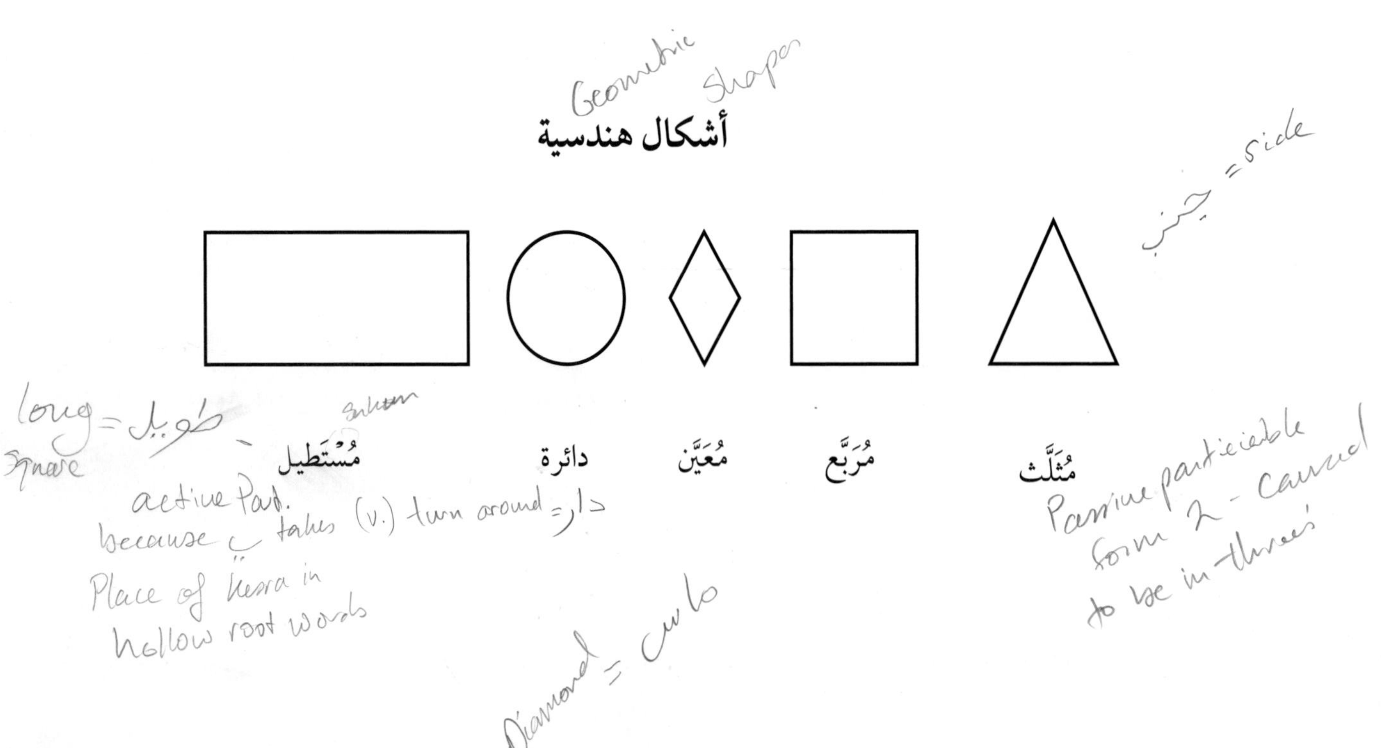

تمرين ١

أجب عن الأسئلة الآتية وفق نص القِراءة:

١- ما الفكرة الرئيسة في نصّ القراءة؟

٢- حدِّد بعض الأفكار الثانويّة.

٣- اكتب عنواناً آخر لهذا الدرس.

تمرين ٢

أكمل الجمل الآتية من نص القراءة:

١- يُبَثّ برنامج أمّ وليد في الساعة ________.

٢- أمّ وليد لدَيْها ________.

٣- مُشاهِدات بَرنامج أمّ وليد من ________.

٤- طَبَق اليوم هو ________.

٥- يُصنع هذا الطَبَق من ________.

٦- يَبقى الطَبَق في الفُرن مُدّة ________.

٧- نَحتاج إلى عَصير الليمون في تَحضير ________.

٨- أين توضع اللوزة ________.

تمرين ٣

للمحادثة: في مجموعات من اثنين، اسأل زميلك:

الطعام المفضَّل، مُكَوّنات هذا الطبق، محليّ أم عالميّ، الأدوات اللازمة لتحضيره، الوقت من اليوم الذي يؤكل فيه عادة، أين يأكله، مع مَن، متى كانت آخر مرة تناوله، مَن كان معه، في أي مناسبة، لماذا يفضِّل هذا الطبق، بعض الأطباق الشائعة في بلدة الطالب، الطبق الذي تحضِّره والدة الطالب بنجاح، وغير ذلك.

تمرين ٤

وافِق بين كُلِّ كَلِمة واكتُب الكَلِمَتين في الوسط:

١	نار		دِمَشقيّ
٢	زُبدة		ساعة
٣	موادّ		مُوَظَّفة
٤	دَقيقة		سَهل
٥	شاميّ		مَوقِد
٦	طِفْل		مَقادير
٧	صَعْب		أمّ
			لَبَن

تمرين ٥

اختَر الكَلِمةَ الّتي لا تُناسِب باقي الكَلِماتِ في كُلِّ مَجْموعةٍ وبَيِّن السَبَب:

١- سُكّر حلوى ثلاثاء هريسة

٢- موَظَّفة ربّة بيت مُذيعة شَجَرة

٣- لَيمون خَلَطَ فارَ دَهَنَ

٤- صينيّة مِلْعَقة شَوكة سِكّين

٥- دائرة لَوْزة مُثَلَّث مُرَبَّع

تمرين ٦

أعد ترتيب الكلمات في كل مجموعة لتشكّل جملاً مُفيدةً:

١- على ضَعي الطاولة الصينيّة

٢- باب اِنتظرنا المَسرَح أمام

٣- الماء عند مئة يغلي حرارة دَرَجة

٤- العربية الطلاّب صُعوبة بعض تكلّم يَجِد في

٥- الجِدار الدِهان جَيّداً حَرِّك ثُمَّ بالفُرشاة ادهن

تمرين ٧

أعد ترتيب الجمل لتُشكِّل فقرة كاملة. الجملة الأولى في مكانها المُناسِب:

ضَعِ الحاسوب الجديد على الطاولة

اِبْدأ بكتابة رسالتك.

ثُمَّ صِلِ الحاسوبَ بالكَهرباء.

أولاً صِل لوحة المفاتيح بالحاسوب.

انتظر دقيقة أو دقيقتين ليُحمِّلَ الحاسوب برامجه.

تمرين ٨

للكتابة: صِفْ طِريقة تَحضير طَبَق يُعجِبك واذْكر الموادّ والأوانيَ التي يجِب استعمالها.

القواعد

1. The Invariable Verb وَجَبَ (يَجِبُ)

Different from other verbs, وَجَبَ (*to be necessary, must*) is invariable. In other words, it agrees only with its subject in gender, not in number.

It is necessary to prepare for the test tomorrow.	يَجِبُ التَحْضيرُ لِلامتِحان مِنَ الآنَ.	١

Example 1 shows وَجَبَ in present tense and uses a يـ prefix because the subject of the sentence (i.e., **التَحْضير**) is masculine. This verb can be used in present tense (i.e., example 2) or in past (i.e., example 3).

It is necessary to correspond with them.	تَجِبُ المُراسَلةُ مَعَهُم.	٢
It was necessary to correspond with them.	وَجَبَتِ المُراسَلةُ مَعَهُم.	٣

The most common use of this verb is in the set phrase يَجِبُ أنْ, which is followed by a present tense verb (i.e., examples 4, 5, and 6).

I must prepare for the test now.	يَجِبُ أنْ أُحَضِّرَ لِلامتِحانِ مِنَ الآنَ.	٤
You (m.) must prepare for the test now.	يَجِبُ أنْ تُحَضر لِلامتِحانِ مِنَ الآنَ.	٥
You (f.) must prepare for the test now.	يَجِبُ أن تُحَضِّري لِلامتِحانِ مِنَ الآنَ.	٦

تَذَكَّروا

In the يَجِبُ أنْ format, the verb يَجِبُ never changes (see examples 4, 5, and 6).

To add emphasis to the يَجِبُ أن phrase, simply add على directly after the verb:

You have to prepare for the test now.	يَجِبُ عَلَيْكَ أن تُحَضِّر لِلامتِحان مِنَ الآنَ.	٧
He has to prepare for the test now.	يَجِبُ عَلَيْه أنْ يُحَضِّر لِلامتِحان مِنَ الآنَ.	٨

مُلاحَظة

How do you say '*shouldn't*' in Arabic? An important characteristic of يَجِبُ أنْ is its ability to express '*should not*' simply by adding لا after يَجِبُ أنْ.

يَجِبُ أنْ + لا = يَجِبُ ألاّ

Notice that the ن disappears when followed by لا and becomes ألا.

I should not be late.	يَجِبُ ألاّ أتأخّر.	أنا	
You (m.s.) should not be late.	يَجِبُ ألاّ تَتأخّر.	أنتَ	
You (f.s.) should not be late.	يَجِبُ ألاّ تَتأخّري.	أنتِ	٩
You (m. pl.) should not be late.	يَجِبُ ألاّ تَتأخّروا.	أنتُم	
We should not be late.	يَجِبُ ألاّ نَتأخّر.	نَحنُ	

As you will notice in example 9, the verb that follows ألاّ is مَنصوب.

At times, you may wish to add emphasis to *should not*. This is done, just as before, by adding على plus a suffixed pronoun.

You (really) should not **be late.**	يَجِبُ عَلَيكَ ألاّ تَتأخّر.	١٠
She (really) should not **be late.**	يَجِبُ عَلَيها ألاّ تَتأخّر.	

تمرين ٩

على ورقة مُنْفصلة ترجم هذه الجمل:

1. I must bring this book with me to school tomorrow.
2. We should not forget our friends.
3. You must write your name on this paper.
4. She had to ride the bus to work.
5. You shouldn't write on the walls.
6. It is necessary to stir the mixture.

2. Uses of the Preposition بِـ

This extremely useful preposition can be used to create adverbials (i.e., quickly, easily, slowly). Simply prefix the بـ to a noun or a verbal noun and voila, instant adverbial.

A dessert that can be prepared quickly.	حَلوى يُمكِنُ تَحْضيرُها بِسُرعةٍ.	بِسُرعة	١
Adil speaks Arabic with ease.	يَتَحَدَّثُ عادل اللُغة العَرَبيّة الفُصحى بِسُهولة.	بِسُهولة	٢
The negotiations are proceeding, although slowly.	تَتَقَدَّمُ المُفاوضات ولكن بِبُطء.	بِبُطء	٣

This preposition was used at the end of our main reading passages, an oft-used expression meaning '*bon appétit.*'

With happiness and health	بِالهَناء والشِفاء	٤

We can also use بِـ with an instrument to mean 'with a, in a, by a':

Cut up the harisa with a knife.	قَطِّعي الهَريسَةَ بِالسِكّين.	
My mother prepared the dessert in the oven.	حَضَّرتْ أمّي الحَلوى بِالفُرنِ.	٥
He arrived by car.	وَصَلَ بِالسيّارةِ.	

تمرين ١٠

على ورقة مُنْفصلة ترجم هذه الجمل:

1. We came by car.
2. She made this dish herself.
3. I clean my teeth with a toothbrush.
4. I did this exercise with difficulty.
5. They carried the refrigerator easily.

3. Descriptive Iḍāfa الإضافة غير الحقيقية

The إضافة is possibly the most sophisticated structure in Arabic. Among its many features is its ability to act as an adjective to describe a noun. Its English equivalent sounds a bit 'formal' or antiquated, but it is very impressive if used in Arabic.

To create this structure, simply put the adjective in front of its modified noun.

A tray of medium size.	صينيّةٌ مُتوسِّطةُ الحَجم.	١

The adjective agrees with the gender of the subject of the sentence, not with its modified noun. In example 1, the adjective مُتوسِّط agreed with صينيّة, not with حَجم. This differs from the manner in which we would have described the tray before learning this structure:

A tray its size (is) medium.	صينيّةٌ حَجمُها مُتوسِّطٌ	٢

Take a look at how to create this structure using the noun-adjective structure that we already know as our starting point.

A boy whose hair is short.	وَلَدٌ قَصيرُ الشَعَرِ.	⇐	وَلَدٌ شَعَرُه قَصيرٌ.	٣
This house's price is expensive.	هذا البَيْتُ غالي الثَمَنِ.	⇐	هذا البَيْتُ ثَمَنُهُ غالٍ.	٤

تمرين ١١

على ورقة مُنْفصلة ترجم هذه الجمل:

1. Her sister has a beautiful face.
2. My brother has many children.
3. Some languages are easy to learn.
4. أحْمَد has large feet.
5. This is a high-priced car.

4. Ordinal Numbers as Numerical Adverbs الأعداد الترتيبية

Ordinal numbers are known as such because they indicate things that have been put in *order*. These numbers (e.g., الأوّل، الثاني، الثالِث) can be used like their counterparts in English (i.e., firstly, secondly, thirdly, etc.). The following table shows cardinal numbers (عَدَدٌ أصليّ), followed by ordinal numbers (عَدَدٌ تَرتيبيّ), and numerical adverbs (ظَرْف تعداديّ):

عَدَدٌ أصليّ	عَدَدٌ تَرتيبيّ	ظَرْف تعداديّ
واحِد / واحِدة	أوّل / أولى	أوّلاً
اِثنانِ	ثانٍ / ثانية	ثانياً
ثَلاثة	ثالِث	ثالِثاً
أربَعة	رابِع	رابِعاً
خَمسة	خامِس	خامِساً

تمرين ١٢

Use numerical adverbs (e.g., أوّلاً، ثانياً، ثالِثاً) to describe the steps in the following process. Rearrange the sentences, beginning each one with the correct numerical adverb. Please provide an appropriate title for the paragraph once completed:

أغْلِقِ الحقيبة واقفلها بالمفتاح.

اِنْزِلْ إلى الشارع لِتنتظِرَ سيارة الأجرة.

أحْضِرْ حقيبة كبيرة.

أحْضِرْ ملابِسك وأمتعتك وضعها في الحقيبة.

اِتّصِلْ بسيارة الأجرة لتأخذَك إلى المطار.

افْتحِ الحقيبة ونظّفْها من الداخل.

تمرين ١٣

للمُحادَثة: اشرح لزميلك في غرفة الصف عمليّة ما من البداية حتّى النهاية مستخدماً الظَرف التعدادي (أوّلاً، ثانياً، ثالثا). بعض المواضيع قد تكون:

١- طريقة طبخ أكلتك المفضَّلة
٢- عمليّة شراء سيّارة
٣- عمليّة شراء حاسوب جديد
٤- عمليّة تعلّم لغة ثانية
٥- عمليّة قيادة سيّارة

5. Demonstratives and ها

The particle **ها** is used to attract the attention of the listener. This particle is very familiar to us since it is actually part of the compound word '*this*' in Arabic:

ها + ذا = هذا

ها + ذِه = هذِه

It can also be used as an independent word as an attention-grabbing particle, like 'here' or 'there' in English:

١	ها هِيَ تَشرَحُ . . .	*Here she is explaining . . .*

It should be noted that when **ها** is used with reference to a noun, ***a separating pronoun*** should be used:

٢	ها هُوَ الأستاذُ يَكتُب على السَبّورة.	*Here's the professor writing on the board.*

تمرين ١٤

على ورقة مُنفصلة تَرجِم هذه الجمل مستخدماً "ها":

1. Here I am, writing to you from Tunis.
2. There he is, driving his new car.
3. Here's my mother, preparing a dessert.
4. There they are, playing basketball.

6. The Imperative Revisited مُراجعة الأمْر

As was mentioned in *Ahlan wa Sahlan* I, the imperative is used only with second person and is formed from the jussive المُضارِع المجْزوم. Consider the following table:

الأمر	المُضارِع المَجْزوم	المُضارِع المَرفوع	الضَمير
اِسألْ	تَسألْ	تَسألُ	أنتَ
اِسألي	تَسألي	تَسألينَ	أنتِ
اِسألا	تَسألا	تَسألانِ	أنتُما
اِسألوا	تَسألوا	تَسألونَ	أنتُم
اِسألْنَ	تَسألْنَ	تَسألْنَ	أنتُنَّ

تمرين ١٥

Use the imperative to express the following ideas in writing:

Example: Ask a man to put the TV on the floor. ⇒ ضَعِ التِلفازَ على الأرض.

1. Ask a woman to wait for you in front of the bus stop (*use* ني *for the direct object*).
2. Ask a few men not to forget to write their names on a sheet of paper.
3. Ask your female students to bring their books tomorrow.
4. Ask your male chauffeur to bring the car to the front of the house.
5. Ask your sister to give you the newspaper.

تمرين ١٦

آ- **أجب عن الأسئلة وفق نص الاستماع:**

١- ماذا تبيع هذه الدِعاية؟

٢- لماذا يشتري الناس شيئاً مثل هذا؟

٣- ما الرياضة الّتي يقوم بها الرجل؟

٤- ما الرياضة الّتي تقوم بها أنت؟

ب- **اكتب «خطأ» أو «صواب» بجانب كل جملة وصحِّح الجمل الخطأ:**

١- المشي إحدى الرياضات.

٢- تريد المرأة أن تبيعِ للرجل درّاجة ثابِتة.

٣- تعرف المرأة قليلاً عن الرياضة.

٤- الرجل لديه درّاجة ثابِتة.

ج- **أكمل الجمل الآتية بالاخيار المناسب وفق نص الاستماع:**

١- رياضة الرجل المفضّلة ______________ .

☐ رُكوبُ الدرّاجة ☐ كرةُ السلّة ☐ الجَرْيُ ☐ المَشْيُ

٢- لا يركب الرجل درّاجة لأنّ ______________ .

☐ الدرّاجةَ غالية ☐ ركوبَ السيارة أحسن.

☐ الشوارعَ فيها سيّارات كثيرة. ☐ الرجلَ لا يحتاج إلى الرياضة.

٣- ركوبَ الدرّاجة جيّد خصوصاً ______________ .

☐ للرِجلَينِ ☐ لليَدَينِ ☐ للقَدَمينِ ☐ للقَلْب

٤- يَجِب أن يتمرّن الرجل ______________ .

☐ ركلّ يوم ☐ثلاثين دقيقة ☐ ٣ مرّات أسبوعياً ☐ ٥ مرّات أسبوعاً

المـُفْرَدات

during	(adv.)			أثناء
to become red in color; to blush	(v.)	اِحْمِرار	(يَحْمَرُّ)	اِحْمَرَّ
to add	(v.)	إضافَة	(يُضيفُ)	أضافَ
until				إلى أنْ
to become cold	(v.)	بَرْد	(يَبْرُدُ)	بَرَدَ
coconut	(n., m.)			جَوْزُ الهِنْد
size, volume	(n., m.)	ج حُجوم / أحْجام		حَجْم
to thicken; to coagulate	(v.)	خُثور	(يَخْثُرُ)	خَثَرَ
to mix, to confuse	(v.)	خَلْط	(يَخْلِطُ)	خَلَطَ
mixture	(n., f.)	خَلَّطات	ج	خَلْطة
yeast, leaven	(n., f.)	خَمائِر	ج	خَميرة
circle	(n., f.)	دَوائِر	ج	دائِرة
to daub, to butter, to paint	(v.)	دَهْن	(يَدْهُنُ)	دَهَنَ
to ask	(v.)	سُؤال	(يَسألُ)	سألَ

سُرْعة	ج سُرْعات/ سُرُعات	(n., f.)	speed; velocity
سَريع		(adj.)	fast, quick
سِكّين	ج سَكاكين	(n., f.)	knife
سَميد		(n., m.)	semolina
شِفاء		(n., m.)	cure, healing, recovery
صَبَّ	(يَصُبُّ) صَبّ	(v.)	to pour, to fill
صَحْن	ج صُحون	(n., m.)	plate
صَعْب		(adj.)	difficult, hard
صُعوبة	ج صُعوبات	(n., f.)	difficulty
طَبَخَ	(يَطْبُخُ) طَبْخ	(v.)	to cook
طَبَق	ج أطْباق	(n., m.)	dish, plate
طَحَنَ	(يَطْحَنُ) طَحْن	(v.)	to grind, to pulverize
طَريقة	ج طرائق	(n., f.)	method, way, manner
عَميق		(adj.)	deep
غَلى	(يَغلي) غَلْيٌ / غَلَيان	(v.)	to boil

to boil, simmer, bubble	(v.)	فَوَران	(يَفورُ)	فارَ
oven	(n., m.)	أفْران	ج	فُرْن
peel, rind, skin, shuck, crust	(n., m.)	قُشور	ج	قِشْر
syrup	(n., m.)			قَطْر
to cut up, cut into pieces	(v.)	تَقْطيع	(يُقَطِّعُ)	قَطَّعَ
to be sufficient, to be enough	(v.)	كِفاية	(يَكْفي)	كَفى
almond	(n., m.)			لَوْز
lemon	(n., m.)			لَيْمون
material, substance, ingredient	(n., f.)	مَوادّ	ج	مادّة
diamond (shape)	(pass. p.)	مُعَيَّنات	ج	مُعَيَّن
measure, quantity, amount	(n., m.)	مَقادير	ج	مِقْدار
suitable, appropriate	(act. p.)			مُناسِب
employee, civil servant	(pass. p.)	مُوَظَّفون	ج	مُوَظَّف
fire, heat	(n., f.)	نيران	ج	نار
to become ripe, mature, well-cooked	(v.)	نَضْج / نُضْج	(يَنْضَجُ)	نَضِجَ

dessert made from semolina	(n., f.)			هَريسة
happiness, good health, well being	(n., m.)			هَناء
vessel, container	(n., m.)	أوْعِية	ج	وِعاء

الدَرْسُ الرابع

Objectives

- Learning to give and get directions
- Incorporating letter-writing phrases
- Introduction to the idiom: بفارغ الصبر
- **Grammar**: creating emphasis with the absolute object, conditions with إنْ, uses of حتّى, tag questions with أَلَيسَ كذلك
- **Culture**: significance of street names, learning how to congratulate someone

رُكنُ المُفْرَداتِ الجَديدةِ

to cross; to pass	اِجْتاز (يَجْتازُ) اِجْتياز
to continue; resume	اِسْتَمَرَّ (يَسْتَمِرُّ) اِسْتِمْرار
to turn	اِنْعَطَفَ (يَنْعَطِفُ) اِنْعِطاف
to reach	بَلَغَ (يَبْلُغُ) بُلوغ
emphasis, assurance (certainly, with certainty)	تأكيد (بالتأكيد)
to intersect with	تَقاطَعَ (يَتَقاطَعُ) تَقاطُع (مَعَ)
to welcome	رَحَّبَ (يُرَحِّبُ) تَرْحيب (بِـ)
to live	عاشَ (يَعيشُ) عَيْش
to cross	عَبَرَ (يَعْبُرُ) عُبور
congratulations!	مَبروك!
distance	مَسافة ج مَسافات

عُنوان ميساء الجديد

مَيساء سيّدةٌ في الثانية والعشرين من عمرها، مُتزوِّجةٌ ولها طفلان. الطفل الأكبر اسمه يوسُف والأصغر رامِز. كانت تسكن في شقّة صغيرة بعيدة عن مكان عمل زوجها فَيْصل وعن منزل أهلها في دِمشَق. في الشهر الماضي وَجَدَ فيصل شقّة جديدة قريبة من عملِه ومن دار أهل ميساء.

عزيزتي ميساء،

سأكون في دمشق يوم ١٠ حزيران.

أنا في شوق إليك وسأزورك بالتأكيد.

إلى اللقاء قريباً

في الأسبوع الماضي اِستلمَت ميساء بطاقة بريديّة من صديقتِها هالة الّتي تعيش في مدينة حَلَب، وقد تكلّمت هالة معها بالهاتف في اليوم نفسه تُخبرها أنّها ستَحضُر إلى دِمشَق بعد أُسبوعَيْن وتُحِبّ أن تزورها.

فَرِحَت ميساء بهذا الخَبَر فَرَحاً عظيماً إذ إنّها لم تَرَ هالة مُنذُ أكثر من سنتين.

تمرين ١

وافِق بين كُلِّ كَلِمة واكتُب الكَلِمَتين في الوسط:

١	عاشَ		وَصَلَ
٢	أهلاً		رِسالة
٣	أهل		ساحة
٤	مشى		مَوقِف
٥	بِطاقة		مَرحباً
٦	طَريق		سَكَنَ
٧	بَلَغَ		شارِع
٨	حافلة		سارَ
			أسرة

كتبَت ميساء هذه الرسالة لهالة تُرحِّب بها وتدُلها على الطريق إلى شقّتها الجديدة.

دِمشَق في ٢٥ أيار ٢٠١٢

بسم الله الرحمن الرحيم

عزيزتي هالة،

أطيب التحية لك من دِمشَق وأحرّ الأشواق. أنتظر زيارتك بفارغ الصبر وأن أراك قريباً كما وعدت. رُبّما لا تعلمين أني انتقلت في الشهر الماضي إلى شقّة جديدة. هي أوسع وأجمل من شقّتي القديمة.

قولي «مبروك» فأنا سعيدة بها جدّاً لأنها قريبة من دار أهلي. إليك عنواني الجديد. الخريطة قد تساعدك على الاهتداء إلى بيتي بسهولة.

أنت تعرفين شارع الفَيْحاء حيث تقع مدرسة خَوْلة الثانوية الّتي درسنا فيها معاً. إن كنت تقفين عند تقاطُع شارعَيْ النهر والفَيْحاء خُذي شارع الفَيْحاء باتجاه الشمال حتّى تبلغي شارع الحُريّة وهو شارع عريض. انعطفي إلى اليسار على شارع الحُريّة وسيري فيه مَسافة مئتَيْ مِتر تقريباً حيث تصِلين إلى شارع الفارابي. انعطفي إلى اليمين وامشي في شارع الفارابي نحوَ الشمال أيضاً. اجتازي شارع جرير واستمري في المشي حتّى تبلُغي شارع ابن خَلدون. هنا انعطفي يميناً وسيري في شارع ابن خَلدون إلى أن تصِلي إلى شارع الرازي حيث تنعطفين يساراً وتمشين فيه نحو ٣٠٠ مِتر. أُعبُري الشارع إلى الجانب الأيسر وادخُلي البناية رقم ١٦٨. اِصعَدي إلى الطابق الرابع إما على الدَرَج أو بالمِصعَد. رقم شقّتي ١٧. عُنواني سهل أليس كذلك؟ سلامي إلى زوجك وإلى لقاء قريب.

المشتاقة ميساء

ملاحظة: إذا كنت عند مَوقِف الحافلات في ساحة الشُهداء فاتجهي شرقاً نحوَ شارع الفارابي وانعطفي فيه يميناً نحوَ الجنوب. امشي فيه قليلاً حتّى يتقاطع مع شارع ابن خَلدون. من هنا تعرِفين الطريق حسب التعليمات أعلاه.

خريطة الطريق إلى شقّة ميساء الجديدة

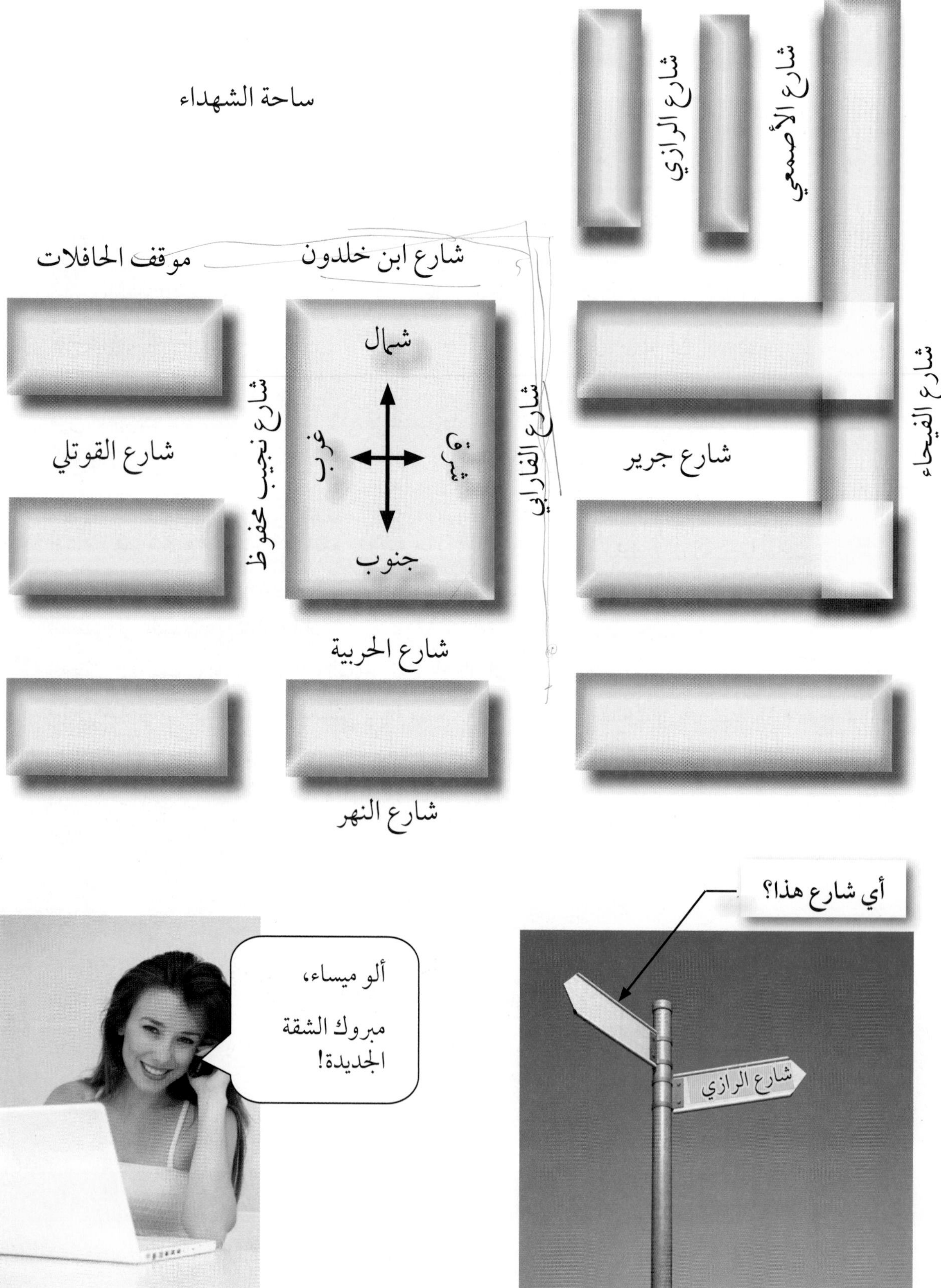

تمرين ٢

اِختَرِ الكَلِمةَ الّتي لا تُناسِب باقي الكَلِماتِ في كُلِّ مَجْموعةٍ وبَيِّن السَبَب:

١- طَريق اِهتداء تقاطُع ساحة

٢- مِتر قَدَم كيلومتر مِصعَد

٣- صَديق عائلة أهل أب

٤- اِستمَرَّ اِتَّجَهَ اِنعطَفَ رَحَّبَ

٥- عَمَلٌ بِناية شَقّة مِصعَد

٦- حافِلة مَوقِف خَريطة راكِب

٧- شَوق ضَيِّق واسِع عَريض

تمرين ٣

أجب عن هذه الأسئلة العامة:

١- هل تستعمل المِصعَد إذا كنت تريد الصُعود إلى الطابق الثاني؟ لماذا؟

٢- صِفْ مكان سكنك (شَقّة أو بيت) والطريق التي تصل منها إلى الجامعة أو إلى أي مكان آخر .

٣- هل أنت سعيد في حياتك؟ لماذا؟

٤- ما العبارة التي تُقال لصديق حين يشتري سيارة جديدة؟

٥- ما المدينة التي تفضِّل أن تعيش فيها؟ ما سبب ذلك؟

٦- إذا كان لديك حيوان أليف كقطّة أو كلب هل تستطيع استئجار أي شقّة تريد؟ ماذا تفعل في هذه الحال؟

تمرين ٤

أجب عن الأسئلة الآتية وفق نصّ القراءة:

١- ما الفكرة الرئيسة في هذا الدرس؟

٢- لماذا كتبَت ميساء رسالة إلى صديقتها؟

٣- ما الأفكار الثانوية في رسالة ميساء؟

٤- مَن هؤلاء الأشخاص: هالة، يوسف، فيصل؟

٥- متى انتقلَت ميساء إلى شقّتها الجديدة؟

٦- لماذا انتقلَت ميساء إلى شقّتها الجديدة؟

٧- ما عنوان ميساء الجديد؟

٨- في أي طابَق توجد شقة ميساء؟

٩- أين مَوقِف الحافلات؟

١٠- لماذا ميساء سعيدة؟ أعطِ السبب أو الأسباب لذلك.

تمرين ٥

أعد ترتيب الكلمات في كل مجموعة لتشكّل جملاً مُفيدةً:

١- مِن	طوابِق	بِنايتُنا	سِتّة	مؤلّفة		
٢- أمام	مِن	المَصرِف	الحافِلة	نَزلتُ		
٣- شارِعَيْ	سامي	والنيل	مَحلّ	عِند	السَلام	تقاطُع
٤- إلى	شمالاً	أوّل	واتّجه	اليمين	شارِع	خُذْ

تمرين ٦

أعد ترتيب الجمل لتُشكِّل فقرة كاملة. الجملة الأولى في مكانها المُناسِب:

١- ابن خالي لديه عائلة مؤلّفة من زوجته ووَلَد وبنتَيْن.

أوّلاً: لأن ذلك الحي مزدحِم.

شقّتُه في الطابَق الرابِع لكنّه لا يستعمِل المِصعَد.

تريد زوجته الانتقال إلى شقّة أكبر في حي قريب من عَمَلِها.

يسكُن وأسرته في بِناية من سبعة طوابِق

ثانياً: لأن الشقُق هناك أغلى بكثير من شقّتهم.

يقول إن صُعود الدَرَج رياضة له.

لكنّه لا يريد الانتِقال لسَبَبَيْن.

1. Giving Directions— The Imperative

When giving directions to someone, we use the imperative form of the verb. Here is a list of some very useful verbs in their imperative to facilitate acquisition:

المَعنى	المُؤنَّث	المُذَكَّر
pass	اِجتازي	اِجْتَزْ
continue	اِسْتَمِرّي	اِسْتَمِرّ
turn	اِنْعَطِفي	اِنْعَطِفْ
head (toward)	اِتّجهي	اِتّجِهْ
walk; go	اِمشي	اِمشِ
cross	أُعْبُري	أُعْبُرْ
go up	اِصْعَدي	اِصْعَدْ
enter	أُدْخُلي	أُدْخُلْ
take	خُذي	خُذْ
go	سيري	سِرْ

تَذَكَّروا

When using the imperative, add a ي to the end of the verb when talking to a female, and a وا when talking to a group of people.

2. Giving Directions—Adverbials and Prepositions

We also make extensive use of adverbs of place and prepositional phrases when giving directions:

to the north	إلى / نَحْوَ الشَمال	شَمالاً
to the south	إلى / نَحْوَ الجَنوب	جَنوباً
to the east	إلى / نَحْوَ الشَرْق	شَرْقاً
to the west	إلى / نَحْوَ الغَرْب	غَرْباً
to the left	إلى اليَمين	يَميناً
to the right	إلى اليَسار	يَساراً

تمرين ٧

للمحادثة: صِف لأحد الزملاء الطريق من مطار المدينة التي تعيش فيها إلى المكان الذي تسكن فيه. إذا لم يكن هناك مطار في بلدتك، صِف الطريق من غرفة الصف إلى بيتك.

3. Letter-Writing Phrases

Certain writing conventions are associated with letter writing. Many people begin their letters with the religious phrase:

١	بِسمِ اللهِ الرَحمنِ الرَحيم.	*In the name of God the Beneficent the Merciful.*

This phrase is, in fact, said out loud before performing any sort of task such as eating, studying, dressing, cooking, setting out to work or on a trip, etc. It is said regardless of the level of formality; it is used in casual as well as formal situations.

مُلاحَظة

The use of religious-sounding phrases or those containing the word الله is not restricted to Muslims. Many Christians, at least in Syria, use such phrases liberally.

Choosing the appropriate term of address is a little intricate; the level of formality and a person's gender must be taken into account.

a. Informal Terms of Address

The most common term of address among people who know each other well translates into English as *dear*, عَزيزي. You may use it or حَبيب with close friends and loved ones.

dear (when used casually in speech it's more like 'buddy').	عَزيزي / عَزيزَتي	٢
my darling, sweetheart	حَبيبي / حَبيبتي	

Another very common and neutral term, أخي / أُختي is used both in speech and writing to address actual brothers and sisters as well as total strangers. While signifying closeness, it remains formal enough to address a colleague. To add more intimacy to this address, we modify it with حَبيب أو عَزيز.

my dear sister/brother	أَخي العَزيز / أُخْتي العَزيزة	٣
my beloved sister/brother	أخي الحَبيب / أُخْتي الحَبيبة	

b. Formal Terms of Address

When addressing a noted individual, such as a university professor or a highly educated person, use quite elaborate terms of address:

The eminent Professor Doctor so-and-so, Esq.,	الأستاذ الفاضِل الدكتور فُلان المُحتَرَم،	٤
Mr. so-and-so, Esq., may God preserve him,	السَيِّد فُلان المُحتَرَم أدامَه الله،	

While it translates literally as 'presence', حَضرَة is used for the high form of أنتَ / أنتِ in both speech and in writing.

High form of أنتَ أو أنتِ *(in speech)*	حَضْرَتُك	
Feminine form (in writing)	حَضرَةُ السَيِّدة إلهام الطَرابيشي المُحتَرَمة.	٥
Masculine form (in writing)	حَضرَة السَيِّد سَعيد الطَرابيشي المُحتَرَم.	

c. The Closing

Certain phrases are used to close the letter; among the most commonly used are:

sincerely	المُخلِص / المُخلِصة	
cordially	المُحِبّ / المُحِبّة	٦
in longing	المُشتاق / المُشتاقة	

القواعد

4. Creating Emphasis Using the Absolute Object المَفْعول المُطلَق

Because Arabic does not have adverbs, we use a device known as المَفعول المُطلَق. The idea here is to turn the verb in a given sentence into a noun so that it can be modified by an adjective. To accomplish this task, we take the مَصْدَر of the verb and then modify it with an adjective.

Maysa rejoiced greatly (a great joy). . . . was very happy	فَرِحَتْ مَيساءُ فَرَحاً عَظيماً.	١

Translated into English properly, example one would read: *Maysa was very happy.* فَرِحَ is the verb of the sentence, and to modify it, we turn it into a noun فَرَح, which can then be modified by an adjective.

Let's take a look at how to form this construction so that we can integrate this into our everyday speech. The cases of مَفعول مُطلَق are highlighted in example two.

He wrote very well.	كَتَبَ كِتابةً جَيِّدةً.	
We walked for a long time.	مَشَينا مَشياً طويلاً.	٢
We used the car very little.	اِستَعمَلنا السَيّارة اِستِعمالاً قليلاً.	

المَفعول المُطلَق can be used as the first term in an إضافة structure as well to create a simile.

She rejoiced like a child (the rejoice of children).	فَرِحَت فَرَحَ الأطفالِ.	٣

You will notice the مَفعول مُطْلَق in example three has no تَنوين by virtue of it being part of a definite إضافة.

تمرين ٨

Translate the following sentences into Arabic making use of المَفعول المُطلَق:

1. She welcomed us warmly.
2. We headed in the wrong direction.
3. We crossed the road correctly.
4. He writes beautifully.
5. The car took a sharp حادّ turn.
6. He repaired the refrigerator well.

5. Expressing Conditional Meaning with إنْ

إنْ (= if) is much like the particle إذا, which we learned indicated a likely event. We may not realize it, but we are very familiar with إنْ since it occurs in one of the most frequently used expressions in Arabic:

God willing; if God wills.	إنْ شاء الله.

You may wonder what the difference is between إذا وإنْ if both particles mean *if.* You may wish to think about them in this way: إذا is slightly more likely to happen than إنْ. For example, one would say:

If (when) morning comes, I will see you.	إذا أتى الصَباحُ أراكَ.

But not:

If (maybe) morning comes, I will see you.	إنْ أتى الصَباحُ أراكَ.

The reason lies in the fact that there is little doubt about the sun rising.

You may recall that إذا is followed by a past tense verb, while the answer clause may have either a past or present tense verb. Four possible verb tense combinations are possible when using إنْ:

١	إنْ كَتَبتَ لي كَتَبتُ لَكَ.	*If you write me, I would write you (past/past).*
٢	إنْ كَتَبتَ لي أكتُبُ لَكَ.	*If you write me, I would write you (past/present).*
٣	إنْ تَكتُبْ لي أكتُبْ لَكَ.	*If you write, I will write you (present/present).*
٤	إن تَكتُبْ لي كَتَبتُ لَكَ.	*If you write me, I would write you (present/past).*

As you see, the meanings of examples 1-4 change slightly regarding the use of past and present tense verbs.

It should be noted that, like إذا, the particle فـ should be attached to the first word in the answer clause. That is to say, if the answer clause begins with سَوْفَ، قَدْ، إنَّ، لَنْ، لا or any particle of this sort, فـ must be attached to it. Let's take a look at instances in which the answer clause includes these particles.

a. Future Time Using سَـ / سَوْفَ

٥	إنْ كَتَبتَ لي فَسوفَ أكتُبُ لَكَ.	*If you write me, I will write you.*

b. Completed Action or Possibility Using قَدْ

٦	إنْ تَكتُبْ لي فقَدْ أكتُبُ لَكَ.	*If you write me, I might write you.*
٧	إنْ حَضَرَ مُتأخِّراً فَقَدْ تأخَّرَ مِن قبل.	*If he is late, (it's no wonder) he's been late before.*

c. Nominal Sentence Introduced by إنَّ

٨	إنْ كُنتُ طَويلاً فإنّ أخي أطول.	*If (you think) I am tall, my brother is taller.*

d. Negative Sentence Introduced by لَنْ، لَيسَ، لا، ما، غير

If you go, I won't go.	إنْ تَذهبي فَلَنْ أذهَبَ.	٩
If you forget my name, you are not my friend.	إنْ نَسيتِ اسمي فَلَستِ صَديقتي.	١٠
If you go out this evening, don't forget your house key.	إنْ تَخرُجي مساءً فَلا تَنْسَيْ مِفتاحَ البَيْت.	١١
If I were to buy a new car, I would want a make other than this one.	إنْ أَرَدتُ شِراءَ سيّارةٍ جَديدةٍ فَغَيرَ هذا النَوعِ أريد.	١٢

e. Imperative in the Answer Clause

If she goes, go with her.	إنْ ذَهَبَت فَاذهَبْ مَعَها.	١٣

f. The Answer Clause as a Nominal Sentence

If they are late, they have their reasons.	إنْ تأخَّروا فَلَهُم أسبابُهُم.	١٤

g. Answer Sentence Introduced by رُبَّما

If you eat fruits and vegetables, perhaps it is better for you.	إنْ تأكلوا الخُضَرَ والفَواكِهَ فَرُبَّما كانَ أحسَنَ لَكُم.	١٥

الخلاصة

- إنْ is used to express somewhat likely conditions.
- When using إنْ, any combination of past and present tense verbs can follow it with little to no time implications.
- When إنْ is followed by a present tense verb, it makes the verb مجزوم.

الخلاصة

Similar to إذا, we attach the particle فَـ to the first word of the إن answer clause when using:

- سَـ / سَوفَ + المُضارِع، قَدْ + الماضي، قَدْ + المُضارِع، فِعل الأمر
- إنَّ + جُملة اسميّة
- لا، لَنْ، لَيْسَ، ما، غَيْر
- رُبَّما

تمرين ٩

Use إنْ to express the conditional meanings of the following sentences:

1. If you arrive late, you won't find me.
2. If you exercise, I will exercise with you.
3. If he went to bed early, he may be ill.
4. If you go to Paris, perhaps I will go with you.
5. If he drops out of school (stops studying), a job (his work) is available for him.
6. If you go to London, visit the zoo.

6. Uses of حَتّى

An extremely important and useful particle to know, حَتّى has four main meanings:

a. Until (Noun + حَتّى)

I waited for her until noon.	١ اِنتَظَرتُها حَتّى الظُهر.

b. Until (Past Tense Verb + حَتّى)

I awaited the plane until it took off.	اِنتَظَرتُ الطائرةَ حَتّى أقلَعَت.	٢

c. In Order to (حَتّى + فِعْل مُضارِع)

He went to the library in order to study.	ذَهَبَ إلى المَكتَبةِ حَتّى يَدرُسَ.	٣

d. Even (including s.th.)

The students came, even/including Khaled.	حَضَرَ الطُلاّبُ حَتّى خالِدٌ.	٤

تمرين ١٠

Use حَتّى to express the meanings of the following sentences:

1. هالة had several courses for dinner, even dessert.
2. My father did not drive a car until he reached fifty.
3. She invited me to lunch in order to talk to me.
4. I stayed at school until five o'clock.
5. They went to the train station to see the president.

7. Reflexive and Emphatic Use of نَفْس

Strictly speaking, نَفْس means *self*, and can be used in conjunction with the preposition بِـ and a pronominal suffix to create *by (his/her) self* = بنفسه / بنفسها. It is used reflexively in that the action is both done and experienced by the subject. It is generally used to emphasize its modified noun.

Ahmad washed the car himself.	غَسَلَ أَحمَدُ السيّارةَ بِنَفسِه.	١
Ahmad himself washed the car.	غَسَلَ أَحمَدُ نَفسُه السيّارةَ.	٢
Ahmad washed the car itself.	غَسَلَ أَحمَدُ السيّارةَ نَفسَها.	٣

w/o ب modify noun directly before it

تمرين ١١

Express the following sentences using حَتّى to convey emphatic and reflexive meanings:

1. فَريد himself told me that the stores were closed.
2. Where do you see yourself in ten years?
3. سامية typed the letter by herself.
4. The taxicab driver himself carried my suitcase to my apartment.

8. Tag Questions

A normal statement is turned into a question using a short interrogative at the end of the sentence. Many such devices are found in English:

He goes to school, doesn't he?

They can speak Arabic, can't they?

Unlike English, Arabic utilizes one set structure: أَلَيْسَ كَذلِكَ, which can loosely be translated as *isn't that right*?

Salma has been to Aleppo, hasn't she?	زارَت سَلمى مَدينةَ حَلَب، أَلَيْسَ كَذلِكَ؟	١
We're going to study math, aren't we?	سَنَدرُسُ الرياضيّاتِ، أَلَيْسَ كَذلِكَ؟	٢

مُلاحَظة

This is a great device to memorize and use in your everyday speech, especially since the Arabic tag, unlike its English counterpart, is invariable.

تمرين ١٢

للمُحادثة: في مجموعات من طالبين أو ثلاثة، اسأل زميلك الأسئلة الآتية وعلى الطالب الذي يجيب عن السؤال أن يحاول استخدام «**حتّى**» و «**أَلَيْسَ كَذلِكَ**» في الإجابة.

مثال: أ- لماذا سُميت هذه المدينة بهذا الاسم؟
ب - حَتّى يجذب أكبر عدد من الناس إليها، فكرة جميلة، أليس كذلك؟

١- لماذا يريد المرء أن يدرس لغة أجنبيّة؟
٢- لماذا يريد المرء السفر إلى باريس / القاهرة / واشنطن؟
٣- لماذا تشاهد الأخبار؟

9. Idioms المُصطَلَحات

In her letter, Maysa uses the phrase بِفارِغِ الصَبرِ. If you consider the meaning of each item separately, the phrase would seem senseless: فارِغ *empty* and صَبَر *patience*. When combined, they mean *a lack of patience, intense anticipation,* or *impatience*. So, whenever you would like to say, "I can't wait for such-and-such", you should use:

أنتظِرُ شيئاً بِفارِغِ الصَبَر.

تَذَوّق الثَقافَة العَرَبِيَّة

مَبروك!

١

A common phrase used in many parts of the Arab world, مَبروك is used in a variety of contexts such as: buying a car; getting a new pair of shoes or a shirt; winning the lottery; passing an exam; getting engaged, married, or a job.

الله يُبارِك فيكَ

This phrase is used in response to مَبروك and means: *may God bless you.*

تَذَوَّق الثقافة العَرَبيَّة

أسماء الشَوارِع

In most Arab towns, as in other parts of the world, streets bear the names of notable people, ideals, and significant events. In the map that Maysa sent to her friend, you can see the names of historical and contemporary figures, literary people, historians, philosophers, religious and political leaders, and so forth. Ideals are also common (e.g., الحُريّة *liberty*, الوَحدة *unity*).

Events are memorialized by naming streets after them (e.g., ١٧ نيسان *Syria's Independence Day*). It is noteworthy that historical figures are represented just as often as contemporary ones, perhaps even more so. For example, in the map of this lesson, only نَجيب محفوظ is a contemporary figure; all the rest are much older: ابن خَلدون 15th century, الرازي 9th century, الفارابي 9th to 10th century, and جَرير 8th century.

تمرين ١٣

أ- املأ الفراغات الآتية حسب نص الاستماع:

عزيزي رياض،

أرجو أن تكون وأسرتك بخير وأن يكون الطقس في عمان جميلاً كما هو في الشام سأكون سعيداً جداً إذا زرتني في دكاني الجديدة حين تأتي إلى دمشق في الشهر القادم. عنوان دكاني ليس ________ أنت تعرف ذلك الجزء من المدينة خصوصاً وأنك ستنزل في دار ابن عمك هيثم ________ من شارع العابد.

تستطيع أن تأتي إلى دكاني مشياً من موقف الحافلات. إذا كنت عند ________ في شارع العابد مع شارع ستة وعشرين أيار ________ نحو الغرب و________ ________ الصالحية و________ في المشي في طريق شارع العابد إلى أن ________ إلى شارع الحرية هنا ________ إلى اليسار و________ في هذا الشارع إلى الجنوب بعد قليل ________ فندق أمية إلى يسارك ________ في المشي وسترى ثانوية ابن خلدون إلى يسارك.

هنا تكون قد ______ إلى شارع ابن رشد ______ إلى اليمين وسر ______ الغرب مسافة خمسين متراً ثم ______ يميناً مرة أخرى في شارع ضيق ______. دكاني في أول هذا الشارع وهي ثاني دكان إلى اليسار.

أرجو أن يكون عنواني سهلاً ______ زيارتك يا أخي بفارغ الصبر وإلى اللقاء سلامي إلى هاني وصفوان.

أخوك المشتاق

ماهر

b. Based on the directions in the recorded passage, draw a line on the map below that traces the trail of the speaker's friend from the starting point to the final destination. Place an X where the speaker's store is located.

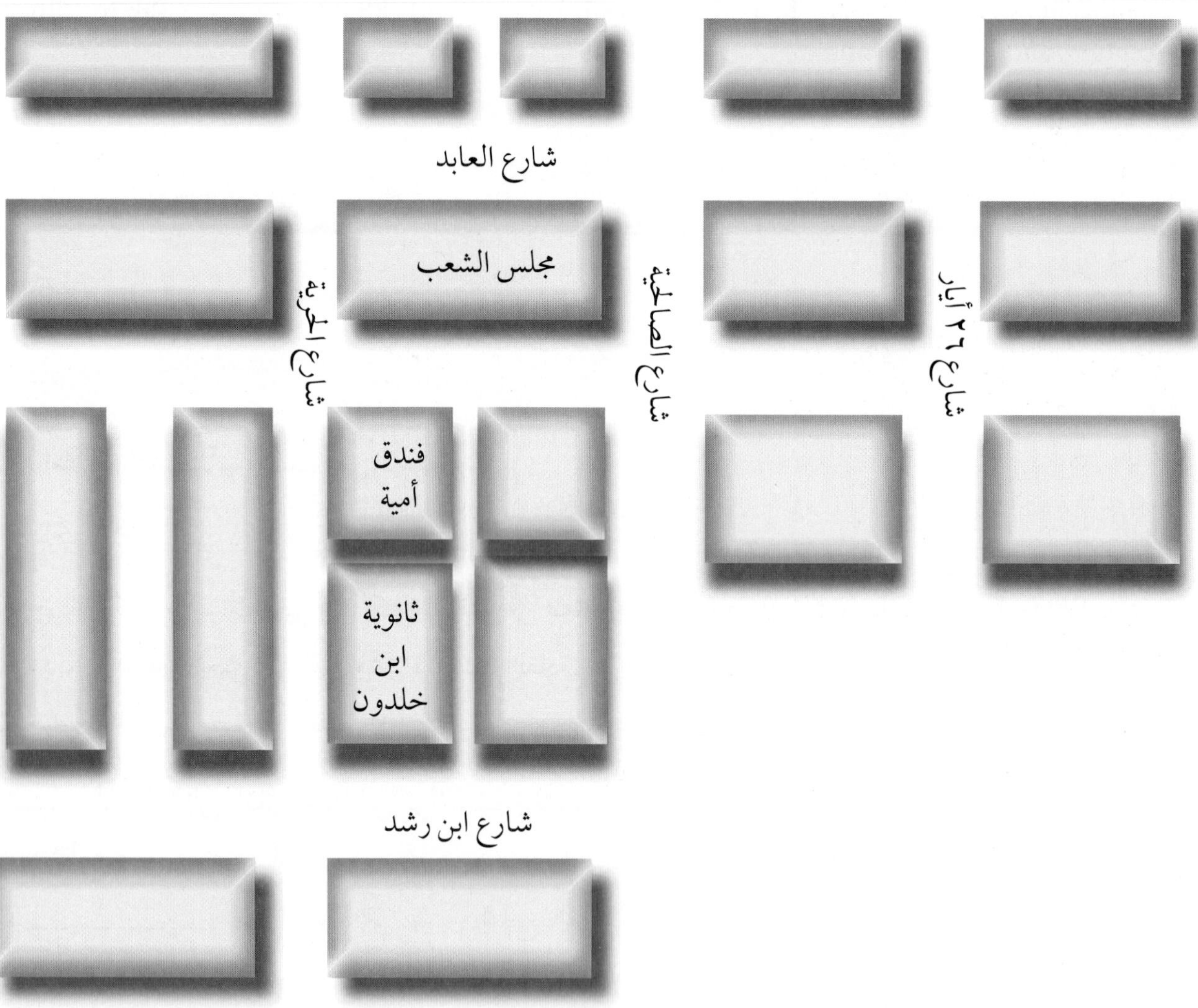

المـُفْرَدات

to cross, pass	(v.)	اِجْتِياز	(يَجتازُ)	اِجتازَ
to continue, resume, go on	(v.)	اِستِمرار	(يَستَمِرُّ)	اِستَمَرَّ
hello (used in answering the telephone)	(int.)			ألو
if	(part.)			إنْ
to turn, swerve, swing	(v.)	اِنعِطاف	(يَنعَطِفُ)	اِنعَطَفَ
to find the right way	(v.)	اِهتِداء	(يَهتَدي)	اِهتَدى
family, one's folks	(n., m.)	أهالٍ	ج	أهل
to reach, get to a place	(v.)	بُلوغ	(يَبلُغُ)	بَلَغَ
assurance (most certainly)	(n., m.)		(بالتأكيد)	تأكيد
to cross, intersect with	(v.)	تَقاطُع	(يَتَقاطَعُ)	تَقَاطَعَ

حَضْرة	ج	حَضَرات	(n., f.)	respectful term of address used with both men and women
رَحَّبَ	(يُرَحِّبُ)	تَرحيب	(v.)	to welcome
شَوق	ج	أشواق	(n., m.)	longing, yearning, desire
صَبَرَ	(يَصبِرُ)	صَبر	(v.)	to be patient, forbearing
صَعِدَ	(يَصعَدُ)	صُعود	(v.)	to climb up
عاشَ	يَعيشُ	عَيش	(v.)	to live
عَبَرَ	(يَعبُرُ)	عُبور	(v.)	to cross, carry across, traverse
عَريض			(adj.)	wide
فارِغ			(act. p.)	empty
فَرِحَ	(يَفرَحُ)	فَرَح	(v.)	to be happy, rejoice
مَبروك			(pass. p.)	congratulations

مِتر	ج	أمتار	(n., m.)	meter (measurement of length)
مَسافة	ج	مَسافات	(n., f.)	distance
نَحوَ			(adv.)	about, approximately, toward
وَعَدَ	(يَعِدُ)	وَعْد	(v.)	to promise

الدَرْسُ الخامِس

Objectives

- Introduction to interview and Q & A techniques
- Requesting and accepting things; getting into and out of conversations
- **Register**: Mixing standard and colloquial elements; suppressing endings
- **Culture**: Family names and their origins
- **Grammar**: Expressing obligation without يَجِب; forming yes/no questions with أ, absolute negation with لا, inquiring about quantity with كَم
- **Revisiting**: Exception, the passive, and adverbs of time

رُكنُ المُفْرَداتِ الجَديدةِ

to conduct	أجْرى (يُجْري) إجْراء
to point (to)	أشار (يُشيرُ) إشارة (إلى)
تكَلّم (مع)	تَحَدَّث (يَتَحَدَّثُ) تَحَدُّث (مع)
come! (imperative)	تعال (للمُذَكّر) تعالي (لِلمؤنَّث)
wing; pavilion	جَناح ج أجْنِحة
to try; to attempt	حاوَلَ (يُحاوِلُ) مُحاوَلة (إلى)
to chat (colloquial)	دَرْدَشَ (يُدَرْدِشُ) دَرْدَشة
to participate	شارَكَ (يُشارِك) مُشارَكة
to interview	قابَلَ (يُقابِل) مُقابَلة
exhibition; fair	مَعْرِض ج مَعارِض
(is it) possible to (+ subjunctive)	مُمْكِن أن (+ فِعل مُضارِع منصوب)

تمرين ١

وافِق بين كُلِّ كَلِمة واكتُب الكَلِمَتين في الوسط:

١	لَحظة		حياة
٢	اِرتَدى		فارِغ
٣	وَفاة		مُراسِل
٤	داخِل		ثانية
٥	مَملوء		اِلتَقى
٦	مُثَلَّجات		وَلَد
٧	قابَل		طَقس
٨	صَبيّ		لَبِسَ
٩	جَوّ		بُوظة
			خارِج

تمرين ٢

اِختَر الكَلِمَةَ الّتي لا تُناسِب باقي الكَلِماتِ في كُلِّ مَجْموعةٍ وبَيِّن السَبَب:

١- مَعرِض	كَريم	جَناح	بِضاعة
٢- وَطَن	فُندُق	زائر	نَوم
٣- عِرْقسوس	شَراب	فِضّة	ثلج
٤- مَوت	اِبتَسَم	ضَحِكَ	سُرور
٥- ظَهْر	يَد	وَجه	طَبَق
٦- دَولة	مَعهَد	بَلَد	قُطر
٧- سائح	مُسَلسَل	بَرنامَج	حَلْقة

بَرنامَج «مع الناس»

أسرة من زَحلة

«مع الناس» بَرنامَج تلفزيونيّ يَعرِض لِلمُشاهِدين مُقابَلات مع أشْخاص يعملون في مَجالات مُختلِفة. في إحدى الحَلَقات قابلَت مُراسِلة التِلفاز، وهي مُذيعة في الوقت نفسِه، عدداً من زُوّار مَعرِض دِمشَق الدَوليّ، وهو مَعرِض تِجاريّ وصِناعيّ يُقام كُلَّ سنة في أواسِطِ الصيفِ في شهرِ تمّوز ويَستمِرّ عَشْرةَ أيّام. تُشارِك في المَعرِض دُوَل عربيّة وأجنبيّة. لِكُلِّ دَولة جَناح خاصّ بِها.

يَزور مَعرِض دِمشَق الدَوليّ مئات الآلاف من الناس من سوريّة ومُدُن البِلاد العربيّة المُجاوِرة وكَذلِكَ من الدُوَل الأجنبيّة.

أمام دُكّان بائع المُثلَّجات (أو البُوظة) أجرَت المُراسِلة مُقابَلة مع أسرة تَزور المَعرِض.

المُراسِلة: مرحباً يا أخ.

الرَجُل: أهلاً

المُراسِلة: هل عندك مانع أن (نُدَردِش) قليلاً؟

الرَجُل: لا أبداً. تَفضّلي.

المُراسِلة: الاسم الكَريم؟

الرَجُل: نَبيل خوري.

المُراسِلة: أهلاً بِك. من أين أنتَ؟

الرَجُل: من زَحلة.

المُراسِلة: أنتَ وَحدك هنا؟

الرَجُل: لا، حَضَرتُ صباح اليوم بالسيّارة مع زوجتي وأولادي.

المُراسِلة: أين هُم؟

الرَجُل: هَناك. (يَلتَفِت ويُنادي زوجتَه). ليلى . . . ليلى . . . تَعالي لَحظة.

سوريا
البحر الأبيض المتوسط
بيروت
زحلة
صيدا
سوريا
صور
فلسطين

نَبيل خوري وزوجته ليلى وابنه غسّان وابنته فَرَح

تَتَقَدَّم نَحوَ المُراسِلة والرَجُل سَيِّدةٌ شابةٌ جَميلةٌ تَرتَدي مَلابِس أنيقة ومَعَها بنت وصَبيّ.

المُراسِلة: مُمكِن أن نَتَعَرَّف عليك؟

السَيِّدة: بِكُلِّ سُرور. اسمي ليلى وهذه ابنَتي فَرَح وهذا ابني غَسّان.

المُراسِلة: أهلاً بِكُم. (تَقتَرِب من الفَتاة الصَغيرة). كَم عُمرُكِ؟

البِنت: سَبْع سْنين (بالنطق العامي)

المُراسِلة: (تُخاطِب الصَبيّ) وأنت؟

الصَبيّ: تسْع سْنين وبعد شهرين بْصير عَشْر سْنين.

المُراسِلة

المُراسِلة: (تَلتَفِت إلى الأب) ما نَوع عَمَلِك يا سَيِّد نَبيل؟

الرَجُل: عِندي مَطعَم في زَحلة.

المُراسِلة: هل تُقَدِّم الطعام العربيّ أم الغربيّ؟

الرَجُل: في الواقِع نُقَدِّم النوعَين. عِندَنا أطباق لُبنانيّة وأطباق غربيّة، لأنَّ عَدَداً كَبيراً من السُيّاح الأجانب يَزورون المَطعَم.

المُراسِلة: هل تُساعِدك زوجتُكَ في العَمَل؟

الرَجُل: (يَبتَسِم ويَلتَفِت إلى زوجته) . . . قليلاً.

السَيِّدة: (تَبتَسِم أيضاً) في الواقِع لا. أنا رَبة بيت.

المُراسِلة: وهل أنتِ سعيدة في حياتِك هكَذا؟

السَيِّدة: نعم أنا سعيدة جِدّاً مع زوجي وأولادي.
أُحاوِل دائماً أن أجعَل جَوّ البيت مُريحاً لَهُم، وكَذلِكَ أُساعِد غسّان وفَرَح بالدِراسة.

عَلَمُ لُبنان

المُراسِلة: هل تَستَمتِعون بزيارة المعرَض؟

الرَجُل: حَتّى الآن نعم. لكِنَّنا لَمْ نَزُر إلاّ جَناحَين فقط.

المُراسِلة: أرجو لَكُم زيارة سعيدة وأُرَحِّب بِكُم مرّة أخرى بِوَطَنِكُم الثاني سوريّة.

ثلاث فتَيات

تنتَقِل المُراسِلة إلى مَكان آخر من المَعرِض وتُقابِل ثلاثَ فَتَيات إحداهُنّ ترتَدي اللِباس الإسلاميّ.

الفَتاة ١

المُراسِلة:	مَساء الخير.
الفَتَيات:	مَساء النور.
المُراسِلة:	مُمكِن أن نَتَحدَّث معاً على شاشة التلفاز؟
الفَتاة ١:	لا مانع. تَفَضَّلي.
المُراسِلة:	أولاً، مُمكِن أن أعرِف من أين الآنِسات؟
الفَتاة ٢:	نَحنُ من هنا، من الشام.
المُراسِلة:	أهلاً. أهذه أول مرّة تَزُرنَ فيها المَعرِض؟
الفَتاة ٢:	زُرناه عِدّة مرّات في سَنوات سابقة. (تُشير إلى الفَتاة الثالثة) لكِن هذه هي المرّة الأولى بالنسبة لَها.
المُراسِلة:	(تَلتَفِت نَحوَ الفَتاة الثالثة) كيف تَجِدين المَعرِض؟ هل يُعجِبك؟
الفَتاة ٣:	مُعظَم الأجنِحة أعجبَتني، خُصوصاً الجَناح المَغربيّ والجَناح السوريّ من الأجنِحة العَربيّة، والفَرنسيّ من الأجنبيّة.
المُراسِلة:	هل تعملْنَ أم تَدرُسنَ؟
الفَتاة ١:	أنا في السنة الثانية في المَعهَد المُتَوسِّط الهَندَسيّ.
الفَتاة ٢:	أنا في السنة الأولى أدرُس الصَيدلة في جامعة دِمشَق.
المُراسِلة:	(لِلفَتاة الثالثة) وهل تَدرُسين أنتِ أيضاً؟
الفَتاة ٣:	لا. أنا أعمَل في مَصنَع مَلابِس داخِليّة.
المُراسِلة:	يبدو أنّكِ تُفَضِّلين العمل على الدراسة.
الفَتاة ٣:	لا. كنتُ أدرُس المُحاسَبة في كُلّيّة التِجارة، لَكِنّي تَركتُ الدِراسة بسَبَب وَفاة والِدي. كان مُوَظّفاً بَسيطاً ولَم يَترُك لَنا راتِباً كافِياً فكان عليّ أن أعمَل. لكِن حين يَكبُر إخوتي سأعود لِلدِراسة إن شاء الله.
المُراسِلة:	أرجو أن تَتَحقَّق رَغبتُكِ، وأتَمَنّى لكُنَّ زيارة مُمتِعة.

الفَتاة ٢

الفَتاة ٣

بائع العِرْقسوس

بائع العِرْقسوس

كان بائع العِرْقسوس يَحمِل على ظَهرِه وِعاءً مَعدِنيّاً كَبيراً فِضيّ اللون مَملوءاً بِشَراب العِرْقسوس وحول وَسَطِه حِزام خاصّ يَضع فيه كؤوساً فِضيّة ويَحمِل بِيدِه اليُسرى إبريقاً فِضيّاً مَملوءاً بِالماء لِيَغسِل بِه الكؤوس بعد أن يَشرَب بِها الناس.

المُراسِلة: مَرحباً يا أخ.

بائع العِرْقسوس: أهلاً يا أختي.

المُراسِلة: مُمكِن أن أسألَك بعض الأسئلة؟

بائع العِرْقسوس: تَفَضَّلي اسألي. لكن اسمحي لي أولاً أن أُقَدِّم هذه الكأس لِلزَبون.

المُراسِلة: طَبعاً. تَفَضَّل.

بائع العِرْقسوس: (يُقَدِّم الكأس لِلزَبون ثُمَّ يَلتَفِت إلى المُذيعة) أنا الآن تَحتَ أمرِك.

المُراسِلة: العَفو. في المَعرِض ناس كثيرون، عرب وأجانب. مَن منهُم يَشتَري العِرْقسوس؟

بائع العِرْقسوس: غالِباً أبناء العَرب، وأحياناً بعض السُيّاح الأجانب.

المُراسِلة: وهذا الخَزّان الذي تَحمِلُه على ظَهرِك، أهو ثَقيل؟

بائع العِرْقسوس: نعم. ثَقيل جِدّاً. يَتَّسِع وهو مَملوء لأكثر من ثمانين كأساً مع الثلج.

المُراسِلة: كَم تَضع فيه من الثلج؟

بائع العِرْقسوس: أكثر من رُبع الخَزّان لأن العِرْقسوس لا يكون لَذيذاً إلا إذا كان مُثَلَّجاً. (يُعيد الزَبون لَهُ الكأس فارغة يَتَناوَلها منه ويُخاطِبه) صَحَّتين (ينطقُها «صَحْتين»).

المُراسِلة: لا أريد أن آخذ من وقتِك أكثر. شُكراً على هذه المَعلومات.

بائع العِرْقسوس: العفو يا أختي. الله مَعك.

سائحة

تمرين ٣

اكتب «خطأ» أو «صواب» إلى جانب كل جملة ثُمَّ صَحِّح الجُمَل الخطأ:

١- ليلى خوري ربة بيت وتُساعِد ابنها وابنتها بالدراسة.

٢- الفتَيات الثلاث حضرنَ إلى المَعرِض من لُبنان.

٣- تَرتدي المُراسِلة اللِباس الإسلامي.

٤- وفاة والد إحدى الفتَيات جعلَتها تَعود للدراسة.

٥- يبيع بائع العِرْقسوس شَرابَه من دُكّانه.

تمرين ٤

أكمل الجمل الآتية بالاختيار المناسب وفق نص القراءة:

١- أجرَت المُراسِلة المُقابِلات في ______________ .

☐ الجَناح المَغربيّ ☐ الجَناح السوري ☐ لُبنان ☐ المَعرِض

٢- تعمل المُراسِلة في ______________ .

☐ المَعرِض ☐ التلفاز ☐ الإذاعة ☐ الجريدة

٣- حضرَت عائلة الخوري من لُبنان ______________ .

☐ بالسيّارة ☐ بالطائرة ☐ بالحافلة ☐ بالقِطار

٤- تُشارِك في مَعرِض دِمشَق ______________ .

☐ دُوَل عربيّة ☐ دُوَل أجنبيّة ☐ دُوَل أوروبيّة ☐ دُوَل عَربيّة وأجنبيّة

٥- تَرتَدي ليلى خوري مَلابِس ______________ .

☐ إسلاميّة ☐ لُبنانيّة ☐ أنيقة ☐ رَخيصة

٦- الفَتاة الثالثة أعجبها الجَناح ______________ .

☐ المَغربيّ ☐ اللُبناني ☐ الأجنبيّ ☐ الأوروبيّ

٧- تعمَل إحدى الفتَيات في مَصنَع لِلمَلابِس ______________ .

☐ الإسلاميّة ☐ الداخِليّة ☐ الأنيقة ☐ العَربيّة

٨- يَحمَل بائع العِرْقسوس على ظَهْرِه ______________ .

☐ ثلجاً ☐ إبريقاً ☐ خزّاناً ☐ زَبوناً

تمرين ٥

أجب عن الأسئلة الآتية وفق نصّ القراءة:

١- ما الفكرة الرئيسة في نص القراءة؟

٢- حَدِّد بعض الأفكار الثانوية.

٣- اكتُبْ عنواناً آخر لهذا الدرس.

٤- متى يُقام مَعرِض دِمشَق الدَولِيّ؟

٥- كَم شخصاً قابَلَت المُراسِلة أمام دُكّان بائع المُثَلَّجات؟

٦- ما عَمَل نَبيل خوري؟

٧- لِماذا لَم يَترُك والد الفَتاة لأسرتِه راتِباً جيِّداً؟

٨- ماذا يَحمَل بائع العِرْقسوس بيدِه؟ لِماذا يَحمَله؟

تمرين ٦

أعد ترتيب الكلمات في كل مجموعة لتشكّل جملاً مُفيدةً:

١	لِلدِراسة	مُريح	المَكتبة	جَوّ			
٢	الإسلاميّ	هَنادي	اللِباس	تَرتَدي	فَتاة		
٣	بِكُلِّ	قامَت	سُرور	بِعملِها	الفَتاة		
٤	الماء	مُثَلَّجاً	أشرَب	إلا	لا		
٥	إلى	ابنه	الأب	نادى	البيت	لِلدُخول	
٦	فَرَنسيّ	المُذيعةُ	مع	أجرَت	سائِح	مُقابَلَةً	
٧	مِن	وأجنبيَة	يَزور	عَربيّة	بِلادٌ	المَعرِض	سُيّاح

تمرين ٧

Speaking: In groups of two: describe a fair or exhibition you went to or a trip you made to an amusement park. Explain what you did while you were there in some detail, what you saw, who you were with, what you liked and didn't like, what the weather was like, and so forth.

Be sure to record all of the information that you get from your partner. Now, for homework, write the story your classmate described to you.

تمرين ٨

هذه المُقابَلة أجراها مُراسِلٌ صَحَفيّ مع فَتاةٍ جامعيّة. تَصوَّر (imagine) أنك تِلكَ الفَتاة واكتُب إجابات الفَتاة عن أسئلة المُراسِل:

المُراسِل: مَرحباً يا آنِسة.

الفَتاة: ____.

المُراسِل: أنا صَحَفيّ أُجري اليوم مُقابَلات مع طُلّاب وطالِبات من الجامعة. مُمكِن أن أتحدّث معكِ؟

الفَتاة: ____.

المُراسِل: ماذا تدرُسين في الجامعة؟

الفَتاة: ____.

المُراسِل: لماذا اِختَرتِ هذا التَخَصُّص؟

الفَتاة: ____.

المُراسِل: ماذا تُريدين أن تَفعلي بعد التَخَرُّج؟

الفَتاة: ____.

المُراسِل: أتعجبك هذه الجامعة؟

الفَتاة: ____.

المُراسِل: لماذا؟

الفَتاة: ____.

المُراسِل: شكراً على سماحك بالمُقابَلة.

الفَتاة: ____.

تمرين ٩

أعد ترتيب الجمل لتُشكِّل فقرة كاملة. الجملة الأولى في مكانها المُناسِب:

١- أخبَرَني صَديقي أن هناك مَعرِضاً لصوَرٍ من البحرين.

بعض الصوَر كانت عن قَرية أثريّة يَبلُغ عُمرُها أكثر من ألفَي (٢٠٠٠) سنة.

أعجبتنا الصوَر كثيراً وتمنّينا لو نذهب إلى البحرين لرؤية تِلكَ القَرية.

وسيُقام هذا المَعرِض في المتحف الوطنيّ بِحَلَب ويبدأ في ١ أيلول.

كما يظهَر في الصوَر أيضاً المكان الذي كان يُخزَّن فيه البَلَح (dates).

في الأول من أيلول ذهبت إلى المَعرِض مع صَديقَيَّ حسام وهِشام.

يظهَر في تِلكَ الصوَر هندسة البيوت في القَرية.

وكان في المَعرِض أكثر من ١٥٠ صورة من تاريخ البحرين القَديم.

تمرين ١٠

للكتابة: تَصوَّر أنك صَحَفيّ تعمل في جريدة أو مَجلّة، أو أنك مُذيع تُقابل شَخصيّات مَشهورة في بَرنامَجك الإذاعي أو التلفزيوني. أجْرِ مُقابَلة مع شَخصيّة عَربيّة أو أمريكيّة (رَجُل أو امرأة) حقيقيّة (real) أو غير حقيقيّة واحصل على مَعلومات عن حياة ذلكَ الشَخص والمَكان الذي يعيش فيه وماذا يعمل وما يُحِبّ ولا يُحِبّ من طعامٍ وشراب وهِواياتِه وأشيائه المُفَضَّلة وإن كان مُتَزوّجاً وإلى أي البِلاد سافَر، وغير ذلِكَ من المَعلومات.

1. Useful Communicative Phrases

a. Terms of Address

You may have noticed that the terms أخ وأخت that we learned in lesson four of this book were used in practice as يا أخ ويا أُخت in the dialogue between the reporter and the beverage vendor. أخ وأُخت are frequently used to address people who know one another well and strangers in writing and in speech.

b. Asking about Someone's Name

When people are asked to introduce themselves formally, the request is usually done in an indirect manner. It was in this vein that the reporter asked her questions, never using the phrase «ما اسمك؟»

Your name? (lit. Your honorable name?)	الاسم الكَريم؟	١
Could we make your acquaintance?	مُمكِن أنْ نَتَعَرَّفَ علَيك؟	٢

c. Calling Someone Over

The imperative word تعالَ is used to ask someone over. While it functions like a verb in the imperative, it really only exists in the imperative.

Come here!	*(m.s.)*	تعالَ	٣
	(f.s.)	تعالي	
	(dual)	تعالا	
	(m.,pl.)	تعالوا	

d. Social Niceties

Expressions used to convey appreciation, compliance, thanks, and approval fall into this category.

Do you have any objection . . . not at all.	هَل عِندَكَ مانِع . . . لا أبداً.	٤
With pleasure.	بِكُلِّ سُرور.	
I would like to welcome you to your new home.	أُرَحِّبُ بِكُم بِوَطَنِكُم الثاني.	
No objection. Go ahead.	لا مانِع. تَفَضَّلي.	
I hope that your desire is fulfilled.	أرجو أن تَتَحَقَّق رَغبَتُك.	
I hope that you have a wonderful visit.	أتَمَنّى لَكُنَّ زِيارةً مُمتِعة.	
At your command; at your service.	تَحتَ أمْرِكَ.	

e. Making Polite Requests and Responses

If you would like to ask someone's permission for something, you could use:

May I . . .; Allow me to . . .	اِسْمَحْ لي . . .	٥
Is it possible . . .?	مُمكِن . . .؟	٦

مُمكِن is taken from the prepositional phrase مِن المُمكِن (= *it is possible*) and, in speech, can be used by itself to ask permission as long as the context is clear. For example, if someone wants to borrow a pen that is lying on a desk and one points to it, the word مُمكِن with a rising intonation signifies the desire to use the pen.

In writing, the word مُمكِن should be followed with أنْ, whereas in casual speech, the أنْ can be dropped.

May I use the pen? (formal)	مُمكِن أنْ أستعمِلَ القَلَم؟	٧
May I use the pen? (informal)	مُمكِن أستعمِل القَلَم؟	٨

The response to such a request, in the affirmative, could be:

Go ahead! (Take it).	تَفَضَّل.	٩
With pleasure.	بِكُلِّ سُرور.	١٠
Certainly; of course; naturally.	طَبْعاً.	١١
No objection (no problem).	لا مانِع.	١٢

The word تَفَضَّل (ex. 8) is a verb in the imperative whose meaning is context sensitive. It has multiple meanings such as *go ahead*; *please*; *by your leave*; *after you*. Example 10, interestingly, comes from the word طَبْع (*nature*), so طَبْعاً literally means *naturally*, but can also signify *sure*, and *of course*.

Example 11 involves a grammatical structure known as لا النافية لِلجِنْس or the لا that negates an entire class, or genus, of something (i.e., absolute negation). Note that the word that it negates is *a noun*, and not *a verb*. This structure should be very familiar to you, since it is used in the شَهادة:

١٣	لا إلهَ إلاّ الله	*There is no deity except God.*

مُلاحَظة

Because لا النافية لِلجِنْس negates the entire class of a noun, it cannot be used with numbers or names, for these specify members of a class, not the entire class.

genus negates

there is no things

تمرين ١١

اِختَر أفضَل إجابة:

١- مُمكِن أن أستعملَ الهاتف؟

☐ العَفو ☐ طَبْعاً ☐ شكراً

٢- إنَّ عَمَلَك هذا مُمتاز!

☐ شكراً ☐ عَفواً ☐ طَبْعاً

٣- أنا تَحتَ أمرِك الآن.

☐ العَفو ☐ إن شاء الله ☐ تَفَضَّل

٤- أعِندك مانع أن نَتَحَدَّث قليلاً؟

☐ لا أبداً ☐ الحَمدُ لله ☐ الله مَعَك

٥- أسَعيدة أنتِ في حياتِك؟

☐ الحَمْدُ لله ☐ العَفو ☐ شكراً

٦- هل ستأتين غَداً إلى العَمَل؟

☐ لا مانع ☐ لا أبداً ☐ إن شاء الله

تمرين ١٢

للمُحادثة: تَصوَّر أنّك مُمثِّل أو مغنٍ مَشهور (أمريكيّ أو عَرَبيّ) ويجب على زميلك أن يُخمّنَ (guess) اسمَكَ دون أن يسألَ السؤالين التاليين: ما اسمك؟ ومَن أنت؟ قد تساعدك الأسئلة الآتية:

١- هل يعيش الآن؟

٢- كم مَدينة سكن في حياته، وأين؟

٣- ماذا عَمِلَ أو يعمل وأين؟

٤- كَمْ عُمُرُه؟

٥- كَمْ أخاً لَه؟

٦- ماذا فعل في حياته؟

القواعد

2. Inquiring about Number and Quantity with كَم

In statements كَم means *many*; *much*, and in questions *how many*; *how much*. In questions, كَمْ is followed by a noun in the singular—unlike English which uses a plural.

Memorize This Formula

كَمْ + singular noun اً

How many siblings do have?		كَمْ أخاً لَكَ؟	
How many children do you have?		كَمْ وَلَداً لَدَيْكِ؟	١
How many books do you want?		كَمْ كِتاباً تُريد؟	

The most difficult aspect of this formula for Americans is in using singular nouns after the question phrase: *How many*?, which, invariably in English will be followed by a plural. So, it may sound to your ear as if you are asking, "How many student are in the room?"—but this is the proper form in Arabic.

a. كَمْ in the إضافة

كَمْ can also be followed by an إضافة, the first noun is in المَرفوع (it takes a ضمة).

How old are you?	كَمْ عُمُرُكِ؟	٢
How old is your son?	كَمْ عُمُرُ ابنِكَ؟	

b. كَمْ in a Prepositional Phrase

كَمْ is modified by the preposition بِـ when asking for a price.

How much is this?	بِكَمْ هذا؟	٣

c. كَمْ When Used with Uncountable Nouns

Uncountable nouns are those nouns that you cannot hold in your hands to count, like air, liquids, time, etc. In order to inquire about how much someone had to drink or how long someone has spent in a particular place, use the structure:

Uncountable Noun Structure

How much coffee did you drink?	كَمْ مِن القَهوةِ شَرِبتِ؟	٤
How long have you been here?	كَمْ مِن الوَقْتِ بَقيتِ هُنا؟	

تمرين ١٣

للمُحادثة: اِسأل زملاءك في غرفة الصف الأسئلة الآتية مُستخدماً "كَمْ" في السؤال. سَجِّل أجوبة الطُلاب الآخرين لِتُخبرَ الأستاذ بِما عَلِمت.

1. How old they are.
2. How many brothers and sisters they have.
3. How much they paid for something.
4. How long they have been in this city.
5. How old their car is.
6. How much sugar they put in their coffee.

3. Expressing Obligation with the Preposition على

In order to say '*have to*' we use the formulas: (على + أنْ + المُضارِع) or (المَصدَر + على):

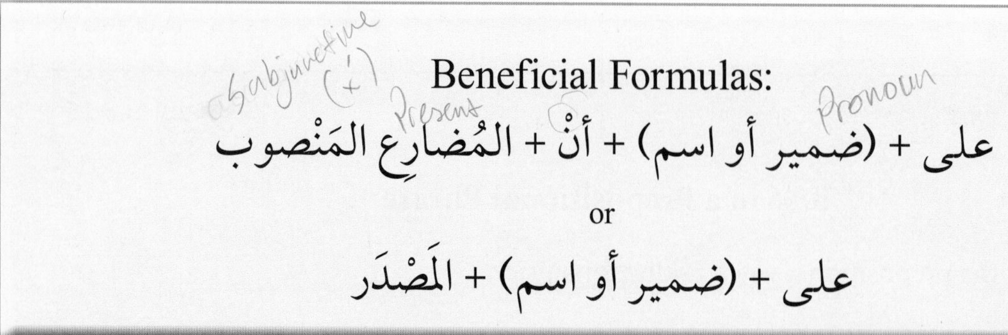

Beneficial Formulas:

على + (ضمير أو اسم) + أنْ + المُضارِع المَنْصوب

or

على + (ضمير أو اسم) + المَصْدَر

I have to speak with you.	عَلَيَّ أنْ أتَكَلَّمَ مَعَكِ.	١
You have to work.	عَلَيكَ أنْ تَعمَل.	

She has to write a letter.	عَلَيها كِتابةُ رِسالةٍ.	٢
He has to wash his car.	عَلَيهِ غَسْلُ سَيّارته.	

How would you say '*had to*'? All you have to do is place كانَ before عَلى:

I had to speak with you.	كانَ عَلَيَّ أنْ أتَكَلَّمَ مَعَكِ.	٣
You had to work.	كانَ عَلَيكَ أنْ تَعمَل.	

تمرين ١٤

Express obligation using prepositional phrases with على:

1. I have to go to the bathroom.
2. Cleaning the apartment is on you.
3. I have to do my homework.
4. We had to wait for them for an hour.

4. Forming Yes/No Questions with أ

a. Prefixed to Nouns, Pronouns, Verbs, and Particles

The most common usage of أ is when you would like to form yes/no questions. This interrogative particle does not affect its modified word structurally in any way.

Is your car Japanese ?(noun)	أسَيّارتُكَ يابانيّةٌ؟	١
Is she your friend? (pronoun)	أهِيَ صَديقتُكِ؟	٢
Do you see that tree? (verb)	أتَرَيْنَ تِلكَ الشَّجَرة؟	٣
Didn't I tell you that he isn't in his office? (particle)	ألَمْ أقُلْ لَكِ إنَّه ليسَ في مَكتَبِه؟	٤

Difference between هَلْ / أ

هَلْ is used exclusively for affirmative statements (ex. 5)

أ is used with affirmative and negative statements (ex. 6)

Do you write with your right or left hand? (affirmative statement)	هَلْ تَكتُبُ بِيَديكَ اليُمنى أم اليُسرى؟	٥
Don't you write with your right hand? (negative statement)	ألا تَكتُبُ بِيدِكَ اليُمنى؟	٦

b. Use of أ in Reprimanding, Expressing Sarcasm, and Wonder

You're going out with that girl while you are married?	أتَخرُجُ مَعَ تِلكَ الفَتاةِ وأنتَ مُتَزَوِّج؟	٧
Don't you see his face? (i.e., he's ugly)	ألا تَرى وَجهَه؟	٨
He walks to work when he has a car?	أيَمشي إلى عَمَلِه وعندَهُ سيّارة؟	٩

c. The Particle That Means 'or' أوْ / أم

Choosing between أوْ and أمْ

أوْ is used for affirmative statements (ex. 10)

أمْ is used with questions (ex. 11)

I write with my right or left hand.	أكتُبُ بيدي اليُمنى أوْ باليُسرى.	١٠
Do you write with your right or left hand?	أبِيدِكِ اليُمنى تكتُبينَ أمْ بِاليُسرى؟	١١

تمرين ١٥

Use أ to express the following sentences in Arabic:

1. Do you walk to school?
2. You're late for your own graduation party حَفلة!
3. Is that your teacher?
4. Didn't he say that we should be there at three o'clock?
5. Did she study political science or international studies?
6. Do you watch TV during finals' week?

مُراجَعة القَواعِد

5. Exception with إلاّ

In affirmative statements the noun that follows إلاّ is مَنصوب.

I saw all of the pavilions except two.	شاهَدتُ كُلَّ الأجْنِحةِ إلاّ جَناحَيْنِ.	١
Hala read the book, save one page.	قرأَتْ هالة الكِتابَ إلاّ صَفحةً.	

When the statement is either negative or interrogative, the case of the noun after إلاّ is context dependent—meaning it strictly follows the natural rules of syntax. Examples of nouns whose case depends on context follow:

a. As Direct Object of a Verb مَنصوب

I drink nothing but water with food.	لا أشرَبُ إلاّ الماءَ مَعَ الطَعام.	٢
I will only sleep an hour.	لَنْ أنامَ إلاّ ساعةً.	

b. As the Subject of the Sentence مَرفوع

You have only this letter to write.	ما عَلَيكَ إلاّ كِتابةُ هذه الرِسالةِ.	٣

c. As Adverbial (حال) مَنصوب

I haven't seen her, except walking = I have always seen her walking.	لَمْ أرَها إلاّ ماشيةً.	٤

d. In a Question مَرفوع

Isn't his name the same as his father's?	هَلْ اِسمُهُ إلاّ مِثلُ اِسمِ أبيه؟	٥

The words that follow إلاّ do not necessarily have to be nouns. Verbs as well as particles can be modified by إلاّ, as you can see in examples 6 and 7.

I never spoke with him one time without him stating, "I'm busy."	ما تَكَلّمتُ مَعَهُ مَرّةً إلاّ قالَ "إنّي مَشغول".	٦
There is no student here who does not have a computer.	ما مِن طالِبٍ هُنا إلاّ لَدَيهِ حاسوب.	٧

تمرين ١٦

Use إلا to express the following sentences in Arabic:

1. I don't go to the movies except with my friends.
2. All the students have arrived except for one.
3. Your wife is nothing but your friend.
4. Every time we stayed by the sea, we went swimming.
5. All the ladies in this photo have dogs with them except one.
6. Every time I call her, her son answers the telephone.

6. Passive Voice (*Refer to AwS I, Lesson 15 pp. 292-295*)

In order to reacquaint ourselves with the passive voice, let's take a sentence in the active voice (example 1) and make it passive to understand what is involved in this process.

The state holds the fair every summer.	١ تُقيمُ الدَولةُ المَعرِضَ كُلَّ صَيفٍ.

The agent of example 1 is الدَولة since it is the entity that is doing the action. As you can see, الدَولةُ is مَرفوع indicating that it is the subject of the sentence. The object that receives the action of the verb المَعرِضَ is مَنصوب being that it is the direct object of the verb. Let's now change that sentence into passive voice.

The fair is held every summer.	٢ يُقامُ المَعرِضُ كُلَّ صَيفٍ.

What has happened is المَعرِضُ has now become the subject of the sentence, thus it is مَرفوع. Additionally, the verb has undergone internal morphological changes, and to understand how to make those changes, we need to take a close look at creating passive verbs.

A passive verb is formed by making certain internal vowel changes. Examine the verbs in the table below in الماضي والمُضارِع, in active مَعلوم and passive مَجهول voices. All verbs in the table are Form I, but these changes can be applied to all forms II – X using the formula given in parentheses in the مَجهول column.

المُضارِع				الماضي			
مَجهول		مَعلوم		مَجهول		مَعلوم	
(ُ + َ)	يُكتَب	(َ + ُ)	يَكتُب	(ُ + ِ)	كُتِب	(َ + َ)	كَتَب
(ُ + َ)	يُشرَب	(َ + َ)	يَشرَب	(ُ + ِ)	شُرِب	(َ + ِ)	شَرِب
(ُ + ا)	يُقال	(َ + و)	يَقول	(ي)	قيل	(ا)	قال
(ُ + ى)	يُسَمّى	(ُ + ي)	يُسَمّي	(ُ + ِ + يَ)	سُمِّيَ	(َ + ى)	سَمّى

تمرين ١٧

اجعلْ هذه الأفعال مبينة لِلمَجهول مَعَ الشكْل كما في المثِال:

مِثال قَطَّعَتْ ⇐ قُطِّعَتْ

١- قابَلَت ______________________

٢- أقامَ ______________________

٣- رَأى ______________________

٤- أحضَروا ______________________

٥- اِستَعْمَلَ ______________________

7. Adverbs of Time ظَرْف الزَمان

The Arabic term ظَرْف literally means *container* or *vessel*, because—metaphorically speaking— it *contains time*. Adverbs of time and place are مَنصوب because they are considered to be direct objects of verbs. In order for a noun to be considered an adverb, it should describe an action or event.

١	حَضَرتُ صَباحَ اليَومِ.	*I came this morning.*

The action حَضَر, in example ١, occurred in the morning of that particular day, thus صَباحَ is مَنصوب. However, if the time of day does not modify (i.e., describe) the verb, then it is treated as a regular noun with its case determined by the context.

٢	أتى الصَباحُ.	*The morning came.*

Types of Adverbs of Time

1. Indeclinable: the adverb is مَنصوب (e.g., حينَ، وَقْتَ، الآنَ، اليَومَ، غَداً، صَباحاً).

2. Declinable: the case marker is determined by context (ex. 2).

Substitutes for Adverbs of Time

a. Demonstratives اسم الإشارة

These are particles that *demonstrate* or *indicate* something and function as adverbs when followed by ظَرف الزمان.

Salma arrived today.	وَصَلَت سَلمى هذا اليَومَ.	٣

b. Verbal Nouns المَصدَر

The مَصدَر must refer to time or duration and must form an إضافة structure with ظرف الزَمان (i.e., it must be مُضاف إليه). The adverb is dropped, since it is understood (وَقتَ). This usage is rare in MSA.

We arrived in town at sunrise.	وَصَلنا المَدينةَ طُلوعَ الشَمسِ.	٤

Example 4 can be understood as:

We arrived in town at the time of sunrise.	وَصَلنا المَدينةَ وقتَ طُلوعِ الشَمسِ.	٥

c. Quantifiers

Words that refer to part or all of an entity comprise this category. Selected examples of quantifiers are:

كُلّ، جَميع، بعض، بِضع، رُبع، ثُلث، نِصْف

Quantifiers function as مُضاف and the adverb that follows as مُضاف إليه.

I walked for the entire day.	مَشَيتُ كُلَّ النَهارِ.	٦

d. Numbers

Like quantifiers and مَصدَر, numbers must be مُضاف and the adverb of time مُضاف إليه.

The fair will go on for three weeks.	يَستَمِرُّ المَعرِضُ ثلاثةَ أسابيعَ.	٧

تمرين ١٨

Use adverbs of time to convey the following meanings in Arabic. Provide inflectional endings to indicate case:

1. Do you walk to school?
2. You're late for your own graduation party حَفلة!
3. Is that your teacher?
4. Didn't he say that we should be there at three o'clock?
5. Did she study political science or international studies?
6. Do you watch TV during finals' week?

8. Register مُستوى لُغويّ

Register can be defined as mixing two codes or varieties. For everyday communication, speakers of Arabic use a colloquial variety known as dialect. Formal situations and school instruction in which oral interaction is required are carried out in MSA الفُصحى. Few speakers of Arabic, however, can maintain constant discourse in the standard variety. Most tend to mix elements from their local colloquial variety (their mother tongue) with standard elements learned at school.

Radio and television interviews (like those presented in this lesson) tend to have a high percentage of standard pronunciation/lexicon/structure. Some speakers can sustain performance in MSA for an extended period of time, and most try to use as much of the standard register as possible in formal settings, but they may lapse into colloquial usage. These lapses may be either in the form of outright use of colloquial words, morphology, or syntax or in the form of dropping inflectional endings.

a. When to Use Colloquial Elements

In the reading passage, the reporter uses the colloquial word for chat دَردَش. Its use may be acceptable in this context because the interaction is oral and rather informal. The verb دَردَش is quite frequently used in such situations. The boy uses colloquial morphology when he prefixes the indicative بـ marker to the present tense verb (ex. 1).

١	بَعد شَهرَين بْصير عشر سنين.	*In two months, I will be ten.*

The verb بْصير is used instead of the standard أصيرُ. The indicative بـ prefix is common to several Arabic dialects. It is prefixed to all indicative forms المُضارِع المَرْفوع. Examples are given for present tense first person:

مَشى ← بِمشي | راح ← بْروح | شَرِبَ ← بِشْرَب

b. When to Drop Inflectional (Case) Endings

One challenging aspect of using MSA orally is the correct use of inflectional endings. These endings mark the cases of nouns and adjectives and the moods of verbs. Only those highly educated in Arabic can master the use of declensional endings; they are, however, mostly markers of accuracy, not of meaning.

Therefore, many educated Arabic speakers drop these endings in speech that is not highly formal, such as interviews. Compare these two versions (examples 1 & 2) of the same sentence from the reading passage, paying attention to the voweling on the word endings.

٢	أنا في السَنَةِ الثانِيَةِ في المَعهَدِ المُتَوَسِّطِ الهَندَسيِّ.	الفُصحى
٣	أنا في السَنَة الثانية في المَعهَد المُتَوَسِّط الهَندَسي.	لُغة المثقَّفين

The first line (ex. 2), when pronounced with all the diacritics, is grammatically accurate and complete; the second line (ex. 3), with the endings dropped, represents how most people would actually say the sentence in a situation that calls for the use of MSA but is not formal enough to warrant full inflection. You may notice that the internal vowels remain the same in examples 2 and 3, while the inflectional endings disappear (ex. 3) in something that is known as pausal form.

It warrants mentioning that the internal vowels do change in certain communicative phrases, such as the one that occurred in our main reading passage:

اللهُ مَعَكِ. ⇐ الله مَعِك.

Notice that the final كسرة of كِ has changed its position and has now become attached to مَع. This is how gender is denoted when dealing with all pronominal suffixes in Arabic varieties.

How do you think you would say the above phrase to a man?

اللهُ مَعَكَ. ⇐ الله مَعَك.

Notice that the final فتحة of كَ has changed position to grace the end of مَعَ.

When the seller also wishes his customer good health, he uses pausal form:

العالمية	الفُصحى
صَحْتين	صَحَّتَيْن

A well-known Arabic saying speaks to the virtues of dropping endings to avoid committing grammatical errors:

٦ سَكِّنْ تَسلَمْ.	*Use a* سكون *and you will be safe (grammatically).*

Nonetheless, those who use Arabic accurately are greatly admired. Sometimes, people try to show the level of their education by the amount of endings integrated into their speech, particularly when they are in a formal situation such as being in front of the camera or on the radio.

تَذَوّق الثَقافَة العَرَبيَّة

ملاحظات في المفردات والكنية

The word أواسِط is the plural of وَسَط meaning *middle*. Let's take a look at this structure in context taken from our main reading passage:

وهو مَعرِض تِجاريّ وصِناعيّ يُقام كُلّ سنة في أواسِطِ الصيف.

In this context, the plural denotes the middle few days/weeks of summer. Similar structures are used to mean the first few of s.th.أوائل (from أوّل) and the last few of s.th. أواخِر (from آخِر).

In the interview with العِرقسوس, the vender uses the expression أبناء العرب (literally "sons of Arabs"). Functionally, however, this phrase simply means *Arabs*. People, especially expatriates, may refer to a woman as بنت عَرَب and to a man as ابن عَرَب meaning that they are Arab.

The family name خوري is quite common in Greater Syria بِلاد الشام among Christians. It means *priest, cleric,* or *minister*. Families bearing this name may not be blood related. One of the most famous of the الخوري is a man by the name of فارس الخوري, who was a writer, statesman, lawyer, and the Prime Minister of Syria. Try to infer the meanings of the underlined words in this short biography about him on the following page:

فارس الخوري سياسي وأديب سوري. وُلِدَ في بلدة الكْفير سنة ١٨٧٧ وتُوفِّيَ في دِمشقَ عامَ ١٩٦٢. عُضوُ المَجمَع العِلميّ بِدِمشَق. صار رئيساً لمجلس النوّاب السوريّ ورئيساً للوزارة عدّة مرّات. شاركَ في وضع الدُستور السوري ومثّلَ سوريّة في هَيئة الأمم المُتّحِدة عامَ ١٩٤٥ كعُضو مؤسِّس.

تمرين ١٩

آ املأ الفراغات الآتية حسب نص الاستماع:

- ممكن أن تقدّمي نفسك؟
- اسمي زينا نِعمة أنا من عَمّان في الأردن لي ثلاثة إخوة لكن ليس لي أخت.
- ماذا تفعلين هنا في الولايات المتحدة؟
- أدرس الموارِدَ البشرية.
- لماذا اخترت هذا ___________؟
- أحب أن أتعامل مع الناس بشكل عام و___________هم.
- ماذا ستفعلين بعد تخرُّجِك؟
- أحب أن أعملَ في ___________ أجنبية في عمّان.
- أأنت وحدك هنا؟
- أخي معي وهو يدرس المحاسبة.
- أتعجبك ___________ في أمريكا بصورة عامة؟
- نعم، كل شيء يبدو سهلاً وأناس يحبون أن يساعدوك.
- ما الشيء الذي ___________ أكثر من سواه؟
- النظامُ واحترامُ الإنسانِ وحقوقِه.
- وما الشيء الذي لا ___________؟
- عدم الاهتمام بما يجري في العالم والاهتمام فقط بالأمور العادية كالرياضة مثلاً.
- ماذا ___________ في الشهور القليلة المقبلة؟
- ___________ أن أتخرّج في الوقت المحدّد وأن أبدأ العمل مباشرةً. وأتمنّى أيضاً أن ___________ وأنجب أولاداً كثيرين وأن أتابع دراستي للحصول على شهادة الدكتوراه وأن أزور عدة بلاد.
- كيف ___________ الناس إلى المرأة العربية في الغرب؟

- يظن كثيرون إنها غير متعلِّمة وخادمة للزوج ولا تخرُج من بيتها. هذه صورة غير صحيحة أبداً هناك ______ و______ و______ والأستاذات الجامعيات والقاضيات والسياسيات وهناك نساء في الأعمال التجارية بل إن هناك وزيرات في الحكومة كما في سورية وبعض البلاد العربية الأخرى.
- وما هي ______؟
- القراءة والرياضات ومشاهدة الأفلام السينمائية.
- ما لونك ______؟
- البنفسجي.
- ما مدينتك ______؟
- روما.
- هل زرتها ولماذا تفضّلينها؟
- نعم، زرتها منذ عامين وأحبها لأنها جميلة ومليئة بالتاريخ وكأنها مُتحفٌ كبير.
- وما طعامك المفضَّل؟
- ______ وأحبّها كثيراً.
- شكراً على ______ وأتمنّى لك حياة ناجحة سعيدة.

ب- أكمل الجمل الآتية بالاخيار المناسب وفق نص الاستماع:

١- يُعجب زينا في الوِلايات المُتّحِدة ______.

☐ النِظام ☐ الطعام ☐ الرياضة ☐ الدِراسة

٢- تَدرُس زينا في الوِلايات المُتحِدة ______.

☐ عِلم الاجتِماع ☐ عِلم الحاسوب ☐ المَوارِد البَشَريّة ☐التِجارة والمُحاسبة

٣- يَنظُر الغَرْب إلى المرأة العربيّة على أنّها ______.

☐ سياسيّة ☐ وزيرة ☐ طَبيبة ☐ ربّة بيت

٤- مِن هِوايات زينا ______.

☐ القِراءة ☐ الدِراسة ☐ السِباحة ☐ المُراسَلة

ج- لَخِّص المُقابَلة مع زينا بحوالي خمسين كَلِمة.

المُفْرَدات

هَلْ				أ
to smile	(v.)	اِبْتِسام	(يَبْتَسِمُ)	اِبْتَسَمَ
to perform, to conduct, to do	(v.)	إجْراء	(يُجْري)	أجرى
to wear	(v.)	اِرْتِداء	(يَرْتَدي)	اِرْتَدى
to point, to indicate, to allude	(v.)	إشارة	(يُشيرُ)	أشارَ
to set up, to found, to convene	(v.)	إقامة	(يُقيمُ)	أقامَ
to approach, to come close, to draw near	(v.)	اِقْتِراب	(يَقْتَرِبُ)	اِقْتَرَبَ
to turn, to pay attention	(v.)	اِلْتِفات	(يَلْتَفِتُ)	اِلْتَفَتَ
a command, an order	(n., m.)	أوامِر	ج	أمْر
neat, elegant	(adj.)			أنيق
left (in terms of direction)	(adj. f.)	يُسْرى	(adj. m.)	أيْسر
to talk to, to speak	(v.)	تَحَدُّث	(يَتَحَدَّثُ)	تَحَدَّثَ
Come here!	(imp.)			تَعالَ
heavy, burdensome, unpleasant	(adj.)	ثُقَلاء	ج	ثَقيل
pavilion, wing	(n., m.)	أجْنِحة	ج	جَناح
to make	(v.)	جَعْل	(يَجْعَلُ)	جَعَلَ

جَوّ	ج	أجْواء	(n., m.)	atmosphere, weather, ambience
حاوَلَ	(يُحاوِلُ)	مُحاوَلة	(v.)	to try, to attempt
حِزام	ج	أحْزِمة	(n., m.)	belt
حَلْقة	ج	حَلَقات	(n., f.)	episode (of a series), link
خاطَبَ	(يُخاطِبُ)	مُخاطَبة	(v.)	to address, to deliver a sermon
داخِل			(act. p.)	inner, inside, interior
دَرْدَشَ	(يُدَرْدِشُ)	دَرْدَشة	(v.)	to chat (colloquial)
دَوْلة	ج	دُوَل	(n., f.)	country, state
راتِب	ج	رَواتِب	(n., m.)	salary
زائر	ج	زُوّار	(act. p.)	visitor
زَبون	ج	زَبائن	(n., m.)	customer, client
سابِق			(act. p.)	former, previous
سائح	ج	سُيّاح / سائحون	(act. p.)	tourist
سَمَحَ	(يَسْمَحُ)	سَماح	(v.)	to allow, to permit
شارَكَ	(يُشارِكُ)	مُشارَكة	(v.)	to participate
صَبِيّ	ج	صِبْية / صِبْيان	(n., m.)	boy
ظَهْر	ج	ظُهور	(n., m.)	back
عَرَضَ	(يَعْرِضُ)	عَرْض	(v.)	to show, to display

licorice root	(n., m.)			عِرْقسوس
to interview, to meet	(v.)	مُقابَلة	(يُقابِلُ)	قابَلَ
generous, honorable	(adj.)	كُرماء / كِرام	ج	كَريم
moment, instant	(n., f.)	لَحَظات	ج	لَحْظة
objection, obstacle, obstruction	(act. p.)	مَوانِع	ج	مانِع
chilled food products; ice cream	(act. p.)	مُثَلَّجات	ج	مُثَلَّج
field, area of specialization	(n., m.)	مَجالات	ج	مَجال
adjacent, neighboring	(act. p.)			مُجاوِر
correspondent, reporter	(act. p.)	مُراسِلون	ج	مُراسِل
comfortable (to give comfort)	(act. p.)			مُريح
exhibition, fair, show	(n., m.)	مَعارِض	ج	مَعْرِض
institution, institute, academy	(n., m.)	مَعاهِد	ج	مَعْهَد
enjoyable, pleasant, interesting	(adj.)			مُمْتِع
full	(adj.)			مَمْلوء
possible	(adj.)			مُمْكِن
to call, to cry out, to shout	(v.)	مُناداة	(يُنادي)	نادى
relationship	(n., f.)	نِسَب	ج	نِسبة

concerning, with regard to				بالنِسبة لِـ
like this, so, thus	(dem.)			هكَذا (هاكَذا)
waist, middle, surroundings	(n., m.)	أوْساط	ج	وَسَط
death	(n., f.)	وَفَيات	ج	وَفاة

الدَرْسُ السادِس

Objectives

- Learning how to describe professions and places
- Reinforcing the ability to use all time frames
- **Grammar**: Introducing the circumstantial adverb الحال
- **Revisiting**: The nominal sentence, كان and its set, the subjunctive, the adverb of time, diptotes, the passive participle, passive voice, and multiple إضافة

رُكنُ المُفْرَداتِ الجَديدةِ

to take (time)	اِسْتَغْرَقَ (يَسْتَغْرِقُ) اِسْتِغْراق
عَمِلَ	اِشْتَغَلَ (يَشْتَغِلُ) اِشْتِغال
to stretch, to extend	اِمْتَدَّ (يَمْتَدُّ) اِمْتِداد
to end	اِنْتَهى (يَنْتَهي) اِنْتِهاء (مِن)
to wander about, to tour	تَجَوَّلَ (يَتَجَوَّلُ) تَجَوُّل
to stop	تَوَقَّفَ (يَتَوَقَّفُ) تَوَقُّف
time, duration of time	زَمَن ج أزْمان / أزمِنة
refugee	لاجئ ج لاجئون
built; based (on)	مَبْني (على)
camp	مُخَيَّم ج مُخَيَّمات
located (reality)	واقِع (الواقِع)

المُفرداتُ الجَديدةُ في صُوَرٍ عَديدةٍ:

تَزَلَّجَ (يَتَزَلَّجُ) تَزَلُّج

قاد (يَقود) قِيادة

غاص (يَغوصُ) غَوص

تَسَلَّقَ (يَتَسَلَّقُ) تَسَلُّق

قَصْر (ج) قُصور

قِمَّة (ج) قِمَم

تمرين ١

اِختَرِ الكَلِمةَ الّتي لا تُناسِب باقي الكَلِماتِ في كُلِّ مَجْموعةٍ وبَيِّنِ السَبَب:

١-	شُرب الماء	تَزَلَّج على الماء	تَسَلَّق جِبال	غَوص في البحر
٢-	حَفلة	هَدوء	رَقْص	غِناء
٣-	آثار	تاريخ	قَديم	حَديث
٤-	قيادة	سَفينة	سَيّارة	شاحِنة
٥-	عَمَل	وَظيفة	شُغل	اِستِراحة

رامي مارتيني في عمّان

رامي مارتيني

رامي مارتيني أخو عَدنان مارتيني، وهو طالب يدرس التِجارة في جامعة حَلَب، ويَشتَغِل أيضاً سائقاً على شاحنة لشَرِكة تَصنَع البَرّادات والغَسّالات في حَلَب، ثاني أكبر المُدُن السوريّة. يَسوق رامي شاحنَتَهُ عادةً مرّةً في الأسبوع إلى دمشق ليَنقُل أجهِزة كَهرَبائية. حينَ يكون في دمشق لا يَنام في الفُندُق عادةً بَلْ في شَقّة أخيه أيمن الّذي يدرس الطِبَّ في جامعة دمشق. أيمن في سنتِه الدِراسيّة الأخيرة، وسيُصبِح طَبيباً بعد بِضعة أشْهُر.

شاحنة

مُنذُ شَهرَين سافر رامي بالشاحنة إلى عمّانَ عاصِمة المَملَكة الأردنيّة الهاشميّة الواقِعة جَنوب سورية، ونَقَلَ بَرّاداتٍ إلى هناك. استغرَقَت الطَريق إلى عمّانَ بالشاحِنة تسع ساعات تقريباً. مرَّ في طريقِه إلى عمّانَ بِمَدينة حَماةَ الواقِعة جَنوب حَلَب، ثُمَّ مَرَّ بِمَدينة حِمصَ، ثُمَّ بدمشقَ وأخيراً بدَرعا آخرِ بَلدة سوريّة قَبلَ الحُدود السوريّة الأردنيّة. تَوَقَّف هناك قليلاً ثُمَّ ساق شاحنتَهُ إلى عمّان.

المَسرَح الروماني «فيلادلفيا»

بَقيَ رامي ثلاثةَ أيّام في عمّان، زارَ خِلالَهُ صَديقَهُ أحمَد نحّاس الّذي يدرُس اللغة الإنكليزيّة في الجامعة الأردنيّة. زارَ مع صديقِه حَرَم الجامعة الأردنيّة. زارَ معَهُ كَذلِكَ المَسرَح الرومانيّ القديم في وَسَط مدينة عمّان والمُسمّى «فيلادلفيا» وهو اسم عمّانَ القديم. يقع هذا المَسرَح على سَفح جبَل الجَوْفة أوّل جبَل سُكِن في عمّان.

جَبَل عمّان

تَجَوَّل رامي وصديقُه في جِبال عمّان السبعة الّتي صارَت كلُّها مَسكونة الآن. بدأ العُمران يَمتَدُّ خارج جَبَل الجَوْفة بعد سنةِ ١٩٤٩ حينَ صارَت عمّان عاصمة الأردنّ عامَ ١٩٤٦. بجانب قِمّة جَبَل الجَوْفة يُوجَد جَبَل التاج وقد سُمِّيَ كَذلِكَ لأَنَّهُ أعلى مِنطقة بعمّان. اِمتَدَّ العُمران إلى جَبَل القَلْعة أوَّلاً، ثُمَّ بدأ يَمتَدُّ إلى جَبَل عمّان حَيْثُ يُوجَد مَجلِس الأمّة وعدد كبير من السِفارات الأجنبيّة وبعض الوِزارات وقَصْر زَهران، قَصْر والدة المَلِك حُسَين.

عمّان عاصمة الأردنّ

ثُمَّ ذهبا إلى جَبَل اللوَيْبدة الَّذي يقع في وَسَط الجِبال الأخرى، وهو ثاني مِنطقة سكنيّة بعد الجَوْفة، وقد بدأ العُمران فيه عامَ ١٩٤٩. تَجَوَّلا أيضاً في جَبَل الحُسيْن، ومَرّا بِمُخيَّم اللاجئين الفلسطينيين الّذي أصبحَ منطقة سَكنيّة اليوم. اِمتَدَّ العُمران كَذلِكَ إلى جَبَلَيْ النُزْهة والقُصور. وعَلِمَ رامي من أحمد أن العُمران اِمتَدَّ إلى خارج عمّان ووصل إلى جَبَل الهاشميّ، حَيْثُ تُوجَد القُصور المَلكيّة على اِمتِداده.

بعد ذلك تَوَجَّه الصديقان إلى حي عَبْدون، حَيْثُ تُوجَد الدُور الفَخمة، وقال أحمد: إنَّ هذا الحي واحد من ثلاثة أحياء حديثة راقيّة بالإضافة إلى أمّ أُذَيْنة ودَيْر غُبار. وجد رامي أنَّ مُعظَم البُيوت مَبنيّة بناء جَميلاً من الحَجَر الأبيض كَما في حَلَب. كان رامي سَعيداً بِنهاية الزيارة هذه. في صباحِ اليوم الثالث قادَ شاحنتَهُ راجِعاً إلى حَلَب ولَمْ يَتَوَقَّف في دمشق.

تمرين ٢

أوّلاً: اقرأ المعلومات في شهادة قيادة رامي مارتيني ثُمَّ اكتُبْ فِقرة تَصِف فيها رامي حَسَب هذه المَعلومات:

الجمهورية العربية السورية | **شهادة قيادة خاصة**

إدارة المرور العامة

الاسم: رامي	المهنة: طالب
الشهرة: مارتيني	رقم الهاتف: ٧٦٥١٦١٣
تاريخ الميلاد: ١٧ آذار ١٩٧٨	رقم الشهادة: ٦٧٥٨٧٣٦٤ ب
مكان الميلاد: حلب	تاريخ الإصدار: ٢٥/٨/١٩٩٦
العنوان: شارع المتنبي، رقم ١٥	تاريخ الانتهاء: ٢٤/٨/٢٠٠٠

ثانيا: إملاء شهادة القيادة الآتية بمَعلومات عن نفسك:

الجمهورية العربية السورية | **شهادة قيادة خاصة**

إدارة المرور العامة

صورتك

الاسم:	المهنة:
الشهرة:	رقم الهاتف:
تاريخ الميلاد:	رقم الشهادة:
مكان الميلاد:	تاريخ الإصدار:
العنوان:	تاريخ الانتهاء:

تمرين ٣

أكمل الجُمَل الآتية حَسَب نص القراءة:

١- ينام رامي في ________ حينَ يكون في دمشق.

٢- تقع ________ بين حماة ودمشق.

٣- درعا بَلدة صغيرة تقع على ________.

٤- لِرامي صديق اسمه ________.

٥- يقع المَسرَح الرومانيّ على ________.

٦- كُلُّ جِبال عمّان ________ الآن.

٧- يُوجَد قَصْر زَهران في جَبَل ________.

٨- صارت عمّان عاصِمة الأردنّ عامَ ________.

تمرين ٤

اكتُب «خطأ» أو «صواب» إلى جانب كُلّ جملة ثُمَّ صَحّح الجُمَل الخطأ:

١- مِهنة رامي سائق.

٢- يدرس رامي التِجارة في جامعة حَلَب.

٣- يَنقُل رامي أجهِزة كَهربائيّة من عمّان إلى حَلَب.

٤- تقع عمّان على عِدّة جِبال.

٥- كان اسم عمّان القديم "المَسرَح".

٦- قِمة جَبَل الجَوْفة أعلى مِنطقة في عمّان.

٧- أمّ أذَيْنة أحد الأحياء الراقيّة في عمّان.

تمرين ٥

أ- وافِق بين كَلِمتين واكتُب الأزواج السبعة في الوسط:

١	اِشتَغَلَ		سينما
٢	الأوَّل		شارع
٣	جِهاز كَهرَبائيّ		سَعيد
٤	طَريق		عَمِلَ
٥	تجوّل		بَرّاد
٦	مَسرَح		سيّارة
٧	شاحِنة		مَشى
			الثاني

ب- وافِق بين كَلِمتين لِتُشَكِل إضافة واكتب العبارات الأربع في الوسط:

١	حَرَمُ		الأمّة
٢	سَفحُ		العربيّة
٣	شَهادةُ		الجامعة
٤	مَجلِسُ		الجَبَل
			القيادة

ج- وافِق بين كُلِّ كَلِمة في العمود الأيمن ومرادفها في العمود الأيسر واكتبها في الوسط:

١	أصبَحَ		عَمِلَ
٢	ساقَ		دار
٣	رَجَعَ		عام
٤	سَنة		صارَ
٥	بَيْت		عادَ
			قادَ

تمرين ٦

In Arabic, describe the relationship among the three people mentioned in the main reading passage and describe their activities and backgrounds in some detail.

رامي مارتيني، أيمن مارتيني، أحمَد نحّاس

تمرين ٧

a. Describe the cities/towns/places you went through on a trip you have made (real or imaginary), giving details about the things you saw, the things that surprised you, or that you still remember for some reason. Try, as well, to describe where some things were in relation to one another to practice using the cardinal directions.

b. Describe a town of your choice that you have visited or lived in in terms of its history, population, different neighborhoods, and tourist attractions.

أماكن هامّة في الأردنّ

خريطة الأردنّ

جَرَش

تقع في شَمال الأردنّ وفيها آثار رومانيّة في حال حَسَنة، كالمَسرَح الرومانيّ الّذي تُقام فيه حَفَلات موسيقية وحَفَلات رَقْص شَعبيّ.

مَسرَح جَرَش الرومانيّ

مادَبا

تقع مادَبا على بُعد ٣٠ كيلومتراً إلى الجَنوب الغَربيّ من عمّان. فيها كَنيسة قديمة وآثار وفُسَيفُساء تعود إلى زَمَن الرومان.

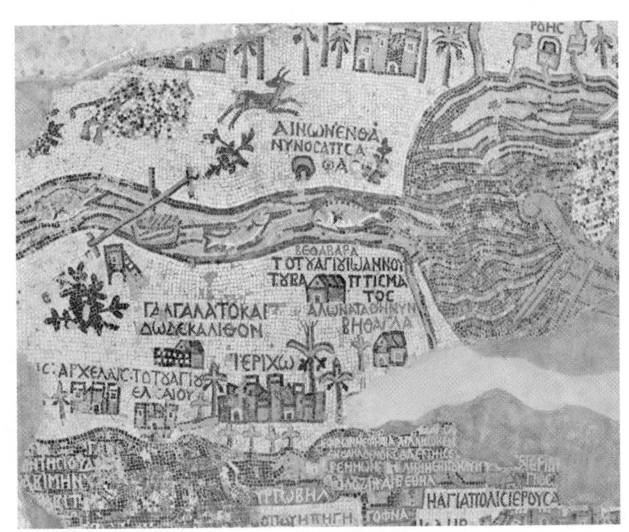

من فُسَيفُساء مادَبا

البَتراء

مدينة قديمة مبانيها مَحفورة في الصَخر الوَرديّ اللون. تقع على بُعد ٢٠٠ كم تقريباً إلى الجَنوب من عمّان. سَكَنَها الأنباط قبلَ الإسلام، وكانت مَركَزاً مُهِمّاً لِلتِجارة والقَوافِل.

العَقَبة

العَقَبة ميناء الأردنّ الوَحيد ويقع على البحر الأحمر. لِلعَقَبة شاطئ رمليّ جميل، وفيها عدد من الفنادق والمطاعِم. يأتيها الأردنيّون والسُيّاح لِلسِباحة وتسلّق الجبال والتزلّج على الماء والغَوص في البحر الأحمر. تَبعُد عن عمّان حوالي ٣٠٠ كيلومترٍ إلى الجَنوب.

ميناء العَقَبة

تمرين ٨

أجِب عن هذه الأسئلة:

١- أين تُوجَد آثار بالفُسَيفُساء؟

٢- من أي شيء بُنيت البَتراء وماذا كانت في التاريخ؟

٣- كيف تُستخدَم آثار جَرَش اليوم؟

٤- ما أهمية العَقَبة؟

٥- لو كنت سائحاً ولدَيك الوقت لِزيارة إحدى تِلكَ الأماكِن في الأردنّ، إلى أي مكان تذهب ولِماذا تفضّله؟

تمرين ٩

للمحادثة: اطلب من زميلك أن يسألَك الأسئلة الست أدناه حول ما فعلته في إحدى الإجازات. استخدم في إجاباتك الكلمات الموجودة في حصيلة المفردات:

تَجوَّلَ (يَتَجوَّلُ) تجوُّل	اِنْتهى (يَنْتَهي) اِنْتِهاء	اِسْتَغْرَقَ (يَسْتَغرِقُ) اِسْتِغْراق
أعْجَبَ (يُعْجِبُ) إعْجاب	تَسَلَّقَ (يَتَسَلَّقُ) تَسَلُّق	تَزَلَّجَ (يَتزَلَّجُ) تزَلُّج

1. Where did you go and with whom?
2. How long did you stay and where?
3. Did you enjoy your vacation?
4. How did you get there?
5. What did you do while you were there?
6. When did you return and how?

القواعد

1. Circumstantial Adverb الحال

الحال is used to modify the verb (action) of a sentence and answers the question *how*?

The student arrived (how?) walking.	جاءَ الطالِبُ ماشياً .	
The plane arrived (how?) coming from Beirut.	وَصَلَتِ الطائرةُ قادِمةً مِن بَيروت.	١
The ambulance took off (how?) quickly.	اِنْطَلَقَتْ سَيّارةُ الإسْعافِ مُسْرِعةً.	

It functions as the adverb of manner in English (e.g., quickly, slowly, ____ly). The most common form of الحال in Arabic is an indefinite noun in the accusative:

اسم + اً (مثال: صباحاً)

Often الحال takes the form of اسم الفاعل in the sentence. Bear in mind though, it could take other forms:

Types of الحال

1. A single word: *derived* (ex. 2 & 3) and *underived* (ex. 4)--(found on page 142)
2. A sentence: *verbal* (ex. 5) *nominal* (ex. 6)--(found on page 142)
3. A clause: *prepositional* (ex. 7) and *adverbial* (ex. 8)--(found on page 143)

a. As an Active Participle اسم الفاعل

Remember that اسم الفاعل takes a form dictated by the وَزن (see *lesson 16 AwS-I*). As you recall, form I takes the shape of the particle فاعل. To derive the remaining active participles (Forms II-X), simply go to the present tense conjugation of that verb and substitute a مُـ for the first letter of the verb and leave the remaining stem as is:

Forming the Active Participle (Forms II-X)
مُـ + فعِل (مِثال: مُراسِل)

He entered the room (how?) smiling.	دَخَلَ الغُرفة مُبْتَسِماً.	٢
He drove his truck (how?) returning to Aleppo.	قادَ شاحِنَتَهُ راجِعاً إلى حَلَب.	

b. As a Passive Participle اسم المَفعول

In form I, اسم المَفعول follows the pattern مَفعول, whereas in forms II-X the form is derived by taking the present tense مُضارِع conjugation of the verb, substituting مُـ for the first letter/short vowel, and then changing the penultimate short vowel to a فَتحة.

Forming the Passive Participle (Forms II-X)
مُـ + فعَل (مِثال: مُسْتَعْمَل)

I found the professor (how?) busy.	وَجدتُ الأُستاذَ مَشْغولاً	٣
She finished the race (how?) tired and exhausted.	اِنْتَهَتْ من السِباق مُرهَقةً مُتعَبةً.	

c. As an Underived Noun

We can also describe the state of a person with الحال and not simply the action.

Ahmad returned to us as a man.	رَجَعَ أحمَد إلَينا رَجُلاً.	٤
My dad works as an instructor.	يَعمَلُ والِدي أُسْتاذاً.	

d. As a Sentence

الحال can be both a verbal (ex. 5) or nominal (ex. 6) sentence.

I found Sami writing a letter.	وَجَدتُ سامي يَكتُبُ رِسالةً.	٥
Sami walked with his hand in her hand.	مَشى سامي ويَدُهُ بيَدِها.	٦

e. As a Clause

Two types of clauses exist, prepositional (ex. 7) and adverbial (ex. 8).

I saw Marwan's car on the street.	شاهَدتُ سيّارةَ مَروانَ في الشارِع.	٧
I saw the moon between the clouds.	رأيتُ القَمَرَ بَيْنَ الغُيوم.	٨

تمرين ١٠

للمُحادَثة: صِفْ زميلك في غُرفة الصف. كيف يجلِس، كيف يكتُب، كيف دخل الصفّ، كيف خرج من البيت، كيف وصل إلى غرفة الصف؟ لا تنسَ غرض هذا التمرين أن تجيب عن السؤال: كيف فعل فلان الفلاني شيئاً ما (مستخدماً أنواع الحال).

تمرين ١١

a. Underline the words that are حال in the following sentences:

١- وصل الطلاّب مُتأخّرين إلى غُرفة الصفّ.

٢- تكلّمنا مع المُذيع وَجهاً لِوجه.

٣- رأت سِهام أمَّها ماشيةً في الشارِع.

٤- ركبوا الطائرة مُسافِرين إلى الجزائر.

٥- سمِعتُ أُغنية فَيروز من الإذاعة.

٦- دخل فَريد الغرفة قائلاً: إنه لن يعمل في هذا البلد بعدَ الآن.

b. Derive the appropriate form of the verb in parentheses to form حال and provide the case endings:

١- ذهبتُ إلى المكتبة. (مشى)

٢- خرجنا من دار السينما. (ضحك)

٣- رأيت أخاك (جلس) في الحديقة.

٤- وصل مازن إلى المطار (حمل) حقيبتين.

c. **Convey the following meanings in Arabic, using حال:**

1. She came into the room running.
2. He arrived thirty minutes late.
3. I put my bicycle between two cars.
4. She stood in front of us reading poetry.

مُراجَعة القَواعِد

2. The Nominal Sentence الجُملة الاسميّة

There are two types of sentences in Arabic: 1) those that start with verbs, known as verbal; and 2) those that start with nouns known as nominal. A nominal sentence is comprised of two parts traditionally known as the subject and the predicate. These parts are known properly in Arabic as المُبتدأ *the topic* (the thing that is being talked about) and الخَبر *the comment* (the description).

The city is big.	المَدينةُ كَبيرةٌ.	١

In example 1, المَدينة is the topic while كَبيرةٌ is the comment on that topic. In the first paragraph of our main reading passage two nominal sentences occurred:

Rami Martini is Adnan's brother.	رامي مارتيني أخو عدنان مارتيني.	٢
Ayman is in his last year of school.	أيمَنُ في سَنتِه الدِراسيّة الأخيرة.	٣

We have shaded المُبتدأ in blue in examples 2 and 3, while the rest of the sentence is considered to be الخبر because it describes the topic.

a. The Topic المُبتدأ

The topics in examples 1-3 are good illustrations of the norm in that they are in nominative case مَرفوع and definite مَعرفة. Exceptions do exist where the topic is indefinite نَكِرة; the following two cases being the most common:

i. **When the topic is modified by an adjective (ex. 4):**

A foreign student is at our university.	طالبٌ أجنَبيٌّ في جامعتِنا.	٤

ii. **When the topic is the first part of an إضافة (ex. 5):**

A housewife presents the program.	رَبّةُ بيتٍ تُقدِّمُ البَرنامَجَ.	٥

b. The Comment الخَبَر

Normally, الخَبر is مَرفوع and نَكِرة when it is a noun. It may function as:

i. A Single Word

The truck is new.	٦ الشاحِنةُ جَديدةٌ.

ii. A Nominal Sentence

The fair has many visitors.	٧ المَعرِضُ زُوّارُهُ كَثيرون.

iii. A Verbal Clause

Khaled speaks French.	٨ خالِدٌ يتَكَلَّمُ الفَرَنْسِيّة.

iv. A Prepositional Phrase

Salma is home.	٩ سَلمى في البيت.

v. An Adverbial Phrase

The sun is behind the clouds.	١٠ الشَمسُ خَلفَ الغُيوم.

c. Preposing the Comment

There are three instances in which the comment can precede the topic.

i. When the topic is نَكِرة and the predicate a clause:

In our house is a man.	١١ في بَيْتِنا رَجُلٌ.
Near the city is a lake.	١٢ قُربَ المَدينةِ بُحَيْرَةٌ.

ii. The topic has an attached referential pronoun:

To make harisa, its own recipe.	١٣ لِصُنعِ الهَريسةِ طَريقَتُها.

iii. The comment is a question word:

Where is your house?	١٤ أينَ بَيتُك؟

d. The Nominal Sentence

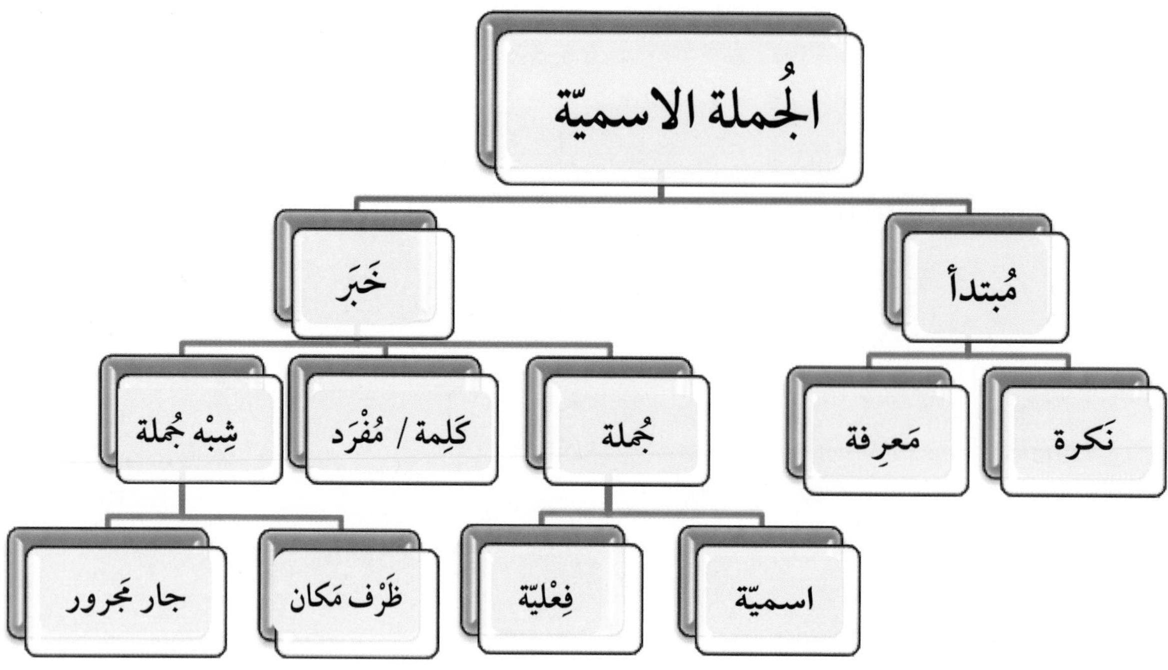

The nominal sentence may begin with one of the so-called defective verbs (كان وأخواتها). They, however, do not make the sentence verbal; rather it remains nominal because they are not verbs that denote action. Take, for example, a sentence lifted from our passage:

Amman became the capital of Jordan.	صارَت عَمّانُ عاصِمةَ الأردُنّ.	١

Example 1 is a nominal sentence with صار, from the set of كان وأخواتها placed at the beginning of the sentence denoting a change of state.

Let us now analyze why كان وأخواتها are not considered verbs. Essentially, when they are added to a subject, the meaning of a sentence remains incomplete:

Khaled came.	جاءَ خالِدٌ.	٢
Khaled was . . .	كانَ خالِدٌ . . .	٣

Example 2 is a full and complete sentence because جاءَ is a verb; whereas example 3 is a fragment—hence the reason this set is known as defective verbs.

A sentence containing كانَ وأخواتها requires a خَبر to complete its meaning:

Khaled was *sick*.	٤ كانَ خالدٌ مَريضاً.

Of course, كانَ puts الخَبر in حالة النَصب. Let's take a look at how كانَ وأخواتها affect الخَبر by examining example 4 without كان.

Khaled is *sick*.	٥ خالِدٌ مَريضٌ.

As we can see, مَريضٌ is مَرفوع because it is الخَبر so it agrees in case with المبتَدأ (= خالد). When we introduce كان وأخواتها into the sentence, the sentence's syntax changes and الخَبر becomes مَنصوب, as you can see in example 1 (عاصِمةً) and in example 4 (مَريضاً).

3. The Set Known as كان وأخواتها

This set contains twelve words:

كانَ، أصبَحَ، أضْحى، ظَلَّ، أمْسَى، باتَ، صارَ، لَيْسَ، مازالَ، مابَرِحَ،ماأنْفَكَّ، مافَتِئَ، مادامَ

These words are divided into four subgroups based on their function and meaning.

a. Verbs That Mean *to become*

Each member of this set determines at what state of the process a transformation occurred. It is interesting to note that they are derived from times of the day.

Verb		Connotation		Time of day
أصْبَحَ	is derived from	صَباح	*morning*	*change early in the process*
أضْحى	is derived from	ضُحى	*forenoon*	
ظَلَّ	is derived from	ظَلٌّ / ظِلٌّ	*daytime*	*to continue*
أمْسى	is derived from	مَساء	*evening*	*change late in the process*
باتَ	is derived from	مَبيت	*nighttime*	

Two other members of this set كانَ and صارَ have slightly different connotations. كانَ, of course, parallels the English copula *to be*, while صارَ (*to become*) signifies a general transformation with no time connotation. All of these verbs conjugate fully in the past (ex. 6), present (ex. 7), and imperative (ex. 8).

The weather was cold. (past)	كانَ الطَقسُ بارِداً	٦
When is the director in his office? (present)	مَتى يكونُ المُديرُ في مَكتَبِه؟	٧
Be at the bus stop at four o'clock. (imperative)	كونوا عِندَ مَوقِفِ الحافِلةِ في الساعةِ الرابِعةِ.	٨

b. The Negative Verb لَيسَ

Use this verb to negate nominal sentences. If you wish to say 'is *not s.th.*', then use لَيسَ. This verb is generally not used to negate verbs; rather, it is usually used to negate anything other than a verb.

Conjugate this verb in exactly the same manner as a past tense hollow verb.

I am not an instructor.	لَسْتُ أستاذاً.	
Iran is not an Arabic country.	لَيسَتْ إيرانُ بَلَداً عَرَبيّاً.	٩
This car is not my car.	هٰذِه السَيّارةُ لَيسَتْ سَيّارَتي.	

c. Verbs That Mean (*to be*) *still* مابَرِحَ، مازالَ، مافَتِئَ، ماانفَكَّ

As you may have noticed, these are compound words in that they are preceded by the negative particle ما followed by a verb. They conjugate in both the past and present, but when they are in the present, use the correct negative particle. In other words, use ما to negate these past tense verbs (ex. 10) and لا to negate them in present tense verbs (ex. 11).

Hala continued to work at the company until she retired.	مازالَتْ هالةُ تَعمَلُ في الشَرِكةِ حَتّى تَقاعَدَتْ.	١٠
Hala is still working at the company.	لاتَزالُ هالةُ تَعمَلُ في الشَرِكةِ.	١١

d. The Verb Meaning *as long as, while, since*: مادامَ

Unlike group 'c' in this section, مادامَ only conjugates in the past like لَيسَ; but it too must be used in conjunction with the negative particle ما.

Why aren't you studying in the university, since you are living in this town?	لِماذا لا تَدرُسينَ في الجامِعةِ مادُمتِ تَسكُنينَ في هٰذِه المَدينةِ؟	١٢

تمرين ١٢

إستعمِل الفِعلَ الماضي الناقِص المُناسِب في تَرجَمةِ الجُمَل الآتية:

1. As long as I'm alive, I will continue learning.
2. هاني is still studying electrical engineering.
3. He was a poor man before he became rich.
4. Gasoline has become very expensive.
5. You don't need a car so long as you live near the university campus.

e. Adverb of Time ظَرف الزَمان

An instance of ظَرف الزَمان occurred in this lesson in an إضافة comprised of a number and an adverb of time. The number in the إضافة functions as an adverb.

The trip took nine hours.	إستَغرَقَتِ الرِحلَةُ تِسعَ ساعاتٍ.	١

تذَكّروا

Adverbs of time are accusative nouns

f. Diptotes المَمنوع من الصَرف

A diptote is a noun that can only take two short vowels (ضَمّة وفَتْحة), as opposed to the usual triptote, which takes all three short vowels in Arabic. Diptotes' nominative case is marked with a ضَمّة as usual, but its accusative and genitive cases are marked by the فتحة. Diptotes do not accept تَنوين (see the grammar review in this book).

Examples of diptotes taken from our passage are presented here for consideration. Note that all of them take a فتحة.

إلى عَمّانَ، في عَمّانَ، اسمُ عَمّانَ القَديم، بعَمّانَ، جامعةُ حَلَبَ، في حَلَبَ، جَنوبَ حَلَبَ، جامِعةُ دِمْشَقَ، في دِمَشْقَ، مَدينةُ حَماةَ، قَصْرُ زَهرانَ

g. Deriving the Passive Participle from Hollow Verbs Form I

Hollow verbs الفعل الأجْوَف are those with long vowels as middle radicals. If the middle vowel in the present tense is either a و (ex. 2) or a ي (ex. 3), then simply substitute a مَـ for the indicative prefix and leave the stem as is.

which was originally:	مَقوول	*said*	مَقول	⇐	يَقول	⇐	قالَ	٢
which was originally:	مَبيوع	*sold*	مَبيع	⇐	يَبيع	⇐	باعَ	٣

If the middle long vowel is the ألف *in the present tense*, it must be replaced by the original vowel as the ألف is never an original vowel. The original vowel must be either a و or a ي.

which was originally:	مَخووف	*feared*	مَخوف	⇐	يَخاف	⇐ خافَ	٤
which was originally:	مَهيوب	*venerable*	مَهيب	⇐	يَهاب	⇐ هابَ	٥

h. Deriving the Passive Participle from Weak Verbs Form I

Weak verbs مُعتلٌ الآخِر are those verbs that have a long vowel as the final radical in their root. When forming the passive participle of these types of verbs, substitute مَـ for the indicative prefix and then double the final radical with a شَدّة.

irrigated	مَرويّ	⇐	يَروي	⇐ رَوى	٦
invited	مَدعُوّ	⇐	يَدعو	⇐ دَعا	٧

i. Deriving the Passive Participle from Hollow Verbs Forms II-X

To create the passive participle for forms II through X simply substitute the indicative prefix ي with a مـُ while placing a فتحة on the penultimate letter.

used	مُسْتَعْمَل	⇐	يَسْتَعْمِلُ	⇐ اِسْتَعْمَلَ	٨

When the penultimate letter is a ي in the imperfect (present) tense, it changes to an ألف when making the passive participle.

advisor	مُستَشار	⇐	يَستَشير	⇐ اِستَشار	٩

When the penultimate letter is an ألف in the imperfect (present) tense, it remains an ألف.

selected	مُختار	⇐	يَختار	⇐ اِختار	١٠

j. Deriving the Passive Participle from Weak Verbs Forms II-X

When the verb in forms II-X is weak, the final و or ي changes into an ألف مقصورة.

equivalent	مُساوى	⇐	يُساوي	⇐ ساوى	١١

تمرين ١٣

Derive the passive participle اسم مَفعول from the following verbs:

١- سَرَّ	٤- تابَعَ	٧- اِهتَدى
٢- ساقَ	٥- داوى	٨- قادَ
٣- مَشى	٦- غادَرَ	٩- نَسِيَ

k. Passive Voice

Remember that no agent is specified in passive voice. Examine example 1:

١١ أَوَّلُ جَبَلٍ سُكِنَ في عَمّان.	*The first mountain that was inhabited in Amman*

The noun that occupies the position after the verb is, in fact, taking the place of the subject of the sentence and is known in Arabic as نائب الفاعِل.

l. Multiple إضافة

When more than two nouns are strung together in a relationship denoting belonging or possession, then you are dealing with a multiple إضافة.

١٢ بِجانِبِ قِمّةِ جَبَلِ الجَوفةِ.	*Next to the summit of Mount Jawfa.*

The noun that occupies the position after the verb is, in fact, taking the place of the subject of the sentence and is known in Arabic as نائب الفاعِل.

مُلاحَظة

The first noun of the إضافة is known as the مُضاف while every noun that follows it (i.e., مُضاف إليه) will always be مَجرور (ex. 12).

تمرين ١٤

آ أجب عن الأسئلة وفق نص الاستماع:

١- ما الفِكرة الرئيسة في نَص الاستِماع؟
٢- اذكُر بعض الأفكار الثانويّة.
٣- مَن سافرَ مع الكاتِب؟
٤- في أية مدينة وأي مكان تسكُن أُخْت الكاتِب؟
٥- ما شَكْلُ شَوارِع المدينة الّتي زارَها؟
٦- ماذا شاهدَ في الشَوارِع؟
٧- ما اسم ابنة أُخْت الكاتِب؟

ب- أكمل الجمل الآتية بالاخيار المناسب وفق نص الاستماع:

١- زارَ الكاتِب مدينة ____________ .

☐ دمشق ☐ أبو ظَبي ☐ الإمارات العربية المُتحدة

٢- كان في اِنتِظار الكاتِب ووالدتِه ______________ .

☐ أُختُه وزوجُها ☐ أختُه وابنتُها ☐ عائلةُ أختِه

٣- يشاهدَ الكاتِب هناك ______________ .

☐ مَبانيَ قديمة ☐ شَوارِعَ حديثة ☐ طائراتٍ ألمانيّةَ ويابانيّة

ج- لَخِّص المُقابَلة مع زينا بحوالى خمسين كَلمة.

المُفْرَدات

اِستَغرَقَ	(يَستَغرِقُ)	اِستِغراق	(v.)	to take (time)
اِمتَدَّ	(يَمْتَدُّ)	اِمتِداد	(v.)	to stretch, to extend
أمّة	ج	أُمَم	(n., f.)	nation, people
اِنتَهى	(يَنتَهي)	اِنتِهاء	(v.)	to end, to expire
بَعُدَ	(يَبعُدُ)	بُعْد (عَن)	(v.)	to be distant, to be far away (from)
تَزَلَّجَ	(يَتَزَلَّجُ)	تَزَلُّج	(v.)	to slide, to ski, to skate
تَسَلَّقَ	(يَتَسَلَّقُ)	تَسَلُّق	(v.)	to climb
تَوَقَّفَ	(يَتَوَقَّفُ)	تَوَقُّف	(v.)	to stop, to stop over
تَجَوَّلَ	(يَتَجَوَّلُ)	تَجَوُّل	(v.)	to wander about, to tour
حَرَم	ج	أحْرام	(n., m.)	campus, sacred possession
حَفْلة	ج	حَفَلات	(n., f.)	party, celebration
راقٍ	ج	راقون	(n., m.)	high-class, upper-class, refined
رومانيٌّ			(adj.)	roman
زَمَن	ج	أزْمُن / أزْمان	(n., m.)	time, period, duration to time

embassy	(n., f.)	سِفارات	ج	سِفارة
foot (of a mountain)	(n., m.)	سُفوحٌ	ج	سَفْحٌ
people, nation	(n., m.)	شُعوب	ج	شَعْب
construction, development	(n., m.)			عُمْرانٌ
to dive	(v.)	غَوْص	(يَغوصُ)	غاصَ
magnificent, splendid, stately	(adj.)			فَخْم
silver	(n., f.)			فِضّة
to drive, to pilot	(v.)	قيادة	(يَقودُ)	قادَ
palace, mansion, castle	(n., m.)	قُصورٌ	ج	قَصْرٌ
summit, peak	(n., f.)	قِمَم	ج	قِمَّةٌ
refugee	(act. p.)	لاجِئون	ج	لاجئٌ
built, constructed	(pass. p.)			مَبْنِيٌّ
council, assembly	(n., m.)	مَجالِسٌ	ج	مَجْلِسٌ
camp	(n., m.)	مُخَيَّماتٌ	ج	مُخَيَّمٌ
inhabited	(pass. p.)			مَسْكون

area, region, zone	(n., f.)	مَناطِق	ج	مِنْطَقةٌ
kingdom	(n., f.)	مَمالِكُ	ج	مَمْلَكَةٌ
Hashemite (ruling family in Jordan)	(adj.)			هاشِمِيٌّ
located, existing	(act. p.)			واقِع

الدَرْسُ السابِع

Objectives

- Introduction to describing an evening out on the town
- Learning how to express and summarize a personal event in a letter
- Reinforcing letter-writing conventions and styles
- **Grammar**: Introducing types of ما, adverbs of manner, the particle ألاّ

رُكنُ المُفْرَداتِ الجَديدةِ

to master (s.th.); to be skilled or proficient at	أجاد (يُجيدُ) إجادة
to apologize	اِعتَذَرَ (يَعتَذِرُ) اِعتِذار
to send	بَعَث (يَبعَثُ) بَعْث
delay; tardiness	تأخير
to invite	دعا (يَدعو) دُعاء
to see	رأى (يَرى) رأي / رؤية
to forgive	سامَح (يُسامِحُ) مُسامَحة
to treat (s.o.)	عامَل (يُعامِلُ) مُعامَلة
to be about (أنْ to do s.th.)	كاد (يَكادُ)
to joke	مَزَح (يَمزَحُ) مَزْح
to spend time (الماضي)	مَضى (يَمضي) مُضِيّ
place of entertainment	مَلهى ج ملاهٍ
to intend	نَوى (يَنوي) نية

تمرين ١

وافِق بين كَلِمتين واكتُب الأزواج السبعة في الوسط:

١	سُرعة		موسيقية
٢	حَلْبة		عُذْر
٣	صَوْت		بَرْق
٤	مُسامَحة		مَسْموع
٥	فِرقة		عامَلَ
٦	ثوب		رَقْص
٧	طاوِلة		مَشْرَب
٨	بار		شاهَدَ
٩	بَعَثَ		مائِدة
١٠	رأى		لِباس
			أرْسَلَ

تمرين ٢

وافِق بين المتضادّات واكتب الأزواج في الوسط:

١	خافِت		خارِج
٢	فائِت		مُقبِل
٣	داخِل		عَجين
٤	شابّ		قَويّ
			فتاة

غادة تَزورُ مَلهىً لَيْليّاً

ملهى ليلي

مضت سنةٌ ونِصف تقريباً على غادة في الولايات المتحدة الأمريكية ولم تَزُرْ ملهىً ليلياً. لكن في عُطلة الأسبوع الفائت دعتها صديقاتُها الأمريكيات ساندي وميليسا وليندا إلى زيارة أحدِ الملاهي الليلية كي ترى ما هو وتعرفَ ما يجري فيه.

في السابعة من مساء السبت حضرت الفتياتُ الثلاث إلى شقّة غادة، وكنَّ يلبسنَ أثواباً أنيقةً لا يلبسنها عادةً إلى الجامعة. دعت غادة صديقاتها إلى شُربِ فنجانِ قهوة عربية قبل الذهاب إلى الملهى. شربت مليسا وليندا القهوة لكن ساندي اعتذرت وقالت: إنَّ القهوةَ العربية ثقيلة جداً بالنسبة لي.

بعد الساعة الثامنة بقليل وصلت الفتيات الأربع إلى ملهىً يُسمّى «الفصول الأربعة». كان اسم الملهى مكتوباً بالنِيون الأحمر والأخضر على لافتةٍ كبيرة. وكان يقف أمام الباب عدد من الشباب والفتيات يتحدّثون قبل الدُخول. وكان صوت الموسيقا مسموعاً إلى خارج الملهى.

في الداخِل كانت الأضواءُ خافِتةً حَول الطاوِلات، لكن فوق حَلْبة الرَقْص كان عدد من الأضواء الباهِرة تومِض بسرعة مِثل البَرق، وكان على حَلْبة الرَقْص بعض الشبابِ والفتيات يرقصون على أنغام موسيقا صاخِبة تكاد تخرِق الآذان. كان بعض الناس يجلسون أمام المَشرَب (البار) على كراسٍ عالية يشربون ويتحدّثون.

حَلْبة رَقْص

فُستُق سودانيّ

وجدت غادة وصديقاتُها طاولة فارِغة بعيدة عن الفِرقة الموسيقية وجلسن إليها. أتت نادِلة شابّة وسألتهن: ماذا تشرَبْن؟ . طلبت ليندا وساندي بيرة أمّا ميليسا فطلبت «بينيا كولادا»، وهو مشروبٌ كحوليّ مكسيكي، وطلبت غادة كولا لأنها لا تتناوَل مشروبات كحولية. أحضرت النادلة المشروبات، وأحضرت معها أيضاً صحناً صغيراً فيه فُستُق سوداني ووِعاءً فيه «تورتيا» وهي رَقائق مُحَمَّصة من عَجين الذُرة.

تقدَّم شابّان من مائدة غادة وصديقاتها، ودعوا مليسا وساندي إلى الرَقْص. اعتذرت ساندي وقالت: إنِّي لا أرقُص، فالتَفَت الشاب إلى ليندا ودعاها إلى الرَقْص فقامت. بقيت غادة وساندي جالستين تراقبان الراقصين وتشربان الشراب وتأكلان التورتيّا والفُستُق السودانيّ.

بعضُ زبائن الملهى الليلي

تمرين ٣

اخترِ الكَلِمةَ الّتي لا تُناسِب باقي الكَلِماتِ في كُلِّ مَجْموعةٍ وبَيِّنِ السَبَب:

١- راقَبَ　　نَوى　　شاهَدَ　　رأى

٢- ضَوء　　وَميض　　بَرْق　　ثَوْب

٣- رَقْص　　تأخير　　مَشرَب　　مَلهى

٤- خَرجَ　　أسِفَ　　سامَحَ　　اِعتَذَرَ

٥- موسيقا　　صاخِب　　عُذْر　　صَوت

بعد زيارة الملهى الليلي كتبت غادة رسالة إلى صديقتِها نَجوى الّتي تعيش مع زوجها في دولة الإمارات العربية المتحدة. وكانت غادة برسالتِها هذه تَرُدُّ على رسالة وصلتها من صديقتها قبل أسبوعين، ووصفت لها في الرسالة زيارتَها للملهى الليلي.

١٦ آذار ٢٠١٢

أختي الحبيبة نجوى.

أبعث لك تحيةً عاطِرةً من أمريكا، وأشكرك على رِسالتِك الّتي وصلتني قبل أسبوعين. أعتذر لعدم الكتابة إليكِ قبل الآن. آسفة يا أختي فقد كنت مشغولة جداً بالدراسة. عندنا الآن عطلة، وسوف أرتاح من الدراسة لمدّة أسبوعين. شوقي إليك كبير. كيف حالك؟ وماذا تفعلين هذه الأيام؟

أمس ذهبت مع صديقاتي الأمريكيات إلى ملهى ليلي في وسط المدينة، وكانت تلك أوّل مرّة أزور فيها ملهى ليلياً. أعجبتني الزيارة لكنّي لا أنوي أنْ أزورَ ملهى آخَر في وقت قريب. كان هناك ناس كثيرون يشربون ويتحدّثون ويرقُصون. أنا لم أرقُصْ لأني لا أُجيدُ الرَقْص. كانت الموسيقا صاخبةً جداً وكنتُ أكاد لا أسمع ما تقول صديقاتي.

إلى اللقاء يا عزيزتي في رسالة مُقبلة. أرجو أن تكتبي إليَّ وألاّ تعامِليني كما عاملتك، فأنا عندي عُذر وهو الدراسة (أنا أمزح وسامحيني مرّة ثانيّة على التأخير). قُبلاتي لك وسلامي إلى مروان.

أختك المخلِصة المُشتاقة

غادة

تمرين ٤

اختَر التكملة المناسبة لهذه الجمل حسب النصّ:

١- اِعتَذَرَت ساندي عن شُرْبِ القهوة العربية لأنَّها ________ .

☐ ثقيلة ☐ رَخيصة ☐ غالية ☐ لذيذة

٢- كانت الفتيات الأربع في ________ قبل الذهاب إلى الملهى الليلي.

☐ الجامعة ☐ المطعم ☐ شقّة غادة ☐ بيت ساندي

٣- كان يوجَد خارجَ المَلهى ________ .

☐ موسيقا صاخِبة ☐ شباب وفتيات ☐ أضواء خافِتة ☐ كراسٍ عالية

٤- يوجَد أمام المَشرَب ________ .

☐ كراسٍ عالية ☐ لافِتة كبيرة ☐ قهوة عربية ☐ طاولة غادة

٥- طلبت غادة ________ .

☐ بيرة ☐ كولا ☐ قهوة ☐ بينيا كولادا

٦- وضعت النادلة الفُستُق السودانيّ في ________ .

☐ صَحْن صَغير ☐ وِعاء كبير ☐ كأس وَسَط ☐ خَزّان صغير

٧- قامت ________ إلى الرَقْصِ مع الشابين.

☐ مليسا وساندي ☐ مليسا وليندا ☐ مليسا وغادة ☐ ساندي وغادة

٨- تعيش نَجوى في ________ .

☐ أمريكا ☐ مصر ☐ دولة الإمارات ☐ لُبنان

٩- الشيء الذّي لم يُعجب غادة في الملهى هو ________.

☐ الموسيقا الصاخِبة ☐ الرَقْص الحديث ☐ المَشروبات الكُحولية

١٠- اعتَذَرَتْ غادة مِن نَجوى بِسبَب ________.

☐ عَدَم الكتابة لها ☐ تأخير الردّ ☐ الذهاب إلى المَلهى

تمرين ٥

أكمل الجمل التالية بالكلمة المناسبة:

١- وصلَت الطائرة إلى المطار بعد __________ ساعة أو أكثر.

☐ خارِج ☐ تأخير ☐ دُخول ☐ ذُرة

٢- يعرف الناس ما __________ في العالم من التلفاز.

☐ يَعتَذِر ☐ يومِض ☐ يَدعو ☐ يَجري

٣- __________ شهران ولم أستلِمْ رسالة من أخي.

☐ مضى ☐ جرى ☐ نوى ☐ رأى

٤- لا يشرب المسلمون عادةً المشروبات __________ .

☐ الأجنبيّة ☐ الكُحوليّة ☐ الفارِغة ☐ المَسموعة

٥- سَلمى في __________ كبير إلى أمِّها.

☐ شَوق ☐ شُرب ☐ ثَوب ☐ بَرق

٦- __________ صديقي إلى حَفلةِ زَواجِه.

☐ دعاني ☐ شاهَدَني ☐ سامَحَني ☐ رآني

٧- يجِب __________ أنسى موعدي مع أستاذي.

☐ لا ☐ ألاّ ☐ إلاّ ☐ أم لا

٨- نريد أنْ نجلِسَ إلى __________ قريبة من الشُبّاك.

☐ رَقيقة ☐ خاصّة ☐ مُحمّصة ☐ مائِدة

تمرين ٦

Conversation: Describe a night that you went out that is similar to our main reading passage. Feel free to discuss things like going to the movies, the theater, a dance club, or your local hangout. Try to describe, in as much detail as possible, what you did there, whom you hung out with, and how late you were allowed to stay out. Also, try to describe your hangout المكان المفضل للتجمع in as much detail as you can.

For Homework: Write the story that you told or that your partner related to you in the same style as our main reading passage.

تمرين ٧

أجِبْ عن الأسئلة التالية حسب النصّ:

١- في أيّ يوم زارت غادة الملهى الليليّ؟

٢- ما اسم الملهى الليلي الّذي زارته غادة؟

٣- ما هو البينيا كولادا؟

٤- مَن مِن صديقات غادة قامت إلى الرَقْص؟

٥- أين تعيش نَجوى؟

٦- مَن هو مَروان؟

تمرين ٨

آ- أعد ترتيب الكلمات في كل مجموعة لتشكّل جملاً مُفيدةً:

١	ليلياً	زارت	صديقات	غادة	ملهى	مع	ثلاث			
٢	مكتوباً	على	كان	اسم	لافِتة	الملهى	كبيرة			
٣	صاخِباً	خافِتةً	جَوّ	والأضواء	الملهى	كان				
٤	أنْ	كادت	تنسى	موعد	سلوى	طائرتِها				
٥	صديقي	الفائت	زَواج	كثيراً	في	في	حفلة	رقصنا	الشهر	
٦	أمام	وَقَفَ	باب	دقائق	المطعم	أيمن	معنا	بِضع	وزوجته	وتحدّثا

b. غادة uses three different forms to apologize in her letter to نجوى. List these three forms.

تمرين ٩

اكتب «صواب» أو «خطأ» إلى جانب كل جملة وصحّح الجمل الخطأ:

١- أتَت غادة إلى أمريكا في سنة ٢٠٠٥.

٢- زارت غادة الملهى الليليّ لأنّها تحبّ الرَقْص.

٣- كانت طاولة غادة وصديقاتها قريبة من الفِرقة الموسيقية.

٤- لم ترقصْ غادة لأنّها لا تعرف الرَقْص.

٥- تناولت الفتيات في الملهى عشاءً لذيذاً.

٦- في الملهى الليلي لم تعجِبْ غادة المشروبات الكحولية.

٧- دَعا شابٌّ غادة إلى الرَقْص فاعتذَرَت.

٨- وصلَت رسالةُ نجوى إلى غادة في أوّل آذار.

تمرين ١٠

أعد ترتيب الجمل لتشكّل فقرة كاملة. الجملة الأولى في مكانها المناسب:

١- علِمتُ من صديقي أنّ مطعماً جديداً اسمه «الصحّة» قد فتح أبوابه.

دخلنا المطعم ووجدنا فيه عدداً كبيراً من الموائد.

طلبتُ كُبّة مع الحمَّص وطلبَت زوجتي دجاجاً مَشوياً.

ثمّ حضر نادِل آخَر وسألنا ماذا نطلب.

يجِب أنْ أقول: إنَّ الطعام كان لذيذاً ولم يكُنْ غالياً.

في يوم الخميس الفائت ذهبنا إلى ذلك المطعم الجديد.

قادتنا النادلة إلى مائدة قريبة من الشبّاك.

وحين وصلنا إليه شاهدنا لافِتة كبيرة كُتِب عليها اسم المطعم بالأضواء.

تمرين ١١

املأ الفراغات الآتية مستخدماً الكلمات المناسبة حسب السياق:

في مدينة دمشق القديمة يوجَد عددٌ من المقاهي الشعبيّة. والمقهى هو مكانٌ لِلرِجالِ فقط ________ فيه الشاي والقهوة (ومن هنا تأتي كلمة «مقهى») ويلعبون الورق وطاولة الزهر. يأتي إلى بعض هذه ________ عددٌ كبير من الزبائن فيضعون لهم كراسيَ على الرصيف في الشارِع ________ يجلسون ويشربون الشاي و________ ويراقبون الناس الّذين يمشون في ________. في هذه المقاهي يتكلّم ________ عادةً مع الزبائن بصوتٍ عالٍ، ويُحضِر لهم ________ يطلبون بِسُرعة كبيرة. لكن إذا أردت ________ تجلِس مدّة طويلةً في مقهى مثل هذا فيجب أنْ تطلبَ ________ قهوةٍ أو شاي أو غير ذلك كلّ نِصْفِ ساعة تقريباً أو ________ أنْ تتركَ المقهى.

القواعد

1. The Different Types of ما

The particle ما serves different linguistic functions; several of which are described in this section.

a. The Relative Pronoun ما الموصولة *what*

This particle is used for non-humans and can be used before pronouns (ex. 1) as well as verbs (ex. 2), and in both cases it relates the same unrestricted meaning *what*. The term "unrestricted" means that when we use it, we are not talking about a certain known and understood object, like we do when we use الذي، التي، الذين.

So you can see what it is . . .	كَيْ ترى ما هو . . .	١
. . . and understand what happens in it.	. . . وتَعرِفَ ما يَجْري فيه.	٢

It is not uncommon to see this type of ما used before a past tense verb. You may ask yourself, "How can I differentiate the referential type of ما from ما النافية that negates past tense verbs?" Examine examples 3 and 4 to see if you can come up with a linguistic rule.

He explained to us what he saw in the museum.	وَصَف لَنا ما شاهَدَ في المُتحَف.	٣
I have not yet visited Cairo.	ما زُرْتُ القاهِرةَ حَتّى الآن.	٤

If you stated that the linguistic rule was that ما النافية begins sentences, you would be partially correct. Look at example 3. There are two verbs used in this sentence: the main verb وَصَف and the second verb شاهَد. In order to use ما الموصولة before a past tense verb, it must precede the second—not the main verb. By extension, we can conclude that ما النافية must precede the main verb in the sentence.

Difference between ما الموصولة وما النافية

1. ما الموصولة must precede a second verb of the sentence (i.e., not the main verb).
2. ما النافية must precede the main verb of the sentence.

b. The Interrogative ما الاستفهامية

This type of ما precedes nouns (ex. 3) and pronouns (ex. 4) and is the first type of ما that we learned when we learned the question: ما اسمك؟.

٥	ما اسمُكَ؟	*What is your name?*
٦	ما هي أرقام هَواتِف الطُلاّب؟	*What are the students' telephone numbers?*

c. The Redundant ما الزائدة

This particle occurred in our main reading passage after the word إذا creating the structure إذا ما. The ما of this structure can be omitted without changing the meaning of the sentence in any way.

٧	وإذا ما أَعْجَبَنا ذلِكَ البَلَد.	*And whether we liked that country.*

Summary of Four Types of ما

Relative pronoun	ما الموصولة
Negative particle	ما النافية
Interrogative particle	ما الاستفهاميّة
Redundant particle	ما الزائدة

تمرين ١٢

A. Read the following passage carefully and then circle all instances of ما الموصولة while underlining ما النافية:

وصلَت أمّ عدنان على خطوط «يو إس إير» الجوية إلى نيويورك من كلمبس في طريقِ عودتِها إلى سورية. ما سافرَت أمّ عدنان على هذه الطائرة مِن قَبل. نزلَت في فندقٍ قريبٍ من وسط المدينة كَيْ تَشتريَ ما تريد مِن ملابس وهدايا وغيرِها وترى ما يجري في هذه المدينة الكبيرة. ما أعجبتها جميع البضائع في السوق لكنَّ بعضَها كان كما تريد تماماً. في ذلك اليوم تحدَّثَت مع سيِّدة أمريكيّة باللغة الفَرنسيّة وكانت سعيدة جدّاً بذلك. دعَتها تلك السيِّدة إلى فنجان قهوة فقبَلَت. قضَت معها أمّ عدنان أكثر من ساعتين ثمَّ ترَكَتها وذهبَت إلى الفندق وما عَرَفَت ما تعمل ولا أين تسكن.

b. Using the different types of ما, express the following in Arabic:

1. عدنان did not study Arabic at the University of Michigan.
2. لينا would like to know what the President does in the White House.
3. What is your telephone number, نجوى ?
4. ليث asked about what is going on upstairs.
5. فاطمة did not stay at the Hilton in New York City.

2. Adverbs of Manner الظرف

ظروف الزمان والمكان in Arabic include such words شمالاً (*place*) and صباحاً (*time*). Other adverbials describe the manner in which a verb is performed, known as الحال. One way of forming الحال is by prefixing the preposition بـِ to certain verbal nouns creating prepositional phrases.

The waiter came quickly.	جاء النادِلُ بِسُرْعةٍ.	١

In example 1, بِسُرْعةٍ is a prepositional phrase comprised of the preposition بـِ and the verbal noun سُرْعة. Not all verbal nouns can be used in this manner, but some of the more frequently used are:

slowly	بِبُطءٍ	*peacefully*	بِسَلامٍ
nicely	بِلُطْفٍ	*quietly*	بِهدوءٍ

3. The Particle ألاّ *not to*

This particle is actually a combination of two particles (أنْ + لا = ألاّ) with the ن disappearing through a process of assimilation. Let's take a close look at how this particle changes the meaning of the sentence. You will place ألاّ where you would normally place أنْ in a sentence.

I should write to my brother.	يَجِبُ أن أكتُبَ رِسالةً إلى أخي.	١
I shouldn't write to my brother.	يَجِبُ ألاّ أكتُبَ رِسالةً إلى أخي.	٢

As you can see in example 2, يَجِبُ ألاّ is a way you can express *shouldn't.*

٣	أرجو أن تَقولَ هذا الشَيء لأحَمد.	*I wish that you would tell that to Ahmed.*
٤	أرجو ألاّ تَقولَ هذا الشَيء لأحَمد.	*I wish that you wouldn't tell that to Ahmed.*

Difference between ألاّ / إلاّ

Notice the difference between these two particles so you do not get confused:

إلاّ = except ألاّ = not to

المُفْرَدات

أجادَ	(يُجيدُ)	إجادة	(v.)	to master, to be skilled or proficient at
آسِف			(act. p.)	sorry
أحْضر	(يُحْضِرُ)	إحْضار	(v.)	to bring
ألاّ	(أنْ + لا)		(part.)	so as not to
اِعتَذَر	(يَعتَذِرُ)	اِعتِذار (عَن)	(v.)	to apologize, to excuse oneself from
بار	ج	بارات	(n., m.)	bar
باهِر			(act. p.)	dazzling, brilliant
بَرْق	ج	بُروق	(n., m.)	lightning
بَعَث	(يَبعَثُ)	بَعْث	(v.)	أرسل
تأخير			(n., m.)	delay, tardiness
ثَوب	ج	أثْواب	(n., m.)	dress
جَرى	(يَجري)	جَرْي	(v.)	to run, to happen, to occur
حَلْبة	ج	حَلَبات	(n., f.)	area; (dance) floor
خارِج			(act. p.)	outside
خافِت			(act. p.)	dim
خَرَق	(يَخْرِقُ)	خَرْق	(v.)	to pierce
داخِل			(act. p.)	inside

entering	(n., m.)			دُخول
to invite	(v.)	دَعْوة	(يَدعو)	دَعا
corn	(n., f.)			ذُرة
to see	(v.)	رؤية	(يَرى)	رأى
to observe, to watch	(v.)	مُراقَبة	(يُراقِبُ)	راقَبَ
to dance	(v.)	رَقْص	(يَرقُص)	رَقَص
flake, thin layer	(n., f.)	رَقائق	ج	رَقيقة
to forgive	(v.)	مُسامَحة	(يُسامِحُ)	سامَح
young man; youth	(n., m.)	شَباب	ج	شابّ
drinking	(n., m.)			شُرْب
longing	(n., m.)	أشْواق	ج	شَوْق
noisy, loud	(act. p.)			صاخِب
a light	(n., m.)	أضْواء	ج	ضَوْء
perfumed; nice	(act. p.)			عاطِر
to treat s.o.	(v.)	مُعامَلة	(يُعامِلُ)	عامَل
dough	(adj.)			عَجين
non-, un-, in-, dis-	(part.)			عَدَم
excuse	(n., m.)	أعْذار	ج	عُذْر

then, so, therefore, thus	(part.)			فَـ
past; last	(act. p.)			فائِت
band, group	(n., f.)	فِرَق	ج	فِرْقة
pistachios (peanuts)	(n., m.)	(فُسْتُق سودانيّ)		فُسْتُق
kiss	(n., f.)	قُبُلات	ج	قُبْلة
almost, on the verge of	(v.)		(يَكادُ)	كادَ
alcohol	(n., m.)		(الكُحول)	كُحول
as, like	(part.)			كَما
sign	(act. p.)	لافِتات	ج	لافِتة
table	(act. p.)	مَوائِد	ج	مائِدة
toasted; roasted	(pass. p.)			مُحَمَّص
to joke	(v.)	مَزْح	(يَمزَحُ)	مَزَح
audible, able to be heard	(pass. p.)			مَسْموع
bar	(n., m.)	مَشارِب	ج	مَشْرَب
drink, refreshments	(pass. p.)	مَشْروبات	ج	مَشْروب
to pass (time), to elapse	(v.)	مُضي	(يَمضي)	مَضى
next; coming	(act. p.)			مُقْبِل
written	(pass. p.)			مَكْتوب

مَلْهى	ج	مَلاهٍ	(n., m.)	place of entertainment
نَغَم	ج	أنْغام	(n., m.)	note, tune, melody
نَوى	(يَنْوي)	نية	(v.)	to intend
نِيون			(n., m.)	neon
وَقَف	(يَقِفُ)	وُقوف	(v.)	to stand, to stop
أوَمَض	(يومِضُ)		(v.)	to flash

الدَرْسُ الثامِن

Objectives

- Introducing Arabic jokes and humorous anecdotes
- Learning to understand and tell jokes; getting a feel for relating an extended anecdote
- **Grammar**: Introducing إذا الفجائية
- Reintroducing the verb of approximation كادَ
- **Revisiting**: المَبني للمَجهول والحال and the particle فـَ

رُكنُ المُفْرَداتِ الجَديدةِ

to send (to)	أرسَلَ (يُرْسِلُ) إرسال (إلى)
to find strange, to be surprised (at)	اِسْتَغْرَبَ (يَسْتَغْرِبُ) اِسْتِغْراب (مِن)
to consume	اِسْتَهْلَكَ (يَسْتَهْلِكُ) اِسْتِهْلاك
to await	اِنْتَظَرَ (يَنْتَظِرُ) اِنْتِظار
to get married (to)	تَزَوَّجَ (يَتَزَوَّجُ) تَزَوُّج (مِن)
to become embroiled in trouble	تَوَرَّطَ (يَتَوَرَّطُ) تَوَرُّط (في)
allergy, sensitivity; allergic (to)	حَساسية (مِن)
to tell (a joke)	حَكَى (يَحْكي) حَكي
especially	خِصّيصاً = خُصوصاً = خاصةً
suddenly	فجأةً = إذا بِـ
to kill; to murder	قَتَلَ (يَقْتُلُ) قَتْل
anxious	قَلِقٌ
joke	نُكْتة ج نُكَت / نِكات

تمرين ١

وافِق بين كَلِمتين واكتُب الأزواج السبعة في الوسط:

١	مُحضَّر		نُقود
٢	رئيس تَحرير		نَظيف
٣	پاوند		مَطبوخ
٤	إرْباً		فَحْص
٥	شِحْنة		رَطل
٦	ثَمَن		دَجاجة
٧	قَذِر		صَحيفة
٨	فَرْخ		ميناء
			قِطَعا

تمرين ٢

اختَرِ الكَلِمةَ الّتي لا تُناسِب باقي الكَلِماتِ في كُلِّ مَجْموعةٍ وبَيِّن السَبَب:

١- لافِتة　　مُستَشفى　　فُنُدق　　سِفارة

٢- مَريض　　عِلاج　　حِذاء　　طَبيب

٣- حَساسية　　حَزِنَ　　جُنَّ　　ماتَ

٤- مُدير تَحرير　　دَجاجة　　عيد الشُكر　　ديك حَبَش

٥- رئيس تَحرير　　ديك مَشوي　　سَفير　　ساعٍ

ابتسِم . . !

نُكَت من هنا وهناك

في ما يلي بعض النِكات المأخوذة من صُحُف عربية بالإضافة إلى مَقالة طريفة لرئيس تَحرير إحدى الجرائد. قد تدُلّ هذه النُكَت على طريقة تفكير العربي وما يجعله يبتسِم.

١

الزوجة: ماذا تفعل لو مُتُّ فَجأةً؟

الزوج: أُجَنُّ من شِدّة الحُزن.

الزوجة: وهل تتزوّج بعدي؟

الزوج: ما دُمتُ سأُجَنُّ فقد أتزوَّج.

٢

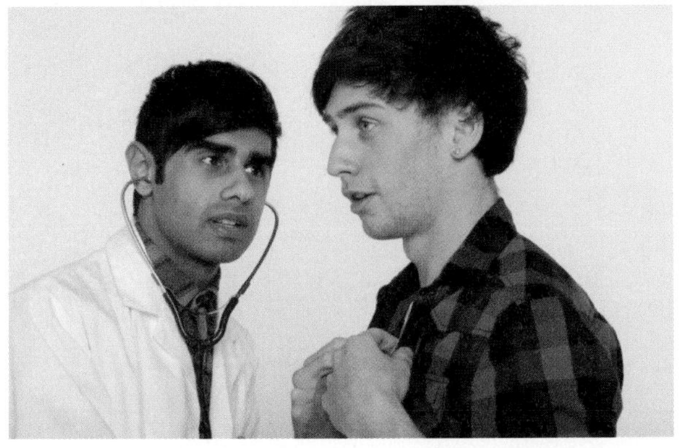

الطَبيب: لقد أجريتُ فَحصاً دقيقاً عليك وكل ما أراه أنك تحتاج إلى الراحة.

المَريض: ولكني أريد عِلاجاً. انظرْ إلى لِساني.

الطبَيب: وهذا أيضاً يحتاج إلى راحة.

٣

المَريض: الحقني يا دكتور! الحساسية تكاد تقتلني.

الطبيب: ارجع إلى البيت وافْتح جميع الشبابيك والأبواب قبل أن تنام.

في اليوم التالي عاد المريض إلى عيادة الطبيب.

الطبيب: هل ذهبَت الحساسية؟

المَريض: لا يا دكتور، ذهب التلفاز والراديو والساعة.

٤

دخل أحد الأشخاص فندقاً قذِراً واستغرب عندما رأى لافتة عند مدخله كُتِبَ عليها «امسح حذاءك» فأضاف إليها «عند خروجك».

امسح حذاءك
عند خروجك

٥

ينتظر الشاب تذكرة عودة

الأوّل: لي صديق ربح تذكرة سفر لأستراليا.

الثاني: وأين هو الآن؟

الأوّل: مازال هناك منذ خمسة أعوام ينتظر أن يربح تذكرة عودة.

٦

الأوّل:	من أين لكَ هذه النقود؟
الثاني:	من الكتابة.
الأول:	وماذا تكتب؟
الثاني:	أكتب رسالة إلى أبي فيُرسِل لي النقود.

عيدُ الشُكر 

بقلم جهاد الخازن

كتب جهاد الخازن في عديد من الصحف العربية، وقد ظهرت المقالة التالية في صحيفة الشرق الأوسط منذ عدة سنوات حين كان رئيس تحريرها. (بتصرّف)

يحتفل الأمريكيون في شهر تشرين الثاني بعيد الشكر وهو عيد يشكرون فيه الله على نعمه عليهم، ويحتفلون به بعشاء عائلي يأكلون فيه ديكاً رومياً (حَبَش) مُحضَّراً على طريقة الأمريكيين الأوائل.

ديك حَبَش

وكنتُ قبل سنوات طويلة في بيروت قد تورّطت في «عيد شكر» لم أخرج منه بغير الصداع. بدأ الأمر بسيطاً، فقد جاءني مدير التحرير وقال: إن في بيروت شِحْنات كبيرة من ديوك الحبش وصلت بمناسبة عيد الشكر لاستهلاك الأمريكيين من سكّان البلد. وإني اشتريت ديك حبش «ثلاثين پاوندا».

أعجبني أن يزن ديك رومي واحد ثلاثين پاونداً. واستدعيت الساعي وطلبت منه أن يذهب إلى السوق المركزية ويشتري لي ديكاً وزنه ١٤ كيلوغراماً.

وغاب الساعي ساعة وساعتين، ثمّ اتصل بي هاتفياً ليقول إنه لا يوجد ديك حبش بهذا الوزن. فكلّ ما رأى في حدود خمسة كيلوغرامات، مع واحد أو اثنين فقط وزنهما حوالي سبعة. لكن بما أنّ مدير التحرير اشترى ديك حبش وزنه ١٥ كيلوغراماً فلا يُعقَل أن يأكل رئيس التحرير فرخة. وطلبت من الساعي أن يصلني بمدير السوق المركزية ففعل. وحكيت له القصّة فقال الرجل إن عنده آخر شحنة من ديوك الحبش في الميناء وسيأخذ الساعي معه ليختار أكبرها.

أحد الأمريكيين الأوائل

وحمل الساعي إلى البيت ديكاً رومياً وزنه ٣٢ رَطْلاً إنكليزياً، ووجدنا أنّه أكبر من كلّ الطناجر الموجودة، بل وأكبر من الفرن. ثمّ رأينا أنّ أفضل طريقة هي أن نقطّعه قطعاً لنستطيع إدخاله الفرن فنأكله مشوياً.

فرخ

وجلسنا نَعدُ النفسَ بعشاء على الطريقة الأمريكية، وإذا بالباب يُدَقّ. وفتحتُ فوجدت صاحب السوق المركزية أمامي، وقد كان قلِقاً بشكل ظاهر. قال الرجل: الديك . . . الديك . . . أين الديك؟ قلتُ إنه في الفرن.

كاد صاحب السوق المركزية يبكي وهو يرى الديك مقطّعاً إرباً. فهمتُ منه أن ذلك الديك كان الوحيد بهذا الوزن وأنّه أُرسِل خصوصاً إلى السفير الأمريكيّ في بيروت ليكون نجم حفلة عيد الشكر في السِفارة.

كادَ الرجُل يَبكي

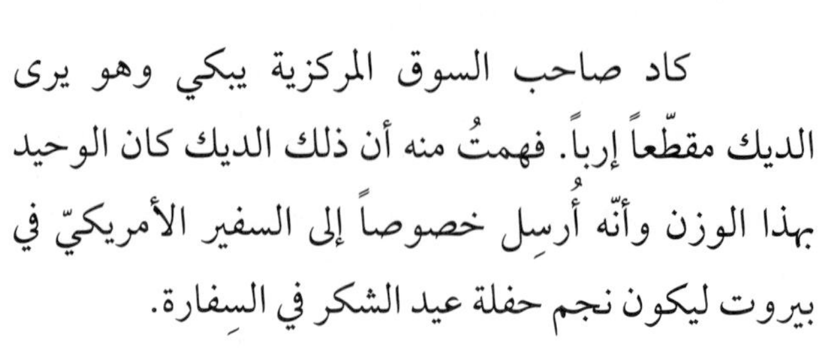

ورأيت مدير التحرير في اليوم التالي وحكيت له القصّة ثمّ عاتبته على توريطي في البحث عن ديك وزنه ثلاثون رَطْلاً مع أنه لا يوجد ديك بهذا الوزن في البلد كلّها. وردّ الرجل باستغراب إنه لم يقُل لي شيئاً من هذا أبداً، فقد قال بالإنكليزية إن الديك «ثلاثون پاونداً» وكان يعني بكلمة « پاوند» ليرة لبنانية لا رَطْلاً إنكليزياً كما فهمتُ، فقد دفع ثلاثين ليرة ثمن ديك وزنه خمسة كيلوغرامات. وكلّ عام وأنتم بخير.

تمرين ٣

للمحادثة:

أ- حاول قدر الإمكان أن تحكي بالعربيّة نكتةً تعرفها جيداً لزميلك في غرفة الصفّ.

ب- احكِ قصّة طريفة لزميلك حدثت معك في الماضي. من الممكن أن تفيدك الأفكار التالية:

١- متى حصلت القصّة الطريفة وكم كان عمرك؟

٢- ماذا كانت ظروفها؟

٣- مَن كان معك؟

٤- ماذا كانت النتيجة؟

٥- هل كنت الوحيد الذي اعتبرت القصّة مضحكة؟

٦- ماذا فكر الناس الآخَرون بالنسبة إليها؟

تمرين ٤

أجِبْ عن الأسئلة التالية حسب النصّ:

١- ما الفكرة الرئيسة في نص "عيد الشكر"؟

٢- حدِّد الأفكار الثانوية في "عيد الشكر".

٣- اكتب عنواناً آخر للنص.

تمرين ٥

اكمل الجمل التالية بالاختيار المناسب وفق نص القراءة:

١- الزوجة في النكتة الأولى ________________ .

☐ مجنونة ☐ ميتة ☐ حزينة ☐ حية

٢- المريض في النكتة الثانية مصاب ________________ .

☐ بالحساسية ☐ بالصداع ☐ بالحزن ☐ بالجنون

٣- يرى الطبيب في النكتة الثالثة أنّ الرجلَ ________________ .

☐ مريض ☐ بخير ☐ حزين ☐ مجنون

٤- يظنّ الرجُل أنّ الفندق ________________ .

☐ رخيص ☐ غال ☐ قَذِر ☐ نظيف

٥- ربِح الصديق تذكرة طائرة ________________ .

☐ ذهاباً وإياباً ☐ ذهاباً فقط ☐ إياباً فقط ☐ إلى بلده

٦- يحصل الشخص الثاني في النكتة السادسة على النقود من ________________ .

☐ الصحيفة ☐ عمله ☐ صديقه ☐ أبيه

٧- ذهب ________________ إلى السوق المركزية لشِراء الديك.

☐ مدير التحرير ☐ ساعي المكتب ☐ رئيس التحرير ☐ السفير الأمريكي

٨- كان احتفال الكاتب بعيد الشكر مصدراً ________________ .

☐ لسرور عظيم ☐ لعشاء ممتاز ☐ لصداع ومشاكل ☐ لحزن شديد

٩- قطّع جهاد الخازن الديك قطعاً كي ________________.

☐ يشويه بالفرن ☐ يأكله قطعاً ☐ يضعه بالطنجرة ☐ ليحتفل بالعيد

١٠- أُرسِل الديك الرومي الّذي شواه الكاتب خِصّيصاً إلى ________________.

☐ السفارة الأمريكية ☐ الأمريكيين في بيروت

☐ الأمريكيين الأوائل ☐ رئيس تحرير الجريدة

تمرين ٦

احكِ قصّة لزميلك بحيث كان عليك أن تعاتب فيها شخصاً ما لسبب ما. قد تفيدك الأفكار التالية:

١- ما الّذي زعّلك؟

٢- كيف حَصَل الشيء المزعج؟

٣- ماذا كان رد فعل الشخص الّذي عاتبته؟

٤- بماذا تشعر الآن بعد أن صار ما صار؟

٥- هل كان هناك أشخاص آخرون رأوا ما حصل؟

٦- متى حدث هذا الحادث وكم كان عمرك؟

تمرين ٧

اكتب «خطأ» أو «صواب» إلى جانب كلّ جملة ثمّ صحّح الجمل الخطأ:

١- سوف يتزوّج الزوج بعد موت زوجته.

٢- حصل مريض الحساسية على علاج نَفَعَه.

٣- يظنّ المريض في النكتة الثالثة أنّه يحتاج إلى علاج.

٤- أرض الشارع أقذر من الفندق حسب رأي أحد الأشخاص.

٥- لا يزال الصديق في أستراليا يعمل فيها.

٦- كان جهاد الخازن يسكن في أمريكا حين كتب هذه المقالة.

٧- يحتفل اللبنانيون بعيد الشكر.

٨- ورّط مدير التحرير الكاتب في أمر الديك الرومي.

تمرين ٨

أعد ترتيب الجمل لتشكّل فِقرة كاملة. الجملة الأولى في مكانها المناسب:

١- أردتُ وثلاثة من أصدقائي أن نقضيَ إجازة الربيع على الشاطئ.

كان القطار موجوداً في المحطة وفيه بعض الركّاب.

استغرقت الرحلة خمس ساعات إذ وصلنا في الساعة الثانية عشرة والنصف.

أولاً اشترينا تذاكر القطار.

صعدنا إلى القطار ووضعنا الحقائب في مكانها.

ركِبنا سيّارة أجرة من المحطة إلى الفندق.

جلستُ إلى جانب الشبّاك وجلس عبد الرحيم مقابلي.

في يوم السفر اتّجهنا إلى محطة القطار بسيّارة أم عبد الرحيم.

أمّا مروان وسعيد فجلسا إلى يسارنا.

وصلنا إلى المحطة في الساعة السابعة، أي قبل موعد القطار بنصف ساعة.

القواعد

1. إذا الفُجائية lo and behold

While different from conditional إذا (*if*) in meaning, إذا الفُجائية is pronounced and spelled exactly the same. However, إذا الفُجائية denotes a sudden or unexpected action.

١	خَرَجنا مِن المَبنى فَإذا بلافِتةٍ تَسقُطُ فَوقَ رؤوسِنا.	*We exited the building and lo and behold a sign fell on top of our heads.*

This construct is usually followed by a بـِ which introduces the thing that unexpectedly happened, as in example 1. As well, this structure is usually preceded by a فَـ (as in example 1) or a وَ as occurred in our reading passages.

٢	جَلَسنا لِلعَشاء وإذا بالبابِ يُدَقُّ	*We sat down for dinner and suddenly there was a knock at the door.*

إذا الفُجائية structure does not necessarily have to followed by the بـِ. Let's take example 2 and remove the بـِ as a model.

٣	جَلَسنا لِلعَشاء وإذا البابُ يُدَقُّ	*We sat down for dinner and suddenly there was a knock at the door.*

This change, as you can see by comparing examples 2 and 3, has had no effect on the meaning of the sentence.

تمرين ٩

Use إذا الفُجائية to translate the following sentences into Arabic:

1. I stepped out of the door and it was raining.
2. The mother went into the bedroom and lo and behold the little child was on the floor.
3. He went to the bank to withdraw (سَحَبَ) some money and it was closed.
4. We arrived at the movie theater, and there was نادية waiting for us.

2. Verbs of Approximation أفعال المُقارَبة

Arabic offers its speakers the ability to express the idea of *almost*; *practically*; or *just about* in verb form:

كادَ، كَرَب، أوشَكَ

While similar to كانَ وأخَواتها, this set requires the second verb to be in the present tense:

The tree almost died.	كادَتِ الشَجَرةُ تموتُ.	١
The tree almost died.	كادَتِ الشَجَرةُ أن تَموتَ.	

As you can see in example 1, كادَ can be followed by a present tense verb, or أنْ followed by a present tense verb without changing the meaning of the sentence.

كاد Negated by ما، لَم، لا *scarcely*, *hardly*

When كادَ is negated with ما، لَم، لا its meaning changes to *hardly* or *scarcely*.

We had hardly finished dinner when the visitors came.	ما كِدْنا نَنتهي مِن العَشاء حتّى أتى الزُوّار.	٣
He had hardly sat down when the phone rang.	لَم يَكَدْ يَجلِسُ حتّى دَقَّ الهاتف.	٢
I can hardly sleep because of the heat.	لا أكادُ أنامُ مِن شِدّةِ الحَرِّ.	٤

تَصريف الفِعْل «كادَ»			
الضَمير	الماضي		المُضارِع
أنا	كِدْتُ	المُتَكَلِّم	أكادُ
نَحْنُ	كِدْنا		نَكادُ
أنْتَ	كِدْتَ	المُخاطَب	تَكادُ
أنْتِ	كِدْتِ		تَكادينَ
أنْتُما	كِدْتُما		تَكادانِ
أنْتُنَّ	كِدْتُنَّ		تَكَدْن
أنْتُم	كِدْتُم		تَكادونَ
هو	كادَ	الغائب	يَكادُ
هِيَ	كادَت		تَكادُ
هُما	كادا		يَكادانِ
هُما	كادَتا		تَكادانِ
هُنَّ	كِدنَ		يَكَدْنَ
هُمْ	كادوا		يَكادونَ

مُلاحَظة

This table can also be used for the conjugation of نامَ interestingly enough.

تمرين ١٠

Convey these meanings in Arabic using كادَ:

1. The day is almost over.
2. No sooner had the film started than the phone rang.
3. I can barely see the ocean from this window.
4. Sami's flight is about to arrive.

3. Verbs in the Passive Voice مَبني للمَجهول

Our main reading passage had multiple instances of verbs in مَبني لِلمَجهول such as the following:

أُرْسِلَ، كُتِبَ، أُجَنُّ، يُدَقُّ

Let's take a look at a couple of examples of these passive verbs from our passage:

> **مُلاحَظة**
>
> يُجَنُّ, like هُرِعَ, only exists in the passive voice.

It was sent specifically to the American Ambassador.	وأنّه أُرسِل خُصوصاً إلى السفير الأمريكيّ	١
He was surprised when he saw a sign at its entrance written on it, "wipe your feet."	واستَغْرَبَ عِنْدَما رأى لافِتةً عِنْدَ مَدْخَلِه كُتِبَ علَيْها "امسح حذاءك"	٢
I would go crazy from intense grief.	أُجَنُّ من شدّة الحُزن.	٣
And suddenly there was a knock at the door.	وإذا بالباب يُدَقُّ.	٤

4. Unlikely Conditions with لَوْ (*if*)

Hypothetical لَوْ is followed by a past tense verb and is used specifically for unlikely situations. From our passage we have:

What would you do if I died suddenly?	ماذا تَفعَلُ لَوْ مُتُّ فَجأةً؟	١

We have to bear in mind that in a statement the answer clause is introduced by لَـ :

If I had known she was in town, I would have visited her.	لَو عَلِمتُ أنّها في المَدينةِ لَزُرتُها.	٢

مُلاحَظة

When you want to express an idea containing *would have*, you will need to use the لَو . . . لَـ structure.

5. The Conjunction فَـ (*so, then, therefore*)

While only one letter in length, this particle is a very powerful tool in speech and writing in that it signals resumption of an earlier thought. It can be translated as *so*, *then*, or *therefore*, but you do not have to translate it at all in some cases.

So, everything he saw was within five kilos.	فَكُلُّ ما رآه في حُدود خَمسةِ كيلو غرامات.

6. The Circumstantial واو الحال (*while; when*)

Let's take a look at an example of واو الحال as it occurred in our main reading passage:

He almost cried when he saw the turkey dismembered.	كادَ يَبكي وهو يرى الديكَ مُقطَّعاً.

The واو here does not indicate a conjunction of thoughts; rather it represents an aspect of time wherein two things are happening simultaneously loosely translated into English as *when*.

تمرين ١١

a. **Identify instances of قَد as it was used in our main reading passages. After identifying them, on a separate sheet of paper indicate whether they denote completed action or possibility.**

b. **Express the following meanings in Arabic using لَم، قَد، لَو، جُنَّ، كادَ.**

1. They may be a little late this evening.
2. She took two aspirin, but they did not do her any good.
3. If I were you, I would participate in the theater festival.
4. He almost went out of his mind with joy.

7. Vocabulary Enhancement توسيع المفردات

بِما أنَّ (*since; because*)

In order to say, "*because* I was . . ." or "*since* . . .", we use بِما أنَّ. This structure is followed by a nominal sentence introduced by either an attached pronoun or a noun.

١	بِما أنَّ المطعمَ مُغلَقٌ، هَل تُحِبّون أن تأتوا إلى بيتي؟	*Since the restaurant is closed, would you like to come to my house?*
٢	بِما أنَّكَ تَتَكَلَّمُ الفَرَنسيّة، مُمكِن أنْ تَقرأ لي هذه الرِسالة؟	*Since you speak French, could you read this letter for me?*

تَذَوَّق الثَقافَة العَرَبيَّة

There is no equivalent for the word *supermarket* in the western, particularly American, sense. Many speakers of Arabic simply use the English word. However, the conventional MSA equivalent is سوق مَركَزيّة meaning *central market.*

تمرين ١٢

آ **أجب عن الأسئلة وفق نص الاستماع:**

١- ما الفكرة الرئيسة في نص الاستماع؟

٢- حدِّد بعض الأفكار الثانوية في النص.

٣- كم رسالة قرأت حنان ذلك اليوم؟ ممَّن؟

٤- لماذا اتصلت حنان بريم؟

٥- مَن هؤلاء الأشخاص؟ سَمر، هَديل، أُبَيّ؟

ب- أكمل الجمل التالية بالاخيار المناسب وفق نص الاستماع:

١- وضعت ريم الرسالة ________________ .

☐ في البريد ☐ على النافذة ☐ تحت الطاولة ☐ على الأرض

٢- وجدَت حنان في الشقّة ________________ .

☐ رسالة من ريم ☐ مكالمتين من سمر وريم

☐ عرسالة من ريم ورسالة من سمر ☐ رسالة من ريم ومكالمة من سمر

٣- أخذَت ريم ________________ معها إلى حفلة عيد الميلاد.

☐ أختها سمر ☐ أباها ☐ صديقتها ☐ ابنها

ج- لَخِّص المُقابَلة مع زينا بحوالى خمسين كَلمة.

د- اكتب «خطأ» أو «صواب» إلى جانب كلّ جملة ثمّ صحِّح الجمل الخطأ:

١- وجدَت حنان رسالة في صندوق البريد.

٢- حضرَت سمر إلى شقّة ريم وأخبرَتها بحفلة عيد الميلاد.

٣- كان الخطأ بسبب والِد ريم (أبيها).

تَذَوّق الثَقافَة العَرَبيَّة

إليكم بعض النكات للمطالعة والتسلية. نتمنّى أن تستمتعوا بقراءتها كما استمتعنا بها.

*****

القاضي للمتهم: كم مرّة حكمتُ عليك سابقاً؟

المتهم: حوالى عشر مرات.

القاضي: إذاً سأحكم عليك الآن بأقصى عقوبة.

المتهم: لماذا يا حضرة القاضي؟ أليس عندكم تنزيلات للزبائن؟

*****

تَذَوَّق الثَقافَة العَرَبيَّة

*****

القاضي للص: هل تعترف بأنك سرقت هذا المحل ثلاث مرّات؟

اللص: نعم يا سيدي، ولكني لم أسرق منه إلا فستاناً واحداً.

القاضي مستغرباً: فستاناً واحداً، في المرّات الثلاث؟

اللص : نعم يا سيدي، ففي المرّتين الأوليين لم يعجب زوجتي لون الفساتين.

*****

المُفْرَدات

small piece of s.th.	(n., f.)	إرَب	ج	إرْبة
to send, to transmit	(v.)	إرسال	(يُرسِلُ)	أرسَلَ
to call, to send for, to summon	(v.)	اِستِدعاء	(يَستَدْعي)	اِستَدعى
to find strange, odd, unusual	(v.)	اِستِغراب	(يَستَغرِبُ)	اِستَغرَبَ
to consume	(v.)	اِستِهلاك	(يَستَهلِكُ)	اِستَهلَكَ
to await	(v.)	اِنتِظار	(يَنتَظِرُ)	اِنتَظَرَ
to cry, to weep	(v.)	بُكاء	(يَبكي)	بَكى
to get married	(v.)	تَزَوُّج	(يَتَزَوَّجُ)	تَزَوَّجَ
to become embroiled in, involved in	(v.)	تَوَرُّط	(يَتَوَرَّطُ)	تَوَرَّطَ
to go crazy, to go mad (passive)	(v.)	جُنون	(يُجَنُّ)	جُنَّ
to edit (also: write, liberate)	(v.)	تَحرير	(يُحَرِّرُ)	حَرَّرَ
to be sad, to mourn	(v.)	حُزْن	(يَحزَنُ)	حَزِنَ
allergy (allergic to)	(n., f.)		(مِن)	حَساسية
to tell, to recount, to narrate	(v.)	حَكي	(يَحكي)	حَكى
specifically	(adv.)			خِصّيصاً
to knock, to bang	(v.)	دَقّ	(يَدِقُّ)	دَقَّ

precise, accurate	(adj.)			دَقيق
doctor, physician (loan word used in colloquial speech)	(n., m.)	دكاتِرة	ج	دُكتور
rest	(n., f.)			راحة
to win	(v.)	رِبْح	(يَربَحُ)	رَبِحَ
mail carrier, janitor	(n., m.)	سُعاة	(الساعي) ج	ساعٍ
cargo, shipment, load	(n., f.)	شِحْنات	ج	شِحْنة
strength, intensity	(n., f.)			شِدّة
owner, proprietor, friend, companion	(act. p.)	أصْحاب	ج	صاحِب
headache	(n., m.)			صُداع
uncommon, funny, novel	(adj.)			طَريف
saucepan, skillet	(n., f.)	طَناجِر	ج	طَنْجَرة
to chide, to scold mildly	(v.)	مُعاتَبة	(يُعاتِبُ)	عاتَبَ
to be reasonable, to comprehend	(v.)	عَقْل	(يَعقِلُ)	عَقَلَ
to be absent	(v.)	غِياب	(يَغيبُ)	غابَ
suddenly	(adv.)			فَجْأةً
to examine, to test	(v.)	فَحْص	(يَفحَصُ)	فَحَصَ
chick	(n., f.)	فِراخ	ج	فَرْخ
to kill, to murder	(v.)	قَتْل	(يَقتُلُ)	قَتَلَ

dirty, filthy	(n., m.)			قَذِر
worried, uneasy, apprehensive	(n., m.)			قَلِقٌ
to be about to do s.th., at the point of, almost	(v.)		(يَكادُ)	كادَ
to catch up, to keep close	(v.)	لَحاق	(يَلحَقُ)	لَحِقَ
tongue, language	(n., m.)	ألسِنة/ ألسُن	ج	لِسان
entrance, foyer, introduction	(n., m.)	مَداخِل	ج	مَدخَل
to wipe off, to erase, to clean	(v.)	مَسْح	(يَمسَحُ)	مَسَحَ
essay, article, editorial	(n., f.)	مَقالات	ج	مَقالة
star	(n., m.)	نُجوم	ج	نَجْم
easy life, blessing	(n., f.)	نِعَم	ج	نِعْمة
money, currency	(n., m.)	نُقود	ج	نَقْد
joke, anecdote	(n., f.)	نُكَت/ نِكات	ج	نُكتة
to get s.o. in trouble	(v.)	تَوريط	(يُوَرِّطُ)	وَرَّط
to weigh	(v.)	وَزْن	(يَزِنُ)	وَزَنَ
bar	(n., m.)	مَشارِب	ج	مَشْرَب
drink, refreshments	(pass. p.)	مَشْروبات	ج	مَشْروب
to pass (time), to elapse	(v.)	مُضي	(يَمضي)	مَضى
next; coming	(act. p.)			مُقْبِل

written	(pass. p.)			مَكْتوب
place of entertainment	(n., m.)	مَلاهٍ	ج	مَلْهى
note, tune, melody	(n., m.)	أنْغام	ج	نَغَم
to intend	(v.)	نية	(يَنْوي)	نَوى
neon	(n., m.)			نِيون
to stand, to stop	(v.)	وُقوف	(يَقِفُ)	وَقَف
to flash	(v.)		(يومِضُ)	أوَمَض

الدَرْسُ التاسِع

Objectives

- Learning to describe vacations and places of interest
- Introduction to historical personalities and events through narration
- **Grammar**: Introduction to prepositional phrases and prepositions that collocate with certain verbs
- **Revisiting**: Expressing reason with لِـ، كَيْ، حَتّى،اسم الفِعْل
- **Culture**: Popular epics and folk heroes; storytelling; shadow puppets; the meaning of the phrase عليه السَّلام

رُكنُ المُفْرَداتِ الجَديدةِ

economy	اقْتِصاد
to discover	اِكْتَشَفَ (يَكْتَشِفُ) اِكْتِشاف
visa (entry, exit)	تأشيرة (دُخول وخُروج)
tradition(s) (habits and traditions)	تَقْليد ج تَقاليد (عادات وتقاليد)
passport	جواز سَفَر
to show, to indicate, to point out	دَلّ (يَدُلُّ) دَلالة
popular	شَعَبيّ (مِن شَعْب = ناس)
to cost	كَلَّف (يُكَلِّفُ) تكليف/ تكلِفة
to represent, to act (actor)	مَثَّلَ (يُمَثِّلُ) تمثيل (مُمَثِّل)
center	مَرْكَز ج مَراكِز
café	مَقْهى (مِن قَهوة)
middle, mid-	مُنْتَصَف (مِن نِصْف)
original	أصليّ
national	وَطَنيّ

تمرين ١

وافِق بين كَلِمتين واكتُب الأزواج السبعة في الوسط:

١	عَثَر		مَسجِد
٢	حارّة		السِريانيّة
٣	شاغِر		قَلعة
٤	جامِع		قِصّة
٥	حِكاية		وَجَد
٦	الآراميّة		فارِغ
٧	حُجْرة		زُقاق
			غُرفة

تمرين ٢

وافِق بين كلمات من العمودين لتشكّل عبارات من مُضاف ومُضاف إليه واكتُب الكَلِمَتين في الوسط:

١	تأشيرة		سَفَر
٢	جواز		الفاتِحة
٣	سيرة		أُجرة
٤	خيال		دُخول
٥	سورة		دِمشق
٦	خُطوط		عَنتَرة
٧	سيّارة		الطيران
٨	مُتحَف		الشيوخ
			الظِلّ

تمرين ٣

اخترِ الكَلِمةَ الّتي لا تُناسِب باقي الكَلِماتِ في كُلِّ مَجْموعةٍ وبَيِّنِ السَبَب:

١-	مَغسلة	غُرفة	مِرحاض	نَبات	حَمّام
٢-	الشام	دار ميسيق	دمشقا	دامسكي	المعادي
٣-	أخبر	تأخّر	قال	تكلّم	تحدّث

مايكل براون يزور دمشق

في عطلة الربيع سافر مايكل براون وصديقاه ويليَم وريتشارد من مِصرَ إلى سورية. هذا ما كتبه لأستاذه في الولايات المتّحدة عن رحلته:

أردتُ أنا وصديقاي ويليَم وريتشارد أن نزور سورية في عطلة الربيع. أوّلاً كان علينا أن نحصل على تأشيرات دخول إلى سورية من السِفارة السورية في حيّ الدُقّي. ثانياً اشترينا تذاكر السفر وقد كلّفَت التذكرة نحو ٢٦٠ دولاراً ذهاباً وإياباً على الخُطوط الجويّة السوريّة. في يوم السفر ركِبت سيّارة أجرة إلى حي الزَمالِك لأصل إلى شقّة ويليم وريتشارد. من هناك ركِبنا سيّارة أجرة أخرى إلى المطار ودفعنا للسائق أربعينَ جُنَيهاً أجرة الركوب.

دمشق

أقلعَت الطائرة في موعدها وكانت الرحلة قصيرة إلى سورية. هبطَت الطائرة في مطار دمشق الدولي بعد ساعتين تقريباً. توجّهنا إلى مركز الجوازات حيث ختم الموظَّف جوازاتنا. خرجنا من مبنى المطار وركِبنا سيّارة أجرة إلى فندق «بِلال»، إذ حصلنا على اسمه من صديقة لنا زارَت دمشق منذ شهور. لكن لم يكن هناك غرفة شاغرة، لذلك ذهبنا إلى فندق آخر قريب من سوق الحَميدية أيضاً. استأجرنا غرفة واحدة بثلاثة أَسرّة. كان في الغرفة مغسلة، لكن الحمّام كان خارجَ الغرفة، وقد كان والحمد لله نظيفاً معظم الوقت.

تحدّثنا مع مدير الفندق وكان شاباً لطيفاً. أخبرَنا أنّ دمشق أقدم مدينة في العالم سُكِنَت دون انقطاع. وقال إن المخطوطات الّتي اكتُشِفَت في إبلا تدُلّ على أن «دامسكي» كانت مدينة ذات اقتصاد قويّ في الألف الثالث قبل الميلاد. وفي الكتابات المصريّة القديمة عرفها المصريون القدماء باسم «دمشقا». وفي منتصف الألف الثاني قبل الميلاد صارت عاصمة المملكة الآراميّة «دار ميسيق» أي الدار المَسقِية. والآراميون هم سُكّان سورية الأصليّون وكانوا يتكلّمون اللغة السريانيّة. ولا يزال سكّان ثلاث قرى في الجبال القريبة من دمشق يتكلّمون السِريانيّة إلى اليوم، وهي مَعْلولا وجَبَعْدين ونَجْعا.

في اليوم الثاني ذهبنا إلى الجامع الأموي. قبل أن ندخل المسجد كان علينا أن نخلَع أحذيتنا. تجوّلنا في المسجِد دون أحذية وكان منظره جميلاً جِداً. لكن كان هناك أعداد كبيرة من الحمام لذلك كان علينا أن نعرف أين نضع أقدامنا.

بعد ذلك تجوّلنا في سوق الحَميدية القريبة من الجامع، ثمّ ذهبنا إلى قصر العَظْم، وهو مُتحَف التقاليد الشعبيّة. المُتحَف موجود في دار دِمشقيّة قديمة كانت دار والي دمشق أسعد باشا العَظْم أيّام الحُكم العُثمانيّ منذ حوالي ٢٩٠ عاماً. يُصوّر المُتحَف الحياة الدِمشقيّة في ذلك الوقت، وكلّ غرفة فيه تُمثّل صورة من صُوَرها: ففي إحدى الغُرَف رأينا كيف كانوا يحضِّرون العروس للعُرس، بما في ذلك ثوب العُرس والحذاء الخشبي الخاص وأدوات التجميل. وفي حجرة أخرى شاهدنا أدوات الطبخ والأواني المستعملة في ذلك الزمن.

ثمّ دخلنا غرفة تحكي قصّة المقهى الشعبيّ، حيث يوجَد «الحَكَواتي» الّذي يقرأ كلّ ليلة جُزْءاً من حكاية طويلة كسيرة «عَنتَرَة» وسيرة «أبو زَيد الهِلالي» وسيرة «الظاهِر بَيْبَرْس». وكان في المقهى شاشة يظهر خلفها دُمى صغيرة تُمثّل قصّة، ويُسمّى هذا التمثيل «خيال الظِلّ». كان هناك أيضاً تمْثالان لرجلين يلعبان «السيجة» وهي لعبة شعبيّة انقرضَت الآن. وفي مكان آخَر شاهدنا حبّة قمح نُقِشَت عليها سورة «الفاتِحة» من القرآن الكريم.

في المساء ذهبنا إلى فندق الميريديان حيث تناولنا القهوة الفرنسيّة مع الـ«كرواسان». اشترينا من الفندق قُمصاناً قطنيّة وكلّف الواحد ٢٥٠ ليرة سوريّة (الدولار الواحد يساوي ٤٧ ليرة تقريباً).

في صباح اليوم التالي توجّهنا إلى مُتحَف دمشق الوَطَنيّ وهو من أحسن المتاحف العربية حيث توجَد فيه آثار سورية وإغريقيّة ورومانيّة وعربيّة إسلاميّة. شاهدنا دِرع صلاح الدين الأيوبي المصنوعة من زَرْد الحديد. أمّا الشيء الّذي أعجبني جدّاً فكان رَقيماً فَخّاريّاً صغيراً بحجم الإصبع نُقِشَت عليه أوّل أبجديّة في العالم. وقد عُثِرَ على هذا الرَقيم في «رأس الشَمْرة» في شمال سورية حيث كانت مملكة أوغاريت.

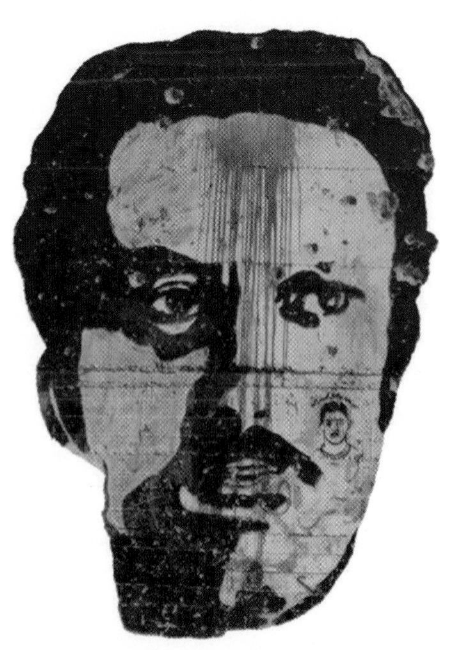

عدنا إلى الفندق ووجدتُ أنّ مدير الفندق قد أحضر لي كتاباً وهو قصّة للكاتبة السورية غادة السمّان وقدّمه لي هدية. وقد كنتُ أخبرتُه أني أريد قِصصاً لها وللكاتب الفلسطينيّ غسّان كنفاني لأني لم أعثر على هذه الكتب في القاهرة. اشتريت من دمشق أيضاً شريطين للمغنّي اللبناني مارسيل خليفة لم أجدهما في القاهرة.»

تمرين ٤

للمحادثة: احكِ قصّة لزميلك عن رحلة قُمت بها إلى بلد آخر أو ولاية أخرى. حاول أن تحكي هذه القصّة بالتفاصيل من أوّلها إلى آخرها قدر ما تستطيع. قد تساعدك الأسئلة الآتية في القيام بالحوار:

١- كيف سافرت إلى هناك؟

٢- متى وصلت ومع مَن؟

٣- ماذا فعلت في ذلك المكان؟

٤- ما الأماكن الّتي زرتها؟

٥- ماذا رأيت هناك؟

تمرين ٥

أجب عن الأسئلة الآتية وفق نص القراءة:

١- ما الفكرة الرئيسة في نص القراءة؟

٢- حدِّد بعض الأفكار الثانوية.

٣- اكتب عنواناً آخر للدرس.

٤- كم تكلّف سيّارة الأجرة من القاهرة إلى المطار؟

٥- صِف الغرفة الّتي حصل عليها مايكل؟

٦- لماذا ذهب مايكل وأصدقاؤه إلى فندق بِلال أوّلاً؟

٧- أين تُحكى اللغة السِريانيّة هذه الأيّام؟

٨- أين أقيم مُتحف التقاليد الشعبية؟

٩- ماذا يُصوِّر مُتحف التقاليد الشعبيّة؟

١٠- ما الّذي أعجب مايكل في مُتحف دمشق الوطنيّ؟

تمرين ٦

اكتب فِقرة عن المواضيع الآتية لا تقلّ عن خمسين كلمة. لا تنسَ ذكر أهمية كلٍ منها من حيث التاريخ والتراث:

١- سوق الحميدية ٢- الحَكَواتي ٣ - رأس الشَمْرة

تمرين ٧

اكتب «خطأ» أو «صواب» إلى جانب كلّ جملة ثمّ صحّح الجمل الخطأ:

١- نزل مايكل براون في فندق بِلال بدمشق.
٢- استأجر مايكل غرفة مع حمّام في الفندق.
٣- دمشق أقدم مدينة في العالم.
٤- أسعد باشا العَظْم والي دمشق في الوقت الحاضر.
٥- شاهد مايكل عمليّة تحضير العروس في مُتحف دمشق الوَطَنيّ.
٦- رأى مايكل أوّل أبجديّة في العالم في رأس الشَمْرة.
٧- أراد مايكل أن يحصل على كتب للكاتبة السورية غادة السمان والكاتب الفلسطينيّ غسّان كَنَفاني.

تمرين ٨

أكمل الجمل الآتية بالاختيار المناسِب وفق نصّ القراءة:

١- سافَر مايكل براون إلى سوريةَ ______________ .
☐ وحده ☐ مع صديق ☐ مع صديقين ☐ مع ثلاثة أصدقاء

٢- حصل مايكل على ______________ دخول قبل سفره.
☐ تأشيرة ☐ جواز ☐ تذكرة ☐ بطاقة

٣- كان على مايكل أن يخلع حذاءه في ______________ .
☐ المطار ☐ الزقاق ☐ السوق ☐ المسجِد

٤- توجَد آثار إغريقيّة في ______________ .
☐ مُتحف التقاليد الشعبيّة ☐ مُتحف دمشق الوَطَنيّ
☐ مسجِد بني أميّة ☐ سوق الحميديّة

تمرين ٩

آ- أعد ترتيب الكلمات في كل مجموعة لتشكّل جملاً مُفيدةً:

١ في أدوات القديمة شاهدنا التجميل المُتحف

٢ ركبت فيه إلى السيّارة الّذي الحي أسكن

٣ العالم أوّل الشَمْرة في في أبجديّة اكتُشِفَتْ رأس

تمرين ١٠

أعد ترتيب الجمل لتشكّل فِقرة كاملة. الجملة الأولى في مكانها المناسب:

١- أراد أسامة وزوجته كريمة السفر من القاهرة إلى بيروت من أجل عطلة الصيف.
سمعا إعلاناً من السمّاعات عن إقلاع طائرتهما.
بعد وزن حقائبهما توجّها إلى مركز الجوازات.
جلست كريمة في مقعد إلى جانب الشبّاك وجلس نديم إلى يسارها.
وصل أسامة وكريمة إلى المطار قبل موعد إقلاع الطائرة بساعتين.
عند انتهائهما من الجوازات جلسا في قاعة الانتظار أمام البوابة رقم ١٨.
كان معهما أربع حقائب.
صعِد الركّاب إلى الطائرة قبل نصف ساعة من موعد إقلاعها.
توجّها أوّلاً إلى مكان وزن الحقائب.
قال الإعلان: "الرجاء من حضرات الركّاب التوجّه إلى البوابة رقم ١٨".

تمرين ١١

اكتب عن زيارةٍ قمت بها إلى مُتحف واشرح المعروضات الموجودة فيه بحوالي مئة كلمة.

القواعد

1. Prepositional Phrases Containing ما

In the main reading passage two prepositional phrases contained ما الموصولة, a particle that means *that/what/which:*

١	حَصَلَ على ما تَمَنّى	*He got what he wished for.*

This type of ما is a great tool to have at your disposal if you wish to refer to something non-specific. Another example of this type of ما occurs in the very useful phrase بِـما في ذلِكَ *including*:

٢	بِما في ذلِكَ ثَوبُ العُرس.	*including the wedding gown.*

> **مُلاحَظة**
>
> بِما في ذلِكَ is an invariable phrase, in that its form remains fixed regardless of what follows.

A similar equally useful phrase to add to your repertoire of expressions is: بِما أنَّ *since, because*:

٣	أنْتَ لا تَحتاجُ إلى تأشيرةِ دُخول إلى ألمانيا بِما أنَّكَ أمريكيّ.	*You do not need an entry visa for Germany, since you are an American.*

Example 3 is a powerful tool that can just as easily be used at the beginning of an argument, changing its meaning to *being that*:

٤	بِما أنَّني لَمْ أفْهَمْ ما حَدَثَ هُنا فَلا أريدُ أن أتَوَرَّطَ فيه.	*Being that I didn't understand what happened here, I don't want to get embroiled in it.*

تمرين ١٢

Use ما الموصولة to translate the following sentences into Arabic.

1. I study Islamic studies including the Qur'an and the Hadith.
2. Being that Damascus is one of the oldest cities, it has relics from different civilizations in it.
3. You will need a car since you live far from campus.
4. I like what you wrote.
5. Have you noticed what I noticed?

2. Prepositions That Collocate with Certain Verbs

Certain verbs have prepositions that accompany them that have an impact on their meaning. For instance, حَصَلَ means *to happen;* while حَصَلَ على means *to obtain.* That means, as speakers of Arabic, we have to be aware of what verbs take which preposition and the ensuing changes in meaning.

المَعنى	حَرْفُ الجَرّ	الفِعْل
He obtained (a degree).	على (شَهادة)	حَصَلَ
He arrived at/from (the airport).	إلى / مِن (المَطار)	وَصَلَ
He paid (me a lira).	لِـ (لي ليرةً)	دَفَعَ
He went to (the marketplace).	إلى (السوق)	ذَهَبَ
He returned to (his house).	إلى (مَنزِله)	عادَ
He offered (me a drink).	لِـ (لي شَراباً)	قَدَّمَ
He traveled to (Aleppo).	إلى (حَلَب)	سافَرَ
He brought (me something).	لِـ (لي شَيْئاً)	أحْضَرَ
He spoke with (me).	مَعَ (مَعي)	تَحَدَّثَ
He told (me).	لِـ (لي)	قالَ
He found (a key).	عَلى (مِفتاح)	عَثَرَ
He stayed at/in (the hotel).	بِـ / في (الفُندُق)	نَزَلَ
He seized upon (it).	عَلى (عَليها)	اِستَولى
He met with (his friend).	بِـ (صَديقِه)	اِلتَقى
He sat at (a table).	إلى (مائِدة)	جَلَسَ

تمرين ١٣

أ- اختر حرف الجَرّ الصحيح من الكلمات بين القوسين حسب الفعل والسياق:

(على ، إلى ، مِن ، لِـ ، مع ، بِـ ، في)

١ - هل يُمْكِنُكِ إحْضار الكتاب ______ ريم؟

٢- لقد سافرت هالة بستاني ______ لبنان.

٣- بعد أن دخلَت الحانوت، جلسَت البنات ______ المائدة (الطاولة).

٤- قَد أَلْتقي ______ رامي أمام المكتبة الرئيسة.

٥ - قبل أن يعود ______ بيته، نزل فريد ______ فندق فخم.

٦- استولى الجيش ______ الحكم (السلطة).

٧ - هل دفعتَ ______ زينب ثمن الحقيبة؟

٨ - متى وصلتِ ______ هذه المدينة؟

٩ - تريد أن تحصلَ ______ شهادة من هذه الجامعة؟

١٠ - كنتُ أريد أن أتكلم ______ المدير.

b. Translate the following sentences into Arabic using the correct preposition:

1. I arrived from London on Saturday.
2. She stayed at her mother's house.
3. I saw him sitting at that table.
4. هالة, did you talk to your husband about buying that watch?
5. What did those men say to you?
6. When did you return home last night, سارة?
7. Did you pay the man?
8. I want to get a car.

مُراجَعة القَواعِد

3. Expressing Reason with لِـ، كَيْ، وحَتّى

If you wish to convey *in order to* (+ verb), then these are three particles that you will want to use. The verb that follows these particles will always be in present tense, just as it would be in English: *in order to eat*.

مُلاحَظة

لِـ / كَيْ / حَتّى can be used interchangeably to mean:

in order to + المُضارِع المَنصوب

١	أتى عَدنانُ إلى أمريكا لِيَدرُسَ / حَتّى يَدرُسَ / كَيْ يَدرُسَ عِلمَ الحاسوب.	*Adnan came to America in order to study computer science.*

The لـ is the only one of these three particles that can be used to modify a مَصدَر. When used as such, it is considered a preposition, but retains the same meaning:

٢	أتى عَدنانُ إلى أمريكا لِدِراسةِ عِلْمِ الحاسوب.	*Adnan came to America in order to study computer science.*

4. Nouns with Verbal Force اسمُ الفِعْل

The two types of اسم الفعْل we are introducing in this section are: 1) the independent words أفٍّ وشَتّان; and 2) the prepositional phrases إليك وعليك.

١	أفٍّ مِن الدُنيا بِدونَك.	*I couldn't stand life without you.*
	شَتّانَ ما بَيْنَ اليَوْمَ والأمسِ!	*What a difference between today and yesterday!*

To form اسم الفِعْل from the prepositional phrases إلى وعلى, just add a personal pronoun:

Here's a letter from me.	إليكَ رِسالةً مِني.	٢
You need to be at the airport at one o'clock.	عَليكَ أنْ تَكونَ في الساعةِ الواحِدةِ بالمَطار.	

تمرين ١٤

Express the following meanings in Arabic using اسمُ الفِعْل or حتّى، لِـ، كَيْ:

1. I have to wash the car on Saturday.
2. هالة bought a book to read about American history.
3. We have to be home at eight in order to watch our favorite television show.
4. Who is going to bring the fruit?

تَذَوّق الثَّقافَة العَرَبيّة

Terms Used to Refer to Prophets of Islam

Traditionally, most Muslims use a phrase after mentioning prophets in writing and speech. For instance, after mentioning the Prophet Muhammad, the most important and last prophet of Islam, one such saying is:

صلّى اللهُ عليهِ وسلّم

Other prophets of Islam, to include Adam, Noah, Abraham, Moses, and Jesus, have another saying associated with them:

عليهِ السّلام

Both sayings are in fact short prayers asking God to bestow peace on the prophet mentioned.

دَوْر المقهى الاجتماعي

Before the advent of the radio, movie theaters, and television, men in Iraq, Syria, Egypt, and elsewhere in the Middle East used to congregate in coffeehouses. It was in these establishments where coffee, tea, and herbal teas made from dried flowers were served. Usually, working men frequented coffeehouses after sunset, while unemployed men spent most of their day there playing cards, backgammon, and dominos. Two main evening attractions brought men to coffeehouses in substantial numbers: the storyteller الحَكَواتي and shadow puppets خيال الظِل. In the next two sections, we introduce both of these important pastimes.

الحَكَواتي

The role of الحَكَواتي is usually played by a literate man who possesses a talent for storytelling and the ability to capture the attention of his audience. Storytellers were masters of suspense, telling stories in installments using pitch variation and gestures to enrich context. The audience would be divided into two groups, each one siding with one of the main characters similar to a football match. An experienced storyteller would stop at a critical point, hoping that the audience would come the following night. Sometimes fights would break out if one character was made to have the upper hand over the other. So, the storyteller had to improvise and strike a balance between the victories on each side.

دَوْر المرأة العربية تاريخياً

You may wonder what women did when men were at coffeehouses. For centuries, up until the First World War, the majority of women were traditional housewives. Particularly in urban areas it was expected that women only leave their home when visiting the public bath about once a week or to take care of urgent matters. However, female relatives and neighbors regularly got together, helping one another in cooking elaborate dishes and preparing food for special occasions such as weddings, engagement parties, celebrations of the birth of babies, etc. In the evening, they told tales and fables, especially the elders to the young. Such tales were passed down orally from mother to daughter virtually verbatim. The women would also play games such as برجيس which historically has been and remains the most popular game for women. Nowadays, however, it is not uncommon to find women sitting alongside of men in modern cafés in the Arab world as you can see in these pictures.

خيال الظِلّ

These figures are crafted of several parts: arms, legs, a body, and a head joined together and attached to long sticks manipulated by actors who stand behind a white cloth screen. The figures are made from thin, stiff, translucent camel hide. The white cloth is backlit by a powerful lantern that casts shadows upon the screen that, from the audience's side, appear like an early form of cartoon. This form of art is not exclusive to the Middle East; in fact it was known in many other parts of the world, such as China, India, and Indonesia, before it appeared in Turkey, Syria, and Egypt. It was introduced to the Middle East about 700 years ago and quickly became popular. Many plays, from the serious to the farcical, were written especially for this venue. Cafés were among the places shadow puppet plays were performed. But performances were also given in village and town squares as well as in homes.

خيال الظِل literally means *shadows of fancy* in reference to the imaginary world created by these figures and the stories associated with them. The plays included action, music, and even songs. The players are led by the shadow master, who knew at least as many plays as the nights of the month of Ramadan, when attending shadow plays was a custom for many people.

Ahmed El-Khoumy "The Last Shadow Master"

تمرين ١٥

آ أجب عن الأسئلة وفق نص الاستماع:

١- ما الفكرة الرئيسة في نص الاستماع؟
٢- حدِّد بعض الأفكار الثانوية في النص.
٣- مِن أيِّ بلد كارول وأصدقاؤها؟
٤- كيف وصلوا إلى عمّان؟
٥- أين شاهدوا النواعير؟

ب- أكمل الجمل التالية بالاختيار المناسب وفق نص الاستماع:

١- بقِيَت كارول في دمشق ________ .
☐ أسبوعاً ☐ ستّة أيّام ☐ عشرةَ أيّام ☐ شهراً

٢- تقع البتراء في ________ .
☐ الشمال ☐ الجنوب ☐ الشرق ☐ الغرب

٣- شاهد الأصدقاء نهرَ العاصي في ________.
☐ مصر ☐ الأردن ☐ سورية ☐ لبنان

٤- يقع مسجِد خالد بن الوليد في ________ .
☐ حِمص ☐ حماة ☐ حَلَب ☐ دمشق

٥- حين وصلوا دمشقَ تَوَجَّهَ الأصدِقاءُ أوّلاً إلى ________.
☐ المُتحف ☐ المطعم ☐ الفُندُق ☐ سوق الحميديّة

ج- لَخِّص المُقابَلة مع زينا بحوالى خمسين كَلمة.

د- اكتب «خطأ» أو «صواب» إلى جانب كلّ جملة ثمّ صحِّح الجمل الخطأ:

١- سافر الأصدقاء بالحافلة إلى البتراء.
٢- زاروا المسجِد الأمويّ بحَلَب.
٣- اشترَت كاسي عُلبةً خشبيّةً من سوق حَلَب.
٤- توقّفوا بحماة في طريق العودة.

Folk Heroes and Tales

Here, we present the three most popular Arabian folk tales for your reading pleasure:

سيرة عَنْتَرَة

The tale of عَنْتَرَة tells the adventures of عَنْتَرَة بن شَدّاد العَبسيّ, a pre-Islamic hero. He was born to an Arab father from a powerful tribe and an Ethiopian slave mother. As pre-Islamic tradition would have it, he did not acquire his father's name and thus was considered a slave. Believing that he had been slighted and discriminated against, he began composing poetry through which he expressed his feelings. A brave and feared warrior and an accomplished poet, he fell in love with his cousin. But this love was forbidden, because any ensuing marriage between a slave and his حبيبة was prohibited. It is believed that it was this unfulfilled love that inspired his best poetry.

When his tribe came under attack and lost much of its wealth to the plundering invading tribes, his father told him he could earn his freedom fighting against the enemy. عَنْتَرَة fought courageously and regained much of what his tribe had lost in the spoils of war becoming a respected military leader. His poetry was so valued that it was placed on the wall of the holy shrine in مَكّة known as الكَعبَة, an honor bestowed on few poets. These poems are called المُعَلَّقات (i.e., *hanging poems*). It is reported through tradition that the Prophet Mohammad once said that of all the Arabs of pre-Islamic times, the only one he would have wanted to meet was عَنْتَرَة. Here is a well-known verse that represents his pride and ideals:

لا تَسْقِني ماءَ الحياةِ بذِلَّةٍ   بَل فَاسْقِني بِالعِزِّ كَأسَ الحَنظَلِ

Traditional Arabic poetry is laid out in two parts called hemistichs شَطْر and each verse known as بَيْت, the same word as *house, home* that we learned so long ago.

glory, power	عِزّ	*elixir of life*	ماء الحياة	*to give water*	سَقى (يَسقي)
rather	بَل	*an extremely bitter plant*	حَنْظَل	*vileness*	ذِلّة

سيرة «أبو زيد الهلالي»

Known to almost all Arabs as the saga of بنو هلال, this epic is distinguished from all other Arab sagas because of its all inclusive nature. It begins in the Najd (central modern-day Saudi Arabia) where the بنو هلال tribe attacked Mecca shortly after it was taken by the Prophet Muhammad in 630. Later, the بنو هلال tribe emigrated to Egypt where they settled in the south. In 1052, they migrated to Tunisia, where some الهلال tribes branched off from the main tribe and ended up settling in Morocco. This epic is divided into five parts detailing the alliance among the tribes of سليم ورباح وهلال who fought to defend the values and honor of الأمّة. Like most epics, tales of military conquests, heroes in times of peace and war and their conquests perpetuate the telling and retelling of السيرة الهلالية recounting the glory days of الأمة.

شعار علم الظاهِر بيبَرْس

According to two French Arabists, Professors Gillum and Beauhas of the University of Paris, this epic is quite possibly the longest in the world, consisting of 36,000 pages! Its French translation is based on a manuscript discovered in Aleppo, Syria, and was completed in 2009 and published in sixty volumes. It is believed that this work will have a greater impact on European and world literature than *A Thousand and One Nights* ألف ليلة وليلة. It recounts a story of بيبرس, a Mamluk king who fought the Crusaders in المَنصورة, Egypt, and Syria, in addition to fighting the Tatars in Palestine. He passed away in Damascus in 1277.

المُفْرَدات

إبْلا			(n., f.)	Ebla (ancient Syrian kingdom discovered in 1976)
إحْدى	(n., f.)	أحَد	(n., m.)	one of
آراميّ			(adj.)	Aramaic
أصْليّ			(adj.)	original, authentic
إغْريقيّ	ج	إغريقيّون	(adj.)	Greek
اِقْتِصاد			(n., m.)	economy
اِكْتَشَفَ	(يَكْتَشِفُ)	اِكْتِشاف	(v.)	to discover
أمَوِيّ	أُمَيّة		(adj.)	Omayyad
اِنْقَرَضَ	(يَنْقَرِضُ)	اِنْقِراض	(v.)	to become extinct
تأشيرة	تأشيرات		(n., f.)	(entry) visa
تَجْميل			(n., m.)	beautification, makeup
تَقْليد	ج	تَقاليد	(n., m.)	tradition, folklore
تَماماً			(adv.)	exactly
ثَوْب	ج	أثْواب	(n., m.)	dress, costume

mosque	(n., m.)	جَوامِع	ج	جامِع
weather, atmosphere, ambiance	(n., m.)	أجْواء	ج	جَوّ
passport	(n., m.)	جَوازات	ج	جَواز
alley, narrow street	(n., f.)	حارات	ج	حارة
grain	(n., f.)	حَبّات	ج	حَبّة
room, chamber	(n., f.)	حُجَرات/ حُجَر	ج	حُجْرة
volume, size	(n., m.)	أحْجام	ج	حَجْم
silk	(n., m.)			حَرير
good	(adj.)			حَسَن
story, tale, narrative	(n., f.)	حِكايات	ج	حِكاية
to rule, to sentence	(v.)	حُكْم	(يَحْكُمُ)	حَكَم
storyteller	(n., m.)	حَكَواتِيّة	ج حَكَواتِيّون/	حَكَواتيّ
ornament, jewelry	(n., m.)	حُليّ	ج	حَلي
pigeon, dove	(n., f.)	حَمامات/ حَمام	ج	حَمامَة
around	(adv.)			حَوْل
life	(n., f.)	حَيَوات	ج	حَياة

special, private	(adj.)			خاصّ
to stamp, to seal	(v.)	خَتْم	(يَخْتِمُ)	خَتَمَ
wood, lumber	(n., m.)	أخْشاب	ج	خَشَب
wooden, of wood	(adj.)			خَشَبِيّ
to take off, to undress	(v.)	خَلْع	(يَخْلَعُ)	خَلَعَ
shadow, reflection	(n., m.)	أخِيلة	ج	خَيال
coat of mail, armor, shield	(n., m.)	دُروع	ج	دِرْع
to show, to indicate, to point out	(v.)	دَلالة	(يَدُلُّ)	دَلَّ
doll, dummy	(n., f.)	دُمىً	ج	دُمْية
inscription, tablet	(n., m.)	رُقُم	ج	رَقيم
chain main	(n., m.)	زُرود	ج	زَرَد
chain mail	(n., m.)		زَرَد الحَديد	زَرَد الحَديد
Syriac, member of the Syrian church	(adj.)			سِريانيّ
biography, history	(n., m.)	سِيَر	ج	سيرة
young man	(n., m.)	شَباب	ج	شابٌّ
vacant, empty, unoccupied	(act. p.)			شاغِر

popular, of the people	(adj.)			شَعْبيّ
shadow, shade	(n., m.)	ظِلال	ج	ظِلٌّ
ottoman	(adj.)			عُثْمانيّ
wedding, marriage	(n., m.)	أعْراس	ج	عُرْس
bride	(n., f.)	عَرائِس	ج	عَروس
groom	(n., m.)	عُرُس / عِرْسان	ج	عَروس
	(n., m.)	عُرُس / عِرْسان	ج	--
courtyard	(n., m.)	أفْنية	ج	فِناء
foot	(n., f.)	أقْدام	ج	قَدَم
story	(n., f.)	قِصَص	ج	قِصّة
wheat	(n., m.)			قَمْح
croissant	(n., m.)			كْرواسّان
to cost	(v.)	تَكْليف/ تكلِفة	(يُكَلِّفُ)	كَلَّفَ
gentle, kind, friendly	(adj.)	لُطفاء	ج	لَطيف
to represent, to exemplify, to act	(v.)	تَمْثيل	(يُمَثِّلُ)	مَثَّلَ
center	(n., m.)	مَراكِز	ج	مَركَز
irrigated, supplied with water	(adj.)			مَسْقيّ

مَقْهى	ج	مَقاهٍ/ المَقاهي	(n., m.)	café
مُنْتَصَف			(pass. p.)	middle, mid-
هَبَطَ	(يَهبُط/ يَهبِطُ)	هُبوط	(v.)	to descend, to land, to drop
والٍ	(الوالي) ج	وُلاة	(n., m.)	ruler, governor
وَطَنيّ	وَطَنيّ		(adj.)	national

الدَرْسُ العاشر

Objectives

- Learning how to relate historical facts in writing and speaking
- Describing significant historical sites and personalities
- Learning facts about Queen Zanobia, Palmyra, and Aleppo
- **مراجعة القواعد**: البدل، كان وأخواتها، إن وأخواتها، الفعل المبني للمجهول، الإضافة الوصفية

رُكنُ المُفْرَداتِ الجَديدةِ

to seize	اِستَولى (يَستَولي) اِستيلاء على
prisoner	أسير ج أسْرى
deity	إله ج آلِهة
cow	بَقَرة ج بَقَرات
to enjoy	تَمَتَّعَ (يَتَمَتَّعُ) تَمَتُّع بِـ
intelligence	ذَكاء
inexpensive	رَخيص
to hit; to strike	ضَرَبَ (يَضْرِبُ) ضَرْب
arch (triumphal arch)	قَوْس ج أقْواس (قَوْس النَصْر)
region, area	مِنطَقة ج مَناطِق
queen	مَلِكة ج مَلِكات
prophet	نَبيّ ج أنبِياء
date palm	نَخيل

تمرين ١

وافق بين كلمات من العمودين واكتبهما في الوسط:

١	الفُرس		تاريخ
٢	ذَهَبٌ		مَضيق
٣	آثار		قِصّة
٤	ظَنَّ		رُبّما
٥	حِكاية		حَسَن
٦	جَيِّد		إيران
٧	قَدْ (يَفْعَل)		فَكَّرَ
			فِضّة

تمرين ٢

اخترِ الكَلِمةَ الّتي لا تُناسِب باقي الكَلِماتِ في كُلِّ مَجْموعةٍ وبَيِّن السَبَب:

١- الحافلة الطائرة السيّارة الجيش القِطار

٢- مَعبَد كَنيسة مَسجِد حَرْب

٣- تَحَدَّثَ عَثَرَ تَكَلَّم حكى

٤- نبيّ مَلِك إمبراطور والي رئيس

٥- مَعبَد بَعْل أعمدة عَظيمة قَلعة حَلَب إله المَطَر

مايكل براون يزور تَدمُر وحَلَب

من أثار تَدمُر

ركِبتُ وأصدقائي الحافلة إلى مدينة تدمُر الأثريّة الواقعة في وسط الصحراء السوريّة على بُعد ٢١٠ كيلومترات من دمشق. قضَينا النهار هناك بين الآثار الكثيرة الّتي تمتدّ على مِساحة ستة كيلومترات مربعة. شاهدنا مَعبَد بَعْل إله المطر والخِصْب لدى الكنعانيين الّذين سكنوا بلاد الشام في الألف الثالثة قبل الميلاد، وزُرنا قَوْس النصر والأعمدة العظيمة والمسرح والحمّامات والشارع الطويل ومجلس الشيوخ والمدافِن. في المساء عُدنا بالحافلة من حَيث أتينا.

بُنيَت تدمُر قديماً على نَبع ماء حار يُسمّى «أفقا» وفيها بساتين النَخيل والزيتون والعنب. وقد كانت تدمُر مركزاً تجاريّاً هامّاً، وتمتّعت بثراء هائل. ثمّ صارت دولة منذ القرن الثالث قبل الميلاد. في عام ٢٦٧ للميلاد هزم ملكها أُذَينة الفُرْس مرّتين ثمّ خلّص إمراطور روما من أسْر الفُرْس فسرَّ ذلك الرومان كثيراً وسمّوه «زعيم المَشرِق». لكنّ أُذَينة اغتيلَ في العام نفسِه واستلمَت زوجتُه زنوبيا الحُكم بعده وصارت مِلكةً هذه الدولة. كانت زنوبيا جميلة الوجه طويلة القامة عظيمة الذكاء واسعة الثقافة، وكانت تتكلّم ثلاث لغات بطلاقة وهي التدمُريّة والمصريّة واليونانيّة.

أرادَت زنوبيا أن تحكُم المِنطقة كلّها، بل أرادَت أن تَستَوليَ على الإمبراطوريّة الرومانيّة وتخلع الإمبراطور أورليان فقد كان مشغولاً بحروب داخليّة وخارجيّة وظنّت أنّ الفرصة مناسبة لذلك. فاستولَت أوّلاً على سوريّة جميعها في عام ٢٧٠ للميلاد ثمّ على مصر فآسيا الصُغرى (تركيا اليوم) ووصلَت جيوشها إلى مضيق البوسفور. وفي عام ٢٧١ م ضَرَبَت نقوداً عليها صورتها وصورة ابنها دون صورة إمبراطور روما. وبذلك جعلَت مملكة تدمر الصغيرة إمبراطوريّة واسعة امتدّت من مصر جنوباً إلى آسيا الصُغرى شمالاً.

آثار رومانية في مدينة تدمر

لكن أورليان إمبراطور روما لم يُعجبْه ذلك، وما كاد ينتهي من حروبه حتّى شكّل جيشاً كبيراً واتّجه به إلى سورية. وعند حِمْص في وسط سورية اِلتَقى بجيش زنوبيا الأوّل وهزمه هناك، ثمّ اِتّجه إلى تدمُر وحاصرها إلى أن سقطَت عام ٢٧٤م. دخل تدمُر واعتقل زنوبيا وأخذها أسيرةً إلى روما، حيث ماتَت هناك بعد سنوات.

مايكل في حلب

سافرنا إلى حلب بالحافلة، وحلب ثانيةُ أكبرِ المُدُنِ السورية وتقع في شمال غرب سورية وتبعُد عن دمشق ٣٥٠ كم. نزلنا هناك في فندق «بارون» الّذي نزلَت فيه الكاتبة البريطانيّة «أغاثا كريستي» والضابط البريطاني المُسمّى «لورنس العرب.» صار الفندق قديماً اليوم، لكننا حصلنا على غرفة جيّدة بثلاثة أسرّة وفيها حمّام أيضاً. زُرنا بعد الظُهر قَلْعة حلب وتجوّلنا في أَسواق المدينة القديمة الّتي تقع حول القَلْعة.

لورنس العرب

قَلْعة حلب

علمتُ شيئاً عن حلب لم أكُن أعرفه من قبل. اِلتقَينا شاباً حلبيّاً في حديقة «السبيل» وتحدّثنا معه بالعربيّة وقد أُعجِبَ كثيراً وقال: «إنكم تتكلّمونها جيّداً.» قال إنّ حلبَ تُعرَف باسم «حلب الشَهْباء» وهذا الاسم له حِكاية. يُقال إن النبيّ إبراهيم عليه السلام نزل بهذه المدينة وحَلَبَ بَقرتَه الشَهْباء أي ذات اللون الرمادي على الجَبَل حَيثُ تقوم قَلْعتُها اليوم، ومن هنا جاء الاسم «حلب الشَهْباء». رُبّما كان هذا صحيحاً.

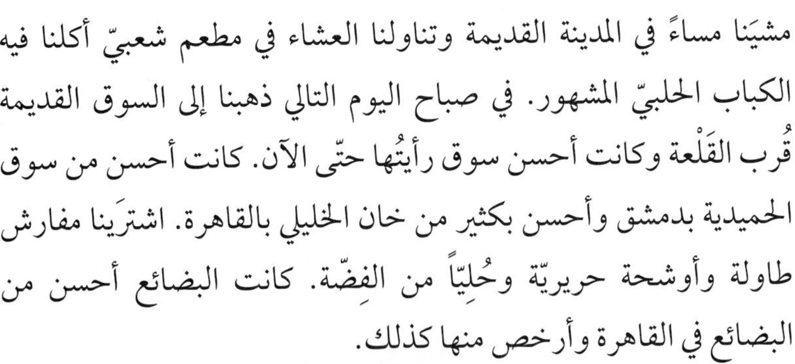

مشيَنا مساءً في المدينة القديمة وتناولنا العشاء في مطعم شعبيّ أكلنا فيه الكباب الحلبيّ المشهور. في صباح اليوم التالي ذهبنا إلى السوق القديمة قُرب القَلْعة وكانت أحسن سوق رأيتُها حتّى الآن. كانت أحسن من سوق الحميدية بدمشق وأحسن بكثير من خان الخليلي بالقاهرة. اشترَينا مفارش طاولة وأوشحة حريريّة وحُلِيّاً من الفِضّة. كانت البضائع أحسن من البضائع في القاهرة وأرخص منها كذلك.

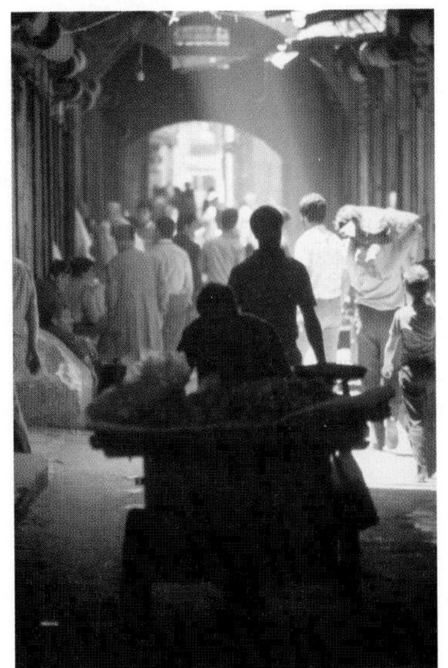

سوق قديمة بحلب

تمرين ٣

وافِق بين كلمات من العمودين لتشكّل عبارات تحوي مُضافاً مُضافاً إليه مثل: «جامعة دمشق»:

١	قَلْعة		بَغل
٢	مَعبَد		الشام
٣	لورَنْس		الشَهباء
٤	فندق		الخليلي
٥	بِلاد		حلب
٦	خان		العرب
			بارون

تمرين ٤

اكتب «خطأ» أو «صواب» إلى جانب كلّ جملة ثمّ صحّح الجمل الخطأ:

١- سافر مايكل وصديقاه إلى تدمُر بالطائرة.

٢- قوس النصر في مدينة حلب.

٣- كان أذَينة زوج زنوبيا.

٤- توفّيت زنوبيا في تَدمُر.

٥- نزل مايكل في فندق «لورنس العرب».

٦- أحسن سوقٍ رآها مايكل كانت سوق خان الخليلي بالقاهرة.

مدينة حلب بالليل

تمرين ٥

للمحادثة: احكِ قِصّة لزميلك عن أوّل مرّة ركبت فيها طائرة. فيما يلي بعض الأسئلة الّتي قد تساعدك في ترتيب الأفكار:

١- كيف شعرت عند وصولك إلى المطار؟

٢- مَن رافقك إلى المطار؟

٣- من أيّ مدينة غادرت؟ وإلى أيّ مدينة توجهت؟

٤- لماذا استقللتَ طائرة ولم تستقلَّ وسيلة أخرى من وسائل النقل؟

٥- كم استغرقتِ الرحلة؟

٦- هل تحدّثت مع أحد ركّاب الطائرة ؟ وماذا قلت له؟

والآن اشرح أحاسيسك بعد هبوط الطائرة. أين نزلت في المدينة؟ وهل حَجَزتَ غرفة في فندق قبل وصولك؟ وكم من الوقت بقيت في هذا المكان؟

تمرين ٦

أجب عن الأسئلة الآتية وفق نص القراءة:

١- ما الفكرة الرئيسة لهذا الدرس؟

٢- حدّد بعض الأفكار الثانويّة.

٣- اكتب عنواناً آخر لهذا الدرس.

٤- كم تبعُد تدمُر عن دمشق؟

٥- ماذا فعل الأصدقاء الأربعة مساءً في حلب؟

٦- لماذا سُمّيَ أُذَينة «زعيم المَشرِق»؟

٧- كيف جعلت زنوبيا مملكتَها إمبراطوريّة؟

٨- لماذا سُمّيت حلب باسم «الشَهباء» وفق قصّة الشاب؟

تمرين ٧

أكمل الجمل الآتية بالاختيار المناسِب وفق نصّ القراءة:

١- سافر مايكل إلى تدمُر ______________ .

☐ بالطائرة ☐ بالسيّارة ☐ بالحافلة ☐ بالقطار

٢- مَعبَد بَعْل في ______________.

☐ دمشق ☐ تدمُر ☐ مُتحف دمشق ☐ مُتحف حلب

٣- نزل مايكل وصديقاه في فندق ______________ .

☐ بارون ☐ أغاثا كريستي ☐ لورنس العرب ☐ حلب

٤- تقع أسواق حلب القديمة حول ______________ .

☐ الشَهباء ☐ القَلْعة ☐ الفندق ☐ خان الخليلي

٥- كانت البضائع في أسواق حلب جيّدة و ______________ .

☐ غالية ☐ قديمة ☐ عظيمة ☐ رخيصة

تمرين ٨

آ- أعد ترتيب الكلمات في كل مجموعة لتشكّل جملاً مُفيدةً:

١ أحمد   يسافرَ   أنّ   علِمتُ   لن   دُبي   إلى

٢ اللغة   تتكلّم   بطلاقة   هالة   الألمانيّة

٣ الذكاء   زعيمة   كانت   عظيمة   زنوبيا

٤ مِن   الصين   الإسلاميّة   امتدّت   الأندلس   الدولة   إلى

٥ بَعْل   سورية   إله   القديمة   يُسمّى   والخِصب   في   كان   المطر

تمرين ٩

أعد ترتيب الجمل لتشكّل فِقرة كاملة. الجملة الأولى في مكانها المناسب:

١- أردتُ أنا وصديقاتي أن نترك المدينة لبضعة أيّام لنستمتع بجو الريف.
غادرنا دمشق في الساعة السابعة صباحاً.
قضينا خمسة أيّام هناك عُدنا بعدها إلى دمشق.
لذلك قرّرنا أن نستأجر حافلة صغيرة مع سائقها تَقِلُّنا إلى الكفرون.
توقّفنا مرّتين في الطريق ووصلنا الكفرون مساء.
استأجرنا داراً كبيرة فيها أربع غرف نوم.
لقد استمتعنا جدّاً بهذه الرحلة، واتّفقنا أن نكرّرها مرّة أخرى.
والكفرون بلدة صغيرة جميلة تقع في الجبال في غرب سورية الأوسط.
قَضينا أيّامنا هناك في زيارة الأماكن الجميلة والمطاعم في الجبال.

تمرين ١٠

للمحادثة: فكّر في وصف لشخص تاريخي بارز مشهور، ثمّ رتّب أفكارك فيه ترتيباً زَمَنيّاً. لا تذكر اسمه أو اسمها، بل صِفْ بالتفصيل هذه الشخصية المختارة لزميلك أو لأستاذك واطلب منهم أن يحزروا اسمها.

تمرين ١١

للكتابة:

١- اكتب تاريخاً مختصراً للبلد الّذي تعيش فيه بما لا يزيد عن ٢٥٠ كلمة. اذكر متى بدأ والدولة أو الدول الّتي تتالت عليه والأحداث الهامّة الّتي مرّ بها وغير ذلك.

٢- اشرح كيف تولدُ الدُوَلُ وتكْبر ثم تموت. أعط مثالاً عن دولة تعرفها مرّت بهذه المراحل من التاريخ.

مُراجَعة القَواعِد

١. البَدَل

حين نستخدم اسماً آخر لشيءٍ ما ولا يزال يفهمه المستمع فهذا ما نعتبره "البَدَل" إذ استبدلنا

١	باريس مدينة النور.	*Paris, the city of lights.*
٢	نيويورك التفاحة الكبيرة.	*New York, the Big Apple.*

نفهم من مثال ١ أن كلمة باريس ومدينة النور تدلان على نفس المدينة كما في مثال ٢ إذ أنَّ نيويورك والتفاحة الكبيرة تدلان على نفس المكان. دعنا الآن نلقي نظرة على جملة وَرَدَت في النص الرئيس:

٣	لكِنَّ أورليانَ إمبراطورَ روما لم يُعجِبْه ذلِكَ.	*But that did not please Aurelian, Emperor of Rome.*

إن كلمةَ إمبراطور تدل على منصب أورليان وتوضّح المقصود ومن حيث القواعد إمبراطورَ منصوبةٌ لأنّها بَدَلٌ مِن أورليان (المُبدَل مِنه) وهو اسم «لكِنَّ». البَدَلُ له حالة (case) المُبدَلِ منه نفسها، فإنْ كان مرفوعاً يكون مرفوعاً مثله، وإنْ كان منصوباً يكون منصوباً مثله وإنْ كان مجروراً يكون مجروراً مثله.

٢. كان وأخواتُها

«كان» فِعلٌ ماضٍ يدخل على الجُملة الاسميّةِ فيَرفَعُ الاسمَ وينصبُ الخَبَرَ. دعنا الآن نتأمل جملة اسميّة وأخرى فيها «كان»:

١ | قَلْعةُ حَلَبَ هامّةٌ. ⇐ كانَتْ قَلعَةُ حَلَبَ هامّةً.

ماذا لاحظتَ يا طالبَ العربية في مثال ١؟ نرى في مثال ١ قَلْعةُ حَلَبَ لا تتغير من حيث الإعراب أما هامّة فتحوّلت من حالة الرفع (هامّةٌ) إلى حالة النصب (هامّةً) بسَببِ دخول كانَتْ على هذه الجملة.

مُلاحَظة

(كانَ، أصبَحَ، أضْحى، أمْسى، باتَ، صارَ، ظَلَّ) تَتَصَرَّفُ في الماضي والمضارع والأمر أمّا "لَيْسَ" فلا تتصرّف إلاّ بالماضي.

انظر إلى مثال ٢:

٢ | أصْبَحَ / يُصْبِحُ / أصْبِحْ

٣. إنَّ وأخواتُها

تدخلُ إنَّ وأخَواتُها على الجملةِ الاسميّة فتَنصُبُ الاسمَ وترفَعُ الخَبَرَ، وهي:

إنَّ	*emphasis*
أنَّ	*emphasis*
كأنَّ	*comparison*
لكِنَّ	*contrast*
لَيْتَ	*wishing*
لَعَلَّ	*hope*

دعنا نقرأ مثالاً مأخوذاً من نص القراءة.

٣ | آثارُ تَدْمُرَ عَظيمةٌ. ⇐ إنَّ آثارَ تَدْمُرَ عَظيمةٌ.

نرى في مثال ٣ حالة آثارُ تغيرت من حالة الرفع (آثارُ) إلى حالة النصب (آثارَ) بسبب دخول إنَّ على هذه الجملة.

٤. الفِعْلُ المَبْنيُّ لِلمَجْهول

الفاعِلُ مَحذوف والمَفْعولُ بِهِ يُصْبِحُ نائِباً لِلفاعِل كما هو في المِثال.

٤ هَزَمَ أورليانُ جَيْشَ زَنوبيا. ⇐ هُزِمَ جَيْشُ زَنوبيا.

فِعْل ⇑ هَزَمَ، **فاعِل** ⇑ أورليانُ، **مَفْعول بِه** ⇑ جَيْشَ، **فِعْل مَبني للمَجهول** ⇑ هُزِمَ، **نائب فاعِل** ⇑ جَيْشُ

نرى في مثال ٤ أن فعل هَزَمَ تحوّل إلى هُزِمَ حين حذفنا أورليانُ (أي الفاعِل) من الجملة، وجيشَ (حالة النصب) صار جَيْشُ (حالة الرفع) عند حذف الفاعِل.

٥. الإضافة الوَصفيّة

هذه إضافة تصِفُ شيئاً أو شخصاً.

٥ | القَلْعةُ عاليةُ الأسوار. أي: القَلعةُ أسوارُها عاليةٌ.

⇑ إضافة وصفية

هذه إضافة تصِفُ شيئاً أو شخصاً.

٦ | كانت المَلِكَةُ عَظيمةَ الذَكاءِ. أيْ: كانَ ذَكاؤُها عَظيماً.

⇑ إضافة وصفية

تمرين ١٢

Translate the following sentences into Arabic using structures that reflect the grammatical categories in this section:

1. I wish the stores were open now.
2. The castle was besieged for two months.
3. هُمام has become a doctor at the age of twenty-four.
4. Our professor is of vast knowledge.
5. رَنا studies law, her favorite subject.
6. The sky is not cloudy.

تمرين ١٣

آ **أجب عن الأسئلة وفق نص الاستماع:**

١- ما موضوع هذا النص؟
٢- ما اسم الكاتبة الكامل؟
٣- مَن كان عند الكاتبة ذلك المساء؟
٤- كيف علمَت الكاتبة أنَّ وِعاء الشجرة انكسر؟
٥- مَن كسر الوِعاء الّذي كانت فيه الشجرة؟
٦- ماذا فعلَت الكاتبة بالشجرة؟

ب- **أكمل الجمل التالية بالاختيار المناسب وفق نص الاستماع:**

١- كاتبة القصّة ________________ .

☐ لبنانيّة ☐ فلسطينيّة ☐ مصريّة

٢- كانت شجرة الكاتبة ________________ .

☐ في حديقة البيت ☐ على سطح الدار ☐ في غرفة الاستقبال

٣- علمَت الكاتبة أنَّ الشجرة لا تزال حيّةً بعد ________________ .

☐ يوم ☐ أسبوع ☐ شهر

٤- وضعت الكاتبة الوِعاء الجديد في ________________ .

☐ الشمس ☐ غرفة النوم ☐ الحديقة

ج- **لَخِّص المُقابَلة مع زينا بحوالى خمسين كَلمة.**

د- اكتب «خطأ» أو «صواب» إلى جانب كلّ جملة ثمّ صحّح الجمل الخطأ:

١- نص الاستماع جزء من قصّة كتبتها الكاتبة.

٢- انكسرت الشجرة حين كان ضيوفها في البيت.

٣- حَمِدت الكاتبة الله أنّ قِطتها لم تَمُت.

آثار مدينة تدمر

المُفْرَدات

إِستَولى	(يَستَولي)	إِستِيلاء (على)	(v.)	to seize, to capture
أسير	ج	أسْرى	(n., m.)	prisoner (of war)
أشهَب	شَهباء	شُهْب	(adj.)	gray
إله	ج	آلِهة	(n., m.)	deity
بَقَرة	ج	بَقَرات	(n., f.)	cow
بوسفور	(مَضيق البوسفور)		(n., m.)	Bosporus (strait)
تَمَتَّعَ	(يَتَمَتَّعُ)	تَمَتُّع (بِـ)	(v.)	to enjoy
حَلَبَ	(يَحْلِبُ / يَحْلُبُ)	حَلْب	(v.)	to milk
ذَكاء			(n., m.)	intelligence, acumen
رَخيص			(adj.)	cheap, inexpensive
رَماديّ			(adj.)	ash colored
شَيْخ	ج	شُيوخ	(n., m.)	an elderly person, chief, senator, religious person
ضَرَبَ	(يَضْرِبُ)	ضَرْب	(v.)	to hit, to strike, to beat
قَوْس	ج	أقْواس (قوس النَصْر)	(n., m.)	bow, arch (triumphal arch)
مَضيق	ج	مَضائِق	(n., m.)	strait, narrow pass

queen	(n., f.)	مَلِكات	ج	مَلِكة
spring, water source	(n., m.)	يَنابيع	ج	نَبْع
prophet	(n., m.)	أنبِياء	ج	نَبيّ
palm, date palm	(n., m.)			نَخيل

سوق قديمة في حلب

الدَرْسُ الحادي عشر

Objectives

- Introduction to media Arabic
- Learning how to report facts, procedures, and events
- Reinforcing narration of past events
- **Grammar**: Introducing واو الحال; introducing the expression لا بُدَّ
- **Revisiting**: The uses of فـ، قَد، لَمْ; the passive voice, negation with لا

رُكنُ المُفْرَداتِ الجَديدةِ

to collide (with)	اصْطَدَمَ (يَصْطَدِمُ) اصْطِدام (بِـ)
to arrest	اعْتَقَلَ (يَعْتَقِلُ) اِعْتِقال
to assure, to assert, to emphasize	أكَّدَ (يُؤَكِّدُ) تأكيد
to head toward	تَوَجَّهَ (يَتَوَجَّهُ) تَوَجُّه
culture	ثَقافة ج ثَقافات
to steal	سَرَقَ (يَسْرِقُ) سَرِقة
procedure, process, operation	عَمَليّة ج عَمَليّات
thief	لِص ج لُصوص
stage	مَرْحَلة ج مَراحِل
to be successful, to pass	نَجَحَ (يَنْجَحُ) نَجاح
hospital	مُسْتَشْفى ج مُسْتَشْفَيات
fair, festival (exhibition)	مِهْرَجان (مَعْرِض)

تمرين ١

وافِق بين كُلِّ كَلِمة واكتُب الكَلِمَتين في الوسط:

١	نِسبة		عُمر
٢	تلميذ		يعني
٣	وزير		جديد
٤	أيْ		لِصّ
٥	مُستجِدّ		مُتَوَسِّط
٦	تعليم		طالب
٧	سرق		مدارس
			دَولة

تمرين ٢

اختَرِ الكَلِمةَ الّتي لا تُناسِب باقي الكَلِماتِ في كُلِّ مَجْموعةٍ وبَيِّن السَبَب:

١-	فارق	عملية	دم	تَخدير	أشعة
٢-	طبيب	مريض	عمود	عيادة	مستشفى
٣-	حادِث	تَخدير	اصطِدام	مرور	سيّارة
٤-	إطفاء	إسعاف	شُرطة	حادِث	كهرباء
٥-	إصابة	لصّ	سرق	سطا	مَسروق
٦-	صُداع	اِلتهاب	مِهرجان	حَساسية	عِلاج

أخبار من الصُحُف العربية

سبعةُ ملايينَ تلميذٍ يتوجّهون إلى المدارسِ في الجزائر

غُرفةُ الصَفّ

بدأ سبعةُ ملايينَ تلميذٍ أي نحوَ رُبع سكان الجزائر، عاماً دراسياً جديداً. من بينهم ستُمئةٍ وخمسةُ آلاف (٦٠٥٠٠٠) تلميذٍ مستجدٍ في المرحلة الابتدائية، وهي مرحلة إجبارية تصل إلى ست سنوات.

وقال السيد وزير التعليم الجزائري إن التعليم يمتصّ ربع ميزانية الدولة. وقال إن نسبة التلاميذ تصل إلى ٨٥٪ من الأطفال الذين أعمارهم بين ست سنوات واثنتي عشرة سنة.

وتصل نسبة التعليم إلى مئة بالمئة في بعض المدن، وتقلّ نسبة تعليم البنات بقليل عن المتوسط القومي، إذ تصل نسبتهن إلى ٨٠٪ فقط.

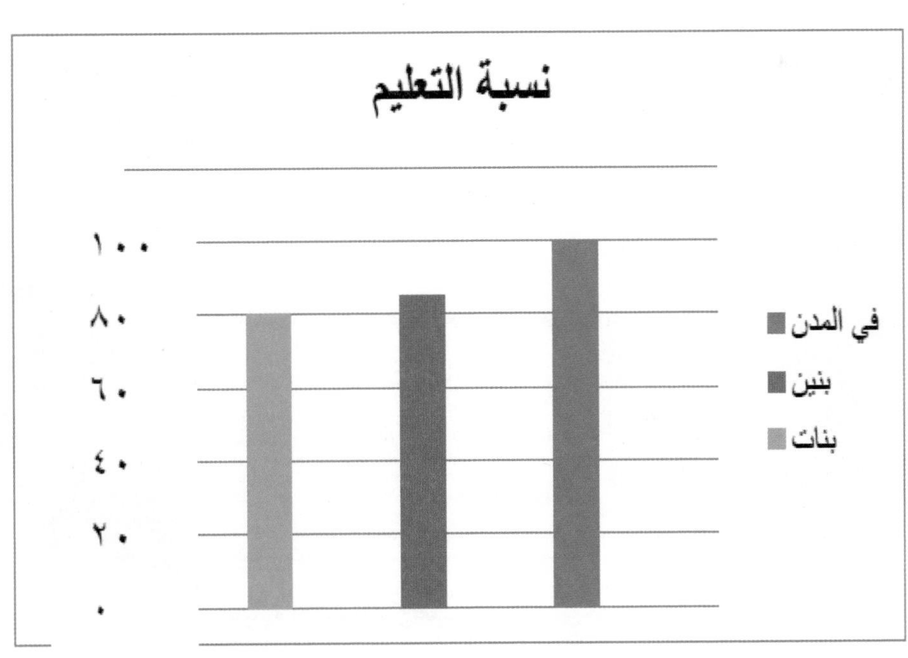

علاجُ اللوزتين بالليزر

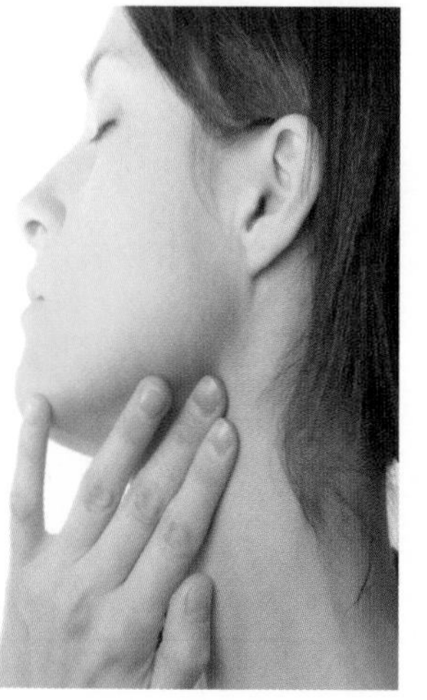

مريضة قبل العملية

باريس. وكالات الأنباء:
توصّل طبيبان فرنسيان إلى تقنية حديثة تُمكّن من علاج اللوزتين باستعمال أشعة الليزر.

ويقول الطبيبان إنه لا بدّ من إجراء عملية تخدير في مكان اللوزتين، ثم تُسلّط أشعة الليزر خلال وقت لا يزيد عن دقيقتين على المساحة التي توجد فيها اللوزتان. لا تسبب هذه العملية سيلان قطرة واحدة من الدم. ويحتاج العلاج بأشعة الليزر إلى ما بين أربع وثماني جلسات بفارق ١٥ يوما على الأقل بين كل جلسة وأخرى.

ويؤكد الطبيبان أن هذه التقنية الجديدة أُجريت على ٢٠٠ شخص وقد حقّقت نجاحا كبيرا. إلا أن ثلاثة أشخاص من هذه المجموعة لم تنفعهم هذه التقنية.

حادثُ مرور

عمود كهربائي

اصطدمت صباحَ اليومِ سيارةٌ خاصة كانت تسير على طريق المطار الدولي بسرعة كبيرة بشاحنة مُتعطّلة تَقف على الجانب الأيمن من الطريق. بدأ الحادث بسيطا إذ اصطدم طرف السيارة الأيمن بجانب الشاحنة، لكن السائق انحرف إلى يسار الطريق ثم إلى اليمين مرة ثانية واصطدم بعمود الكهرباء. سقط العمود على السيارة واشتعلت النار بها. هُرِع الناس لمساعدة السائق وحملوه خارجَ السيارة. وبعد دقائقَ حضرت سيارة الإطفاء ثم وصلت

سيارة الإسعاف ونقلت السائق إلى المستشفى.

سيارة إسعاف

عمليةُ سطو

حلي

سطا لِص ليلةَ أمس على شقة رجل وزوجته وهما في دار السينما. سرق اللِص جهاز التلفزيون وجهاز الراديو ومسجلة مع ساعتين غاليتين، كما سرق عددا من حُليّ السيدة ومبلغ ٢٢٥ دينارا كان موجودا في الخِزانة. اعتُقل اللص بالصُدفة في الساعة السادسة من صباح اليوم، إذ كان يركب سيارة أجرة إلى خارج المدينة، وقد وقع لها حادث مرور. أصيب بالحادث سائق سيارة الأُجرة واللص إصابات شديدة. تبيّن للشرطة أن الأشياء الموجودة مع الرجل مسروقة فاتّصلوا بصاحبها وأعادوها له.

لِص

مكتبةٌ نسائيةٌ في جُدّة

أنشأت الجمعية النسائية أول مكتبة نسائية في جدة تضُم آلاف الكتب في جميع فنون المعرفة. تقدّم المكتبة خدماتها للقارئات بأحدث الطرق باستخدام أقراص الليزر لتقديم المعلومات.

مَعرِضُ الكتاب

نظّمت مكتبة الأسد في دمشق معرِض الكتاب السابع. شارك في المعرِض ٣١١ دارا للنشر من ١٩ دولة عربية وأجنبية. وقد بلغ عدد العناوين في المعرض اثنين وعشرين ألفا وخمسمئة عنوان (٢٢,٥٠٠) في العديد من فنون المعرفة.

معرِضُ الخط العربي

أقيم في مدينة الجزائر خلال شهر تشرين الأول الماضي معرِضٌ للفنان رابح بو عنيفة. ضمّ المعرِض أربعين لوحة حول الخطّ العربي تصوّر جمال الأحرف والكلمات العربية.

مِهرجان الفنون المسرحية

أقيم في مدينة بنغازي في ليبيا المِهرجان الرابع للفنون المسرحية، وقد شارك في المهرجان عدد من الدول العربية.

تمرين ٣

أجب عن الأسئلة الآتية وفق نص القراءة:

١- ما الفكرة الرئيسة في هذا الدرس؟

٢- عدّد الأفكار الثانوية في النصوص.

٣- لخّص النص «علاج اللوزتين بالليزر» بما لا يزيد عن عشرين كلمة.

٤- اكتب عنوانا آخر للنص «عملية سطو».

تمرين ٤

أكمل الجمل الآتية بالاختيار المناسِب وفق نصّ القراءة:

١- تبلغ نسبة التلاميذ في المرحلة الابتدائية بالجزائر ______________ من الأطفال بهذه السن.

☐ ٨٠٪ ☐ ٨٥٪ ☐ ١٠٠٪

٢- تُسلّط أشعة الليزر على اللوزتين لمدة ______________.

☐ دقيقتين ☐ أقل من دقيقتين ☐ أكثر من دقيقتين

٣- يستغرق علاج اللوزتين بأشعة الليزر ______________ على الأقل.

☐ أربعة أيام ☐ ١٥ يوماً ☐ شهرين

٤- اشتعلت النار ______________.

☐ بعمود الكهرباء ☐ بالسيارة ☐ بالشاحنة

٥- سطا اللص على ______________.

☐ محل تجاريّ ☐ سيارة أجرة ☐ شقة رجل وزوجته

٦- أنشأت الجمعية النسائية أول ______________.

☐ معرض للخط العربي ☐ مهرجان للفنون المسرحية ☐ مكتبة نسائية

٧- ضمّ معرض الخط العربي ______________.

☐ ٤٠ لوحة ☐ ٦٠ لوحة ☐ ٢٠ لوحة

٨- أقيم في الجزائر معرض ______________.

☐ الكتاب العربي ☐ الخط العربي ☐ الفنون المسرحية

تمرين ٥

اكتب «خطأ» أو «صواب» إلى جانب كلّ جملة ثمّ صحّح الجمل الخطأ:

١- التعليم في الجزائر إجباري.

٢- لا يسيل دم المريض أثناء علاجه بأشعة الليزر.

٣- جميع الناس يستفيدون من العلاج بأشعة الليزر.

٤- حملت سيارة الإطفاء السائق إلى المستشفى.

٥- وقع حادث سيارة للص وجرى اعتقاله.

تمرين ٦

أجب عن الأسئلة التالية وفق نص القراءة وبحسب ما تعلم:

١- كم يكلِّف التعليم في دولة الجزائر ؟

٢- ما عدد سكان الجزائر بحسب ما جاء في النص؟

٣- لو كنت تحتاج إلى عملية في اللوزتين هل تعالجها بأشعة الليزر؟ لماذا؟

٤- ما نسبة المرضى الّذين تنفعهم عملية الليزر؟

٥- كيف ساعد الناس سائق السيارة الّتي اصطدمت بعمود الكهرباء؟

٦- ماذا سرق اللص من الشقة؟

تمرين ٧

You have just witnessed a traffic accident. One person plays the role of a police officer taking a report, and the other plays the role of a witness to the accident. Things you may wish to mention are:

1. The time of the accident.
2. How the accident occurred.
3. Was anyone injured, how?
4. When did the ambulance arrive?
5. Was anyone taken to the hospital?
6. What happened at the hospital?

تمرين ٨

آ- أعد ترتيب الكلمات في كل مجموعة لتشكّل جملاً مُفيدةً:

١	عيادتِه	في	يُعالج	المرضى	الطبيبُ				
٢	ألاّ	عن	١٠٠ كيلومتر	يجب	سرعة	تزيد	بالساعة	السيارات	
٣	متعطِّل	أخي	الهاتف	عفواً	يا	هذا			
٤	فهُرِعتُ	سمعتُ	يُدق	لأفتحَهُ	البابَ				
٥	مِن	على	رِجلِها	الأرضِ	الطفلةُ	وسال	الدمُ	سقطت	فأصيبَت

تمرين ٩

أعد ترتيب الجمل لتشكّل فِقرة كاملة. الجملة الأولى في مكانها المناسب:

١- عَلِمَ المُراسلُ الصَّحَفيّ من الشرطة أن النار قد اشتعلت في شَقّة.

بعد خروج رجال الإطفاء من الشَقّة، دخلها المراسل فوجد الجدران سوداء اللون.

وكان رجال الإطفاء يحاولون إطفاء النار بالماء.

ثم هُرِع المراسل بعد ذلك عائداً إلى صحيفته كي يكتبَ الخبر وينشره.

التقط بعض الصور للشقة من الداخل قبل أن يغادرَها.

حين وصل إلى العُنوان كانت إحدى سيارات الإطفاء تقف أمام المنزل.

وكانت مياهٌ سوداءُ قذرة على الأرض والأثاث.

فركب سيارته وهُرِع إلى العنوان الّذي حصل عليه من الشرطة.

بعد حوالي رُبعِ ساعة نجح رجال الإطفاء في إطفاء النار وغادروا الشَقة.

في الطريق إلى الشَقة سمع سيارات الإطفاء تتجه إليها.

القَواعِد

1. The *Wāw* of Manner or Circumstance واو الحال

Used in both colloquial and MSA, this type of واو creates an adverbial situation that usually denotes *when* or *while*. We were introduced to this type of واو in the previous lesson when we learned that واو الحال begins a full and complete sentence. Three types of واو الحال are described in the following examples.

a. As a Nominal Sentence with No Referential Pronoun

I walked when the sun was in the middle of the sky.	مَشَيتُ والشَمسُ في وَسَطِ السَماءِ.	١
We completed the task with the TV on.	أكمَلنا الواجب والتِلفازُ مفتوح.	

b. As a Nominal Sentence Beginning with an Independent Referential Pronoun

The man entered the office smiling.	دَخَلَ الرَجُلُ المَكْتَبَ وهو يبْتَسِمُ.	٢
We drank the coffee when it was hot.	شَرِبْنا القَهوةَ وهي ساخِنةٌ.	

An instance of this type of واو occurred in our reading passage:

A burglar broke into their apartment while they were at the movies.	سَطا لِصٌّ على شَقّتِهِما وهُما في دار السينَما.

c. As a Verbal Sentence in the Past

Generally قد is used with واو الحال in affirmative sentences (e.g., ex. 3), but واو الحال may also occur in a negative sentence (e.g., ex. 4).

Suad came after having passed the exam.	جاءت سُعادُ وقد نَجَحَت في الامتحان.	٣
Suad came, but we did not know of her arrival.	جاءت سُعادُ وما عَلِمنا بوُصولِها.	٤

An instance of this type of واو occurred in our reading passage:

He was riding in a taxi cab after it had been involved in an accident.	كان يَركَبُ سَيّارةَ أُجرةٍ وقَد وَقَعَ لَها حادِث.

تمرين ١٠

Use واو الحال to express the following meanings in Arabic:

1. سامي met an old friend while he was on his way to work.
2. She went to sleep with the TV on.
3. I saw them while they were walking.
4. He walked to school when the weather was cold.

2. The Expression لابُدَّ *must; necessary; inevitable*

Usually لابُدَّ is followed by من + مَصدَر resulting in the following structure:

Forming the لابُدَّ Structure

لابُدَّ من + مَصدَر (مِثال: لابُدَّ مِن شُرْبِ الماء)

This expression is composed of absolute لا and the noun بُدَّ, which when used together mean *necessary, must*. When using this expression, you can either use المَصدَر after مِن (ex. 1), or you can introduce a verb by using أَنْ (ex. 2).

It is necessary to administer an anesthetic.	لابُدَّ مِن إجراءِ عَمَليّةِ تخدير.	١
It is necessary that an anesthetic be administered.	لابُدَّ مِن أنْ تُجرى عَمَليّةُ تخدير.	٢

You may have noticed that the verb in ex. 2 is passive, but it could just as easily have been active:

It is necessary that the doctor administer the anesthesia.	لابُدَّ مِن أنْ يُجرِيَ الطَبيبُ عَمَليَّةَ تَخدير.	٣

The agent of the sentence could be moved right after لابُدَّ, but, keep in mind, it must be modified by the preposition لِـ, which is attached to the agent as a prefix:

It is necessary for the doctor to perform the anesthesia.	لابُدَّ لِلطَبيبِ مِن أنْ يُجرِيَ عَمَليَّةَ تَخدير.	٤

تمرين ١١

Convey these meanings in Arabic using لابُدَّ. Try to avoid literal translation:

1. She must prepare for her trip to Paris.
2. It is necessary for them to find a new apartment.
3. It is inevitable that you obtain a passport if you want to travel abroad.
4. There is no way the doctor can operate without giving an anesthetic to the patient.

مُراجَعةُ القَواعِد

3. Verbs in the Passive Voice مَبني للمَجهول

Our main reading passage had multiple instances of verbs in مَبني لِلمَجهول:

أُقيمَ، تُسَلَّطُ، هُرِعَ، اِعتُقِلَ، أُصيبَ

Let's take a look at a couple of examples of these passive verbs in context:

> **مُلاحَظة**
>
> هُرِعَ *to hasten, to hurry* (only exists in the passive voice.)

The laser beam is directed at the tonsils.	تُسَلَّطُ أشعّةُ الليزَر على اللَّوزتين.	١
An Arabic calligraphy exhibit was held.	أُقيمَ مَعرِضٌ لِلخطِّ العَرَبيّ.	٢

In order to create verbs مَبني لِلمَجهول simply follow the following formulas:

Past Tense Formula for مَبني لِلمَجهول

فُعِلَ (_ُ_ِ_َ)

Present Tense Formula for مَبني لِلمَجهول

يُفْعَل (يـُ_ْ_َ_)

4. The Particle قَد and Its Variations

Remember that this particle carries two very different meanings in usage. When used after a past tense verb قَد carries the meaning of an auxiliary verb (i.e., *has, had, have*, etc.):

I called the airport, and they said the airplane had arrived.	اِتَّصلتُ بالمَطار وقالوا إنَّ الطائرةَ قَد وَصَلَت.	١

After a *present tense* verb قَد denotes possibility (i.e., *might, may*):

Reema may/might study medicine.	قَد تَدرُسُ ريما الطِبَ.	٢

You will certainly encounter this particle in its many guises in your readings—it may have a فـَ، وَ، أو لَـ prefixed to it, but these prefixes do not change the function of قد in any way:

فَقَد، وَقَد، لَقَد

5. The Negative Particle لَم

This particle is used to negate the past tense, but requires that a present tense verb in the jussive follow it.

The treatment benefited the patient.	نَفَعَ العِلاجُ المَريضَ.	١
The treatment did not benefit him.	لَمْ يَنْفَعْه العِلاجُ.	٢

Notice that the verb in example 2 takes a سكون since it is in مَجزوم. Using the particle لَمْ is generally considered more eloquent than using ما + الماضي, but they express the same exact meaning.

The treatment did not benefit him.	ما نَفَعَه العِلاجُ.	٣

Compare examples 2 and 3. Notice that both sentences render the same meaning, but they are structured somewhat differently.

تمرين ١٢

a. From the main reading passage, list two past tense passive verbs and one present passive verb.

b. Translate these sentences into Arabic using قَد، لَمْ، هُرِعَ:

1. We might travel to Jordan to see the ancient Roman ruins in جَرَش.
2. They have lived in Casablanca for two years.
3. We arrived at the theater when the concert was over.
4. The little girl rushed to open the door for her father.

تمرين ١٣

آ   **أجب عن الأسئلة وفق نص الاستماع:**

١- اكتب عُنواناً لهذه القصّة.

٢- اذكر الفكرة الرئيسة.

٣- عدّد الأفكار الثانوية.

٤- أعطِ مَعنى هذين الفعلين والاسمين من القصّة: أمسَكَ، هَرَبَ، سُلَّم، سَطْح.

٥- هل كانت السيّدة سعيدة في نِهايةِ القصّة؟ كيف عَرَفت ذلك؟

ب- **أكمل الجمل التالية بالاختيار المناسب وفق نص الاستماع:**

١- كان الأولاد يلعبون __________ .

☐ على الشجرة   ☐ على السَطْح   ☐ أمام الدار   ☐ في الدار

٢- رأى رجُل الإطفاء __________ على السَطْح.

☐ رجُلاً   ☐ قِطَّةً   ☐ فالسُلَّمَ   ☐ الدارَ

٣- كان مع رِجال الإطفاء __________.

☐ شُرطي   ☐ لِصّ   ☐ وَقْت   ☐ سُلَّم

٤- رأت أمّ عادل قِطَّتَها في أعلى __________ .

☐ الشجرة   ☐ السَطْح   ☐ السُلَّم   ☐ الدار

٥- وَجّه رجُلُ الإطفاءِ سؤالاً إلى __________ .

☐ الأولاد   ☐ الرَجُل   ☐ السيّدة   ☐ الشُرطة

٦- كان اللِصّ ينتظِر __________ ليدخُلَ الدار.

☐ الشُرطي   ☐ السيِّدة   ☐ النَهار   ☐ الليل

ج- **لَخِّص المُقابَلة مع زينا بحوالى خمسين كَلمة.**

د- **اكتب «خطأ» أو «صواب» إلى جانب كلّ جملة ثمّ صحِّح الجمل الخطأ:**

١- كانت قِطّةُ السيّدة على سَطح الدار.

٢- عَلِمَت السيّدة من الأولادِ مَكانَ قِطَّتِها.

٣- اتَّصَلَتِ السيّدةُ بالشُرطةِ لِمُساعَدَتِها في مُشكِلة قِطَّتِها.

٤- حاولَ اللِصُّ أنْ يهرُبَ مِن رجُلِ الإطفاء.

٥- اعتَقَلَ رجُلُ الإطفاءِ اللِصَّ.

٦- استطاعت القِطَّةُ أنْ تَنزِلَ بِنَفسِها.

ه- **أكمل الجمل التالية وفق نص الاستماع:**

١- حضر رِجال الإطفاء كي _________________.

٢- وجدت السيّدة قطّتَها تجلِس _________________.

٣- حاول الرجُل أنْ يهرب لكن _________________.

٤- اقتادت الشُرطة اللِصّ إلى _________________.

٥- كان الرجُل ينتظِر على السطْح حتى _________________.

المُفْرَدات

إجْباريّ			(adj.)	compulsory
إسْعاف	ج	إسعافات	(n., m.)	first aid
اِشتَعَلَ	(يَشتَعِلُ)	اِشتِعال	(v.)	to catch fire
أشِعّة			(n., f.)	rays, beams
أصابَ	(يُصيبُ)	إصابة	(v.)	to hit, to injure
اِصْطَدَمَ	(يَصْطَدِمُ)	اِصْطِدام بـ	(v.)	to collide with
أطفَأ	(يُطفِئُ)	إطفاء	(v.)	to extinguish, to put out a fire
أعادَ	(يُعيدُ)	إعادة	(v.)	to return (s. th.)
اِعتَقَلَ	(يَعتَقِلُ)	اِعتِقال	(v.)	to arrest
أكَّدَ	(يُؤَكِّدُ)	تأكيد	(v.)	to assert, to emphasize
اِمتَصَّ	(يَمتَصُّ)	اِمتِصاص	(v.)	to absorb
اِنحَرَفَ	(يَنحَرِفُ)	اِنحِراف	(v.)	to veer, to turn to one side
أيْ			(part.)	namely, that is to say
بُدّ	(لابُدّ)			necessary, inevitable (used with لا)
بَلَغَ	(يَبلُغُ)	بُلوغ	(v.)	to amount to, to reach
تَبَيَّنَ	(يَتَبَيَّنُ)	تَبين	(v.)	to become clear, to be evident
تَقنية			(n., f.)	technology
تِلميذ	ج	تَلاميذ	(n., m.)	pupil
تَوَجَّهَ	(يَتَوَجَّهُ)	تَوَجُّه	(v.)	to head toward
تَوَصَّلَ	(يَتَوَصَّلُ)	تَوَصُّل	(v.)	to attain, to arrive, to achieve
ثَقافة	ج	ثَقافات	(n., f.)	culture, intellectualism

session, meeting, gathering	(n., f.)	جَلَسات	ج	جَلْسة
society, association	(n., f.)	جَمعيّات	ج	جَمْعِيّة
accident	(act. p.)	حَوادِث	ج	حادِث
to anesthetize, to numb	(v.)	تَخدير	(يُخَدِّرُ)	خَدَّرَ
blood	(n., m.)	دِماء	ج	دم
to flow, to stream, to run	(v.)	سَيَلان	(يَسيلُ)	سالَ
to steal	(v.)	سَرِقة	(يَسرِقُ)	سَرَقَ
to burglarize, to break into	(v.)	سَطْوٌ	(يَسْطو)	سَطا
to focus, to put in power	(v.)	تَسْليط	(يُسَلِّطُ)	سَلَّطَ
speaker (i.e., radio-stereo speaker)	(n., f.)	سَمّاعات	ج	سَمّاعة
chance, happenstance	(n., f.)	صُدَف	ج	صُدْفة
to join, to gather, to combine	(v.)	ضَمّ	(يَضُمُّ)	ضَمَّ
extremity, edge, limb	(n., m.)	أطراف	ج	طَرَف
operation, procedure, process	(n., f.)	عَمَليّات	ج	عَمَلِيّة
pole, post	(n., m.)	أعْمِدة / عَواميد	ج	عَمود
difference, distinction, disparity	(act. p.)	فَوارِق	ج	فارِق
art, type, kind, variety	(n., m.)	فُنون / أفْنان	ج	فَنّ
artist	(adj.)	فَنّانون	ج	فَنّان
disc, tablet	(n., m.)	أقْراص	ج	قُرْص
drop (of s.th.)	(n., f.)	قَطَرات	ج	قَطْرة
national	(adj.)			قَوْميّ
thief, robber, burglar	(n., m.)	لُصوص	ج	لِصّ

tonsils	(n., f.)	لَوْزات (اللَوزَتان)	ج	لَوزة
laser	(n., m.)			لِيزَر
amount of money	(n., m.)	مَبالَغ	ج	مَبْلَغ
broken, out of order	(act. p.)			مُتَعَطِّل
average, medium, intermediate	(act. p.)			مُتَوَسِّط
group; set	(pass. p.)	مجموعات	ج	مجموعة
stage, phase	(n., f.)	مَراحِل	ج	مَرْحَلة
traffic	(n., m.)			مُرور
new, recent	(act. p.)	مُسْتَجِدّون، مُسْتَجِدّات	ج	مُسْتَجِدّ
hospital	(n., m.)	مُستَشفَيات	ج	مُسْتَشفى
stolen	(pass. p.)			مَسْروق
knowledge	(n., f.)	مَعارِف	ج	مَعْرِفة
to enable, to make possible	(v.)	تمكين	(يُمَكِّنُ)	مَكَّنَ
festival, fair	(n., m.)	مِهْرَجانات	ج	مِهْرَجان
budget	(n., f.)	ميزانيّات	ج	ميزانيّة
news	(n., m.)	أنباء	ج	نَبَأ
to succeed, to pass, to be successful	(v.)	نَجاح	(يَنجَحُ)	نَجَحَ
to spread, to publish	(v.)	نَشر	(يَنشُرُ)	نَشَرَ
to organize, to put in order	(v.)	تَنظيم	(يُنَظِّمُ)	نَظَّمَ
to be useful, to benefit	(v.)	نَفْع	(يَنفَعُ)	نَفَعَ
to hurry, to hasten, to rush	(v.)	هَرَع	(يُهْرَعُ)	هُرِعَ
agency (news)	(n., f.)	وَكالات	ج	وَكالة

الدَرْسُ الثاني عشر

Objectives

- Describing feelings, places, and situations
- Learning storytelling devices for narration
- Introducing idiomatic expressions: بِالمُناسَبة، خَيرُها بِغَيرِها، لِحُسْنِ الحَظّ، لا مِن مُجيب
- **Revisiting**: the نون of dual and plural إضافة, adjectives containing doubled consonants, describing circumstance with بِـ, assimilation, doubled verbs negated with لم

- **مراجعة القواعد**: أعجب، جمع المؤنث السالم، الاسم الموصول، اسم المَفعول، الأسماء الخمسة، أفعال الشُروع والرَجاء والمُقارَبة

رُكنُ المُفْرَداتِ الجَديدةِ

to realize	أدْرَكَ (يُدْرِكُ) إدْراك
to take a break (from)	اِرتاح (يَرْتاحُ) اِرتياح (مِن)
except (for)	بِاستِثْناء
invitation	دَعْوة ج دَعَوات
vicious	شَرِسٍ ج شَرِسون
to happen upon, to meet by coincidence	صادَفَ (يُصادِفُ) مُصادَفة
to pressure s.th.	ضَغَطَ (يَضْغَطُ) ضَغْط
to hang, to suspend	عَلَّقَ (يُعَلِّقُ) تَعليق
unlucky, ill-fated	مَنحوس ج مَناحيس
result	نَتيجة ج نَتائج
to threaten	هَدَّدَ (يُهَدِّدُ) تَهْديد

تمرين ١

وافِق بين كلمات من العمودين لها علاقة في المعنى واكتُب الكَلِمَتين في الوسط:

١	إجازة		بِسرعة
٢	غَضِبَ		مُسدَل
٣	مَزرعة		عُطلة
٤	مُغلَق		عَرِقَ
٥	بِبطءٍ		حَنِقَ
٦	بدأ		ريف
			شَرَعَ

تمرين ٢

وافِق بين كلمات من العمودين لتشكّل عبارات من مُضاف ومُضاف إليه:

١	عَدّاد		دَعوة
٢	مَحطّة		البيت
٣	مُحرِّك		المَسافة
٤	جَرَس		الوقود
			السيّارة

تمرين ٣

اخترِ الكَلِمةَ الّتي لا تُناسِب باقي الكَلِماتِ في كُلِّ مَجْموعةٍ وبَيِّن السَبَب:

١-	أسرة	عامِل	جَدّ	أولاد
٢-	سِتارة	سيّارة	جَرّار	شاحِنة
٣-	أشجار	مَزرعة	نُباح	ريف
٤-	غَضَب	حَنَق	غَيْظ	فَرَح
٥-	عُطلة	قَهوة	شاي	فِنجان

دعوة مَنحوسة

كتب لي صديقي عبد الرحمن التِلمْسانيّ رسالة يدعوني فيها إلى قضاء يومَي الخميس والجمعة معه ومع أسرته في داره الريفيّة الّتي تقع وَسَطَ مَزرعته الكبيرة قُرب دمشق. فرِحتُ بهذه الدعوة فَرَحاً شديداً لأني أحتاج إلى إجازة حقيقيّة أسترخي فيها في مكان هادئ وإلى إنسان أتحدّث معه، لأني أشعر بوحدة شديدة بعد سفر زوجتي والأولاد إلى بيروت لزيارة بيت جدّهم.

مَزرعة

عدت من عملي مُبكِّراً يوم الخميس وتناولت الغداء. بعد العصر بقليل ركِبتُ سيّارتي وانطلقتُ إلى دار صديقي على طريق ريفيّة تحفّ بها الأشجار من الجانبين. أعجبني هذا المنظر وتذكّرتُ العطلة السابقة الّتي قضَيتُها في تلك المنطقة الرائعة. لم أصادِف سيّارات كثيرة على الطريق باستثناء بعض الجرّارات والشاحنات. بعد حوالي ساعة وصلت مَزرعة صديقي أبي مروان، وأوقفتُ سيّارتي في فناء واسع إلى يمين الدار.

جرّار

كَلبٌ شَرِسٌ مَربوطٌ بِجنزير

أطفأت مُحرِّك السيّارة ونظرتُ من النافذة فإذا بي أرى كلباً كبيراً شَرِساً يستقبلني بنُباحِهِ المُخيف. بقيتُ داخِل السيّارة ولم أجرؤ أن أفتح الباب. لكن لحُسن الحَظّ لاحظتُ أنَّ الكلب مَربوط بجنزير قويّ، فارتحتُ لذلِك ونزلتُ من السيّارة واقتربت من البيت. إلاّ أني لاحظتُ أنَّ جميع الأنوار مطفأة في المنزل وأن الشبابيكَ مُغلَقةٌ وبعضَ الستائرِ مسُدَلة.

مشيتُ نحو الباب وضغَطتُ على الجَرَس ولم يجِب أحد. ضغَطتُ على الزرّ ولِمُدّة أطول ولا مِن مُجيب. قرعتُ الباب بقوة بيدي وحصلت على النتيجة نفسها. وفي هذه الأثناء لم يتوقّف ذلك الكلب اللعين عن النُباحِ لحظةً واحدةً مّما زاد من ارتباكي.

جَرِس الباب

نظرتُ حولي فوجدتُ صحيفة الصباح مازالت على عَتَبة الباب لم يرفعْها أحد، فأدركتُ أنّ أبا مَروان وأسرته ليسوا في البيت. غضِبتُ لذلك غَضَباً شديداً وكِدتُ أقرِّرُ وأنا في منتهى الحَنَق أن أقاطِع هذا الصديق لأنّه نسيَ موعدي معه. وفي الحال كتبتُ له رسالةً عاتبتُه فيها عِتاباً شديداً.

علّقتُ الرسالة على الباب ثمّ توجّهتُ نحو سيّارتي لأعودَ إلى المدينة وإذا بي أجد ذلك الكلب الضخم يقِف إلى جانب باب السيّارة وينظر إليَّ نظرةَ تهديد. استغربتُ ذلك جداً. «تُرى كيف استطاع أن يصل إلى السيّارة وهو مَربوط بذلك الجِنزير القويّ؟» ألقيتُ نظرةً أخرى على الجِنزير وتبيّن لي أنّه جنزير طويل. وبدأ الكلب ينبح بِشراسة أشدّ وأقوى فارتجف قلبي من الخوف، وتراجعتُ ببطء ودرتُ حول السيّارة والكلب يتبعني، ولّما وصلتُ بابَ السائقِ فتحتُه بسرعة وقفزتُ إلى داخل السيّارة وأغلقتُ الباب خلفي.

عزيزي أبو مروان،
حضرت حسب دعوتك ولم أجدك.
عسى أن تكون بخير. تمنيت أن أشرب
عندك فنجان شاي. لكن لا بأس،
خيرها بغيرها.
بالمناسبة، كلبك لا يحبّني ولا أحبّه،
وكان استقباله لي أسوأ استقبال.
أخوك رياض

مَحطّة وُقود

لعنتُ أبا مروان ألف لعنة على هذه الدعوة المَنْحوسة. ثمّ أدرتُ مُحرِّك السيّارة وشتَمتُ الكلب من خلف زُجاج النافذة منفِّساً عن حَنَقي، وتوجّهتُ إلى دمشق في الظلام. وقبل أن أصل إلى داري رأيت أن أملأ خزّان سيّارتي بالوقود، فتوقّفتُ من أجل ذلك عند مَحطّة وقود. وبينما كان العامل يملأ الخزّان بالوقود مددتُ يدي إلى العُلبة الّتي أمامي وفتحتُها لأتناول ورقة وقلماً كي أكتب الرقم الّذي سجّله عدّاد المسافة وإذا برسالة الدعوة الّتي بعثها لي أبو مروان بالعُلبة.

أخي العزيز رياض،

يسرّني أن أدعوك إلى داري الريفية لقضاء يومي الخميس والجمعة ٦ و ٧ تموز.

أرجو أن تستطيع الحضور.

أخوك

أبو مروان

تناولتُ الرسالة وشعرتُ بالحَنَق يعود إليَّ ثانيةً، وشرعتُ أقرأها والغيظ يتزايد داخلي. وفجأةً شعرتُ بالخَجَل الشديد وتصبّب العَرَقُ من جبيني، إذ اكتشفتُ من الرسالة أنّ موعد الدعوة ليس هذا الأسبوع بل الأسبوع المُقبِل.

تمرين ٤

للمحادثة: احكِ قصةً لزميلك تصف فيها موقفاً أحسست فيه بارتباك وخوف. قد تفيدك الأفكار التالية:

١- ما الّذي سَبَّب الإحساس بالخوف؟

٢- أين كنت؟

٣- كيف تورّطت في ذلك الموقف؟

٤- ماذا قرّرت أن تفعل؟

٥- صِف حالك في الموقف، هل كنت خائفاً أو مُرتَبِكاً؟

٦- كيف خلّصت نفسك من الموقف؟

تمرين ٥

أجب عن الأسئلة التالية وفق نص القراءة:

١- ما الفكرة الرئيسة لهذا الدرس؟

٢- حدِّد بعض الأفكار الثانويّة.

٣- اكتب عنواناً آخر لهذا الدرس.

٤- مَن صاحِبُ الدعوة؟

٥- لماذا سُمّيت الدعوة "مَنحوسة"؟

٦- أين قضى كاتب القصّة إجازته السابقة؟

تمرين ٦

اكتب «خطأ» أو «صواب» إلى جانب كلّ جملة ثمّ صحِّح الجمل الخطأ:

١- انطلق الكاتب إلى منزل صديقه كي يشرب فنجان شاي.

٢- شعر الكاتب بوحدة شديدة على الطريق الريفيّة.

٣- لم يكُن هناك أحد في دار السيّد التِلمساني.

٤- قضى الكاتب ليلة يوم الخميس في مَحطّة الوقود.

تمرين ٧

آ- أعد ترتيب الكلمات في كل مجموعة لتشكّل جملاً مُفيدةً:

١	من	سيّارتي	الوقود	يتّسع	ليترا	خزّانُ	لخمسين
٢	شديد	لأمي	أشعر	وأبي	بشوق	وإخوتي	
٣	كلّ	مفتوحة	اِقتربتُ	البيت	وجدتُ	لمّا	من	النوافذ
٤	الريف	زُهَير	صغيرة	قضى	قرية	في	إجازة	في

تمرين ٨

أكمل الجمل الآتية بالاختيار المناسِب وفق نصّ القراءة:

١- فرِح كاتب القصّة بالدعوة ____________.

☐ لأنّ زوجته وأولاده في بيروت ☐ لأنّه يحتاج إلى إجازة

☐ لأنّه لم يزر تلك المنطقة من قبل ☐ لأنَّ صديقه يسكن دارا ريفية

٢- ترك الكاتب عمله يوم الخميس ____________.

☐ صباحاً ☐ ظهراً ☐ عصراً ☐ مساءً

٣- شاهد الكاتب ____________ على جانبي الطريق.

☐ أشجاراً ☐ شاحنات ☐ جرّارات ☐ سيّارات

٤- ظنَّ الكاتب أنَّ صديقه قد ____________.

☐ نسيَ الكلبَ في فِناءِ الدار ☐ كتب له رسالةَ دعوة

☐ ترك بابَ الدارِ مفتوحاً ☐ نسيَ موعدَهُ معه

٥- استطاع الكلب أن يقترب من سيّارةِ الكاتبِ لأنّه ____________.

☐ كان مربوطاً بجِنزير طويل ☐ كلب شَرِس

☐ كلب قوي ☐ لم يكن مَربوطاً

٦- شتم الكاتب الكلب كي ____________.

☐ يعود إلى مكانه ☐ يتوجّه إلى المدينة ☐ ينفِّس عن غضبه ☐ يدخل السيّارة

٧- توقّف الكاتب قبل أن يصل إلى منزله في ____________.

☐ الطريق الريفية ☐ مزرعة صديقه ☐ مكان هادئ ☐ محطّة وقود

تمرين ٩

للمحادثة: تصوّر أنك رياض بالقصة في هذا الدرس. احكِ لزميلك ما يجب أن تفعل بعد أن اكتشفتَ خطأَك في محطّة الوقود.

تمرين ١٠

للكتابة:

١- تصوّر أنّك رياض واكتب رسالة إلى أبي مروان تعتذر فيها عن الرسالة الّتي تركتها وتصف فيها ما حدث معك أمام بيته ذلك اليوم.

٢- اكتب رسالة إلى صديق أو (صديقة) تدعوه إلى بيت أسرتك الواقع على شاطئ بحيرة لقضاء عطلة نهاية الأسبوع. صف في الرسالة ما تستطيعان أن تفعلا معاً في تلك العطلة.

تمرين ١١

أكمل القصّة التالية بكلمات من هذا الدرس ثمَّ أعط معنى الكلمات الّتي تحتها خط. لخّص القصّة بعد ذلك بحوالي ثلاثين كلمة:

Fill in the blanks with words from this lesson then provide the meanings of the underlined words. After you are through, provide a summary in Arabic in around thirty words:

عملتُ ساعاتٍ طويلةً في الأسبوع الماضي وشعرتُ أني أريد أن أنام متأخرة يوم الجمعة. لذلك حين اتّصلَت بي صديقتي نور ودعتني لقضاء يوم الجمعة في مزرعة والدها ________ وقلتُ لها آسفة وإني أريد أن أنامَ ولن أستطيعَ الذهابَ معها. في ليلة يوم الخميس ________ النوافذ في بيتي و________ الستائر كي لا أسمع أيَّ صوتٍ من خارج البيت. في الصباح وقبل ________ السادسة استيقظتُ على صوت ________ الهاتف. رفعتُ السّماعة وأنا نصف نائمة وكان ________ خطأ. عدتُ إلى السرير وحاولت أن أنام. لكن بعد دقائق سمعتُ ________ كلبٍ من الطريق. بقي الكلب تحت نافذتي ينبَحُ أكثر من عشر دقائق وشعرتُ بـ________ شديد. بعد قليل ذهب ________ وأغمضتُ عينيَّ واسترخيتُ. مضت بضع ________ وإذا بي أسمع شخصاً ________ بابي بقوة، فهُرِعتُ إلى البابِ لأرى ما يجري، وإذا بشرطي يقف بالباب. سألني إن كنت ________ بالشرطة لأشكوَ كلباً. قلت لا، فاعتذر الشرطي وذهب. في تلك اللحظة ذهب عني ________ تماماً ولم أحبَّ أن أرجعَ إلى السرير. تذكّرتُ دعوة نور، فهُرِعتُ إلى ________ واتصلتُ بها راجيةً أنّها ما زالت في البيت. رنّ جرسُ هاتفها عدّة مرّات ولا من ________ وتبيّن لي أنّها قد ذهبت إلى ________ . . . خَيرُها بـ________.

Idioms

An idiom is an expression used in a particular way and setting that usually has a figurative meaning. After being in use for an extended period of time, an idiom becomes frozen—its intended meaning becomes more pragmatic, not necessarily literal. Consider the following idiomatic expressions and try to incorporate them into your everyday speech.

بالمُناسَبة

Use this expression when you want to say *by the way*. It literally means, *with suitability, in relationship.*

خيرُها بِغَيرِها

This expression means something on the order of *better luck next time*, or *how about a raincheck*. The phrase literally means *may the good of this occasion be transferred to another*. It is usually said when you miss some sort of opportunity or when you are disappointed by the result of your actions, but you hope to do better in the future when the opportunity presents itself. The meaning of the idiom changes depending on the context in which it is used. In our main reading passage the speaker intended to say "I hope to come again," because he missed his friend that evening and the socially appropriate thing to do is to promise another visit.

لِحُسْنِ الحَظ

You can use this phrase anytime you want to say *fortunately*. Its literal and pragmatic meanings are almost the same, in that if translated literally it means *for good fortune.*

لا مِن مُجيب

This idiom is used when an action does not receive the expected response: if, for instance, you knocked on a door and there was no answer.

تمرين ١٢

أكمل الجمل بهذه العبارات:

(بِالمُناسَبة، خَيرُها بِغَيرِها، لِحُسْنِ الحَظّ، ولا مِن مُجيب)

١- أردتُ أن ألتقي بك حين كنتَ تزور أخاك، لكنّي لم أستطِع الحُضور ________.

٢- انتهيتُ من قراءة ذلك الكتاب الّذي أعجبك ________ مؤلّفه جزائريّ وليس مغربيّاً.

٣- قرعتُ باب شقّة أحمد أكثر من ستّ مرّات، ________.

٤- حين عدت مِن عملي مساءً تبيَّن لي أنّي نسيتُ مِفتاح البيت في المكتب ________ وصل زوجي بعدي بخمس دقائق.

تمرين ١٣

Elicit the following idiomatic expressions from your classmates using these questions:

(لِحُسْنِ الحَظ ، لِسوءِ الحَظ ، بالمُناسَبة ، خَيْرُها بغَيرِها ، لا مِن مُجيب)

1. Did you have a good rest over the weekend?
2. Did you stop by my house last night?
3. Did you watch any TV yesterday?
4. Did you call me yesterday?
5. Did you finish your Arabic homework?

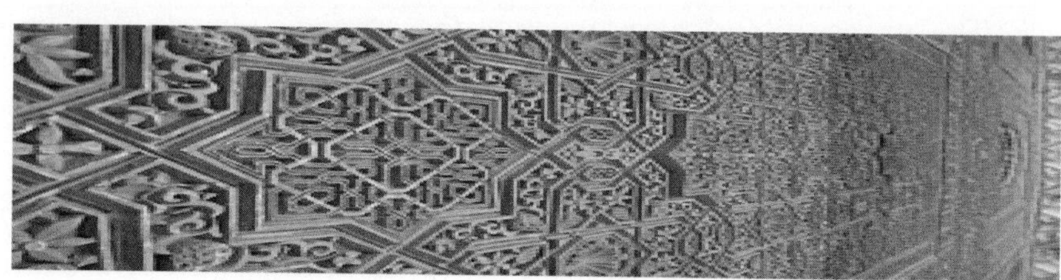

تمرين ١٤

أعد ترتيب الجمل لتشكّل فِقرة كاملة. الجملة الأولى في مكانها المناسب:

١ - يسكن عمي في قرية بعيدة في الريف ولم أزرْهُ منذ أشهر.
غادر القطار المَحطّة في موعده.
وصل القطار إلى مَحطّة بلدة عمي بعد ثلاث ساعات تقريباً.
لذلك اشتريتُ تذكرة قطار إلى بلدته ذهاباً وإياباً.
نزلتُ من العربة وكان عمي في انتظاري بالمَحطّة مع ابنه.
وصعدتُ إلى إحدى العربات وجلستُ إلى جانب النافذة.
قضيتُ في دار عمي خمسة أيّام استمتعتُ بها استمتاعاً عظيماً.
فقرّرتُ أن أزورَه وأقضيَ معه بضعة أيّام في الريف.
في صباحِ يوم الخميس ذهبتُ إلى مَحطّة القطار.
وفي الطريق شاهدتُ مزارعَ كثيرةً من نافذة القطار.
ركِبنا شاحنة ابن عمي الصغيرة وانطلقنا إلى دار عمي في المزرعة.

القَواعِد

1. Pronunciation Tip Concerning مِن وعَن

The preposition مِنْ is pronounced *min* with a سكون when it precedes words that do not have a definite article:

min dimashq	مِنْ دِمَشق	١
min aathār tadmur	مِنْ آثارِ تَدمُر	

When مِن precedes words that have a definite article it is pronounced *mina:*

mina s-sūqi	مِنَ السوقِ	٢
mina l-madīna	مِنَ المَدينة	

The pronunciation patterns of عَنْ are very similar to that of مِن in that a short vowel is introduced to facilitate fluency. The difference between the two prepositions, however, is the short vowel that is introduced before definite articles for عَنِ is a كسر, not the فتح used for مِن.

ᶜan riḥlatihā	عَنْ رِحلَتِها	٣
ᶜani r-riḥlati	عَنِ الرِحلةِ	

تَذَوَّق الثَّقافَة العَرَبِيَّة

Certain times of the day are named due to their association with formal prayer times:

Morning prayer	صَلاةُ الصُبْحِ / صَلاةُ الفَجْرِ
Midmorning prayer	صَلاةُ الضُحى
Noon prayer	صَلاةُ الظُهْرِ
Midafternoon prayer	صَلاةُ العَصْرِ
Sunset prayer	صَلاةُ المَغْرِبِ
Evening prayer	صَلاةُ العِشاءِ

2. The Verb of Hope عَسى

عَسى is one of three verbs that express hope:

عَسى، حَرى، اِخلَوْلَق

Only عَسى is typically used in MSA, with حَرى وأخلَوْلَق being relegated to the domain of philologists. عَسى is used to mean *perhaps, might, could be,* or *I hope*:

The train might be late.	عَسى القِطارُ أنْ يَتأخَّرَ.	١

You can see in example 1 عَسى functions just like a member of كانَ وأخَواتُها in that it has a subject قطارُ and predicate أنْ يَتَأَخَّرَ. Let's take a look at a sentence in which عَسى occurred in our main reading passage:

I hope that you are well.	عَسى أنْ تكونَ بِخَيْر.	٢

You may have wondered if this verb can be used without أنْ introducing the predicate. In fact, it can:

Perhaps the train will arrive soon.	عَسى القِطارُ يَصِلُ قَريباً.	٣
Perhaps it will arrive soon.	عَساه يَصِلُ قَريباً.	٤

As you can see in example 4, this verb is very flexible in that it can take an attached pronomial suffix. A common phrase that does not incorporate أنْ into the predicate reads:

I hope you are all right.	عَساكَ بِخَيْر.	٥

3. Verbs of Beginning أفعال الشُروع

One of twelve Arabic verbs that denote the infinitive *to begin*, شَرَعَ (and its set) function in a manner similar to كانَ وأخَواتُها in that they introduce a nominal sentence with a subject and predicate. These verbs can be used interchangeably without changing meaning or sentence structure. Of the most frequently used أفعال الشُروع are:

أخَذَ، شَرَعَ، هَبَّ، قامَ، أنْشأَ، جَعَلَ، بَدَأَ

١ شَرَعَ الأستاذُ يَشرَحُ الدَرْسَ.	*The teacher started to explain the lesson.*

مُلاحَظة

أفعال الشُروع do not require أنْ to introduce الخَبر

The reason that أفعال الشُروع do not require أنْ is that these verbs refer to an action taking place in the present, whereas أنْ denotes future tense.

أفعال الشُروع are distinguished from other verbs in that when they introduce a مَصدَر it is preceded by a preposition. Let's consider example 1 but change يَشرَحُ into a مَصدَر:

٢ شَرَعَ الأستاذُ بِشَرْحِ الدَرْسِ.	*The teacher started explaining the lesson.*

You may have noticed that بَدَأ of the members of أفعال الشُروع was used in our main reading passage and follows all of the rules mentioned in this section:

٣ وبدأ الكَلْبُ يَنْبَحُ	*The dog started to bark.*

تمرين ١٥

استخدِم (بَدَأ، شَرَعَ، عَسى) لتُكمِل الجُمَل التالية. يجب أن يطابِق الفعِل الفاعِل:

١- ____________ الكتب تصل المكتبة في الأسبوع المُقبِل.

٢- ____________ أختي بشِراء الأثاث لبيتها الجديد.

٣- ____________ـها تنجح في دراستِها.

٤- ____________ الطلاّب يصلون الجامعة للعام الدراسي الجديد.

٥- ____________ـني أجد شقّة أكبر من شقّتي.

تمرين ١٦

Translate the following sentences into Arabic using verbs of beginning and hope:

1. I hope the plane arrives on time.
2. She started speaking Arabic at the age of fifteen.
3. Perhaps he will come back next week.
4. The students in my class began to correspond by email with students from the Arab world in Arabic.

مُراجَعةُ القَواعِد

4. The Disappearing نون of Dual and Plural مُضاف

As you know, an إضافة is comprised of two parts: مُضاف ومُضاف إليه. The first noun can take any case, but all nouns following the first must be مَجرور. Dual nouns are marked with an ان for حالة الرفع and يْنَ for حالتا النَصْب والجر. Sound masculine plurals are marked with ونَ for حالة الرَفْع and ـينَ for حالتا النَصْب والجر.

> **مُلاحَظة**
>
> The نون that indicates dual or plural nouns completely disappears when acting as المُضاف

The (two) days: Thursday and Friday	يَومَيْ الخَميس والجُمعة	
Hala's (two) parents	والدا هالة	١
The school's teachers	مُعَلِّمو المَدرَسة	

5. The Verb أَعْجَبَ

This form IV verb resembles the concept *to please* in English in that the action is done by the object that is pleasing. Consider an excerpt from our main reading passage:

Swimming pleases me.	تُعْجِبُني السِباحةُ.	٢

Here, in both Arabic and English, السِباحة is doing the action while the person who enjoys swimming أنا is the direct object, (when أنا is a direct object, it becomes ني).

6. The Case Marking of the Sound Feminine Plural

Sound feminine plurals are created by simply changing the تاء مَربوطة into ات. You may have noticed that there is a discrepancy in case markings when sound feminine plurals are in حالتا النَصْب والجَر.

I passed by many cars.	صادَفتُ سيّاراتٍ كثيرةً.	١

It would seem that سيّارات being that it is the direct object of the verb صادَفْتُ should be in حالة النَصْب, and in theory it is. The rule states sound feminine plurals take كسرة or تنوين بالكسر in accusative and genitive cases. As you can see in example 1, the adjective كَثيرةً remains loyal to the grammatical case of being in حالة النَصْب.

I looked at many cars.	نَظرتُ إلى سيّاراتٍ كَثيرةٍ.	٢

As you might have guessed, the modified adjective كَثيرةٍ takes the same case marker as its noun سيّاراتٍ in that both are in حالة الجَر.

7. The Use of Restrictive Relative Pronouns

Relative pronouns (الّذي، الّتي، الّذينَ) agree in number and gender with their modified noun, while the dual forms of relative pronouns (اللذان، اللتان) agree in case as well.

مُلاحَظة

Relative pronouns are only used if the noun that they modify is definite

I know all of the people who came.	أعرِفُ كُلَّ الأشْخاصِ الّذينَ حَضَروا.	١
I know people who came without an invitation.	أعرِفُ أشْخاصاً حَضَروا دونَ دَعوة.	٢

When example 1 and 2 are compared, you will notice that the relative pronoun is retained in the English translation even though it is absent in the Arabic source text.

8. إذا الفُجائية

This particle, not to be confused with conditional إذا (= *if*) introduces an unexpected action that translates into English as *lo and behold.* إذا الفُجائية takes either a و or a فـ as its prefix while the pronoun following it (usually) has an attached بـِ.

I looked out the window and lo and behold I saw a huge dog!	نَظَرتُ مِن النافِذةِ فإذا بي أرى كَلْباً كَبيراً.

9. Forming the Superlative out of Adjectives with Doubled Consonants

Certain words in the Arabic language have the same letter for their second and third letters of the root. This might seem to pose a problem when forming the superlative or comparative structures, but in reality it is quite simple.

من صيَغ اسم التَفضيل			
جَديد	⇐	ليس أجْدَد	أجَدُّ
لَذيذ	⇐	ليس ألذَذ	ألَذُّ
شَديد	⇐	ليس أشْدَد	أشَدُّ
عَزيز	⇐	ليس أعْزَز	أعَزُّ

As you can see through these examples, all one has to do to create the superlative/comparative degree from adjectives with doubled second and third radicals is 1) place a أ before the adjective; 2) remove the ي and final radical; and 3) place a شَدّة on the final radical.

10. Passive Participles اسم المَفعول

Because several instances of the passive participle occurred in this lesson, we thought it would be a good idea to review how to derive it from the trilateral verb in form I. This table offers examples of passive participles in forms I-X that might help you in identifying and forming اسم المَفعول:

أوزان اسم المَفعول			
written	مَكتوب	مَفعول	I
camp	مُخَيَّم	مُفَعَّل	II
being accountable	مُحاسَب	مُفاعَل	III
closed	مُغلَق	مُفْعَل	IV
learned, acquired	مُتَعَلَّم	مُتَفَعَّل	V
attainable	مُتَناوَل	مُتَفاعَل	VI
---	لا يوجَد	مُنفَعَل	VII
believed; belief	مُعْتَقَد	مُفْتَعَل	VIII
reddish	مُحْمَرّ	مُفعَلّ	IX
used	مَستَخْدَم	مُستَفْعَل	X

مُلاحَظة

Passive participles in forms II-X are formed by ensuring a فتح is placed on the penultimate letter following the form:

مُـــ ـَـــ ـــ

11. The Five Nouns الأسماء الخمسة

أَبٌ، أَخٌ، حَمٌ، فَمٌ، ذو

a. When Acting as the مُضاف

These five nouns receive special treatment in Arabic grammar since their last radical inflects with a long vowel. When in nominative case they take a و (the long vowel equivalent of the ضَمّ), in accusative they take an ا (the long vowel equivalent of the فَتْح), while in the genitive they take a ي (the long vowel equivalent of كَسر).

الأسماء الخمسة			
في حالة الرَّفْع	الضَمّ	⇐	ـو
في حالة النَصْب	الفَتْح	⇐	ا
في حالة الجَر	الكَسر	⇐	ـي

Abu Marwan lives on a farm.	يَعيشُ أبو مَروان في مَزرَعةٍ.	١
I visited Aba Marwan.	زُرْتُ أبا مَروان.	٢
I wrote to Abi Marwan.	كَتَبتُ إلى أبي مَروان.	٣

مُلاحَظة

When these five nouns act as المُضاف they are quite easy to deal with as long as you follow the pattern:

حالةُ الرَفْع	حالةُ النَصْب	حالةُ الجَر
___ + و	___ + ا	___ + ي

b. When Not Acting as the مُضاف

When these nouns are in the singular and not the مُضاف, they inflect like any other noun in Arabic:

This is a father and his daughter.	هذا أبٌ وابنتُه.	٤
I saw a father and his daughter.	رأيتُ أباً وابنتَه.	٥
I passed by a father and his daughter.	مَرَرتُ بأبٍ وابنتِه.	٦

Why would you think that all of these nouns shown in examples 4-6 take تَنوين? If you said because they are indefinite, you are correct.

Let us now direct our attention to dual form for these nouns, something that occurs much more frequently in Arabic than you might initially think since many people have two brothers.

c. When أخٌ Is in Dual Form المُثَنَّى

Using أخ as our model, we can see how the other nouns in this set behave in المُثَنّى.

The two brothers came by.	جاءَ الأخَوانِ.	٧
I saw the two brothers.	رأيتُ الأخَوَينِ.	٨
I wrote to the two brothers.	كَتَبتُ إلى الأخَوَينِ.	٩

مُلاحَظة

When stating that you have two brothers, follow this model:

لي أخَوان

To form this, simply add the dual انِ to the base أخو.

d. When أَخٌ Acts as the مُضاف in Dual Form

When dealing with المُثَنّى in the إضافة we must remember to drop the final ن. Let's take a look at المُثَنّى with a first-person pronomial suffix added:

My two brothers came by.	جاءَ أخَوايَ.	١٠
You saw my two brothers.	رأيت أخَوَيَّ.	١١
I wrote to my two brothers.	كَتَبتُ إلى أخَوَيَّ.	١٢

If pronominal suffixes are added to المُثَنّى, they will follow the pattern illustrated in examples 13-15:

Your two brothers came by.	جاءَ أخَواكَ.	١٣
I saw your two brothers.	رأيتُ أخَوَيْكَ.	١٤
I wrote to our two brothers.	كَتَبتُ إلى أخَوَيْنا.	١٥

e. The Marking for the Plural of the Five Nouns

All of these nouns have broken plurals, but luckily, when in the plural, they have regular markings:

جَمْعُ الأسماء الخمسة		
أَبٌ	⇄	آباء
أَخٌ	⇄	إخْوة
حَمٌ	⇄	أحْماء
فَمٌ	⇄	أفواه
ذو	⇄	أذواء

Examine these sentences that illustrate the three cases with plural nouns:

These are brothers of yours.	هؤلاء إخوَةٌ لَكُم.	١٦
We saw our fathers doing that.	شاهَدنا آباءَنا يَفعَلونَ ذلِكَ.	١٧
I heard this from the mouths of scholars.	سَمِعتُ ذلِكَ مِن أفواهِ العُلَماء.	١٨

مُلاحَظة

ذو can only be used when it is مُضاف:

Adnan is (a man) of wealth (= wealthy).	عَدنانُ ذو مالٍ.	١٩
Adnan is of precise appointments (= punctual).	عَدنانُ ذو مواعيدَ دَقيقةٍ.	٢٠

مُلاحَظة

فَمٌ cannot be declined like the other four nouns unless the final م is dropped, leaving the letter فـ.

The noun فَم occurs naturally in an idiomatic expression said in appreciation of something nice someone has said, especially in public:

May your mouth be safe! (literal); *Bravo! Well said! (functional)*	سَلِمَ فوكَ!

تمرين ١٧

اِختَر التكملة المناسبة لهذه الجمل المحتوية على الأسماء الخمسة:

١- وصل ________ على الطائرةِ نفسِها.

☐ الأخوانِ ☐ الأخَوَيْنِ ☐ الأخانِ ☐ الأخَينِ

٢- تِلكَ سيّارةُ ________ سَعيد.

☐ أب ☐ أبا ☐ أبو ☐ أبي

٣- لا أعلِم لماذا وضعَت القلمَ في ______________.

☐ فِها ☐ فيها ☐ فاها ☐ فوها

٤- أتعرِفُ الرَجلَ ______________ الشَعرِ الأسوَد.

☐ ذو ☐ ذا ☐ ذي ☐ ذوا

٥- هذا ______________ وأختُه.

☐ أخٌ ☐ أخو ☐ أخا ☐ أخي

٦- هذا الطعامُ سيذهب لِمَلءِ ______________ أطفالِ العالَم.

☐ أفهام ☐ أفياه ☐ أفواه ☐ فُواه

تمرين ١٨

Translate the following sentences into Arabic using الأسماء الخمسة:

1. This letter is for your father.
2. I have a brother who lives in Alaska.
3. Are these your two brothers?
4. How many brothers do you have?
5. هاني is a man with many problems.

12. Describing Circumstance with بِـ

This preposition is regularly used to describe the circumstance in which an action is performed and readily translates into English as an adverb. Its literal meaning is *with*, connoting something on the order of *with + verb* like *with speed* (= *quickly*); or *with slowness* (= *slowly*).

The dog started to bark viciously (with viciousness).	بَدَأَ الكَلْبُ ينبَحُ بِشَراسة.	١
I opened it quickly (with speed).	فَتَحتُه بِسُرعةٍ.	٢

13. Verbs of Beginning, Hope, and Approximation

أفعال الشُروع والرَجاء والمُقارَبة

We would like to introduce three rules to these verbs that might quite possibly make using them easier:

i. كادَ conjugates in the past (ex. 1) and present (ex. 2):

The temperature almost reached ٩٦ degrees.	كادَت الحَرارةُ تَصِلُ إلى ٩٦ دَرَجة.	١
Problems almost never end.	تَكادُ المَشاكِلُ لا تَنتَهي.	٢

ii. Verbs of beginning do not require أنْ to introduce the predicate:

Students started to arrive on campus.	بَدَأَ الطُلّابُ يَصِلونَ إلى حَرَمِ الجامِعةِ.	٣

iii. The use of أنْ to introduce the predicate of عَسى and كادَ is optional and has no impact on meaning:

Perhaps the plane will arrive on time.	عَسى الطائِرةُ تَصِلُ في مَوعِدِها.	٤
Perhaps the plane will arrive on time.	عَسى الطائِرةُ أنْ تَصِلَ في مَوعِدِها.	٥

تمرين ١٩

اختَرِ التكملة المناسبة لهذه الجمل المحتوية على أفعال الشُروع والرَجاء والمُقارَبة:

١- كادَت ريما ________ مَوعِدَ طَبيبِ الأسنان.

☐ نَسِيَت ☐ أن تَنسى ☐ نِسيان

٢- شَرعَت مدينة بيروت ________ شوارع جديدة.

☐ تَبني ☐ أنْ تَبني ☐ بَنَت

٣- عساكَ ________ في هذا الكتاب ما تريد.

☐ أنْ تجِد ☐ وجدتَ ☐ وُجود

٤- بدأنا ________ إلى أصدقائنا دَعَوات لحفلة تخرُّج سميرة.

☐ نكتبُ ☐ أنْ نكتبَ ☐ نكتبَ

تمرين ٢٠

Conversation: Find out who in class (is) _______________, by using the following grammatical structures:

(عسى، عساني، عساك، كاد، كِدْتُ، كِدْتَ، بدأ، شرع)

1. almost got into an accident this morning
2. started studying Arabic last year
3. hoping to graduate next year
4. almost ready to graduate
5. about to buy a house
6. about to move to another residence

14. Assimilation

When a preposition ends in a ن and the following particle begins with a م assimilation takes place creating a new graphic representation.

about what	عَمّا	⇐	عَنْ + ما
of what	مِمّا	⇐	مِنْ + ما
from whom	مِمَّن	⇐	مِنْ + مَن

15. Doubled Verbs Negated with لَمْ

Past tense verbs negated with لم are in the jussive case مَجزوم. When dealing with a doubled verb, مَجزوم takes a different short vowel (a فَتْح instead of a سَكون). Consider the following examples:

يَدُلَّ	لَمْ
يَمُرَّ	
يَظُنَّ	
يَرُدَّ	
يَمُدَّ	

تمرين ٢١

آ أجب عن الأسئلة وفق نص الاستماع:

١- ما الفكرة الرئيسة في نص الاستماع؟

٢- حدِّد بعض الأفكار الثانوية.

٣- اكتب عنواناً لهذه القصّة.

٤- صِف طقس ذلك اليوم.

٥- لماذا اضطرّ الزوج إلى الخروج مساءً في ذلك اليوم؟

٦- صِف حال الزوج حين عاد إلى البيت.

ب- أكمل الجمل التالية بالاختيار المناسب وفق نص الاستماع:

١- خرج الرجل إلى السوق ______________ .

☐ لأنّ الطقس حارّ وماطر ☐ لأنّه لم يخرج طول النهار

☐ لأنّ أصدقاءَه سيحضرون ☐ لأنّه يريد زيارة بعض الأصدقاء

٢- عُمْرُ نبيل ______________ .

☐ سنتان ☐ أربع سنوات ☐ ست سنوات ☐ عشر سنوات

٣- وضع الرجل ابنَه في السيّارة ______________ .

☐ على كرسي ☐ على الأرض ☐ في المقعد الأماميّ ☐ إلى جانبه

٤- أوقف الرجل سيّارته ______________ .

☐ أمام ☐ مُقابِل ☐ خلف ☐ جانب

٥- نسي الرجل مفاتيحه في ______________ .

☐ السيّارة ☐ البيت ☐ الدكّان ☐ الطريق

٦- كان على الشرطة أن تكسر زجاج نافذة السيّارة لأن ______________ .

☐ الرجل كان خارج السيّارة ☐ المفاتيح كانت مع الرجل

☐ الطِفل كان في السيّارة ☐ الناس حاولوا أن يفتحوا السيّارة

ج- لَخِّص المُقابَلة مع زينا بحوالى مئة كَلمة.

د- اكتب «خطأ» أو «صواب» إلى جانب كلّ جملة ثمّ صحِّح الجمل الخطأ:

١- ظنت الزوجة أنّ خروجَ زوجِها مساءً شيء حسن.
٢- ذهب الابن إلى السوق لشراء الحلوى لوالديه.
٣- كسر الناس زجاج نافذة السيّارة لأنّ الرجل أوقفها في الشارع المقابل.
٤- وصل الأصدقاء إلى دار الزوجين في موعدهم.

المُفْرَدات

إبهام	ج	أباهيم	(n., m.)	thumb
إجازة	ج	إجازات	(n., f.)	vacation
أدارَ	(يُديرُ)	إدارة	(v.)	to start (s.th.), to turn (s.th.) on
أدرَكَ	(يُدْرِكُ)	إدْراك	(v.)	to attain, to reach, to realize
أُذُن	ج	آذان	(n., f.)	ear
اِرتاحَ	(يَرتاحُ)	اِرتياح (مِن)	(v.)	to take a break (from)
اِرتَبَكَ	(يَرتَبِكُ)	اِرتِباك	(v.)	to be embarrassed/confused
اِرتَجَفَ	(يَرتَجِفُ)	اِرتِجاف	(v.)	to tremble, to shiver, to shudder
اِستِثناء	ج	اِستِثناءات	(n., m.)	exception
اِستَرخى	(يَستَرخي)	اِستِرخاء	(v.)	to relax
اِنطَلَقَ	(يَنطَلِقُ)	اِنطِلاق	(v.)	to disembark, to set out for
أنْف	ج	أنوف	(n., m.)	nose
أوقَفَ	(يوقِفُ)	إيقاف	(v.)	to stop, to park
بِنْصِر	ج	بَناصِر	(n., m.)	ring finger
بَينَما			(conj.)	while, whereas
تَراجَعَ	(يَتَراجَعُ)	تَراجُع	(v.)	to retreat, to withdraw
تُرى	يا تُرى		(excl.)	I wonder
تَزايَدَ	(يَتَزايَدُ)	تَزايُد	(v.)	to intensify, to grow greater
تَصَبَّبَ	(يَتَصَبَّبُ)	تَصَبُّب (عَرَقاً)	(v.)	to flow, to pour forth, (to sweat)
جَبين	ج	جِباه / أجْبُن	(n., m.)	forehead

to dare, to have courage	(v.)	جُرأة	(يَجرُؤُ)	جَرُؤَ
tractor	(n., m.)	جَرّارات	ج	جَرّار
bell, ringer	(n., m.)	أجْراس	ج	جَرَس
chain	(n., m.)	جَنازير	ج	جِنزير
eyebrow	(n., m.)	حَواجِب	ج	حاجِب
fortune, luck, lot, fate	(n., m.)	حُظوظ	ج	حَظّ
real	(adj.)			حَقيقيّ
to be furious, to be full of rage	(v.)	حَنَق	(يَحنَقُ)	حَنِقَ
to fear, to dread, to be afraid / scared	(v.)	خَوْف	(يَخافُ)	خافَ
to be ashamed, embarrassed	(v.)	خَجَل	(يَخجَلُ)	خَجِلَ
cheek	(n., m.)	خُدود	ج	خَدّ
little finger	(n., m.)	خَناصر	ج	خِنصر
to turn, to revolve	(v.)	دَوَران	(يَدورُ)	دارَ
to invite, to call, to summon	(v.)	دُعاء	(يَدعو)	دَعا
invitation	(n., f.)	دَعَوات	ج	دَعْوة
arm	(n., f.)	أذْرُع	ج	ذِراع
chin	(n., m.)	ذُقون	ج	ذَقْن
wonderful	(adj.)			رائع
to pick up, to raise, to lift	(v.)	رَفْع	(يَرفَعُ)	رَفَعَ
to increase	(v.)	زِيادة	(يَزيدُ)	زادَ
glass	(n., m.)			زُجاج

button, push button	(n., m.)	أزْرار	ج	زِرّ
leg, thigh	(n., f.)	سيقان	ج	ساق
drape, curtain	(n., f.)	سَتائِر	ج	سِتارة
to write down, to register	(v.)	تَسجيل	(يُسَجِّلُ)	سَجَّلَ
moustache	(n., m.)	شَوارِب	ج	شارِب
to curse, to swear, to call names	(v.)	شَتْم	(يَشتُمُ)	شَتَمَ
intense, powerful	(adj.)	أشِدّاء	ج	شَديد
vicious, fierce	(adj.)	شَرِسون	ج	شَرِس
to begin, to start, to commence	(v.)	شُروع	(يَشْرَعُ)	شَرَعَ
to feel, to have a feeling	(v.)	شُعور	(يَشعُرُ)	شَعَرَ
hair	(n., m.)	أشْعار	ج	شَعْر
to come across, to meet by chance	(v.)	مُصادَفة	(يُصادِفُ)	صادَفَ
huge, great	(adj.)	ضِخام	ج	ضَخْم
to press, to push, to pressure	(v.)	ضَغْط	(يَضغَطُ)	ضَغَطَ
doorstep, threshold	(n., f.)	عَتَبات	ج	عَتَبة
meter, counter	(n., m.)	عَدّادات	ج	عَدّاد
to perspire, to sweat	(v.)	عَرَق	(يَعرَقُ)	عَرِقَ
midafternoon	(n., m.)	أعْصار	ج	عَصر
box, case, carton	(n., f.)	عُلَب	ج	عُلبة
to hang, to spend, to attach	(v.)	تَعليق	(يُعَلِّقُ)	عَلَّقَ
neck	(n., m.)	أعْناق	ج	عُنُق

to get angry, to be furious	(v.)	غَضَب	(يَغضَبُ)	غَضِبَ
to break off a relationship, to interrupt	(v.)	مُقاطَعة	(يُقاطِعُ)	قاطَعَ
to decide	(v.)	تَقرير	(يُقرِّرُ)	قَرَّرَ
to knock, to rap	(v.)	قَرْع	(يَقرَعُ)	قَرَعَ
to spend (time), to pass (time)	(v.)	قَضاء	(يَقضي)	قَضى
shoulder	(n., f.)	أكْتاف	ج	كَتِف
palm (of a hand)	(n., m.)	كُفوف / أكُفّ	ج	كَفّ
to notice, to take note	(v.)	مُلاحَظَة	(يُلاحِظُ)	لاحَظَ
to curse, to damn	(v.)	لَعْن	(يَلعَنُ)	لَعَنَ
curse	(n., f.)	لَعَنات	ج	لَعْنة
cursed, damned, detested, evil	(adj.)	مَلاعين	ج	لَعين
responder	(n., m.)	مُجيبون	ج	مُجيب
engine, motor	(n., m.)	مُحَرِّكات	ج	مُحَرِّك
frightening, intimidating	(adj.)			مُخيف
to stretch (out), to reach, to extend	(v.)	مَدّ	(يَمُدُّ)	مَدَّ
tied, bound, fastened	(pass. p.)			مَربوط
drawn (a curtain)	(pass. p.)			مُسدَل
turned off, extinguished	(pass. p.)			مُطفَأ
to fill, to fill up	(v.)	مَلْء	(يَملأُ)	مَلأَ
the extreme, the utmost	(n., m.)			مُنتَهى
unlucky, unfortunate, ill-fated	(pass. p.)	مَناحيس	ج	مَنحوس

نَبَحَ	(يَنبَحُ)	نُباح	(v.)	to bark
نَتيجة	ج	نَتائِج	(n., f.)	result, outcome
نَفَّسَ	(يُنَفِّسُ)	تَنفيس	(v.)	to vent (frustrations)
مُنَفِّس			(act. p.)	s.o. venting
نور	ج	أنوار	(n., m.)	light (not dark)
هَدَّدَ	(يُهَدِّدُ)	تَهديد	(v.)	to threaten
وَحدة			(n., f.)	loneliness, being alone
وَقود			(n., m.)	fuel

الدَرْسُ الثالِث عشر

Objectives

- Introduction to the use of hypothetical speech
- Learning to describe wishes, desires, hopes, and dreams
- Grammar: Feminine superlative adjectives, the verb جَعَل, verbs that only occur in the passive

- **مراجعة القواعد:** المُضارع المَرفوع والمنصوب والمجزوم، إذا، لو، الاسم الموصول، كاد

رُكنُ المُفْرَداتِ الجَديدةِ

to inform	أخْبَرَ (يُخْبِرُ) إخْبار
to be forced (to)	اُضْطُرَّ (يُضْطَرُّ) اِضْطِرار (إلى)
instead (of)	بَدَلاً (مِن)
to remember	تَذَكَّرَ (يَتَذَكَّرُ) تَذَكُّر
to be matched, to be in agreement	تَطابَقَ (يَتَطابَقُ) تَطابُق
fortune, riches	ثَرْوة ج ثَرَوات
to dream	حَلَم (يَحْلُمُ) حُلْم
opinion	رأيٌ ج آراء
to compare, to contrast	قارَنَ (يُقارِنُ) مُقارَنة
lately	مُؤَخَّراً
factory	مَعْمَل
surprising	مُفاجِئ
lottery	يانَصيب

تمرين ١

وافِق بين كُلِّ كَلِمة في العمود الأيمن ومضادتها في العمود الأيسر واكتبهما في الوسط:

١	مُسِنّ		حُزْن
٢	ذَهاب		صَحيح
٣	سَعادة		مَقعَد
٤	فَقير		شاب
٥	مَريض		إياب
			غني

تمرين ٢

وافِق بين كلمات من العمودين واكتب الأزواج الستة في الوسط:

١	موقِف		يانصيب
٢	أجر		جوارِب
٣	حِذاء		سَفَر
٤	مُساعَدة		حافِلة
٥	سَحْب		دواء
٦	مَريض		إعانة
			نُقود

حلم وحقيقة

سهام عاملةٌ بسيطة في معمل صغير للجوارِب. لم تتخرّج من المدرسة الثانوية لأنها تركَتها كي تساعدَ أباها في مصروف البيت، فراتبه قليل لا يكفي أسرته الكبيرة. سهام فتاةٌ شابة في الثامنةَ عشْرةَ من عمرها وهي أكبر إخوتها وأخواتها. لها أخوان وثلاث أخوات ما زالوا في المدرسة.

تركب الحافلة تحلم بربح اليانصيب

تعمل سهام ثماني ساعات في اليوم، ستّةَ أيّام في الأسبوع. تركَب الحافلة كلّ يوم صباحاً من موقفٍ قُربَ دارها إلى المعمل وتستغرق رحلة الذهاب ثلاثة أرباع الساعة ومثلها في الإياب. خلال الرحلة لا تنظر سهام إلى الركّاب الآخرين ولا إلى الطريق بل تحلُم دوماً أحلاماً حلوة. تحلُم أحياناً أنها عادَت إلى المدرسة تدرس وتمرح مع صديقاتها، وتحلُم أيضاً أنّ صاحِب المعمل أُعجِب بعملها وجعلها مُراقِبة على العاملات ورفع راتبها خمسين بالمئة. كانت تقول بينها وبين نفسها: «لو كنت صاحبة المعمل لَرفعتُ أجور العاملات وجعلتهُنَّ يعملْنَ خمسة أيّام في الأسبوع بدلاً من ستّة».

«ماذا أعمل لو ربحت الجائزة الكبرى»

بدأت سهام مؤخّراً شراء بِطاقة يانصيب مرّة في الأسبوع، ومنذ ذلك الوقت صارَت أحلامها تدور حول الأمور الّتي تنوي أن تفعلها إذا ربِحَت الجائزة الكُبرى. قالَت لِنفسها: «إذا ربِحتُ الجائزة الكُبرى فَسأشتري لنفسي مَلابِس أنيقة وأحذية غالية وحُلِيّاً، وربّما اشتريتُ سيّارة أذهب بها إلى عملي . . . لكن لا، لن أعمل بعد أن أربح الجائزة الكُبرى. سأذهب بالسيّارة إلى صديقاتي أزورهُنَّ وإلى السوق أشتري منها كلّ ما يُعجِبني. وربّما أسافر إلى أوروبا وأرى روما وباريس ولندن. إذا ربِحتُ الجائزة الكُبرى فسوف أكون أسعد فتاة على وجه الأرض».

في يوم من الأيّام في طريق العودة إلى دارها توجّهَت نحوَ دُكّان أبي خليل كَعادتها كَيْ تَشتريَ بِطاقة يانصيب. لكنّها توقّفَت أوّلاً أمام الواجهة الزُجاجية لتقارن الرقم الرابح برقم بطاقتها. فإذا بالرقمين يتطابقان. غمرها شعور غريب وكاد يُغمى عليها من الفَرَح، وركضَت بأقصى سرعة إلى البيت لتُخبِر أمّها وأباها وإخوتها.

تشتري كلّ ما تتمنّاه

مساء ذلك اليوم جلسَت في سريرها تفكّر ماذا تفعل بهذه الثروة المفاجئة. أتنزل إلى السوق قبل كلّ شيء في اليوم التالي وتشتري كلّ ما كانت تتمنّاه؟ ثمّ قالَت في نفسها: « يجب أوّلاً أن أساعد أهلي. سأشتري لهم داراً وأثاثاً». ثمّ تذكّرَت خالها المريض الّذي اُضطُرَّ أن يترك عمله، وهو بحاجةٍ شديدةٍ إلى المساعدة. «سأبعث له مبلغاً من المال كَيْ يشتريَ الدواء ويصرفَ على أسرتِه ونفسِه. هناك أيضاً جارتنا أمّ خالد، وهي امرأة مُسنّة وفقيرة. سأستأجر لها خادمة تساعدها في البيت وتطهو لها طعامها».

حَسَبَت سهام المبلغ اللازم لكلّ ذلك فوجدَت أنّه لا يكاد يكفي لشِراء بيت وأثاث لأهلها ومساعدة خالها وإعانة أمّ خالد. ولن يبقى لها شيء من المال لشِراء المَلابِس الجديدة والأحذية الغالية والحُليّ والسيّارة والسَفَر إلى أوروبا الذّي وعدَت نفسَها به.

حُليّ

في صباح اليوم التالي كانَت سهام تجلِس في مقعدها بالحافلة في طريقها إلى مَعمَل الجوارِب تحلُم بالمَلابِس وبالأحذية وبالحُليّ وبالسيّارة الّتي سوف تشتريها وبالبُلدان الأوروبية الّتي سوف تزورها إذا ربِحَت في السحب مرّة ثانية.

تمرين ٣

اختَرِ الكَلِمةَ الّتي لا تُناسِب باقي الكَلِماتِ في كُلِّ مَجْموعةٍ وبَيِّن السَبَب:

١-	موقِف	راكِب	حافِلة	سائق	دواء
٢-	مُدير	خال	عامِل	مُراقِب	مَعمَل
٣-	بيت	دار	أثاث	سَرير	نَفْس
٤-	مَصروف	أسرة	أمّ	أب	إخوة

تمرين ٤

للمحادثة: اِحكِ قصة لزميلك تشرح رأيك في رَبْح اليانصيب. قد تساعدك الأسئلة التالية في القيام بالحوار:

١- ما رأيك في رَبْح جائزة اليانصيب الكبرى والحصول على ثروة مفاجئة؟

٢- هل تعتقد بأن الحصول على الأموال فجأةً وبدون تعب شيءٌ إيجابي أم سلبي في حياة الإنسان؟ ولماذا؟

٣- كم مرّة تشتري بطاقات يانصيب في الأسبوع أو الشهر؟

٤- على أيّ شيءٍ تصرف مالَك؟

٥- هل رَبِحت في اليانصيب في حياتك؟ متى وماذا ربحت؟

٦- ما أحلامك في حياتك؟

تمرين ٥

أجب عن الأسئلة التالية وفق نص القراءة:

١- ما الفكرة الرئيسة لهذا الدرس؟

٢- هات بعض الأفكار الثانويّة من القصّة.

٣- لماذا لا تنظر سهام إلى الطريق أو الركّاب الآخرين حين تكون في الحافلة؟

٤- متى ستكون سهام أسعد فتاة على وجه الأرض؟

٥- ماذا فعلَت سهام بالمال الّذي ربِحَته؟

تمرين ٦

اكتب «خطأ» أو «صواب» إلى جانب كلّ جملة ثمّ صحّح الجمل الخطأ:

١- جَعلَ صاحبُ المَعْمل سهام مراقبة.

٢- أمّ خالد هي خالة سهام الغنيّة.

٣- تساعد سهام أباها في مصروفِ البيت.

٤- زارت سهام بلدانا أوربية.

٥- سوف تشتري سهام أحذية غالية.

تمرين ٧

أكمل الجمل الآتية بالاختيار المناسِب وفق نصّ القراءة:

١- أكمَلَت سهام تعليمها ____________.

☐ الابتدائي ☐ الإعدادي ☐ الثانوي ☐ الجامعي

٢- لوالد سهام ____________.

☐ ولَدان وأربع بنات ☐ ثلاث بنات وولدان

☐ ثلاث بنات وثلاثة أولاد ☐ بنتان وأربعة أولاد

٣- إذا ربِحَت سهام الجائزة الكُبرى باليانصيب فسوف ____________.

☐ تعود إلى المدرسة ☐ تعيش في أوروبا

☐ تساعد أهلها ☐ تصبح مراقبة على العاملات

٤- حصلَت سهام على بطاقة اليانصيب الرابحة من ____________.

☐ جارتها أم خالد ☐ دكّان أبي خليل

☐ مَعمَل الجوارِب ☐ خالها المَريض

٥- يحتاج خال سهام إلى ____________.

☐ دواء ☐ سيّارة ☐ بطاقة يانصيب ☐ خادمةً

٦- تعمل سهام ____________ ساعة في الأسبوع.

☐ ٣٠ ☐ ٤٠ ☐ ٤٨ ☐ ٥٦

تمرين ٨

آ- أعد ترتيب الكلمات في كل مجموعة لتشكّل جملاً مُفيدةً:

١ اليانصيب جديدةً إذا داراً فسوف ربِحتُ أشتري في

٢ شهرياً خمسمئة هل مبلغ دولار يكفيك مصروفاً؟

٣ لنفسه هذه ماهر أن قال يجب السنة أتخرّج

٤ دول الدول الفقيرة الغنية العالم مساعدة إلى تحتاج

تمرين ٩

أولاً: أعد ترتيب الجمل لتشكّل فِقرة مترابطة (الجملة الأولى في مكانها المناسب). ثانياً: ترجم الفقرة إلى اللغة الإنكليزية. ثالثاً: اكتب عنواناً بالعربية لهذه القصّة. رابعا: ابحث عن معاني الكلمات الّتي تحتها خط في قائمة المفردات:

١- كان هشام معجباً جداً بفتاة اسمها دانة من أيّام المدرسة وشعر أنه يحبّها وتمنّى أن يتزوّجَها.

لذلك اتّصل بأبيها وشرح له قصّته وقال له إنّه يودّ الزواج من ابنته.

فلمّا طلبها هشام خطيبةً له وافقَت، ووافقَت أسرتها أيضاً.

لكن المشكلة أنه كان فقيراً ودانة من أسرة غنية فلم يفكّر بخطبتها.

لكنّ دانة أعجبها هشام بعد التعرّف عليه وشعرَت أنها قد أحبّته.

فسألها أبوها إن كانت تحبّ أن تراه حتّى تتعرّف عليه أكثر.

وافقَت دانة أن ترى هشاماً وأن يخرجا معاً لتعرف شعورها نحوه.

ردّ الأب أنّه يجب أن يسأل ابنته دانة أوّلاً.

فخرجا إلى المُتنزّهات معاً وإلى المطاعم وأحياناً إلى دار السينما.

حين تخرّج من الجامعة حصل على عمل جيّد في مصرف وبسرعة نجح في عمله.

لمّا سألها أبوها عن رأيها بهشام قالَت له إنها لا تعرفه جيّداً.

بعد أن نجح بعمله قال لنفسه إنّه يجِب أن يطلبها من أسرتها زوجةً له.

Idioms

بَيْني وبَيْنَ نَفْسي

Use this expression when you want to say literally '*between me and myself* or any variation of *to s.o.'s self* similar to what occurred in our main reading passage when Sihām thought:

كانَتْ تقولُ بَيْنَها وَبَيْنَ نَفْسِها: "لَوْ كُنْتُ صاحِبَةَ المَعْمَلِ لَرَفَعْتُ أجورَ العامِلات . . ."

Sihām would say *to herself,* "If I were the factory owner, I would raise workers' wages . . ."

بَدَلاً من

This very useful expression means *instead of.* Some very useful derivations of this phrase are: بَديل *alternate, substitute*; تَبادَلَ *to exchange*; and اِسْتَبْدَلَ بِـ meaning *to substitute s.th. for s.th. else.*

"... and made them work five days instead of six."	". . . وجعلتهُنَّ يعملْنَ خمسة أيّام في الأسبوع بدلاً من ستّة"

في يَوْمٍ مِنَ الأيّام

You should use this expression whenever you want to say *one day* as in: *one day I went to the mall.*

One day on her way home . . .	في يوم من الأيّام في طريق العودة إلى دارها . . .

تمرين ١٠

للمحادثة: تصوّر أنك سهام بالقصّة في هذا الدرس. اِحكِ لزميلك ما تريد أن تفعل بعد أن اكتشفت أنّ الحظ قد حالفك في رَبْح الجائزة الكبرى في اليانصيب.

القَواعِد

1. Verbs Only Used in the Passive أُضْطُرَّ

In this book, we have introduced certain verbs that only occur in the passive:

هُرِعَ / جُنَّ

Two others occurred in this lesson:

He was forced to quit his job.	١ أُضْطُرَّ أنْ يَتْرُكَ عَمَلَهُ.
She almost fainted from joy.	٢ كادَ يُغْمى عليها مِنَ الفَرَح.

Verbs, like أُضْطُرَّ, conjugate in a way that is slightly different from "regular" verbs. As with all doubled verbs, the شَدّة over their last radical is spelled out in first المُتَكَلِّم and second المُخاطَب person. Examine the table below.

المُضارِع		الماضي	
أُضْطَرُّ	المُتَكَلِّم	أُضْطُرِرْتُ	أنا
نُضْطَرُّ		أُضْطُرِرْنا	نَحْنُ
تُضْطَرُّ	المُخاطَب	أُضْطُرِرْتَ	أنْتَ
تُضْطَرِّينَ		أُضْطُرِرْتِ	أنْتِ
تُضْطَرّانِ		أُضْطُرِرْتُما	أنْتُما
تُضْطَرَرْنَ		أُضْطُرِرْتُنَّ	أنْتُنَّ
تُضْطَرّونَ		أُضْطُرِرْتُم	أنْتُمْ
يُضْطَرُّ	الغائب	أُضْطُرَّ	هو
تُضْطَرُّ		أُضْطُرَّت	هِيَ
تُضْطَرّانِ		أُضْطُرَّتا	هُما
يُضْطَرّانِ		أُضْطُرّا	هُما
يُضْطَرَرْنَ		أُضْطُرِرْنَ	هُنَّ
يُضْطَرّونَ		أُضْطُرّوا	هُمْ

2. Feminine Superlative Nouns

Unlike the masculine superlative form أفْعَل, feminine superlative nouns form the pattern:

فُعْلى

One feminine superlative noun occurred in our main reading passage:

If she won the grand prize.	إذا ربِحَتْ الجائزةَ الكُبرى.	١

Let's compare masculine superlative nouns with their feminine counterparts:

my oldest sister	أخْتي الكُبْرى	*my oldest brother*	أخي الأكْبَرُ	٢
top speed	السُرْعة القُصْوى	*the farthest mosque*	المَسْجِد الأقْصى	٣
low temperature	دَرَجةُ الحَرارةِ الصُغْرى	*young boy*	الوَلَدُ الصَغير	٤

3. Doubly Transitive Verbs الأفعال المُتَعدِّيةُ لِمَفْعولَيْن

Certain verbs take two objects, similar to the English direct and indirect objects: (e.g., I gave John a book). *Book* is the direct object of *gave* and *John* is the indirect object. This sentence can be rephrased as: *I gave a book to John*, in which we can clearly see the direct object is *book*, while *John* is now the object of the preposition *to*.

Let's consider the verb أعْطى and how it functions within sentences.

I gave your friend your phone number.	أعْطَيْتُ صَديقَكَ رَقْمَ هاتِفِك.	١
I gave your phone number to your friend.	أعْطَيْتُ رَقْمَ هاتِفِكَ لِصَديقِك.	٢

Similar to our English example, our Arabic examples 1 & 2 illustrate the direct رَقْمَ هاتفك and indirect صَديقَك objects. By placing the direct object next to the doubly transitive verb, we create a situation that requires the introduction of a prepositional phrase: لِصَديقِك just as we did in our English example *I gave a book to John.*

This short list contains الأفعال المُتَعدِّيةُ لِمَفْعولَيْن with which we are familiar:

ظَنَّ، جَعَلَ، عَلِمَ، وَجَدَ، أعْطى، سأل

Let's examine a sentence that occurred in our main reading passage:

The boss made the worker a supervisor.	جَعَلَ صاحِبُ العَمَلِ العامِلَةَ مُراقِبةً.	٣

In example 3, we find that صاحِبُ العَمَلِ is the subject, العامِلةَ is the direct object, while مُراقِبةً is the indirect object.

مُراجَعةُ القَواعِد

4. Moods of the Present Tense (Imperfect)
المُضارِع المَرفوع والمَنصوب والمَجزوم

These three moods appear in our main reading passage in the following sentences:

She rides the bus.	مُضارِع مَرفوع	تَركَبُ الحافِلةَ.	١
In order to help her father.	مُضارِع مَنصوب	كَي تُساعِدَ أباها.	٢
She didn't graduate from school.	مُضارِع مَجزوم	لَمْ تَتَخَرَّجْ مِنَ المَدْرَسةِ.	٣

تَذَكَّروا

Verbs that follow these five particles will always be in المُضارِع المَنصوب:

أَنْ، لَنْ، كَيْ، حَتّى، لِـ

5. Conditional Sentences جُمَل الشَرْط

The conditional sentence in Arabic distinguishes between likely conditions using إذا and unlikely hypothetical conditions using لَوْ. Because of the nature of this lesson's topic, both of these conditional devices were used. Let's take a look at them in context:

If I win the jackpot, I will buy expensive clothes.	فَسأشتري مَلابِسَ غالِيةً.	إذا رِبِحتُ الجائزةَ الكُبرى	١
	answer clause	condition clause	

If I were the boss, I would raise the workers' pay.	لَرَفعتُ أجورَ العامِلات.	لَوْ كُنتُ صاحِبةَ المَعمَلِ	٢
	answer clause	condition clause	

As you can see, conditional clauses—whether using إذا or لَوْ—are comprised of two parts: the condition الشَّرْط and its answer جَواب الشَّرْط. One major difference between the answer clauses between إذا and لَوْ is their particle:

مُلاحَظة

answer	+ فَـ +	condition	إذا +
answer	+ لَـ +	condition	لَوْ +

6. Relative Pronouns الاسم الموصول

As can be seen by their name, relative pronouns are considered nouns أسماء in traditional Arabic grammar. These nouns have to agree in person, number, gender, and case.

مُلاحَظة

الاسم المَوصول is only used when its modified noun is definite.

Since the modified noun صَديقي is definite, introducing the subordinate clause requires a relative pronoun, in this case الّذي since we are dealing with a masculine singular noun. But, what if صَديقي were indefinite صَديق and we still wanted to introduce a subordinate clause? Consider the following:

I wrote to my friend [who] works in Kuwait.	كَتَبْتُ إلى صَديقٍ يَعمَلُ في الكُوَيت.	١

Unlike English, which still requires the use of a relative pronoun, Arabic requires that the relative pronoun be omitted.

Because of the variety of relative pronouns in Arabic, their use may be a bit confusing. We hope that the following chart will facilitate memorization and integration of the relative pronouns into your repertoire.

الأسماءُ المَوصولةُ			
الجَمْع	المُثنّى	المُفْرَد	
الّذينَ	اللّذانِ / اللّذَيْنِ	الّذي	المُذَكّر
اللاّتي / اللّواتي	اللّتانِ / اللّتَيْنِ	الّتي	المُؤنّث

The relative pronouns in the table above are known as *restrictive* in that they refer to a specific object.

Arabic enjoys two relative pronouns that are non-restrictive as well:

Non-Restrictive Relative Pronouns	
who (for humans)	مَنْ
what (for non-human)	ما

These pronouns are considered non-restrictive because they do not refer to any specific entity.

Do you know who will come today?	هَلْ تَعْرِفينَ مَن سَيَحْضُرُ اليَوْمَ؟	٣
I cannot read what I wrote.	لا أسْتَطيعُ أنْ أقرأ ما كَتَبْتُ.	٤

7. The Verb of Approximation كادَ

This verb indicates an action about to take place. Similar to كانَ, it introduces a nominal sentence:

Snow was about to fall.	كادَ الثَلْجُ أنْ يَنْزِلَ.	١
She almost fainted from joy.	وَكادَ يُغمَى عَلَيْها مِنَ الفَرَح.	

Grammatically speaking, الثَلْجُ is the subject of example 1 while أنْ يَنْزِلَ is the predicate. Note that كادَ, like كانَ, can be used in present tense as well:

His salary is hardly adequate for his family.	لا يَكادُ راتِبُه يَكفي أسرتَه.	٢
It is hardly enough to buy a house and furniture for her family.	لا يَكادُ يَكفي لِشراءِ بَيْتٍ وأثاثٍ لأهْلِها.	٣

8. إذا الفُجائية

This particle introduces an unexpected action that translates into English as *lo and behold*. إذا الفُجائية takes either a و or a فـَ as its prefix while the pronoun following it (usually) has an attached بِـ.

And lo and behold the two numbers matched!	فإذا بالرَقَمَيْنِ يَتطابَقانِ!

تمرين ١١

أعد ترتيب الكلمات في كلّ جملة لتشكّل جملاً صحيحةً وفق القواعد أعلاه ثمّ ترجمها إلى الإنكليزيّة:

١- فإذا فتحتُ يقِف بصديقي هناك البابَ

٢- مِن الجديدَ تعرِفون الأستاذَ أتانا هل تونس الّذي

٣- رئيس مَن أحمد جعل نعرِف هذا النادي لا

٤- مُعتدِلٌ بلدٍ أعملَ في أنْ طقسُه أحبّ

٥- هذا أكاد لا أحداً في أعرِف المكان

٦- ما المُتحف أعجبني رأيت كلّ في

٧- أكتب لي لَها إذا فسوف كتبَتْ

٨- عَمَلِها سامية حتّى لَمْ إلى تَصِلْ الآن

٩- لَلبِستُ الطقسَ عرفتُ أنّ حارٌّ لَوْ قميصاً

١٠- يسكن معهم في هل الشقّة مَن تعرِفون؟

تمرين ١٢

Conversation: Find out who in class (is) ________________, by using the following grammatical structures:

(أُضْطُرّ، أعطى، إذا، لَوْ، كادَ، إذا الفُجائية)

1. was forced to quit their job to study.
2. gave a friend notes for class.
3. made someone smile/laugh today.
4. was looking for something and suddenly found it.
5. almost didn't come to class today.

تمرين ١٣

آ **انظر الكلمات الجديدة أوّلاً في المفردات (أنشأ، بَعْد، دَهشة، مُتَحَرِّك) ثمّ أجب عن الأسئلة وفق نص الاستماع:**

١- حدِّد الفكرة الرئيسة في نص الاستماع.

٢- حدِّد بعض الأفكار الثانوية.

٣- في أيّ سنة تقريباً دخل التلفاز إلى دار الكاتب؟

٤- مَن أنشأ محطّة التلفاز؟

٥- ماذا كان أوّل برنامج شاهده هو وأسرته؟

٦- من شاهد التلفاز مع الأسرة في الليلة الأولى؟

ب- **لَخِّص المُقابَلة مع زينا بحوالى مئة كَلمة.**

ج- **اكتب «خطأ» أو «صواب» إلى جانب كلّ جملة ثمّ صحّح الجمل الخطأ:**

١- اشترى الأب تلفازاً لأسرته لأنّ أصدقاءهم وأقاربهم كان لديهم أجهزة تلفاز.

٢- شاهدت الأسرة أخباراً محلية فقط على التلفاز في الليلة الأولى.

٣- وافق الوالد على أن يشاهد أولاده التلفاز في المساء فقط.

٤- كانت مدّة الإرسال نحو عشر ساعات كلّ يوم.

٥- كانت دهشتهم بالتلفاز مثل فرحهم به.

د- **أكمل الجمل وفق نص الاستماع:**

١- سمع أولاد الأسرة أنّ ________________.

٢- رجا الأولاد أباهم أنْ ________________.

٣- كانت الأسرة تشاهد التلفاز في الظلام لأنهم كانوا يظنّون ________________.

٤- بدأ الإرسال التلفزيوني في شهر ________________.

المُفْرَدات

أخْبَرَ	(يُخْبِرُ)	إخْبار	(v.)	to tell, to inform
اِضْطُرَّ	(يُضْطَرُّ)	اِضْطِرار (إلى)	(v.)	to be compelled, to be forced (to)
أعان	(يُعينُ)	إعانة	(v.)	to help, to assist, to aid
أُغْمِيَ	(يُغْمى)	إغْماء	(v.)	to lose consciousness, to faint
بَدَلاً (مِن)	(بَدَلاً (مِن)		(adv.)	instead (of)
بَعَثَ	(يَبْعَثُ)	بَعْث	(v.)	to send, to dispatch
تَذَكَّرَ	(يَتَذَكَّرُ)	تَذَكُّر	(v.)	to remember
تَطابَقَ	(يَتَطابَقُ)	تَطابُق	(v.)	to match, to fit, to agree
ثَرْوة	ج	ثَرَوات	(n., f.)	fortune, riches
جار	ج	جيران	(n., m.)	neighbor
حَسَبَ	(يَحْسُبُ)	حِساب	(v.)	to calculate, to reckon
حَلَمَ	(يَحْلُمُ)	حُلْم	(v.)	to dream
حُلوٌ			(n., m.)	sweet, beautiful
خِطْبة			(n., f.)	engagement, betrothal, courtship
خَطيب	ج	خُطَباء	(n., m.)	suitor, fiancé
خَطيبة	ج	خَطيبات	(n., f.)	fiancée

during	(adv.)		خِلالَ	خِلالَ
medicine	(n., m.)	أدْوِية	ج	دَواء
opinion, point of view	(n., m.)	آراء	د	رَأْيٌ
to run, to race	(v.)	رَكْض	(يَرْكُضُ)	رَكَضَ
to spend, to expend	(v.)	صَرْف (على)	(يَصْرِفُ)	صَرَفَ
guest, visitor	(n., m.)	ضُيوف	ج	ضَيْف
to cook	(v.)	طَهْو / طَهْي	(يَطْهو)	طَها
strange, stranger	(adj.)	غُرَباء	ج	غَريب
to flood, to inundate, to fill	(v.)		(يَغْمُرُ)	غَمَرَ
to compare, to contrast	(v.)	مُقارَنة	(يُقارِنُ)	قارَنَ
far, distant	(n., m.)	قُصْوى	أقْصى	قاصٍ
biggest, greatest, eldest	(n., f.)	كُبْرَيات	ج	كُبْرى
lately	(adv.)			مُؤَخَّراً
money, wealth	(n., m.)	أمْوال	ج	مال
park, recreation ground	(n., m.)	مَنازه	ج	مُتَنَزَّه
supervisor, observer	(act. p.)	مُراقِبون	ج	مُراقِب
to rejoice, to be merry	(v.)	مَرَح	(يَمْرَحُ)	مَرِحَ

مُسِنّ	ج	مُسِنّون	(act. p.)	elderly, old
مَصْروف	ج	مَصاريف	(pass. p.)	expenditure, allowance
مَعْمَل	ج	مَعامِل	(n., m.)	factory, plant
مُفاجِئ			(adj.)	sudden, unexpected, surprising
واجِهة	ج	واجِهات	(n., f.)	store window, façade
وافَقَ	(يُوافِقُ)	مُوافَقة	(v.)	to agree, to consent
وَدَّ	(يَوَدُّ)	وُدّ	(v.)	to like, to want
يانَصيب			(n., m.)	lottery

الدَرْسُ الرابِعِ عشر

إبراهيم عبد القادر
المازني

Objectives

- Learning to express humor through reading two pieces of literature
- Incorporating the use of idioms and similes تشبيه
- Working with adverbials using بـِ with a مَصدَر
- Introducing connectors; turns of phrase; phrasal verbs اِنْقَطَع لـِ، اِنْقَطَع عَن
- **Grammar**: Multiple مُضاف and multiple مُضاف إليه, assimilated verbs مِثال
- **مراجعة القواعد**: الإضافة غير الحقيقية، أفعال البدء، اسم التفضيل، الفعل الأجوف

رُكنُ المُفْرَداتِ الجَديدةِ

to resume	اِستأنَفَ (يَسْتأنِفُ) اِسْتِئناف
to grab	أمسَكَ (يُمسِكُ) إمساك
to produce	أَنْتَجَ (يُنْتِجُ) إنْتاج
to establish	أنشأ (يُنشِئُ) إنْشاء
talkative	ثَرْثار ج ثَرْثارون
secret	سِرّ ج أَسْرار
to tie, to link, to attach	رَبَطَ (يَربِطُ) رَبْط
to fill up, to sate	شَبِعَ (يَشبَعُ) شَبَع
to settle, to resolve	فَضَّ (يَفُضُّ) فَضّ
to think (about)	فَكَّرَ (يُفَكِّرُ) تَفْكير (في)
axis	مِحْوَر ج مَحاوِر
contemporary	مُعاصِر ج مُعاصِرون
dispute	نِزاع ج نِزاعات

تمرين ١

وافِق بين كلمات من العمودين لهما معنيان متشابهان (similar) واكتب الأزواج الستة في الوسط:

١	وَقود		بَسالة
٢	سَيْر		بُقْعة
٣	مُغْتَبِط		أدْرَكَ
٤	شَجاعة		بَنزين
٥	مَكان		شارِع
٦	طَريق		سَعيد
			مَشي

تمرين ٢

وافِق بين كلمات من العمودين لتشكِّل عبارة واحدة:

١	نُجوم		النفس
٢	لَوْح		ماء
٣	بِئر		الظُهر
٤	مِحوَر		نَفط
٥	راضي		العَجَلة
٦	مُنشرِح		ثَلج
			الصَدْر

قصّتان قصيرتان

هاتان القِصّتان القصيرتان بقلم اثنين من أشهر الكتّاب المِصريين في النصف الأوّل من القرن العشرين الّذين قدّموا الكثير للأدب العربيّ الحديث، إبراهيم عبد القادر المازنيّ ومُصطفى لُطفي المَنفَلوطيّ، وقد كان أحدهما معاصرا للآخر. القصّة الأولى تصِف شيئاً وهو سيّارة المازنيّ الّتي امتلكها ربّما في الثلاثينات من القرن العشرين، والقصّة الأخرى تصِف صورة لشخص رسمها المنفلوطيّ للحلاّق جرَت أحداثها أثناء الحرب الروسية اليابانية. وكلاهما تعبّران عن روح الفُكاهة الّتي اتّصف بها الكاتبان.

تمرين ٣

للنقاش قبل قراءة القصّة:

١- ما البلاد العربية الّتي تُنتج النِفط؟

٢- ما أوّل بلد عربيّ ظهر فيه النِفط وصار يصدِّره بكَميّات تجارية؟

٣- أين تقع المَوصِل؟

٤- ما المادّة الّتي تحتاج إليها السيّارة حتّى تسير؟

٥- كيف تختلف سيّارات اليوم عن سيّارة المازني؟

السيّارة الملعونة

بقلم إبراهيم عبد القادِر المازني

يُعتبَر المازني أحد الآباء المؤسسين للكتابة العربية الحديثة وُلِدَ عام ١٨٨٩ في القاهرة، وعمل مدرّساً وصحفيّاً ثمّ انقطع للأدب، فأنتج أكثر من عشرين كتاباً أشهرها "صندوق الدنيا" و"عَوْد على بَدْء" و"حصاد الهشيم" و"قَبْض الريح". توفّي المازني في آب عام ١٩٤٩.

كانت لي سيّارة كبيرة أرتني النجوم في الظهر. ذلك أنّها كانت تستنفِد من البَنزين والزيت كلّ ما هو معروض في طريقها منها، ثمّ لا تشبع، حتّى فكّرتُ أن أربِط خزّانها بآبار المَوصِل.

آبار نِفط

ثمّ إنّ خزّان الماء كان يغلي كالمِرجَل بعد دقائق قليلة من السير فتبدو لي علامة الخَطَرِ الحمراء، فأقف وأغيّر لها الماء ثمّ أستأنف السير وهكذا.

هذا في الشتاء، فكيف بها في الصيف؟ ولهذا صِرتُ أشتري لها الثلج وأحشو به خزّانها بدلاً من الماء، ولا أركَبها إلاّ ومعي ذخيرة كافية من ألواح الثلج على المقاعد الخلفية.

وقد أكون سائراً مغتبِطاً، راضي النفس منشرِح الصَدْر وإذا بصوت يقول: كركركركر . . . وإذا بإحدى العجلتين خرجَت من مِحورها وذهبت تجري وحدها في الطريق!

تمرين ٤

أجب عن الأسئلة التالية وفق نص القراءة:

١- في أي قطر عربيّ عاش وعمِل المازني؟

٢- ما المِهنة الّتي اختارها المازني في النهاية وماذا عمِل قبل ذلك؟

٣- ما "قبض الريح"؟

٤- ما الأشياء الّتي كانت تستنفدها سيّارة المازني؟

تمرين ٥

اخترِ الكَلِمةَ الّتي لا تُناسِب باقي الكَلِماتِ في كُلِّ مجموعةٍ وبيِّن السَبَب:

١- مُنشرِح   مُدرّس   صحافي   كاتب

٢- زيت   وَقود   بَنزين   ثَلْج

٣- ماء   ذَخيرة   بئر   مِرجَل

٤- حلاّق   نِزاع   شَعر   رأس

٥- أسطول   مُدمِّرة   حَرب   زَبون

تمرين ٦

أكمل الجمل الآتية بالاختيار المناسِب وفق نصّ القراءة:

١- كتب المازني أكثر من ______________ كتاباً.

☐ اثني عشر ☐ عشرين ☐ ثلاثين ☐ أربعين

٢- ربّما كانت سيّارة المازني من ______________ القرن العشرين.

☐ عشرينات ☐ ثلاثينات ☐ أربعينات ☐ خمسينات

٣- كان الكاتب يتوقّف كلّ بضع دَقائق ______________.

☐ ليملأ خزّان الوقود ☐ ليملأ خزّان الماء

☐ ليُصلّح العجلة ☐ ليضع ألواح الثلج على المَقعَد الخلفيّ

٤- فكّر المازني أن يربِط خزّان سيّارته بآبار المَوصِل كَيْ ______________.

☐ لا يتوقّف عند محطات الوقود ☐ لا يغلي الماء في خزّانها

☐ تشبع من الزيت والبنزين ☐ يبقى مغتبِطاً وهي تسير

٥- ظنّ المازني أنّ ماء السيّارة يغلي ______________.

☐ في الشتاء كما في الصيف ☐ في الصيف أكثر من الشتاء

☐ في الصيف أقلّ من الشتاء ☐ في الصيف فقط

تمرين ٧

اكتب «خطأ» أو «صواب» بجانب كلّ جملة وصحّح الجمل الخطأ:

آ- ١- خرجَت عجلة السيّارة من محورها عندما بدَت علامة الخطر الحمراء.

٢- كان المازني يضع الثلج في خزّان السيّارة بدلاً من الماء في الصيف.

ب- **هات كلمات أو عبارات من القصّة تتعلّق بكلّ من الكلمات الآتية. يدلّ الرقم على عدد الكلمات أو العبارات المتعلّقة بكلّ منها:**

١- سعيد (٣)

٢- وقود (٣)

٣- سيّارة (٨)

٤- فصول السنة (٢)

تمرين ٨

للمحادثة: في رأيك ما بعض المفردات والجمل الّتي استخدمها المازني لتحقيق غرضه في إدخال روح الفُكاهة في القصّة؟ أعطِ أسباباً تدعم رأيك في ما تعتبره مضحكاً أو غير ذلك.

الحلاّق الثرثار

المنفلوطيّ (١٨٧٦ - ١٩٢٤) أديب مصريّ درس في الأزهر وكتب العديد من القِصَص القصيرة والروايات الطويلة في أوائل القرن العشرين، وهذه القصّة القصير واحدة منها.

تمرين ٩

للنقاش قبل قراءة القصّة:

١- هل تعلم متى وقعَت الحرب الروسية اليابانية؟
٢- هل الشخص الّذي يقصّ لك شعرك رجل أم امرأة؟
٣- هل حلاّقك ثرثار كما يظنّ كثير من الناس؟
٤- عن أي شيء يتحدّث حلاّقُك؟
٥- كم زبونا يتّسِع حانوتُ حلاّقِك في وقت واحد؟
٦- صِفْ حانوتَ حلاّقِك من الداخل باختصار (briefly).

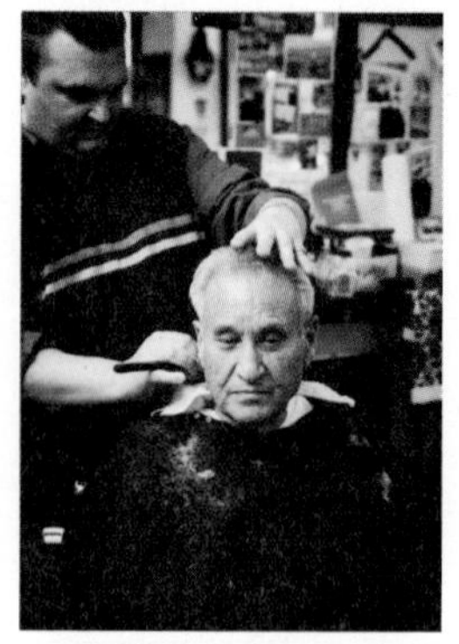

يحلق الحلاّق رأس الزبون

حدّثني أحد الأصدقاء أنّه دخل في أيّام الحرب الروسية اليابانية حانوتَ حلاّقٍ معروفٍ بالثرثرة ليحلق له رأسه، وكان عنده جماعة من زائريه، فأجلسه على كرسي أمام المرآة وأمسك بالموسى وأنشأ يحلق له رأسه حلقاً غريباً لا عهد له بمثله من قبل، فكان يحلق بُقْعة ويترك إلى جانبها أخرى مستطيلة أو مستديرة وأخرى مُثلثة أو مُربّعة، حتّى ريع الرجل وظنّ أنّ الحلاّقَ أصابه مسٌّ من الجُنون، فارتعد بين يديه وخاف أن يمتدّ به جنونه إلى ما لا تُحمد عُقباه واعتُقل لسانه فلَمْ يستطِع أن يسألَه عن سرِّ عملِه.

فلما انتهى الحلاّق من أشكالِه الهندسية ورسومِه الجغرافية حتّى التفت إلى جلسائه وقال لهم وكأنه يتمِّم حديثاً سابقاً بينه وبينهم، "لأجل فضّ النزاع بيننا قد رسمت لكم خريطة الحرب الروسية اليابانية في رأس الزبون. هنا طوكيو وهنا بور آرثَر، وفي هذا الخط مرّ الأسطول الروسيّ. وفي هذه البُقعة تلاقى الأسطولان."

بعض الصور للحرب الروسية اليابانية

وهنا أخذ يتكلّم بحدّة وحماسة عن شجاعة اليابانيين وبسالتهم، ثُمَّ أردف كلامه بقوله، وفي هذه البُقْعة ضرب اليابانيون الروسَ الضربةَ القاضية وضرب بِجُمع يده أمّ رأسِ الزبون فقام صارخاً يُوَلوِل ويُهَروِل مكشوفَ الرأس يلعن السياسة والسياسيين والروس واليابانيين والناس أجمعين.

الطرّاد الروسي في الحرب الروسية اليابانية

تمرين ١٠

أجب عن هذه الأسئلة وفق القصّة:

١- ما الفكرة الرئيسة في قصّة "الحلاّق الثرثار".

٢- ما بعض الأفكار الثانوية؟

٣- في أي بلد وقعَت هذه القصّة في رأيك؟

٤- ماذا كانت تحوي أخبار ذلك الوقت الّذي حدثَت فيه القصّة؟

٥- لماذا ظنّ الزبون أنّ الحلاّق قد جُنّ؟

٦- صِف شكل الزبون حين خرج من حانوت الحلاّق.

تمرين ١١

أ أكمل الجمل بكلمات مناسبة وفق النصّ:

١- حدثَت هذه القصّة ________________.

☐ للمنفلوطي ☐ لصديق الكاتب ☐ لحلاّق الكاتب

٢- هذه القصّة عن ________________.

☐ زبون أحد الحلاّقين ☐ الحرب الروسية اليابانية ☐ الحلاّقين

٣- رسم الحلاّق خريطة على ________________.

☐ مِرآةِ حانوته ☐ دفترِ جلسائه ☐ رأسِ زَبونِه

٤- لم يسأل الزَبونُ الحلاّقَ عن سبب حلقه الغريب لأنّ ________________ .

☐ الحلاّقَ لا يتكلّم اليابانية ☐ لِسانَ الزبونِ ارتبط

☐ جلساءَه في الحانوت ☐ يبقى مغتبِطاً وهي تسير

ب- بيّن إن كانت الجمل الآتية صواباً أو خطأ وفق النصّ وصحِّح الخطأ منها:

١- كان الرجال في زمن كتابة هذه القصّة يمشون في الشارع مكشوفي الرأس.

٢- كان الحلاّق من الّذين يعجبهم الجيش الروسي.

٣- كان موضوع النِقاشِ بين الحلاق وجلسائه الحرب الروسية اليابانية.

٤- كان الحلاّق وزبونه وحدهما في الحانوت.

٥- اختلف الحلاّق وجلساؤه على أحد أمور الحرب العالمية الأولى.

تمرين ١٢

للمحادثة:

أ- تخيَّل أنّ عندك سيّارة مثل سيّارة المازني بالقصّة الأولى في هذا الدرس. اِحكِ لزميلك ما تريد أن تفعل بعد أن أرتْكَ سيارتُك النجومَ في عزِّ الظهر. إذا اخترت بيعها فكيف تقنع الشارِيَ المحتمل أنّها سيّارة صالحة للشراء. وإذا اخترت الاحتفاظ بها فماذا تفعل حتّى تجعلَها تسير أحسن؟

ب- تخيّل أن حلاقك حَلَقَ لك رأسك حلقاً غريباً لا عهد لك بمثله من قبل. اِحكِ لزميلك ما تفعل لو كان لتسريحتك أشكال هندسية لم تطلبها.

تمرين ١٣

أعد ترتيب الكلمات في كلّ جملة لتشكّل جملاً صحيحةً وفق القواعد أعلاه ثمّ ترجمها إلى الإنكليزيّة:

١- عام العالمية ١٩٣٩ قامَت الثانية الحرب

٢- رسم المسيح صورة داڤينشي وهو مع العشاء أصحابه يتناول

٣- رئيساً أنْ محامياً عمل يكون لِنكَن قبل

٤- آلاف العراق منذ الناس النفط عرف في السنين

٥- قصيراً رانية طويلاً يحبّه تقصّ بينما شعرها زوجها

تمرين ١٤

أعد ترتيب الجمل لتشكّل فِقرة كاملة. الجملة الأولى في مكانها المناسب:

١- كان عدد من الناس يجلسون في مقهى إلى جانب الطريق.
لحسن الحظّ لم يُصَب أحد من الزبائن.
فجأةً ظهرَت قطّة أمام إحدى السيّارات فانحرف السائق إلى اليمين.
استمرَّت السيّارة في السير على الرصيف ودخلَت المقهى.
إلاّ أنّ الواجهة الزجاجية وعدداً من الطاولات والكراسي تحطّمَت.
لكنّ السائق لم يستطِع أن يوقف السيّارة فصعِدَت على الرصيف.
وكان هناك سيّارات تسير في وسط الشارع أمام المقهى.

Idioms

أرَتْني النُجوم في الظُهْر

All languages contain expressions peculiar to them. As you recall, idioms usually cannot be understood from the individual words that make up the expression. For instance, *out of the blue* cannot be understood by looking up each individual word; rather, it is the combination of these words that creates the idiom's meaning. المازني uses the idiom أرَتْني النُجوم في الظُهْر to indicate that unusual trouble, hardship, or distress was caused by something not of your own doing. Literally it means *x caused me to see stars at noon*, which is improbable. This idiom is used in both colloquial and formal speech.

القَواعِد

1. Similes التشبيه

A simile is a figure of speech in which two essentially unlike things are compared, often in a phrase, and usually introduced by *like* or *as* (e.g., *I'm as hungry as a horse*; *I feel like a million bucks*). To create this situation in Arabic we use:

as	كـَ
like	مِثْل
as though	كأنَّ
to be like	حاكى
looks most like	أشْبَهُ

In **المازني's** story about his car, we were introduced to the simile:

The radiator would boil like a caldron.	خزّانُ الماءِ كانَ يَغْلي كَالمِرْجَلِ.

Let's take a look at each one of the similes above in context:

He walks like a peacock.	يَمشي كَالطاووس.
His memory is as deep as the sea.	ذاكِرَتُهُ مِثْلُ البَحْرِ عُمْقاً.
As if her eyes were as blue as the sea.	كأنَّ عينَيْها البَحْرُ في زرقتِه.
Her figure is like a reed.	حاكى قَوامُها عودَ الخَيْزُران.
The place is like paradise.	هذا المَكانُ أشْبَهُ بالجَنّةِ.

2. Expressing Humor

The authors of both of these short stories used several devices to infuse humor into their writing including exaggeration, action verbs, dramatic events, and imagery. Consider the following examples:

a. Exaggeration

Authors use hyperbole to dramatize the situation:

It would use gas and oil, all that was available to it along the way, and it was still not sated.	كانَتْ تَسْتَنْفِدُ مِنَ البَنْزِين والزَيْتِ كُلَّ ما هوَ مَعْروضٌ في طَريقِها مِنْهُما ثُمَّ لا تَشْبَع.	١
I thought about hooking its gas tank up to Mosul's oil wells.	فَكَّرْتُ أنْ أرْبِطَ خَزّانَها بآبارِ المَوْصِل.	٢

b. Action Verbs

These authors created humor by using unexpected verbs:

I stuffed it [the ice] in its radiator instead of water.	أَحْشو بِهِ خَزّانَها بَدَلاً مِنَ الماءِ.	٣

The humor here is created by combining two seemingly incongruous things: the verb *stuffing* with *radiator.*

c. Dramatic Actions

The authors dramatize the events that unfold within the story to create humor.

And lo and behold the wheel came off its axle and started off down the road on its own.	وإذا بإحْدى العَجَلَتَيْنِ خَرَجَتْ مِنْ مِحْوَرِها وذَهَبَتْ تَجْري وَحْدَها في الطَريق.	٤
With his clenched fist he hit the crown of the patron's head.	وضَرَبَ بِجُمْعِ يَدِهِ أمَّ رأسِ الزَبون.	٥
So he started screaming and wailing as he rushed out.	فَقامَ صارِخاً يُوَلْوِلُ وَيُهَرْوِلُ.	٦

d. Imagery

These two authors create humorous images and scenes by virtue of their incongruence with normality:

Then the radiator would boil like a caldron.	ثُمَّ إنَّ خَزّانَ الماءِ كانَ يَغْلي كَالمِرْجَل.	٧
A sufficient arsenal of blocks of ice on the back seat.	ذَخيرةٌ كافيَةٌ مِن أَلْواحِ الثَلْج على المَقاعِدِ الخَلْفِيّة.	٨
He took to giving the man a strange haircut.	أَخَذَ يَحْلِقُ لَهُ رأسَهُ حَلْقاً غريباً.	٩
The man was frightened.	ريعَ الرَجُل.	١٠
He became tongue-tied.	أُعْتُقِلَ لِسانُهُ.	١١

3. Cause and Effect

Describing cause and effect is a characteristic of coherent discourse. Initially, the speaker/writer describes a situation in which a stimulus produces a response. In Arabic several particles indicate *effect*—three of which were used in our main reading passages.

until	حَتّى
because of this	لِهذا
consequently	لِذلِكَ
so, consequently	فَـ
looks most like	أشْبَهُ

The following examples are taken from our main reading passages:

It would use gas and oil, all that was available to it along the way, still was not sated until I thought about hooking its gas tank up to Mosul's oil wells.	كانَتْ تَسْتَنفِدُ مِنَ البَنْزينِ والزَيْتِ كُلَّ ما هُوَ مَعروض في طَريقِها مِنْهُما، ثُمَّ لا تَشْبَع، حَتّى فَكَّرْتُ أنْ أربطَ خَزّانَها بِآبارِ المَوْصِل.	١
Because of this, I started buying it ice and stuffing it in its radiator.	ولِهذا صِرْتُ أشْتَري لَها الثَلْجَ وأحْشو بِهِ خَزّانَها.	٢

٣	لكن لم يكن هناك غرفة شاغرة، لذلك ذهبنا إلى فندق آخر.	*But, there were no rooms available, so we went to another hotel.*
٤	ثُمَّ إنّ خَزّانَ الماءِ كانَ يَغْلي كَالمِرْجَلِ بَعْدَ دَقائقَ قَليلةٍ مِنَ السَيْرِ فَتَبْدو لي عَلامةُ الخَطَرِ الحَمْراء.	*Then, the radiator would boil like a caldron just a few minutes after taking off, consequently the warning light came on.*
٥	فكانَ يَحْلِقُ بُقْعةً ويَتْرُكُ أخرى حَتّى ريعَ الرَجُلُ.	*Then he would cut a patch and leave another until the man got scared.*

تمرين ١٥

The paragraph below is chock full of cause and effect devices. Translate the paragraph into Arabic using these four connectors:

لِذلِكَ، لِهذا، حَتّى، فَـ

> My bedroom was too hot to sleep in, so I got up, went to the window, and opened it. But the noises from the street kept me from falling back to sleep. Therefore, I decided to read. So, I went to the bookshelf to choose my favorite book. I took to reading until I fell asleep.

4. Describing Circumstance Using بِـ and المَصْدَر

Used in both colloquial and MSA, the بِـ + المَصْدَر combination can be translated in English as an adverb, or the *adjective + ly* combination (i.e., quickly, slowly, etc.). In the second short story, المنفلوطي uses بِحِدّة to mean *excitedly*:

١	وَهُنا أَخَذَ يَتَكَلَّمُ بِحِدَّةٍ وَحَماسةٍ عَنْ شَجاعةِ اليابانيين وبَسالتِهِم.	*Here, he took to talking excitedly and enthusiastically about the courage and bravery of the Japanese.*

مُلاحَظة

When using a series of adverbs consecutively, the preposition is only prefixed to the first, as in example 1.

Here, we present a list of these useful devices to add to your repertoire:

moderately	باعتِدال	in short, briefly	باخْتِصار
quickly	بِسُرعة	regularly	بانتِظام
politely	بِتَهْذيب	modestly	باحتِشام
respectfully	باحتِرام	recklessly	بِرُعونة

Let's take a look at each of these adverbials in context:

باخْتِصار	إلَيْكُمُ الأخْبار باخْتِصارٍ شَديدٍ.
بانتِظام	أدْرُسُ اللُّغَةَ العَرَبيّةَ بانْتِظام.
باحتِشام	هُنا في هذا العَمَلِ، نَلْبَسُ باحتِشام.
بِرُعونة	قالَ لي أبي "لا تسُقْ بِرُعونة!"
باعتدال	ثَمةَ نَظَرية تَقول: الشوكولاتة مُفيدةٌ لِلقَلْبِ باعتدال.
بِسُرعة	قالَتِ الأمُّ لأوْلادِها: "يللاّ بِسرْعة!"
بِتَهْذيب	سَمع الرَجُلُ النُكتةَ فَضحِكَ بِتَهْذيب.
باحْتِرام	تَكَلَّمَ الطالِبُ مَعَ أُستاذِهِ باحْتِرامٍ.

تمرين ١٦

Conversation: Find out what each person does ________________, by using the following adverbials:

(باخْتِصار، بانْتِظام، باحْتِشام، بِرُعونة، باعْتِدال، بِسُرْعة، بِتَهْذيب، باحْتِرام)

Write your results on a separate sheet of paper and be prepared to share them with the class.

5. Connectors and Indicating Transition

Connectors function as devices to indicate transition from one idea to another or one sentence to the next. They provide cohesion to a text by binding sentences and thoughts together. In this section we highlight three important connectors that were used quite extensively in المازني's story:

فـَ، وَ، ثُمَّ

While you are certainly familiar with these connectors, it is time to start incorporating them into your discourse in a seamless fashion. This means that you have to understand and recognize their function in very precise terms. Let's examine a single sentence taken from المازني's story:

ثُمّ إنّ خزّانَ الماءِ كان يغلي كالمِرجَلِ بعد دقائقَ قليلةٍ من السيرِ فتبدو لي علامةُ الخَطَرِ الحمراءُ فأقفُ وأغيّرُ لها الماءَ ثُمّ أستأنِفُ السيرَ، وهكذا.

> **مُلاحَظة**
>
> فـَ، وَ، ثُمَّ
>
> These particles serve three functions:
>
> 1) Conjunctions (e.g., and);
> 2) Transition devices (e.g., so, or then)
> 3) Dummy particles (i.e., those that appear at the beginning of sentences and have no function)

تمرين ١٧

Copy the following passage down on a separate sheet of paper. Identify the connectors in the following passage and indicate whether they are conjunctions (c), transition devices (t), or dummy particles (p):

ولمّا وصل القطارُ إلى المحطّةِ توجّه الركّابُ نحوَه بسرعة وصَعِدوا إلى العربات وجلسوا في مقاعدِهم. ثمّ صَعِد إلى القطارِ موظّفٌ يسمّى "الجابي" وعمله هو جمعُ التذاكرِ أو بيعُها للركّاب. ولم يكن مع أحد الركّاب تذكرة، فقال له الجابي إنّه يمكن أن يشتريَ واحدة منه وطلب ثمناً مرتفعاً للتذكرة. فرفض الراكب شراء التذكرة بهذا السعر المرتفع وقال إنها أرخص من ذلك في شباك التذاكر. وطلب الجابي منه إمّا أن يشتري التذكرة أو ينزل من القطار. فاضطُرّ الراكبُ أن يشتريَ التذكرة بالسعر المرتفع لأن الوقت كان متأخراً ولم يكن يريد التأخّرَ عن عمله.

6. Phrasal Verbs انقطع لِـ، اِنقطع عن

A phrasal verb is a combination of a *verb* + (preposition / direct object / prepositional phrase / إضافة). This section concerns itself with verbs that are followed by certain prepositions, and when those prepositions change, the meaning of the verb phrase changes with them.

to dedicate o.s. to s.th.; to apply o.s. to s.th.	اِنقَطَعَ إلى الكِتابةِ.	١
to dissociate o.s. from; to break up or part with	اِنقَطَعَ عَنْ أصْحابِه.	٢
to desist, to abstain from, to cease	اِنْقَطَعَ عَنِ التَدْخين.	٣

7. Multiple إضافة (مُضاف إليه)

The إضافة structure may have multiple مُضاف إليه, but it can only have one مُضاف. Let's take a look at a multiple إضافة:

This is the statistics professor's husband's car.	هذه سيّارةُ زوجِ أستاذةِ مادةِ الإحصاءِ.	١

Example 1 is a straight forward four-part مُضاف إليه. Another example of multiple إضافة occurred in the last paragraph of the second story and is worth mentioning since the pattern it follows is different from its semantic equivalent in English.

He took to talking excitedly about the courage and bravery of the Japanese.	أخَذَ يَتَكَلَّمُ بِحِدَّةٍ عَنْ شَجاعةِ اليابانيينَ وبَسالتِهِم.	٢

As you can see, the English structure in example 2 is quite different from its Arabic counterpart:

English: *courage and bravery of the Japanese*

as opposed to

Arabic: *courage of the Japanese and their bravery*

It would be considered an awkward (and somewhat weak) structure if there were two مُضاف: (e.g., شُجاعة وبسالة اليابانيين), although you will see this weaker structure used in media Arabic since this venue has been highly influenced by the English structure.

8. The Assimilated Verb مِثال

Verbs that begin with a و or a ي are known as assimilated verbs because the semivowel assimilates into the ت in form VIII افْتَعَلَ. This means that the ت of form VIII becomes doubled and therefore takes a شَدّة. Consider the following three examples:

Theoretical non-assimilated		افْتَعَلَ (VIII)		فَعَلَ (I)	
اِوْتَصَلَ	*to get in touch*	اِتَّصَلَ	*to connect*	وَصَلَ	١
اِوْتَصَفَ	*to be characterized by*	اِتَّصَفَ	*to describe*	وَصَفَ	٢
اِوْتَضَحَ	*to become clear*	اِتَّضَحَ	*to be clear*	وَضَحَ	٣

تَذَكَّروا

Assimilated verbs undergo other changes as well. For instance, they lose the semivowel in the present tense and the imperative:

الماضي	المُضارِع	الأمْر
وَصَلَ	يَصِلُ	صِلْ
وَصَفَ	يَصِفُ	صِفْ
وَجَدَ	يجِدُ	جِدْ

مُراجَعةُ القَواعِد

9. الإضافة غير الحقيقية

المازني chose to use this structure in his short story to indicate how happy and joyful he was while driving the car only to have the wheel start making an awful racket:

١	وَقَدْ أكونُ سائراً مُغْتَبِطاً، راضِيَ النَّفْسِ مُنْشَرِحَ الصَّدْرِ وإذا بِصَوْتٍ يَقولُ: كَرْكَرْكَرْكَرْ	*I was going along delighted, content, cheerful when lo and behold a sound emerged: creak, creak, creak, creak . . .*

As you can see in example 1, المازني used two إضافة غير حقيقية back-to-back to create a powerful image in the reader's mind of how happy the driver was.

10. Verbs of Beginning أفعال الشُروع

A number of أفعال الشُروع exist in Arabic; among those most frequently used are:

بَدَأَ، اِبْتَدَأَ، شَرَعَ، جَعَلَ، أَخَذَ، أَنْشَأَ، طَفِقَ

Of this set, the two highlighted were used in الحلاّق الثرثار.

He started speaking excitedly.	أخَذَ يَتَكَلَّمُ بِحِدَّةٍ.	١
He began to give him a strange haircut, one never before seen.	وَأَنْشَأَ يَحْلِقُ لَهُ رَأْسَهُ حَلْقاً غَريباً لا عَهْدَ لَهُ بِمِثْلِهِ مِنْ قَبْلُ.	٢

11. The Use of Plural Superlatives

Certain superlatives have a plural, among them are:

المَعنى	الجَمْع	المُفْرَد
first few of s.th.	أوائِل	أوَّل
last few of s.th.	أوَاخِر	آخِر
middle; central	أواسِط	أوْسَط

In order to use them effectively in our speech, we have to know how they function in context. Examine these examples:

The first few days of the month.	في أوائِلِ الشَهرِ.	١
The middle of this week.	في أَواسِطِ هذا الأسْبوعِ.	٢
The last few days of summer.	في أواخِرِ الصَيفِ.	٣

تمرين ١٨

Conversation: Find out who in class ________________, by using the following structures:

(أَواسِط، اِنْقَطَعَ لِـ / عَن، مِثْل، أَشْبَهُ، أَخَذَ، أَنْشَأَ، أوائِل)

1. has stopped smoking.
2. looks like their father/mother.
3. started working out at the beginning of this year.
4. has applied themselves to their studies.
5. works the last few days of each week.

12. The Passive Form of Hollow Verbs الفِعْلُ الأَجْوَف

Verbs with a long middle vowel, such as قال، باعَ، راعَ change to قِيلَ، بِيعَ، رِيعَ in the passive. When we are dealing with form III verbs فاعَلَ, however, the أَلِف turns into a واو:

was watched	شوهِدَ	⇐	شاهَدَ
was met	قوبِلَ	⇐	قابَلَ
was pursued	طورِدَ	⇐	طارَدَ

تمرين ١٩

Using context as a clue, fill in the blanks with the appropriate word or phrase. Be sure to use the appropriate conjugation of the verbs:

(أَواسِط، أَخَذَ، قابَلَ، حَمْراء اللَون، باعَ، لاحَظَ، طويلة الشَعر، جَعَلَ، صَغير الأَنْف)

١- لقد ________________ سيّارتُه بِخمسمئة ألف ليرة تقريباً.

٢- سترجِع أختي وعائلتها من المغرب في ________________ الشتاء.

٣- بعد تخرُّجهم من الجامعة ________________ يعملون في تعليم الرياضيات.

٤- اشترَت وفاء سيّارةً ________________ لِتذهب بها إلى عملها.

٥- ________________ أمي أنّ البريد لا يصل قبل الساعة العاشرة.

تمرين ٢٠

آ أكمِل الجمل الآتية بالاختيار المناسب وفق نصّ الاستماع:

١- عمر الجمعية ________.

☐ أقلّ من ثلاث سنوات ☐ ثلاث سنوات ☐ أكثر من ثلاث سنوات

٢- ترعى الجمعية أكثر من ________.

☐ ١٠٠ ☐ ٥٠٠ ☐ ٦٠٠٠

٣- تساعد الجمعية الأشخاص الّذين هم ________ الثامنة عشرة.

☐ في سنِّ ☐ تحت سنِّ ☐ أعلى من سنِّ

ب- اكتب «خطأ» أو «صواب» إلى جانب كلّ جملة ثمّ صحِّح الجمل الخطأ:

١- تساعد الجمعية الأفراد الّذين ليس لهم أباء أو أمّهات.

٢- لهذه الجمعية مدير من بغداد.

٣- يسكن الأشخاص الّذين تساعدهم الجمعية في مبنى الجمعية.

ج- أكمل الجمل وفق نص الاستماع:

١- توفّر الجمعية لهؤلاء الأشخاص فرصة إتمام ________.

٢- تقدّم الجمعية العناية ________.

٣- حصل بعض مَن تساعدهم الجمعية على عمل في الشركات ________.

د- أجِب عن الأسئلة وفق نصّ الاستماع:

١- ما هدف الجمعية؟

٢- ماذا فعل بعض الأيتام بعد تخرُّجهم من المدرسة؟

٣- كيف يكون الإنسان مواطناً صالحاً وفق النصّ؟

المُفْرَدات

أُمّ	ج	أمَّهات	(n., f.)	center, middle, most significant
اِتّسَعَ	(يَتّسِعُ)	اِتِّساع	(v.)	to accommodate
اِتَّصَفَ	(يَتَّصِفُ)	اِتِّصاف	(v.)	to be characterized, to be distinguished by
أجْمَع	ج	أجْمَعون	(act. p.)	all, the whole of, entire
أخَذَ	(يأخُذُ)	أخْذ	(v.)	to start, to begin, to take
اِرْتَعَدَ	(يَرْتَعِدُ)	اِرْتِعاد	(v.)	to tremble, to shake, to shudder
أرْدَفَ	(يُرْدِفُ)	إرْداف	(v.)	to add, to follow up with
أرى	(يُري)		(v.)	to show, to demonstrate
اِسْتَأنَفَ	(يَسْتَأنِفُ)	اِسْتِئناف	(v.)	to resume, to continue, to recommence
اِسْتَنْفَدَ	(يَسْتَنفِدُ)	اِسْتِنْفاد	(v.)	to exhaust, to consume, to deplete
أُسْطول	ج	أساطيل	(n., m.)	fleet, navy
اِلتَفَتَ	(يَلتَفِتُ)	اِلْتِفات	(v.)	to turn, to turn around
اِمتَدَّ	(يَمْتَدُّ)	اِمْتِداد	(v.)	to extend, to spread out
أنْتَجَ	(يُنْتِجُ)	إنْتاج	(v.)	to produce
أنشأ	(يُنشِئُ)	إنْشاء	(v.)	to begin, to start, to build, to compose
بِئْر	ج	آبار	(n., m.)	well (water/oil)

courage	(n., f.)			بَسالة
still, then, after that	(particle)			بَعْدُ
spot, stain, patch	(n., f.)	بُقَع	ج	بُقْعة
gasoline	(n., m.)			بَنْزين
to complete, to conclude, to finish	(v.)	تَتْميم	(يُتَمِّمُ)	تَمَّمَ
chatty, garrulous, talkative	(n., m.)	ثَرثارون	ج	ثَرْثار
companion, friend, associate	(n., m.)	جُلَساء	ج	جَليس
group, company, party	(n., f.)	جَماعات	ج	جَماعة
shop, store	(n., m.)	حَوانيت	ج	حانوت
sharpness, acuteness	(n., f.)			حِدّة
to report, to relate, to converse with	(v.)	تَحْديث	(يُحَدِّثُ)	حَدَّثَ
to fill	(v.)	حَشو	(يَحْشو)	حَشا
barber, hairdresser	(n., m.)	حَلاّقون	ج	حَلاّق
enthusiasm, ardor, zeal, fervor	(n., f.)			حَماسة
to praise, to laud, to commend, to extol	(v.)	حَمْد	(يَحْمَدُ)	حَمِدَ
reservoir, tank, dam	(n., m.)	خَزّانات	ج	خَزّان
danger, peril, hazard, risk	(n., m.)	أَخْطار	ج	خَطَر

astonishment, amazement, surprise	(v. n.)			دَهْشة
supply, hoard, provisions, ammunition	(n., f.)	ذَخائِر	ج	ذَخيرة
satisfied, content, pleased	(act., p.)	رُضاة	ج	راضٍ
to frighten, to scare, to alarm	(v.)	رَوْع	(يَروعُ)	راعَ
to tie, to bind, to link	(v.)	رَبْط	(يَرْبِطُ)	رَبَطَ
spirit, soul, essence	(n., f.)	أرْواح	ج	روح
oil	(n., m.)	زُيوت	ج	زَيْت
secret, mystery	(n., m.)	أسْرار	ج	سِرّ
to get full, to sate	(v.)	شَبَع	(يَشْبَعُ)	شَبِعَ
bravery, courage, boldness, valor	(n., f.)			شَجاعة
form, shape	(n., m.)	أشْكال	ج	شَكْل
chest, breast, bosom	(n., m.)	صُدور	ج	صَدْر
to export	(v.)	تَصْدير	(يُصَدِّرُ)	صَدَّرَ
to fix, to repair	(v.)	تَصْليح	(يُصَلِّحُ)	صَلَّحَ
wheel	(n., f.)	عَجَلات	ج	عَجَلة
end, issue, effect, outcome, consequence	(n., f.)	ج عَواقِب	ج عُقْبى / عاقِبة	عُقْبى / عاقِبة
knowledge, treaty, decree	(n., m.)	عُهود	ج	عَهْد

غَيَّرَ	(يُغَيِّرُ)	تَغْيير	(v.)	to change, to alter, to modify
فَضَّ	(يَفُضُّ)	فَضّ	(v.)	to settle, to resolve
فُكاهة	ج	فُكاهات	(n., f.)	humor, joke, fun
فَكَّرَ	(يُفَكِّرُ)	تَفْكير (في)	(v.)	to think (about)
قاضٍ	(الضَربة القاضية)	(الضَربة القاضية)	(adj.)	deadly, lethal, fatal (knockout blow)
قامَ	(يَقومُ)	قِيام	(v.)	to rise, to get up, to stand up
قَصَّ	(يَقُصُّ)	قَصّ	(v.)	to cut, to narrate
كافٍ			(adj.)	adequate, enough
مُتَحَرِّك			(act. p.)	moving, movable, mobile
مِثْل	ج	أمْثال	(n., m.)	similar, like, equal, analogous
مِحْوَر	ج	مَحاوِر	(n., m.)	axis, axle, pivot
مِرْجَل	ج	مَراجِل	(n., m.)	boiler, caldron
مَسّ	(مِن الجُنون)		(n., m.)	touched (with insanity, madness, mania)
مُسْتَدير			(adj.)	round, circular
مُعاصِر	ج	مُعاصِرون	(act. p.)	contemporary
مَعْروض			(pass. p.)	shown, displayed
مُغْتَبِط	ج	مُغْتَبِطون	(adj.)	glad, delighted

مَقْعَد	ج	مَقاعِد	(n., m.)	seat
مَكْشوف			(pass. p.)	uncovered, bare, exposed
مَلْعون	ج	مَلاعين	(pass. p.)	cursed, damned, evil, wicked
مُنْشَرِح	(الصَدْر)		(adj.)	cheerful, in high spirits
موسى	ج	أمْواس	(n., m.)	straight razor, razor blade
نِزاع	ج	نِزاعات	(n., m.)	dispute, controversy
نَفْس	ج	أنْفُس / نُفوس	(n., f.)	soul, spirit, psyche, mind
هَرْوَلَ	(يُهَرْوِلُ)	هَرْوَلة	(v.)	to jog, to trot, to hurry, to hasten
وَلْوَلَ	(يُوَلْوِلُ)	وَلْوَلة	(v.)	to wail, to howl, to lament

الدَرْسُ الخامِس عشر

Objectives

- Introduction to Naguib Mahfouz, Nobel Prize winner in Literature
- Introduction to religious debates and differences through short story
- **Grammar**: Compound question particles
- **Culture**: Children's nicknames, terms parents and children use when addressing each other
- **Idiomatic expressions**: جَديرٌ بالذِكْر، ما لَبِثَ أنْ، لا دَخْلَ لِـ، على الرَغْم مِن
- Using colloquial structures in MSA writing

رُكنُ المُفْرَداتِ الجَديدةِ

to take the initiative	بادَرَ (يُبادِرُ) مُبادَرة
experience(s)	تَجْرِبة ج تَجارِب
upbringing (raising a child)	تَربية
to think, to reason	تَفَكَّرَ (يَتَفَكَّرُ) تَفَكُّر
heaven, paradise	جَنّة ج جنّات، جِنان
movement	حَرَكة ج حَرَكات
dialogue	حِوار ج حِوارات
in spite of	بِالرَغْمِ مِن
necessary	ضَروريّ
equal to, tantamount to	عِبارة عن
vague	غامِض
discussion	مُناقَشة ج مُناقَشات

تمرين ١

وافِق بين كلمات من العمودين لكل زوج منها معنيان متشابهان أو لهما علاقة بعضها ببعض.

١	بَلى		نوبل
٢	حُجرة		حصل على
٣	دِين		سماء
٤	جائزة		نعم
٥	سورة		حيرة
٦	جنّة		إسلام
٧	نال		غرفة
			قرآن

تمرين ٢

وافِق بين كلمات متعاكسة في المعنى من العمودين.

١	نعم		شقيّ
٢	مَرِضَ		هتف
٣	جميل		زُجاجة
٤	هُدنة		كَلا
٥	صَمَتَ		شُفِيَ
٦	مُؤَدَّب		حَرْب
٧	جنّة		قَبيح
			نار

تمرين ٣

اختَرِ الكَلِمةَ الّتي لا تُناسِب باقي الكَلِماتِ في كُلِّ مَجْموعةٍ وبَيِّن السَبَب:

١-	الله	نبي	دين	جَنّة	سخرية
٢-	يا	كلاّ	نعم	بلى	
٣-	فَصْل	فُسحة	مَفرَش	مدرّسة	تربية
٤-	كَفَر	تثاءب	صَدّقَ	خَلَقَ	عَبَدَ

جَنّة الأطفال

تمثال نجيب محفوظ في شارع ٢٦ يوليو في القاهرة بمصر

هذه القصّة من مجموعة قصص صدرَت لنجيب محفوظ بعنوان «خمّارة القطّ الأسود». والجدير بالذكر أنّ نجيب محفوظ هو أوّل كاتب عربيّ ينال جائزة نوبل للأدب، وكان ذلك عام ١٩٨٨. وهذه القصّة عبارة عن حوار بين أب وابنته.

تمرين ٤

للنقاش قبل قراءة القصّة:

١- اذكر بعض الاختلافات والتشابهات بين الديانتين الإسلامية والمسيحية.

٢- ما الأديان الرئيسة في الولايات المتّحدة الأمريكية؟

٣- هل يتعلّم التلاميذ الدين في المدارس العامة في الولايات المتّحدة؟ لماذا؟

٤- أي البلاد العربية تتمتّع بنسبة لا بأس بها من المسيحيين؟

٥- ما الطوائف المسيحية الرئيسة في البلاد العربية؟

الطفلة (ط)　　بابا . . .

الأب (أ)　　نعم.

ط　أنا وصاحبتي نادية دائماً مع بعض.

أ　طبعاً يا حبيبتي فهي صاحِبتك.

ط　في الفصل، في الفُسحة، وساعة الأكل.

أ　شيء لطيف، وهي بنت جميلة ومؤدَّبة.

ط　لكن في درس الدين أدخل أنا في حجرة وتدخل هي في حجرة أخرى.

لحظ الأم فرآها تبتسم رغم انشغالها بتطريز مَفرَش. فقال وهو يبتسم:

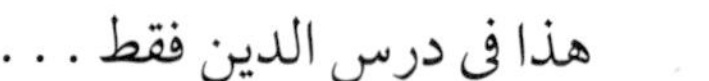

أ　هذا في درس الدين فقط . . .

ط　لِمَ يا بابا؟

أ　لأَنّك لك دين وهي لها دين آخر.

ط　كيف يا بابا؟

أ　أنت مسلمة وهي مسيحية.

ط　لِمَ يا بابا؟

أ　أَنت صغيرة وسوف تفهمين فيما بعد.

ط　أنا كبيرة يا بابا.

أ　بل صغيرة يا حبيبتي.

ط　لِمَ أنا مسلمة؟

عليه أن يكون واسع الصدر وأن يكون حَذِراً ولا يكفر بالتربية الحديثة عند أوّل تجربة. قال:

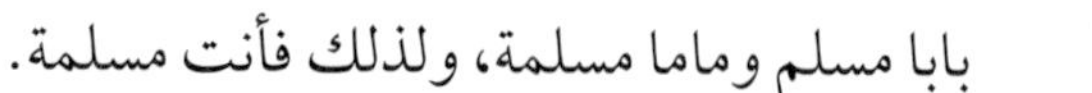

أ　بابا مسلم وماما مسلمة، ولذلك فأنت مسلمة.

ط　ونادية؟

أ　باباها مسيحي وأمّها مسيحية ولذلك فهي مسيحية.

ط　هل لأن باباها يلبس نظّارة؟

أ　كلاّ، لا دخل للنظّارة في ذلك، ولكن لأن جدّها كان مسيحياً كذلك.

وقرّر أن يتابع سلسلة الأجداد إلى ما لا نهاية حتّى تضجر وتتحوّل إلى موضوع آخر، لكنها سألت:

ط من أحسن؟

وتفكّر قليلاً ثمّ قال:

أ المسلمة حسنة والمسيحية حسنة.

ط ضروري واحدة أحسن.

أ هذه حسنة وتلك حسنة.

ط هل أعمل مسيحية لنبقى دائماً معاً؟

أ كلاّ يا حبيبتي، هذا غير ممكن. كلّ واحدة تظلّ كباباها وماماها.

ط ولكن لِمَ؟

حق أنّ التربية الحديثة طاغية . . . وسألها:

أ ألا تنتظرين حتّى تكبَري؟

ط لا يا بابا.

أ حسن. أنت تعرفين الموضة. واحدة تحبّ موضة وواحدة تفضّل موضة، وكونك مسلمة هو آخِر موضة، لذلك يجب أن تبقي مسلمة.

ط يعني أنّ نادية موضة قديمة؟

الله يقطعك أنت ونادية في يوم واحد. الظاهر أنّه يُخطئ رغم الحذر وأنّه يُدفع بلا رحمة إلى عُنق زجاجة، وقال:

أ المسألة مسألة أذواق، ولكن يجب أن تبقى كلّ واحدة كباباها وماماها.

ط هل أقول لها إنّها موضة قديمة وإني موضة جديدة؟

فبادرها:

أ   كلّ دين حسن، المسلمة تعبد الله والمسيحية تعبد الله . . .

ط   ولِمَ تعبده هي في حجرة وأعبده أنا في حجرة؟

أ   هنا يُعبد بطريقة وهناك يُعبد بطريقة . . .

ط   وما الفرق يا بابا؟

أ   ستعرفينه في العام القادم أو الذّي يليه، وكفاية أن تعرفي الآن أنّ المسلمة تعبد الله والمسيحية تعبد الله.

ط   ومن هو الله يا بابا؟

وأخذ، وفكّر ملياً، ثمَّ سأل مستزيداً من الهُدنة:

أ   ماذا قالت "أبلة" في المدرسة؟

ط   تقرأ السورة وتعلّمنا الصلاة، ولكني لا أعرف. فمَن هو الله يا بابا؟

فتفكّر وهو يبتسم ابتسامة غامضة، وقال:

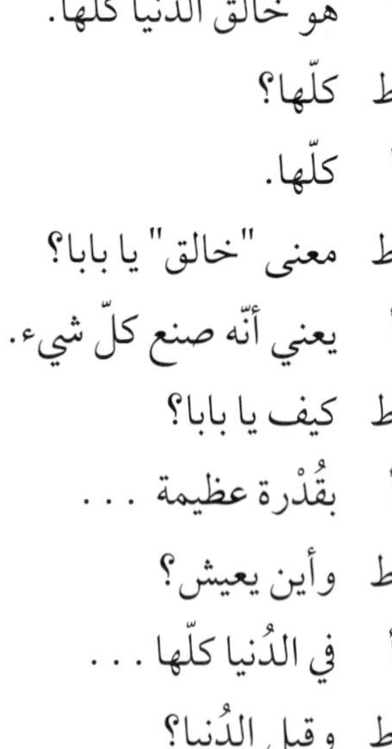

أ   هو خالق الدُنيا كلّها.

ط   كلّها؟

أ   كلّها.

ط   معنى "خالق" يا بابا؟

أ   يعني أنّه صنع كلّ شيء.

ط   كيف يا بابا؟

أ   بقُدْرة عظيمة . . .

ط   وأين يعيش؟

أ   في الدُنيا كلّها . . .

ط   وقبل الدُنيا؟

أ فوق . . .

ط في السماء؟

أ نعم.

ط أريد أن أراه.

أ غير مُمكِن.

ط ولو في التلفزيون؟

أ غير ممكن أيضاً.

ط ألَمْ يرَهُ أحد؟

أ كلاّ.

ط وكيف عرفت أنّه فوق؟

أ هو كذلك.

ط مَن عرف أنّه فوق؟

أ الأنبياء.

ط الأنبياء؟

أ نعم . . . مثل سيّدنا محمّد . . .

ط وكيف يا بابا؟

أ بقُدرة خاصّة به.

ط عيناه قويتان؟

أ نعم.

ط لِمَ يا بابا؟

أ الله خلقه كذلك.

ط لِمَ يا بابا؟

وأجاب وهو يروِّض نفاد صبره:

أ هو حرّ يفعل ما يشاء.

ط وكيف رآه؟

أ عظيم جدّاً، قوي جدّاً، قادر على كلّ شيء . . .

ط مثلك يا بابا؟

غار حِراء حيث نزل الوحي على النبي محمَّد

فأجاب وهو يداري ضحكه:

أ لا مثيل له.

ط ولِمَ يعيش فوق؟

أ الأَرض لا تسعه ولكنّه يرى كلّ شيء.

سرحَت قليلاً ثمَّ قالت:

ط ولكن نادية قالت لي إنّه عاش على الأرض.

أ لأنّه يرى كلّ مكان، فكأنّه يعيش في كلّ مكان.

ط وقالَت لي إنّ الناس قتلوه!!

أ ولكنّه حيّ لا يموت.

ط نادية قالت إنّهم قتلوه.

أ كلاّ يا حبيبتي، ظنّوا أنّهم قتلوه، ولكنّه حيّ لا يموت.

ط وجدّي حيّ أيضاً؟

أ جدّك مات.

ط هل قتله الناس؟

أ كلاّ، مات وحده.

ط كيف؟

أ مرض ثمَّ مات.

ط وأختي ستموت لأنّها مريضة؟

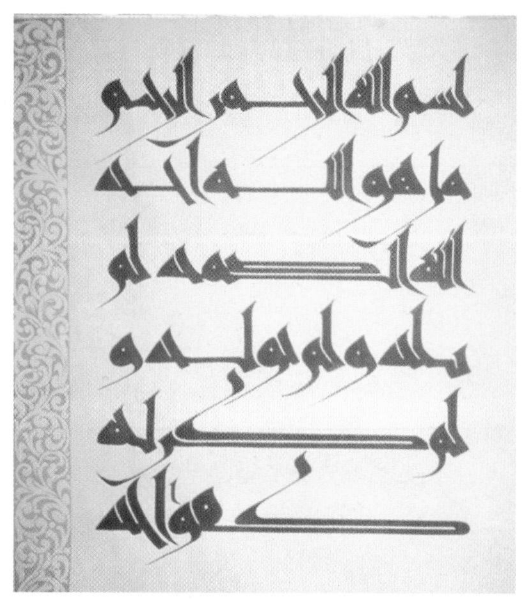

وقطّب قائلاً وهو يلحظ حركة احتجاج آتية من ناحية الأمّ.

أ كلاّ، ستشفى إن شاء الله.

ط ولِمَ مات جدّي؟

أ مرِض وهو كبير.

ط وأنت مرضت وأنت كبير فلمْ تمُت.

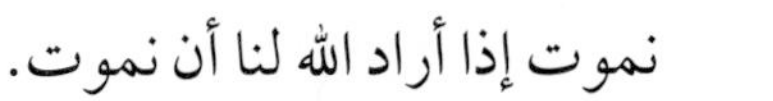

ونهرَتها أمّها ، فنقلت عيناها بينهما في حيرة، فقال هو:

أ نموت إذا أراد الله لنا أن نموت.

ط ولِمَ يريد الله أن نموت؟

أ هو حرّ يفعل ما يشاء.

ط والموت حلو؟

أ كلاّ يا عزيزتي. . .

ط ولِمَ يريد الله شيئاً غير حلو؟

أ هو حلو ما دام الله يريده لنا.

ط ولكنّك قلت إنّه غير حلو.

أ أخطأت يا حبيبتي . . .

ط ولِمَ زعلت ماما لمّا قلت إنّك ستموت؟

أ لأن الله لم يرد ذلك بعدُ.

ط ولِمَ يريده يا بابا؟

أ هو يأتي بنا إلى هنا ثمَّ يذهب بنا.

ط لِمَ يا بابا؟

أ لَنعمل أشياء جميلة هنا قبل أن نذهب.

ط ولِمَ لا نبقى؟

أ لا تتّسِع الدنيا للناس إذا بقوا.

ط ونترك الأشياء الجميلة؟

أ سنذهب إلى أشياء أجمل منها.

ط أين؟

أ فوق.

ط عند الله؟

أ نعم.

ط ونراه؟

أ نعم.

ط وهل هذا حلو؟

أ طبعاً.

ط إذن يجب أن نذهب.

أ لكنّنا لم نفعل أشياء جميلة بعدُ.

ط وجدّي فعل؟

أ نعم.

ط ماذا فعل؟

أ بنى بيتاً وزرع حديقة.

ط وتوتو ابن خالي ماذا فعل؟

وتجهّم وجهه لحظةً، واسترق إلى الأمّ نظرةً مشفِقةً ثمّ قال:

أ هو أيضاً بنى بيتاً صغيراً قبل أن يذهب.

ط لكن لولو جارنا يضربني ولا يفعل شيئاً جميلاً.

أ ولد شقيّ.

ط ولكنّه سيموت . . .

أ إلا إذا أراد الله . . .

ط رغم أنّه لا يفعل أشياء جميلة؟

أ الكلّ يموت، فمَن يفعل أشياء جميلة يذهب إلى الله ومَن يفعل أشياء قبيحة يذهب إلى النار.

وتنهّدت ثمّ صمتَت، فشعر بمدى ما حلّ به من إرهاق. ولَمْ يدرِ كم أصاب وكم أخطأ. وحرّك تيّار الأسئلة علامات استفهام راسبة في أعماقه. ولكنّ الصغيرة ما لبثَت أن هتفَت:

ط أريد أن أبقى دائماً مع نادية.

فنظر إليها مستطلِعاً، فقالَت:

ط حتّى في درس الدين.

وضحك ضحكةً عاليةً، وضحكَت أمّها أيضاً، وقال وهو يتثاءب:

أ لَمْ أتصوّر أنّه من الممكن مناقشة هذه الأسئلة على ذلك المستوى.

فقالَت المرأة: ستكبر البنت يوماً فتستطيع أن تدلي لها بما عندك من حقائق.

والتفت نحوها بحدّة ليرى ما ينطوي عليه قولها من صدق أو سخرية فوجد أنّها قد انهمكَت مرّة أخرى بالتطريز.

تمرين ٥

للمحادثة:

تخيّل أنّك الأب في جنّة الأطفال فكيف تجيب عن أسئلة البنت البسيطة والمعقَّدة في آنٍ واحد والّتي تكاد تكون فلسفية. في مجموعات من اثنين، يمثِّل طالب من طلاّب الصف دورَ البنت في حين يمثِّل الثاني دور الوالد.

تمرين ٦

أجب عن هذه الأسئلة وفق القصّة:

١- ما الفكرة الرئيسة في هذه القصّة وما هي بعض الأفكار الثانوية؟
٢- ما عمر البنت في رأيك؟
٣- أي نوع من التربية يتّبع الأب في تربيته؟ صِفه كما يبدو لك من القصّة.
٤- لماذا يريد الأب من ابنته أن تنتظر حتّى تكبَر؟
٥- ماذا حاول الأب أن يفعل حتّى تضجر ابنته من السؤال؟
٦- هل شرح الأب لابنته الفرق بين المسلمين والمسيحيين في عبادة الله؟ كيف؟
٧- من هو "سيِّدنا محمّد"؟
٨- كيف استطاع الأنبياء رؤية الله حسب قول الوالد؟
٩- كيف فسّر الأب الموت لابنته؟
١٠- هل تظنّ أنَّ الأمَّ تعجبها مناقشة فكرة الموت؟ كيف تعرف ذلك؟
١١- ماذا أثارت أسئلة البنت في ذهن الأب؟

تمرين ٧

أ- **أكمل الجمل الآتية بكلمات مناسبة وفق النصّ.**

١- البنت دائماً مع صاحبتها إلاّ في ____________.

☐ درس الدين ☐ الفُسحة ☐ ساعة الأكل

٢- كانت الأمّ خلال حديث الأب مع ابنته ____________.

☐ تطرّز ☐ في المطبخ ☐ نائمة

٣- نادية ____________.

☐ بنت الجيران ☐ ابنة خال البنت ☐ صديقة البنت

٤- تتعلّم البنت في المدرسة ________ .

☐ الصلاة والعبادة ☐ الموضة الحديثة ☐ الفرق بين الأديان

٥- يعيش الله حسب رأي الأب ________.

☐ في السماء ☐ على الأرض ☐ في كلّ مكان

٦- لولو ________.

☐ ابن الجيران ☐ ابن خال البنت ☐ صاحب البنت

٧- يذهب الّذين يفعلون أشياء جميلة إلى ________.

☐ الأرض ☐ النار ☐ الجنّة

٨- الفرق بين المسيحية والإسلام في القصّة هو في ________.

☐ الموضة ☐ طبيعة الله ☐ معنى الموت

ب- بيّن إن كانت الجمل الآتية صواباً أو خطأ وفق النصّ وصحّح الخطأ منها

١- نادية مسيحية لأن أباها يلبس نظّارة.

٢- يؤمن المسيحيون بأنّ الله عاش على الأرض.

٣- الإسلام والمسيحية مثل الموضة يتّبعها الناس وفقاً لأذواقهم.

٤- المسلمون والمسيحيون يعبدون الله.

٥- الله هو خالق الدنيا بالنسبة للأب.

٦- لَمْ يرَ اللهَ أحد من البَشَر.

٧- يعيش الله في السماء لأنّه قادر على كلّ شيء.

٨- جدّ الطفلة لا يزال حياً.

٩- من الأشخاص الّذين لم يفعلوا أشياء جميلة في القصّة ابن خال البنت.

ج- اختر عنواناً مناسباً للنصّ من العناوين الآتية، وبرّر اختيارك له وعدم اختيارك للأخرى.

١- اختلافات بين المسيحية والإسلام.

٢- الدين الإسلامي أحدث الأديان.

٣- لا فرق بين الناس بسبب الدين.

٤- لم يعِش الله على الأرض ولم يقتله البشر.

تمرين ٨

أكمل الجمل الآتية بكلمات مناسبة وفق النصّ.

١- دار ______________ بين طالبة من صفّنا وشاب حول الدين.

☐ احتجاج ☐ حوار ☐ موضوع ☐ انشغال

٢- تعلّمت سُها الـ ______________ من أمّها.

☐ حقيقة ☐ جائزة ☐ قدرة ☐ تطريز

٣- ما الـ______________ بين مدينتَي لندن وباريس.

☐ فرق ☐ هُدنة ☐ حركة ☐ عبارة

٤- حين ______________ أخي أخذناه إلى الطبيب.

☐ حرّك ☐ تفكّر ☐ مَرِض ☐ نال

٥- كنت في ______________ أمس، هل أذهب إلى السينما أم أدرس.

☐ حَيْرة ☐ فُسحة ☐ تربية ☐ إرهاق

تمرين ٩

أعد ترتيب الكلمات في كلّ جملة لتشكّل جملاً صحيحةً وفق القواعد أعلاه ثمّ ترجمها إلى الإنكليزيّة:

١- ذهب ومات إلى عملاً الجنّة عمل إذا الإنسان حسنا

٢- أوّل الكريم الفاتحة سورة سورة القرآن هي في

٣- أفعل أريد ما أنا حرّ إنسان

٤- الطعام تأكل الفواكه أن تفضّل بعد أمّي

٥- سأقابله بالرغم يوم انشغالي من بالدراسة الخميس

تمرين ١٠

أعد ترتيب الجمل لتشكّل فِقرة كاملة. الجملة الأولى في مكانها المناسب:

١- تثاءبت الطفلة الصغيرة وفتحت عينيها في سريرها صباحاً.
لكنّها فكّرت أن أمّها لن تتركها تبقى في البيت دون مدرسة.
ثمَّ تخرُج مع صاحباتها إلى الملعب وتلعب معهنّ.
لم يعجبْها ما ستفعل ذلك اليوم فقررّت أن تبقى في البيت.
وفي المدرسة ستدخل غرفةّ الدرس وتتعلّم القراءة وبعض الأغاني.
أوّلاً ستلبس ملابسها وتذهب إلى المدرسة.
لذلك تظاهرت أنّها مريضة ولا قدرة لها على الذهاب إلى المدرسة.
قبل أن تنهض من السرير فكّرت فيما ستفعل ذلك اليوم.
وفي نهاية النهار سوف تعود إلى دارها متعبة.

رُكن التعبيرات المتداولة على الألسن

كَونُك + خبَرَ مَنصوب

Use this expression when you want to say *because so and so is . . . ; due to the fact that . . . ; because . . . .* It occurred in our main reading passage as:

كَوْنُكِ مُسْلِمةً هُوَ آخِر موضة، لِذلِكَ يَجِبُ أنْ تَبْقِي مُسْلِمةً.

الله يَقْطَعُك

This expression has the literal meaning of *May God take you!*, but is commonly used when s.o. is fed up with someone else. An instance of this expression occurred in our text:

الله يَقْطَعُكِ أنْتِ ونادية في يَوْمٍ واحِد.

لا مَثيلَ له

You can use this phrase anytime you want to say *unrivaled,* or *incomparable*. The father in the story used this expression when his daughter asked him: مِثْلَكَ يا بابا؟ to which he answered:

لا مَثيلَ لَهُ.

جَديرٌ بالذِكْر / والجَدير بالذِكْرِ

This expression holds the meaning *it is worth mentioning*. It is a wonderful expression to add to your linguistic arsenal and comes in handy when introducing information related to the topic at hand. Found in most every field of discourse, it is commonly used in journalistic Arabic. This expression occurred in the introduction of the short story by Naguib Mahfouz.

وَالجديرُ بِالذِكْرِ أنّ نَجيب مَحْفوظ هُوَ أوّلُ كاتِبٍ عَرَبِيٍّ يَنالُ جائزةَ نوبل لِلأدَب.

ما لَبِثَ أنْ

An expression frequently found literature, ما لَبِثَ أنْ connotes *it wasn't long before; no sooner did . . . than*. Mahfouz used this expression in the following manner:

وَلٰكِنَّ الصَغيرةَ ما لَبِثَتْ أنْ هَتَفَت . . .

لا دَخْلَ لِـ . . . في

If you ever wish to argue that something mentioned *has nothing to do with the topic at hand*, use this expression. Mahfouz uses it in the following manner:

لا دَخْلَ لِلنَظّارةِ في ذٰلِك.

تَذَوَّق الثَقافَة العَرَبِيَّة

Terms Children Use to Address Their Parents

Much like the terms in the West, children address their parents using ماما and بابا. Unlike their Western counterparts, however, parents also use these same terms to refer to their children. A mother refers to all of her children (male and female) as ماما and the father refers to his children as بابا. A father might say the following to his son or daughter:

لا تَتَأخَّرْ / لا تتأخّري، بابا.

This sentence should be translated as: "Don't be late, son," and not: "Don't be late, dad." Translations should be context dependent, not literal.

Another popular term is دادا, which is used to address a sibling, regardless of sex.

تَذَوَّق الثَقافَة العَرَبِيَّة

Children's Nicknames

It is not unusual for children to acquire nicknames based on the first letter of their names. For example, if a boy were to be named is تَوفيق, his nickname might be توتو. If a girl is named لُبنى or لَيْلى her nickname could be لولو, and if her name is مَيْساء her nickname could be ميمي.

Generally, once children become adolescents, they normally stop using their nicknames.

القَواعِد

1. Ellipsis الحَذْف

Sometimes a phrase is not used in its entirety. Instead, the main word in the phrase is used to express the entire phrase. We have seen examples of this in the past in particular when using the word مُمْكِن, wherein other words in the phrase were omitted.

Prescriptive Form		Reduced Form
هل مِنَ المُمْكِنِ أنْ أسْتَعْمِلَ الهاتِفَ؟	⇦	مُمْكِن أسْتَعْمِل الهاتِف؟

We saw a couple of examples of this type of reduction in جَنّة الأطفال:

Prescriptive Form		Reduced Form
مِنَ الضُروريّ أنْ تكونَ واحدةٌ أحْسَنَ. *One must be better!*	⇦	ضَروري واحدة أحْسَن.
عَلى الرَغْمِ مِنَ الحَذَرِ. أو بالرَغْمِ مِنَ الحَذَرِ. *In spite of being cautious.*	⇦	رَغْم الحَذَر.

2. Compound Question Words

Some question words combine with a preposition or another particle as either a prefix or a suffix. The combined meaning of the compound word reflects the meaning of both words. Our main reading passage contained three such words:

> ألا is made up of the interrogative particle أ and the negative particle لا. It is used with present tense verbs to create negative questions like *don't . . . aren't:*

Can't you wait until you are older?	ألا تَنْتَظِرين حَتّى تكبُري؟	١

Much like example 1, ألَمْ consists of the interrogative particle أ followed by the negative particle لَمْ, which is followed by المُضارِع المَجْزوم and has the meaning of *haven't* or *hasn't* as in example 2:

Hasn't anyone seen him?	أَلَمْ يَرَهُ أحدٌ؟	٢

لِمَ is a contracted form of لماذا, which is a combination of the preposition لِـ and the question word ماذا literally meaning *for what,* but conveying *why*:

Why, papa?	لِمَ يا بابا؟	٣

Of course, other combinations of these prepositions + interrogative particle exist as can be seen in the following tables:

with what	= بِمَ / بِما	ب + ماذا
about what	= عَمَّ / عَما	عَن + ما
from whom	= مِمَّن	مِن + مَن
of what	= مِمَّ	مِن + ما
about whom	= عَمَّن	عَن + مَن
until when	= إلامَ	إلى + مَتى
to what	= إلامَ	إلى + ماذا

Let's take a look at these compound particles in context:

بِما	فَتَسْتَطيعُ أنْ تُدْلي لَها بِما عِنْدَكَ مِنْ حقائق.
عَمَّ	عَفواً يا أخي، أعْتَذِرُ عَمَّ فَعَلْتُ.
مِمَّن	مِمَّن هذه الرسالة؟
مِمَّ	مِمَّ تَتألَّفُ قاعِدة المُعطيات؟
عَمَّن	عَمَّن تَتَحَدَّث؟
إلامَ	إلامَ تَبْقى هُنا؟
إلامَ	إلامَ تَرْمُزُ تِلْكَ الحُروفُ؟

تمرين ١١

Select the appropriate compound question words from the previous section to complete the following sentences. As a follow-up exercise, translate the sentences into English.

١- ____________ وصلتَ متأخّراً؟

٢- ____________ اشتريت تلك السيّارة القديمة؟

٣- ____________ تريدين أن تكتبي لوالديك؟

٤- ____________ يتحدّث هذا الخبر؟

٥- ____________ تبحثون؟

٦- ____________ تنظر؟

٧- ____________ أقُلْ لك إنّه ليس هنا؟

٨- ____________ تتألّف السوق الأوروبية؟

3. Colloquialisms

Because the passage in this lesson is a dialogue, it contains a number of structures and expressions that are used in colloquial Arabic that we will now look at closely.

Her papa, her mama	باباها، ماماها	١
Should I convert to Christianity?	هل أعمل مسيحيّة؟	٢
May God take you and Nadia.	الله يقطعِك أنت ونادية	٣

مُلاحَظة

In example 3 the father asks God to take his daughter and her friend on the same day. While this expression may seem extreme when translated literally, the functional usage of the invocation simply expresses displeasure or annoyance toward the person to whom it is addressed.

fashion (moda)	موضة	٤
Older sister (Turkish *abla),* also used to refer to and address female teachers in Egypt.	أبلة	٥
To be upset or annoyed (with).	زَعِلَ مِن	٦

مُلاحَظة

زَعِلَ in example 6 is actually a standard verb originally meaning *to be bored* or *fed up*. It is quite frequently used in colloquial Arabic now to entail *to be upset.* Make sure that you use the preposition مِن to mean *with*, and **not** مع.

تمرين ١٢

أ- **أجِب عن الأسئلة وفق نصّ الاستماع:**

١- ما الموادّ المدرسية الّتي كانت تعجب هاني كثيراً؟
٢- بِمَ كان يحلم هاني حين كان صبياً؟
٣- لماذا ذهبت هناء إلى المسرح وحدها؟
٤- هل تحقّق حلم هاني؟
٥- اكتب عنواناً لهذه القصّة.

ب- **اكتب «خطأ» أو «صواب» إلى جانب كلّ جملة ثمّ صحّح الجمل الخطأ:**

١- عمِل هاني طبيباً بعد تخرّجه من الجامعة.
٢- زوجة هاني ربّة بيت.
٣- بدأت المسرحية في الساعة الثامنة مساء.
٤- كانت هناء تعرف أنّ زوجَها واحدٌ من الممثّلين.
٥- لم يكن هاني يذهب إلى المسرح والسينما كثيراً.
٦- كانت هناء تلتفت نحو الباب لأنّ زوجها كان يقف عند الباب.

ج- **أكمِل الجمل الآتية بالاختيار المناسب وفق نصّ الاستماع:**

١- اهتمّ هاني بالعلوم حين كان في ____________.

☐ المدرسة ☐ الجامعة ☐ العيادة ☐ المسرح

٢- فتح هاني ____________.

☐ عيادة ☐ مسرحاً ☐ بيتاً ☐ علبة

٣- حَلَم هاني بأنْ يصبح ____________.

☐ صبياً ☐ طبيباً ☐ ممثّلاً ☐ صيدلياً

٤- كان هاني يقول النِكات أمام ____________.

☐ زوجته ☐ أصدقائه ☐ الناس في المسرح ☐ المرآة

٥- جلست هناء وحدها في المسرح لأنّ زوجها كان ____________.

☐ متأخّراً ☐ على المسرح ☐ في العيادة ☐ في البيت

٦- تُرفع الستارة في المسرح عادةً ____________.

☐ في الساعة الثامنة ☐ في الساعة التاسعة ☐ بعد المسرحية ☐ بالمناسبات

المُفْرَدات

اِحْتَجَّ	(يَحْتَجُّ)	اِحْتجاج (على)	(v.)	to protest, to object (to)
أخطأ	(يُخْطِئُ)	خَطأ	(v.)	to err, to make a mistake
أدْلى	(يُدلي)	إدلاء (بِـ)	(v.)	to express, to declare
إرْهاق			(n., m.)	exhaustion, fatigue
اِستَرَقَ	(يَسْتَرِقُ)	اِسْتِراق (نَظرة)	(v.)	to steal (a glance)
اِسْتَزادَ	(يَسْتَزيدُ)	اِسْتِزادة	(v.)	to ask for more
اِنْشَغَلَ	(يَنْشَغِلُ)	اِنْشِغال (بِـ)	(v.)	to be busy, to be preoccupied
اِنطَوى	(يَنْطَوي)	اِنْطِواء (على)	(v.)	to involve, to imply, to include
اِنْهَمَكَ	(يَنهَمِكُ)	اِنْهِماك (في)	(v.)	to be absorbed with, to be engrossed in
بابا			(n., m.)	papa (daddy)
بادَرَ	(يُبادِرُ)	مُبادَرة	(v.)	to take the initiative, to begin
بَلى		affirmative particle after negation		نَعَم
تَثاءَبَ	(يَتَثاءَبُ)	تَثاؤُب	(v.)	to yawn
تَجْرِبة	ج	تَجارِب	(n., f.)	experiment, test, trial, experience
تَجَهَّمَ	(يَتَجَهَّمُ)	تَجَهُّم	(v.)	to frown, to scowl
تَحَوَّلَ	(يَتَحَوَّلُ)	تَحَوُّل	(v.)	to change, to alter, to shift, to transform
تَربية			(n., f.)	education, upbringing, cultivation
تَطْريز			(n., m.)	embroidery
تَفَكَّرَ	(يَتَفَكَّرُ)	تَفَكُّر	(v.)	to think (about), to reason
تَنَهَّدَ	(يَتَنَهَّدُ)	تَنَهُّد	(v.)	to sigh

current, flow, trend, tendency	(n., m.)	تَيّارات	ج	تَيّار
prize, award	(n., f.)	جَوائِز	ج	جائزة
worthy, meriting	(n., m.)			جَدير
paradise, heaven	(n., f.)	جَنّات / جِنان	ج	جَنَّة
غُرْفة	(n., f.)	حُجَرات	ج	حُجْرة
cautious, wary	(adj.)			حَذِر
free, independent	(n., m.)	أحْرار	ج	حُرٌّ
to move, to drive, to stimulate	(v.)	تَحريك	(يُحَرِّكُ)	حَرَّكَ
movement, motion	(n., f.)	حَرَكات	ج	حَرَكة
fact, reality	(n., f.)	حَقائِق	ج	حَقيقة
to befall, to descend upon, to afflict	(v.)	حَلّ	(يَحُلُّ)	حَلّ
dialogue, conversation	(n., m.)	حِوارات	ج	حِوار
confusion, perplexity	(n., f.)			حَيْرة
to create	(v.)	خَلْق	(يَخْلُقُ)	خَلَقَ
tavern, wine shop	(n., f.)	خَمّارات	ج	خَمّارة
to humor, to indulge, to flatter, to hide	(v.)	مُداراة	(يُداري)	داري
concern, business, relevance	(n., m.)			دَخْل
to know, to have knowledge, to be aware of	(v.)	دِراية	(يَدْري)	دَرى
world, worldly existence	(n., f.)			دُنْيا
religion	(n., m.)	أدْيان	ج	دين
mentioning, citing	(n., m.)			ذِكْر

taste, liking, inclination	(n., m.)	أذْواق	ج	ذَوْق
deposit, sediment, residue	(n., m.)			راسِب
in spite of	(prep.)		(بالرَغْمِ مِن)	رَغْمَ
to tame, to housebreak	(v.)	تَرْويض	(يُرَوِّضُ)	رَوَّضَ
bottle, flask, vial	(n., f.)	زُجاجات	ج	زُجاجة
to be annoyed, to be upset (with)	(v.)	زَعَل (مِن)	(يَزْعَلُ)	زَعِلَ
ridicule, scorn, derision, mockery	(n., f.)		سُخرية	سُخرية
to be lost in thought, to daydream	(v.)	سُروح	(يَسْرَحُ)	سَرَحَ
chapter in the Qur'an	(n., f.)	سُوَر	ج	سورة
to heal, to cure	(v.)	شِفاء	(يَشْفي)	شَفى
scoundrel, rascal	(n., m.)			شَقيّ
friend (in Egyptian colloquial)	(act. p.)	أصْحاب	ج	صاحِب
patience, forbearance, tolerance	(n., m.)			صَبر
truth, truthfulness, sincerity	(n., m.)			صِدْق
to be silent, to stop talking, to shut up	(v.)	صَمْت	(يَصْمُتُ)	صَمَتَ
to be dissatisfied, to be bored, to be annoyed	(v.)	ضَجَر	(يَضْجَرُ)	ضَجِرَ
essential, necessary	(adj.)			ضَروريّ
prevailing, oppressive person	(n., m.)	طُغاة	ج	طاغٍ
apparent, visible, obvious	(adj.)			ظاهِر
tantamount to, equivalent to	(n., f.)		عِبارة (عَن)	عِبارة (عَن)

to worship	(v.)	عِبادة	(يَعْبُدُ)	عَبَدَ
depth	(n., m.)	أعْماق	ج	عُمْق
obscure, vague, unclear	(act. p.)			غامِض
difference, distinction	(n., m.)	فُروق	ج	فَرْق
recess, intermission, picnic (Egypt)	(n., f.)	فُسَح	ج	فُسْحة
classroom (Egypt)	(n., m.)	فُصول	ج	فَصْل
to prefer, to favor	(v.)	تَفْضيل	(يُفَضِّلُ)	فَضَّلَ
coming, next, following	(act. p.)	قادِمون	ج	قادِم
ugly, unsightly, repulsive	(adj.)			قَبيح
power, faculty, strength	(n., f.)	قُدُرات	ج	قُدْرة
to frown, to scowl	(v.)	تَقْطيب	(يُقَطِّبُ)	قَطَّبَ
to be irreligious, not to believe in God	(v.)	كَفْر / كُفْر	(يَكْفُرُ)	كَفَرَ
not at all, by no means	negative particle			كَلاّ
to linger, to remain	(v.)	لَبْث	(يَلْبَثُ)	لَبِثَ
to notice, to look, to observe	(v.)	لَحْظ	(يَلْحَظُ)	لَحَظَ
well-behaved, well-mannered, polite, courteous	(pass. p.)	مُؤَدَّبون	ج	مُؤَدَّب
mama (mommy)	(n., f.)			ماما
like, similar, equal	(n., m.)	مُثُل	ج	مَثيل
extent, range, scope	(n., m.)			مَدى
to be ill, to get sick	(v.)	مَرَض	(يَمْرَضُ)	مَرِضَ
inquiring	(act. p.)			مُسْتَطلِعاً
level, standard	(n., m.)	مُسْتَوَيات	ج	مُسْتَوى

compassionate	(n., m.)			مُشْفِق
bedspread, bed cover, tablecloth	(n., m.)	مَفارِش	ج	مَفْرَش
a long period of time	(n., m.)			مَليّ
discussion	(n., f.)	مُناقَشات	ج	مُناقَشة
fashion (Italian *moda*)	(n., f.)	موضات	ج	موضة
subject, topic, theme, item	(n., m.)	مَواضيع	ج	مَوْضوع
to obtain, to get, to win	(v.)	نَوْل	(يَنالُ)	نال
to be used up, to be exhausted	(v.)	نَفاد	(يَنْفَدُ)	نَفِدَ
to keep moving	(v.)	تَنْقيل	(يُنَقِّلُ)	نَقَّلَ
to reproach, to scold, to chide	(v.)	نَهْر	(يَنْهَرُ)	نَهَرَ
to shout, to cry, to yell, to exclaim	(v.)	هُتاف	(يَهْتِفُ)	هَتَفَ
quietness, peace, truce, armistice	(n., f.)	هُدُنات	ج	هُدْنة

الدَرْسُ السادِس عشر

Objectives

- Introduction to Loris Maher—medical, political, and social pioneer
- Introduction to the biographical interview and learning to emulate it
- Learning historical facts about the Ottoman Empire and the French mandate in Syria
- Learning cohesive devices for extended rhetoric: Connectors
- **Revisited Structures:** The elative خَير, restrictive and non-restrictive relative pronouns, the simile, nouns with verbal meaning

رُكنُ المُفْرَداتِ الجَديدةِ

to prove, to establish, to verify	أَثْبَتَ (يُثْبِتُ) إثْبات
to influence, to impact	أَثَّرَ (يُؤَثِّرُ) تأثير (في/ على)
mandate	اِنْتِداب
at that time	آنذاك (آن + ذاكَ)
to be immersed	اِنْغَمَسَ (يَنْغَمِسُ) اِنْغِماس
as, like, similar to	بِمثابة
to nominate s.o. for s.th.	رَشَّحَ (يُرَشِّحُ) تَرْشيح
to treat	عالَجَ (يُعالِجُ) مُعالَجة
member	عُضْوٌ ج أعْضاء
to compensate	عَوَّضَ (يُعَوِّضُ) تَعْويض
issue	قَضية ج قَضايا
to confront, to face	واجَهَ (يُواجِهُ) مواجَهة

تمرين ١

وافِق بين كلمات من العمودين لهما عكس المعنى واكتب الأزواج في الوسط.

١	غَنيّ		نام
٢	مَرَض		أخَذَ
٣	وفاة		أُنْثى
٤	اِستيقظ		حَرَم
٥	أعطى		وِلادة
٦	اِعتزّ		صحّة
٧	ذَكَرٌ		ذَلَّ
			فَقير

تمرين ٢

وافِق بين كلمات لها علاقة بعضها ببعض واكتب الأزواج في الوسط.

١	السُلّ		صَحيفة
٢	مُنظَّمة		زيت
٣	مقالة		وحيد
٤	صليب		محفِّز
٥	عثماني		رأى
٦	دُهن		جمعية
٧	شَهِدَ		تركيّ
٨	مُنفرِد		الكوليرا
			المسيحية

تمرين ٣

اختَرِ الكَلِمةَ الّتي لا تُناسِب باقي الكَلِماتِ في كُلِّ مَجْموعةٍ وبَيِّن السَبَب:

١-	غذاء	متخلّف	خُضر	طعام
٢-	نقطة	رضيع	ولد	طفل
٣-	وزّع	أعطى	قدّم	افتتح
٤-	عاطفة	حُبّ	عدم	غضب

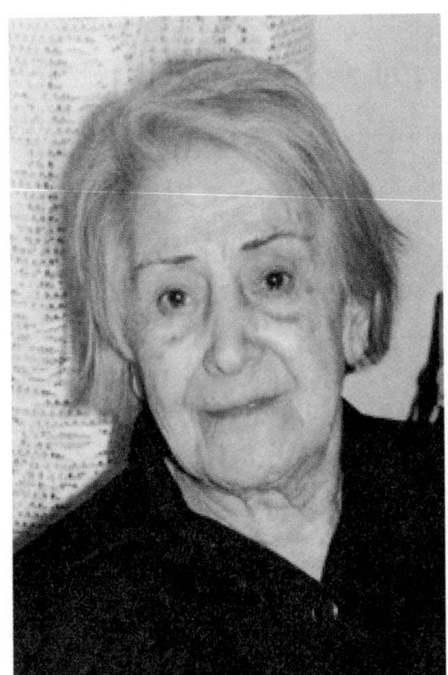

أوّل جامعية

وطبيبة ومرشّحة نيابية

عن مجلّة سيّدتي بتصرّف (العدد ١٠٢٢)

ولدت لوريس ماهر في دمشق سنة ١٩٠٦. إنّها أوّل امرأة في الوطن العربيّ تدخل الجامعة لدراسة الطب وتتخرّج طبيبة وهي أوّل عربيّة ترشِّح نفسها للمجلِس النيابيّ السوريّ. إنّ الدكتورة لوريس ماهر مؤلِّفة إلى جانب عملها بالطب، كما أنّها دخلت عالم التجارة مع والدها حيث أسّسا شركة لطعام الأطفال. في ما يلي مقابلة أجراها الصحافيّ علي طه مع الدكتورة ماهر عام ٢٠٠٠ ميلادي.

تمرين ٤

للنقاش قبل قراءة القصّة:

١- ماذا تتخيّل حين تسمع عبارة "الحركة النسائية"؟

٢- متى بدأت الحركة النسائية في بلدك؟ ومَن قادها؟

٣- هل حقّقت أمريكا المساواة بين الجنسين من حيث الراتب والمنصب في رأيك؟

٤- ماذا تعرف عن الوضع النسائي في الشرق الأوسط؟

٥- ما التحدّيات التي قد تواجهها لو كنت الفتاة الوحيدة بين الشباب في جامعتك؟

لوريس ماهر مع شقيقها وعائلته

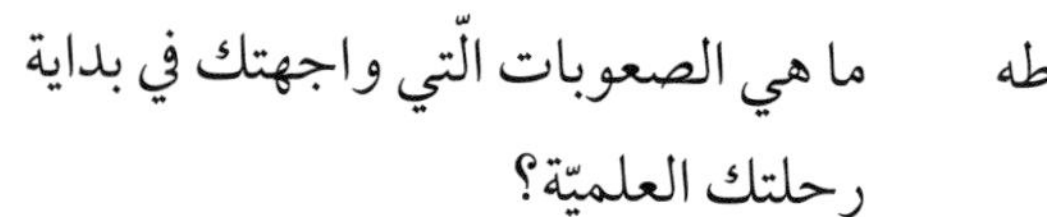

طه　ما هي الصعوبات الّتي واجهتك في بداية رحلتك العلميّة؟

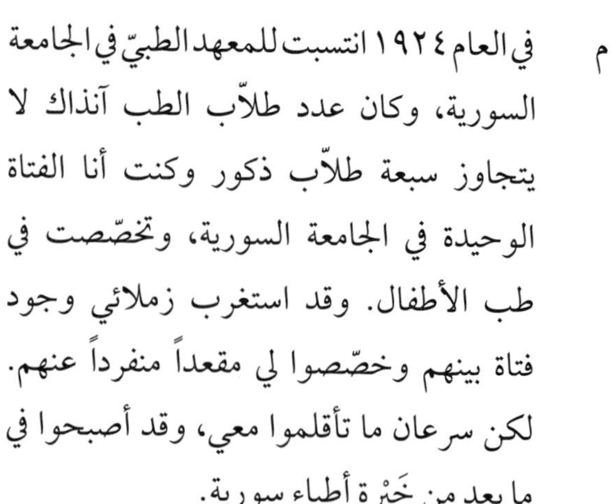

ل م　في العام ١٩٢٤ انتسبت للمعهد الطبيّ في الجامعة السورية، وكان عدد طلاّب الطب آنذاك لا يتجاوز سبعة طلاّب ذكور وكنت أنا الفتاة الوحيدة في الجامعة السورية، وتخصّصت في طب الأطفال. وقد استغرب زملائي وجود فتاة بينهم وخصّصوا لي مقعداً منفرداً عنهم. لكن سرعان ما تأقلموا معي، وقد أصبحوا في ما بعد من خَيْرة أَطِباء سورية.

طه　هل عارضت أسرتك دخولك الجامعة؟ وكيف نظر المجتمع السوريّ لك في البداية؟

ل م　كانت أسرتي خير داعم لي، وكان والدي يريد أن أدرس الصيدلة، إذ إنّه كان أوّل من حصل على شهادة علميّة في مجال الصيدلة في سورية، وقد كان رئيس "دار الاستحضارات الطبيّة" في إدارة الصحّة والإسعاف العام في دمشق أيّام الحكم العثمانيّ. لكنني فضّلتُ الطب وأثبتُ للمجتمع أنّ المرأة قادرة على العطاء كالرجل، خصوصاً أنّني كنت دائماً الأولى على دُفعتي في كلّيّة الطبّ. والحقيقة أنّ نظرة المجتمع لم تكن متخلّفة في ذلك الوقت لأنّ المجتمع اعتبر دخولي الجامعة أمراً طبيعياً. وبعد تخرُّجي من الجامعة عام ١٩٢٩ سافرتُ إلى باريس وتخصّصتُ لمدّة ثلاث سنوات في طبّ الأطفال.

طه　وماذا عملتِ بعد عودتك من فرنسا؟

ل م　عملت في مجال الطبّ طبعاً حيث افتتحتُ عيادة خاصة للأطفال في زمن الانتداب الفرنسيّ حيث شهدَت سورية زيادة في الفقر والمرض وتكرّرَت حوادث الوفيات نتيجة الإصابة بمرض السِلّ والكوليرا وغيرهما من الأمراض. وبما أنّني لم أُرْزَق بأطفال فقد كنت أعتبر كلّ طفل عالجتُه بمثابة ابني لأني كنت مدفوعة بعاطفة الأمومة الّتي حُرِمتُ منها طيلة حياتي لكنّ الله عوّضني عن ذلك بانغماسي في عالم الأطفال الّذي أنساني ألم عدم الإنجاب.

حفلة تخرُّج لوريس ماهر عام ١٩٢٩

ط‍ه أسّستِ خلال فترة الحرب العالميّة الثانية مع والدك شركة "سيريلاك" السورية (Syrielac أي الحليب السوري). كيف كانت هذه التجربة؟

ل م لم تكن شركة للربح بل كانت عملاً خيرياً إنسانيّاً يهدف إلى تصنيع الأغذية البديلة الّتي كانت تصلنا من شركات أوروبيّة والّتي انقطعت منتجاتها عن بلادنا بسبب الحرب، فقُمنا بتصنيع خمسة أصناف غذائيّة للأطفال الرُضّع وُزِّعَت في سورية ولبنان ووصل بعضها حتّى فرنسا. لقد لبّينا بذلك حاجات الأطفال في بلادنا. وقد كانت الكلّيّة الفرنسيّة في بيروت تستورد منا هذه الموادّ وتوزّعها على أطفال لبنان، وكان أكثر من نصف منتجاتنا يوزّع مجّاناً على المحتاجين والفقراء.

ط‍ه هل أثّر زواجك من الصحافي الراحل جورج فارس على عملك؟

ل م على العكس تماماً. فبعد زواجي منه زاد نشاطي، حيث كان يساعدني على نشر موضوعات علميّة في جريدة "صدى سورية" الّتي أسّسها والّتي كانت تصدر بالفرنسيّة. كما ساعدني على نشر مقالات في جريدته "بردى" الّتي كانت تصدر بالعربيّة، وكان دائماً محفّزاً لي على العمل حتّى وفاته.

الدكتورة لوريس ماهر تعزف على البيانو

ط‍ه كنتِ أوّل امرأة تُرشِّح نفسها للمجلس النيابيّ السوريّ، فكيف دخلت هذه التجربة؟

ل م كانت تجربة غنيّة جدّاً بالنسبة لي رغم أني لم أنجح في حملتي الانتخابيّة. لقد كان هدفي الدخول إلى المجلس للدفاع عن قضايا الطفل، إلا أنّ النجاح لم يحالفْني في ذلك لكنّه حالفَني في محبة الأطفال.

ط‍ه وما هي أهم النشاطات الاجتماعيّة الّتي تقومين بها؟

ل م أنا عضوة في جمعيات الإسعاف الخيريّ والدفاع المدنيّ، ولي مشاركات في جمعية "نقطة الحليب" السورية الّتي تسعى إلى مساعدة المحتاجين والأطفال الفقراء حيث توزّع عليهم الحليب بالمجّان. كما أنّني عضوة في جمعية "أطّباء بلا حدود" وفي منظّمة الصليب الأحمر الدوليّة.

ط‍ه ما هي أهم مساهماتك الفكريّة في مجال الطبّ؟

ل م كتبت عدّة مقالات في صحف عربيّة وفرنسيّة وألّفت ثلاثة كتب باللغة الفرنسيّة، وأنا أعتزّ بكتابي الّذي صدر عام ١٩٣٥ بالفرنسيّة تحت عنوان "تمريض الأطفال ودور القائمات على ذلك" لأنّه لاقى رواجاً جيّداً بين أطبّاء فرنسا.

طه عمرك الآن أربع وتسعون سنة. ما نصيحتك للمرأة حتّى تحافظ على صحتها؟

ل م أنصحها بهذه الأشياء: الرياضة والعمل والتفكير، وتناول الخُضَر الطازجة والماء بكثرة، وتناول السكريات والدهون باعتدال، والحصول على الراحة الكافية، والنوم المبكّر والاستيقاظ المبكّر.

تمرين ٥

للمحادثة:

أ- تخيّل أنك مراسل كالمراسل الّذي أجرى المقابلة مع الدكتورة لوريس ماهر مكلَّفٌ بالحصول على معلومات كافية لكتابة مقالة تُشبِه المقالة أعلاه، بينما طالب آخر يتخيّل أنّه شخصيّة تاريخيّة أو معاصرة بارزة تفاصيلها معلومة له حتّى يسترسل في أجوبته. يجري الطالب "المراسل" مقابلة شفوية مع هذه الشخصية التاريخية.

للكتابة: يقوم الطالب "المراسل" والطالب الذي يمثل الشخصية التاريخية بكتابة المقابلة معاً.

تمرين ٦

أجب عن هذه الأسئلة وفق القصّة:

١- ما علاقة سورية بالدولة العثمانيّة؟
٢- متى بدأ ومتى انتهى الانتداب الفرنسيّ على سوريّة؟
٣- هل للمرأة السورية حقوق مثل حقوق الرجل في رأيك؟
٤- حدّد الفكرة الرئيسة في النصّ أعلاه وبعض الأفكار الثانوية.
٥- ما الصعوبات الّتي واجهت الطفل خاصّة بسبب الحرب والانتداب؟
٦- أعطِ عنواناً آخر للدرس.

تمرين ٧

أ- **أكمل الجمل الآتية بكلمات مناسبة وفق النصّ.**

١- كان والد لوريس ماهر ________________ .

☐ طبيباً ☐ عثمانياً ☐ صيدلياً ☐ رئيساً

٢- كاتب نصّ المقابلة في هذا الدرس ________________.

☐ لوريس ماهر ☐ جورج فارس ☐ علي طه ☐ والد لوريس

٣- صار زملاء لوريس من ____________ الأطبّاء في سورية.

☐ أحسن ☐ أكثر ☐ أقلّ ☐ أصعب

٤- كان والد لوريس موظّفاً حكوميّاً أيّام ______________ .

☐ الحكم العثمانيّ ☐ الانتداب الفرنسيّ ☐ الحرب الثانية ☐ الحكم السوريّ

٥- «سيريلاك» هو اسم ____________.

☐ شركة سورية ☐ طبيب فرنسيّ ☐ جمعية خيريّة ☐ طعام فرنسيّ

٦- نشرت لوريس ماهر مقالات في مجلّة ______________.

☐ طبيّة ☐ زوجها ☐ فرنسيّة ☐ الجامعة

٧- «الإسعاف الخيري» اسم ______________.

☐ منظّمة دوليّة ☐ جمعية خيريّة ☐ دائرة حكوميّة ☐ شركة صيدلانيّة

٨- نشرت لوريس ماهر ______________.

☐ كتاباً واحداً ☐ كتابين ☐ ثلاثة كتب ☐ أربعة كتب

٩- تنصح لوريس المرأة بـ ______________.

☐ تناول اللحوم ☐ شرب الكثير من الماء ☐ النوم بعد الظهر ☐ طبخ الخضر

ب- بيّن إن كانت الجمل الآتية صواباً أو خطأ وفق النصّ وصحّح الخطأ منها

١- انتُخِبَت الدكتورة لوريس ماهر نائبة في المجلس النيابيّ السوريّ.

٢- ظلّت لوريس ماهر تجلس منفردة في قاعة الدرس طيلة دراستها الجامعيّة.

٣- لم يرَ المجتمع السوريّ مانعاً في دخول المرأة في مجال الطبّ في بداية القرن العشرين.

٤- أنجبَت لوريس عدّة أولاد.

٥- "نقطة الحليب" إحدى منتجات سيريلاك.

تمرين ٨

أعد ترتيب الكلمات في كلّ جملة لتشكّل جملاً صحيحةً وفق القواعد أعلاه ثمّ ترجمها إلى الإنكليزيّة:

١- في صباحاً السادسة أستيقظ الساعة

٢- العمل قادر أثبت على والدراسة أنّه أخي معاً

٣- في المرشَّحَ انتخبتُ الماضيّة الانتخابات المستقِلّ

٤- عمل فريد عن فَقْره جيّد حصل عوَّضه على سَنَواتِ

٥- على العثمانيّة في الحرب الدولة استولى ممتلكات العالميّة المنتصرون الأولى

تمرين ٩

أعد ترتيب الجمل لتشكّل فِقرة كاملة. الجملة الأولى في مكانها المناسب:

١- انتَسَبَت سلمى إلى جمعية خيريّة لتساعد الفقراء.
لكنّ سلمى لم تنسَ أنْ ترسل للجمعية مالاً كلّ شهر.
بقيَت سلمى عُضوة في الجمعية إلى أن انتقل عمل زوجها إلى مدينة أخرى.
وشعرَت بأنّها يجب أن تساعد هؤلاء الناس.
فزارَت شركات كبيرة تطلب منهم مالاً لمساعدة هؤلاء الفقراء.
وقد تعرّفَت من خلال عملها على عدد من هذه الأسَر المحتاجة.
وكان عملها التعرّف على الأسَر الفقيرة.
وقد تبرّعَت الشركات بالمال والمنتجات لمساعدتِهم.

تمرين ١٠

للنقاش قبل قراءة القصّة:

١- ماذا تعرف عن كلمة "الانتداب" من حيث مفهومها السياسيّ؟

٢- متى أُسِّسَت الدولة العثمانيّة وأين وقعت؟

٣- متى وكيف انتهت الدولة العثمانيّة؟

الإمبراطوريّة العثمانيّة

أسّس هذه الدولة عثمان الأوّل في القرن الثالث عشر في ما يُعرَف اليوم بتركيّا كواحدة من الدُوَيْلات التركيّة المتعدِّدة في بلاد الأناضول. توسّعَت الدولة بسرعة وامتدَّت إلى جميع أنحاء تركيّا وإيران وبلاد الشام ومصر وشمال إفريقيا وأوربا بما في ذلك اليونان والبلقان. في عام ١٣٥٣ فتح محمّد الثاني مدينة القسطنطينيّة عاصمة الدولة البيزنطيّة وسمّاها إستنبول وجعلها عاصمة الدولة. وصلَت الإمبراطوريّة العثمانيّة إلى أوجها حين استولى سليم الأوّل على سورية ومصر سنة ١٥١٧ وأعلن نفسه خليفة المسلمين. بدأت الدولة تضعف في أواخر القرن السادس عشر وفقدَت أجزاء كثيرة منها إلى أن انتهت تماماً بعد الحرب العالميّة الأولى وبدأ تاريخ الجمهوريّة التركيّة الحديثة.

يقع معظم تركيّا الحديثة في آسيا الصغرى وجزء صغير منها في أوروبا. عاصمتها أنقرة ونظامها السياسي جمهوريّ ديموقراطيّ. يحدّها من الشرق إيران وأرمينيا.

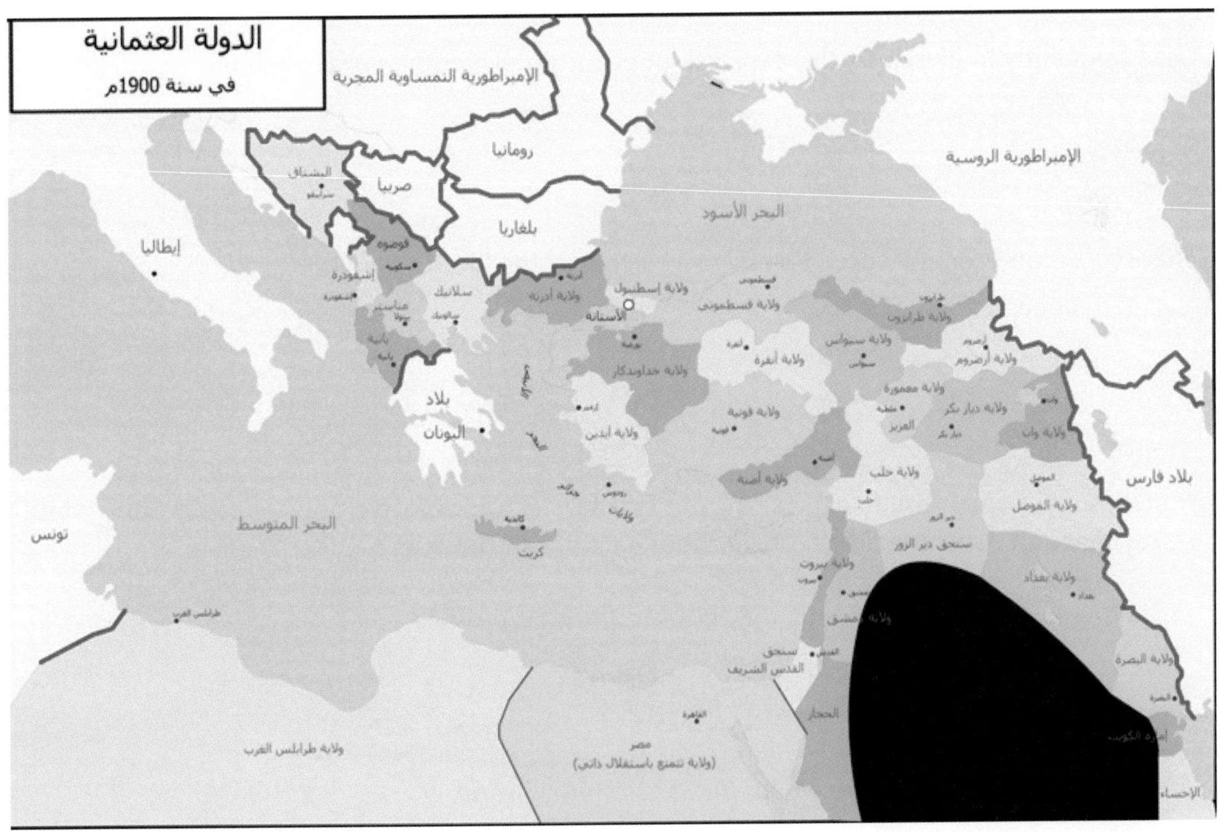

الانتداب الفرنسيّ على سورية

الانتداب نظام أحدثته الدول المنتصرة في الحرب العالميّة الأولى في عصبة الأمم (وهي المنظَّمة الّتي سبقت الأمم المتّحدة) بحيث تشرف الدول المنتصرة على ممتلكات ألمانيا والدولة العثمانيّة بعد هزيمتها في الحرب. كانت سورية ولبنان من نصيب فرنسا، ودخلَت القوّات الفرنسيّة سورية عام ١٩٢٠، لكنّ السوريين رفضوا الانتداب وحاربوه بقوة إلى أن استطاعوا تحقيق الاستقلال عام ١٩٤٦ بعد انتهاء الحرب العالميّة الثانية.

رُكن التعبيرات المتداولة على الألسن

إلى جانب + اسم

This expression is a synonym for علاوةً على, and بالإضافة إلى conveying the meaning *in addition to* or *besides*.

إنّ الدُكْتورة لوريس ماهِر مُؤَلِّفةٌ إلى جانِبِ عَمَلِها بالطِبّ.

سُرعانَ ما

Used frequently in literature, this expression means *no sooner than* or *before long.*

لكِنْ سُرعانَ ما تأَقْلَموا مَعي.

لَبّى حاجة

This expression should be used if you want to convey the idea *to fulfill the need.*

لَقَدْ لَبَّينا بِذلِكَ حاجاتِ الأَطْفالِ في بِلادِنا.

(لم) يُحالِفني النَجاح / الحَظّ

Sometimes you may wish to express the notion that *s.o. was lucky* (or not) *doing s.th.* In Arabic, we say that *luck / success allied s.o.* Check out its usage in context:

إلا أنَّ النَجاحَ لَمْ يُحالِفْني في ذلِكَ.

جَميع أَنْحاء + مَكان / كافة أَنْحاء + مكان

Use this phrase to express *throughout the land/country/world.*

تَوَسَّعَتِ الدَوْلَةُ بِسُرْعةٍ وامْتَدَّتْ إلى جَميعِ أَنْحاءِ تُرْكيّا وإيرانَ وبِلادِ الشامِ ومِصْرَ . . .

بِما في ذلِكَ

This expression comes in handy when you want to indicate that *s.th. is included* within s.th. bigger.

وَشَمالِ إفْريقيا وأوربا بِما في ذلِكَ اليونانَ وَالبَلْقان.

القَواعِد

1. Connectors أدواتُ الرَبْط

Well-crafted, higher-level discourse, whether written or spoken, is characterized by a sound use of connectors. These cohesive devices tie sentences together that occur within a text, creating seamless paragraphs. Dr. Maher instinctively used many of these devices to bind her sentences together in extemporaneous speech. Let's take a close look at these sayings so that we can integrate them into our personal speech patterns.

أدواتُ الرَبْط

بِما أنّ . . . فَـ

because; due to the fact that

وَبِما أنّني لَمْ أُرْزَقْ بِأطْفالٍ فَقَدْ كُنْتُ أعْتَبِرُ كُلَّ طِفْلٍ عالَجْتُه بِمَثابةِ ابْني.

كَما أنّ

just as; in addition

. . . كَما أنّني عُضْوةٌ في جَمْعيةِ «أطِبّاءُ بِلا حُدود»

إلاّ أنّ

but, however (think of it as an elegant form of لكِنّ)

لَقَدْ كانَ هَدَفي الدُخولَ إلى المَجْلِسِ لِلدِفاعِ عَنْ قَضايا الطِفْلِ، إلاّ أنَّ النَجاحَ لَمْ يُحالِفْني.

إذ إنّ

for, since (think of it as an elegant form of لأنّ)

كانَتْ أسْرَتي خَيْرَ داعِمٍ لي، وَكانَ والِدي يُريدُ أنْ أدْرُسَ الصَيْدَلة، إذ إنَّهُ كانَ أوَّلَ مَنْ حَصَلَ عَلى شَهادةٍ عِلْميّةٍ في مَجالِ الصَيْدَلةِ في سوريّة.

أدواتُ الربْط

حَيْثُ

where; when (in statements, not a question particle)

عَملْتُ في مجالِ الطبِّ طَبْعاً حَيْثُ افْتَتَحْتُ عيادةً خاصّةً لِلأطْفالِ في زَمَنِ الانْتِدابِ الفَرَنْسيّ حَيْثُ شَهِدَتْ سورية زيادةً في الفقْرِ والمَرَضِ.

نَتيجَةَ + مُضاف إليه

as a result of . . .

وَتكَرَّرَتْ حوادِثُ الوَفَياتِ نَتيجةَ الإصابةِ بِمَرَضِ السِلِّ والكوليرا وَغَيْرِهما مِنَ الأمْراضِ.

وَالحَقيقة أنَّ

really, actually

وَالحَقيقة أنَّ نَظْرةَ المُجْتَمَعِ لَمْ تكُنْ مُتَخَلِّفةً في ذلِكَ الوَقْتِ.

خُصوصاً

especially

خُصوصاً أنّني كُنْتُ دائِماً الأولى على دُفْعَتي في كُلّيّةِ الطِبّ.

بَلْ

in fact, rather

لَمْ تكُنْ شَرِكةً لِلربْحِ بَلْ كانَتْ عَمَلاً خَيْرياً إنسانيّاً.

تمرين ١١

a. Use the connectors in the word list below to connect the following pairs of sentences. Each connector can only be used once. Note that you may need to make slight modifications such as adding a pronominal suffix to some of them (e.g., كما أنّنا).

بِما أنَّ	لأنَّ	كَما أنَّ	إلاّ أنَّ	إذ إنَّ	والحقيقة	و	فـَ
حَتّى	خُصوصاً	لكنَّ	إلى جانِبِ	حَيْثُ	قَدْ	نَتيجة	بَل

١- درس الهندسة. لم يعمل في مجال الهندسة.

٢- رانية ليسَت مِن حلب. هي من الموصل.

٣- ذهبَت مَها إلى حمص لتدرس في جامعة تشرين. يسكن أخوها هناك.

٤- ذهبنا لزيارة الأقصُر في الشتاء. الطقس مناسِب.

٥- عمِل بالتجارة. وعمِل بالتعليم.

٦- لم تعُد تلعب الرياضة. هي مريضة.

٧- لا أعلم من أين أتى بالمال. أخوه لا يعلم ذلك.

٨- الرياضة جيّدة. إنها ممتعة.

b. Create a paragraph using the connectors in this section. The paragraph could be about anything, but we would suggest writing a short (auto)-biography or a historical synopsis of the area in which you are currently residing so that you can use our new vocabulary in context.

مُراجَعةُ القَواعِد

2. The Elative

Superlative pronouns take the أفْعَل form while simply adding a مِن after it creates the comparative (i.e., أفْعَل مِن). Let's take a close look at two elative forms that occurred in our main reading passage.

١	أوَّلُ سَيِّدةٍ.	*The first* lady

Example one follows the أفْعَل pattern while creating an إضافة structure. But, there is another occurrence of the elative in our passage. This one, however, does not follow the أفْعَل pattern.

The best physicians	خَيْرَةُ الأطِّباء	٢

As you can see, خَيْر + اسْم create a superlative construction meaning *the best*. Two very well-known and oft-used idiomatic phrases contain this type of elative:

The less said the better.	خَيْرُ الكَلام ما قَلّ ودَلّ.	٣
Moderation in all things (is best).	خَيْرُ الأُمورِ أوْسَطُها.	٤

3. Relative Pronouns الاسم الموصول

Both types of relative pronouns occur in our passage: restrictive (الّذي، الّتي، الّذينَ) and non-restrictive (مَن، ما).

a. Restrictive Relative Pronouns اسمُ الموصول الخاص

> **تَذَكَّروا**
>
> Restrictive relative pronouns (in red in examples 1 & 2) refer to a specific noun (in blue) and agree with their noun in absolutely everything: case, number, and gender.

لكِنَّ اللهَ عَوَّضَني عَنْ ذلِكَ بانْغِماسي في عالَمِ الأطْفالِ الّذي أنْساني ألَمَ عَدَمِ الإنْجابِ.	١
لأني كُنْتُ مَدْفوعَةً بِعاطِفَةِ الأمومةِ الّتي حُرِمْتُ مِنْها طيلةَ حَياتي	٢

In example 1, عالم is definite by virtue of being المُضاف of a definite إضافة (i.e., عالَمِ الأطْفال) and therefore, we use الّذي in order to describe the type of the children's world (i.e., الّذي أنْساني ألَمَ عَدَمِ الإنْجابِ). In example 2 الأمومة is made definite by use of the definite article.

b. Non-Restrictive Relative Pronouns

These pronouns modify a noun that has no specific number or gender.

٣ | كان والِدُها أوّلَ مَن حَصَلَ على شَهادة عِلْميّة.

The referent (or antecedent) in example 2 is of unknown gender or number (i.e., it could be a man, woman, or a group of people).

تَذَكَّروا

Non-restrictive relative pronouns may be combined with prepositions:

مِن + مَن	⟸	مِمَّن
مِن + ما	⟸	مِمّا
عَنْ + ما	⟸	عَما

تمرين ١٢

Use the appropriate relative noun:

(ما، مَن، الّذي، الّتي، اللّذان، اللّذين، اللّتان، اللّتين، الّذين، اللاّتي)

١- هل تعرف تلك السيّدة ____________ تقف بالباب؟

٢- حضر جميع العمّال ____________ يعملون في فترة الصباح.

٣- هي لا تريد أن تفعل ____________ أفعل.

٤- مَن هما الرجلان ____________ تكلّمت معهما؟

٥- اتصلتُ بكلّ ____________ زارني في العيد.

٦- إنّ الطالبات ____________ نجحْن بالامتحان سيدخلن الجامعة.

٧- ما اسم المدينتين ____________ تقعان متقابلتين على ضفّتَيْ نهر الدانوب؟

٨- هل تذكر عنوان الكتاب ____________ قرأته في الشهر الماضي؟

4. Forming Similes with كـ

We can use both مِثْلَ and كـ to form a simile, just as لوريس ماهر did in her interview and نجيب محفوظ did in our last lesson in his short story جَنّةُ الأطْفال.

١	المَرأةُ قادِرةٌ عَلى العَطاء كَالرَجُلِ.
٢	كُلُ واحِدةٍ تَظَلُّ كَباباها وماماها.
٣	مِثْلَ سَيِّدِنا مُحَمّد؟

تمرين ١٣

أ- أجِب عن الأسئلة وفق نصّ الاستماع:

١- ما الفكرة الرئيسة في نصّ الاستماع وما هي بعض الأفكار الثانوية؟
٢- أين تقع المنيا؟
٣- ماذا كان يعمل والد هُدى؟
٤- ماذا حدث في مصر عام ١٩١٩؟
٥- كم كان عمرها حين توفيت؟

ب- اكتب «خطأ» أو «صواب» إلى جانب كلّ جملة ثمّ صحّح الجمل الخطأ:

١- كانت هُدى شعراوي تعرف لغتين.
٢- كان زوجها عُضْواً في الجمعية التشريعية.
٣- صارت هُدى غنيّة بسبب زوجها.

ج- افعل ما هو مطلوب.

١- بيّن المقصود من عبارة "ذكرى فقيدة العروبة".
٢- لخّص النصّ بحواليْ ثلاثين كلمة.
٣- اكتب عنواناً للنصّ دون استخدام اسم تلك السيّدة.

د- **أكمِل الجمل الآتية بالاختيار المناسب وفق نصّ الاستماع:**

١- ثار المصريون ضد ______________ عام ١٩١٩.

☐ الإنكليز ☐ الأتراك ☐ الفرنسيين ☐ الملك

٢- كانت هُدى شعراوي أوّل مصريّة مسلمة تخرج إلى الشارع ______________.

☐ ماشية ☐ سياسية ☐ سافرة ☐ تشريعية

٣- ألّفت هُدى شعراوي جمعية ______________.

☐ العمل الخيريّ ☐ الاتّحاد النسائيّ ☐ الأدب العربيّ ☐ المجلس النيابيّ

٤- أصدرَت هُدى شعراوي مجلّة ______________.

☐ العروبة ☐ المرأة ☐ النساء ☐ المصريّة

هـ- **لخِّص نصّ الاستماع بحوالى مئة كِلمة.**

المُفْرَدات

أَثْبَتَ	(يُثْبِتُ)	إثْبات	(v.)	to prove, to establish, to verify
أَثَّرَ	(يُؤَثِّرُ)	تأثير (في/ على)	(v.)	to affect, to influence, to impact
أحْدث	(يُحْدِثُ)	إحْداث	(v.)	to create, to produce
اِسْتِحضار	ج	اِسْتِحضارات	(n., m.)	preparation, formulation, compound
اِسْتَيْقَظَ	(يَسْتَيْقِظُ)	اِسْتِيقاظ	(v.)	to wake up, to awaken, to rise
أَشْرَفَ	(يُشْرِفُ)	إشْراف (على)	(v.)	to supervise, to oversee, to manage
اِعْتَدَلَ	(يَعْتَدِلُ)	اِعْتِدال	(v.)	to be moderate
اِعْتَزَّ	(يَعْتَزُّ)	اِعْتِزاز (بـِ)	(v.)	to be proud of, to take pride in
اِفْتَتَحَ	(يَفْتَتِحُ)	اِفْتِتاح	(v.)	to have a grand opening, to inaugurate
أَلَّفَ	(يُؤَلِّفُ)	تأليف	(v.)	to compose, to compile
أمّة	ج	أُمَم	(n., f.)	nation
اِنْتِداب			(n., m.)	mandate
اِنْتَسَبَ	(يَنْتَسِبُ)	اِنْتِساب (إلى)	(v.)	to join, to be associated (with)
أَنْجَبَ	(يُنْجِبُ)	إنْجاب	(v.)	to beget, to give birth
آنذاك	(آنَ + ذاك)	(آنَ + ذاك)	(adv.)	then, at that time
إنسان			(n., m.)	human being
اِنْغَمَسَ	(يَنْغَمِسُ)	اِنْغِماس	(v.)	to be immersed, to be submerged
أَوْج			(n., m.)	highest point, acme, peak, climax
بَديل	ج	بُدَلاء	(n., m.)	alternative, alternate, substitute

as, like, similar to	(prep. ph.)			بِمَثابةِ
to exceed, to surpass	(v.)	تَجاوُز	(يَتَجاوَزُ)	تَجاوَزَ
to recur, to be repeated	(v.)	تكرُّر	(يَتَكَرَّرُ)	تَكَرَّرَ
to expand, to spread	(v.)	تَوَسُّع	(يَتَوَسَّعُ)	تَوَسَّعَ
need, want, necessity	(n., f.)	حاجات	ج	حاجة
to ally with	(v.)	مُحالَفة	(يُحالِفُ)	حالَفَ
to deprive, to dispossess	(v.)	حِرْمان	(يَحْرِمُ)	حَرَمَ
campaign, attack, offensive	(n., f.)	حَمَلات	ج	حَمْلة
elite, choice, pick	(n., f.)			خَيْرة
supporter	(act. p.)	داعِمون	ج	داعِم
to defend, to protect	(v.)	دِفاع / مُدافَعة (عن)	(يُدافِعُ)	دافَعَ
group, class, set	(n., f.)	دُفُعات	ج	دُفْعة
fat, grease	(n., m.)	دُهون	ج	دُهْن
role, part	(n., m.)	أدْوار	ج	دَوْر
male	(n., m.)	ذُكور	ج	ذَكَر
the late, the deceased	(act. p.)	راحِلون	ج	راحِل
to bestow by God, sustenance, daily bread	(v.)	رِزْق	(يَرْزُقُ)	رَزَقَ
to nominate, to run (candidate)	(v.)	تَرْشيح	(يُرَشِّحُ)	رَشَّحَ
infant, newborn	(n., m.)	رُضَّع	ج	رَضيع
popularity, currency, marketability	(n., m.)			رَواج
increase, increment, addition	(n., f.)	زِيادات	ج	زِيادة
to contribute, to take part	(v.)	مُساهَمة	(يُساهِمُ)	ساهَمَ

no sooner than, at which point	(n. w /verbal meaning)		سُرْعانَ ما	سُرْعانَ ما
tuberculosis	(n., m.)			سُلّ
to witness	(v.)	شَهادة	(يَشْهَدُ)	شَهِدَ
sign of the cross, cross	(n., m.)	صُلْبان	ج	صَليب
category, sort, type, kind	(n., m.)	أصْناف	ج	صِنْف
to weaken, to lose strength	(v.)	ضَعْف	(يَضْعُفُ)	ضَعُفَ
throughout, during, all through	(n., f.)			طيلةَ / طَوالَ
to oppose, to resist, to object	(v.)	مُعارَضة	(يُعارِضُ)	عارَضَ
emotion, passion	(n., f.)	عَواطِف	ج	عاطِفة
to treat, to remedy, to cure, to medicate	(v.)	مُعالَجة	(يُعالِجُ)	عالَجَ
nonexistence, nothingness, absence, lack	(n., m.)			عَدَم
League (of Nations)	(n., f.)			عُصْبة (الأمَم)
member	(n., m.)	أعْضاء	ج	عُضْو
giving, gift, grant, donation	(n., m.)			عَطاء
to compensate, to make up for	(v.)	تَعْويض	(يُعَوِّضُ)	عَوَّضَ
nourishment, nutrient	(n., m.)	أغْذية	ج	غِذاء
period, interval of time	(n., f.)	فَتَرات	ج	فَتْرة
poverty, need, destitution	(n., m.)			فَقْر
capable, competent, powerful, able	(act. p.)	قادِرون	ج	قادِر
issue, cause, affair	(n., f.)	قَضايا	ج	قَضيّة
to meet, to encounter	(v.)	مُلاقاة	(يُلاقي)	لاقى

لَبّى	(يُلَبّي)	تَلْبية	(v.)	to respond to, to comply
مُتَخَلِّف	ج	مُتَخَلِّفون	(act. p.)	backward, retarded, falling behind
مُجْتَمَع	ج	مُجْتَمَعات	(pass. p.)	society, community
مُحْتاج	ج	مُحْتاجون	(pass. p.)	needy, poor, destitute, wanting
مُحَفِّز	ج	مُحَفِّزون	(act. p.)	motivator, stimulator, incentive
مَدْفوع			(pass. p.)	driven forward, propelled, motivated
مُرَشَّح			(pass. p.)	nominated, candidate
مَرَّضَ	(يُمَرِّضُ)	تَمْريض	(v.)	to nurse, to tend
مُنْتَصِر	ج	مُنْتَصِرون	(act. p.)	victor, conqueror, victorious
مُنَظَّمة	ج	مُنَظَّمات	(pass. p)	organization
مُنْفَرِد	ج	مُنْفَرِدون	(act. p.)	alone, solitary, isolated
نَشاط	ج	أَنْشِطة	(n., m.)	activity, vigor, liveliness
نَصيب	ج	نُصُب/ أنصِبة	(n., m.)	share, portion, cut
نَصيحة	ج	نَصائح	(n., f.)	advice, counsel
نُقْطة	ج	نُقَط / نِقاط	(n., f.)	point, drop, period
نِيابيّ			(adj.)	parliamentary, representative
هَدَف	ج	أَهْداف	(n., m.)	target, aim, goal
هَزيمة	ج	هَزائِم	(n., f.)	defeat, rout
واجَهَ	(يُواجِهُ)	مُواجَهة	(v.)	to face, to encounter, to oppose, to confront
وَزَّعَ	(يُوَزِّعُ)	تَوْزيع	(v.)	to distribute, to dispense; to disburse

الدَرْسُ السابِع عشر

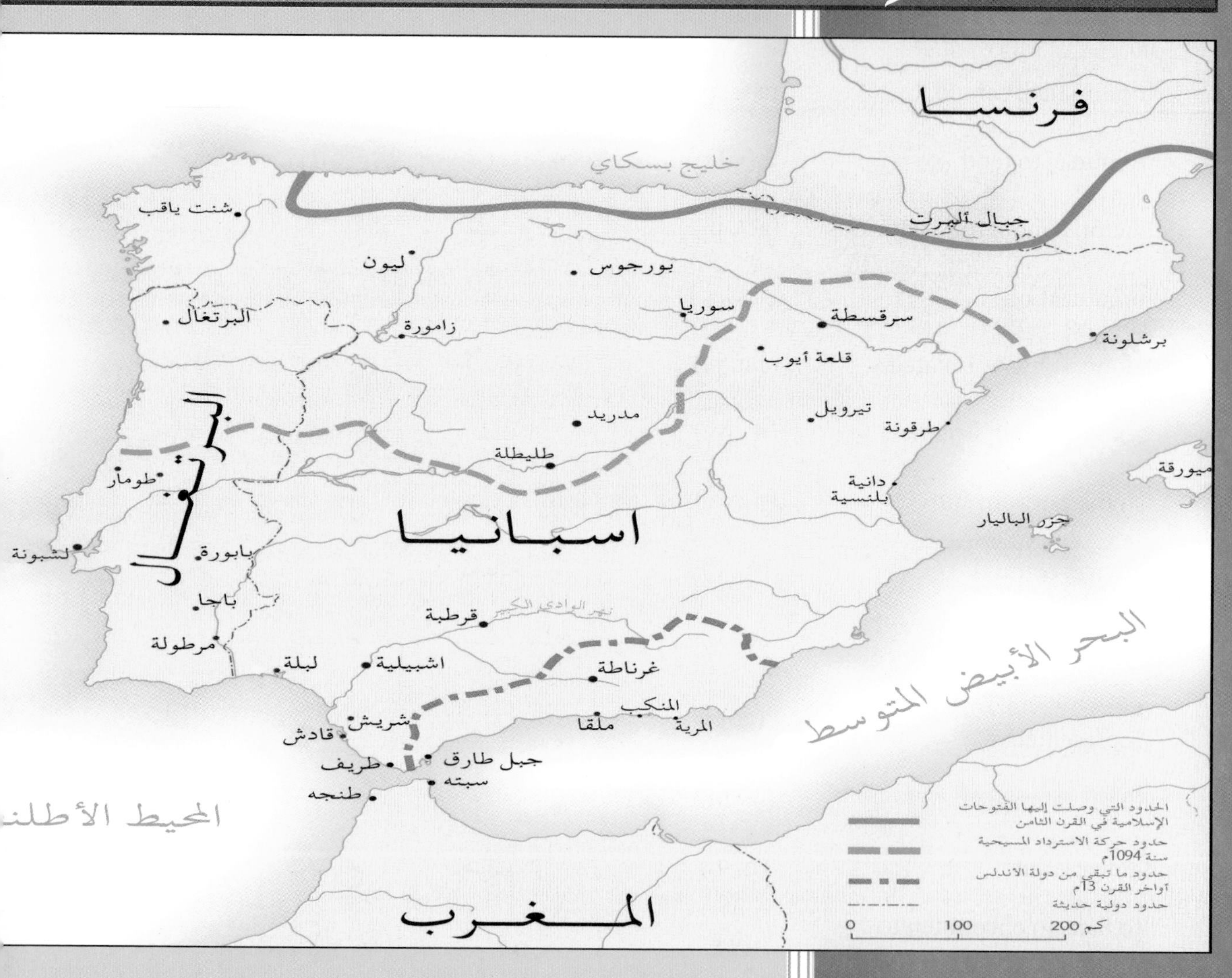

Objectives

- Introduction to Andalusia: its history, culture, and lasting impact on Spanish
- Learning historical events and how to describe them
- **Culture**: Andalusian poetry المَوَشّحات; فيروز singing a selected Andalusian poem
- **Grammar**: Diminutive nouns, collocation, spelling of ابن, and synonyms
- **مُراجَعة القواعد**: اسمُ التَفضيل، والمبني للمجهول

رُكنُ المُفْرَداتِ الجَديدةِ

to recognize, to acknowledge	اِعْتَرَفَ (يَعْتَرِفُ) اِعْتِراف (بِـ)
to withdraw	اِنْسَحَبَ (يَنْسَحِبُ) اِنْسِحاب
to be distinguished	تَمَيَّزَ (يَتَمَيَّزُ) تَمَيُّز
to dispute, to contend	تَنازَعَ (يَتَنازَعُ) تَنازُع
to compete against one another, to rival	تَنافَسَ (يَتَنافَسُ) تَنافُس
to revolt, to rebel	ثارَ (يَثورُ) ثَوْرة ثَوْرات
to review	راجَعَ (يُراجِعُ) مُراجَعة
faction, sect	طائِفة ج طَوائِف
enemy, foe	عَدوّ ج أعْداء
to conquer	فَتَحَ (يَفْتَحُ) فَتْح (فَتَحَ بَلَداً)
poem, ode	قَصيدة ج قَصائِد
battle	مَعْرَكة ج مَعارِك
to break out (war / rebellion)	نَشِبَ (يَنْشَبُ) نُشوب (الحَرْب / الثَوْرة)

تمرين ١

وافِق بين كلمات لها علاقة بعضها ببعض، واكتب الأزواج في الوسط.

١	جيش		جدار
٢	قصر		حيوان
٣	موسيقا		ملِك
٤	معركة		مُزخرَف
٥	خليفة		فنّ
٦	سور		عسكريّ
٧	نافورة		ماء
٨	أسَد		قلعة
٩	طول		عرْض
			حَرب

تمرين ٢

اخترِ الكَلِمةَ الّتي لا تُناسِب باقي الكَلِماتِ في كُلِّ مَجْموعةٍ وبَيِّن السَبَب:

١- قلعة سفح قاعة قصر

٢- ضَعف قائد عسكريّ جيش

٣- معركة حملة دولة ثَوْرة

٤- ثقافة علوم موسيقا سقوط

تمرين ٣

للنقاش قبل قراءة القصّة:

١- هات معلوماتك عن الأندلس.

٢- مَن فتح الأندلس ومَتى؟

٣- كيف أثّر العرب في الثقافة الإسبانية وتراثها؟

الأندلس

لمحة تاريخيّة

الأندلس هو الاسم الّذي أطلقه العرب على إسبانيا بعد الفتح الإسلاميّ عام ٧١١ للميلاد على يد موسى بن نُصَيْر والي شمال إفريقيا الأمويّ. بعث موسى أحد قادتهِ الأمازيغيين (أطلِق عليهم اسم البربر كذلك)، طُرَيْف بن مالك، سراً في حملة استطلاعيّة إلى إسبانيا حيث نزل في بلدة صغيرة حملت اسمه فيما بعد «طُرَيْفة». وفي السنة التالية أرسل أفضل قادتهِ طارق بن زياد على رأس جيش من ٧٠٠٠ من الأمازيغ. وفي سنة ٧١٢ قاد موسى بن نُصَيْر بنفسِه جيشاً من ١٨٠٠٠ مقاتل معظمهم من العرب، وفتح إشبيلية بعد فترة قصيرة. وإشبيلية أغنى مدن الأندلس وأصبحت عاصمتها الأولى. وقد كتب عبد العزيز بن موسى بن نُصَيْر إلى أقاربِه وأصدقائِه في الشام عن البلاد الجديدة ممّا جعل أكثر من ١٣٠٠٠ شخص يأتون إلى الأندلس.

تمثال مُعاوية بن هشام في إسبانيا

حكم الأمويون الأندلس من دمشق بواسطة حاكمهم في شمال إفريقيا حتّى سنة ٧٥٠ حين سقطت دولتهم أمام العباسيين وقُتِلَ معظمهم. لكن عبد الرحمن بن مُعاوية بن هشام أحد أفراد الأسرة الأمويّة نجا من الموت وفرّ إلى الأندلس حيث أسّس هناك دولة أمويّة مستقلّة عام ٧٥٦. إلاّ أنّ هذه الدولة ظلّت تعترف بالخلافة الإسلاميّة في بغداد لمدّة قرنين تقريباً. وفي عام ٩٢٩ أعلن الأمير الأمويّ الثامن عبد الرحمن الناصر الخلافة.

أروقة مسجد قرطبة الرائعة الجمال

وشهدت الأندلس وعاصمتها قُرطُبة عصرها الذَهبيّ خلال الخلافة الأمويّة في الأندلس. إلاّ أنّ ضعَف الحُكّام ونشوب ثورات متعدِّدة بين عامي ١٠٠٩ و١٠٣١ أدّى إلى سقوط الخلافة الأمويّة في الأندلس وانتقال الحكم إلى ملوك دوَيْلات صغيرة سُمِّيَت الطوائف. تميّز حكم ملوك الطوائف بالتنازع فيما بينهم وبتعاونهم مع أعدائهم بعضهم ضد بعض وبضعفهم أمام الممالك الإسبانيّة في الشمال وفقدانهم الكثير من الأراضي لأعدائهم. لكن بالرغم من ضعفهم السياسيّ والعسكريّ فقد ازدهرت العلوم والفنون لتنافُس هؤلاء الملوك في اجتذاب العلماء والفنّانين والأدباء إلى قصورهم.

أدّى الضعف المُزمِن والتنازع بين الملوك إلى سقوط طُلَيْطُلة عام ١٠٨٥. واستعان ملوك الطوائف بالمرابطين حكّام المغرب الّذين حكموا منطقة واسعة من الجزائر إلى السنغال، ودخل يوسف بن تاشفين زعيم المرابطين الأندلس، وبعد أن لمس التنازع بين ملوك الطوائف وغضب الناس عليهم أزاحهم واستولى على الحكم. ثمَّ ثار الناس على المرابطين وطلبوا العون من الموحّدين في المغرب. وما كان حال الموحّدين أفضل من حال المرابطين فقد هُزِموا في معركة العُقاب أمام المسيحيين سنة ١٢١٢ وبدأوا ينسحبون بالتدريج وتساقطت المُدُن الأندلسيّة الواحدة تِلوَ الأخرى حيث لم يبقَ سِوى مملكة غَرناطة في عام ١٢٦٠. استمرّت غَرناطة قائمةً رغم ضعَفها والخطر المُحدِق بها أكثر من قرنين من الزمان. وفي العام ١٤٩١ وصلت جيوش الملك فردينان والملكة إيزابيلا إلى أبواب المدينة. وفي اليوم الثاني من كانون الثاني سنة ١٤٩٢ خرج آخر ملوك بني الأحمر محمّد أبو عبد الله منها وبذلك انتهت الدولة الإسلاميّة في الأندلس.

يطلّ قصر الحمراء على مدينة غرناطة

التراث الأندلسيّ

ترك العرب والمسلمون آثاراً واضحة في شبه الجزيرة الإيبيريّة، في أسماء الأماكن وفي اللغة والعمارة والموسيقا والفلسفة والعلوم. فاسم ميناء Algeciras مثلاً في جنوب إسبانيا اليوم يرجع إلى اسم «الجزيرة الخضراء» الّذي أطلقه الفاتحون العرب على البلاد لدى وصولهم إليها. واسم Gibraltar يرجِع إلى «جَبَل طارِق» نسبةً إلى طارِق بن زياد، ومدينة غَرناطة هي Granada اليوم، وكذلك قُرطُبة Cordoba وطُلَيْطُلة Toledo.

في الجدول إلى اليسار بعض أسماء الأماكن الإسبانيّة الأخرى ذات الأصل العربيّ. لاحِظْ أنّ المَقطَع Guada- يُقصد به الكلمة العربيّة «وادي» والّتي تعني أيضاً «نهر».

أسماء بعض الأماكن بإسبانيا ذات الأصل العربيّ		
الكلمة الإسبانيّة	الأصل العربيّ	المعنى
Albufera	البُحَيْرة	*the lake*
Alborg	البُرْج	*the tower*
Alcázar	القَصر	*the palace*
Alhambra	الحَمْراء	*red castle*
Almeida	المائِدة	*the dining table*
Almadán	المَيْدان	*the field*
Almenara	المَنارة	*lighthouse; minaret*
Almansil	المَنزِل	*stopping place; house*
Guadalcazar	وادي القَصر	*river of the palace*
Guadahorra	وادي المَغارة	*cave river*
Guadalquivir	الوادي الكَبير	*great river*
Guadalahara	وادي الحَجَر	*stony river*
Guadilimar	الوادي الأحْمَر	*red river*
Alqueria	القَرْية	*the village*
Medinaceli	مَدينةُ سالم	*the city of Salim*
Almazara	المِعْصَرة	*(olive) oil press*
Arrecife	الرَصيف	*sidewalk*
Alcantara	القَنْطَرة	*the bridge*

قصر الحمراء

بُنيَ قصر الحمراء على قِمة تلّ يطلّ على غَرناطة آخر مدينة سقطت في الأندلس. والقصر عبارة عن قلعة تضمّ قصر الملك ومجموعة من الأبهاء والقاعات تحيط بها من الجانبين دواوين الدولة. وهناك أيضاً حمّام ومسجد. بُدئَ ببنائِه في القرن الثالث عشر واستمرّ البناء حتّى القرن الرابع عشر. ومن أهمّ أجزائه الأبهاء والأقواس القائمة على أعمدة رخاميّة أمّا البحرات والنوافير فتُضفي جمالاً وروعةً على القصر وأبهائه من النور المنعكِس عنها، وبخاصّة في قاعة السباع.

وقد كتب مؤلِّفون كثيرون عن الأندلس ونظم الشعراء القصائد فيها وسمّاها العرب «الفِردَوس المفقود». ومن الّذين وصفوا قصر الحمراء في الأندلس حديثاً سامي الكيّالي وهو أديب سوريّ وُلِدَ في حلب سنة ١٨٩٨ وأصدر جريدة «الحديث» عام ١٩٢٧ وكتب عدّة كتب ومثّل سورية في اليونيسكو. إليك ما كتب عن قصر الحمراء في غَرناطة.

داخل قصر الحمراء

«إنّني اليوم في كَنَف الحمراء. أقلعةٌ هي أم قصر، أم عدّة قصور؟ إنّها قلعة وقصور وحدائق قامت على هضبات تحيط بها قِمَم عالية صعبة المنحدَر، تتدفّق في سفحها الشماليّ مياه نهر «حِدرو» قُبَيْل التقائه بنهر التاج. وقد حُصِّنَ القصر بأسوار غُطِيَت بالمرمر.

سُمِّيَت الحمراء لأنّ أسوارها وجدرانها تضرب إلى الحمرة وربّما جاءت هذه التَسمية من لون التُربة الّتي قامت عليها ومعظمها مبنيّ من الخَزَف والكِلس والحصباء. دخلتُ قصر الحمراء وفي ذهني حشد من المعلومات عن ماضيه وحاضره، عن «بَهو السِباع» و«بهو البركة» و«قاعة الأختين» و«قاعة بين سراج». فمن هذه القاعات والأبهاء يتكوّن قصر الحمراء. اخترتُ المدخل إلى «باب العدل» وهو مدخل تعلوه قُبّة ضخمة برتقاليّة اللون تضرب إلى الحمرة ذو أروقة تعصف بها الرياح. أمّا برج العدل نفسه فهو أحد الأبراج الأربعة الّتي يتكوّن منها مدخل الحمراء. وقد بُنيَت واجهَتُه من عَقْدَيْن على شكْل حَدْوة الفَرس.

تتوسط نافوة بهو السِباع

وأعظم أبهاء قصر الحمراء بهو السِباع، إذ يبلغ طوله مئة قدم وعرضه خمسين، وأنت حين تسير بين أروقته الّتي قامت على أكثر من مئة عمود مَرمَريّ تقف مشدوهاً بتناسقها الجميل، وبعقودها المُزخرَفة، ولعلّ أظهر ما في البهو النافورة الّتي تحمل اثني عشر أسداً من المَرمَر الأبيض، يقذف كلّ منها المياه من فمه.

المَوَشّحات الأندلسيّة

المُوَشّح نوع من أنواع الشِعر فيه حريّة أكبر للشاعر في نَظْم الكلمات وهو من اختراع أهل الأندلس. نُظِمَ الكثير من شعر الموشّحات وغنّاه المغنون والمغنيات وصارت له شعبيّة كبيرة في شمال إفريقيا وبلاد الشام. وكان من أحسن الشعراء الوزير أبو عبد الله بن الخطيب شاعر الأندلس الّذي نظم الأبيات التالية: (غناء المغنية اللبنانيّة السيدة فيروز وتلحين الأخوين رحباني).

استمع إليها في التسجيل المرفق مع الكتاب عدّة مرّات، وحاول فهم هذه الأبيات بالاستعانة بمعجم عربيّ لتعرف ماذا يدور بين الحبيب وحبيبته. راجع الترجمة الإنكليزيّة في آخر صفحة من هذا الدرس.

أروقة بهو السباع القائمة على أعمدة كثيرة

لَو كانَ قَلْبي مَعي ما اختَرْتُ غَيْرَكُمْ ولا رَضيتُ سِواكُم في الهَوى بَدَلا

لَكِنَّهُ رَغِبٌ فيمَن يُعذِبُهُ ولَيْسَ يَقْبَلُ لا لَوْماً ولا عَتَباً

يا مَن حَوى وَرْدَ الرياضِ بِخَدِّهِ وحَكى قَضيبَ الخَيْزَرانِ بقدِّه

دَعْ عَنكَ ذا السَيْفَ الّذي جَرَّدْتَهُ عَيْناكَ أمْضى مِن مَضارِبِ حَدِّهِ

كُلِّ السُيوفِ قَواطِعٌ إنْ جُرِّدَتْ وحُسامُ لَحْظِكَ قاطِعٌ في غِمْدِهِ

إنْ شِئْتَ تَقْتُلُني فأنتَ مُحَكِّمٌ مَن ذا يُطالِبُ سَيِّداً في عَبْدِهِ؟

جاءَت مُعَذِبَتي في غَيْهَبِ الغَسَقِ كَأنَّها الكَوكَبُ الدُرِّيُّ في الأُفقِ

فَقُلْتُ: نَوَّرتِني يا خَيرَ زائِرَةٍ أما خشيتِ مِنَ الحُرّاسِ في الطُرُقِ؟

فَجاوَبَتْني ودَمْعُ العَيْنِ يَسْبقُها مَن يَرْكَبِ البَحْرَ لا يَخشى مِنَ الغَرَقِ

لَو تَعلَمينَ بِما أجِنُّ مِنَ الهَوى لَعَذَرْتِ أو لَظَلَمتِ إنْ لَم تَعذُري

لا تَحسَبي أنّي هَجَرتُكِ طائِعاً حَدَثٌ لَعَمْرُكِ رائِعٌ أنْ تُهجَري

ما أنتِ والوَعدَ الّذي تَعِدينَني إلاّ كَبَرقِ سَحابَةٍ لَم تَمطِرِ

تمرين ٤

Poems in general, and these verses in particular, are full of rhetorical devices such as those we have studied. Try to find examples of similes and metaphors in the lines above, write them down on a separate sheet of paper, and then translate their meanings into English. Compare your translation with the English translation found on the last page of this lesson right after the vocabulary list.

We offer a modest explanation of the poem to help frame your translation.

تَذَوَّق الثَقافَة العَرَبيَّة

The first two lines are the words said by the female sweetheart, who starts off by addressing her suitor in a formal manner as evidenced by the use of plural forms غَيْرَكُمْ and سِواكُم, suggesting that he might be a man of high stature and importance.

Lines 3-6 extol the charming characteristics of the lover. Check for similes in these lines. Bear in mind that the last six lines are from the suitor's perspective.

تمرين ٥

للمحادثة:

أ- صِفْ لزميلك في غرفة الصف زيارة قمت بها إلى مكان رائع الجمال وحاوِل أن تحكي هذه القصة بأسلوب يشبه أسلوب سامي الكيّالي الأديب السوري الّذي كتب الوصفَ أعلاه عن قصر الحمراء في هذا الدرس.

للكتابة:

ب- حاوِل أن تنظم قصيدة مثل القصيدة أعلاه مع العلم بأن قصيدتك قد تكون فيها حرية أكبر من القصائد التقليديّة.

تمرين ٦

أجب عن هذه الأسئلة وفق القصّة.

١- حدِّد الفكرة الرئيسة في نصّ "لمحة تاريخيّة".
٢- اذكر الأفكار الثانويّة.
٣- من كان حاكم شمال إفريقيا وقت فتح الأندلس؟
٤- في أي عام دخلت أوّل حملة إسلاميّة إلى الأندلس وما كان هدفها؟
٥- ما اسم أوّل عاصمة للأندلس، وهل كانت الأندلس دولة مستقلّة؟
٦- متى كان عصر الأندلس الذهبيّ؟
٧- عدِّد بعض الأسباب الّتي أدّت إلى ضَعف الحكم وبالتالي إلى سقوط الأندلس.
٨- متى انتهت الدولة الأندلسيّة؟
٩- ما الدرس الّذي يمكن أن يتعلّمه عرب اليوم من عرب الأندلس؟
١٠- أُسْرد تاريخ بلدة أو دولة من اختيارك باختصار.

تمرين ٧

أكمل الجمل الآتية بكلمات مناسبة وفق نصّ «لمحة تاريخيّة»:

١- نزل طُرَيْف بن مالك بإسبانيا ____________.

☐ مبكّراً ☐ سرّاً ☐ ضعيفاً ☐ مهزوماً

٢- كانت ____________ أوّل عاصمة للعرب في الأندلس.

☐ طُلَيْطُلة ☐ غَرناطة ☐ قُرطُبة ☐ إشبيلية

٣- سقطت الخلافة الأمويّة في الأندلس في العام ________.

☐ ٧١٢ ☐ ١٠٠٩ ☐ ١٠٣١ ☐ ١٠٨٥

٤- حكم ملوك الطوائف ________.

☐ دوَيْلات صغيرة ☐ المغرب العربيّ ☐ الجزائر والسنغال ☐ الدولة الأمويّة

٥- كانت ________ آخر مملكة عربيّة بالأندلس.

☐ غَرناطة ☐ دولة الموحّدين ☐ إشبيلية ☐ دولة المرابطين

تمرين ٨

أ- **أجب عن هذه الأسئلة وفق القصّة.**

١- حدِّد الفكرة الرئيسة في نصّ «قصر الحمراء»:

٢- اذكر الأفكار الثانويّة في نصّ «قصر الحمراء»:

٣- من كتب أحد النصوص وما أهم عمل له في رأيك؟

٤- لماذا أُطْلِقَ اسم «الحمراء»: على القصر؟

٥- ما اسم أكبر أبهاء القصر؟

ب- **بيّن إن كانت الجمل الآتية صواباً أو خطأ وفق النصّ وصحِّح الخطأ منها.**

١- قاد موسى بن نُصير أوّل حملة عسكريّة إلى إسبانيا.

٢- حكم العبّاسيّون الأندلس حوالي قرنين من الزمن.

٣- أعلن عبد الرحمن الناصر الأمير الأمويّ الخلافة في الأندلس.

٤- انتصر المسلمون على الأمراء المسيحيين في معركة العُقاب.

٥- دخل الجيش الإسبانيّ غرناطة عام ١٤٩٢.

تمرين ٩

أ- أكمل الجمل الآتية بكلمات مناسبة وفق نصّ «قصر الحمراء»:

١- ينبعِث الجمال في قاعة السِباع بخاصة من ________________.

☐ الأبهاء ☐ البحرات والنوافير ☐ دواوين الدولة ☐ الحمّام

٢- يقع قصر الحمراء وسط ________________ .

☐ نهرين كبيرين ☐ جبال منحدرة ☐ عدّة قلاع ☐ هضبات عالية

٣- سُمّي أحد أجزاء قصر الحمراء ________________.

☐ بهو البِركة ☐ نهر التاج ☐ قُمة المنحدر ☐ التُربة الحمراء

٤- دخل الكاتب القصر من باب ________________ .

☐ الكلس ☐ النافورة ☐ السِباع ☐ العدل

٥- تحمل النافورة اثني عشر ________________.

☐ قدماً ☐ أسداً ☐ بهواً ☐ رجلاً

ب- بيّن إن كانت الجمل الآتية صواباً أو خطأ وفق النصّ وصحّح الخطأ منها.

١- تمّ بناء قصر الحمراء في القرن الثالث عشر.

٢- مثّل الكيّالي الأندلس في اليونيسكو.

٣- بُنِيَ قصر الحمراء على شكل حَدْوة الفَرس.

٤- يحوي بهو السِباع أكثر من مئة عمود مرمريّ.

٥- يتكوّن مدخل القصر من أكثر من عشرة أبراج.

تمرين ١٠

أعد ترتيب الكلمات في كلّ جملة لتشكّل جملاً صحيحةً وفق القواعد أعلاه ثمّ ترجمها إلى الإنكليزيّة:

١- رأسِ من والي مقاتل على البلادِ جيشٍ خرج ألفَي

٢- الاقتصاد لكن يتحسّن والفنون والآداب لم انتهاء ازدهرت الحرب العلوم بعد

٣- بالإضافة مِن أحياء تتكوّن المدينة إلى ستّة التجاريّة السوق رئيسة تلك

٤- الأندلسيّة بن الشِعريّة لسانُ الخطيب الدينِ نظم القصائد أجمل الوزير

تمرين ١١

أعد ترتيب الجمل لتشكّل فِقرة مترابطة. الجملة الأولى في مكانها الصحيح.

١ صار مُعاوية بن أبي سُفيان والي الشام في عهد الخليفة الثاني عمر بن الخطاب.

٢ وكان الأمويّون يفضّلون العرب على غيرهم من المسلمين.

٣ وهكذا سقطت الدولة الأمويّة عام ٧٥٠ وانتقلت العاصمة إلى بغداد وقُتِلَ معظم الأمويّين.

٤ لذلك ظهرت معارضة شديدة ضدّ الأمويّين خصوصاً بين غير العرب في الجزيرة والعراق وفارس.

٥ لكنّ أحد أفراد الأسرة الأمويّة (عبد الرحمن بن مُعاوية) نجا من الموت وفرّ إلى الأندلس حيث أسّس دولة أمويّة هناك عام ٧٥٦.

٦ وفي عام ٧٦١ تمكّن مُعاوية من تأسيس الدولة الأمويّة ونقل العاصمة إلى دمشق.

٧ وقد استطاع مُعاوية الاستيلاء على الحكم في عهد عليّ بن أبي طالب الخليفة الرابع.

٨ وتحالَف العبّاسيّون أعداءُ الأمويّين مع الفرس وثاروا عليهم.

٩ قاوم الخليفة مروان الثاني الثورة على دولته طوال أيّام حكمه (من ٧٤٤ إلى ٧٥٠) لكنّ الثورة العبّاسيّة كانت أقوى منه.

رُكن التعبيرات المتداولة على الألسن

سَقَطَ أمامَ

سَقَطَتْ دولَتُهُم أمامَ العَبّاسيّينَ.	*to fall before (at the hands of)*

بالتَدريج / تَدريجيّاً

وبَدَأوا يَنْسَحِبونَ بالتَدْريجِ.	*gradually*

الواحِدةُ تِلْوَ الأخْرى

تساقَطَتِ المُدُنُ الأنْدَلُسيّة الواحِدةُ تِلْوَ الأخْرى	*one after another*

تُضْفي + مفعول به + على

تُضْفي جمالاً ورَوْعةً على القَصْرِ وأبْهائِه.	*imparting s.th. on*

القَواعِد

1. Diminutive Nouns التصغير

The diminutive allows a speaker to create a tiny or "wee" degree of a particular word. The Arabic diminutive follows three forms depending on the number of letters in the root.

a. Triliteral: Three-Letter Root

Comprised of a three-letter root, these diminutives take the form:

فُعَيْل (ة)			
lake	بُحَيْرة	⇐	بَحْر
garden	جُنَيْنة	⇐	جَنّة
a little after	بُعَيْدَ	⇐	بَعْدَ
puppy	كُلَيْب	⇐	كَلْب
town	كُوَيْت	⇐	كوت
name., m.	حُسَين	⇐	حَسَن
name, f.	أُمَيْمة	⇐	أمّ
name., m.	عُبَيْدُ الله	⇐	عَبْدُ الله

b. Quadriliteral: Four-Letter Root

فُعَيْعِل (ة)			
name, m.	سُلَيْمان	⇐	سَلْمان
booklet	كُتَيِّب	⇐	كِتاب
town	قُنَيْطِرة	⇐	قَنْطَرَة
name, f.	سُلَيْمى	⇐	سَلْمى
name, m.	مُحَيْسِن	⇐	مُحْسِن

c. Five-Letter Root

فُعَيْعِيل(ة)			
birdie	عُصَيْفير	⇐	عُصْفور

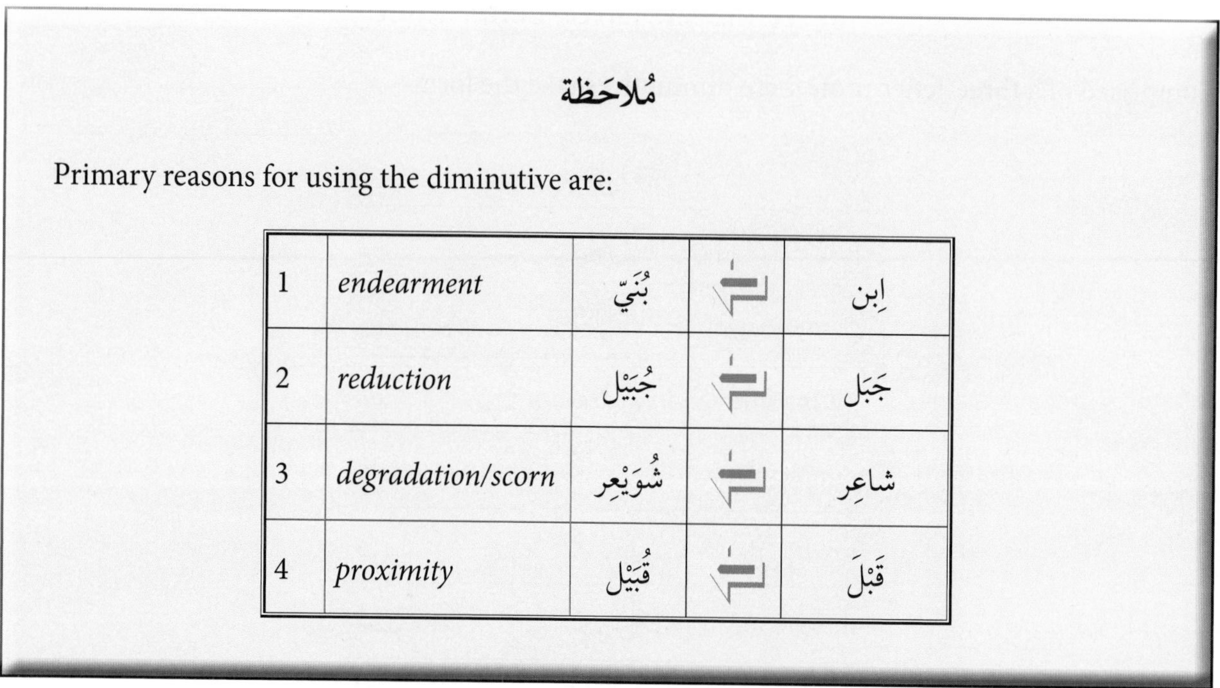

مُلاحَظة

Primary reasons for using the diminutive are:

1	*endearment*	بُنَيّ	⇐	اِبن
2	*reduction*	جُبَيْل	⇐	جَبَل
3	*degradation/scorn*	شُوَيْعِر	⇐	شاعِر
4	*proximity*	قُبَيْل	⇐	قَبْلَ

In the reading passage, دُوَيْلات is used to refer to petty states:

وانْتِقالُ الحُكْمِ إلى مُلوكِ دُوَيْلاتٍ صَغيرةٍ سُمّيت الطَوائف.

It should be noted that many of the diminutive examples cited in grammar books are archaic and have fallen out of use.

2. Collocation التَلازُم اللَفْظيّ

Certain words tend to co-occur with other words; for example *bar* in *bar of soap*, *steel bar*, *bar of chocolate*. Co-occuring words can be anything from verbs, prepositions, or even adjectives (e.g., remind s.o. of s.th., mad at s.o., amenable to s.th.). We find the same phenomenon in Arabic as can be seen in our main reading passages. For instance, تَصَبَّبَ immediately triggers the use of عَرَقاً, while سامَحَك is most often followed by الله (a phrase usually intended as a reprimand but quite literally means *May God forgive you*).

Let's take a look at the verb ضَرَبَ and how different collocations influence its meaning:

ضَرَبَ		
	الباب	*to knock*
	عُمْلة	*to mint*
	مَثَلاً	*provide an example*
ضَرَبَ ⇐	إلى + لَوْن	*a hue of*
	خَيْمةً	*to pitch a tent*
	أخماساً بِأسداس	*to rack one's brain*
	السَلام	*to salute*

تمرين ١٢

وافق من العمودين بين كلمات وردت في نصوص القراءة يتلازم بعضها مع بعض عادة.

١	تدفّق		أغنيّة
٢	عَصَفَت		اسماً
٣	نظم		العدوّ
٤	لحّن		عموداً
٥	أطْلق		الشِعر
٦	نَشِبَت		النهر
٧	فتح		الريح
٨	هزم		بلداً
			الحرب

3. Synonyms المترادفات

Synonyms are words that have the same or nearly the same meaning as another word or words. المترادفات rarely, if ever, have exactly the same meaning. This means that we, as speakers of Arabic, must take great care to choose the precise word that we intend, as المترادفات cannot be used interchangeably. In this lesson, several words occurred that have synonyms or near-synonyms (e.g., سور / جِدار / حائط).

تمرين ١٣

هات مُرادِفات عربيّة للكلمات الآتية، وردت في نصوص القراءة.

١ مُؤلِّف: ________	٢ أتى: ________
٣ عادَ: ________	٤ بَعَثَ: ________
٥ تِلْوَ: ________	٦ فَرْد: ________
٧ مَسْجِد: ________	٨ رُخام: ________
٩ عَقْد: ________	١٠ جَمال: ________
١١ استمرّ: ________	١٢ سنة: ________

تمرين ١٤

اختر كلمات من النصوص أعلاه تتناسب والفِئات التالية.

مِثال: (مدرسة) مادّة، طالب، أستاذ، كتاب، دراسة، اختبار، امتحان، قراءة، كتابة، مبنى، غرفة صف

١- (عِمارة) ________

٢- (حكومة) ________

٣- (عسكريّ) ________

٤- (جماعات دينيّة وعرقيّة وطائفيّة) ________

٥- (أدَب) ________

مُراجَعةُ القَواعِد

4. The Elative اِسْمُ التَفْضيل

Elatives use the أَفْعَل form followed by another noun in an إضافة structure.

١ | وفي السَنَةِ التاليةِ أرْسَلَ أفْضَلَ قادَتِهِ طارِقَ بْنَ زياد عَلى رأسِ جَيْشٍ مِنْ ٧٠٠٠ مِنَ الأمازيغ..

In example 1 we see that أفْضَل closely follows the أفْعَل pattern and acts as a مُضاف with قادَته playing the role of مُضاف إليه. The comparative form in Arabic is very similar to that of the elative, with one important exception: the comparative is followed by مِن (i.e., أفْعَل مِن).

٢ | وَما كانَ حالُ المُوَحِّدينَ أفْضَلَ مِنْ حالِ المُرابِطينَ.

As you can see أفْضَل + مِن creates the comparative and in example 2 means *better than*.

5. The Passive مَبْني لِلمَجْهول

We use this structure when we do not wish to mention the agent or subject of the verb. The ضَمّة + كَسْرة sequence that occurs in perfect verbs allows us to recognize and functionally use this structure in our speech:

قَتَلَ	⇐	قُتِلَ	*was killed*	حَكَمَ الأمويّون الأنْدَلُسَ حَتّى سَنَةِ ٧٥٠ حين سَقَطَتْ دَوْلَتُهم أمامَ العَبّاسيّينَ وَقُتِلَ مُعْظَمُهم.
حَصَّنَ	⇐	حُصِّنَ	*was fortified*	وَقَدْ حُصِّنَ القَصْرُ بأسْوارٍ غُطِّيَتْ بالمَرمَر.
غَطّى	⇐	غُطِّيَ	*was covered*	
سَمّى	⇐	سُمِّيَ	*was named*	سُمِّيَت الحَمْراءُ لأنَّ أسْوارَها وجُدْرانَها تَضْرِبُ إلى الحُمْرة.
بَدَأَ	⇐	بُدِئَ	*was started*	بُدِئَ بِبِنائه في القَرْنِ الثالِثَ عَشَرَ.
نَظَمَ	⇐	نُظِمَ	*was composed*	نُظِمَ الكَثيرُ مِنْ شِعْرِ المُوَشَّحات.

If, however, the perfect verb contains long vowels such as an ا or a ى, then these long vowels turn into a ي:

بَنى	⇐	بُنِيَ	was built	بُنِيَ قَصْرُ الحَمْراء عَلى قِمةِ تلٍّ.
				وَقَدْ بُنِيَتْ واجِهتُهُ مِنْ عقدَيْنِ عَلى شَكْلِ حَذْوةِ الفَرَس.

تمرين ١٥

In the reading passages—to include the verses of poetry—identify the eleven instances of the elative and six instances of the passive (other than those found in the previous examples).

تمرين ١٦

أ- **أجِب عن الأسئلة وفق نصّ الاستماع:**

١- ما الفكرة الرئيسة في النص؟ عدِّد بعض الأفكار الثانوية.

٢- اكتب عنواناً للنصّ.

٣- إلى أين اتّجهت السفينة؟

٤- ماذا سُمِّي عبد الرحمن بن مُعاوية؟

ب- **اكتب «خطأ» أو «صواب» إلى جانب كلّ جملة ثمّ صحِّح الجمل الخطأ:**

١- استولى الملك ويتزا على ممتلكات سارة.

٢- طلب الخليفة من والي شمال إفريقيا مساعدة سارة للحصول على حقّها.

٣- التقت سارة بالأمير عبد الرحمن عند زيارتها لدمشق.

٤- جعل عبد الرحمن عاصمته إشبيليّة.

٥- تزوّجت سارة وعاشت في شمال إفريقيا.

ج- **لَخِّص نصّ الاستماع بحوالَيْ مئة كِلمة.**

د- أكمِل الجمل الآتية بالاختيار المناسب وفق نصّ الاستماع:

١- لسارة ____________.

☐ عَمّ واحد ☐ عَمّان ☐ ثلاثة أعمام ☐ أربعة أعمام

٢- ذهبت سارة إلى دمشق ____________.

☐ لتتعرّف على الخليفة ☐ لتطلب المساعدة ☐ لتتزوّج رجلاً ☐ لزيارة عمّها

٣- وُلِدَ لسارة ____________.

☐ ولد واحد ☐ ولدان ☐ ثلاثة أولاد ☐ أربعة أولاد

٤- تزوّجت سارة من ____________.

☐ عبد الرحمن بن مُعاوية ☐ عيسى بن مزاحم

☐ ابن هشام ☐ والي شمال إفريقيا

٥- سكنت سارة وزوجها في ____________.

☐ دمشق ☐ قرطبة ☐ إشبيليّة ☐ شمال إفريقيا

تَذَوَّق الثَقافَة العَرَبيَّة

The Spelling of ابن

The word ابن is spelled with همزة وصل, whose seat is an ألف. When this word is in its initial position in the sentence or phrase, the ألف is retained. However, if the word occurs in the middle of a sentence or phrase, the ألف is dropped.

ابْنُ خَلْدون

عَبْدُ الرَحْمنِ بنُ خَلْدون

المُفْرَدات

to attract	(v.)	اِجْتِذاب	(يَجتَذِبُ)	اِجْتَذَبَ
to invent	(v.)	اِختِراع	(يَختَرِعُ)	اِختَرَعَ
to lead (to)	(v.)	تأدية (إلى)	(يُؤَدِّي)	أدّى
man of letters, educated, refined	(n., m.)	أُدَباء	ج	أديب
to remove, to drive away, to banish	(v.)	إزاحة	(يُزيحُ)	أزاحَ
to flourish, to prosper, to thrive	(v.)	اِزدِهار	(يَزدَهِرُ)	اِزدَهَرَ
exploration, reconnaissance, investigation	(v.)	اِستِطلاع	(يَستَطلِعُ)	اِستَطلَعَ
to seek the help of	(v.)	اِستِعانة	(يَستَعينُ)	اِستَعانَ
lion	(n., m.)	أُسود	ج	أَسَد
to allot generously, to grant	(v.)	إضفاء	(يُضْفي)	أَضْفى
to launch, to fire	(v.)	إطلاق	(يُطلِقُ)	أطلَقَ
to name, to give a name				أطلَقَ اسماً على
to recognize, to acknowledge, to confess	(v.)	اِعتِراف (بـِ)	(يَعتَرِفُ)	اِعتَرَفَ
to withdraw, to retreat	(v.)	اِنسِحاب	(يَنسَحِبُ)	اِنسَحَبَ
to be reflected	(v.)	اِنْعِكاس	(يَنْعَكِسُ)	اِنْعَكَسَ
Berber of North Africa	(n., m.)	بَرْبَر	ج	بَرْبَري

tower, castle	(n., m.)	أبراج / بُروج	ج	بُرْج
hall, parlor	(n., m.)	أبْهاء	ج	بَهْوٌ
to pour forth, to gush	(v.)	تَدَفُّق	(يَتَدَفَّقُ)	تَدَفَّقَ
soil	(n., f.)			تُرْبة
to translate	(v.)	تَرْجَمَة	(يُتَرْجِمُ)	تَرْجَمَ
to fall down, to rain down from everywhere	(v.)	تَساقُط	(يَتَساقَطُ)	تَساقَطَ
to cooperate	(v.)	تَعاوُن	(يَتعاوَنُ)	تَعاوَنَ
to be created, to be formed	(v.)	تَكَوُّن	(يَتَكَوَّنُ)	تَكَوَّنَ
after	(prep.)	(الواحِد تِلْوَ الآخَر)		تِلْوَ
to be distinguished, to be set apart	(v.)	تَمَيُّز	(يَتَمَيَّزُ)	تَمَيَّزَ
to dispute, to contend, to rival	(v.)	تَنازُع	(يَتَنازَعُ)	تَنازَعَ
to be well-coordinated, symmetrical	(v.)	تَناسُق	(يَتَناسَقُ)	تَناسَقَ
to compete, to rival	(v.)	تَنافُس	(يَتَنافَسُ)	تَنافَسَ
to revolt, to rebel	(v.)	ثَوْرة	(يَثورُ)	ثارَ
governor, ruler	(n., m.)	حُكّام	ج	حاكِم
horseshoe	(n., f.)	حَذَوات	ج	حَذْوة
crowd, gathering, assembly	(n., m.)	حُشود	ج	حَشْد

pebbles, gravel	(n., f.)			حَصْباء
to fortify, to strengthen	(v.)	تَحْصين	(يُحَصِّنُ)	حَصَّنَ
pottery, porcelain, ceramics	(n., m.)			خَزَف
governmental office, chancellery	(n., m.)	دَواوين	ج	ديوان
gold	(n., m.)			ذَهَب
mind, intellect	(n., m.)	أذْهان	ج	ذِهْن
to review, to go over	(v.)	مُراجَعة	(يُراجِعُ)	راجَعَ
marble	(n., m.)			رُخام
colonnade, portico	(n., m.)	أرْوِقة	ج	رِواق
beauty, charm, splendor, fear, alarm	(n., f.)			رَوْعة
wall, fence	(n., m.)	أسْوار	ج	سور
to shade (into a color)	(v.)	ضَرْب (إلى)	(يَضْرِبُ)	ضَرَبَ
a shade of red				ضارِبٌ إلى الحُمرة
faction, sect	(n., f.)	طَوائِف	ج	طائِفة
enemy, foe	(n., m.)	أعْداء		عَدوّ
breadth, width	(n., m.)	عُروض	ج	عَرْض
military, soldier	(adj.)			عَسْكَريّ

to storm, to blow violently	(v.)	عَصْف	(يَعصِفُ)	عَصَفَ
arch, vault	(n., m.)	عُقود	ج	عَقْد
building, architecture	(n., f.)	عَمارات		عَمارة
to cover, to wrap, to conceal	(v.)	تَغطية	(يُغَطِّي)	غَطَّى
to conquer	(v.)	فَتْح (فَتَحَ بَلَداً)	(يَفتَحُ)	فَتَحَ
to flee, to run away	(v.)	فِرار	(يَفِرُّ)	فَرَّ
individual, member	(n., m.)	أفْراد	ج	فَرْد
paradise	(n., m.)	فَراديس	ج	فِرْدَوْس
horse, mare	(n., m.)	أفْراس	ج	فَرَس
to lose	(v.)	فُقْدان	(يَفقِدُ)	فَقَدَ
dome	(n., f.)	قِباب / قُبَب	ج	قُبّة
to throw, to cast	(v.)	قَذْف	(يَقذِفُ)	قَذَفَ
century; horn	(n., m.)	قُرون	ج	قَرْن
poem, ode	(n., f.)	قَصائِد	ج	قَصيدة
fortress, castle	(n., f.)	قِلاع	ج	قَلعة
lime, limestone	(n., m.)			كِلْس
side, shadow, shelter	(n., m.)	أكْناف	ج	كَنَف

to compose, to set to music	(v.)	تَلحين	(يُلَحِّنُ)	لَحَّنَ
glimpse, brief insight	(n., f.)	لَمَحات	ج	لَمْحة
author, writer	(n., m.)	مُؤَلِّفون	ج	مُؤَلِّف
imminent, encircling, surrounding	(act. p.)			مُحْدِق
attached, enclosed	(pass. p.)			مُرفَق
marble	(n., m.)			مَرْمَر
chronic, enduring	(act. p.)			مُزمِن
decorated	(pass. p.)			مُزَخْرَف
independent	(act. p.)			مُسْتَقِلّ
baffled, confused, perplexed	(n., m.)	مَشْدوهون	ج	مَشْدوه
battle	(n., f.)	مَعارِك	ج	مَعْركة
lost	(pass. p.)			مَفْقود
warrior, fighter, combatant	(act. p.)	مُقاتِلون	ج	مُقاتِل
slope, incline, descent (of river)	(pass. p.)	مُنحَدَرات	ج	مُنْحَدَر
reflected	(act. p.)			مُنْعَكِس
fountain	(n., f.)	نَوافير / نافورات	ج	نافورة
to survive	(v.)	نَجاة	(يَنْجو)	نَجا

to break out (war / rebellion)	(v.)	(يَنشَبُ) نُشوب (الحَرْب/ الثَّوْرة)		نَشِبَ
to arrange, to organize, to compose (verse)	(v.)	نَظْم	(يَنْظِم)	نَظَمَ
hill	(n., f.)	هِضاب / هَضَبات	ج	هَضْبة

If my heart had been with me I would not have chosen another
But he is desirous of one who torments him
Oh to those whose cheeks are roses in an oasis

Put away that sword you have unsheathed

All swords cut when unsheathed

If you want, kill me, for you are the judge

My tormentor came at the darkness of twilight
I said: you fill me with light, oh finest of visitors

She answered me with a tear preceding it

If you only knew how crazy in love I am, you would have apologized
Do not think that I have forsaken you willfully
You and the promise that you made me are no more

I would not have been content to love anyone else other
Who does not accept blame nor chide

And whose slim body; a bamboo shoot

Your eyes are sharper than the cutting edge of a sword
But your eyes cut when sheathed
Who would question what a master does to his slave?

As if she were a brilliant star on the horizon

Weren't you afraid of the guards on the streets?
Whosoever rides the seas doesn't fear drowning

Or felt guilty if you hadn't apologized

By your life, it was an awful event that you were forsaken
Than lightning from a cloud that doesn't bring rain

الدَرْسُ الثامِن عشر

Objectives

- Learning about philosophy and how to describe and explain abstract ideas
- Introduction to Averroes: his philosophy and his exegeses
- Learning about Averroes and his lasting impact on the West, life achievements, and intellectual pursuits
- **مُراجَعة القواعد:** ضَمائِر النَصْب المُنْفَصِلة، والاسمُ المَقصور

رُكنُ المُفْرَداتِ الجَديدةِ

to accuse	اِتَّهَمَ (يَتَّهِمُ) اِتِّهام (بِـ)
to embrace	اِعتَنَقَ (يَعْتَنِقُ) اِعْتِناق
to be distinguished	اِمْتازَ (يَمْتازُ) اِمْتِياز
to support	أَيَّدَ (يُؤَيِّدُ) تأييد
proof	بُرْهان ج بَراهين
to translate	تَرْجَمَ (يُتَرْجِمُ) تَرْجَمة
argument, debate	جَدَل
difference, dispute	خِلاف ج خِلافات
poison	سَمّ ج سُموم
to believe	صَدَّقَ (يُصَدِّقُ) تَصْديق
fight, struggle	صِراع ج صِراعات
ideology, dogma, tenet	عَقيدة ج عَقائِد
status	مَنزِلة

تمرين ١

واِفِق بين كلمات تتشابه بالمعنى واكتب كلّ اثنتين في الوسط.

١	توفّي		استمرّ
٢	قانون		عالَم
٣	حَقّ		آية
٤	قصر		دُفِن
٥	شرح		شَرْع
٦	كَوْن		تفسير
٧	دام		بَلاط
٨	سورة		صَدَّق
			نظريّة

تمرين ٢

واِفِق بين كلمات من العمودين لا تتوافق بالمعنى واكتب الكلمتين في الوسط:

١	اتّهم		إيمان
٢	رَضِيَ		فِكْر
٣	حُبّ		باطِن
٤	مخالِف		عفا (عن)
٥	كُفْر		أيّد
٦	ظاهِر		كُرْه
٧	غِذاء		مُلائِم
٨	هاجم		غَضِب
			سُمّ

تمرين ٣

اخترِ الكَلِمةَ الّتي لا تُناسِب باقي الكَلِماتِ في كُلِّ مَجْموعةٍ وبَيِّن السَبَب:

١-	مذهب	طريقة	مدفَن	نظرّية
٢-	صِراع	شَرْع	فِقْه	قاضٍ
٣-	فَكَّرَ	فَهِم	اعتقَد	دَفَن
٤-	فَلْسفة	تهافُت	تفسير	فِقْه
٥-	لخَّص	نَشَأ	تُوفِّيَ	وُلِد
٦-	خَلَقَ	صَنَعَ	مَنَعَ	جَعَلَ

تمرين ٤

للنقاش قبل قراءة القصّة:

١- ماذا تعرف عن ابن رشد المسمى (Averroes) في الغرب؟
٢- أين استقرّ العرب المسلمون في أوروبا؟
٣- كيف ساهم العرب المسلمون في نظرك بالحضارة الغربية؟
٤- هل زرت جنوب إسبانيا أو قرأت عنه؟ ماذا يميزه عن باقي أوروبا؟

ابن رُشد
فيلسوف ومفكّر أندلسيّ

تمثال ابن رشد في مدينة قرطبة

هو أبو الوليد محمّد بن أحمد بن رُشد وُلِد في قرطبة عام ١١٢٦ للميلاد وتُوفّي في مَرّاكُش عام ١١٩٨ ودُفِن فيها، لكنّه نُقِل بعد ثلاثة أشهر ليُدفَنَ في مدفَن أسرتِه في مدينتِه قُرطُبة حيث كان جدُّه قاضياً فيها وكذلك والده.

نشأ ابن رشد على حُبِّ العلم واللغة والأدب، وامتاز في علم الطبّ وقد أخذه عن أبي مروان البَلَنسي وعن أبي جَعفَر هارون وألّف فيه كتاب «الكُلّيّات». ودرس أيضاً الفِقْه مثل والدِه وجدِّه، إلاّ أنّ الفلسفة كانت أهمّ ما عُنِيَ به أبو الوليد واشتُهِرَ بها في المغرب

ابن رشد لوحة أثينا من الفنان رافاييل ١٥٠٩

العربيّ ومشرِقه وفي أوروبا حيث عرفه الأوروبيّون باسم Averroes. وكان على صلة بالفيلسوف ابن طُفَيْل الّذي عرّفه على الخليفة أبي يعقوب يوسف في المغرِب الّذي عيّنه في سنة ١١٦٩ قاضيَ إشبيليّة ثمّ قاضيَ قرطبة حوالَيْ عام ١١٧١، ثمّ تلاه ابنه المنصور وعيّنه قاضيَ القُضاة بقرطبة في أواخِر حياته.

لكن ابن رشد مرّ بمشكلة كبيرة، ففي عام ١١٩٥ أيّام حُكْم الخليفة المنصور اتّهمه أعداؤه ومعظمهم من علماء الدين بالكُفر وصدّقهم الخليفة وأبعده بعد أن كان مقرَّباً منه وحرّم قراءة الكتب الفلسفيّة. والسبب في كُرْه أعدائه له هو أنّ آراء ابن رشد كانت مخالفة لآرائهم وأنّ بعضها كان مخالِفاً للعقيدة الإسلاميّة. وبما أنّ المنصور كان يسير إلى الحرب ضدّ الفونس الثامن مَلِك قِشتالة أراد أن يُرضيَ الرأي العام في الأندلس، لكنّه حين عاد إلى مرّاكش وابتعد عن جوّ التنازُع في الأندلس رَضيَ عن ابن رشد وعفا عنه ودعاه إلى بَلاطه، إلاّ أنّ عودته إلى الحياة العامة لم تَدُمْ طويلاً، وتُوفّي أبو الوليد بعد بضعة أشهر.

أعماله

إنّ أهمّ عمل قام به ابن رشد هو شرح كتب أرسطو وتفسيرها، وكذلك تلخيص بعض الكتب والمقالات وشرحها لأرسطو وأفلاطون وبطليموس وجالينوس والفارابي وابن سينا وابن باجة. فقد لخّص كتاب «الجمهوريّة» لأفلاطون وشرح ولخّص لأرسطو كتباً عديدة. كما لخّص تسع مقالات من كتاب «الحيوان».

وكان لابن رشد مقالات عديدة أصليّة في المَنطِق وعلم النفس والعقل والفَلَك والحِكمة والجَدَل الفلسفيّ والطبّ والفِقه وعلم الكلام. وله كتب منها «الكلّيّات» في الطبّ و«بداية المُجتَهِد ونهاية المُقتَصِد» في الفِقْه و«فصل المقال» في علم الكلام و«تهافُت التهافُت» في الفلسفة، وهذا الكتاب الأخير ردّ على كتاب «تهافُت الفلاسفة» لأبي حامِد الغزالي

شروح ابن رشد لكتاب أرسطو «عن الروح»

الّذي هاجم فيه الفلسفة والفلاسفة. جدير بالذِكر أنّ «تهافُت التهافُت» كُتِب بعد كتابة «تهافُت الفلاسفة» بحواليَ قرن من الزمان في ١١٨٠ م تقريباً.

تأثيره في الغرب

تعرّف الغرب على أرسطو وأفكاره من خلال شروح ابن رشد الّتي تُرجِمَت إلى اللاتينيّة، فهي أوّل من عرّف الغرب بالفِكر اليونانيّ القديم والتفكير الفلسفيّ. واعتنق العديد من المفكِّرين الأوروبيّين نظريّات ابن رشد وتكوّن حولها مذهب «الرُشديّة» نسبةً له وقام حول هذا المذهب صِراع عَنيف في أوروبا. فقد هاجمت الكنيسة الرشديّين وحرّم أسقُف باريس القول بهذه النظريّات، كما ألّف توما الأكويني رسالة ضدّ أفكاره.

النقاش بين توما الأكويني وابن رشد

فلسفته

حاول ابن رشد الوِفاق بين الدين والفلسفة أو بين الإيمان والعقل وذلك بالإجابة عن أسئلة هامّة كموقِف الدين من الفلسفة، والتوافق بين الشرع والفلسفة، وقِدَم العالَم، وعِلْم الله بالجزئيات، والبَعث الجسماني، وسنعرض هنا رأيه في السؤالين الأولين. أمّا بالنسبة لموقِف الدين من الفلسفة فأكّد ابن رشد أنّ الشرع يطلب دراسة الفلسفة وعلوم المنطِق لأنّ الفلسفة إنّما هي النظر بالموجودات والتفكير بها وأنّ هذا النظر يُرينا إيّاها مصنوعات لها صانع وهو الله. وأيّد أبو الوليد رأيه بآيات من القرآن:

* أوَ لَمْ يَنْظُرُوا في مَلَكوتِ السَّماواتِ وَالأرْضِ وَمَا خَلَقَ اللهُ مِن شَيْءٍ؟ * الأعراف ١٨٥

* أفَلا يَنْظُرُونَ إلىَ الإبِلِ كَيْفَ خُلِقَتْ وَإلىَ السَّماءِ كَيْفَ رُفِعَتْ * الغاشية ١٧

* وَيَتَفَكَّرونُ في خَلْقِ السَّماواتِ وَالأرْضِ * آل عمران ١٩١

بعض الفلاسفة الإغريقيين المشاهير

أمّا في ما يتعلّق بالتوافق بين الشرع والفلسفة فقد رأى أنّ لا خِلاف بينهما لأنّ الإسلام حقّ ونتيجة التفكير الفلسفيّ حقّ، والحقُّ لا يكون ضدّ الحقّ. إلاّ أنّ للشرع في رأيه ظاهراً وباطِناً، ظاهِراً سهل يفهمه جميع الناس، وباطِناً صعباً لا يفهمه سِوى الفلاسفة ويفهم بعضه المتكلّمون. ويعتقِد أنّ هناك ثلاثة أنواع من الناس: البُرهانيّون والجدَليّون والخطابيّون. والبُرهانيّون هم الفلاسفة، والجدليّون هم المتكلّمون كالمُعتزِلة الّذين يقتربون من الحقّ ولا يبلغونَهُ، والخطابيّون هم عامّة الناس. ويعتقد أنّ العِلم كالغِذاء، «قد يكون رأي هو سُم في حقّ نوع من الناس، وغذاء في حقّ نوع آخر. فمَن جعل الآراء كلّها مُلائِمة لكلّ نوع من أنواع الناس بمنزلة مَن جعل الأشياء كلّها أغذية لجميع الناس.» فإذا أدّى النظر البرهانيّ إلى معرفة اتّفقت وظاهر الشرع فلا خِلافَ بين الشرع والفلسفة. أمّا إذا أدّى النظر البُرهانيّ إلى معرفة تخالُف الشرع، فهي إنما تُخالِف ظاهِرَه لا باطنَه، ويمكن أن نصل إلى الباطِن بتأويل هذا الظاهِر أي بشرحه وتفسيره، وبذلك يتمّ التوافق.

تمرين ٥

للمحادثة:

أوّلاً: صِفْ لزميلك في غرفة الصف ما فهمت من تفسيرات ابن رشد في ما يتعلّق بالعلاقة بين الدين والفلسفة.

ثانياً: اشرح لزميلك سبب إثارة خلافات بين ابن رشد والخليفة المنصور، وماذا حدث في نهاية المطاف؟

للكتابة: حاوِل أن تُرتِّب أفكارك حول عقائد ابن رشد كما وردت في النصّ أعلاه واكتب ما استوعبت من قراءة النصّ عن تاريخه وشخصيّته وكتبه وفلسفته.

تمرين ٦

أجب عن هذه الأسئلة وفق القصّة:

١- ما أهم شيء عرفته من النصّ عن ابن رُشد؟

٢- اذكر أمرين تراهما هامّين في حياة ابن رُشد.

٣- اذكر ثلاثة على الأقلّ من كتاباته.

٤- كيف أثّر أبو الوليد بالغرب؟

٥- بأي شيء اتُّهِم ابن رُشد؟

تمرين ٧

أ- **أكمل الجمل الآتية بأفضل إجابة وفق نصّ القراءة:**

١- تُوفّيَ ابن رُشد عن ________ .

☐ ٤٦ عاماً ☐ ٦٨ عاماً ☐ ٧٠ عاماً ☐ ٧٢ عاماً

٢- اشتُهر ابن رشد ________ .

☐ حاكماً وزعيماً ☐ فيلسوفاً وطبيباً ☐ عالماً بالفَلَك ☐ بالشِعر والأدب

٣- أبعد الخليفة ابن رُشد كي يُرضيَ ________ .

☐ ملِك قشتالة ☐ أهل المغرب ☐ أفلاطون ☐ الرأي العام

٤- من أعمال ابن رشد الأصليّة ________ .

☐ تهافُت التهافُت ☐ تهافُت الفلاسفة ☐ الحيوان ☐ الجمهوريّة

٥- **تكوّن في أوروبا** ________ الرُشديّة من المفكّرين الّذين اعتقدوا بأفكار ابن رُشد.

☐ فِكر ☐ نظريّة ☐ مذهب ☐ شَرع

٦- اعتقد ابن رُشد أنّ ________ بين الدين والفلسفة ممكن.

☐ الخلاف ☐ الشَرع ☐ الوِفاق ☐ المَنطِق

٧- من الأمور الهامّة الّتي حاول ابن رشد الإجابة عن أسئلة حولها ________ .

☐ البعث ☐ القرآن ☐ الفلسفة ☐ الإبل

٨- ________ سورة من سُوَر القرآن.

☐ الآيات ☐ البعث ☐ السماوات ☐ الأعراف

٩- الشَرع والفلسفة كِلاهما ________ .

☐ بُرهان ☐ حقّ ☐ ظاهِر ☐ باطِن

ب- **بيّن إن كانت الجمل الآتية صواباً أو خطأ وفق النصّ وصحّح الخطأ منها**

١- انحدر ابن رُشد من أسرة من القضاة.
٢- تعلّم بن رشد الطب في جامعة أوروبيّة.
٣- إنّ سبب غضب الخليفة على ابن رشد هو خروجه عن العقيدة الإسلاميّة.
٤- تُوفِّيَ ابن رُشد ودُفِن في قرطبة.
٥- كانت الكنيسة ضدّ أفكار ابن رُشد.
٦- يرى ابن رشد أنّ القرآن يدعو الإنسان إلى التفكير وبالتالي فهو لا يتعارض مع الفلسفة.
٧- يفهم عامّة الناس والفلاسفة وغيرهم كلّ الأمور.

تمرين ٨

اِختَر كلمات من النصوص أعلاه تتناسب والفِئات التالية.

١- فُروع المعرفة والدراسة disciplines: ____________________
٢- الأسرة: ____________________
٣- مَناصِب positions: ____________________
٤- أدوات الربط بالفقرة الثانية من "فلسلفته": ____________________

تمرين ٩

أعد ترتيب الجمل لتشكّل فِقرة مترابطة. الجملة الأولى في مكانها الصحيح:

١- وُلِد ابنُ خَلِّكان في عام ١٢١١ م بالعراق من أسرة البرامِكة المشهورة.
ولا يوجَد إلاّ كتاب الواقِدي بهذه الأهمّيّة.
عيَّنه السلطان بيبَرس قاضيَ القُضاة في دمشق بعد أن صار عالِماً معروفاً.
ويُعتبَر كتابه هذا مرجعاً هامّاً في تاريخ الشخصيّات العربيّة والإسلاميّة.
درس علوم الدين في حلب ودمشق والقاهرة.
وهي الأسرة الّتي كان منها وُزَراء هارون الرشيد.
وهذا الكتاب يحوي سيَرَ أكثر من ٨٠٠ رجل مشهور.
ألّف ابن خَلِّكان "كتاب وَفَيات الأعيان".

رُكن التعبيرات المتداولة على الألسن

على صِلةٍ بِـ

وَكانَ (ابْن رُشْد) عَلى صِلةٍ بالفَيْلَسوفِ ابْن طُفَيْل.	*in touch with*

مِن خِلالِ

تَعَرَّفَ الغَرْبُ عَلى أَرَسطو وَفَهْمِهِ مِنْ خِلالِ شُروحاتِ ابْنِ رُشد.	*via, by way of, through, from*

نسبةً لـ / بالنِسْبَةِ لِـ

توَتكَوَّنَ حَولَها مَذْهَبُ "الرُّشْديّة" نِسْبَةً لَهُ. أمّا بالنسْبَةِ لِمَوْقِفِ الدينِ مِنَ الفَلْسَفَةِ فَـ . . .	*with regards to, in respect to*

في ما يَتعَلَّقُ بـ

أمّا في ما يَتعَلَّقُ بالتوافُقِ بَيْنَ الشَرْعِ والفَلْسَفِةِ فَقَدْ رأى أنَّ لا خِلافَ بَيْنَهُما.	*concerning, regarding*

ما دامَ طَويلاً / لَم يَدُمْ طَويلاً

إلاّ أنّ عَودَتَه إلى الحَياةِ العامّةِ لَمْ تَدُمْ طَويلاً.	*did not last long*

في أواخِر + تَوقيت

في أَواخِرِ حَياتِه.	*at the end of; the final stages of*

بما أنَّ

بِما أنّ المَنصورَ كانَ يَسُ إلى الحَرْبِ ضِدّ الفونْس الثامِن.	*since, because*

جَديرٌ بالذِكْرِ أنّ

جَديرٌ بالذِكْرِ أنّ "تهافُت التَهافُت" كُتِبَ بعْدَ كِتابةِ "تَهافُت الفَلاسِفة".	*it's worth mentioning; it is worthy to mention*

تمرين ١٠

أعد ترتيب الكلمات في كل مجموعة لتشكّل جملاً مُفيدةً:

١ أستاذي لي النسبيّة لم فشرحها أفهم لأينشتاين النظريّة

٢ بغرناطة في ونشأ طُفَيل ببلدة وُلِد الأندلس ابن آش

٣ مِن ابنتِه على جارنا رَنا عِماد خِلال تعرّفنا أبي

٤ تنجح توافق عملها أن حاولَت بين ودراستها لَمى فَلَمْ

٥ نجيب إلى مؤلّفات كبيرٌ الأجنبيّة محفوظ اللغاتِ عددٌ تُرجِمَ من

مُراجَعةُ القَواعِد

1. Independent Accusative Pronouns ضَمائِر النَصْب المُنْفَصِلة

When attempting to use a sentence that has both a direct and an indirect pronoun ascribed to one verb (e.g., *I gave it to her*), we have to use a base on which to hang our direct pronoun. Consider the following scenario:

١
آدَم: مَن أعْطاكَ تِلْكَ الحَقيبة؟
نوح: أُخْتي أعْطَتْني إيّاها.

As can be seen in example 1, we use إيّا to form a base which can accept most any attached pronoun. Examine the following table:

	مؤنّث		مُذكّر	
المُخاطَب	إيّاكَ	أنْتَ	إيّاكِ	أنْتِ
	إيّاكُما	أنْتُما	إيّاكُما	أنْتُما
	أيّاكُم	أنْتُم	إيّاكُنَّ	أنْتُنَّ
الغائب	إيّاها	هِيَ	إيّاه	هُوَ
	إيّاهما	هُما	إيّاهما	هُما
	إيّاهُنَّ	هُنَّ	إيّاهُم	هُم

This construction serves as direct objects of verbs, especially when the object precedes the verb as it does in the opening prayer of the Qur'an:

٢ | إِيّاكَ نَعْبُدُ وَإِيّاكَ نَسْتَعِينُ

تمرين ١١

Translate the following sentences into Arabic, using independent accusative pronouns.

1. I asked him for his book, so he gave it to me.
2. She cut the apple up and fed it to them.
3. We asked him about the photographs from his trip, and he showed them to us.

2. Defective Nouns الاسم المقصور

You may have wondered why قاضٍ *judge* was spelled without its ياء when it was indefinite, but retains its ياء when definite(القاضي) .

This noun belongs to a set of nouns known as الاسم المقصور all of which end in a ياء, and behave in following manner: when definite they retain their ياء and when indefinite the ياء disappears and تنوين كسر takes its place. The ياء is also restored when in dual form (قاضيان) or when it is the first part of an إضافة (e.g., قاضي القضاة).

تمرين ١٢

أ- **أجب عن الأسئلة وفق نصّ الاستماع:**

١- ما الفكرة الرئيسة في النصّ؟
٢- حدِّد فكرتين ثانويتَيْن في النصّ.
٣- لماذا أمَرَ الخليفة بقتل ابن المُقفّع؟
٤- ما أعمال ابن المُقَفّع المذكورة بالنصّ؟

ب- **اكتب «خطأ» أو «صواب» إلى جانب كلّ جملة ثمّ صحّح الجمل الخطأ:**

١- كان ابن المُقَفَّع من الزرادشتيين أوّل حياته.
٢- صار ابن المُقفّع وزيراً للمنصور.
٣- قُتِلَ ابنُ المُقفّع بسبب هجومه على الخليفة في قِصَصه.
٤- والي البصرة هو الّذي قتل ابنَ المُقفّع.

ج- لَخِّص نصّ الاستماع بحوالَيْ مئة كِلمة.

د- أكمِل الجمل الآتية بالاختيار المناسب وفق نصّ الاستماع:

١- عبد الله بن المُقَفَّع مؤلِّف ____________ .

☐ فارسيّ ☐ عربيّ ☐ إسلاميّ ☐ هنديّ

٢- ترجم ابن المُقَفَّع "كليلة ودِمْنة" من ____________.

☐ الفهلويّة ☐ الهنديّة ☐ العربيّة ☐ المانويّة

٣- قصّة كليلة ودِمْنة ____________.

☐ حيوانيّة ☐ فارسيّة ☐ عربيّة ☐ سياسيّة

٤- كان المنصور ____________.

☐ ملكاً ☐ حاكِماً ☐ خليفةً ☐ قاضياً

المُفْرَدات

أَرْضى	(يُرْضي)	إِرْضاء	(v.)	to try to satisfy, to please
اِبْتَعَدَ	(يَبْتَعِدُ)	اِبتِعاد (عَن)	(v.)	to draw away from, to withdraw
أَبْعَدَ	(يُبْعِدُ)	إِبْعاد	(v.)	to banish, to expel, to deport
اِتَّهَمَ	(يَتَّهِمُ)	اِتِّهام	(v.)	to accuse
أَرِسْطو	أَرِسْطوطاليس		(name)	Aristotle
أُسْقُف	ج	أَساقِفة	(n., m.)	bishop
أَصْليّ			(adj.)	original, authentic, genuine
اِعْتَنَقَ	(يَعْتَنِقُ)	اِعْتِناق	(v.)	to embrace, to convert
أَفْلاطون			(name)	Plato
اِمْتازَ	(يَمْتازُ)	اِمْتِياز	(v.)	to excel, to surpass, to be distinguished
إِيّا	(ضمير النصب)		(pron.)	base form of the accusative separate pronoun
آية		آيات	(n., f.)	sign, wonder, *Quranic* verse
أَيَّدَ	(يُؤَيِّدُ)	تأييد	(v.)	to support, to back
إيمان			(n., m.)	faith, belief
بُرْهان	ج	بَراهين	(n., m.)	proof
بَطْليموس	ج	بَطالِسة	(name)	Ptolemy
بَعَثَ	(يَبْعَثُ)	بَعْث	(v.)	resurrection (from death)
بَلاط	ج	أَبْلِطة	(n., m.)	royal court
تَرْجَمَ	(يُتَرْجِمُ)	تَرْجَمة	(v.)	to translate
تَعَلَّقَ	(يَتَعَلَّقُ)	تَعَلُّق (بِـ)	(v.)	to be related (to), to be concerned (with)

to fall, to plunge	(v.)	تَهافُت	(يَتَهافَتُ)	تَهافَتَ
congruity, agreement, conformity	(n., m.)			تَوافُق
Galen	(name)			جالينوس
argument, debate, dispute	(n., m.)			جَدَل
the minor details, the particulars	(n., f.)			الجُزئيّات
to prohibit	(v.)	تَحْريم	(يُحَرِّمُ)	حَرَّمَ
difference, disparity, incongruence	(n., m.)	خِلافات	ج	خِلاف
to last, to continue, to persist	(v.)	دَوام	(يَدومُ)	دامَ
to bury, to conceal	(v.)	دَفْن	(يَدْفِنُ)	دَفَنَ
to be satisfied, to consent, to agree	(v.)	رِضىً (عن)	(يَرْضى)	رَضِيَ
to move along, to walk, to operate	(v.)	سَيْر / مَسير	(يَسيرُ)	سارَ
poison	(n., m.)	سُموم	ج	سُمّ
except	(part.)			سِوى
canonical law of Islam	(n., m.)			شَرْع
to believe	(v.)	تَصْديق	(يُصَدِّقُ)	صَدَّقَ
fight, struggle	(n., m.)	صِراعات	ج	صِراع
number of, large quantity	(n, m.)		(مِن)	عَديد
to forgive, to excuse	(v.)	عَفْو (عن)	(يَعْفو)	عَفا
reason, rationality	(n., m.)			عَقْل
article of faith, tenet, dogma, ideology	(n., f.)	عَقائِد	ج	عَقيدة
violent	(adj.)			عَنيف

to appoint	(v.)	تَعيين	(يُعَيِّنُ)	عَيَّنَ
to explain, to expound, to explicate	(v.)	تَفْسير	(يُفَسِّرُ)	فَسَّرَ
understanding, jurisprudence	(n., m.)			فِقْه
thinking, thought	(n., m.)	أفْكار	ج	فِكْر
astronomy	(n., m.)			فَلَك
judge, magistrate, justice	(n., m.)	قُضاة	ج	قاضٍ
to hate, to detest, to loathe	(v.)	كُرْه / كَراهة / كَراهية		كَرِهَ
to renege one's faith, to blaspheme God	(v.)	كُفْر	(يَكْفُرُ)	كَفَرَ
scholastic theology	(n., m.)	(عِلم الكَلام)		كَلام
to summarize, to abridge	(v.)	تَلْخيص	(يُلَخِّصُ)	لَخَّصَ
contradictory, conflicting, divergent	(act. p.)	مُخالِفون	ج	مُخالِف
doctrine, creed, movement, trend	(n., m.)	مَذاهِب		مَذْهَب
thinker	(act. p.)	مُفَكِّرون	ج	مُفَكِّر
close companion, favorite	(pass. p.)	مُقَرَّبون	ج	مُقَرَّب
suitable	(act. p.)			مُلائِم
status, rank, position	(n., f.)			مَنزِلة
logic	(n., m.)			مَنْطِق
theory	(n., f.)	نَظَريّات	ج	نَظَريّة
to attack, to assail	(v.)	مُهاجَمة	(يُهاجِمُ)	هاجَمَ
harmony, concord, conformity	(n., m.)			وِفاق

الدَرْسُ التاسِع عشر

Objectives

- Introduction to proverbs—history and context
- Learning how to use proverbs and similes and their appropriate settings
- Introducing idioms: familial and descriptive and those offering wisdom and advice
- **Grammar**: using رُبَّما and compound particles عَمّا، إنّما، مّما
- **مُراجَعة القواعد**: أنواع «ما»، واسم التفضيل «خَير وخَيْرٌ مِن»، وأنواع «لا»

رُكنُ المُفْرَداتِ الجَديدةِ

to respect	اِحْتَرَمَ (يَحْتَرِمُ) اِحْتِرام
sign, indication	بادِرة ج بَوادِر
to use frequently	تَداوَلَ (يَتَداوَلُ) تَداوُل
legacy, heritage, lore	تُراث
to be extreme	تَطَرَّفَ (يَتَطَرَّفُ) تَطَرُّف
moral constitution, moral character	خُلُق ج أخْلاق
to throw, to shoot	رَمى (يَرْمي) رَمْي
satisfaction, contentment, conviction	قَناعة ج قَناعات
disaster, calamity	مُصيبة ج مَصائِب
intended	مَقْصود
to implement	نَفَّذ (يُنَفِّذُ) تَنْفيذ
to occur, to be mentioned	وَرَدَ (يَرِدُ) وُرود

تمرين ١

وافِق بين كلمات لها معانٍ متعاكسة واكتب الأزواج في الوسط:

١	حِلم		صَديق
٢	طارَ		جِلد
٣	شَبّ		عاقِل
٤	حَرب		هُدوء
٥	عَدوّ		غَضَب
٦	عاميّ		شابَ
٧	جاهِل		فَصيح
٨	ضَجيج		سلام
			وَقَعَ

تمرين ٢

وافِق بين كلمات من العمودين لها معانٍ متشابهة واكتب الأزواج في الوسط:

١	حِكمة		سَيِّدتي
٢	اختار		حَضارة
٣	أسّد		مِثل
٤	ناقة		أخذ
٥	مَولاي		مَثَل
٦	عير		شِبْل
٧	خَيْر		أفضَل
٨	شَرْوى		حَمير
			جَمَل

تمرين ٣

اخترِ الكَلِمةَ الّتي لا تُناسِب باقي الكَلِماتِ في كُلِّ مَجْموعةٍ وبَيِّن السَبَب:

١-	غَضَب	حُزْن	ناقة	فَرَح
٢-	فائدة	ناس	أمّة	قَوم
٣-	فِكْر	رَذاذ	تُراث	حَضارة
٤-	شِبْل	أسَد	حِمار	رَحى
٥-	مقال	فُصحى	خُدعة	عاميّة

تمرين ٤

للنقاش قبل قراءة القصّة:

١- ما وظيفة الأمثال في اللغة في رأيك؟

٢- هل لكل تعبير عربي مقابله بالإنجليزيّة؟ لماذا أو لماذا لا في رأيك؟

٣- اذكر بعض الأمثلة العربية التي تعرفها.

هكذا قالت العرب

الأمثال هي أقوال يتداولها الناس يوميّاً على مرّ السنين وهي تدلّ على طريقة تفكيرهم وكيف ينظرون إلى أنفسهم وإلى العالم. كلّ مَثَل من هذه الأمثال المختارة في هذا الدرس يحمل في طواياه جُزءاً من الحضارة العربيّة ومن الفكر العربيّ ومن الشعور العربيّ. بعبارة أخرى، الأمثال تنبئ عمّا في التُراث والعقل والقلب. بعض هذه الأمثال قديم جداً ويعود إلى ما قبل الإسلام إلاّ أنّها لا تزال مستعملة إلى يومنا هذا كلاماً وكتابةً.

والأمثال كالشِعر، هي كلمات قليلة تحمل معانيَ كثيرة. لذلك فإنّ كلّ مَثَل يرد وإلى جانبه المعنى المقصود باختصار أو المناسبة الّتي قيلَ فيها. لاحِظ أنّ الأمثال مكتوبة بالخط العريض لتمييزها، وهي مصنَّفة حسب مواضيعها كالمعاملات والأسرة والحكمة والنصيحة والتشبيه. هناك المئات من الأمثال والأقوال لدى الناطقين بالعربيّة، وقد اختير بعضها فقط لهذا الدرس. يجدر بالذِكر أنّ العاميّات العربيّة فيها كثير من الأمثال والأقوال والحِكَم أيضاً، لكن تمّ اختيار الفصيح منها فقط.

الأسرة

١ **الولدُ سِرُّ أبيه**. يُقالُ حين يُستَدَلُّ على صفات الأب من خلال صفات الابن، لأنّ الابن عادةً يكون مثل أبيه.

٢ **مَن شابَه أباهُ فما ظَلَم**. من الطبيعيّ أن يشبه الإنسان والده إمّا في الشكل أو السلوك.

٣ **إنّ هذا الشِبلَ مِن ذاكَ الأسَد**: يُقالُ عن الشخص الّذي يُشبِه والِدَه، بخاصّة إنْ كان الشَبَه في أَرْمٍ جيّد، لأنّ صورة الشِبْلِ (ابن الأسَد) وصورة الأسد لدى العرض صورتان حسنتان.

التَشبيه

٤ **كُلٌّ يُغَنّي على لَيْلاه**. يُقالُ عند اختلاف الناس بآرائهم حيث يحاول كلٌّ منهم تأييد رأيِه بقوة، فهم كالّذين يُغنّون أغانيَ مختلفة في وقت واحد، ولا يهتمّ أحدهم بما يقوله الآخرون.

٥ **كالمُسْتَجير مِنَ الرَمْضاءِ بالنارِ**. يُقالُ حين يحاول الإنسان الهروب من مشكلة فَيقعُ في أخرى أسوأ منها وأخطر، أي كمَن يحاول الهروب من شدة الحرّ بالقفز في النار.

٦ **كَأنَّ على رُؤوسِهِمُ الطَيْر**. يُستَعمَل لوصف جَماعة من الناس يجلسون في مجلِس بصَمْت تامّ وكأنّ طيراً يجلس فوق رأس كلٍّ منهم، ولا يريدون أن يتحرّكوا حتّى لا تطير الطيور.

٧ **أسمَعُ جَعْجَعةً ولا أرى طَحناً**. يُقالُ حين يكثُر الكلام وتَقِلُّ الأفعال، أي حين يعِدُ أحدهم مستَمِعيه بأشياء كثيرة دون تنفيذ ما يقول. والصورة مأخوذة من طاحونة القمح حيث يُصدِر حَجَر الرَحى صوتاً عاليّاً حين يدور لطحن القمح، فإذا لم يكن هناك قمح يطحن فلا فائدة من الدوران والصوت العالي أو الضجيج (الجعْجعة).

الوَصْف

٨ **أنْ تسمَعَ بالمُعَيْديِّ خَيرٌ مِن أنْ تَراه**. يُقالُ حين تكون سُمْعة الشخص أفضل من شكله. والقصّة وراءه هي أنّ النُعمان بن المُنذِر آخر ملوك اللّخميين في الحيرة بالعراق (حَكَمَ من ٥٨٠ إلى ٦٠٢ م) سمِع أنّ أحدَ الأعراب كان يستولي على أموال الناس ولا يحترم أملاكهم ولا يخاف أحداً فأمَر النُعمان بحبسه. ولمّا اعتُقِل المُعَيْديّ أراد أن يرى هذا الرجل الّذي أدخل الخوف في قلوب الناس ولم يَخَف أحداً. فأحضروه أمامه وكان قصيراً جدّاً وقد أكلت آثار الجُدَريّ وجهه، فقال هذا القول. لكنّ المُعَيْديّ لم يسكت بل قال للملك: «يا مولاي، أخطأت بحكمك، لأن الرجل يُقَوّم بقلبه ولسانه.» وكان يقصد بذلك الشجاعة والفصاحة. أعجبَ الملك بهذا الردّ وضمّه إلى بلاطه مستشاراً ونديماً.

٩ **لا ناقةَ لي في هذا ولا جَمَل**. يُقالُ للتعبير عن عدم وجود علاقة لشخص بأمر ما، والصورة تمثّل شخصاً كأنّه ينظر إلى مجموعة من الإبل ويقول إنه لا يملك منها شيئاً.

١٠ **لا يَملِكُ شَرْوى نَقير**. يُقالُ للتَعبير عن الفقر الشديد، والشَرْوى معناها «المِثْل» والنَقير جزءٌ صغير من نُواة التَمْرة، أي أنّه شديد الفقر لا يملِك حتّى الشيء الّذي لا قيمة له.

١١ **الجُنون فنون**. يُقالُ لوصف سلوكٍ غير عاديّ، أي أنّ الجُنون أو مخالفة العادي لَهُ أشكال عديدة.

١٢ **لا في العيرِ ولا في النَفير**. يُقالُ في وصف شخص لا يصلُح لشيء. والصورة تمثّل مجموعتين: ((العير)) هي القافلة من الحمير، ولكن لما كثر استعمالها أصبحت الكلمة تطلق على كل قافلة تحمل الميرة (أي الأطعمة والبضائع)، أما ((النفير)) فهم القوم الذين ينفرون للقتال. في أصل المثل المقصود بكلمة العير عير قريش التي أقبلت مع أبي سفيان من الشام محملة بالأطعمة وغيرها، وأنه أريد بكلمة النفير الناس الذين خرجوا مع عُتْبة بن ربيعة من مكة لإنقاذ القافلة من أيدي المسلمين، حيث وقعت على إثرها معركة بدر، فمن لم يكن في أحد الجمعين، أي لم يكن في القافلة ولا في الذين هبوا لنجدتها، قيل عنه: لا في العير ولا في النفير، أي لا يعدّ من الرجال، ثم صارت مثلاً يُضرب لكل رجل صغير الشأن مستهان به، إلا أنه أحسن من الحمير.

١٣ **رُبَّ رَمْيةٍ مِن غيرِ رامٍ**. يُقالُ في وصفِ عمل جيّدٍ لم يأتِ بالاستِعداد أو التحضير الجيّد له إنّما جاء نتيجة الصُدْفة.

النصيحة

١٤ **إذا أطعَمْتَ فأشبِعْ وإذا ضَرَبْتَ فأوْجِعْ**. يجب إعطاء كلّ شيء حقّه. مثلاً إنْ ذهبت في نُزهة فاستمتع بها وإذا قمت للعمل فاعمل بجدّ وإذا بدأت الدراسة فَأَعْطها كلّ وقتك.

١٥ **الحِلْمُ عند الغَضَب والعَفْوُ عِندَ المَقْدِرة**: يُقالُ في صِفات الإنسان النبيل، فهو يصبر ويهدّئ نفسه إذا غضِب ويعفو عن عدوّه حين ينتصر عليه. وقصّة هذا القول أنّ مُعاوية بن أبي سُفيان والي الشام (في القرن السابع) سُئِلَ عن معنى النُبْل فقال هذا القول.

١٦ **الجارُ قَبْلَ الدار**. يُقالُ لنصْح شخص في اختيار جيرانه قبل أن يختار داره، وهذا يُعبِّر عن أهميّة الجار في العلاقات الاجتماعيّة عند العرب.

١٧ **لِكُلِّ مَقامٍ مَقال**. اختيار الكلمة المناسبة لقولها في المكان المناسب، أي أنّ كلّ مناسبة تحتاج إلى نوع خاصّ من الكلام يختلف عمّا هو مطلوب في مناسبات أخرى. فحين يتكلّم الإنسان أمام مجموعة من الناس في حفل كبير يستعمل العربيّة الفُصحى وإذا تكلّم مع صديقه يستخدم العاميّة. وهو يستعمل النكتة والفكاهة في حفلةٍ مثلاً ويكون جادًا وقت الحُزن.

١٨ **خالِفْ تُعْرَف**. يُقالُ عن الشخص الّذي يحبّ أن يكون مشهوراً أو معروفاً، وذلك بسلوكه سلوكاً مُخالِفاً لسلوك معظم الناس.

١٩ **مَن حَفَرَ حُفْرةً لأخيهِ وَقَعَ فيها**. للتحذير مِن نتائج العمل السيّئ نحو الناس الآخرين، فالعمل السيّئ لا يعود على صاحبه إلا بالسوء.

٢٠ **لا تَنْهَ عَنْ خُلُقٍ وتأتيَ مِثْلَهُ**. يُقالُ في ضرورة تناسُب الأقوال مع الأفعال، أي لا تطلب من الآخرين الامتناع عن فعل شيء ثمّ تفعله أنت.

٢١ **مَن جَدَّ وَجَدَ**. يُقالُ لتشجيع الناس على الجِدّ بالعمل، فالجِدّ يؤدّي للنجاح. أي أنّك إذا عملت بجِدّ وجدت النجاح أمامك.

٢٢ **خَيْرُ الأمورِ أوْسَطُها**. يُقالُ في تفضيل الطريق الوسط والابتِعاد عن التَطَرُّف، فالوسَط هو الأفضل.

٢٣ اتَّقِ شَرَّ مَن أحسَنْتَ إلَيْه. إن العمل الحسن نحو الآخرين قد لا يعود عليك بالشيء الحَسَن دائماً، أي يجب على المرء أن يحذَر الناس حتّى الّذين أحسن إليهم.

٢٤ **خَيْرُ الكلام ما قَلَّ ودلّ**. إنّ أحسن الكلام هو المختَصَر المُفيد، أي الكلام القليل ذو المعنى الواضح.

٢٥ إذا كنتَ في قَوْم فاحلِبْ في إنائهم. تدلّ هذه النصيحة على أنّه من الأحسن أن يكون سلوكُ المرءِ ولباسَه وكلامَه مثلاً مشابهاً لسلوك الناس الّذين يعيش بينهم.

٢٦ **القَناعةُ كَنْزٌ لا يَفنى**. يُقالُ لنصح المرء في القبول بما لديه وعَدَم النَظَر إلى ما لدى الآخرين، لأن القبول بما لديه يجعله يشعر وكأن ما لديه كلُّ شيء.

٢٧ **أعذَرَ مَن أنذَر**. لا لوم على فعل سبقه إنذار.

٢٨ **بَلَغَ السَيْلُ الزُبى**. للتحذير من خطر قادم تبدو بَوادِرُه. والسيل يمثّل الخطر المتوقّع والزُبى (جمع زُبْيَة وهي المكان المرتفع) تمثّل الخطر. فحين يصل ماء السيل إلى الزُبى فكلّ مكان أضحى في خطر. ويُستعمَل هذا القول أيضاً للتعبير عن نفاد الصبر.

الحِكمة

٢٩ **زامِرُ الحَيِّ لا يُطْرِب**. ينظر الناس إلى ما لدى غيرِهم ويرَوْنَ فيه شيئاً جميلاً، بينما لا يرَوْنَ الشيء نفسه جميلاً إذا كان عندهم. والصورة هنا لعازِف المِزمار من أهل الحي الّذي لا يَطرَب له الناس، أي لا يعجبون بعزفه لأنّه منهم، لكن لو قام بالعزف نفسه زامر من حَيّ آخَر أو من بلد آخر لَطَرِب له الناس.

٣٠ **الطُيوُر على أشكالِها تَقَع**. يخالط الناس مَن هم مِثلُهم، فالطيّب يخالط الطيّبين والسيّئ يخالط السيّئين.

٣١ **ينضَحُ الإناءُ بما فيه.** لا يستطيع المرء أن يعطي ما لا يملك. فالعالِم يمكن أن يعطيَك عِلماً كثيراً، لكن الجاهِل لا يستطيع ذلك ولو حاول. والصورة لإناء فخّاريّ فيه سائل يرشَحَ منه، فلا يمكن للإناء أن يرشح إلا مِن هذا السائل ولا شيءِ سواه.

٣٢ **سبَقَ السيفُ العَذَل**. يُقالُ حين يفعل الإنسان شيئاً ويريد أن يلوم نفسه أو غيره على ما حدث، أي أنّ الفعل قد وقع ولا فائدة من اللوم (أي العَذَل).

٣٣ **رُبَّ أخٍ لكَ لم تَلِدْهُ أمُك**. يُقالُ عن الصديق الّذي هو أقرب إليك من أخيك. أي أنّ هناك ناساً مخلصين لك ليسوا من أفراد أسرتك لكنهم يعاملونك كإخوانك.

٣٤ **مَصائِبُ قَوْمٍ عِندَ قَوْمٍ فوائدُ**. يُقالُ حين يستفيد بعض الناس من مصيبة أصابت غيرهم.

٣٥ **لا يفُلُّ الحَديد إلاّ الحَديد**. حول ضرورة استعمال قوّة مُماثِلة لصدِّ قوّة أخرى، فنحن نحتاج إلى الحديد أو إلى ما هو أقوى منه ليؤثّر بالحديد.

٣٦ **مَن شَبَّ على شيءٍ شابَ عليه**. الأمور التّي يتعلّمها الإنسان في صِغَره تبقى معه طَوال حياته من سن الطفولة إلى أن يصبح شيخاً.

٣٧ **مَن عاشَرَ قَوْماً أربَعين يوماً صار مِنهم**. يُقالُ عن تأثير الحياة بين مجموعة من الناس لمدّة من الزمن على سلوك المرء، فإذا عاش بينهم حوالي أربعين يوماً يصبح سلوكه مثل سلوكهم.

٣٨ **ما حَكَّ جِلْدَكَ مثلُ ظُفُرك** . يدلّ على أهميّة الاعتماد على النفس، أي أن ما تفعله بنفسك أفضل ممّا يمكن أن يفعله الآخرون لك.

٣٩ **ومعظَمُ النارِ مِن مُسْتَصْغَرِ الشَرَر**. المشاكل الكبيرة سببها أمور صغيرة، كالنار أو الحريق الّذي يشبّ بسبب شَرَر بسيط.

٤٠ **عَدوٌّ عاقِل خَيْرٌ مِن صَديقٍ جاهِل**. عن أهميّة الحِكمة والعقل، لدرجة أنّ العدوّ قد يكون أفضل بالنسبة لك من الصديق إن كان هذا العدوّ عاقلاً وكان الصديق جاهلاً.

٤١ **الحربُ خُدْعة**. لا تعتمد الحرب على استخدام القوّة فقط بل على الخدعة ربّما أكثر.

٤٢ **أوّلُ الغَيْثِ قَطْرٌ**. الأمور الكبيرة تبدأ بداية بسيطة كالمطر الغزير الّذي يسبقه رذاذ خفيف.

تمرين ٥

اكتب رقم المَثَل المناسب لكلّ من الجمل الآتية بين القوسين:

١- تحذير الناس من إساءة بعضهم إلى بعض، والإساءة تعود على صاحبها. (_______)

٢- مظهر الشخص قد لا يدلّ على حقيقة ذلك الشخص. (_______)

٣- تبرير أي عمل على أنّه مقبول بسبب الحرب. (_______)

٤- مجموعة من الناس أفرادها مختلفون بالرأي، ولا يحاول بعضهم فهم آراء بعضهم الآخر.. (_______)

٥- وصف شخص على أنّه لا يصلح لأي عمل. (_______)

٦- قول ينصح الناس باستعمال كلمات تناسب الموقف الّذي هم فيه. (_______)

٧- توقّع قدوم الخير بناءً على أشياء تدل عليه. (_______)

٨- من المؤكّد أنّ هذا الطفل من ذلك الأب. (_______)

٩- وصف سلوك غير طبيعيّ وغير مقبول. (_______)

١٠- سيستفيد بعض الناس من المشاكل الّتي تصيب غيرهم من الناس. (_______)

تمرين ٦

اِختَرَ الأمثال العربيّة من الدرس الّتي توافق الأمثال الإنكليزيّة التالية، واكتب رقم المثل العربيّ بين القوسين:

1. Much ado about nothing / all talk, no action. (________)
2. With friends like these, who needs enemies? (________)
3. Birds of a feather flock together. (________)
4. Like father, like son. (________)
5. To each his own. (________)
6. When in Rome, do as the Romans do. (________)
7. Out of the frying pan into the fire. (________)
8. He hasn't a red cent to his name. (________)
9. Constant dripping wears away stone. (________)

تمرين ٧

اكتب إلى جانب كلّ من الكلمات الآتية الكلمة الّتي لها معنى مشابه:

١- غَيث ______________________

٢- أضحى ______________________

٣- رَشَحَ ______________________

٤- تَبيين ______________________

٥- انتصر (على) ______________________

٦- خالَطَ ______________________

٧- سَكَتَ ______________________

رُكن التعبيرات المتداولة على الألسن

بِعِبارةٍ أخرى

بِعِبارةٍ أخرى، الأمْثالُ تُنبِئُ عَمّا في التُراثِ والعَقْلِ والقَلْب.	*in other words*

إلى يَوْمِنا هذا

(الأمْثال) لا تَزالُ مُسْتَعمَلةً إلى يَوْمِنا هذا كَلاماً وكِتابةً.	*to this very day*

يَجْدُرُ بالذِكْرِ

يَجْدُرُ بالذِكْرِ أنّ العاميّاتِ العَرَبيّةَ فيها كَثيرٌ مِن الأمْثالِ والأقْوالِ.	*it is worthy of mentioning*

نَفادُ الصَبْرِ

وَيُسْتَعمَلُ هذا القَوْلُ أيضاً لِلتَعبيرِ عَنْ نَفادِ الصَبْرِ.	*losing patience*

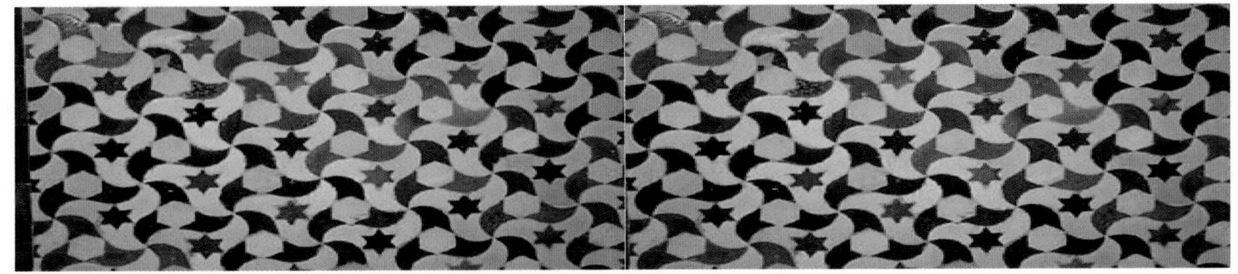

القَواعِد

1. The Preposition رُبَّ *many a*

This preposition has become arcane, falling out of usage in MSA. As you may have noticed, it occurred in two of our parables, numbers 13 and 33:

١	رُبَّ رَمْيةٍ مِن غيرِ رام (١٣)
٢	رُبَّ أخٍ لكَ لم تَلِدْهُ أمُّك (٣٣)

It does, however, occur quite frequently when collocated with ما creating the compound رُبَّما meaning *perhaps*. This word may be followed by nouns (ex. 3), verbs (ex. 4), or prepositional phrases (ex. 5).

Perhaps his mother is sick.	رُبَّما أمُّه مَريضة.	٣
I might buy a convertible.	رُبَّما أشْتَري سَيّارةً مَكْشوفةً.	٤
Perhaps it is in your pocket.	رُبَّما في جَيْبِك.	٥

2. Compound Particles إنّما، مِمّا، عَمّا

Some particles and prepositions may be combined together to form a single word. Those that we are concerned with in this section involve a particle + ما.

nothing but, rather, much more	إنَّما	⇐	إنَّ + ما
of what, from what	مِمّا	⇐	مِن + ما
about what, what about	عَمّا	⇐	عَنْ + ما

We offer a few examples of these compound particles in context:

I don't know what he is asking about.	لا أعْلَمُ عَمّا يَسأل.
What is chewing gum made of?	مِمَّ تُصْنَعُ العِلْكة؟
Believers are nothing but brothers.	إنَّما المُؤْمنونَ إخْوة.
Hard workers are nothing but successful.	إنَّما يَنْجَحُ المُجِدّون.

مُلاحَظة

The particle إنَّما may be followed by a verb, something that is not allowed with إنَّ.

مُراجَعةُ القَواعِد

3. Types of ما

As you may have noticed through our many encounters with it, there are many different types and functions of ما. The first ما we were exposed to was of course its interrogative function. Let's take a look at that as well as five other types:

١	ما الاسْتِفْهاميّة	ما اسْمُك؟	*What's your name?*
٢	ما النافيّة	ما اتَّصَلَتْ سَلْمى بَعْدُ.	*Salma hasn't called yet.*
٣	ما المَوصولة	لا أعْلَمُ ما يُريدُ.	*I don't know what he wants.*
٤	ما التَعَجُّبيّة	ما أحْسَنَ الطَقْسَ!	*How nice the weather is!*
٥	ما الزائِدة	أيْنَما تَذْهَبْ أذْهَبْ.	*Wherever you go, I go.*
٦	ما الكافّة	قَلَّما أذْهَبُ إلى السينَما.	*I rarely go to the movies.*
		رُبَّما نراه في الحَفْلة.	*We might see him at the party.*

مُلاحَظة

Example 5 ما الزائِدة occurs when ما is suffixed to a conditional particle.

ما الكافّة in example 6 occurs when ما is suffixed to certain verbs and particles, altering their normal syntactic function within the sentence.

4. The Elative خَيْر

Although it doesn't follow the base form of the superlative/comparative in Arabic, خير can function as both—a fact we encountered when reading the parables:

١	خَيْرُ الأمورِ أوْسَطُها.
٢	خَيْرُ الكلامِ ما قَلَّ ودلّ.
٣	أنّ تسمَعَ بالمُعَيْديِّ خَيْرٌ مِن أنْ تراه.
٤	عَدوٌّ عاقِل خَيْرٌ مِن صَديقٍ جاهِل.

As you can see in examples 1 and 2, خير functions as a superlative and behaves just as the superlative أفْعَل form by creating an إضافة structure with the following noun. While in examples 3 and 4, it functions as a comparative taking the preposition مِن to form: خَيْر مِن.

5. Types of لا

Functioning differently in five different contexts, لا is a particle that enjoys a wide syntactic range.

a. Negative Particle

As a negative particle, لا negates imperfect verbs (ex. 1) and sometimes even perfect verbs (ex. 2) when used in the context of *neither*.

My brother does not work in construction.	لا يَعْمَلُ أخي في البِناء.	١
Hadia neither wrote nor called.	هادية لا كَتَبَتْ ولا اِتَّصَلَت.	٢

In order to create the *neither . . . nor* structure, we use لا . . . وَلا in both MSA and dialects. Fortunately this لا . . . وَلا structure also applies to nouns as well, as we see in examples 3 and 4:

Rami is neither tall nor short.	رامي لا طَويلٌ وَلا قَصيرٌ.	٣
We returned neither tired nor hungry.	رَجَعْنا لا تَعبينَ وَلا جائعينَ.	٤

b. Negative 'not' Construction

In this context, لا is used to set two things in opposition to one another (e.g., this *not* that):

Hand me the book, not the magazine.	أَعْطِني الكِتابَ لا المَجَلَّةَ.	٥
A man called, not a woman.	اِتَّصَلَ رَجُلٌ لا امْرأةٌ.	٦

مُلاحَظة

As can be seen in examples 5 and 6, the لا had no syntactical impact on the sentences. The direct object المَجَلّة remained حالة النَّصْب while the subject of example 6 remained حالة الرَّفْع.

c. The Negative Response to a Question: لا

- Do you have any objection to chatting a little?	- هَلْ عِنْدَكَ مانِع نُدَرْدِش قليلاً؟	٧
- No.	- لا.	

d. لا نافية لِلجِنْس

This لا negates a whole class of nouns:

There is no deity except God.	لا إلهَ إلاّ الله.	٨
It's necessary to buy a larger house.	لا بُدَّ مِنْ شِراءِ دارٍ أكْبَر.	٩

e. Negation of the Imperative لا الناهِية

This type of لا is simply a negative command:

Don't write on the wall!	لا تَكْتُبْ على الجِدارِ!	١٠
Don't be late!	لا تَتأخَّري!.	١١

مُلاحَظة

The verb following لا الناهية is مَجزوم

تمرين ٨

قبل الاستماع إلى النصّ، راجع الكلمات التالية:

measure of weight	قِنْطار	measure of weight	دِرْهَم
eloquent	يَبيع	silence	سُكوت
to pardon	عَفا	to postpone	أجّل
النِهاية	خاتَم	to be in labor	تَمَخَّضَ

أجب عن الأسئلة وفق نصّ الاستماع:

١- هناك مثل في نص الاستماع قريب بالنعنى والقصد من مثل في مجموعة الأمثال في هذا الدرس. ما هما المثلان؟

٢- اكتب بين القوسين رقم المَثَل العربيّ الوارد في نص الاستماع الّذي يشبه أحد الأمثال الإنكليزيّة الآتية:

a. Speech is silver, but silence is golden. (__________)
b. A bird in the hand is worth two in the bush. (__________)
c. Actions speak louder than words. (__________)
d. Prevention is better than cure. (__________)
e. Cleanliness is next to godliness. (__________)
f. Let bygones be bygones. (__________)
g. Out of sight, out of mind. (__________)
h. A tempest in a teapot. (__________)

٣- ما المَثَل الإنكليزيّ الّذي ينصح الناس بالقيام بأعمالهم دون تأخيرها إلى الغد؟ ما المثل العربيّ الّذي يحمل نفس المعنى؟

٤- أي مثل يبيّن أنّ الإنسان يتعلّم من خطئه (في الأصل حديث شريف)؟

المُفْرَدات

اِحْتَرَمَ	(يَحتَرِمُ)	اِحتِرام	(v.)	to respect, to honor, to revere
اِستَدَلَّ	(يَستَدِلُّ)	اِستِدْلال	(v.)	to seek information, to obtain information
أضْحى			(v.)	to become, to turn into
أمَرَ	(يأمُرُ)	أمر (بـِ)	(v.)	to order, to command, to instruct
إناء	ج	آنِية / أوانٍ	(n., m.)	vessel, container
أنْبأ	(يُنبِئُ)	إنْباء	(v.)	to inform, to tell
اِنتَصَرَ	(يَنتَصِرُ)	اِنتِصار	(v.)	to triumph, to prevail, to win, to defeat
اِهْتَمَّ	(يَهْتَمُّ)	اِهْتِمام (بـِ)	(v.)	to be concerned (with)
أوْجَعَ	(يُوجِعُ)	إيجاع	(v.)	to hurt, to cause pain
بادِرة	ج	بَوادِر	(n., f.)	sign, indication, precursor
تامّ			(adj.)	full, complete, whole, total, perfect
تَداوَلَ	(يَتَداوَلُ)	تَداوُل	(v.)	to make frequent use, to exchange
تُراث	ج	تُراثات	(n., m.)	legacy, inheritance
تَطَرَّفَ	(يَتَطَرَّفُ)	تَطرُّف	(v.)	to go to extremes, to hold an extreme position
جاهِل	ج	جَهَلة / جُهّال / جُهَلاء	(act. p.)	ignorant, fool, foolish
جِدّ			(n., m.)	seriousness, earnestness, diligence
جَدُرَ	(يَجْدُرُ)	جَدارة (بـِ)	(v.)	to be worthy (of)
جُدَريّ			(n., m.)	smallpox
جَعْجَعة			(n., f.)	clamor, noise, din, racket
حَبَسَ	(يَحْبِسُ)	حَبْس	(v.)	to hold in custody, to detain

millstone	(n., m.)		(رَحى)	حَجَر
iron, steel	(adj.)			حَديد
civilization	(n., f.)	حَضارات	ج	حَضارة
to dig a hole, to excavate	(v.)	حَفْر	(يَحفِرُ)	حَفَرَ
to scratch, to scrape, to rub	(v.)	حَكّ	(يَحُكُّ)	حَكَّ
chivalry, patience, reason	(n., m.)			حِلْم
donkey	(n., m.)	حَمير	ج	حِمار
to mix with, to associate with	(v.)	مُخالَطة	(يُخالِطُ)	خالَطَ
to contradict, to disagree with	(v.)	مُخالَفة	(يُخالِفُ)	خالَفَ
deception, cheating	(n., f.)	خُدَع	ج	خُدعة
moral constitution, moral character	(n., m.)	أخْلاق	ج	خُلُق
better than	(n., m.)		خَيْر مِن	خَيْر مِن
many a . . .	(prep.)			رُبّ
drizzle	(n., m.)			رَذاذ
to exude, to ooze, to seep, to leak	(v.)	رَشْح	(يَرْشَحُ)	رَشَحَ
scorching heat (archaic usage)	(n., f.)			رَمْضاء
to throw, to shoot	(v.)	رَمْي	(يَرْمي)	رَمى
piper, player of a wind instrument	(act. p.)	زامِرون	ج	زامِر
to precede, to arrive before	(v.)	سَبْق	(يَسبِقُ)	سَبَقَ
to be silent, to be quiet	(v.)	سَكوت	(يَسْكُتُ)	سَكَتَ
to behave, to act	(v.)	سُلوك	(يَسْلُكُ)	سَلَكَ

reputation, standing, renown	(n., f.)			سُمْعة
flood, torrent	(n., m.)	سُيول	ج	سَيْل
to become gray-haired	(v.)	شَيْب	(يَشيبُ)	شابَ
to resemble	(v.)	مُشابَهة	(يُشابِهُ)	شابَهَ
to grow up, to be a youth	(v.)	شَباب	(يَشِبُّ)	شَبّ
lion cub	(n, m.)	أشْبال	ج	شِبْل
comparison, simile	(v.)	تَشبيه	(يُشَبِّهُ)	شَبَّهَ
similar to, like	(n., m.)			شَرْوى
to be silent, to be quiet	(v.)	صَمْت	(يَصْمُتُ)	صَمَتَ
noise, clamor	(n., m.)			ضَجيج
to grind, to mill, to pulverize	(v.)	طَحْن	(يَطحَنُ)	طَحَنَ
to be moved (mostly with joy)	(v.)	طَرَب	(يَطْرَبُ)	طَرِبَ
fold, conviction	(n., f.)	طَوايا	ج	طَويّة
fingernail, toenail, claw	(n., m.)	أظْفار / أظافِر	ج	ظِفْر / ظُفُر
to do injustice, to do wrong, to act tyrannically	(v.)	ظُلم	(يَظلِمُ)	ظَلَمَ
to associate with, to mix with	(v.)	مُعاشَرة	(يُعاشِرُ)	عاشَرَ
abundant, copious	(adj.)			غَزير
abundant rain	(n., m.)	غُيوث	ج	غَيْث
to dent, to blunt	(v.)	فَلّ	(يَفُلُّ)	فَلَّ
to perish	(v.)	فَناء	(يَفْنى)	فَنِيَ
to accept, to consent	(v.)	قَبول	(يَقْبَلُ)	قَبِلَ
drip, drop	(n., m.)			قَطْر

to jump, to leap	(v.)	قَفْز	(يَقفِزُ)	قَفَزَ
satisfaction, contentment, conviction	(n., f.)	قَناعات	ج	قَناعة
to evaluate, to assess, to rectify	(v.)	تَقويم	(يُقَوِّمُ)	قَوَّمَ
people, nation	(n., m.)	أقْوام	ج	قَوْم
as if, as though	(conj.)			كَأنَّ
treasure	(n., m.)	كُنوز	ج	كَنْز
to blame, to reproach, to admonish	(v.)	لَوْم	(يَلومُ)	لامَ
proverb	(n., m.)	أمْثال	ج	مَثَل
summed up, abbreviated, summarized	(pass. p.)			مُختَصر
seeker of refuge or asylum	(act. p.)	مُسْتَجيرون	ج	مُستَجير
consultant, counsel, adviser	(pass. p.)	مُسْتَشارون	ج	مُسْتَشار
listener	(act. p.)			مُسْتَمِع
classified, sorted	(pass. p.)			مُصَنَّف
misfortune, calamity, disaster	(act. p.)	مَصائِب	ج	مُصيبة
treatment, social intercourse	(n., f.)	مُعامَلات	ج	مُعامَلة
article, essay, way of speaking	(n., m.)	مَقالات	ج	مَقال
standing, rank, position, prestige	(n., m.)	مَقامات	ج	مَقام
power, strength, capacity	(n., f.)	مَقدِرات	ج	مَقدِرة
intended	(pass. p.)			مَقصود
to own, to possess	(v.)	مُلْك / مَلْك / مِلْك	(يَمْلِكُ)	مَلَكَ
occasion, opportunity	(n., f.)	مُناسَبات	ج	مُناسَبة

master, lord, chief	(n., m.)	مَوالٍ	ج	مَوْلى
to distinguish	(v.)	تَمْييز	(يُمَيِّزُ)	مَيَّزَ
she-camel	(n., f.)	نوق / ناقات	ج	ناقة
to reveal, to impart	(v.)	إنْباء	(يُنْبِئُ)	أنْبأ
noble, highborn, magnanimous	(n., m.)	نُبَلاء	ج	نَبيل
companion, confidant	(n., m.)	نُدَماء	ج	نَديم
picnic, excursion, stroll, promenade	(n., f.)	نُزهات	ج	نُزهة
to exude, to ooze, so seep, to leak	(v.)	نَضْح	(يَنْضَحُ)	نَضَح
to execute, to carry out, to implement	(v.)	تَنْفيذ	(يُنَفِّذُ)	نَفَّذَ
tiny spot on a date pit	(n., m.)			نَقير
to forbid, to prohibit, to prevent	(v.)	نَهي	(يَنْهى)	نَهى
date pit, nucleus, kernel	(n., f.)	نَوَيات	ج	نَواة
to escape, to flee	(v.)	هُروب	(يَهْرُبُ)	هَرَبَ
to occur, to appear, to be found	(v.)	وُرود	(يَرِدُ)	وَرَدَ
to describe	(v.)	وَصْف	(يَصِفُ)	وَصَفَ
to promise	(v.)	وَعْد (بِـ)	(يَعِدُ)	وَعَدَ

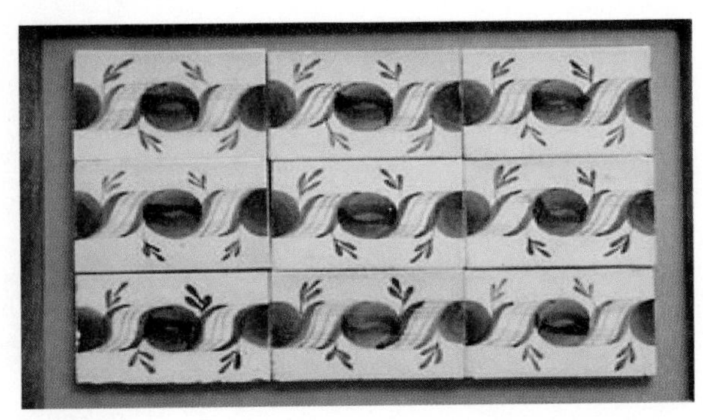

الدَرْسُ العِشْرون

Objectives

- Introduction to modern poetry
- Incorporating the use of idiomatic phrases and poetic devices
- Introducing connectors; turns of phrase:

بلا حَسَبٍ ولا نَسَب، كانَ ومازالَ، وبِطَبيعةِ الحال، وبالأخَصّ، حَلَّ مَحَلَّ، مَحْروم مِن، ومِنْ ثَمَّة

- **مراجعة القواعد:** expressing *one of s.th*، ما الزائدة، جملة بصيغة كلمة

رُكنُ المُفْرَداتِ الجَديدةِ

to strive (to)	سَعى (يَسْعى) سَعي (إلى)
hometown	مسقط الرأس
to dedicate, devote o.s. (to)	كرّسَ (يكرّس) تكْريس
accompanied by	بصُحْبَةِ + اسم
unique, extraordinary	فَذّ ج أفذاذ
mosaic	فُسَيْفُساء
fancy, misconception	وَهَم ج أوْهام
misgiving, notion	هاجِس ج هَواجِس
talent(s)	مَوْهِبَة ج مَواهِب
to be suitable (for)	لاقَ (يَليقُ) لَيْق (بِـ)
fantasy, imagination	مُخَيِّلَة ج مُخَيِّلات
mind	خاطِر ج خَواطِر
to circulate	تَداوَلَ (يَتَداوَلُ) تَداوُل

تمرين ١

وافِق بين كلمات من العمودين لهما معنيان متشابهان (similar) واكتب الأزواج الستة في الوسط:

١	لاقَ		تَصَوَّرات
٢	مُخَيِّلة		بال
٣	سَعى (إلى)		مَكانة
٤	هَزَمَ		ناسَبَ
٥	خاطِر		ميزة
٦	مَنْزِلة		تَغَلَّب (على)
			حاوَلَ

تمرين ٢

وافِق بين كلمات من العمودين لتشكِّل عبارة واحدة:

١	كانَ		الحال
٢	بِطَبيعة		مَحَلَّ
٣	حَلَّ		وَمازالَ
٤	وَمِن		المِثال
٥	بِلا حَسَب		ثَمّة
			وَلا نَسَب

تمرين ٣

للنقاش قبل قراءة الموضوع

١- ما انطباعاتك تجاه الشعر بشكل عام والشعر العربي بشكل خاص؟

٢- ما أهمية الشعر العربي بالنسبة للعرب بصورة عامة والمجتمع العربي بصورة خاصة في رأيك؟

٣- ما مقابل الشعر العربي في الغرب إن وُجِدَ؟

نُبذةٌ عن الشِعر العربي

إن كلّ أمة تسعى إلى استبقاء عاداتها وتقاليدها وتراثها بشكل من الأشكال ونمط من الأنماط وكانت العرب تعتمد على تدوين الشعر من أجل ذلك بما يتوفر فيه من سهولة حفظ الكلام وتداوله. يُقال إن الشعر ديوان العرب إذ إنه كان ومازال يُخلِّد آثارها ومآثرها منذ ظهور الحضارة العربية حتى يومنا هذا. وبطبيعة الحال مرّ الشعر العربي بمراحل عدة شهِد فيها نمواً وتطوّراً عظيمين، الأمر الذي أدى إلى إلقاء اسم على كل طور تَبَعاً للعصور التي توالت عليه وهي كالآتي: العصر الجاهلي وعصر صدر الإسلام والعصر الأمويّ، والعصر العباسي والعصر العثماني وينتهي إلى العصر الحديث وهو الذي نهتم به ها هنا في هذا الدرس وبالأخص الشاعرَيْن الكبيرَيْن محمود درويش ونزار قباني.

محمود درويش (١٣ آذار/ مارس ١٩٤١ - ٩ آب/ أغسطس ٢٠٠٨)

ولد عام ١٩٤١ في قرية البروة الفلسطينية وبعد مرور سبعة أعوام على ولادته غادر هو وأسرته بصحبة اللاجئين الفلسطينيين إلى لبنان وبقيت فيه عاماً واحداً وسُرعان ما عادت خِلسةً متسللةً إلى فلسطين لتجد مسقط رأسه مهدوماً مدمَّراً وقد حلت محلَّه قرية زراعية إسرائيلية ((آحيهود)) التي صارت قريته الجديدة. وقد عاش هذه الفترة الزمنية محروماً من الجنسية إذ كانت أسرته تخشى التعرُّض إلى النفي مجدداً. وبعد تخرجه من الثانوية العامة انتسب إلى الحزب الشيوعي الإسرائيلي وعمل صحافياً للحزب إلا أنه لم يتخلَ عن وفائه لفلسطين وقد اعتقلته السلطات الإسرائيلية عدة مرات في الفترة ما بين عام ١٩٦١ و١٩٧٢ بتهم تتعلق بأقواله ونشاطاته السياسية ومن ثمّة انتقل إلى الاتحاد السوفييتي وفي أواخر العام نفسه أي ١٩٧٢ لجأ إلى مصر حيث التحق بمنظمة التحرير الفلسطينية . وبعد إقامة قصيرة في باريس حصل على إذن للعودة إلى إسرائيل للقيام بزيارة لأمه المريضة وقد استأذن من الكنيست أن يسمح له بالبقاء في وطنه المحبوب، وإذا به يسمح له بذلك. ومنذ ذلك الحين حتى وفاته عام ٢٠٠٨ كرّس محمود درويش حياته لقضية تحرير الأراضي الفلسطينية بواسطة قلمه الفذ المبدع، وهذا سبب من الأسباب التي جعلته يُعتبَر من أروع الشعراء العرب المعاصرين.

تمرين ٤

اخترِ الكَلِمةَ الّتي لا تُناسِب باقي الكَلِماتِ في كُلِّ مَجْموعةٍ وبَيِّن السَبَب:

١-	شِعْر	فسيفساء	قَصيدة	نَثر
٢-	مُحاصَرة	هَواجِس	أوْهام	مُخَيِّلات
٣-	لاقَ	لاءَمَ	ناسَبَ	سَلَبَ
٤-	حَطَّمَ	دَمَّرَ	سَعى	فَتَكَ
٥-	مَنْزِل	بَيْت	مَثوى	مَنْزِلة

تمرين ٥

أكمل الجمل الآتية بالاختيار المناسِب وفق نصّ القراءة:

١- كانت العرب تعتمد على ______________ من أجل تخليد تراثها.

☐ نظم الشعر ☐ النقش في الصخر ☐ كتابة النثر ☐ التجارة

٢- يتمتّع الشِعر العربي بسهولة ______________ .

☐ القراءة ☐ الحفظ ☐ النظم ☐ الإلقاء

٣- عادت أسرة درويش إلى فلسطين ______________ .

☐ مرفوعةَ الرأس ☐ سعيدةً ☐ حزينةً ☐ متسللةً

٤- عند عودة أسرة درويش وجدت قريتها ______________ .

☐ سليمة ☐ مدمّرة ☐ قَذِرة ☐ متطورة

٥- أُعتُقِلَ درويش عدة مرات بتهم تتعلق بـ ______________ .

☐ أقواله ونشاطاته ☐ التسلُّل إلى إسرائيل ☐ السعي في القتل ☐ الابتزاز

في ما يلي نقدِّم بعض المقاطع الشعرية التي نظَمها الشاعر الفلسطيني محمود درويش.

أنا من هناك

أنا من هناك . ولي ذكرياتٌ. وُلدْتُ كما تُولدُ الناسُ. لي والدةْ
وبيتٌ كثيرُ النوافِذِ. لي إخوَةٌ. أصدقاءُ. وسِجنٌ بنافذةٍ باردةْ.
ولي مَوْجةٌ خَطفتْها النوارِسُ. لي مَشْهَدي الخاصُّ. لي عُشْبَةٌ
زائدةْ.
ولي قَمَرٌ في أقاصي الكلام، ورِزْقُ الطيورِ، وزيتونَةٌ خالدةْ.
مَرَرْتُ على الأرضِ قَبْلَ مُرورِ السُّيُوفِ على جَسَدٍ حوَّلوهُ إلى
مائدةْ.
أنا من هناكَ. أُعيدُ السَّماء إلى أُمِّها حينَ تبْكي السَّماءُ على أُمِّها،
وأبْكي لِتَعْرفَني غَيْمةٌ عائدةْ.
تعلَّمتُ كُلَّ كلامٍ يليقُ بمحكَمَةِ الدَّمِ كَيْ أكسر القاعِدةْ.
تَعَلَّمْتُ كُلَّ الكلامِ، وفكَّكْتُهُ كَيْ أُرَكِّبَ مُفْرَدَةً واحِدةْ
هي :الوَطَنُ

تمرين ٦

هات كلمات أو عبارات من قصيدة «أنا من هناك» التي تتعلّق بكلّ من الكلمات الآتية.

١- والدة	٥- أبديّ	٩- لِسان
٢- شبابيك	٦- غَير	١٠- سَحاب
٣- أصْحاب	٧- طاولة	١١- أساس
٤- إضافية	٨- أرْجَعَ	١٢- الأمة

تمرين ٧

للكتابة: أجب عن الأسئلة الآتية وفق نص قصيدة «أنا من هناك»

١ - تحدث عن الرموز المذكورة في القصيدة مثل « سِجن ونوارس وعشبة وقمر».
٢ - تأمل البيت الآتي: «أُعيدُ السَماءَ إلى أُمِّها حينَ تبْكي السَماءُ على أُمِّها». تحدث عن أهميته في السياق.
٣ - لَخِّص القصيدة في جملة واحدة.

مقطع من قصيدة «الجدارية»
هَزَمَتْكَ يا موتُ الفنونُ جميعُها.
هَزَمَتْك يا موت الأغاني في بلاد الرافدين.
مِسَلَّةُ المصريّ، مقبرةُ الفراعنةِ،
النقوشُ على حجارة معبدٍ هَزَمَتْكَ
وانتصرتْ، وأفْلَتَ من كمائنك
الخُلُودُ . . .

تمرين ٨

للكتابة: أجب عن الأسئلة الآتية وفق نص قصيدة «الجدارية»

١ - ما الذي تغلّب على الموت حسب ما جاء في القصيدة؟
٢ - ما الفكرة الأساسية التي يركز عليها درويش؟
٣ - ما المقصود من ذكر الآثار الفرعونية القديمة في القصيدة؟
٤ - لَخِّص القصيدة في فقرة واحدة.

مقطع من قصيدة «حالة حصار»	
١	٢
الشهيدُ يُحاصِرُني كُلَّما عِشْتُ يوماً جديداً	الشهيدُ يُحاصِرُني: لا تَسِرْ في الجنازة
ويسألني: أَين كُنْت ؟	إلاّ إذا كُنْتَ تعرفني. لا أُريد مجاملةً
أَعِدْ للقواميس كُلَّ الكلام الذي كُنْتَ	من أَحَدْ.
أَهْدَيْتَنيه،	الشهيد يُحَذِّرُني: لا تُصَدِّقْ زغاريدهُنَّ.
وخفِّفْ عن النائمين طنين الصدى	وصدّق أَبي حين ينظر في صورتي باكياً:
الشهيدُ يُعَلِّمني: لا جماليَّ خارجَ حريتي.	كيف بدَّلْتَ أدوارنا يا بُنيّ، وسِرْتَ أَمامي.
الشهيدُ يُوَضِّحُ لي: لم أفتِّشْ وراء المدى	أنا أوّلاً، وأنا أوّلاً !
عن عذارى الخلود، فإني أُحبُّ الحياةَ.	الشهيدُ يُحَاصرني: لم أُغيِّرْ سوى موقعي.
على الأرض، بين الصُنَوْبرِ والتين،	وأَثاثي الفقيرِ.
لكنني ما استطعتُ إليها سبيلاً، ففتَّشْتُ	وَضَعْتُ غزالاً على مخدعي،
عنها بآخر ما أملكُ: الدم في جَسَدِ	وهلالاً على إصبعي،
اللازوردْ.	كي أُخفِّف من وَجَعي!

تمرين ٩

للكتابة: أجب عن الأسئلة الآتية وفق نص قصيدة «حالة حصار»

١- ما أوامر الشهيد لمستمعيه؟

٢- ما حجة الشهيد لأن يستشهد حسب رأي درويش؟

٣- إلى ماذا يفتقر الشهيد في حياته وبمَ يتمتع؟

٤- كيف يصوّر درويش حالة الشهيد من حيث العائلة؟

٥- لَخِّص القصيدة في فقرة واحدة.

بطاقة هُوِيَّةْ

١	٢
سَجِّلْ!	سجّل!
أنا عربي.	أنا عربي.
ورَقْمُ بطاقتي خمسون ألفْ.	أنا اسمٌ بلا لَقَبِ.
وأطفالي ثمانيةٌ.	صبُورٌ في بلادٍ كُلُّ ما فيها
وتاسِعُهم ... سيأتي بعد صيفْ!	يعيش بفَوْرةِ الغضبِ.
فهل تغضبْ؟	جذوري ..
	قبل ميلاد الزمان رستْ.
	وقبل تفتُّحِ الحِقَبِ.
سَجِّل!	وقبل السَرْوِ والزيتونْ
أنا عربي.	.. وقبل تَرَعْرُعِ العشبِ.
وأعمل مع رفاق الكَدْح في محجرْ.	أبي ... من أُسرة المِحراث.
وأطفالي ثمانيةٌ.	لا من سادةٍ نُجُبِ.
أسلُّ لهم رغيفَ الخبزِ،	وجدّي كان فلاحاً.
والأثوابَ والدفترْ	بلا حَسَبٍ . . . ولا نَسبِ!
من الصخر ..	يُعَلمني شموخ النَفْس قبل قراءة الكتبِ
ولا أتوسَّلُ الصدقات من بابِكْ	وبيتي، كوخُ ناطورٍ
ولا أصغُرْ	من الأعوادِ والقصبِ.
أمام بَلاط أعتابك.	فهل تُرضيك منزلتي؟
فهل تغضبْ؟	أنا اسمٌ بلا لقبِ!

٣	٤
سجّل!	سجّل!
أنا عربي.	أنا عربي.
ولونُ الشعر فحميٌّ.	سَلَبْتَ كروم أجدادي
ولونُ العين بنّيٌّ.	وأرضاً كنتُ أفلحها
وميزاتي:	أنا وجميعُ أولادي
على رأسي عقالٌ فوق كوفِيَّةْ	ولم تترك لنا ... ولكل أحفادي
وكفّي صلبةٌ كالصخر ...	سوى هذي الصخور ..
تخمشُ من يلامسها.	فهل ستأخذها
وعنواني	حكومتكم ... كما قيلا!؟
أنا من قريةٍ عزلاءَ ... منسيَّةْ.	إذن!
شوارعها بلا أسماء.	
وكل رجالها ... في الحقل والمحجرْ.	سجّل ... برأس الصفحة الأولى!
فهل تغضب؟	أنا لا أكره الناسَ
	ولا أسطو على أحدٍ.
	ولكني ... إذا ما جعتُ
	آكلُ لحمَ مُغتَصِبي.
	حذارِ ... حذارِ ... من جوعي
	ومن غضبي !!

تمرين ١٠

للكتابة: أجب عن الأسئلة الآتية وفق نص قصيدة «بطاقة هوية»:

١- صف موقف المتكلم كما تتخيّله.

٢- ما الأبعاد الثقافية والاجتماعية المذكورة في القصيدة؟

٣- اذكر مقوِّمات الهُويَّةِ العربية بشكل عام والهُوِيَّة الفلسطينية بشكل خاص.

تمرين ١١

في القاموس:

ابحث في قاموسك عن الكلمات الآتية المأخوذة من قصيدة «**بطاقة هُوِيَّة**». يدل الرقم جنب الكلمة على القطعة التي ظهرت فيها الكلمة وستجدها مظللة بالأحمر في النص أعلاه. إن لم تجدها في القاموس ماذا تستطيع أن تستنبط معنوياً من السياق أو من الوزن؟

((أسلُّ – ١، محجر – ١، الصدقات – ١، أصْغُر –١، رَسَت – ٢، كوخ ناطور– ٢))

تمرين ١٢

للمحادثة:

- بعد قراءة هذه المختارات من أعمال محمود درويش، ما الأبعاد الاجتماعية والسياسية والثقافية التي يتطرق إليها في قصائده بصورة عامة في رأيك؟
- ما انطباعاتك حول أسلوب كتابة درويش؟
- ما الأفكار المتكررة في قصائد درويش إن وُجِدَت؟

نزار قباني

ولد نزار قباني عام ١٩٢٣ لأسرة دمشقية عريقة. نود هنا أن نفسح المجال ليتحدث نزار إلينا عن نشأته:

«ولدت في دمشق في آذار (مارس) ١٩٢٣ في بيت وسيع، كثير الماء والزهر، من منازل دمشق القديمة، والدي توفيق القباني، تاجر وجيه في حيه، عمل في الحركة الوطنية ووهب حياته وماله لها. تميز أبي بحساسية نادرة وبحبه للشعر ولكل ما هو جميل. ورث الحس الفني المرهف بدوره عن عمه أبي خليل القباني الشاعر والمؤلف والملحن والممثل وباذر أول بذرة في نهضة المسرح المصري. امتازت طفولتي بحب عجيب للاكتشاف وتفكيك الأشياء وردها إلى أجزائها ومطاردة الأشكال النادرة وتحطيم الجميل من الألعاب بحثا عن المجهول الأجمل. عنيت في بداية حياتي بالرسم. فمن الخامسة إلى الثانية عشرة من عمري كنت أعيش في بحر من الألوان. أرسم على الأرض وعلى الجدران وألطخ كل ما تقع عليه يدي بحثا عن أشكال جديدة. ثم انتقلت بعدها إلى الموسيقا ولكن مشاكل الدراسة الثانوية أبعدتني عن هذه الهواية».

نعم، تربّى نزار في حي مئذنة الشحم، أحد أحياء دمشق القديمة ودرس في مدرسة الكلية العلمية وبعد تخرجه منها التحق بكلية الحقوق بالجامعة السورية. عمل في وزارة الخارجية السورية إثر تخرجه وعاش حياته متنقلاً من سفارة إلى أخرى إلى أن تعيّن سكرتيراً ثانياً في سفارة سورية في الصين واستمر في منصبه الدبلوماسي حتى عام ١٩٦٦. وفي أثناء هذه الفترة صار يكتب الشعر التقليدي ثم انتقل إلى الشعر العمودي. يعتبر قباني من أروع الشعراء المعاصرين إن لم يكن أروعهم من حيث نظم شعر الحب. إلا أن هزيمة ١٩٦٧ تركت آثاراً عميقة في وجدانه نقلته من كتابة شعر الحب إلى كتابة شعر السياسة والمقاومة. عاش أواخر حياته في لندن بعد أن قضى خمسين عاماً ونيّفاً في كتابة قصائد الحب والسياسة والثورة.

وفي هذا الباب نقدّم لك قصيدة «إلى أمي». بقلم الشاعر الكبير نزار قباني ومن ثَمَّ نوفر لك بعض الكلمات التي قد تفيدك في استيعاب معناها:

أوصى (يُوصي) إيصاء (بِـ)	to advise	ضَجِرَ (يَضْجَرُ) ضَجَر (مِن)	to be discontent
تَخت ج تُخوت	bed	عَبير	fragrance, scent
جانِحة ج جَوانح	bosom, heart, soul	عَبِقَ (يَعْبَقُ) عَبَق	to linger on (a scent)
جَثا (يَجْثو) جُثو	to kneel	عَريشة	trellis
جَرْجَرَ (يُجَرْجِرُ) جَرْجَرة	to drag	عَضَّ (يَعَضُّ) عَضّ	to bite
حَدَقَة ج حَدَقات	pupils (of the eye)	غَدا (يَغْدو) غَدوة	to become
خاطِر ج خَواطِر	mind	غَمَرَ (يَغْمُرُ) غُمورة (بِـ)	to lavish (upon)
خَبَأَ (يَخْبَأُ) خَبْء	to hide, to conceal	كَسا (يَكْسو) كِسوة	to clothe, to cover
خُرافيّ	fictitious, legendary	مُثوى ج مَثاوٍ	abode, dwelling
خَرْبَشَ (يُخَرْبِشُ) خَرْبَشة	to scratch	مَدْمَع ج مَدامع	tear ducts
دَلَّلَ (يُدَلِّلُ) تَدْليل	to pamper	مَشْتَل ج مَشاتِل	nursery, arboretum
رِحاب	courtyard	نَثَرَ (يَنْثِرُ) نَثْر / نِثار	to scatter, to sprinkle
بِرِفْق	gently	نَشَلَ (يَنْشُلُ) نَشْل	to pick up
سَقى (يَسْقي) سَقي	to give s.o. a drink	نُعمى	happiness

دنانيراً منَ الذهبِ	أشعة الشمس التي تتخلل أوراق الشجرة فتسقط كأنها قطع ذهبية دائرية الشكل لامعة
كوم صَبّارة	*A pile of five peeled prickly pears chilled on a block of ice. People go out to eat them mostly at night in late summer.*
ساحة النجمة	*Star Square where five streets intersect. This is the neighborhood in New Damascus where Nizar's family moved from Old Damascus. The building that they occupied overlooked this square.*
فَيروزُ عَينَيه	*Nizar, like his father, was blue-eyed (Turquoise color).*
عَروسة السكر	*A doll-like candy for kids. It comes in different colors and tastes like crunchy marshmallows.*
جانِرك	*A fruit not unlike a small plum. They are green, crunchy, and have a sour taste.*

إلى أمي	
١	٢
صباحُ الخير ... يا حلوة ...	أنا وحدي ...
صباحُ الخير ... يا قديستي الحلوة	دخانُ سجائري يَضْجر ومني مقعدي يَضْجر
مضى عامان يا أمي	وأحزاني عصافيرٌ ...
على الولد الذي أبحر	تُفتش - بعدُ - عن بَيْدر
برحلته الخرافيَّةْ	عرفت نساء أوروبا ...
وخبأ في حقائبهِ ...	عرفت عواطف الإسمنت والخشبِ
صباح بلاده الأخضر	عرفت حضارة التعبِ ...
وأنجمها، وانهرها، وكل شقيقها الأحمر	وطُفتُ الهند، طُفتُ السند،
وخبَّأ في ملابسهِ	طُفت العالم الأصفر ولم أعثَر ...
طرابيناً من النعناع والزعترْ	على امرأة تَمْشُط شعريَ الأشقر
وليلكةً دمشقيةً ...	وتحمل في حقيبتها ...
	إليَّ عرائس السُّكَّر
	وتكسوني إذا أعرى
	وتنشُلني إذا أعثُر
	أيا أمي ...
	أنا الولد الذي أبحر
	ولا زالت بخاطرهِ ...
	تعيش عروسةُ السكّر
	فكيف ... فكيف يا أمي
	غدوتُ أباً ...
	ولم أكبُر ...

٣	٤
سلاماتٌ .	فلُّ دمشقَ
سلاماتٌ .	تسكنُ في خواطرنا
إلى بيتٍ سقانا الحُبَّ والرحمة	مآذنُها ... تُضيءُ على مراكبنا
إلى أزهارك البيضاءِ . . . فرحةِ (ساحة النجمة)	كأنَّ مآذنَ الأُمويِّ...
إلى تَخْتي ...	قد زُرِعت بداخلنا ...
إلى كُتبي ...	كأنَّ مشاتل التفاحِ ...
إلى أطفال حارتنا ...	تَعبَق في ضمائرنا
وحيطانٍ ملأناها ...	كأنَّ الضوءَ والأحجارَ
بفوضى من كتابتنا ...	جاءت كلُّها معنا
إلى قطط كسولاتٍ	أتى أيلول أماه ...
تنام على مشارفنا	وجاء الحزنُ يحمل لي هداياهُ
وليلكةٍ معرشةٍ	ويترك عند نافذتي
على شباك جارتنا	مدامعهُ وشكواهُ
مضى عامان ... يا أمي	أتى أيلول ... أين دمشق ؟
ووجه دمشقَ،	أين أبي وعيناهُ
عصفورٌ يخربش في جوانحنا	وأين حريرُ نظرته ؟
يَعَضُّ على ستائرنا ...	وأين عبيرُ قهوته ؟
وينقرنا ...	سقى الرحمن مثواهُ .
برفق من أصابعنا ...	وأين رحابُ منزلنا الكبيرُ ...
مضى عامان ... يا أمي	وأين نُعماهُ؟
وليلُ دمشقَ	وأين مدارج الشمشيرِ ...

٤	٥
تضحك في زواياهُ	صباحُ الخير، من مدريد
وأين طفولتي فيهِ؟	ما أخبارها الفُلَّة ؟
أجرجر ذيل قطتهِ	بها أوصيك يا أماه ...
وآكل من عريشتهِ	تلك الطِّفلة الطِّفلة
وأقطف من (بنفشاهُ)	فقد كانت أحب حبيبةٍ لأبي ...
دمشق . دمشقُ .	يُدللها كطفلتهِ
يا شعراً	ويدعوها إلى فِنْجان قهوتهِ
على حدَقات أعيننا كتبناهُ	ويسقيها . . .
ويا طفلاً جميلاً ...	ويُطعمها . . .
من ضفائرهِ صلبناهُ	ويغمُرها برحمته . . .
جَثَوْنا عند رُكبتهِ ...	ومات أبي
وذُبنا في محبتهِ	ولا زالت تعيش بِحُلْم عودتهِ
إلى أنْ في محبتنا قتلناهُ	وتبحث عنه في أرجاء غرفتهِ
	وتسأل عن عباءتِهِ ...
	وتسأل عن جريدته ...
	وتسأل – حين يأتي الصيفُ –
	عن فيروز عينيهِ ...
	لتنثرَ فوق كفَّيْهِ ...
	دنانيراً من الذهب ...

تمرين ١٣

للكتابة: أجب عن الأسئلة الآتية وفق نص قصيدة «إلى أمي»:

١- تَحَدَّثْ عن الرموز الّتي وجدتها في القصيدة مثل: «الولد، الرحلة، الأم، شجرة الفل»:

٢- في القطعة الأولى ما أهمية أبيات «وخبّأ في حقائبه صباح بلاده الأخضر وأنجمها، وأنْهُرها، وكل شقيقها الأحمر»: في هذا السياق؟

٣- في القطعة الثانية شبّه نزار أحزانه بالعصافير، ما العلاقة بين الكلمتين في رأيك؟

٤- في القطعة الثانية ماذا حدث للولد وكيف صار هذا؟

٥- في القطعة الرابعة، ما العلاقة بين «دمشق والأم»: بالقصيدة في رأيك؟

٦- ما المقصود من آخر بيت القصيدة «إلى أنْ في محبتنا قتلناه»:

وفي هذا الباب نقدّم لكم قصيدة «دمشق . . . مهرجان الماء والياسمين»: مكتوبة بخط يد نزار قباني وقبل أن تتذوقوا جمالها وإناقتها نوفر لكم بعض المفردات قد تكون مفيدة:

اكتظّ / يَكْتَظُّ / اِكْتِظاظ	*to be overcrowded*	عِلْمُ العَروض	*metrics, prosody*
ثدي	*a breast*	الغوطة	*fertile oasis of southern Damascus*
حَنْجَرة	*throat*	فُسَيْفُساء	*mosaic*
حِياكة	*weaving*	فصيل ج فصائل	*genus, species*
رِحْم أو رَحِم	*womb*	محْصول	*crop, yield*
رَشَّ / يَرُشّ / رَشّ	*to spray, to sprinkle*	مخيّلات	*imagination*
الرمان	*pomegranate*	مَسامات	*pores*
السَفَرْجَل	*quince (tree whose fruit resembles pears)*	مشيمة (حَبَل مشيمة)	*placenta (umbilical cord)*
صَدَف	*mother-of-pearl*	مُطَعَّم بـ	*to be inlaid with*
صَفْصافة	*willow tree*	نَوْل ج أنوال	*loom*
ضَفائر	*braid, plait*	هاجِس ج هَواجِس	*notions, misgivings*
عاشق	*lover*	هلوَسات	*hallucinations*

fancy, imagination	وَهَم ج أوْهام	to cover (as jasmine does a trellis)	عرّش / يُعَرِّش / تعريش
a small bucket of licorice drink chilled and made fresh	سَطْل عِرقسوس	Arabism, the Arab character	عُروبة
a Sufi philosopher from Andalusia who preached in Damascus	الشيخ محيي الدين بن عربي	a coffee pot	رَكوة قهوة

دمشقُ .. مهرجانُ الماءِ والياسمين

نزار قباني

١

لا أستطيعُ أن أكتبَ عن دمشق، دونَ أن يُعرِّشَ الياسمينُ على أصابعي.

ولا أستطيعُ أن أنطقَ اسمَها، دونَ أن يكتظَّ فمي بعصيرِ المشمشِ، والرمّانِ، والتوتِ، والسفرجلْ.

ولا أستطيعُ أن أتذكّرها، دونَ أن تحطَّ على جدارِ ذاكرتي ألفُ حمامةٍ.. وتطيرَ ألفُ حمامةْ..

٢

كلُّ أطفال العالم، يقطعُونَ لهم حبلَ مشيمتهم عندما يُولَدون.

إلا أنا... فإنَّ حبلَ مشيمتي لم يزل مشدوداً الى رَحِمِ دمشق،

منذ ٢١ آذار ١٩٢٣.

إنها معجزةٌ طبيّةٌ، أن يبقى طفلٌ من الأطفال يبحثُ عن ثدي

أمّه سبعينَ عاماً...

٣

أنا مسكونٌ بدمشقَ، حتى حينَ لا أسكنُها.

أولياؤُها، مدفونونَ في داخلي.

حاراتُها تتقاطعُ فوقَ جَسَدي.

وقططُها، تعشقُ.. وتتزوّجُ.. وتتركُ أطفالَها عندي.

٤

دمشقُ، ليستْ صورةً منقولةً عن الجنَّة.

إنّها الجنّة.

وليستْ نُسْخةً ثانيةً للقصيدةْ..

إنّها القصيدةْ.

وليستْ سيفاً أمويّاً على جدار العروبةْ..

إنّها العروبَةْ.

٥

لا تطلبوا مِنّي أوراقي الثُّبُوتِيَّة.

فأنا محصولٌ دمشقيٌّ مئةً بالمئة..

كما الحنطةُ ، والخوخُ ، والرمّانُ ، والجانَرْكُ ،

واللوزُ الأخضرُ في بساتينِ الغُوطَة.

وكما البروكار ، والأغباني ، والداماسكو ، وأباريقِ النحاسْ ،

والخزائنُ المطعّمةُ بالصَدَف ، التي هي جزءٌ من تاريخي..

ومن جهازِ عُرْسِ أُمّي..

٦

اللغةُ التي أكتُبُ بها أيضاً ، هيَ محصولٌ دمشقيٌّ

فلو فتحتُ ثقباً صغيراً في أبجديّتي.. لانفجرتْ نوافيرُ الماءْ..

وطلعتْ من مسامات حُروفي..

رائحةُ النرْجسِ ، والريحان ، والزَعْتَر البريِّ ، والطرخُونْ ....

٧

سافرتُ كثيراً .. حتى وصلتُ الى حائطِ الصينِ العظيم.

ولكنَّ حمائمَ الجامعِ الأمويِّ لا تزالُ تطلعُ من جيوبي حيثما اتّجهت ،

ولا تزالُ القططُ الشاميّةُ تموءُ تحت سريري في كلِّ فندقٍ أنزلُ فيه .

ولا تزالُ رائحةُ الخُبّيزة والقرنفل تطلعُ لي من كلِّ حقيبةٍ أفتحُها...

٨

أنا خاتمٌ من صياغة دمشقْ .
نسيجي لغويٌّ من حياكة أنواليها .
صوتٌ شعريٌّ خرجَ من حنجرتها .
رسالةُ حُبٍّ مكتوبةٌ بخطِّ يدها .
سحابةٌ من القِرْفَة واليانسون ، تتجوَّلُ في أسواقها .
شجرةُ فُلٍّ تركَتْها أمّي على نافذتي ،
ولا تزالُ تُطْلِعُ أقمارَها البيضاءَ .. كلَّ عامْ ..

٩

في أسفاري ، تمرُّ بي أوهامٌ كثيرة .
فأتصوَّرُ مرةً أنني سَفَرْجلةْ .
ومرةً ، أنني رغيفُ خبزٍ مرقوقْ .
أو سطلُ عرقسوسٍ ، أو كومُ صبارةٍ مثلَّجةٍ في ليالي الصيف ..
إنّني أعرفُ أنَّ كلَّ هذه الهواجس هي هواجسُ طفوليّة ،
وأنَّ كلَّ هذه التهلوسات ، هي هلوساتُ عاشقْ ..
ولكنْ .. لن أسمحَ لأحَدٍ أن يُلغيَ مخيلتي .
ولن أسمحَ لأحدٍ أن يمنعني من أن أكونَ عنقودَ عنب ..
أو ركوةَ قهوةٍ .. أو سِرْبَ سنونو .. أو قطّةً شاميةً فرحيّةَ العينينْ ..
أو نافورةَ ماءٍ تقولُ الشعرَ ، دون أن يعلّمها أحدٌ علمَ العَروضْ ...

١٠

وبعدُ.. وبعدْ..

فبصدور هذا الكتاب الذي يحمل عنوانَ: (دمشق.. نزار قباني).

أشعرُ أنّ حُلُماً قديماً من أحلامي قد تحقّقْ.

وهو أن أصبحَ ذاتَ يومٍ جزءاً من تاريخِ دمشقْ.

قطعةَ فُسَيْفِساءٍ على جدرانِ الجامعِ الأمويّ.

خاتماً مشغولاً بالفيروز في (سوق الصاغة).

صفصافةً تغسلُ ضفائرَها بمياه (عَيْن الفيجَة).

فصيلاً من فصائل نَعْناعٍ، وطرخونٍ، ومُشْمُشٍ، وسَفَرْجلٍ.

باباً خشبيّاً واطئاً يوزّعُ تذاكرَ الدُخولِ إلى الجنّةْ...

تلميذاً من تلاميذ الشيخ محي الدين بن عربي.

بيتاً من الشعر لأبي الطيّب المتنبّي محفوراً على سُقوفِ قاعاتها..

نافورة ماءٍ، ترشُّ دفاترنا المدرسيّة بحبرها الأزرقِ كلَّ صباحْ.

تمرين ١٤

للكتابة: أجب عن الأسئلة الآتية وفق نص قصيدة «بدمشق . . مهرجان الماء والياسمين»:

١- اذكر سبب عدم قدرة نزار على نطق اسم دمشق.

٢- بمَ يرتبط نزار إلى دمشق؟

٣- كيف يصوّر نزار دمشقَ في القطعة الرابعة؟

٤- ماذا تشمل بساتين الغوطة بالنسبة لنزار؟

٥- ماذا سيحدث لو فتحتَ ثقباً صغيراً في أبجدية اللغة العربية؟

٦- في رأي نزار، ماذا يفتقر حائط الصين العظيم؟

٧- في القطعة التاسعة يذكر نزار هواجسه وهلوساته، ما هي؟ ولماذا تعتقد أنه يشبه نفسه بهذه الأشياء بالذات؟

٨- كيف صار نزار قطعة فسيفساء دمشق؟

٩- ماذا يتمنى نزار أن يصبح ذات يومٍ حسب القطعة العاشرة؟ إلامَ ترمز هذه الأشياء في رأيك؟

تمرين ١٥

أ- ترجم القطعة الثامنة.

ب- اختر موضوعاً يمكن أن تُنظَمَ قصيدة فيه. تستطيع إذا أردت أن تقلّد أسلوب كتابة شاعر من الشاعرين الموجودين في هذا الدرس أو غيرهما.

رُكن التعبيرات المتداولة على الألسن

بلا حَسَبٍ ولا نَسَبِ

وجَدي كانَ فَلاّحاً بِلا حَسَبٍ . . . ولا نَسَبِ | *not to be of noble descent*

كانَ ومازالَ

يُقال إن الشعر ديوان العرب إذ إنه كان ومازال يُخلِّد آثارها ومآثرها | *it was and continues to be*

وبطبيعة الحال

وبطبيعة الحال مرّ الشعر العربي بمراحل عدة | *by the very nature of the case, as is only natural*

وبالأخصّ

وإنما العصر الحديث الذي نهتم به ها هنا في هذا الدرس وبالأخصّ الشاعرَيْن الكَبيرين | *and in particular*

حَلَّ مَحَلَّ

وقد حلت محله قرية زراعية إسرائيلية «آحيهود» التي صارت قريته الجديدة. | *to take the place of*

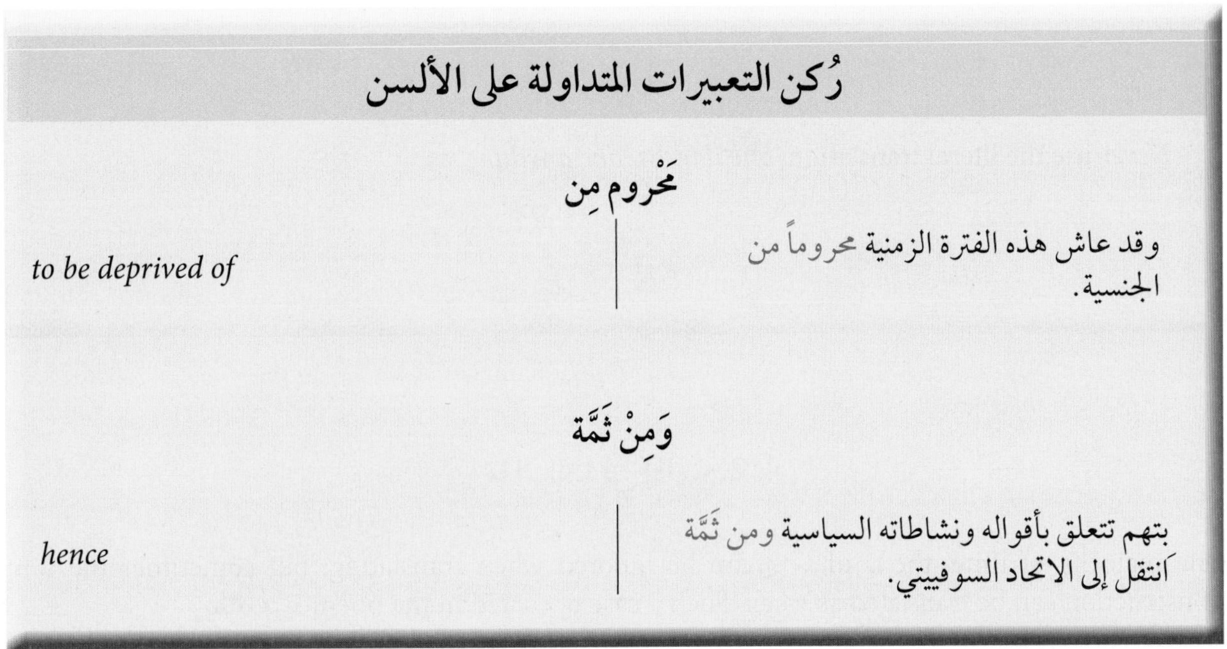

رُكن التعبيرات المتداولة على الألسن

مَحْروم مِن

وقد عاش هذه الفترة الزمنية محروماً من الجنسية.	*to be deprived of*

وَمِنْ ثَمَّة

بتهم تتعلق بأقواله ونشاطاته السياسية ومن ثَمَّة انتقل إلى الاتحاد السوفييتي.	*hence*

مُراجَعةُ القَواعِد

1. Expressing 'one of something'

Arabic allows its speakers a convenient and eloquent way to express *one of s.th.* or *in a certain s.th.* by using the following formula:

مُفْرَد + مِنَ + الجَمْع

١	شَكْلٌ مِنَ الأشْكالِ	*In a certain way*
٢	وَنَمَطٌ مِنَ الأنْماطِ	*With a certain design*

That is to say, if you want to express *one day I* ______, then you will use this formula:

٣	في يَوْمٍ مِنَ الأيّامِ . . .	*One day, on a certain day . . .*

تَذَكَّروا

Never use the literal translation '*one day*' or '*one anything*' as:

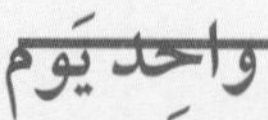

ما الزائدة في إذا ما .2

The majority of time, the ما of إذا ما can be ignored when translating; but sometimes the إذا ما construction can be translated as *when*. Such a case occurred in the poem بطاقة هوية :

But, when I get hungry, I eat the flesh of my rapist.	ولكني ... إذا ما جعتُ آكل لحم مُغتصبي	٣
But, if I get hungry, I will eat the flesh of my rapist.		٤

3. Sometimes a Word Is a Sentence in Arabic

Arabic, as a language, has the ability to express complete ideas in a single word. Consider the following example taken from القطعة الأولى من حالة حصار :

Return all of the words that you presented me to the dictionaries.	أَعِدْ للقواميس كُلَّ الكلام الذي كُنْتَ أَهْدَيْتَنِيه،	٥

If we take a closer look at this verb, we can better see the heavy semantic load this verb is carrying:

ه	ي	تَ	أهْدَيْ	⇐	أَهْدَيْتَنِيه
مَفْعول بِهِ ثانٍ	مَفْعول بِه	فاعِل	فِعْل ماضٍ	⇐	جملة
it	*to me*	*you*	*to present a gift*	⇐	*You presented me with it.*

تمرين ١٦

آ **أكمِل الجمل الآتية بالاختيار المناسب وفق نصّ الاستماع:**

١- في القصيدة يقول أدونيس إنه لا يريد ________.

☐ هويةً ☐ حُبّاً ☐ وَطَناً

٢- وقالَ أيضاً في القصيدة إنه يريد أن نكون ________.

☐ أفكاراً ☐ لُغاتٍ ☐ وضوحاً

٣- ابتكر أبو نُوّاس ________.

☐ قِيَم المدينة والحياة المدنية ☐ قِيَم الشكّ والتساؤل ☐ قِيَم البحث عن الحقيقة

ب- **اكتب «خطأ» أو «صواب» إلى جانب كلّ جملة ثمّ صحِّح الجمل الخطأ:**

١- أدونيس أكثر الشعراء إثارةً للجدل.

٢- تقتصر شهرة أدونيس على منطقة الشرق الأوسط.

٣- ترعرع أدونيس في ظروف سلسة هينة.

ج- **أكمل الجمل وفق نص الاستماع:**

١- أسّسَ أدونيس مجلّتي ________ و ________.

٢- الحداثة ليست مجرد شكل وإنما هي ________.

٣- ترفض العرب العقل الذي ابتكر ________.

د- **أجِب عن الأسئلة وفق نصّ الاستماع:**

١- متى دخل أدونيس المدرسة؟

٢- حسب أقوال أدونيس لماذا لم تستطع الحداثة الشعرية العربية تأسيس أرضية ثابتة؟

٣- في رأي أدونيس، لِمَ لَمْ يدرك الوطن العربي الحداثة حتى اليوم رغم ظهورها في العصر العباسي؟

المُفْرَدات

اِسْتَبْقى	(يَسْتَبْقي)	اِسْتِبْقاء	(v.)	to preserve, to retain
أَفْلَتَ	(يُفْلِتُ)	إفْلات	(v.)	to slip away
اكتظّ	(يَكْتَظُّ)	اِكْتِظاظ	(v.)	to be overcrowded
اِنْتَزَعَ	(يَنْتَزِعُ)	اِنْتِزاع	(v.)	to remove
أَهْدى	(يُهْدي)	إهْداء	(v.)	to give a gift
أوصى	(يُوصي)	إيصاء (بِـ)	(v.)	to advise
بُعْد	ج	أَبْعاد	(n., m.)	dimension
بَنْفَش			(n., m.)	pansy (flower)
بَيْدَر	ج	بَيادِر	(n., m.)	threshing floor
تَداوَلَ	(يَتَداوَلُ)	تَداول	(v.)	to circulate, to be in circulation
تَرَعْرَعَ	(يَتَرَعْرَعُ)	تَرَعْرُع	(v.)	to flourish
ثدي	ج	أَثْداء	(n., m./f.)	breast
ثَمّة				there (is, are) هُناكَ
جانِحة	ج	جَوانح	(act. p.)	bosom, heart, soul
جَثو	(يَجْثو)	جُثو	(v.)	to kneel
جَرْجَرَ	(يُجَرْجِرُ)	جَرْجَرة	(v.)	to drag
جُموح			(n., m.)	recalcitrance, defiance; willfulness
حارة	ج	حارات	(n., f.)	neighborhood
حاصَرَ	(يُحاصِرُ)	مُحاصَرة	(v.)	to lay siege, to blockade

خاطِر	ج	خَواطِر	(act. p.)	mind
حَدَقَة	ج	حَدَقات	(n., m.)	pupils (of the eye)
حَذارِ	(مِن)			beware, watch out (for)
حِقْبة	ج	حِقَق / أحْقاب	(n., m.)	long period of time
حَنْجَرة	ج	حَناجِر	(n., f.)	throat
حِياكة			(n., f.)	weaving
خَبَأ	(يَخْبَأُ)	خَبْء	(v.)	to hide, to conceal
خُرافيّ			(adj.)	fictitious, legendary
خَرْبَشَ	(يُخَرْبِشُ)	خَرْبَشة	(v.)	to scratch
خُلْسَةً			(n., f.)	stealthily, unnoticeably
دَلَّلَ	(يُدَلِّلُ)	تَدْليل	(v.)	to pamper, to dote on
دَوَّنَ	(يُدَوِّنُ)	تَدْوين	(v.)	to record, to write down
رِحاب			(n., m.)	courtyard
رَحِم	ج	أرْحام	(n., f.)	womb
رَشَّ	(يَرُشُّ)	رَشّ	(v.)	to spray, to sprinkle
بِرِفْق			(phrase)	gently
رُمّان			(n., m.)	pomegranate
زهو			(adj.)	arrogantly
سَفَرْجَل			(n., m.)	quince (tree whose fruit resembles pears)
سَقى	(يَسْقي)	سَقي	(v.)	to give s.o. a drink

to plunder	(v.)	سَلْب	(يَسْلُبُ)	سَلَبَ
executioner	(n., m.)	سيّافون	ج	سيّاف
haughty	(n., m.)			شُموخ
mother of pearl, sea shell	(n., m.)	أصْداف	ج	صَدَف
willow tree	(n., f.)			صَفْصافة
to be discontent, to be displeased	(v.)	ضَجَر (مِن)	(يَضْجَرُ)	ضَجِرَ
braid, pigtail, tress, lace	(n., f.)	ضَفائِر	ج	ضَفيرة
to wander, to circle around	(v.)	طَوْف	(يَطوفُ)	طافَ
lover	(act. p.)	عاشِقون	ج	عاشق
to linger on (a scent)	(v.)	عَبَق	(يَعْبَقُ)	عَبِقَ
scent, fragrance				عَبير
doorstep, threshold	(n., f.)	أعتاب	ج	عَتَبة
to become	(v.)	غَدوة	(يَغْدو)	غَدا
to cover (as a vine does a trellis)	(v.)	تَعْريش	(يُعَرِّشُ)	عرّش
trellis	(n., f.)			عَريشة
Arabism, to have the Arabic character	(n., f.)			عُروبة
doll	(n., f.)	عَرائِس (السكر)	ج	عَروسة
to bite	(v.)	عَضّ	(يَعَضُّ)	عَضَّ
metrics, prosody				عِلْمُ العَروض
to lavish (upon)	(v.)	غُمورة (بِـ)	(يَغْمُرُ)	غَمُرَ

Ghouta (name of fertile oasis in southern Damascus)	(n., f.)			الغوطة
stallion, strong man, luminary	(n., m.)	فُحول(ة)	ج	فَحْل
mosaic	(n., m.)			فُسَيْفُساء
genus	(n., m.)	فَصائِل	ج	فصيل
jasmine	(n., m.)			فلٌّ
to cultivate, to till	(v.)	فَلْح	(يَفْلَحُ)	فَلَحَ
toil, labor, drudgery	(v.)			كَدْح
vineyard	(n., m.)	كُروم	ج	كَرْم
to clothe, to cover	(v.)	كِسوة	(يَكْسو)	كسا
ambush	(n., f.)	كَمائِن	ج	كَمين
to be suitable (for)	(v.)	لَيْق (بِـ)	(يَليقُ)	لاقَ
lilac	(n., f.)			لَيْلكة
minaret	(n., f.)	مآذِن	ج	مِئذَنة
infiltrated	(act. p)			مُتَسَلِّل
abode, dwelling	(n., m.)	مَثاوٍ	ج	مُثوى
crop, yield	(pass. p.)			مَحْصول
bed chamber	(n., m.)	مَخادِع	ج	مَخْدَع
imagination, fantasy	(n., f.)	مُخَيِّلات	ج	مُخَيِّلة
tear duct	(n., m.)	مَدامِع	ج	مَدْمَع
pores	(n., m.)	مَسامّات	ج	مَسامّ

obelisk	(n., f.)	مِسَلّات	ج	مِسَلّة
nursery, arboretum	(n., m.)	مَشاتِل	ج	مَشْتَل
placenta	(n., f.)	مَشايم	ج	مَشيمة
umbilical cord				حَبَلُ مِشيمة
inlaid (with)	(pass. p)		بِـ	مُطَعَّم
components	(n., m.)	مُقَوِّمات	ج	مُقَوِّم
status, position, standing	(n., f.)	مَنازِل	ج	مَنْزِلة
talent	(n., m.)	مَواهِب	ج	مَوْهِبة
distinguishing feature	(n., f.)	ميزات	ج	ميزة
guard, keeper, warden	(n., m.)	نَواطير	ج	ناطور
to scatter, to sprinkle	(v.)	نَثْر / نِثار	(يَنْثُرُ)	نَثَرَ
to pluck out	(v.)	نَتْف	يَنْتِفُ	نَتَفَ
to pick up	(v.)	نَشْل	(يَنْشُلُ)	نَشَلَ
star	(n., m.)	أَنْجُم	ج	نَجْم
happiness	(n., m.)			نُعمى
river	(n.)	أَنْهُر	ج	نَهْر
sea gull	(n., m.)	نَوارِس	ج	نَوْرَس
loom	(n., m.)	أَنْوال	ج	نَوْل
medal	(n., m.)	نياشين	ج	نيشان
notions, misgivings	(n., m.)	هَواجِس	ج	هاجِس

to neutralize, to defeat	(v.)	هَزْم	(يَهْزِمُ)	هَزَمَ
hallucination, vision	(n., f.)	هَلْوَسات	ج	هَلْوَسَة
fancy, imagination, misconception	(n., m.)	أوْهام	ج	وَهَم

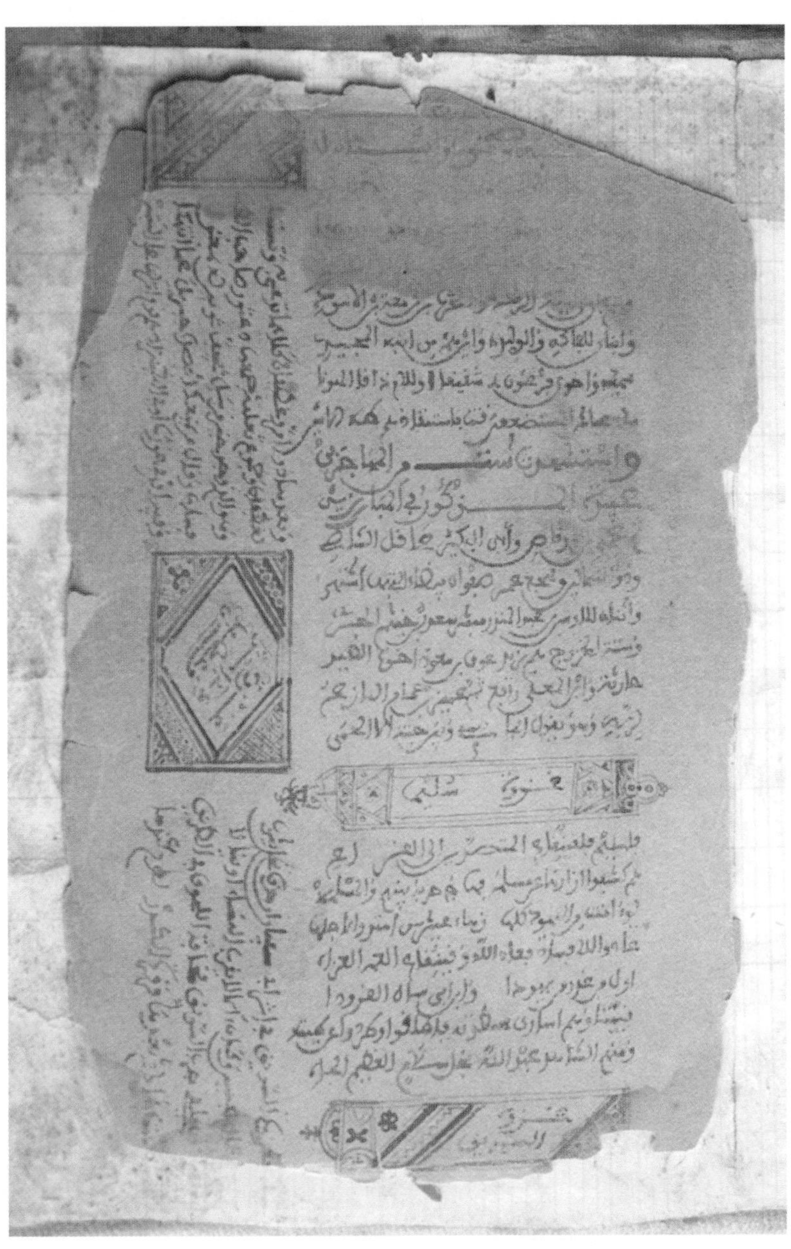

مقطع من قصيدة موريتانية

مُراجَعَةُ القَواعِدِ

لِكِتابِ أهْلاً وَسَهْلاً الجُزءُ الثاني

Objectives

• Cases of the Noun	حالاتُ الاِسْمِ العَرَبيّ •
• The Nominal Sentence	الجُمْلَةُ الاسْميّةُ •
• The Verbal Sentence	الجُمْلَةُ الفِعْليّةُ •
• Pronouns	الضَمائِر •
• The Permutative	البَدَل •
• The إضافة	الإضافة •
• Diptotes	المَمْنوعُ مِنَ الصَّرْفِ •
• Comparative and Superlative Nouns	اِسْمُ التَفْضيل •
• Number-Noun Agreement	تَطابُقُ العَدَدِ والاسْمِ المَعدود •
• Adverbials	الظُروف •
• The Verb	الفِعْل •
• Derivation	الاِشْتِقاق •
• Negation	النَفْي •
• Dictionary of Grammatical Terms	مُعجَم مُصْطَلَحات القَواعِد •

مُلاحَظة

This review presents Arabic grammar from an Arabic, not Western, perspective. Western terminology, however, is used to describe the categories.

القَواعِد

1. Cases of the Noun حالاتُ الاسم

Nouns can be in one of three cases: nominative, genitive, or accusative.

a. The Nominative Case حالةُ الرَفْع

The nominative case is marked by:

جَمْعُ المُذَكَّر السالم	مُثَنّى	نكِرة	مَعرِفة
ونَ	انِ	تَنْوين ضَمّة	ضَمة
مُعَلِّمونَ	مُعَلِّمان	مُعَلِّمٌ	المُعَلِّمُ

A noun is مَرْفوع when it is:

i. المُبْتَدأ - the subject (a.k.a. *topic*) of a nominal sentence:

١ | الطالِبُ مُتَأخِّرٌ.

ii. الخَبر - the predicate (a.k.a. *comment*) of a nominal sentence:

٢ | الطالِبُ مُتَأخِّرٌ.

iii. اسْم كانَ - The subject of a nominal sentence introduced by كان:

٣ | كانَ الطالِبُ مُتَأخِّرٌ.

iv. خَبَر إنَّ - The predicate of a nominal sentence introduced by إنَّ:

٤ | إنَّ الطالِبَ مُتَأخِّرٌ.

v. الفاعِل في جملة فعلية - The noun of agent فاعِل of a verbal sentence:

٥ | وَصَلَ الطالِبُ

vi. نائِب الفاعِل - The substitute of فاعِل after a passive verb:

٦ | بُنِيَتِ الأَهْراماتُ مُنْذ أَكْثَر مِنْ أَرْبعةِ آلافِ سَنة.

b. The Genitive Case حالةُ الجَر

The genitive case is marked by:

جَمْعُ المُذَكَّر السالم	مُثَنّى	نكِرة	مَعرِفة
ـينَ	ـَيْنِ	تَنْوين كَسْرة	كَسْرة
مُعَلِّمينَ	مُعَلِّمَيْنِ	مُعَلِّمٍ	المُعَلِّمِ

A noun is مَجرور when it is:

i. The object of a preposition

١ في الجامَعةِ.

ii. The second (or following) member of الإضافة

٢ مِفْتاحُ بابِ غُرْفَةِ الصَفِّ.
غُرْفَةُ المُدَرِّسينَ

c. The Accusative Case حالةُ النَصْب

The accusative case is the most varied of the three noun cases and since we are only dealing with three cases, the easiest way to identify the accusative is by process of elimination: if it is not nominative or genitive, it is accusative مَنْصوب.

جَمْعُ المُذَكَّر السالم	مُثَنّى	نكِرة	مَعرِفة
ـينَ	ـَيْنِ	تَنْوين فَتْحة	فَتْحة
مُعَلِّمينَ	مُعَلِّمَيْنِ	مُعَلِّماً	المُعَلِّمَ

The most frequently occurring reasons for being حالةُ النَصْب are illustrated in example here:

i. المَفْعول به – Direct object of the verb:

١ | كَتَبْنا رَسائِلَ.

ii. خَبَرَ كانَ – The predicate of a nominal sentence introduced by كانَ:

٢ | كانَ الطالِبُ مُتَأَخِّراً.

iii. اسم إنَّ – The subject of a nominal sentence introduced by إنَّ:

٣ | إنَّ الطالِبَ مُتَأَخِّرٌ.

iv. الظَرْف – Adverbials:

٤ | وَصَلْتُ صَباحاً.

v. التَمييز – Nouns of specification:

٥ | اِشْتَرَيْتُ خَمْسَةَ عَشَرَ قَلَماً.

vi. الاسْتِثْناء – Exception created after إلاّ and ما عدا in positive sentences:

٦ | قَرَأَ أَحْمَدُ الكُتُبَ إلاّ واحِداً.

2. The Nominal Sentence الجُمْلَةُ الاسمِيَّة

Nominal sentences are those sentences that begin with a noun and are comprised of a subject and a predicate:

١ | أَحْمَدُ طالِبٌ.

Both words in example 1 are nouns in حالةُ الرَفْع and combine together to create an equational sentence. The مُبْتَدأ is أَحْمَدُ while the خَبر is طالِبٌ.

تَذَكَّروا

- **Definite words like أَحْمَدُ only take one ضَمّة**
- **Indefinite words like طالِبٌ take تَنْوين ضَمّة**

a. Nominative Sentences with كانَ وَأخَواتها

When speaking in past or future time, a member of the set of كانَ is used as a copula (*to be*):

٢	كانَ أَحْمَدُ طالِباً.
٣	سَيَكونُ أَحْمَدُ طالِباً.

Every member of the set of كانَ has the same syntactic effect on the other words in the sentence. They make the predicate (a.k.a. the comment) مَنْصوب.

أخوات كانَ

أَصْبَحَ، أَمْسَى، أَضْحى، ظَلَّ، صارَ، باتَ، مادامَ، لَيْسَ، مازالَ

to become	صارَ
	أَصْبَحَ
	أَمْسَى
	أَضْحى
	باتَ
to continue	ظَلَّ
to remain	مازالَ
to continue to, as long as	مادامَ
negates nouns and adjectives	لَيْسَ

b. Nominative Sentences with إنَّ وأخواتها

Every member of the set of إنَّ has the same syntactic effect on the other words in the sentence. They make the subject (a.k.a. the topic) مَنْصوب.

أخوات إنَّ	
behold, truly	إنَّ
that + (noun)	أنَّ
as if	كَأنَّ
but, however	لكِنَّ
if only, if it were only so	لَيْتَ
perhaps, maybe	لَعَلَّ

٤ | إنَّ أحْمَدَ طالِبٌ.

The predicate طالِبٌ remains unchanged in that it remains in المَرْفوع.

The subject of a sentence introduced by either كانَ or إنَّ may be an attached pronoun:

They were students.	كانوا طُلاّباً.	٥
He is a student.	إنَّهُ طالِبٌ.	٦

The ending suffixed to كانَ in example 5 is the type of pronoun suffixed to verbs; whereas in example 6, the ending suffixed to إنَّ is a pronoun suffixed to nouns and prepositions (see § 4b Attached Pronouns).

Positions of the subject and predicate: Some sentences have the order of the subject and predicate reversed. The most common instances in which the predicate is preposed are:

i. When the Predicate is a Prepositional Phrase

I have a car. (literally: with me a car.)	عِنْدي سَيّارة.	٧
In my room, a telephone.	في غُرْفَتي هاتِفٌ.	٨

> **مُلاحَظة**
>
> The sentences that have an indefinite subject will also fall into the category of sentences that have preposed predicates (ex. 8). So, when you want to say, "there is a *whatever* in *wherever*," in Arabic we say, "in *wherever* is a *whatever*" thereby avoiding breaking the rule that states *we should not start a sentence with an indefinite noun.*

ii. When the Predicate is a Question Word

Who is your brother?	مَنْ أخوك؟	٩
Where is Fez?	أَيْنَ فاس؟	١٠

iii. When the Predicate is an Adverb

This is (radio) Cairo.	هُنا القاهِرة.	١١
In front of my house, a tree.	أمامَ بَيْتي شَجَرةٌ.	١٢

3. The Verbal Sentence الجُمْلةُ الفِعْليّة

Verbal sentences have two basic components: الفِعْل the verb and الفاعِل *the agent* (*doer of the action*).

Ahmed came.	جاءَ أَحْمَدُ.	١

The sentence in example 1 is obviously complete, because we are dealing with *regular* or *sound* verbs. There are certain verbs, however, that are defective in that they do not involve action. Their meaning is incomplete without a predicate:

Ahmed was . . .	كانَ أَحْمَدُ. . .	٢

Here, we offer a table illustrating the set of defective verbs and its many members:

أَفْرادُ المَجْموعة	الفِعْل الناقِص
أَصْبَحَ، أَمْسَى، أَضْحى، ظَلَّ، صارَ، باتَ، مادامَ، لَيْسَ، مازالَ	كانَ وَأَخَواتُها
كادَ، أَوْشَكَ، كَرَبَ	أَفْعالُ المُقارَبةِ
عَسَى، حَرى، اخْلَوْلَقَ	أَفْعالُ الرَجاءِ
أَخَذَ، شَرَعَ، هَبَّ، قامَ، أَنْشأَ، طَفِقَ، جَعَلَ	أَفْعالُ الشُروعِ

Direct Object of the Verb

If the verb is transitive, that is, it takes an object, then a noun or a pronoun may function as a direct object مَفْعول.

حالةُ النَصْبِ	
رأى أَحْمَدُ مُعَلِّماً.	نَكِرة
رأى أَحْمَدُ المُعَلِّمَ.	مَعْرِفة
رأى أَحْمَدُ مُعَلِّمَيْنِ.	مُثَنَّى
رأى أَحْمَدُ مُعَلِّمينَ.	جَمْعُ المُذَكَّرِ السالِمِ

مُلاحَظة

It is possible that both the فاعِل and the مَفعول بِهِ be pronouns:

I saw her in the library.	رأَيْتُها في المَكتَبة.

The word رأَيْتُها is not merely a verb, but a complete sentence as well:

ـها	ـتُ	رأَيْـ
مَفْعول بِهِ	فاعِل	فِعْل

تمرين ١

Identify and list at least three instances of each category listed in the table below. Your answers might include pronouns:

سافر سامي وزوجُه حَنينٌ في الشَهرِ الماضي إلى مدينة اللاذقية. اللاذقيّة ميناءٌ على الساحلِ السوريِّ وتقعُ في شَمال غربِ سورية. وصلا المدينةَ مساءً ونزلا في فندقٍ على البحْرِ. كان الطقسُ جميلاً ذلك اليوم. وضع الزوجانِ حقائبَهُما في الغرفةِ ثمّ ذهبا إلى المطعم. طلبَت حَنينُ سمكاً أمّا سامي فطلب كُبّةً وأطعِمةً أخرى. أحضَرَ النادِلُ قهوةً شرِباها بعدَ الطعام. سامي وحَنينٌ يظنّانِ أنَّ طعامَ ذلك المَطعمِ جيِّدٌ.

خَبر	مُبتَدأ	مَفعول بِه	فاعِل	فِعْل

تمرين ٢

Provide the correct endings (the short vowels) for the words in the parentheses with respect to context and explain your choices if necessary:

مِثال: قادَتْ رِحابُ (السيّارة) إلى عَمَلِها.

جواب: سيّارةَ: منصوب بالفتحة لأنها معرفة ومفعول بِه.

١- مَروانُ وأخوهُ (يعمَلُ) سائِقَيْن.

٢- (الجامِعة) قريبةٌ من بيتي.

٣- أبوها (طبيب) في مدينةِ تونس.

٤- اشترى أخي (حاسوب).

٥- كانَ (الأستاذ) (مُتَأخِّر) صباحَ اليوم.

٦- سوف تكون (هالة) (أمّ) في شهرِ حَزيران.

٧- (ماء) البحرِ (بارِد) في الشِتاءِ.

٨- إنَّ (السَماء) (غائِمَة) اليوم.

٩- صار أخي (طبيب) في الخامسةِ والعشرينَ من عمرِه.

١٠- يعملُ (زوجها) مهندساً.

١١- استأجرتُ (شقّة) قُرْبَ السوق.

١٢- أسكنُ قريباً من (موقِف) الحافِلة.

4. Pronouns الضَمائِر

Pronouns are considered to be definite in Arabic, in that they refer to specific entities. There are three types of pronouns: *separate, attached*, and *understood*:

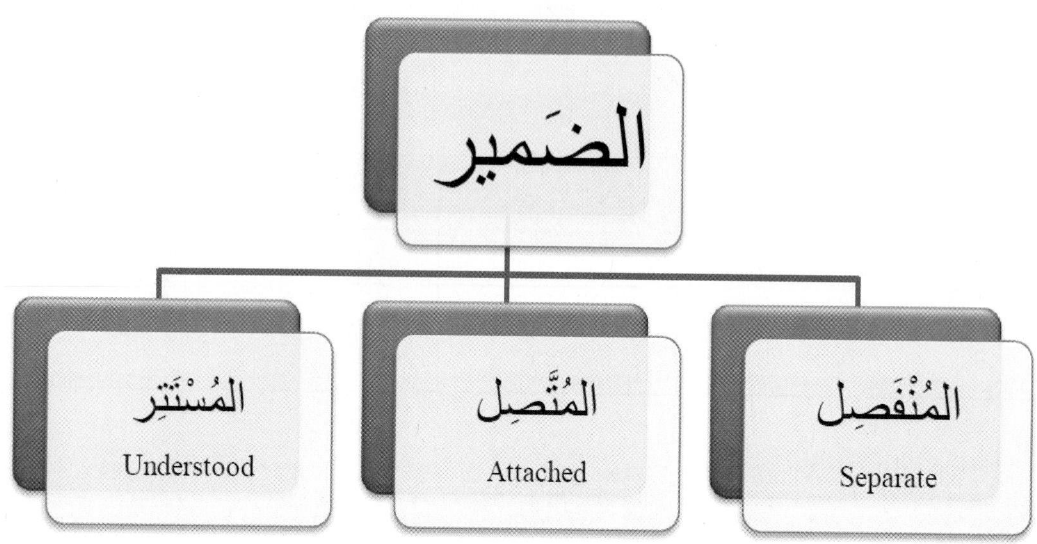

a. Separate (Independent) Pronouns الضَمائِر المُنفَصِلة

These nominative pronouns are listed according to voice in the following table:

غائِب	مُخاطَب	مُتَكَلِّم	
هُوَ، هِيَ	أَنْتَ، أَنْتِ	أنا	مُفْرَد
هُما	أَنْتُما	----	مُثَنّى
هُم، هُنَّ	أَنْتُم، أَنْتُنَّ	نَحنُ	جَمْع

b. Attached Pronouns الضَمائِر المُتَّصِلة

Pronouns which attach to nouns, particles, prepositions, and verbs are known as الضمائِر المُتَّصِلة. They may be nominative رَفْع, accusative نَصْب, or genitive جَرّ.

i. Nominative Pronouns

When a pronoun serves as the agent الفاعِل, then it is considered to be nominative. There are six attached nominative pronouns:

الضَمائِر المُتَّصِلة المَرْفوعة							
الألِف	دَرَسا	يَدْرُسانِ	أُدْرُسا				
الواو	دَرَسوا	يَدْرُسونَ	أُدْرسوا	لَمْ يَدْرُسوا			
التاء	دَرَسْتَ	دَرَسْتُ	دَرَستَ	دَرَسْتِ	دَرَسْتُما	دَرَسْتُمْ	دَرَسْتُنَّ
النون	تَدْرُسْنَ	يَدْرُسْنَ	أُدْرُسْنَ				
الياء	تَدْرُسينَ	أُدْرُسي	لَمْ تَدْرُسي				
نا	دَرَسْنا						

ii. Accusative Pronouns

Accusative pronouns can be suffixed to transitive verbs where they function as the object of the verb, or they can be suffixed to members of the set of إنَّ.

الضَمائِر المُتَّصِلة المَنْصوبة					
	الحَرْف	الأمْر	الماضي	المَجْزوم	
الياء	إنّي	دَرِّسْني	دَرَّسَني	----	
الكاف	إنَّكَ	----	دَرَّسَكَ	لَمْ يُدَرِّسْكَ	(أو كِ، كُما، كُم، كُنَّ)
الهاء	إنَّه	دَرِّسْهُ	دَرَّسَهُ	لَمْ يُدَرِّسْهُ	(أو ها، هُما، هُم، هُنَّ)
نا	إنَّنا	دَرِّسْنا	دَرَّسَنا	لَمْ يُدَرِّسْنا	

iii. Genitive Pronouns

Genitive pronouns can be suffixed to prepositions as its object and nouns as a member following the مُضاف.

الضمائِر المُتَّصِلة المَجرورة			
	حَرْفُ الجَرّ	الضَمير المِلكي	
الياء	إليَّ	كِتابي	
الكاف	إليكَ	كِتابُك	أو كِ، كما، كُم، كُنَّ
الهاء	إلَيْه	كِتابُهُ	أو ها، هُما، هُم، هُنَّ
نا	إلَيْنا	كِتابُنا	

5. The Permutative البَدَل

In Arabic, البَدَل means *substitution* and grammatically speaking indicates a situation where a noun stands for another noun. This *substitute* noun takes the same case and gender of the original noun.

١	نَزَلْتُ بِالقاهِرَةِ عاصِمَةِ مِصرَ.	*I stayed in Cairo, the capital of Egypt.*

القاهِرة and عاصِمَة مِصر both connote the same city, thus one is a بَدَل of the other and can be substituted for one another without losing meaning. As can be seen in example 1, they agree in case in that they are both مَجرور بالكَسْرة.

تمرين ٣

Identify the noun or nouns functions as بَدَل in each of the following sentences while providing the appropriate ending on each.

١- هذا سامر زميل أخي.

٢- رأيتُ أمسِ الطالبَيْنِ أحمد وصديقه.

٣- سافرنا إلى مدينة اللاذقيّة ميناء سورية الأوّل.

٤- قرأنا القرآن كتاب المسلمين المقدّس.

٥- ثناء زوجة أخي تعمل مديرة مدرسة.

٦- يدرس سالم في جامعة دمشقَ، أوّل جامعة سوريّة.

٧- زرنا "تايم سكوير" مركز مدينة نيويورك.

6. الإضافة

A possessive construct of two or more nouns occurring back-to-back, without anything separating them, is known as الإضافة:

The student's book. / The book of the student.	كِتابُ الطالِبِ.	١
A student's book. A book of a student.	كِتابُ طالِبٍ	٢

This structure is governed by certain rules:

i. المُضاف

The first noun of an إضافة is known as المُضاف, which in examples 1 and 2 is كِتاب. As you may have noticed in your experience reading Arabic texts, the مُضاف can be any of the three cases depending on context. The first noun المُضاف is the focus of the phrase, while the following members of the إضافة illustrate a possessive relationship with the first.

Take, for instance, كتاب in examples 1 and 2. The book belongs to either the student or a student depending on the definiteness of the second member of the إضافة known as المُضاف إليه. If you would like to change who the book (or whatever noun) belonged to, simply change the مُضاف إليه and *voila*, you have changed ownership.

ii. المُضاف Must be Indefinite

The مُضاف is always indefinite; whereas the مُضاف إليه can be definite or indefinite.

iii. The Disappearing نون of المُضاف

The مُضاف loses the final نون in dual and plural suffixes:

غُرْفَتا نَوْمٍ	⇐	غُرْفَتانِ	٣
مُهَنْدِسو الشَرِكَةِ	⇐	مُهَنْدِسون	٤

iv. المُضاف Does not Take تَنْوين

The مُضاف cannot take تَنْوين.

v. حالةُ الجَرّ for All Members of المُضاف إلَيْه

The مُضاف إليه and all members of a complex إضافة that follow it will be مَجْرور.

vi. The Definiteness of الإضافة

The إضافة is definite if:

1. The last noun in the phrase has a definite article.	شُبّاكُ السَيَّارةِ.
2. It has an attached pronoun.	شُبّاكُ سَيَّارتِها.
3. It is a proper name.	شُبّاكُ سَيَّارةِ زَيْنَب.

vii. The Indefiniteness of الإضافة

The إضافة is indefinite if the last noun is indefinite:

1. The last noun in the phrase does not have a definite article.	شُبّاكُ سَيَّارةٍ.

مُلاحَظة

An إضافة can have more than one مُضاف إليه:

٦	مُديرُ مَكْتَبِ رَئيسِ جامِعَةٍ.	نَكِرة
٧	مُديرُ مَكْتَبِ رَئيسِ الجامِعَةِ.	مَعْرِفة

This multiple إضافة will be indefinite if the last noun is indefinite and *vice versa*.

تمرين ٤

Underline the مُضاف in the following sentences while placing two lines under the مُضاف إليه. Please provide the appropriate markers for every إضافة.

١- مَشَيْنا عَلى شاطِئِ البَحْر.
٢- هذا فُنْدُقٌ ينامُ فيهِ سائقو الشاحِنات.
٣- وَصَلَتْ طائِرة رئيس الجُمْهورية مَساءً.
٤- تاريخ مَدينة دِمَشق قديم جِدّاً.
٥- اِنْتَظَرْتُ أمامَ غُرْفة أستاذ العربيّة.
٦- هذا بَيْت أستاذنا.
٧- إنّها طالبة جامعة.

7. Diptotes المَمْنوعُ مِنَ الصَّرْفِ

Indefinite nouns and plurals that do not fully inflect are known as diptotes. These are nouns that only accept two of the three short vowels when declined (i.e., الفَتْحة والضَمّة). They differ from regular nouns in two respects:

i. They never take تَنْوين when they are indefinite:

١	جاءَتْ سُعادُ	*not* سُعادٌ

ii. Plural diptotes take فَتْحة for both accusative and genitive cases. When they are definite, however, they decline fully just like regular nouns:

	مَرْفوع	مَنصوب	مَجْرور
٢	مَدارِسُ	مَدارِسَ	مَدارِسَ
٣	المَدارِسُ	المَدارِسَ	المَدارِسِ

Certain proper names are diptotes such as عَمّان:

٤	هذِهِ عَمّانُ .	مَرْفوع بالضَمّة
٥	شاهَدْتُ عَمّانَ .	مَنْصوب بالفَتْحة
٦	وَصَلْتُ إلى عَمّانَ .	مَجْرور بالفَتْحة

مُلاحَظة

Adjectives modifying diptotes agree with the case of the noun regardless of its marker. Compare the endings of عَمّان and its adjective:

٧	هذهِ عَمّانُ الجَديدةُ .	مَرْفوع بالضَمّة
٨	شاهَدُ عَمّانَ الجَديدةَ .	مَنْصوب بالفَتْحة
٩	وَصَلْتُ إلى عَمّانَ الجَديدةِ .	عَمّان مَجْرور بالفَتْحة والجَديدةِ مَجْرور بالكَسْرة

How to Identify a Diptote

ends with اء	صَحْراء
has the pattern مَفاعِل *or* مَفاعيل *as a plural*	مَصابيح أو مَدارِس
is a masculine noun ending with ة	أُسامة
is a feminine noun that either ends with ة *or without*	سُعاد أو كريمة
is a foreign name	إبراهيم
is a compound name	بَعْلَبَك
ends with ان	عَدنان أو مَروان
has a verb pattern	أَحْمَد أو يَزيد
is patterned after أَفْعَل *and* فَعْلان	أَخْضَر أو عَطْشان
is a number patterned after فُعال *or* مَفْعَل	مَثْنى أو رُباع
is patterned after فُعَل	عُمَر أو أُخَر (جمع أُخرى)

تَذَكَّروا

Diptotes are fully declinable when they are definite. A noun is definite if:

the definite article is prefixed to it	في الصَحْراءِ.	١٠
it has an attached pronoun	في صَحْرائِنا.	١١
it is the first word of a definite إضافة	في صَحْراءِ العِراق.	١٢

تمرين ٥

Underline all diptotes in each sentence and provide the appropriate inflectional endings for all nouns and adjectives:

١- أخَذَني صَديقي عادِل لِزيارة مَصانِع السَيّارات في مِصْر.
٢- سافَرَتْ لَيْلى مَعَ ميخائيل إلى صَوْفَر في لُبْنان.
٣- قَدَّمَتِ الفَتاة الطَعام إلى رَجُل جَوْعان.
٤- دَرَسْتُ في المَدارِس الحُكوميّة.
٥- اِلْتَقَطْنا هذِهِ الصورة في صَحْراء الأرْدُنّ.
٦- كَتَبْتُ إلى عَدْنان رِسالة طَويلة.
٧- مَرَرْنا بِحِمْص بَعدَ الظُهْر.
٨- هَل أنتَ صَديقُ عَدنان؟
٩- دَرَسَتْ سَميحَةُ في مَدارِس خاصَّة.

8. Comparative Adjectives (the Elative) اسمُ التَفْضيل

Fortunately, comparative and superlative nouns share the same base form:

أفْعَل

a. Superlative

The superlative forms an إضافة with the noun that follows it:

December is the coldest month of the year.	كانونُ الأوَّلُ أبْرَدُ شَهْرٍ في السَّنةِ.	١

b. Comparative

Place a مِن after the base form أفْعَل to create the comparative:

Today is colder than yesterday.	اليَوْمُ أبْرَدُ مِن أمْسِ.	٢

c. Adjectives and Colors in Superlative / Comparative

Colors and certain adjectives do not lend themselves well to the pattern أفْعَل.

i. Comparative Adjectives

In order to create the comparative degree with certain adjectives, other adjectives that lend themselves well to this pattern (i.e., كَثير، قَليل، شَديد) are used in combination with the noun derived from the original word:

Today is rainier than yesterday.	اليَوْمُ أكْثَرُ مَطَراً مِن أمْسِ.	مَطَر (n.)	⇐	ماطِر (adj.)	٣

مُلاحَظة

Note that in example 3, the أفْعَل + اسم structure ceases to be an إضافة because it specifies 'what there is more of'. Nouns of specificity التمييز are accusative.

ii. Superlative + Adjective Structures

difficulty	صُعوبة	*difficult*	صَعْب	٤
Spanish is less difficult than Arabic.		الإسبانيّة أقَلُّ صُعوبةً من العَرَبيّةِ.		

ease	سُهولة	easy	سَهْل	٥
Future relations between the two countries will not be as easy as they are currently.		العَلاقاتُ المُسْتَقْبَلِيّةُ بَيْنَ البَلَدَيْنِ سَتكون أقلّ سُهولةً ممّا هِيَ عليهِ الآن.		

We follow the same process when dealing with colors:

redness	حُمْرة	red	أحْمَر	٦
My car is more red than yours.		سَيّارَتي أشَدُّ حُمْرةً مِنْ سَيّارَتك.		

تَذَكَّروا

Those adjectives with a doubled final radical take the form:

أجَدّ

not أجْدَد

My car is newer than your car.	سَيّارَتي أجَدُّ مِنْ سَيّارَتِك.	٧

تمرين ٦

Form the comparative based on context. Verbal nouns are provided in the leftmost column for your convenience:

١- طَقْسُ هَوائي / جَميل / طَقْس / في أمريكا	جَمال
٢- مرسيدس / غالٍ / دودج	غَلاء
٣- حَديقَتي / أخْضَر / حَديقَتك	خُضْرة
٤- الكُبّةُ / لَذيذ / طَبَق سوريّ	لَذّة
٥- هُدى / مُتَأخِر / لَيْلى عَن الصَفّ	تَأخُّر
٦- الأمْطارُ في السُعوديّة / قَليل / الأمْطارِ في لُبْنان	قِلّة
٧- القاهِرةُ / كَبير / مَدينةٍ في الوَطَنِ العَرَبيّ	كُبر
٨- سَيّارةُ أخْتي / صَغير / سَيّارَتي	صُغْر

9. Number–Noun Agreement تَطابُقُ العَدَدِ والاسمِ المَعدود

When a number is used with a noun, a gender and number relationship exists and must be taken into consideration. Let's take a look at this complex relationship and try to make some sense out of it:

a. Numbers 1 and 2

Numbers one and two behave as adjectives following their modified noun and agreeing in everything.

Numbers to indicate singular and dual nouns need not be mentioned:

I have a car, but my brother has two.	عِندي سَيّارةٌ ولكِنَّ أخي عِنْدَهُ سَيّارتانِ.

If they are mentioned, it is for emphasis:

I have one car, but my brother has two cars.	عِندي سَيّارةٌ واحِدةٌ ولكِنَّ أخي عِنْدَهُ سَيّارتانِ اثْنَتانِ.

b. Numbers 3-10

These numbers have reverse gender agreement with the singular of the modified noun. That is, if the noun is feminine in its singular form, then the number will be masculine, and *vice versa*. Consider the following examples:

١	خَمْسَةُ طُلاّبٍ.
٢	خَمْسُ طالِباتٍ.

Since طالب, the singular of طُلاّب, in example 1 is masculine, then the number is feminine—in that it takes a تاء مَرْبوطة. Likewise, the singular of طالبات is طالِبة, meaning the number should be masculine—meaning that it does not take a تاء مَربوطة.

c. Numbers 11-12

Much like numbers 1 and 2, numbers 11 and 12 agree in gender with the singular noun they modify. These numbers are always in the accusative case with the modified noun appearing in indefinite, singular, accusative form:

٣	أحَدَ عَشَرَ طالِباً.
٤	إحْدى عَشْرَةَ طالِبةً.

d. Numbers 13-19

These numbers are invariable in case—they are accusative regardless of their syntactic position in the sentence. Just as is the case with 3-9, the singles digit has reverse gender agreement with the modified noun in its singular, while the tens digit agrees with it.

٥	أعْرِفُ ثَلاثَةَ عَشَرَ طالِباً.
٦	أعْرِفُ ثَلاثَ عَشْرَةَ طالِبةً.

e. Numbers 20, 30, 40 etc.

Simply take a cardinal number (e.g., ثَلاث) and then add ونَ when nominative and ينَ when accusative or genitive to produce the multiples of ten 30-90.

٧	عِنْدي ثَلاثون كِتاباً.	مَرْفوع
٨	اِشْتَرَيْتُ ثَلاثينَ كِتاباً.	مَنْصوب
٩	قُمْتُ بِقِراءةِ ثَلاثينَ كِتاباً.	مَجْرور

f. Numbers 21, 22; 31, 32; 41, 42 etc.

Like numbers one and two, the singles digits agree in gender with their modified noun in its singular:

١٠	في الكِتابِ واحِدٌ وعِشْرونَ دَرْساً واثْنَتانِ وتِسْعُونَ صَفْحَةً.

g. Numbers 23-29, 33-39, 43-49 etc.

Like numbers three through ten, the singles digits have reverse gender agreement with their modified noun in its singular:

١١	سَكَنْتُ في ثَلاثٍ وعِشْرينَ وِلايةً.
١٢	تَزَوَّجَتْ أختي وَسِنُّها سِتَّةٌ وعِشْرونَ عاماً.

h. Numbers 100, 200, 1000, 2000 etc.

These numbers form an إضافة with their modified noun.

١٣	يُقارِبُ عُمْرُ جَدّي مِئةَ سَنةٍ.
١٤	في الحَديقةِ أرْبَعُمِئةِ شَجَرةٍ.

مُلاحَظة

Since مئة and ألف form an إضافة with their modified noun, the numbers 200 and 2,000 lose their final نون. As well, an ا marks nominative case while a ي marks genitive and accusative cases:

I have 200 books.	عَنْدي مِئَتا كِتابٍ.	١٥
I bought 200 books, each one for 200 lira.	اِشْتَرَيْتُ مئَتَيْ كِتابٍ بمِئَتَيْ لَيْرةٍ لِكُلٍّ واحِدٍ.	١٦

تمرين ٧

اكتب الأعدادَ التاليةَ بِالكَلِمات كَما في المِثالين:

اِشتَرَيْتُ ١٥ دَفْتَراً. — اِشتَرَيْتُ خَمْسَةَ عَشَرَ دفتَراً.

عِنْدي ١٥ شَجَرَةً في حَديقَتي. — عِنْدي خَمسَ عَشْرَةَ شَجَرَةً في حَديقَتي.

١- وُلِدَ عَبْدُ الرحْمن في عام ١٩٤٣.

٢- في صَفِّنا ٣ طالِباتٍ أجنَبيّات.

٣- عاشَ أحمَدُ ٢٠ سَنةً في تِلِمسان.

٤- في القَدَم ١٢ بوصةً.

٥- اِشْتَرَيْتُ بَرّادي بِـ ٢٠٠٠ لَيْرةٍ.

٦- في شَقَّتي ٢ غُرفَة نَوم.

٧- بَقينا ١٥ يَوماً في المَغرِبِ على ساحِلِ المُحيطِ الأطلَسيّ.

٨- اِشترى غَسّانُ قَميصاً بِـ ١١ دولاراً.

٩- عِندَ أختي (١) اِبن فَقَط.

10. Adverbials الظَرْف

In Arabic grammars, adverbials serve as objects of verbs describing time ظرف زَمان (ex. 1), place ظرف مكان (ex. 2), and manner/circumstance حال (ex. 3):

I arrived in Alexandria in the evening.	وَصَلْتُ الإسكَندَريَّةَ مَساءً.	١
The wind is blowing southerly.	تَهُبُّ الرياحُ جَنوباً.	٢
Salma came to school on foot.	أتَتْ سَلمى إلى الجامِعَةِ ماشِيَةً.	٣

تَذَكَّروا

Some words which behave like prepositions are also adverbs:

خَلْفَ، أمامَ، قَبْلَ، بَعْدَ، نَحْوَ

I live behind the grocery store.	أسْكُنُ خَلْفَ دُكّانِ البَقّال.	٤

Adverbs may be *declinable* مُتَصَرِّف taking different endings based on their position in the sentence or *indeclinable* غَيْر مُتَصَرِّف, in which they do not change their form.

a. Declinable Adverbs of Time مُتَصَرِّف

These adverbs behave syntactically just like a regular noun:

مُضاف	مَساءُ الخَيْرِ.	٥
مُبْتَدأ	مَساؤُكُمْ سَعيد.	٦
ظَرْف	وَصَلَ صَديقي مَساءً.	٧
فاعِل	طابَ مَساؤُكُم.	٨

b. Indeclinable Adverbs of Time غير مُتَصَرِّف

The endings of these adverbs never change regardless of syntax. Some of the more frequently used indeclinable adverbs are:

إذْ، بَيْنَما، قَطّ، لَدى

٩	لَمْ أتكَلَّمْ مَعَ سامي قَطُّ.	*I have not spoken with Sami, ever.*

تمرين ٨

اختَرِ الكلمة المناسبة مِن بين الكلمات الأربع:

١- زُرْنا أصدِقاءَنا ________________.

☐ المَساءُ ☐ مَساءٍ ☐ المَساءِ ☐ مَساءً

٢- تَقَعُ شَقَّتي ________________ مَوقِفِ الحافِلَةِ.

☐ قُرْبَ ☐ قُرْبُ ☐ قُرْبِ ☐ قُرْبٍ

٣- دَخَلَ / مَروانُ الغُرفَةَ ________________.

☐ ضاحِكٌ ☐ ضاحِكٍ ☐ ضاحِكاً ☐ ضِحْكٌ

11. Relative Pronouns الأسماءُ المَوصولة

In Arabic grammars, adverbials serve as objects of verbs describing time (ex. 1), place (ex. 2), and manner (ex. 3):

الأسْماءُ المَوْصول			
	مُفْرَد	مُثَنَّى	جَمْع
مُذَكَّر	الَّذي	اللّذانِ / اللّذَيْنِ	الَّذينَ
مُؤَنَّث	الَّتي	اللّتانِ / اللّتَيْنِ	اللاّتي / اللّواتي

a. Restrictive Relative Pronouns

These relative pronouns are generally translated into English as *who*, *that*, or *which*.

Relative pronouns are only used when the referential noun is definite:

I wrote to my friend who lives in Kuwait.	كَتَبْتُ إلى صَديقي الّذي يَعْمَلُ في الكُوَيْت.	١

The word صَديقي is made definite by the attached pronoun ي *my*.

مُلاحَظة

Unlike English, if the noun is indefinite, no relative pronoun is used:

I wrote to my friend [who] lives in Kuwait.	كَتَبْتُ إلى صَديقٍ يَعْمَلُ في الكُوَيْت.	٢

b. Non-Restrictive Relative Pronouns

These relative pronouns are generally translated into English as *who(m)*, *that*, or *what*.

who	مَن
what / that	ما

Do you know who is coming today?	هَلْ تَعْرِفينَ مَنْ سَيَحضُرُ اليَوْمَ؟	٣
I can't read what I wrote.	لا أسْتَطيعُ أنْ أقرأُ ما كَتَبتُ.	٤

مُلاحَظة

Unlike English, if the noun is indefinite, no relative pronoun is used:

Did you see the new cars that arrived this week?	هَلْ شاهَدْتِ السَيّاراتِ الجَديدةَ الّتي وَصَلَتْ هذا الأُسْبوعِ؟	٥
These are the books that I bought.	هذِهِ هِيَ الكُتُبُ الّتي اِشْتَرَيْتُها.	٦

In example 5 we see that the singular of السَيّارات is السَيّارة, which is feminine, requires the use of الّتي, whereas in example 6 الكُتُب has the singular of الكِتاب, which is feminine, but its plural still requires the feminine form الّتي since:

- *All non-human plurals are treated as feminine singular!*

تمرين ٩

أكمل الجمل الآتية بكلمات مناسبة وفق النصّ.

١- هَل قَرَأتِ الكِتابَ ____________ وَصَلَ إلى المكتَبَةِ هذا الأسبوع.

☐ الّذي ☐ الّتي ☐ الّذين ☐ اللاّتي

٢- أنا لا أسْمَعُ الأخبارَ ____________ لا تُعجِبُني.

☐ الّذي ☐ الّتي ☐ مَنْ ☐ اللاّتي

٣- مَنْ هُما الفَتاتانِ ____________ تَجلِسانِ هُناك.

☐ الّتي ☐ اللّتانِ ☐ اللّتَيْنِ ☐ اللاّتي

٤- كانَ هُنا ____________ يُريدُ أنْ يَتَكَلَّمَ مَعَك.

☐ الّذي ☐ الّتي ☐ مَنْ ☐ ما

٥- هؤلاء هُم الطلاّب ____________ وَصَلوا بِالطائِرةِ أمس.

☐ الّتي ☐ الّذينَ ☐ اللّتَيْنِ ☐ مَنْ

٦- آكُلُ ____________ يُعجِبُني مِن طَعام.

☐ الّذي ☐ الّتي ☐ ما ☐ مَنْ

12. The Verb الفِعْل

Understanding the verb system in Arabic is a major step toward understanding the structure of the Arabic word in general. On the following page you will find a verb tree that the authors hope will aid in organizing your thoughts about the inner workings of the Arabic verb system.

Note: Twelve conjugation tables of verbs representing the categories found in the verb tree on the following page can be found in Appendix A. Those verbs are conjugated in the past, present, and imperative along with active and passive forms.

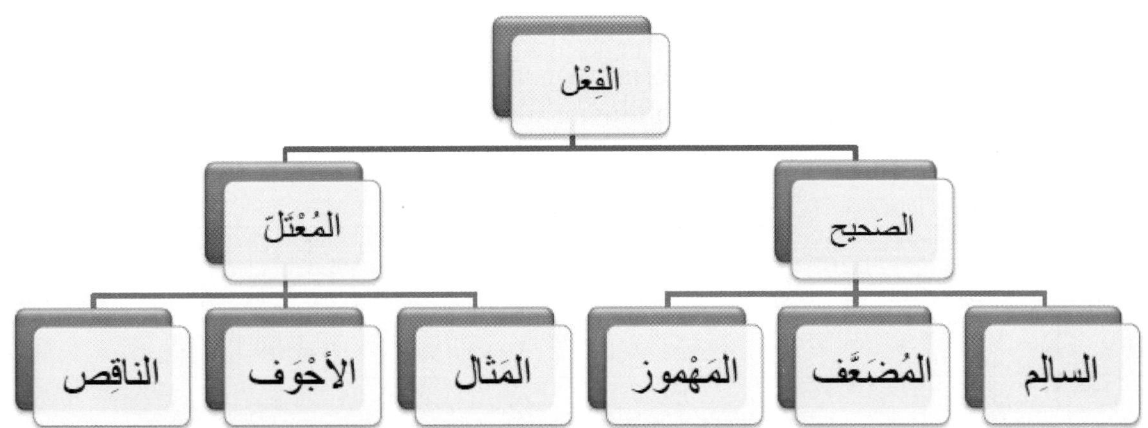

The table below defines the words found in this verb tree as well as most of the words you might need to know to describe the Arabic verb. Each category in the table is explained in detail throughout this section starting from the right and moving left من الشَكْل إلى البِناء:

البِناء *voice*	التَرْكيب *structure*	الوَظيفة *function*	الزَمَن *tense*	التَصْريف *conjugation*	النَوْع *kind*	الشَكْل *form*
مَعْلوم *active*	صَحيح *sound*	لازِم *intransitive*	الماضي *past*	المُتَكَلِّم *first person*	ناقِص *defective*	مُجَرَّد *basic form*
مَجْهول *passive*	مُعْتَلّ *weak*	مُتَعَدٍ *transitive*	المُضارِع *present*	المُخاطَب *second person*	تامٌّ *complete*	مَزيد *augmented*
			الأمْر *imperative*	الغائِب *third person*		أوزانُ الفِعل *verb forms*

a. Form (Basic and Augmented Verbs)

The Arabic verb can be either in a basic, stripped form مُجَرَّد or augmented مَزيد, meaning that it's the *root form + extra letters.*

i. Basic Verbs

The majority of basic verbs are comprised of three basic letters (triliteral), but there are quadriliteral verbs as well such as: بَرْمَجَ *to program* and بَعْثَرَ *to scatter.*

ii. Augmented Verb Forms

These derived verbs fall into ten patterns. Each of these patterns or forms lends a specific meaning to the root verb. There are nine common forms that are labeled with roman numerals in Western dictionaries and grammars. The meaning of the form is found below the Roman numerals in the table below:

فَعَّلَ	فاعَلَ	أَفْعَلَ	تَفَعَّلَ	تَفاعَلَ	اِنْفَعَلَ	اِفْتَعَلَ	اِفْعَلَّ	اِسْتَفْعَلَ
II	III	IV	V	VI	VII	VIII	IX	X
causative	*reciprocal (mutual action)*	*causative*	*reflexive of II*	*reflexive of III*	*passive*	*reflexive of I*	*colors and defects*	*to seek the root*

b. Kind (Sound and Defective Verbs) الفِعْلُ التام والناقِص

i. Defective or Incomplete Verbs

Verbs that are ناقِص impart incomplete meaning to the sentence if the predicate is not introduced (e.g., كانَ).

مُلاحَظة

Incomplete verbs are a closed system of verbs which include:

كانَ وأخَواتُها

أفعال المُقارَبَةِ والرَّجاءِ والشُّروعِ

ii. Sound or Complete Verbs

Verbs that are تامّ impart a complete meaning to the sentence without the need for a predicate or a direct object (e.g., جاءَ).

c. Conjugation: التَّصْريف

Each verb form from I to X can be conjugated according to person, number and gender in the present, past, and imperative.

d. Tense: الزَمَن

The Arabic verb has three tenses: past, present, and imperative.

i. Past الماضي

Known as the 'perfect' tense in most Western grammars, this tense refers to a complete action, which is perfect in the sense that nothing else needs to be done to the action.

ii. Present المُضارِع

Known as 'imperfect', this tense refers to an incomplete action, which is imperfect in the sense that something needs to be done to complete the action.

iii. Imperative الأمر

Unlike English, the imperative is considered a tense because the action is performed in the future. It is used for making requests and giving commands. It is formed by taking a conjugated present tense verb and deleting the prefix:

help me!	ساعِدْني!	ساعِدْ	⇐	يُساعِدُ	١
get used to (it)!	تَعَوَّدْ عليْهِ!	تَعَوَّدْ	⇐	يَتَعَوَّدُ	٢

If the letter after the prefix is a consonant, then an initial أ must be added, such as is the case with Form I verbs:

How to tell what short vowel you need to put on your imperative verbs:

If the past tense verb has four letters, the initial أ takes a فَتْحة.	أعْطِ	⇐	أعْطى
If the present tense verb has a كَسْرة or a فَتْحة on the middle letter, then the initial إ takes a كَسْرة.	اِجْلِسْ اِذْهَبْ	⇐	يَجْلِسُ يَذْهَبُ
If the present tense verb has a ضَمّة on the middle letter, then the initial ا takes a ضَمّة.	اُدْخُلْ	⇐	يَدْخُلُ

تَصْريفُ الفِعْلِ بِالماضي والمُضارِعِ (المَرْفوع والمَنْصوب والمَجْزوم) والأمْر					
الضَمير	الماضي	المُضارع			الأمْر
		المَرْفوع	المَنْصوب	المَجْزوم	
أنا	كَتَبْتُ	أكْتُبُ	أكْتُبَ	أكْتُبْ	
نَحْنُ	كَتَبْنا	نَكْتُبُ	نَكْتُبَ	نَكْتُبْ	
أنْتَ	كَتَبْتَ	تَكْتُبُ	تَكْتُبَ	تَكْتُبْ	أُكْتُبْ
أنْتِ	كَتَبْتِ	تَكْتُبينَ	تَكْتُبي	تَكْتُبي	أُكْتُبي
أنْتُما	كَتَبْتُما	تَكْتُبانِ	تَكْتُبا	تَكْتُبا	أُكْتُبا
أنْتُم	كَتَبْتُم	تَكْتُبونَ	تَكْتُبوا	تَكْتُبوا	أُكْتُبوا
أنْتُنَّ	كَتَبْتُنَّ	تَكْتُبْنَ	تَكْتُبْنَ	تَكْتُبْنَ	أُكْتُبْنَ
هُوَ	كَتَبَ	يَكْتُبُ	يَكْتُبَ	يَكْتُبْ	
هِيَ	كَتَبَتْ	تَكْتُبُ	تَكْتُبَ	تَكْتُبْ	
هُما	كَتَبا	يَكْتُبانِ	يَكْتُبا	يَكْتُبا	
هُما	كَتَبَتا	تَكْتُبانِ	تَكْتُبا	تَكْتُبا	
هُم	كَتَبوا	يَكْتُبونَ	يَكْتُبوا	يَكْتُبوا	
هُنَّ	كَتَبْنَ	يَكْتُبْنَ	يَكْتُبْنَ	يَكْتُبْنَ	

e. Function اللازِمُ والمُتَعَدِّي

A verb may be either transitive مُتَعَدٍّ or intransitive لازِم.

i. المُتَعَدِّي

Transitive verbs require a direct object to complete a thought:

١	زارَ صَديقي مَسْرَحَ راديو سيتي.	*My friend visited Radio City Theater.*

ii. لازِم

Intransitive verbs do not require a direct object to complete a thought:

٢	جاء أخي.	*My friend came.*

f. Structure السالم والمُعتلّ

i. Sound Verbs

Arabic verbs that are comprised strictly of consonants are known as صَحيح *sound* (e.g., كَتَبَ، ذَهَبَ).

مُلاحَظة

Sound verbs also include those verbs that contain a هَمْزة in all positions:

الفِعْلُ المَهْموز	
أَكَلَ	*initial*
سألَ	*medial*
قَرَأَ	*final*

ii. Weak Verbs

Arabic verbs that contain one or more long vowels are known as مُعْتَلّ *weak*. Of these verbs, there are three types:

الفِعْلُ المثال	وَصَلَ
الفِعْلُ الأجْوَف	قال
الفِعْلُ الناقِص	نَسِيَ

g. Voice البِناء

Arabic enjoys two voices: مَعلوم *active* and مَجْهول *passive.*

i. مَعْلوم

A verb is مَعْلوم if the agent is specified:

١	وَصَلَتِ الطائِرةُ.	*The plane arrived.*

Because we know who or what did the arriving (i.e., الطائِرةُ), we consider the verb مَعْلوم *active.*

ii. مَجْهول

A verb is مَجْهول if the agent is not specified:

٢	حُمِلَتْ إلى السَّرير.	*She was carried to bed.*

Who carried her to bed? We cannot answer this question because the agent or the doer of the action remains unknown. If we cannot tell who or what did the action, then we are dealing with a مَجْهول verb.

The Arabic verb is made passive by internal vowel changes both in the past and present. Let's take a look at the inner workings of some verbs to better understand how they are formed and how we can apply that knowledge to our language production.

الماضي				المُضارِع			
مَعلوم		مَجهول		مَعلوم		مَجهول	
كَتَب	(ـَ + ـَ)	كُتِب	(ـِ + ـُ)	يَكتُب	(ـُ + ـَ)	يُكتَب	(ـَ + ـُ)
شَرِب	(ـِ + ـَ)	شُرِب	(ـِ + ـُ)	يَشرَب	(ـَ + ـَ)	يُشرَب	(ـَ + ـُ)
قال	(ا)	قيل	(ي)	يَقول	(و + ـَ)	يُقال	(ا + ـُ)
سَمّى	(ى + ـَ)	سُمِّيَ	(يَ + ـِ + ـُ)	يُسَمّي	(ي + ـُ)	يُسَمّى	(ى + ـُ)

تمرين ١٠

اِختَرْ شَكْلَ الفِعْلِ المُناسِب:

١- أصدِقائي الأعِزّاء، أخبِروني مَتى ______________ إلى مَحَطَّةِ القِطار.

☐ تَصِلُ ☐ تَصِلينَ ☐ تَصِلْنَ ☐ تَصِلونَ

٢- ______________ الأهْراماتُ مُنْذُ آلافِ السِنين.

☐ بَنَت ☐ بُنِيَت ☐ تُبْنَى ☐ تَبْني

٣- شُكْراً ______________ مِن فَضْلِكُم.

☐ اِجْلِسْ ☐ اِجْلِسوا ☐ يَجْلِسونَ ☐ جَلَسوا

٤- طَرَقَ المُوَظَّفُ على بابِ المُدير. فقالَ المُديرُ لَهُ: ______________.

☐ اِدْخِلْ ☐ اَدْخَلْ ☐ اُدْخُلْ ☐ تَدْخُلْ

٥- ______________ هذه السَيّارةُ في عامِ ٢٠١٠.

☐ صُنِعَتْ ☐ صَنَعَتْ ☐ تَصْنَعُ ☐ تُصْنَعُ

تمرين ١٠

A very productive aspect of Arabic is its derivational system that allows speakers to derive various nouns from a common root. This is accomplished by prefixing, infixing, and suffixing certain letters to fit patterns. Each of these patterns imparts a semantic nuance to the root while simultaneously creating a function for the newly formed noun.

الأسْماءُ المُشْتَقّة							
الرقم	الوَزَن	الفِعْل	المَصْدَر	إسْمُ الفاعِل	إسْمُ المَفْعول	مَعنى الجَذَر	مَعنى الوَزَن
I	فَعَلَ	كَتَبَ	كِتابة	كاتِب	مَكْتوب	*to write*	*root*
II	فَعَّلَ	دَرَّسَ	تَدْريس	مُدَرِّس	مُدَرَّس	*to teach*	*causative, intensive*
III	فاعَلَ	حارَبَ	مُحارَبة	مُحارِب	مُحارَب	*to fight*	*reciprocal*
IV	أَفْعَلَ	أعْطى	إعْطاء	مُعْطٍ	مُعْطى	*to give*	*causative*
V	تَفَعَّلَ	تَعَلَّمَ	تَعَلُّم	مُتَعَلِّم	مُتَعَلَّم	*to learn*	*reflexive of II*
VI	تَفاعَلَ	تَقاعَدَ	تَقاعُد	مُتَقاعِد	مُتَقاعَد	*to retire*	*reflexive of III*
VII	اِنْفَعَلَ	اِنْكَسَرَ	اِنْكِسار	مُنْكَسِر	-------	*to be broken*	*passive*
VIII	اِفْتَعَلَ	اِرْتَفَعَ	اِرْتِفاع	مُرْتَفِع	مُرْتَفَع	*to rise*	*reflexive of I*
IX	اِفْعَلَّ	اِحْمَرَّ	اِحْمِرار	مُحْمَرّ	-------	*to redden*	*color or defect*
X	اِسْتَفْعَلَ	اِسْتَأْجَرَ	اِسْتِئْجار	مُسْتَأْجِر	مُسْتَأْجَر	*to rent*	*to seek the root*

تمرين ١١

Select the appropriate pattern for the verb in the parentheses based on the meaning provided:

١ (حَسَنَ) ____________ الطَقْسُ. — *reflexive*

٢ (فَهِمَ) ____________ سامي عَنْ مَوْعِدِ الطائِرة. — *seek the meaning of the verb*

٣ (لَعِبَ) ____________ أخاهُ الصَغير. — *reciprocal action*

٤ (كَسَرَ)	___________ المِصْباحُ.	*passive*
٥ (صَفَرَ)	___________ أوْراقُ الأشْجارِ.	*acquire the characteristic of the verb*
٦ (رَفَعَ)	___________ دَرَجَةُ الحَرارَةِ.	*action occurred of its own accord*

الأسماء المُشْتَقَّة مِنَ الفِعْلِ الثُلاثيّ		
اسْمُ الفاعِل	فاعِل	*denotes the agent (performer) of the action*
اسْمُ المَفْعول	مَفْعول	*refers to the recipient, or experience, of the action*
اِسْمُ التَفْضيل	أفْعَل (مِن)	*indicates the elative or comparative degree*
اِسْمُ المَكان والزَمان	مَفْعَل(ة)، مَفْعِل(ة)	*describes the place or time when an action occurred*
اِسْمُ الآلة	مَفْعَل، مِفْعال، مَفْعلة، فَعّال، فاعول، فَعّالة	*represents a tool or device*
الصِفةُالمُشَبَّهة	فَعيل، فَعْلان، أفْعَل	*denotes a permanent characteristic in the entity described*

13. Active Participle اِسْمُ الفاعِل

Definition: اِسْمُ الفاعِل is the doer of the action; the agent.

Derivation: There are two means of deriving the active participle:

a. Form I: Triliteral

From the triliteral, unincreased Form I verb, the active participle takes the pattern:

	الماضي		اِسْمُ الفاعِل
فاعِل	كَتَبَ	⇐	كاتِب
	طَلَبَ	⇐	طالِب

مُلاحَظة

When dealing with الفِعْلُ الأَجْوَف with a long middle radical of ا the derived active participle will have a هَمْزة على كُرْسيّ ياء:

قائِل	قالَ
صائِم	صامَ
نائِم	نامَ

b. Form I: Quadriliteral

From the quadriliteral (four-letter) and augmented verbs, the active participle is derived from the present tense conjugation by replacing the prefix يـ with مُـ.

اِسْمُ الفاعِل		المُضارِع		الماضي
مُنْتَصِر	⇐	يَنْتَصِرُ	⇐	اِنْتَصَرَ
مُسْتَمِع	⇐	يَسْتَمِعُ	⇐	اِسْتَمَعَ

If, however, the penultimate (next to last) letter is a ياء or an ألف, those long vowels remain exactly as they were in المُضارِع:

اِسْمُ الفاعِل		المُضارِع		الماضي
مُخْتار	⇐	يَخْتارُ	⇐	اِخْتارَ
مُسْتَضيف	⇐	يَسْتَضيفُ	⇐	اِسْتَضافَ

14. Passive Participle اِسْمُ المَفْعول

Definition: اِسْمُ المَفْعول is the recipient of the action.

Derivation: There are two ways to derive the اِسْمُ المَفْعول

a. Form I: Triliteral

From the triliteral, unincreased Form I verb, the passive participle takes the pattern مَفْعول, which is formed by adding a مَـ to the beginning of the root and a واو before the final letter. Make sure that the initial ميم takes a فَتْحة. Consider the examples:

اِسْمُ المَفْعول		الماضي	
مَحْمول	⇐	حَمَلَ	مَفْعول
مَسْكون	⇐	سَكَنَ	

مُلاحَظة

When the middle letter of a hollow verb is an ألف, then the penultimate letter of the derived noun will be either a واو or a ياء.

That which is said: utterance	مَقول	قالَ
That which is sold	مَبيع	باعَ
That which is awed: awe-struck	مَهيب	هابَ

b. The Quadriliteral and Increased Verb Passive Participle

Form the quadriliteral and increased verb passive participle by referring to the present tense (imperfect) conjugation of the verb and replacing the prefix ياء with a مُـ. Be sure to add a فَتْحة on the penultimate letter as in the examples:

اِسْمُ المَفْعول		المُضارِع		الماضي	
مُجَمَّل	⇐	يُجَمِّل	⇐	جَمَّلَ	مَفْعول
مُسْتَبْعَد	⇐	يَسْتَبْعِدُ	⇐	اِسْتَبْعَدَ	

i. If the penultimate letter is a ياء, then change it to an ألف:

اِسْمُ المَفْعول		المُضارِع		الماضي	مَفْعول
مُسْتَشار	⇐	يَسْتَشيرُ	⇐	اِسْتَشارَ	

ii. When the penultimate letter is an ألف it is retained:

اِسْمُ المَفْعول		المُضارِع		الماضي	مَفْعول
مُخْتار	⇐	يَخْتارُ	⇐	اِخْتارَ	

15. Adjective الصِفةُ المُشَبّهة

Definition: Unlike English, الصفةُ المُشَبّهة is considered a noun in Arabic and denotes a permanent characteristic in the modified noun.

Derivation: Only intransitive verbs can serve as fodder for deriving الصفةُ المُشَبّهة with the condition that these verbs are transitive. We use only two verb patterns to derive these adjectives فَعِل وفَعُل. Let's take a closer look at both of these types of verbs and their associated adjectival derivations:

المَنعى	المؤنَّث	الصِفّة		الوَزَن	الأَصْل
tired	تَعِبةٌ	تَعِبٌ	⇐	فَعِلٌ	فَعِلَ
happy	فَرِحةٌ	فَرِحٌ	⇐		
blue	زَرْقاء	أَزْرَق	⇐	أَفْعَل	
blind	عَمْياء	أعْمى	⇐		
cross-eyed	حَوْلاء	أَحْوَل	⇐		
thirsty	عَطْشانة	عَطْشان	⇐	فَعْلان	
hungry	جَوْعانة	جَوْعان	⇐		

المَنعى	المؤنَّث	الصِفّة		الوَزَن	الأصْل
big	كَبيرة	كَبير	⇐	فَعيل	فَعُلَ
small	صَغيرة	صَغير	⇐		
good	حَسَنة	حَسَن	⇐	فَعَل	
moist	رَطْبة	رَطْب	⇐	فَعْل	
coward	جَبانة	جَبان	⇐	فَعال	
brave	شُجاعة	شُجاع	⇐	فُعال	
rigid	صُلْبة	صُلْب	⇐	فُعْل	

16. Nouns of Place and Time اسْمُ المَكان والزَمان

Definition: These nouns denote the time or place of the action.

Derivation: اسْمُ المَكان والزَمان has two patterns: مَفْعَل ومَفْعِل. The form مَفْعَل is derived from present tense (imperfect) verbs whose middle letter has a فَتْحة (ex. يَعْمَل) or a ضُمّة (ex. يَدْرُس); while the مَفْعِل form is derived from imperfect verbs whose middle letter has a كَسْرة.

a. Nouns of the Pattern مَفْعَل

المَنعى	اسْمُ المَكان والزَمان	المُضارِع		الماضي	الوَزَن
factory	مَصْنَع	يَصْنَع	⇐	صَنَعَ	مَفْعَل
factory	مَعْمَل	يَعْمَل	⇐	عَمِلَ	
school	مَدْرَسة	يَدْرُس	⇐	دَرَسَ	
office	مَكْتَب	يَكْتُب	⇐	كَتَبَ	

If you have فَعْل أجوَف where the present tense has a واو as the middle letter, its middle letter will be an ألف as a noun of time and place:

المَنعى	اسْمُ المَكان والزَمان	المُضارِع		الماضي	الوَزَن
field	مَجال	يَجول	⇐	جالَ	مَفْعَل
place of visiting: tourist attraction	مَزار	يَزور	⇐	زارَ	

When the last letter is a vowel, an ألف مَقْصورة will grace the end of اسْمُ المَكان والزَمان

المَنعى	اسْمُ المَكان والزَمان	المُضارِع		الماضي	الوَزَن
goal, target	مَرْمى	يَرْمي	⇐	رَمى	مَفْعَل
anchorage, mooring	مَرْسى	يَرْسو	⇐	رَسا	

There are of course exceptions to this rule and, in this case, eleven such exceptions exist. Notable examples are: مَشْرِق *orient*, مَغْرِب *occident*, and مَسْجِد *mosque*.

المَنعى	اسْمُ المَكان والزَمان	المُضارِع		الماضي	الوَزَن
council	مَجْلِس	يَجْلِس	⇐	جَلَسَ	مَفْعِل
residence	مَنْزِل	يَنْزِل	⇐	نَزَلَ	
exhibition	مَعْرِض	يَعْرِض	⇐	عَرَضَ	

If the first letter of the triliteral is a واو, then the second letter in the noun will also be a واو:

المَنعى	اسْمُ المَكان والزَمان	المُضارِع		الماضي	الوَزَن
appointment	مَوْعِد	يَعِد	⇐	وَعَد	مَفْعِل
stove, burner	مَوْقِد	يَقِد	⇐	وَقَدَ	
place, location	مَوْضِع	يَضَع	⇐	وَضَعَ	

When the middle letter in the triliteral verb is an ألف that was a ياء originally, then the ألف will become a ياء in the noun of time or place:

المَعنى	اسْمُ المَكان والزّمان	المُضارِع		الماضي	الوَزْن
summer resort	مَصيف	يَصيف	⇐	صافَ	مَفْعِل
night stay	مَبيت	يَبيت	⇐	باتَ	

17. Nouns of Instrument اِسْمُ الآلة

Definition: These nouns denote an instrument, device, or machine.

Derivation: Six different patterns are associated with اِسْمُ الآلة:

المَعنى	اِسْمُ الآلة	المُضارِع		الماضي	الوَزْن	
file, rasp	مِبْرَد	يَبْرُد	⇐	بَرَدَ	مِفْعَل	١
scalpel	مِشْرَط	يَشْرُط	⇐	شَرَطَ		
scissors	مِقَصّ	يَقُصّ	⇐	قَصَّ		
key	مِفْتاح	يَفْتَح	⇐	فَتَحَ	مِفْعال	٢
saw	مِنْشار	يَنْشُر	⇐	نَشَرَ		
lamp	مِصْباح	يَصْبَح	⇐	صَبَحَ		
plow	مِحْراث	يَحْرُث	⇐	حَرَثَ		
spoon	مِلْعَقة	يَلْعَق	⇐	لَعِقَ	مِفْعَلة	٣
broom	مِكْنَسة	يَكْنُس	⇐	كَنَسَ		
tractor	جَرّار	يَجُرّ	⇐	جَرَّ	فَعّال	٤
counter	عَدّاد	يَعُدّ	⇐	عَدَّ		

المَنعى	اِسْمُ الآلة	المُضارِع		الماضي	الوَزن	
car	سَيّارة	يَسير	⇐	سار	فَعّالة	٥
washing machine	غَسّالة	يَغْسِل	⇐	غَسَلَ		
refrigerator	ثلاّجة	يَثْلُج	⇐	ثَلَجَ		
computer	حاسوب	يَحْسُب	⇐	حَسَبَ	فاعول	٦
fax	ناسوخ	يَنْسَخ	⇐	نَسَخَ		

As you might imagine, there are exceptions to how اِسْمُ الآلة is derived, such as سَكّين *knife*, قَلَم *pen*, فأس *ax*, شَوْكة *fork*, دَرْع *armor*.

تمرين ١٢

1. **After reading the passage below, list the different derived nouns الاسم المُشتق in their appropriate categories in the cells under أمثلة. As well, identify the triliteral root from which they are derived as in the example:**

زُهَيْر عامِلٌ في مخبزٍ شعبيّ قديم. ينهض من النوم في الساعة الرابعة صباحَ كلِّ يوم ليذهبَ إلى عمله. يرتدي ملابسَه ويشرب كوبَ شاي ثمّ يخرج إلى موقِفِ الحافلة الأقربِ إلى داره لأنه يجب أن يكونَ في عملِه قبل شروقِ الشمس. ينظر إلى ناحية المشرِق ولا يرى إلاّ ظلاماً.

لم يتأخّر زُهَيْر يوماً عن موعِدِه. هو أقدمُ عامِلٍ في المخبز ويعتمد عليه صاحب العمل إلى حَدٍّ كبير في صُنعِ الخبزِ «المَعروك» أيامَ رمضان، فهو النوع المفضّل من الخبز عند كثيرٍ من الناس في ذلك الشهر.

اعتاد الناسُ شراءَ أحسن أنواع الخبز من هذا المحلِّ، فهو مصنوع من القمحِ الصُلب المزروعِ في حَورانَ. يضع زُهَيْر القمحَ المطحونَ في العجّانة، ثمّ يجعله بعد ذلك أقراصاً يضعها في الموقِد حتّى تنضُجَ وتصبحَ خبزاً.

الجذر	المثل من النص	الاسمُ المُشتَق
		اِسمُ الفاعِل
		اِسمُ المَفعول
		اِسمُ المَكان
		أِسمُ الزَمان
		الصفة المشبّهة
		اِسمُ التَفْضيل
		اِسمُ الآلة

2. **List three words you have not seen before from the passage on the previous page. Look up their meanings in a dictionary and then write them down next the list of unknown words.**
3. **Provide the general meaning of the passage in English.**

18. Negation النَّفيُ

We negate verbs, nouns, and adjectives in Arabic by using particles, nouns, or the defective verb (لَيْسَ). Certain particles of negation do not affect the structure of the following word, while others affect the words they modify. Let's take a close look at these negative particles and their respective influence on their modified words:

١. دون

This noun serves as an *adverb of place* and denotes various meanings depending on context. While not considered a negative particle, it is included here due to its negative denotation. At times, it co-occurs with the preposition بـ creating بِدون and is therefore in حالة الجر. Alone, it is حالة النصب. Consider the following examples:

He lived without his family	عاشَ بِدونِ أسْرَتِه.	١
We passed through Cairo without visiting the pyramids.	مَرَرْنا بِالقاهِرَةِ مِن دونِ أنْ نَزورَ الأهرامات.	٢

٢. غَير

This noun forms an إضافة with the following noun. Just as with دونَ, this is not considered to be a negative particle *per se*; although it imparts a negative sense.

Hāla is not tall.	هالةُ غَيْرُ طَويلَةٍ. .	٣

٣. لا

The particle لا serves three distinct functions:

i. When it negates a negative verb, it changes the verb to حالة الجزم:

Don't write on the wall.	لا تَكْتُبْ على الجِدار.	٤

ii. When it negates a present tense verb (e..g, يَدْرُسُ), **it has no effect on the verb:**

ᶜadnān does not study medicine.	لا يَدْرُسُ عَدنانُ الطِبَّ.	٥

iii. The particle لا can also negate an entire class of something (example 6). The noun it modifies in this case is مَنْصوب.

There are no Japanese students in our class.	لا طُلّابَ يابانِيّينَ في صَفِّنا.	٦

4. لَمْ

While this particle negates present tense verbs, it relates a past tense negative sense. The resulting modified verb is مُضارِع مَجْزوم.

Hānī's plane has not arrived.	لم تَصِلْ طائرةُ هاني.	٧

5. لَمّا

As with لم, the verb that follows لَمّا is in مُضارِع مَجْزوم but relates a past tense negative sense—only this time it serves the meaning of something not occurring—*yet.*

Hānī's plane did not yet arrive.	لَمّا تَصِلْ طائرةُ هاني.	٨

6. لَنْ

This particle is followed by مُضارِع مَنصوب, but it relates a future tense negation.

I will not read this book again.	لَنْ أقْرأَ هذا الكِتابَ ثانيةً.	٩

تَذَكَّروا

Make sure that you do not use سَوْفَ أو سَـ after لَنْ.

لَيْسَ .7

This defective verb is used with nominative sentences and causes its subject to be مَرْفوع while its predicate is مَنْصوب:

١٠	لَيْسَ الرَّجُلُ كَنَدِيّاً كما ادّعى.	*The man is not a Canadian as he claimed.*

ما .8

Very possibly the easiest of the past tense negative particles to use, ما is logically followed by a past tense verb and does not affect it in any way. Most Modern Arabic varieties use this particle in everyday speech to negate past tense verbs. It can also be used to negate present tense verbs as you can see in example 10.

١١	ما شاهَدْتُ مِثْلَ هذا الجَمال.	*I have not seen such beauty.*
١٢	«وما تَدْري نَفْسٌ بِأَيِّ أَرْضٍ تَموت؟»	*"No one knows in what land he is to die."*

الخلاصة

There are two types of negative particles:

1. Those that negate a verbal sentence (لَمْ، لَمّا، لَنْ، لا)
2. The defective verb لَيْسَ that negates a nominal sentence

- An entire genus of something can be negated by لا الناهية للجنس
- The words دونَ and غَيْرَ are not negative particles, but they convey a negative sense.

تمرين ١٣

Negate the following sentences using the appropriate particles mentioned in this section. Make appropriate changes where needed.

١- سَأسْكُنُ في هذِهِ الشَقَّةِ في السَنَةِ المُقْبِلةِ.

٢- زُرْنا باريس في الصَيْفِ الماضي.

٣- أحْضِرْ درّاجَتَكَ إلى داخِلِ الغُرفَةِ مِن فَضْلِك.

٤- تَعيشُ أُمُّ وَليد مَعَ ابنَتِها مَها هذِهِ الأيّام.

٥- أريدُ هذِهِ المَجَلَّةَ. (لا تستعملْ "لا")

٦- بَيْتي بَعيدٌ عَنِ الجامِعَةِ.

٧- سَوْفَ يُسافِرُ مَعَ صَديقَيْنِ .

٨- سَيّارَتُها حَمْراء.

٩- رأيْتُ مِثْلَ هذا المَنْظَر.

١٠- عِنْدَهُما مالٌ كَثيرٌ.

١١- هذِهِ الطاوِلَةُ في مَكانِها. (لا تستعمل "لَيْسَ")

١٢- سَوْفَ تَعْمَلُ بِالمُسْتَشْفى بَعْدَ تَخَرُّجِها.

مخطوط قواعد قديم مصدره وعنوانه مجهولان

مُعجَمُ مُصْطَلَحاتِ القَواعِد

المصطلح	الأمثلة	المعنى
المَصْدَر	كِتابة، تَكْسير، اِسْتِثْمار	Verbal noun
الضَمير	أنا، نَحْنُ، أنْتَ، أنْتُم	Pronoun
اِسْمُ العَلَم	مازِن، دِمَشْق، سُعاد	Proper noun
اِسْمُ الفاعِل	كاتِب، مُؤَلِّف، خَبّاز	Active participle
اِسْمُ الإشارة	هذا، أولائِكَ، تِلْكَ	Demonstrative
اِسْمُ الجِنْس	كِتاب، شُبّاك، حاسوب	Concrete and abstract nouns
اِسْمُ المَفْعول	مَكْتوب، مُخْتَصر	Passive participle
الاِسْمُ المَوْصول	الّذي، الّتي، الّذينَ	Relative noun
اِسْمُ العَدَد	أربَعة، سَبْعةَ عَشر	Numbers
الصِفةُ المُشَبَّهَة	شُجاع، كَريمٌ، حَسَنٌ	Adjectival noun
أدوات الاستِفهام	أينَ، كَم، مَتى، هَل	Question particles
اِسْمُ الفِعْل (لَهُ مَعنى الفِعلْ)	سَرْعانَ، آهِ، إلَيْكَ	Nouns with verbal force
اِسْمُ المُبالَغَة	عَلاّمة، صِدّيق، عليم	Intensive noun
اِسْمُ شَرْط	إذا، لَمّا، مَنْ، ما، مَتى	Conditional noun

Diminutive noun	كُلَيب، شُجَيْرة، كُتَيِّب	اِسْمُ التَصغير
The five special nouns	أبٌ، أخٌ، ذو، فو، حَمٌ	الأسْماء الخَمْسة
Comparative / superlative	أكْثر، أجْمل، أشَدّ	اِسْمُ التَفْضيل
Referent to other nouns	كَذا، فُلانُ، بِضْعُ	الكِناية
Adverb of place	وَراءَ، غَرْبَ، مَدينةٌ	ظَرْفُ المَكان
Noun of place	مَجْلِس، مَكتَب، مَوْرِد	اِسْمُ المَكان
Adverb of time	الآنَ، أمسِ، مُنْذُ	ظَرْفُ الزَمان
Noun of time	مَوْعِد، مَغيب	اِسْمُ الزَمان
Noun of instrument	سِكّين، مُحَرِّك، سَيّارة	اِسْمُ الآلة
Noun of frequency	سَفْرة، نَومة	اِسْمُ المَرّة
Relative adjective	عَرَبيّ، أمريكيّ	اِسْمُ النِسْبة
Jussive case	لَمْ أذْهَبْ	حالةُ الجَزْم / المَجْزوم
Nominative case	الرَجُلُ	حالةُ الرَفْع / المَرْفوع
Accusative case	قَرأ الكِتابَ	حالةُ النَصْب / المَنْصوب
Genitive case	في البَيْتِ	حالةُ الجَرّ / المَجْرور

Nouns	مَدْرَسة، اِمْرأة، كِتاب	اِسْمُ ج أسْماء
Particles	فـ، لِـ، عِند	حَرْف ج حُروف
Definite article	الـ	أداةُ التَعْريف
Conditional	إذا + فعل ، لَوْ + فَعَلَ	الشَرْط
Conditional phrase	لَوْ كُنْتَ الرئيس لَـ . . .	جُمْلةٌ شَرْطيّةٌ
Conditional particle	إذا، إنْ حَيْثُما، كَيْفَما، مَا، مَنْ، مَهْمَا، لَو	أداة شَرْط
Apposition	الأخ، الأستاذ، الدكتور، جلالة الملك	البَدَل
Indeclinable	إذْ، بَيْنَما، قَطّ، لَدى	المَبْني
Specificity	ذِراعٌ جوخاً، اِشترَيْتُ قنطاراً قُطْناً	التَمْييز
Plural	طاولات، رِجال، مدارس	جَمْع
Singular	طاوِلة، رَجُل، مدرسة	مُفْرَد
Broken plural	حقائب، دفاتر، حواسيب	جَمْع تكْسير
Sound masculine plural	مُدَرِّسون، مُهَنْدِسون	جَمْع مُذَكَّر سالم
Sound feminine plural	سَيّارات، جامِعات، تفّاحات	جَمْع مُؤنَّث سالم
Nominal sentence	إنَّ المدينة كبيرة، هو أستاذ	جُملةُ اِسْميّة

Verbal sentence	قَرَأَ الطالبُ الكتابَ	جُمْلة فِعْليّة
ḥāl accusative	قائلاً، مُبتَسِماً، نائماً	الحال
Alphabet	أ، ب، ت، ث، ج، ح، خ	حُروف الهِجاء
Phrase	عند الباب، بمثابة	شِبْه الجُمْلة
Predicate	المعرِض زواره كثيرون، النَصْرُ قَريبٌ	الخَبر
Past tense	ذَهَبَ، نَسِيَ، اِشْتَرى	الفِعْلُ الماضي
Intransitive verb	جَلَسَ، جاء، خَرَجَ	الفِعْلُ اللازِم
Transitive verb	زارَ، تَبَنّى، قَدَّمَ	الفِعْلُ المُتَعَدّي
Present tense	يأكُلُ، ينامُ، يَسْتَنْتِجُ	الفِعْلُ المُضارِع
Weak verb	وَعَدَ، قالَ، مضى	الفِعْلُ المُعَتَلّ
Passive voice	وُلِدَ، اُعْتُقِلَ، يُقالُ	الفِعْلُ المَبني لِلمَجْهول
Active voice	دَرَسَ، كَتَبَ، اِنْتَقَلَ	الفِعْلُ المَبْني لِلمَعْلوم
لا of negation	لا تذهَبْ، لا تتأخَّرْ	لا الناهية
لا of negation	لا أريدُ، لا أعْتَقِدُ	لا النافية
Subject or topic	الوَلَدُ جميلٌ، الدَرْسُ سَهْلٌ	المُبْتَدأ

المُثَنّى	والِدانِ، أَخَوانِ	Dual form
إضافة	مِفْتاحُ السَيّارةِ، جَريدةُ الطالِبِ	Possessive construct
المُضاف	مِفْتاحُ السَيّارةِ، جَريدةُ الطالِبِ	First member of إضافة
المُضاف إليه	مِفْتاحُ السَيّارةِ، جَريدةُ الطالِبِ	Second member of إضافة
المَفْعول بِهِ	أَكَلَ تُفاحةً، فَتَحَ البابَ	Direct object
المَمْنوع مِنَ الصَرْف	عَدنان، زَيْنَب، حَمْزَة، إبراهيم، عُمَر، مِصْر، يَزيد	Diptote
نائِبُ الفاعِل	سُرِقَتِ السَيّارةُ، حوصِرَ جَيْشُ الأعداء	Deputy agent
الصِفة / النَعْت	جَميل، كَبير، خَفيف	Adjective

المُعجَم

Vocabulary items are listed in alphabetical order. Verbs are listed in their third person masculine singular past tense form, followed by its present tense in parentheses, and then its verbal noun. Nouns are followed by their plurals indicated by the letter ج (abbreviation of جمع). Nouns starting with a definite article are listed according to the first letter of the word that follows the article. Active and passive participles are listed as independent nouns. Some consonants may have two short vowels shown indicating two different pronunciations. The lesson in which a word first appears is listed next to its English meaning in brackets.

أ

[5] هَلْ				أ
to smile [5]	(v.)	اِبْتِسام	(يَبْتَسِمُ)	اِبْتَسَمَ
to draw away from, to withdraw [18]	(v.)	اِبتِعاد (عَن)	(يَبْتَعِدُ)	اِبْتَعَدَ
to banish, to expel, to deport [18]	(v.)	إِبْعاد	(يُبْعِدُ)	أَبْعَدَ
Ebla (ancient Syrian kingdom discovered in 1976) [9]	(n., f.)			إِبْلا
thumb [12]	(n., m.)	أَباهيم	ج	إِبهام
to head toward [1]	(v.)	اِتِّجاه	(يَتَّجِه)	اِتَّجَهَ
to accommodate [14]	(v.)	اِتِّساع	(يَتَّسِعُ)	اِتَّسَعَ
to complete, to conclude, to finish [14]	(v.)	تَتْميم	(يُتَمِّمُ)	تَمَّمَ
to be characterized, to be distinguished by [14]	(v.)	اِتِّصاف	(يَتَّصِفُ)	اِتَّصَفَ
to accuse [18]	(v.)	اِتِّهام	(يَتَّهِمُ)	اِتَّهَمَ
to prove, to establish, to verify [16]	(v.)	إِثْبات	(يُثْبِتُ)	أَثْبَتَ

to affect, to influence, to impact [16]	(v.)	تأثير (في/ على)	(يُؤَثِّرُ)	أثَّرَ
during [3]	(adv.)			أثناء
to master, to be skilled or proficient at [7]	(v.)	إجادة	(يُجيدُ)	أجادَ
vacation [12]	(n., f.)	إجازات	ج	إجازة
compulsory [11]	(adj.)			إجْباريّ
to cross, pass [4]	(v.)	اِجْتِياز	(يَجتازُ)	اِجتازَ
to attract [17]	(v.)	اِجْتِذاب	(يَجتَذِبُ)	اِجْتَذَبَ
to perform, to conduct, to do [5]	(v.)	إجْراء	(يُجْري)	أجرى
all, the whole of, entire [14]	(act. p.)	أَجْمَعون	ج	أَجْمَع
to need, to have to [2]	(v.)	اِحْتِياج إلى	(يَحْتاج)	اِحْتاجَ
to protest, to object (to) [15]	(v.)	اِحْتجاج (على)	(يَحْتَجُّ)	اِحْتَجَّ
to respect, to honor, to revere [19]	(v.)	اِحترام	(يَحتَرِمُ)	اِحْتَرَمَ
one of [9]	(n., m.)	أحَد	(n., f.)	إحْدى
to create, to produce [16]	(v.)	إحْداث	(يُحْدِثُ)	أحْدث
to bring [7]	(v.)	إحْضار	(يُحْضِرُ)	أحْضر
to become red in color; to blush [3]	(v.)	اِحْمِرار	(يَحْمَرُّ)	اِحْمَرَّ
to tell, to inform [13]	(v.)	إخْبار	(يُخْبِرُ)	أخْبَرَ
to invent [17]	(v.)	اِختِراع	(يَختَرِعُ)	اِختَرَعَ
to start, to begin, to take [14]	(v.)	أخْذ	(يأخُذُ)	أخَذَ

to err, to make a mistake [15]	(v.)	خَطأ	(يُخْطِئُ)	أخطأ
to lead (to) [17]	(v.)	تأدية (إلى)	(يُؤَدِّي)	أدّى
tool, implement, instrument [2]	(n., f.)	أدَوات	ج	أداة
to start (s.th.), to turn (s.th.) on [12]	(v.)	إدارة	(يُديرُ)	أدارَ
to attain, to reach, to realize [12]	(v.)	إدْراك	(يُدْرِكُ)	أدرَكَ
man of letters, educated, refined [17]	(n., m.)	أُدَباء	ج	أديب
since, because [2]	(part.)			إذْ
to express, to declare [15]	(v.)	إدلاء (بِـ)	(يُدلي)	أدْلى
ear [12]	(n., f.)	آذان	ج	أُذُن
to show, to demonstrate [14]	(v.)		(يُري)	أرى
Aramaic [9]	(adj.)			آراميّ
small piece of s.th. [8]	(n., f.)	إرَب	ج	إرْبة
to take a break (from) [12]	(v.)	اِرتياح (مِن)	(يَرتاحُ)	اِرتاحَ
to be embarrassed/confused [12]	(v.)	اِرتِباك	(يَرتَبِكُ)	اِرتَبَكَ
to tremble, to shiver, to shudder [12]	(v.)	اِرتِجاف	(يَرتَجِفُ)	اِرتَجَفَ
to wear [5]	(v.)	اِرْتِداء	(يَرْتَدي)	اِرْتَدى
to tremble, to shake, to shudder [14]	(v.)	اِرْتِعاد	(يَرْتَعِدُ)	اِرْتَعَدَ
to add, to follow up with [14]	(v.)	إرْداف	(يُرْدِفُ)	أرْدَفَ
Aristotle [18]	(name)	أرِسْطوطاليس		أرِسْطو

to send, to transmit [8]	(v.)	إرسال	(يُرسِلُ)	أرسَلَ
to try to satisfy, to please [18]	(v.)	إرْضاء	(يُرْضي)	أرْضى
exhaustion, fatigue [15]	(n., m.)			إرْهاق
to remove, to drive away, to banish [17]	(v.)	إزاحة	(يُزيحُ)	أزاحَ
to flourish, to prosper, to thrive [17]	(v.)	اِزدِهار	(يَزدَهِرُ)	اِزدَهَرَ
to support; to cheer [1]	(v.)	مؤازَرة	(يُؤازِر)	آزَرَ
to resume, to continue, to recommence [14]	(v.)	اِسْتِئناف	(يَسْتَأنِفُ)	اِسْتَأنَفَ
to preserve, to retain [20]	(v.)	اِسْتِبْقاء	(يَسْتَبْقي)	اِسْتَبْقى
exception [12]	(n., m.)	اِستِثناءات	ج	اِستِثناء
preparation, formulation, compound [16]	(n., m.)	اِسْتِحضارات	ج	اِسْتِحضار
to call, to send for, to summon [8]	(v.)	اِستِدعاء	(يَستَدْعي)	اِستَدعى
to seek information; to obtain information [19]	(v.)	اِستِدْلال	(يَستَدِلُّ)	اِستَدَلَّ
to ask for more [15]	(v.)	اِسْتِزادة	(يَسْتَزيدُ)	اِسْتَزادَ
to relax [12]	(v.)	اِستِرخاء	(يَستَرخي)	اِستَرخى
to steal (a glance) [15]	(v.)	اِسْتِراق (نَظرة)	(يَسْتَرِقُ)	اِستَرَقَ
exploration, reconnaissance, investigation [17]	(v.)	اِستِطلاع	(يَستَطلِعُ)	اِستَطلَعَ
to seek the help of [17]	(v.)	اِستِعانة	(يَستَعينُ)	اِستَعانَ
to find strange, odd, unusual [8]	(v.)	اِستِغراب	(يَستَغرِبُ)	اِستَغرَبَ
to take (time) [6]	(v.)	اِستِغراق	(يَستَغرِقُ)	اِستَغرَقَ

to benefit, make use of [1]	(v.)	اِسْتِفادة (مِن)	(يَسْتَفيد)	اِسْتَفادَ
to receive [2]	(v.)	اِسْتِلام	(يَسْتَلِم)	اِسْتَلَمَ
to continue, resume, go on [4]	(v.)	اِستِمرار	(يَستَمِرُّ)	اِستَمَرَّ
to exhaust, to consume, to deplete [14]	(v.)	اِسْتِنْفاد	(يَسْتَنفِدُ)	اِسْتَنْفَدَ
to consume [8]	(v.)	اِستِهلاك	(يَستَهلِكُ)	اِستَهلَكَ
to seize, to capture [10]	(v.)	اِستِيلاء (على)	(يَستَولي)	اِستَولى
to wake up, to awaken, to rise [16]	(v.)	اِسْتِيقاظ	(يَسْتَيْقِظُ)	اِسْتَيْقَظَ
lion [17]	(n., m.)	أُسود	ج	أَسَد
fleet, navy [14]	(n., m.)	أساطيل	ج	أُسْطول
first aid [11]	(n., m.)	إسعافات	ج	إسْعاف
to please, to make happy [2]	(v.)	إسْعاد	(يُسْعِد)	أَسْعَدَ
sorry [7]	(act. p.)			أَسِف
bishop [18]	(n., m.)	أساقِفة	ج	أُسْقُف
prisoner (of war) [10]	(n., m.)	أَسْرى	ج	أسير
to point, to indicate, to allude [5]	(v.)	إشارة	(يُشيرُ)	أشارَ
sign, signal [1]	(n., f.)	إشارات	ج	إشارة
to catch fire [11]	(v.)	اِشتِعال	(يَشتَعِلُ)	اِشْتَعَلَ
to supervise, to oversee, to manage [16]	(v.)	إشْراف (على)	(يُشْرِفُ)	أَشْرَفَ
rays, beams [11]	(n., f.)			أَشِعّة

blond [2]	(color)	شُقْر	/ شَقراء ج	أشْقر
gray [10]	(adj.)	شُهْب	شَهباء	أشهَب
to hit, to injure [11]	(v.)	إصابة	(يُصيبُ)	أصابَ
finger [2]	(n., f.)	أصابِع	(أو أصْبُع) ج	إصْبَع
to become [2]	(v.)		(يُصْبِح)	أصْبَحَ
to collide with [11]	(v.)	اِصْطِدام بـ	(يَصْطَدِمُ)	اِصْطَدَمَ
original, authentic [9]	(adj.)			أصْليّ
to add [3]	(v.)	إضافَة	(يُضيفُ)	أضافَ
to become, to turn into [19]	(v.)			أضْحى
to be compelled, to be forced (to) [13]	(v.)	اِضْطِرار (إلى)	(يُضْطَرُّ)	اِضْطُرَّ
to allot generously, to grant [17]	(v.)	إضفاء	(يُضْفي)	أضْفى
to launch, to fire [17]	(v.)	إطلاق	(يُطلِقُ)	أطلَقَ
to name, to give a name [17]				أطلَقَ اسماً على
to extinguish, to put out a fire [11]	(v.)	إطفاء	(يُطفِئُ)	أطفَأ
to return (s. th.) [11]	(v.)	إعادة	(يُعيدُ)	أعادَ
to help, to assist, to aid [13]	(v.)	إعانة	(يُعينُ)	أعان
beginning, as of, effective from [1]	(adv.)			اِعتِباراً (مِن)
to be moderate [16]	(v.)	اِعْتِدال	(يَعْتَدِلُ)	اِعْتَدَلَ
to apologize, to excuse o.s. from [7]	(v.)	اِعتِذار (عَن)	(يَعتَذِرُ)	اِعتَذَر

to recognize, to acknowledge, to confess [17]	(v.)	اِعتِراف (بـِ)	(يَعتَرِفُ)	اِعتَرَفَ
to be proud of, to take pride in [16]	(v.)	اِعْتِزاز (بـِ)	(يَعْتَزُّ)	اِعْتَزَّ
to arrest [11]	(v.)	اِعتِقال	(يَعتَقِلُ)	اِعتَقَلَ
to embrace, to convert [18]	(v.)	اِعْتِناق	(يَعْتَنِقُ)	اِعْتَنَقَ
to announce [1]	(v.)	إعْلان	(يُعْلِن)	أعْلَنَ
Greek [9]	(adj.)	إغريقيّون	ج	إغْريقيّ
to close [1]	(v.)	إغلاق	(يُغْلِق)	أغْلَقَ
to lose consciousness, to faint [13]	(v.)	إغْماء	(يُغْمى)	أُغْميَ
to have a grand opening, to inaugurate [16]	(v.)	اِفْتِتاح	(يَفْتَتِحُ)	افْتَتَحَ
Plato [18]	(name)			أفْلاطون
to slip away [20]	(v.)	إفْلات	(يُفْلِتُ)	أفْلَتَ
to set up, to found, to convene [5]	(v.)	إقامة	(يُقيمُ)	أقامَ
to approach, to come close, to draw near [5]	(v.)	اِقْتِراب	(يَقْتَرِبُ)	اِقْتَرَبَ
economy [9]	(n., m.)			اِقْتِصاد
to discover [9]	(v.)	اِكْتِشاف	(يَكْتَشِفُ)	اِكْتَشَفَ
to be overcrowded [20]	(v.)	اِكْتِظاظ	(يَكْتَظُّ)	اكتظّ
to assert, to emphasize [11]	(v.)	تأكيد	(يُؤَكِّدُ)	أكَّدَ
so as not to [7]	(part.)		(أنْ + لا)	ألاّ
deity [10]	(n., m.)	آلِهة	ج	إله

اِلْتَفَتَ	(يَلْتَفِتُ)	اِلْتِفات	(v.)	to turn, to pay attention [5]
أَلَّفَ	(يُؤَلِّفُ)	تأليف	(v.)	to compose, to compile [16]
ألو			(int.)	hello [4]
أليف			(adj.)	tame, domesticated, friendly [2]
إِلَيْكَ			(prep.)	take! here you go [1]
إلى أنْ				until [3]
أُمّ	ج	أمَّهات	(n., f.)	center, middle, most significant [14]
أمّة	ج	أمَم	(n., f.)	nation [1]
اِمْتَحَنَ	(يَمْتَحِنُ)	اِمْتِحان	(v.)	to examine, to test [2]
اِمتَدَّ	(يَمْتَدُّ)	اِمتِداد	(v.)	to stretch, to extend [6]
اِمْتازَ	(يَمْتازُ)	اِمْتِياز	(v.)	to excel, to surpass, to be distinguished [18]
اِمتَصَّ	(يَمتَصُّ)	اِمتِصاص	(v.)	to absorb [11]
أمْر	ج	أوامِر	(n., m.)	a command, an order [5]
أَمَرَ	(يأمُرُ)	أمَر (بِـ)	(v.)	to order, to command, to instruct [19]
أمَل	ج	آمال	(n., m.)	hope [2]
أمَوِيّ	أُمَيّة		(adj.)	Omayyad [9]
إنْ			(part.)	if [4]
أنْبأ	(يُنبِئُ)	إنْباء	(v.)	to inform, to tell [19]
أنْبأ	(يُنْبِئُ)	إنْباء	(v.)	to reveal, to impart [19]

to produce [14]	(v.)	إنْتاج	(يُنْتِجُ)	أَنْتَجَ
mandate [16]	(n., m.)			اِنْتِداب
to remove [20]	(v.)	اِنْتِزاع	(يَنْتَزِعُ)	اِنْتَزَعَ
to join, to be associated (with) [16]	(v.)	اِنْتِساب (إلى)	(يَنْتَسِبُ)	اِنْتَسَبَ
to spread [2]	(v.)	اِنْتِشار	(يَنْتَشِر)	اِنْتَشَرَ
to triumph, to prevail, to win, to defeat [19]	(v.)	اِنتِصار	(يَنتَصِرُ)	اِنتَصَرَ
to await [8]	(v.)	اِنتِظار	(يَنتَظِرُ)	اِنتَظَرَ
to end, to expire [6]	(v.)	اِنتِهاء	(يَنتَهي)	اِنتَهى
to beget, to give birth [16]	(v.)	إنْجاب	(يُنْجِبُ)	أَنْجَبَ
to veer, to turn to one side [11]	(v.)	اِنحِراف	(يَنحَرِفُ)	اِنحَرَفَ
then, at that time [16]	(adv.)		(آنَ + ذاك)	آنذاك
human being [16]	(n., m.)			إنسان
to withdraw, to retreat [17]	(v.)	اِنسِحاب	(يَنسَحِبُ)	اِنسَحَبَ
to begin, to start, to build, to compose [14]	(v.)	إنْشاء	(يُنشِئ)	أنشأ
to be busy, to be preoccupied [15]	(v.)	اِنْشِغال (بِـ)	(يَنْشَغِلُ)	اِنْشَغَلَ
to disembark, to set out for [12]	(v.)	اِنطِلاق	(يَنطَلِقُ)	اِنطَلَقَ
to involve, to imply, to include [15]	(v.)	اِنْطِواء (على)	(يَنْطَوي)	اِنطَوى
to turn, swerve, swing [4]	(v.)	اِنعِطاف	(يَنعَطِفُ)	اِنعَطَفَ
to be reflected [17]	(v.)	اِنْعِكاس	(يَنْعَكِسُ)	اِنْعَكَسَ

to be immersed, to be submerged [16]	(v.)	اِنْغِماس	(يَنْغَمِسُ)	اِنْغَمَسَ
nose [12]	(n., m.)	أنوف	ج	أنْف
to be absorbed with, to be engrossed in [15]	(v.)	اِنْهِماك (في)	(يَنْهَمِكُ)	اِنْهَمَكَ
neat, elegant [5]	(adj.)			أنيق
to find the right way [4]	(v.)	اِهتِداء	(يهتَدي)	اِهتَدى
to be concerned (with) [19]	(v.)	اِهْتِمام (بِـ)	(يَهْتَمُّ)	اِهْتَمَّ
to give a gift [20]	(v.)	إهْداء	(يُهْدي)	أهْدى
family, one's folks [4]	(n., m.)	أهالٍ	ج	أهل
highest point, acme, peak, climax [16]	(n., m.)			أوْج
to hurt, to cause pain [19]	(v.)	إيجاع	(يُوجِعُ)	أوْجَعَ
to advise [20]	(v.)	إيصاء (بِـ)	(يُوصي)	أوصى
to stop, to park [12]	(v.)	إيقاف	(يوقِفُ)	أوقَفَ
to flash [7]	(v.)		(يومِضُ)	أوَمَض
namely, that is to say [11]	(part.)			أيْ
base form of the accusative separate pronoun [18]	(pron.)	(ضمير النصب)		إيّا
sign, wonder, Quranic verse [18]	(n., f.)	آيات		آية
to support, to back [18]	(v.)	تأييد	(يُؤَيِّدُ)	أيّدَ
left (in terms of direction) [5]	(adj. f.)	يُسْرى	(adj. m.)	أيْسر
faith, belief [18]	(n., m.)			إيمان

wherever [1]				أَيْنَما

ب

chapter, column (in a newspaper) [2]	(n., m.)	أبواب	ج	باب
papa (daddy) [15]	(n., m.)			بابا
to take the initiative, to begin [15]	(v.)	مُبادَرة	(يُبادِرُ)	بادَرَ
sign, indication, precursor [19]	(n., f.)	بَوادِر	ج	بادِرة
bar [7]	(n., m.)	بارات	ج	بار
dazzling, brilliant [7]	(act. p.)			باهِر
necessary, inevitable (used with لا) [11]			(لابُدّ)	بُدّ
instead (of) [13]	(adv.)		بَدَلاً (مِن)	بَدَلاً (مِن)
alternative, alternate, substitute [16]	(n., m.)	بُدَلاء	ج	بَديل
Berber of North Africa [17]	(n., m.)	بَرْبَر	ج	بَرْبَري
to become cold [3]	(v.)	بَرْد	(يَبْرُدُ)	بَرَدَ
tower, castle [17]	(n., m.)	أبراج / بُروج	ج	بُرْج
lightning [7]	(n., m.)	بُروق	ج	بَرْق
to program [2]	(v.)	بَرْمَجة	(يُبَرْمِج)	بَرْمَجَ
proof [18]	(n., m.)	بَراهين	ج	بُرْهان
courage [14]	(n., f.)			بَسالة

simple, easy, plain, modest [1]	(adj.)			بَسيط
Ptolemy [18]	(name)	بَطالِسة	ج	بَطْليموس
championship [1]	(n., f.)	بُطولات	ج	بُطولة
[7] أرسل	(v.)	بَعْث	(يبعَثُ)	بَعَث
resurrection (from death) [18]	(v.)	بَعْث	(يَبْعَثُ)	بَعَثَ
to be distant, to be far away (from) [6]	(v.)	بُعْد (عَن)	(يبعُدُ)	بَعُدَ
still, then, after that [14]	(particle)			بَعْدُ
dimension [20]	(n., m.)	أبْعاد	ج	بُعْد
cow [10]	(n., f.)	بَقَرات	ج	بَقَرة
spot, stain, patch [14]	(n., f.)	بُقَع	ج	بُقْعة
to cry, to weep [8]	(v.)	بُكاء	(يَبكي)	بَكى
[15] نَعَم	(affirmative particle after negation)			بَلى
royal court [18]	(n., m.)	أبْلِطة	ج	بَلاط
to reach, get to a place [4]	(v.)	بُلوغ	(يَبلُغُ)	بَلَغَ
as, like, similar to [16]	(prep. ph.)			بِمَثابةِ
gasoline [14]	(n., m.)			بَنْزين
ring finger [12]	(n., m.)	بَناصر	ج	بِنْصر
amethyst (violet variety of quartz) [20]	(n., m.)			بَنْفَش
brown [2]	(adj.)			بُنّيّ

hall, parlor [17]	(n., m.)	أبْهاء	ج	بَهْوٌ
Bosporus (strait) [10]	(n., m.)		(مَضيق البوسفور)	بوسفور
well (water/oil) [14]	(n., m.)	آبار	ج	بِئْر
threshing floor [20]	(n., m.)	بَيادِر	ج	بَيْدَر
while, whereas [12]	(conj.)			بَينما

ت

to pursue [2]	(v.)	مُتابَعة	(يُتابِع)	تابَعَ
delay, tardiness [7]	(n., m.)			تأخير
(entry) visa [9]	(n., f.)		تأشيرات	تأشيرة
assurance (most certainly) [4]	(n., m.)		(بالتأكيد)	تأكيد
full, complete, whole, total, perfect [19]	(adj.)			تامّ
to become clear, to be evident [11]	(v.)	تَبين	(يَتَبَيَّنُ)	تَبَيَّنَ
to yawn [15]	(v.)	تَثاؤُب	(يَتَثاءَبُ)	تَثاءَبَ
to exceed, to surpass [16]	(v.)	تَجاوُز	(يَتَجاوَزُ)	تَجاوَزَ
experiment, test, trial, experience [15]	(n., f.)	تَجارِب	ج	تَجْرِبة
beautification, makeup [9]	(n., m.)			تَجْميل
to frown, to scowl [15]	(v.)	تَجَهُّم	(يَتَجَهَّمُ)	تَجَهَّمَ
to wander about, to tour [6]	(v.)	تَجَوُّل	(يَتَجَوَّلُ)	تَجَوَّلَ
to talk to, to speak [5]	(v.)	تَحَدُّث	(يَتَحَدَّثُ)	تَحَدَّثَ

to control [1]	(v.)	تَحَكُّم (في)	(يَتحكَّم)	تَحَكَّمَ
to bear, to endure, to assume responsibility [2]	(v.)	تَحَمُّل	(يَتحمَّل)	تَحَمَّلَ
to change, to alter, to shift, to transform [15]	(v.)	تَحَوُّل	(يَتحوَّلُ)	تَحَوَّلَ
greeting—to say 'greetings from __' [2]	(n., f.)	تَحِيّات	ج	تَحِيَّة
to specialize [2]	(v.)	تَخَصُّص	(يَتخصَّص)	تَخَصَّص
to make frequent use, to exchange; to circulate [19]	(v.)	تَداوُل	(يَتَداوَلُ)	تَداوَلَ
to pour forth, to gush [17]	(v.)	تَدَفُّق	(يَتَدَفَّقُ)	تَدَفَّقَ
to remember [13]	(v.)	تَذَكُّر	(يَتَذَكَّرُ)	تَذَكَّرَ
I wonder [12]	(excl.)		يا تُرى	تُرى
legacy, inheritance [19]	(n., m.)	تُراثات	ج	تُراث
to retreat, to withdraw [12]	(v.)	تَراجُع	(يَتَراجَعُ)	تَراجَعَ
to correspond (with) [2]	(v.)	تَراسُل (مع)	(يَتَراسَل)	تَراسَلَ
soil [17]	(n., f.)			تُرْبة
education, upbringing, cultivation [15]	(n., f.)			تَربية
to translate [17]	(v.)	تَرْجَمَة	(يُتَرْجِمُ)	تَرْجَمَ
to flourish [20]	(v.)	تَرَعْرُع	(يَتَرَعْرَعُ)	تَرَعْرَعَ
to leave, to abandon [2]	(v.)	تَرْك	(يَتْرُك)	تَرَكَ
to intensify, to grow greater [12]	(v.)	تَزايُد	(يَتَزايَدُ)	تَزايَدَ
to slide, to ski, to skate [6]	(v.)	تَزَلُّج	(يَتَزَلَّجُ)	تَزَلَّجَ

to get married [8]	(v.)	تزوُّج	(يَتزوَّجُ)	تزَوَّجَ
to fall down, to rain down from everywhere [17]	(v.)	تَساقُط	(يَتَساقَطُ)	تَساقَطَ
to climb [6]	(v.)	تَسلُّق	(يَتَسلَّقُ)	تَسلَّقَ
entertainment [2]	(n., f.)	ج تَسْلِيات/ تَسالٍ		تَسْلِيَة
to flow, to pour forth, (to sweat) [12]	(v.)	تَصبُّب (عَرَقاً)	(يَتصَبَّبُ)	تَصبَّبَ
to match, to fit, to agree [13]	(v.)	تَطابُق	(يَتطابَقُ)	تَطابَقَ
to go to extremes, to hold an extreme position [19]	(v.)	تَطرُّف	(يَتَطرَّفُ)	تَطَرَّفَ
embroidery [15]	(n., m.)			تَطْريز
to be acquainted [2]	(v.)	تَعارُف	(يَتعارَف)	تَعارَفَ
come here! [5]	(imp.)			تَعالَ
to cooperate [17]	(v.)	تَعاوُن	(يَتعاوَنُ)	تَعاوَنَ
to be related (to), to be concerned (with) [18]	(v.)	تَعلُّق (بِـ)	(يَتعَلَّقُ)	تَعلَّقَ
to think (about), to reason [15]	(v.)	تَفكُّر	(يَتفَكَّرُ)	تَفكَّرَ
to cross, intersect with [4]	(v.)	تَقاطُع	(يَتَقاطَعُ)	تَقَاطَعَ
tradition, folklore [9]	(n., m.)	تَقاليد	ج	تَقْليد
technology [11]	(n., f.)			تَقنية
to recur, to be repeated [16]	(v.)	تَكرُّر	(يَتكَرَّرُ)	تَكرَّرَ
cost, expense [2]	(n., f.)	تَكْلِفات	ج	تَكْلِفة
to be created, to be formed [17]	(v.)	تَكوُّن	(يَتَكوَّنُ)	تَكوَّنَ

pupil [11]	(n., m.)	تَلاميذ	ج	تِلميذ
exactly [9]	(adv.)			تَماماً
to enjoy [10]	(v.)	تَمَتُّع (بِـ)	(يَتَمَتَّعُ)	تَمَتَّعَ
to wish, to desire [2]	(v.)	تَمَنٍّ	(يَتَمَنّى)	تَمَنّى
after [17]	(prep.)	(الواحِد تِلْوَ الآخَر)		تِلْوَ
to be distinguished, to be set apart [17]	(v.)	تَمَيُّز	(يَتَمَيَّزُ)	تَمَيَّزَ
to dispute, to contend, to rival [17]	(v.)	تَنازُع	(يَتَنازَعُ)	تَنازَعَ
to be well-coordinated, symmetrical [17]	(v.)	تَناسُق	(يَتَناسَقُ)	تَناسَقَ
to compete, to rival [17]	(v.)	تَنافُس	(يَتَنافَسُ)	تَنافَسَ
to eavesdrop, listen secretly [1]	(v.)	تَنَصُّت	(يَتَنَصَّتُ)	تَنَصَّتَ
to sigh [15]	(v.)	تَنَهُّد	(يَتَنَهَّدُ)	تَنَهَّدَ
to fall, to plunge [18]	(v.)	تَهافُت	(يَتَهافَتُ)	تَهافَتَ
congruity, agreement, conformity [18]	(n., m.)			تَوافُق
to head toward [11]	(v.)	تَوَجُّه	(يَتَوَجَّهُ)	تَوَجَّهَ
to become embroiled in, involved in [8]	(v.)	تَوَرُّط	(يَتَوَرَّطُ)	تَوَرَّطَ
to expand, to spread [16]	(v.)	تَوَسُّع	(يَتَوَسَّعُ)	تَوَسَّعَ
to attain, to arrive, to achieve [11]	(v.)	تَوَصُّل	(يَتَوَصَّلُ)	تَوَصَّلَ
to stop, to stop over [6]	(v.)	تَوَقُّف	(يَتَوَقَّفُ)	تَوَقَّفَ

ث

to revolt, to rebel [17]	(v.)	ثَوْرة	(يَثورُ)	ثارَ
breast [20]	(n., m./f.)	أثْداء	ج	ثدي
chatty, garrulous, talkative [14]	(n., m.)	ثَرثارون	ج	ثَرْثار
fortune, riches [13]	(n., f.)	ثَرَوات	ج	ثَرْوة
culture, intellectualism [11]	(n., f.)	ثَقافات	ج	ثَقافة
hole, perforation [2]	(n., m.)	ثُقوب	ج	ثُقْب
heavy, burdensome, unpleasant [5]	(adj.)	ثُقلاء	ج	ثَقيل
there (is, are) هُناكَ [20]				ثَمّة
dress [7]]	(n., m.)	أثْواب	ج	ثَوب
current, flow, trend, tendency [15]	(n., m.)	تَيّارات	ج	تَيّار

ج

neighbor [13]	(n., m.)	جيران	ج	جار
mosque [9]	(n., m.)	جَوامِع	ج	جامِع
Galen [18]	(name)			جالينوس
bosom, heart, soul [20]	(act. p.)	جَوانح	ج	جانِحة
ignorant, fool, foolish [19]	(act. p.)	جَهَلة / جُهّال / جُهَلاء	ج	جاهِل
prize, award [15]	(n., f.)	جَوائِز	ج	جائزة
forehead [12]	(n., m.)	جِباه / أَجْبُن	ج	جَبين

to kneel [20]	(v.)	جُثو	(يَجْثو)	جَثو
seriousness, earnestness, diligence [19]	(n., m.)			جِدّ
to be worthy (of) [19]	(v.)	جَدارة (بِـ)	(يَجْدُرُ)	جَدُرَ
smallpox [19]	(n., m.)			جُدَريّ
argument, debate, dispute [18]	(n., m.)			جَدَل
worthy, meriting [15]	(n., m.)			جَدير
to run, to happen, to occur [7]]	(v.)	جَرْي	(يَجري)	جَرى
tractor [12]	(n., m.)	جَرّارات	ج	جَرّار
to drag [20]	(v.)	جَرْجَرة	(يُجَرْجِرُ)	جَرْجَرَ
bell, ringer [12]	(n., m.)	أَجْراس	ج	جَرَس
to dare, to have courage [12]	(v.)	جُرأة	(يَجْرُؤُ)	جَرُؤَ
the minor details, the particulars [18]	(n., f.)			الجُزئيّات
clamor, noise, din, racket [19]	(n., f.)			جَعْجَعة
to make [5]	(v.)	جَعْل	(يَجْعَلُ)	جَعَلَ
skin [2]	(n., m.)	جُلود	ج	جِلْد
session, meeting, gathering [11]	(n., f.)	جَلَسات	ج	جَلْسة
companion, friend, associate [14]	(n., m.)	جُلَساء	ج	جَليس
group, company, party [14]	(n., f.)	جَماعات	ج	جَماعة
society, association [11]	(n., f.)	جَمعيّات	ج	جَمْعِيّة
to beautify [1]	(v.)	تَجْميل	(يُجَمِّل)	جَمَّلَ

recalcitrance, defiance; willfulness [20]	(n., m.)			جُموح
to go crazy, to go mad (passive) [8]	(v.)	جُنون	(يُجَنُّ)	جُنَّ
paradise, heaven [15]	(n., f.)	جَنّات / جِنان	ج	جَنَّة
pavilion, wing [5]	(n., m.)	أجْنِحة	ج	جَناح
chain [12]	(n., m.)	جَنازير	ج	جِنزير
public [1]	(n., m.)	جَماهير	ج	جُمْهور
atmosphere, weather, ambience [5]	(n., m.)	أجْواء	ج	جَوّ
passport [9]	(n., m.)	جَوازات	ج	جَواز
mobile [1]	(n., m.)			جَوّال
coconut [3]	(n., m.)			جَوْزُ الهِنْد

ح

need, want, necessity [16]	(n., f.)	حاجات	ج	حاجة
eyebrow [12]	(n., m.)	حَواجِب	ج	حاجِب
accident [11]	(act. p.)	حَوادِث	ج	حادِث
alley, narrow street [9]	(n., f.)	حارات	ج	حارة
to lay siege, to blockade	(v.)	مُحاصَرة	(يُحاصِرُ)	حاصَرَ
to preserve, to protect [2]	(v.)	مُحافَظة	(يُحافِظ)	حافَظَ
governor, ruler [17]	(n., m.)	حُكّام	ج	حاكِم
to ally with [16]	(v.)	مُحالَفة	(يُحالِفُ)	حالَفَ

(for time) to come, approach, draw near [1]	(v.)	حَين	(يحين)	حانَ
shop, store [14]	(n., m.)	حَوانيت	ج	حانوت
to try, to attempt [5]	(v.)	مُحاوَلة	(يُحاوِلُ)	حاوَلَ
grain [9]	(n., f.)	حَبّات	ج	حَبّة
to hold in custody, to detain [19]	(v.)	حَبْس	(يَحْبِسُ)	حَبَسَ
umbilical cord [20]				حَبَلُ مِشيمة
room, chamber [9]	(n., f.)	حُجَرات/ حُجَر	ج	حُجْرة
millstone [19]	(n., m.)		(رَحى)	حَجَر
size, volume [3]	(n., m.)	حُجوم / أحْجام	ج	حَجْم
sharpness, acuteness [14]	(n., f.)			حِدّة
to report, to relate, to converse with [14]	(v.)	تَحْديث	(يُحَدِّثُ)	حَدَّثَ
pupils (of the eye) [20]	(n., m.)	حَدَقات	ج	حَدَقة
horseshoe [17]	(n., f.)	حَدَوات	ج	حَدْوة
iron, steel [19]	(adj.)			حَديد
beware, watch out (for) [20]			(مِن)	حَذارِ
cautious, wary [15]	(adj.)			حَذِر
free, independent [15]	(n., m.)	أحْرار	ج	حُرٌّ
guarding, watching [2]	(n., f.)			حِراسة
to edit (also: write, liberate) [8]	(v.)	تَحرير	(يُحَرِّرُ)	حَرَّرَ
to move, to drive, to stimulate [15]	(v.)	تَحريك	(يُحَرِّكُ)	حَرَّكَ

movement, motion [15]	(n., f.)	حَرَكات	ج	حَرَكة
campus, sacred possession [6]	(n., m.)	أحْرام	ج	حَرَم
to deprive, to dispossess [16]	(v.)	حِرْمان	(يَحْرِمُ)	حَرَمَ
to prohibit [18]	(v.)	تَحْريم	(يُحَرِّمُ)	حَرَّمَ
silk [9]	(n., m.)			حَرير
belt [5]	(n., m.)	أحْزِمة	ج	حِزام
to be sad, to mourn [8]	(v.)	حُزْن	(يَحْزَنُ)	حَزِنَ
allergy (allergic to) [8]	(n., f)		(مِن)	حَساسية
to calculate, to reckon [13]	(v.)	حِساب	(يَحْسُبُ)	حَسَبَ
good [9]	(adj.)			حَسَن
to fill [14]	(v.)	حَشو	(يَحْشو)	حَشا
crowd, gathering, assembly [17]	(n., m.)	حَشود	ج	حَشْد
pebbles, gravel [17]	(n., f.)			حَصْباء
to fortify, to strengthen [17]	(v.)	تَحْصين	(يُحَصِّنُ)	حَصَّنَ
civilization [19]	(n., f.)	حَضارات	ج	حَضارة
respectful term of address used with both men and women [4]	(n., f.)	حَضَرات	ج	حَضْرة
fortune, luck, lot, fate [12]	(n., m.)	حُظوظ	ج	حَظّ
to dig a hole, to excavate [19]	(v.)	حَفْر	(يَحفِرُ)	حَفَرَ
party, celebration [6]	(n., f.)	حَفَلات	ج	حَفْلة
long period of time [20]	(n., m.)	حِقَق / أحْقاب	ج	حِقْبة

to realize, to fulfill, to make something come true [2]	(v.)	تَحْقيق	(يُحَقِّق)	حَقَّق
fact, reality [15]	(n., f.)	حَقائِق	ج	حَقيقة
real [12]	(adj.)			حَقيقيّ
to scratch, to scrape, to rub [19]	(v.)	حَكّ	(يَحُكُّ)	حَكَّ
to tell, to recount, to narrate [8]	(v.)	حَكي	(يَحكي)	حَكى
story, tale, narrative [9]	(n., f.)	حِكايات	ج	حِكاية
to rule, to sentence [9]	(v.)	حُكْم	(يَحْكُمُ)	حَكَم
storyteller [9]	(n., m.)	حَكَواتِيّون/ حَكَواتِيّة	ج	حَكَواتيّ
to befall, to descend upon, to afflict [15]	(v.)	حَلّ	(يَحُلُّ)	حَلّ
barber, hair dresser [14]	(n., m.)	حَلاّقون	ج	حَلاّق
to milk [10]	(v.)	(يَحْلِبُ / يَحْلُبُ) حَلْب		حَلَبَ
area; (dance) floor [7]	(n., f.)	حَلَبات	ج	حَلْبة
episode (of a series), link [5]	(n., f.)	حَلَقات	ج	حَلْقة
to dream [13]	(v.)	حُلْم	(يَحْلُمُ)	حَلَمَ
chivalry [19]	(n., m.)			حِلْم
sweet, beautiful [13]	(n., m.)			حُلوٌ
ornament, jewelry [9]	(n., m.)	حُليّ	ج	حَلي
donkey [19]	(n., m.)	حَمير	ج	حِمار
enthusiasm, ardor, zeal, fervor [14]	(n., f.)			حَماسة
pigeon, dove [9]	(n., f.)	حَمامات/ حَمام	ج	حَمامَة

to protect [1]	(v.)	حِماية	(يَحْمي)	حَمى
to praise, to laud, to commend, to extol [14]	(v.)	حَمْد	(يَحْمَدُ)	حَمِدَ
campaign, attack, offensive [16]	(n., f.)	حَمَلات	ج	حَمْلة
throat [20]	(n., f.)	حَناجِر	ج	حَنْجَرة
to be furious, to be full of rage [12]	(v.)	حَنَق	(يَحْنَقُ)	حَنِقَ
dialogue, conversation [15]	(n., m.)	حِوارات	ج	حِوار
around [9]	(adv.)			حَوْل
life [9]	(n., f.)	حَيَوات	ج	حَياة
weaving [20]	(n., f.)			حِياكة
confusion, perplexity [15]	(n., f.)			حَيْرة

خ

outside [7]	(act. p.)			خارِج
special, private [9]	(adj.)			خاصّ
to address, to deliver a sermon [5]	(v.)	مُخاطَبة	(يُخاطِبُ)	خاطَبَ
mind [20]	(act. p.)	خَواطِر	ج	خاطِر
to fear, to dread, to be afraid / scared [12]	(v.)	خَوْف	(يَخافُ)	خافَ
dim [7]	(act. p.)			خافِت
to mix with, to associate with [19]	(v.)	مُخالَطة	(يُخالِطُ)	خالَطَ
to contradict, to disagree with [19]	(v.)	مُخالَفة	(يُخالِفُ)	خالَفَ

to hide, to conceal [20]	(v.)	خَبْء	(يَخْبَأُ)	خَبَأ
to stamp, to seal [9]	(v.)	خَتْم	(يَخْتِمُ)	خَتَمَ
to thicken; to coagulate [3]	(v.)	خُثور	(يَخْثُرُ)	خَثَرَ
to be ashamed, embarrassed [12]	(v.)	خَجَل	(يَخْجَلُ)	خَجِلَ
cheek [12]	(n., m.)	خُدود	ج	خَدّ
to anesthetize, to numb [11]	(v.)	تَخدير	(يُخَدِّرُ)	خَدَّرَ
deception, cheating [19]	(n., f.)	خُدَع	ج	خُدعة
service [1]	(n., f.)	خَدَمات	ج	خِدمة
fictitious, legendary [20]	(adj.)			خُرافيّ
to scratch [20]	(v.)	خَرْبَشة	(يُخَرْبِشُ)	خَرْبَشَ
to pierce [7]	(v.)	خَرْق	(يَخْرِقُ)	خَرَق
reservoir, tank, dam [14]	(n., m.)	خَزّانات	ج	خَزّان
pottery, porcelain, ceramics [17]	(n., m.)			خَزَف
wood [2]	(n., m.)	أَخْشاب	ج	خَشَب
wooden, of wood [9]	(adj.)			خَشَبيّ
to specify, allocate, designate [1]	(v.)	تَخْصيص	(يُخَصِّص)	خَصَّصَ
specifically [8]	(adv.)			خِصّيصاً
penmanship, calligraphy, handwriting, line [1]	(n., m.)	خُطوط	ج	خَطّ
engagement, betrothal, courtship [13]	(n., f.)			خِطْبة
danger, peril, hazard, risk [14]	(n., m.)	أَخْطار	ج	خَطَر

suitor, fiancé [13]	(n., m.)	خُطَباء	ج	خَطيب
fiancée [13]	(n., f.)	خَطيبات	ج	خَطيبة
difference, disparity, incongruence [18]	(n., m.)	خِلافات	ج	خِلاف
during [13]	(adv.)		خِلالَ	خِلالَ
stealthily, unnoticeably [20]	(n., f.)			خُلْسَةً
to mix, to confuse [3]	(v.)	خَلْط	(يَخْلِطُ)	خَلَطَ
mixture [3]	(n., f.)	خَلّطات	ج	خَلْطة
to take off, to undress [9]	(v.)	خَلْع	(يَخْلَعُ)	خَلَعَ
to create [15]	(v.)	خَلْق	(يَخْلُقُ)	خَلَقَ
moral constitution, moral character [19]	(n., m.)	أخْلاق	ج	خُلُق
cellular [1]	(adj.)			خَلَويّ
tavern, wine shop [15]	(n., f.)	خَمّارات	ج	خَمّارة
yeast, leaven [3]	(n., f.)	خَمائِر	ج	خَميرة
little finger [12]	(n., m.)	خَناصر	ج	خِنصر
shadow, reflection [9]	(n., m.)	أخِيلة	ج	خَيال
better than [19]	(n., m.)		خَيْر مِن	خَيْر مِن
elite, choice, pick [16]	(n., f.)			خَيْرة

د

داخِل			(act. p.)	inner, inside, interior [5]
دارَ	(يَدورُ)	دَوَران	(v.)	to turn, to revolve [12]
دارى	(يُداري)	مُداراة	(v.)	to humor, to indulge, to flatter, to hide [15]
داعِم	ج	داعِمون	(act. p.)	supporter [16]
دافَعَ	(يُدافِعُ	دِفاع / مُدافَعة (عن)	(v.)	to defend, to protect [16]
دامَ	(يَدومُ)	دَوام	(v.)	to last, to continue, to persist [18]
دائِرة	ج	دَوائِر	(n., f.)	circle [3]
دَخْل			(n., m.)	concern, business, relevance [15]
دُخول			(n., m.)	entering [7]]
دَخَّن	(يُدَخِّن)	تَدْخين	(v.)	to smoke [1]
دَرى	(يَدْري)	دِراية	(v.)	to know, to have knowledge, to be aware of [15]
دَرْدَشَ	(يُدَرْدِشُ)	دَرْدَشة	(v.)	to chat (colloquial) [5]
دَرَّس	(يُدَرِّس)	تَدْريس	(v.)	to teach [2]
دِرْع	ج	دُروع	(n., m.)	coat of mail, armor, shield [9]
دَعا	(يَدعو)	دَعْوة	(v.)	to invite [7]
دِعاية	ج	دِعايات	(n., f.)	advertisement [1]
دَعْوة	ج	دَعَوات	(n., f.)	invitation [12]
دَفّ	ج	دُفوف	(n., m.)	tambourine [2]

to push [1]	(v.)	دَفْع	(يَدْفَع)	دَفَعَ
group, class, set [16]	(n., f.)	دُفُعات	ج	دُفْعة
to bury, to conceal [18]	(v.)	دَفْن	(يَدْفِنُ)	دَفَنَ
to knock, to bang [8]	(v.)	دَقّ	(يَدِقُّ)	دَقَّ
precise, accurate [8]	(adj.)			دَقيق
doctor, physician (loan word used in colloquial speech) [8]	(n., m.)	دكاتِرة	ج	دُكتور
to show, to indicate, to point out [9]	(v.)	دَلالة	(يَدُلُّ)	دَلَّ
to pamper, to dote on [20]	(v.)	تَدْليل	(يُدَلِّلُ)	دَلَّلَ
blood [11]	(n., m.)	دِماء	ج	دم
doll, dummy [9]	(n., f.)	دُمىً	ج	دُمْية
world, worldly existence [15]	(n., f.)			دُنْيا
paint [2]	(n., m.)			دِهان
astonishment, amazement, surprise [14]	(v. n.)			دَهْشة
to daub, to butter, to paint [3]	(v.)	دَهْن	(يَدْهُنُ)	دَهَنَ
fat, grease [16]	(n., m.)	دُهون	ج	دُهْن
medicine [13]	(n., m.)	أدْوِية	ج	دَواء
role, part [16]	(n., m.)	أدْوار	ج	دَوْر
country, state [5]	(n., f.)	دُوَل	ج	دَوْلة
to record, to write down [20]	(v.)	تَدْوين	(يُدَوِّنُ)	دَوَّنَ
religion [15]	(n., m.)	أدْيان	ج	دين

governmental office, chancellery [17]	(n., m.)	دَواوين	ج	ديوان
supply, hoard, provisions, ammunition [14]	(n., f.)	ذَخائِر	ج	ذَخيرة

ذ

corn [7]]	(n., f.)			ذُرة
arm [12]	(n., f.)	أذْرُع	ج	ذِراع
chin [12]	(n., m.)	ذُقون	ج	ذَقْن
intelligence, acumen [10]	(n., m.)			ذَكاء
mentioning, citing [15]	(n., m.)			ذِكْر
male [16]	(n., m.)	ذُكور	ج	ذَكَر
gold [17]	(n., m.)			ذَهَب
mind, intellect [17]	(n., m.)	أذْهان	ج	ذِهْن
taste, liking, inclination [15]	(n., m.)	أذْواق	ج	ذَوْق

ر

to see [7]	(v.)	رؤية	(يَرى)	رأى
opinion, point of view [13]	(n., m.)	آراء	د	رَأْيٌ
salary [5]	(n., m.)	رَواتِب	ج	راتِب
wonderful [12]	(adj.)			رائع
to review, to go over [17]	(v.)	مُراجَعة	(يُراجِعُ)	راجَعَ
rest [8]	(n., f.)			راحة

the late, the deceased [16]	(act. p.)	راحِلون	ج	راحِل
deposit, sediment, residue [15]	(n., m.)			راسِب
to correspond [2]	(v.)	مُراسَلة	(يُراسِل)	راسَل
satisfied, content, pleased [14]	(n., m.)	رُضاة	ج	راضٍ
to frighten, to scare, to alarm [14]	(v.)	رَوْع	(يَروعُ)	راعَ
high-class, upper-class, refined [6]	(n., m.)	راقون	ج	راقٍ
to observe, to watch [7]]	(v.)	مُراقَبة	(يُراقِبُ)	راقَبَ
many a . . . [19]	(prep.)			رُبّ
to win [8]	(v.)	رِبْح	(يَربَحُ)	رَبِحَ
to tie, to bind, to link [14]	(v.)	رَبْط	(يَرْبِطُ)	رَبَطَ
courtyard [20]	(n., m.)			رِحاب
to welcome [4]	(v.)	تَرحيب	(يُرَحِّبُ)	رَحَّبَ
womb [20]	(n., f.)	أرْحام	ج	رَحِم
marble [17]	(n., m.)			رُخام
cheap, inexpensive [10]	(adj.)			رَخيص
drizzle [19]	(n., m.)			رَذاذ
to bestow by God, sustenance, daily bread [16]	(v.)	رِزْق	(يَرْزُقُ)	رَزَقَ
to spray, to sprinkle [20]	(v.)	رَشّ	(يَرُشُّ)	رَشَّ
to exude, to ooze, to seep, to leak [19]	(v.)	رَشْح	(يَرْشَحُ)	رَشَحَ
to nominate, to run (candidate) [16]	(v.)	تَرْشيح	(يُرَشِّحُ)	رَشَّحَ

رَضِيَ	(يَرْضى)	رِضىً (عن)	(v.)	to be satisfied, to consent, to agree [18]
رَضيع	ج	رُضَّع	(n., m.)	infant, newborn [16]
رَغْمَ	(بالرَغْمِ مِن)		(prep.)	in spite of [15]
برِفْق			(phrase)	gently [20]
رَفَعَ	(يرفَعُ)	رَفْع	(v.)	to pick up, to raise, to lift [12]
رَقَص	(يَرقُص)	رَقْص	(v.)	to dance [7]]
رَقيقة	ج	رَقائق	(n., f.)	flake, thin layer [7]]
رَقيم	ج	رُقُم	(n., m.)	inscription, tablet [9]
رَكَضَ	(يَرْكُضُ)	رَكْض	(v.)	to run, to race [13]
رَغْبة	ج	رَغَبات	(n,, f.)	desire [10]
رَماديّ			(adj.)	ash colored [10]
رُمّان			(n., m.)	pomegranate [20]
رَمْضاء			(n., f.)	scorching heat (archaic usage) [19]
رَمى	(يَرْمي)	رَمْي	(v.)	to throw, to shoot [19]
رَواج			(n., m.)	popularity, currency, marketability [16]
رِوايّة	ج	رِوايات	(n., f.)	novel [2]
رِواق	ج	أرْوِقة	(n., m.)	colonnade, portico [17]
روح	ج	أرْواح	(n., f.)	spirit, soul, essence [14]
رَوَّضَ	(يُرَوِّضُ)	تَرْويض	(v.)	to tame, to housebreak [15]
رَوْعة			(n., f.)	beauty, charm, splendor, fear, alarm [17]

roman [6]	(adj.)			رومانيٌّ

ز

to increase [12]	(v.)	زِيادة	(يَزيدُ)	زادَ
piper, player of a wind instrument [19]	(act. p.)	زامِرون	ج	زامِر
visitor [5]	(act. p.)	زُوّار	ج	زائر
customer, client [5]	(n., m.)	زَبائن	ج	زَبون
glass [12]	(n., m.)			زُجاج
bottle, flask, vial [15]	(n., f.)	زُجاجات	ج	زُجاجة
button, push button [12]	(n., m.)	أزْرار	ج	زِرّ
chain mail [9]	(n., m.)	زُرود	ج	زَرَد
chain mail [9]	(n., m.)			زَرَد الحَديد
to be annoyed, to be upset (with) [15]	(v.)	زَعَل (مِن)	(يَزْعَلُ)	زَعِلَ
time, period, duration of time [6]	(n., m.)	أزْمُن / أزْمان	ج	زَمَن
arrogantly [20]	(adj.)			زهو
clothing, apparel, uniform [1]	(n., m.)	أزْياء	ج	زِيّ
increase, increment, addition [16]	(n., f.)	زِيادات	ج	زِيادة
oil [14]	(n., m.)	زُيوت	ج	زَيْت

س

سابِق			(act. p.)	former, previous [5]
سارَ	(يَسيرُ)	سَيْر / مَسير	(v.)	to move along, to walk, to operate [18]
ساعٍ (الساعي)	ج	سُعاة	(n., m.)	mail carrier, janitor [8]
ساق	ج	سيقان	(n., f.)	leg, thigh [12]
سالَ	(يَسيلُ)	سَيَلان	(v.)	to flow, to stream, to run [11]
سألَ	(يَسألُ)	سُؤال	(v.)	to ask [3]
سامَح	(يُسامِحُ)	مُسامَحة	(v.)	to forgive [7]
ساهَمَ	(يُساهِمُ)	مُساهَمة	(v.)	to contribute, to take part [16]
سائح	ج	سُيّاح / سائحون	(act. p.)	tourist [5]
سَبَقَ	(يَسبِقُ)	سَبْق	(v.)	to precede, to arrive before [19]
سِتارة	ج	سَتائِر	(n., f.)	drape, curtain [12]
سَجَّلَ	(يُسَجِّلُ)	تَسجيل	(v.)	to write down, to register [12]
سَحَبَ	(يَسْحَب)	سَحْب	(v.)	to pull [1]
سُخرية	سُخرية		(n., f.)	ridicule, scorn, derision, mockery [15]
سِرّ	ج	أَسْرار	(n., m.)	secret, mystery [14]
سَرَحَ	(يَسْرَحُ)	سُروح	(v.)	to be lost in thought, to daydream [15]
سَرَقَ	(يَسرِقُ)	سَرِقة	(v.)	to steal [11]
سُرْعة	ج	سُرْعات/ سُرُعات	(n., f.)	speed, velocity [3]

no sooner than, at which point [16]	(n. w/verbal meaning)			سُرْعانَ ما
Syriac, member of the Syrian church [9]	(adj.)			سِريانيّ
fast, quick [3]	(adj.)			سَريع
to burglarize, to break into [11]	(v.)	سَطْوٌ	(يُسْطو)	سَطا
embassy [6]	(n., f.)	سِفارات	ج	سِفارة
foot (of a mountain) [6]	(n., m.)	سُفوحٌ	ج	سَفْحٌ
quince (tree whose fruit resembles pears) [20]	(n., m.)			سَفَرْجَل
price [1]	(n., m.)	أسْعار	ج	سِعْر
to give s.o. a drink [20]	(v.)	سَقي	(يَسْقي)	سَقى
to be silent, to be quiet [19]	(v.)	سَكوت	(يَسْكُتُ)	سَكَتَ
knife [3]	(n., f.)	سَكاكين	ج	سِكّين
tuberculosis [16]	(n., m.)			سُلّ
to plunder [20]	(v.)	سَلْب	(يَسْلُبُ)	سَلَبَ
to focus, to put in power [11]	(v.)	تَسْليط	(يُسَلِّطُ)	سَلَّطَ
to behave, to act [19]	(v.)	سُلوك	(يَسْلُكُ)	سَلَكَ
poison [18]	(n., m.)	سُموم	ج	سُمّ
speaker (i.e., radio-stereo speaker) [11]	(n., f.)	سَمّاعات	ج	سَمّاعة
to allow, to permit [5]	(v.)	سَماح	(يَسْمَحُ)	سَمَحَ
reputation, standing, renown [19]	(n., f.)			سُمْعة
semolina [3]	(n., m.)			سَميد

easy, plain [1]	(n., m.)			سَهْل
easiness, facility [1]	(n., f.)			سُهولة
except [18]	(part.)			سِوى
wall, fence [17]	(n., m.)	أسْوار	ج	سور
chapter in the Qur'an [15]	(n., f.)	سُوَر	ج	سورة
executioner [20]	(n., m.)	سيّافون	ج	سيّاف
biography, history [9]	(n., m.)	سِيَر	ج	سيرة
flood, torrent [19]	(n., m.)	سُيول	ج	سَيْل
Ceylon (old name for Sri Lanka) [1]	(name)			سيلان

ش

young man; youth [7]]	(n., m.)	شَباب	ج	شابّ
to become gray-haired [19]	(v.)	شَيْب	(يَشيبُ)	شابَ
to resemble [19]	(v.)	مُشابَهة	(يُشابِهُ)	شابَهَ
moustache [12]	(n., m.)	شَوارِب	ج	شارِب
to participate [5]	(v.)	مُشارَكة	(يُشارِكُ)	شارَكَ
screen [1]	(n., f.)	شاشات	ج	شاشَة
vacant, empty, unoccupied [9]	(act. p.)			شاغِر
to grow up, to be a youth [19]	(v.)	شَباب	(يَشِبُّ)	شَبّ
to get full, to sate [14]	(v.)	شَبَع	(يَشْبَعُ)	شَبِعَ

شِبْل	ج	أشْبال	(n, m.)	lion cub [19]
شَبَّهَ	(يُشَبِّهُ)	تَشبيه	(v.)	comparison, simile [19]
شَتَمَ	(يَشتُمُ)	شَتْم	(v.)	to curse, to swear, to call names [12]
شَجاعة			(n., f.)	bravery, courage, boldness, valor [14]
شَجَّعَ	(يُشَجِّع)	تَشْجيع	(v.)	to support, cheer [1]
شِحْنة	ج	شِحْنات	(n., f.)	cargo, shipment, load [8]
شَدَّة	ج	شَدَّات	(n., f.)	to pull tight, to tie, to tighten [2]
شِدّة			(n., f)	strength, intensity [8]
شَديد	ج	أشِدّاء	(adj.)	intense, powerful [12]
شُرْب			(n., m.)	drinking [7]
شَرِس	ج	شَرِسون	(adj.)	vicious, fierce [12]
شَرَعَ	(يَشْرَعُ)	شُروع	(v.)	to begin, to start, to commence [12]
شَرْع			(n., m.)	canonical law of Islam [18]
شَرْوى			(n., m.)	similar to, like [19]
شَعْب	ج	شُعوب	(n., m.)	people, nation [6]
شَعْبيّ			(adj.)	popular, of the people [9]
شَعَرَ	(يَشعُرُ)	شُعور	(v.)	to feel, to have a feeling [12]
شَعْر	ج	أشْعار	(n., m.)	hair [12]
شِعْر	ج	أشْعار	(n., m.)	poetry [2]
شَفَة	ج	شِفاه	(n., f.)	lip [1]

شَفى	(يَشْفي)	شِفاء	(v.)	to heal, to cure [15]
شِفاء			(n., m.)	cure, healing, recovery [3]
شَقيّ			(n., m.)	scoundrel, rascal [15]
شَكْل	ج	أشْكال	(n., m.)	form, shape [14]
شَمِلَ	(يَشْمَل)	شَمْل	(v.)	to contain, comprise [1]
شَمَلَ	(يَشْمُل)	شُمول	(v.)	to contain, comprise [1]
شُموخ			(n., m.)	haughty [20]
شَهِدَ	(يَشْهَدُ)	شَهادة	(v.)	to witness [16]
شَوق	ج	أشواق	(n., m.)	longing, yearning, desire [4]
شَيْخ	ج	شُيوخ	(n., m.)	an elderly person, chief, senator, religious person [10]

ص

صاحِب	ج	أصْحاب	(act. p.)	owner, proprietor, friend, companion [8]
صاخِب			(act. p.)	noisy, loud [7]]
صادَفَ	(يُصادِفُ)	مُصادَفة	(v.)	to come across, to meet by chance [12]
صالح			(act. p.)	suitable, fit, appropriate [1]
صَبَّ	(يَصُبُّ)	صَبّ	(v.)	to pour, to fill [3]
صَبَرَ	(يَصبِرُ)	صَبر	(v.)	to be patient, forbearing [4]
صَبر			(n., m.)	patience, forbearance, tolerance [15]
صَبِيّ	ج	صِبْية / صِبْيان	(n., m.)	boy [5]

plate [3]	(n., m.)	صُحون	ج	صَحْن
newspaper [1]	(n., f.)	صُحُف	ج	صَحيفة
headache [8]	(n., m.)			صُداع
chest, breast, bosom [14]	(n., m.)	صُدور	ج	صَدْر
to export [14]	(v.)	تَصْدير	(يُصَدِّرُ)	صَدَّرَ
mother of pearl, sea shell [20]	(n., m.)	أَصْداف	ج	صَدَف
to believe [18]	(v.)	تَصْديق	(يُصَدِّقُ)	صَدَّقَ
truth, truthfulness, sincerity [15]	(n., m.)			صِدْق
chance, happenstance [11]	(n., f.)	صُدَف	ج	صُدْفة
fight, struggle [18]	(n., m.)	صِراعات	ج	صِراع
to spend, to expend [13]	(v.)	صَرْف (على)	(يَصْرِفُ)	صَرَفَ
difficult, hard [3]	(adj.)			صَعْب
to climb up [4]	(v.)	صُعود	(يَصعَدُ)	صَعِدَ
difficulty [3]	(n., f.)	صُعوبات	ج	صُعوبة
willow tree [20]	(n., f.)			صَفْصافة
to repair [2]	(v.)	تَصْليح	(يُصَلِّح)	صَلَّح
sign of the cross, cross [16]	(n., m.)	صُلْبان	ج	صَليب
to be silent, to stop talking, to shut up [15]	(v.)	صَمْت	(يَصْمُتُ)	صَمَتَ
to design, decide, be determined [1]	(v.)	تَصْميم	(يُصَمِّم)	صَمَّمَ
brass disc, cymbals [2]	(n., f.)	صُنوج	ج	صَنْج

صِنْف	ج	أصْناف	(n., m.)	category, sort, type, kind [16]

ض

ضَرَبَ	(يَضْرِبُ)	ضَرْب	(v.)	to hit, to strike, to beat [10]
ضَجِرَ	(يَضْجَرُ)	ضَجَر	(v.)	to be dissatisfied, to be bored, to be annoyed [15]
ضَجيج			(n., m.)	noise, clamor [19]
ضَخْم	ج	ضِخام	(adj.)	huge, great [12]
ضَرَبَ	(يَضْرِبُ)	ضَرْب (إلى)	(v.)	to shade (into a color) [17]
ضَرْبٌ إلى الحُمْرة				a shade of red [17]
ضَروريّ			(adj.)	essential, necessary [15]
ضَعُفَ	(يَضْعُفُ)	ضَعْف	(v.)	to weaken, to lose strength [16]
ضَفيرة	ج	ضَفائِر	(n., f.)	braid, pigtail, tress, lace [20]
ضَغَطَ	(يَضغَطُ)	ضَغْط	(v.)	to press, to push, to pressure [12]
ضَمَّ	(يَضُمُّ)	ضَمّ	(v.)	to join, to gather, to combine [11]
ضَوْء	ج	أضْواء	(n., m.)	a light [7]
ضَيْف	ج	ضُيوف	(n., m.)	guest, visitor [13]

ط

طاغٍ	ج	طُغاة	(n., m.)	prevailing, oppressive person [15]
طافَ	(يَطوفُ)	طَوْف	(v.)	to wander, to circle around [20]
طالَعَ	(يُطالِع)	مُطالَعة	(v.)	to read, browse [1]

faction, sect [17]	(n., f.)	طَوائِف	ج	طائِفة
to cook [3]	(v.)	طَبْخ	(يَطْبُخُ)	طَبَخَ
dish, plate [3]	(n., m.)	أطْباق	ج	طَبَق
to grind, to pulverize [3]	(v.)	طَحْن	(يَطْحَنُ)	طَحَنَ
to be moved (mostly with joy) [19]	(v.)	طَرَب	(يَطْرَبُ)	طَرِبَ
extremity, edge, limb [11]	(n., m.)	أطْراف	ج	طَرَف
uncommon, funny, novel [8]	(adj.)			طَريف
way, road [1]	(n., m.)	طُرُق أو طُرُقات	ج	طَريق
method, way, manner [3]	(n., f.)	طرائق	ج	طَريقة
fold, conviction [19]	(n., f.)	طَوايا	ج	طَويّة
throughout, during, all through [16]	(n., f.)			طيلةَ / طَوالَ

ظ

fingernail, toenail, claw [19]	(n., m.)	أظْفار / أظافِر	ج	ظِفْر / ظُفُر
shadow, shade [9]	(n., m.)	ظِلال	ج	ظِلّ
to do injustice, to do wrong, to act tyrannically [19]	(v.)	ظُلم	(يَظلِمُ)	ظَلَمَ
saucepan, skillet [8]	(n., f.)	طَناجِر	ج	طَنْجَرة
to cook [13]	(v.)	طَهْو / طَهْي	(يَطْهو)	طَها
apparent, visible, obvious [15]	(adj.)			ظاهِر
back [5]	(n., m.)	ظُهور	ج	ظَهْر

ع

عاتَبَ	(يُعاتِبُ)	مُعاتَبة	(v.)	to chide, to scold mildly [8]
عارَضَ	(يُعارِضُ)	مُعارَضة	(v.)	to oppose, to resist, to object [16]
عاشَ	يَعيشُ	عَيش	(v.)	to live [4]
عاشَرَ	(يُعاشِرُ)	مُعاشَرة	(v.)	to associate with, to mix with [19]
عاشق	ج	عاشِقون	(act. p.)	lover [20]
عاطِر			(act. p.)	perfumed; nice [7]
عاطِفة	ج	عَواطِف	(n., f.)	emotion, passion [16]
عالَجَ	(يُعالِجُ)	مُعالَجة	(v.)	to treat, to remedy, to cure, to medicate [16]
عامَلَ	(يُعامِلُ)	مُعامَلة	(v.)	to treat s.o. [7]
عِبارة (عَن)			(n., f.)	tantamount to, equivalent to [15]
عَبَدَ	(يَعْبُدُ)	عِبادة	(v.)	to worship [15]
عَبَرَ	(يَعبُرُ)	عُبور	(v.)	to cross, carry across, traverse [4]
عَبِقَ	(يَعْبَقُ)	عَبْق	(v.)	to linger on (a scent) [20]
عَبير			(n., m.)	scent, fragrance [20]
عَتَبة	ج	عَتَبات	(n., f.)	doorstep, threshold [12]
عُثْمانيّ			(adj.)	Ottoman [9]
عَجَلة	ج	عَجَلات	(n., f.)	wheel [14]
عَجين			(adj.)	dough [7]

عَدّاد	ج	عَدّادات	(n., m.)	meter, counter [12]
عَدَم			(n., m.)	nonexistence, nothingness, absence, lack [16]
عَدَم			(part.)	non-, un-, in-, dis-[7]
عَدوّ	ج	أعْداء	(n., m.)	enemy, foe [17]
عَديد	(مِن)		(n, m.)	number of, large quantity [18]
عُذْر	ج	أعْذار	(n., m.)	excuse [7]
عُرْس	ج	أعْراس	(n., m.)	wedding, marriage [9]
عرّش	(يُعَرِّشُ)	تَعْريش	(v.)	to cover (as a vine does a trellis) [20]
عَروس	ج	عَرائِس	(n., f.)	bride [9]
عَروس	ج	عُرُس / عِرْسان	(n., m.)	groom [9]
--	ج	عُرُس / عِرْسان	(n., m.)	
عَرَضَ	(يَعْرِضُ)	عَرْض	(v.)	to show, to display [5]
عَرْض	ج	عُروض	(n., m.)	breadth, width [17]
عَرِقَ	(يَعرَقُ)	عَرَق	(v.)	to perspire, to sweat [12]
عِرْقسوس		(عِرْق سوس)	(n., m.)	licorice root [5]
عُروبة			(n., f.)	Arabism, to have the Arabic character [20]
عَروسة	ج	عَرائِس (السكر)	(n., f.)	doll [20]
عَريشة			(n., f.)	trellis [20]
عَريض			(adj.)	wide [4]
عَزَف	(يَعْزِف)	عَزْف (على)	(v.)	to play an instrument [2]

military, soldier [17]	(adj.)			عَسْكَريّ
League (of Nations) [16]	(n., f.)			عُصْبة (الأمَم)
midafternoon [12]	(n., m.)	أعْصار	ج	عَصر
period, era [1]	(n., m.)	عُصور	ج	عَصْر
modern [1]	(adj.)			عَصْريّ
to storm, to blow violently [17]	(v.)	عَصْف	(يَعصِفُ)	عَصَفَ
to bite [20]	(v.)	عَضّ	(يَعَضُّ)	عَضَّ
member [16]	(n., m.)	أعْضاء	ج	عُضْو
perfume, fragrance [1]	(n., m.)	عُطور	ج	عِطْر
giving, gift, grant, donation [16]	(n., m.)			عَطاء
to forgive, to excuse [18]	(v.)	عَفْو (عن)	(يَعْفو)	عَفا
end, issue, effect, outcome, consequence [14]	(n., f.)	ج عَواقِب		عُقْبى / عاقِبة
arch, vault [17]	(n., m.)	عُقود	ج	عَقْد
to be reasonable, to comprehend [8]	(v.)	عَقْل	(يَعقِلُ)	عَقَلَ
reason, rationality [18]	(n., m.)			عَقْل
article of faith, tenet, dogma, ideology [18]	(n., f.)	عَقائِد	ج	عَقيدة
treatment, therapy [2]	(n., m.)	عِلاجات	ج	عِلاج
grade, mark [2]	(n., f.)	عَلامات	ج	عَلامة
box, case, carton [12]	(n., f.)	عُلَب	ج	عُلبة
to hang, to spend, to attach [12]	(v.)	تَعليق	(يُعَلِّقُ)	عَلَّقَ

عِلْمُ العَروض				metrics, prosody [20]
عَمارة		عَمارات	(n., f.)	building, architecture [17]
عُمْرانٌ			(n., m.)	construction, development [6]
عُمْق	ج	أعْماق	(n., m.)	depth [15]
عَمَليّة	ج	عَمَليّات	(n., f.)	operation, procedure, process [11]
عَمود	ج	أعْمِدة/ عَواميد	(n., m.)	pole, post [11]
عَميق			(adj.)	deep [3]
عُنُق	ج	أعْناق	(n., m.)	nexk [12]
عَنيف			(adj.)	violent [18]
عَهْد	ج	عُهود	(n., m.)	knowledge, treaty, decree [14]
عود	ج	أعْواد	(n., m.)	lute [2]
عَوَّضَ	(يُعَوِّضُ)	تَعْويض	(v.)	to compensate, to make up for [16]
عَيْن	ج	عُيون	(n., m.)	spring (of water) [1]
عَيَّنَ	(يُعَيِّنُ)	تَعيين	(v.)	to appoint [18]

غ

غابَ	(يَغيبُ)	غِياب	(v.)	to be absent [8]
غاصَ	(يَغوصُ)	غَوْص	(v.)	to dive [6]
غامِض			(act. p.)	obscure, vague, unclear [15]
غَدا	(يَغْدو)	غَدوة	(v.)	to become [20]

nourishment, nutrient [16]	(n., m.)	أغْذية	ج	غِذاء
strange, stranger [13]	(adj.)	غُرَباء	ج	غَريب
abundant, copious [19]	(adj.)			غَزير
to get angry, to be furious [12]	(v.)	غَضَب	(يَغضَبُ)	غَضِبَ
to cover, to wrap, to conceal [17]	(v.)	تَغطية	(يُغَطِّي)	غَطَّى
to boil [3]	(v.)	غَلْيٌ / غَلَيان	(يَغلي)	غَلى
to flood, to inundate, to fill [13]	(v.)		(يَغْمُرُ)	غَمَرَ
to lavish (upon) [20]	(v.)	غُمورة (بِـ)	(يَغْمُرُ)	غَمُرَ
name of fertile oasis in southern Damascus [20]	(n., f.)			الغوطة
abundant rain [19]	(n., m.)	غُيوث	ج	غَيْث
to change, to alter, to modify [14]	(v.)	تَغْيير	(يُغَيِّرُ)	غَيَّرَ

ف

then, so, therefore, thus [7]	(part.)			فَـ
to boil, simmer, bubble [3]	(v.)	فَوَران	(يَفورُ)	فارَ
empty [4]	(act. p.)			فارِغ
difference, distinction, disparity [11]	(act. p.)	فَوارِق	ج	فارِق
past; last [7]	(act. p.)			فائِت
to open [1]	(v.)	فَتْح	(يَفْتَح)	فَتَحَ
to conquer [17]	(v.)	فَتْح (فَتَحَ بَلَداً)	(يَفتَحُ)	فَتَحَ

period, interval of time [16]	(n., f.)	فَتَرات ج	فَتْرة
suddenly [8]	(adv.)		فَجْأةً
to examine, to test [8]	(v.)	فَحْص (يَفحَصُ)	فَحَصَ
earthenware, clay [2]	(n., m.)		فَخّار
magnificent, splendid, stately [6]	(adj.)		فَخْم
stallion, strong man, luminary [20]	(n., m.)	فُحول(ة) ج	فَحْل
to flee, to run away [17]	(v.)	فِرار (يَفِرُّ)	فَرَّ
to be happy, rejoice [4]	(v.)	فَرَح (يَفرَحُ)	فَرِحَ
chick [8]	(n., f.)	فِراخ ج	فَرْخ
individual, member [17]	(n., m.)	أفْراد ج	فَرْد
paradise [17]	(n., m.)	فَراديس ج	فِرْدَوْس
horse, mare [17]	(n., m.)	أفْراس ج	فَرَس
difference, distinction [15]	(n., m.)	فُروق ج	فَرْق
band, group [7]	(n., f.)	فِرَق ج	فِرْقة
oven [3]	(n., m.)	أفْران ج	فُرْن
pistachio (peanuts) [7]	(n., m.)	(فُسْتُق سودانيّ)	فُسْتُق
recess, intermission, picnic (Egypt) [15]	(n., f.)	فُسَح ج	فُسْحة
to explain, to expound, to explicate [18]	(v.)	تَفْسير (يُفَسِّرُ)	فَسَّرَ
mosaic [20]	(n., m.)		فُسَيْفُساء
classroom (Egypt) [15]	(n., m.)	فُصول ج	فَصْل

فصيل	ج	فَصائِل	(n., m.)	genus [20]
فَضَّ	(يَفُضُّ)	فَضّ	(v.)	to settle, to resolve [14]
فِضّة			(n., f.)	silver [6]
فَضَّلَ	(يُفَضِّلُ)	تَفْضيل	(v.)	to prefer, to favor [15]
فَضيحَة	ج	فَضائح	(n., f.)	scandal [2]
فَقَدَ	(يَفقِدُ)	فُقْدان	(v.)	to lose [17]
فَقْر			(n., m.)	poverty, need, destitution [16]
فِقْه			(n., m.)	understanding, jurisprudence [18]
فُكاهة	ج	فُكاهات	(n., f.)	humor, joke, fun [14]
فَكَّرَ	(يُفَكِّرُ)	تَفْكير (في)	(v.)	to think (about) [14]
فِكْر	ج	أفْكار	(n., m.)	thinking, thought [18]
فُلّ			(n., m.)	jasmine [20]
فَلَّ	(يَفُلُّ)	فَلّ	(v.)	to dent, to blunt [19]
فَلَحَ	(يَفْلَحُ)	فَلْح	(v.)	to cultivate, to till [20]
فَلَك			(n., m.)	astronomy [18]
فِلم	ج	أفْلام	(n., m.)	film, movie [2]
فَنّ	ج	فُنون / أفْنان	(n., m.)	art, type, kind, variety [11]
فَنِيَ	(يَفْنى)	فَناء	(v.)	to perish [19]
فَنّان	ج	فَنّانون	(adj.)	artist [11]
فِناء	ج	أفْنية	(n., m.)	courtyard [9]

ق

قادَ	(يَقودُ)	قيادة	(v.)	to drive, to pilot [6]
قادِر	ج	قادِرون	(act. p.)	capable, competent, powerful, able [16]
قادِم	ج	قادِمون	(act. p.)	coming, next, following [15]
قابَلَ	(يُقابِلُ)	مُقابَلة	(v.)	to interview, to meet [5]
قارِئ	ج	قُرّاء	(act. p.)	reader [2]
قارَنَ	(يُقارِنُ)	مُقارَنة	(v.)	to compare, to contrast [13]
قاصٍ	أقْصى (.m)	قُصْوى (.f)	(n.)	far, distant [13]
قاضٍ	(الضَربة القاضية)		(adj.)	deadly, lethal, fatal (knockout blow) [14]
قاطَعَ	(يُقاطِعُ)	مُقاطَعة	(v.)	to break off a relationship, to interrupt [12]
قاعة	ج	قاعات	(n., f.)	large room, hall [1]
قامَ	(يَقومُ)	قِيام	(v.)	to rise, to get up, to stand up [14]
قُبّة	ج	قِباب / قُبَب	(n., f.)	dome [17]
قَبِلَ	(يَقْبَلُ)	قَبول	(v.)	to accept, to consent [19]
قُبْلة	ج	قُبْلات	(n., f.)	kiss [7]
قَبيح			(adj.)	ugly, unsightly, repulsive [15]
قَتَلَ	(يَقتُلُ)	قَتْل	(v.)	to kill, to murder [8]
قُدْرة	ج	قُدُرات	(n., f.)	power, faculty, strength [15]
قَدَم	ج	أقْدام	(n., f.)	foot [9]

dirty, filthy [8]	(n., m.)			قَذِر
to throw, to cast [17]	(v.)	قَذْف	(يَقذِفُ)	قَذَفَ
to decide [12]	(v.)	تَقرير	(يُقَرِّرُ)	قَرَّرَ
disc, tablet [11]	(n., m.)	أَقْراص	ج	قُرْص
to knock, to rap [12]	(v.)	قَرْع	(يَقرَعُ)	قَرَعَ
century; horn [17]	(n., m.)	قُرون	ج	قَرْن
peel, rind, skin, shuck, crust [3]	(n., m.)	قُشور	ج	قِشْر
to cut, to narrate [14]	(v.)	قَصّ	(يَقُصُّ)	قَصَّ
story [9]	(n., f.)	قِصَص	ج	قِصّة
palace, mansion, castle [6]	(n., m.)	قُصورٌ	ج	قَصْرٌ
poem, ode [17]	(n., f.)	قَصائِد	ج	قَصيدة
to spend (time), to pass (time) [12]	(v.)	قَضاء	(يَقضي)	قَضى
issue, cause, affair [16]	(n., f.)	قَضايا	ج	قَضيّة
cat [2]	(n., f.)	قِطَط	ج	قِطّة
to frown, to scowl [15]	(v.)	تَقْطيب	(يُقَطِّبُ)	قَطَّبَ
syrup [3]	(n., m.)			قَطْر
drip, drop [19]	(n., m.)			قَطْر
drop (of s.th.) [11]	(n., f.)	قَطَرات	ج	قَطْرة
to cut up, cut into pieces [3]	(v.)	تَقْطيع	(يُقَطِّعُ)	قَطَّعَ
to jump, to leap [19]	(v.)	قَفْز	(يَقفِزُ)	قَفَزَ

heart [2]	(n., m.)	قُلوب	ج	قَلْب
fortress, castle [17]	(n., f.)	قِلاع	ج	قَلعة
worried, uneasy, apprehensive [8]	(n., m.)			قَلِقٌ
summit, peak [6]	(n., f.)	قِمَم	ج	قِمَّةٌ
wheat [9]	(n., m.)			قَمْح
satisfaction, contentment, conviction [19]	(n., f.)	قَناعات	ج	قَناعة
bow, arch (triumphal arch) [10]	(n., m.)	أقْواس (قوس النَصْر)	ج	قَوْس
to evaluate, to assess, to rectify [19]	(v.)	تَقويم	(يُقَوِّمُ)	قَوَّمَ
people, nation [19]	(n., m.)	أقْوام	ج	قَوْم
national [11]	(adj.)			قَوْميّ

ك

to correspond with [2]	(v.)	مُكاتَبة	(يُكاتِب)	كاتَبَ
almost, on the verge of [7]	(v.)		(يَكادُ)	كادَ
adequate, enough [14]	(adj.)			كافٍ
as if, as though [19]	(conj.)			كَأنَّ
biggest, greatest, eldest [13]	(n., f.)	كُبْرَيات	ج	كُبْرى
shoulder [12]	(n., f.)	أكْتاف	ج	كَتِف
alcohol [7]	(n., m.)		(الكُحول)	كُحول
toil, labor, drudgery [20]	(v.)			كَدْح

كَرِهَ		كُرْه / كَراهة / كَراهية	(v.)	to hate, to detest, to loathe [18]
كَرْم	ج	كُروم	(n., m.)	vineyard [20]
كْرواسّان			(n., m.)	croissant [9]
كَريم	ج	كُرماء / كِرام	(adj.)	generous, honorable [5]
كسا	(يَكْسو)	كِسوة	(v.)	to clothe, to cover [20]
كَفّ	ج	كُفوف / أكُفّ	(n., m.)	palm (of a hand) [12]
كَفَرَ	(يَكْفُرُ)	كَفْر / كُفْر	(v.)	to be irreligious, not to believe in God [15]
كَفى	(يَكْفي)	كِفاية	(v.)	to be sufficient, to be enough [3]
كَلاّ			negative particle	not at all, by no means [15]
كَلام	(عِلم الكَلام)		(n., m.)	scholastic theology [18]
كَلْب	ج	كِلاب	(n., m.)	dog [2]
كِلْس			(n., m.)	lime, limestone [17]
كَلَّفَ	(يُكَلِّفُ)	تَكْليف/ تكلِفة	(v.)	to cost [9]
كَما			(part.)	as, like [7]]
كَمّاشة	ج	كَمّاشات	(n., f.)	pliers [2]
كَمين	ج	كَمائِن	(n., f.)	ambush [20]
كَنْز	ج	كُنوز	(n., m.)	treasure [19]
كَنَف	ج	أكْناف	(n., m.)	side, shadow, shelter [17]
كوتشينة			(n., f.)	card game in Egypt [2]

ل

لاجئٌ	ج	لاجِئون	(act. p.)	refugee [6]
لاحَظَ	(يُلاحِظُ)	مُلاحَظَة	(v.)	to notice, to take note [12]
لافِتة	ج	لافِتات	(n., f.)	sign, billboard [1]
لاقَ	(يَليقُ)	لَيْق (بـِ)	(v.)	to be suitable (for) [20]
لاقى	(يُلاقي)	مُلاقاة	(v.)	to meet, to encounter [16]
لامَ	(يَلومُ)	لَوْم	(v.)	to blame, to reproach, to admonish [19]
لاءَمَ	(يُلائِم)	مُلاءَمة	(v.)	to be suitable, appropriate [1]
لَبّى	(يُلَبّي)	تَلْبية	(v.)	to respond to, to comply [16]
لَبِثَ	(يَلْبَثُ)	لَبْث	(v.)	to linger, to remain [15]
لَحَظَ	(يَلْحَظُ)	لَحْظ	(v.)	to notice, to look, to observe [15]
لَحْظة	ج	لَحَظات	(n., f.)	moment, instant [5]
لَحِقَ	(يَلحَقُ)	لَحاق	(v.)	to catch up, to keep close [8]
لَحَّنَ	(يُلَحِّنُ)	تَلحين	(v.)	to compose, to set to music [17]
لَخَّصَ	(يُلَخِّصُ)	تَلْخيص	(v.)	to summarize, to abridge [18]
لَدى			(prep.)	at, by (= عِنْدَ) [2]
لِسان	ج	ألسِنة/ ألسُن	(n., m.)	tongue, language [8]
لِصّ	ج	لُصوص	(n., m.)	theif, robber, burglar [11]
لَطيف	ج	لُطفاء	(adj.)	gentle, kind, friendly [9]

لَعَنَ	(يَلعَنُ)	لَعْن	(v.)	to curse, to damn [12]
لَعْنة	ج	لَعَنات	(n., f.)	curse [12]
لَعين	ج	مَلاعين	(adj.)	cursed, damned, detested, evil [12]
لَمحة	ج	لَمَحات	(n., f.)	glimpse, brief insight [17]
لَوْز			(n., m.)	almond [3]
لَوزة	ج	لَوْزات (اللَوزَتان)	(n., f.)	tonsils [11]
لِيزَر			(n., m.)	laser [11]
لَيْلكة			(n., f.)	lilac [20]
لَيْمون			(n., m.)	lemon [3]

م

ماجِسْتير			(n., m.)	master's degree [2]
مادّة	ج	مَوادّ	(n., f.)	material, substance, ingredient [3]
ماعِز	ج	مَواعِز	(act. p.)	goat [2]
مال	ج	أمْوال	(n., m.)	money, wealth [13]
ماما			(n., f.)	mama (mommy) [15]
مانِع	ج	مَوانِع	(act. p.)	objection, obstacle, obstruction [5]
مائِدة	ج	مَوائِد	(act. p.)	table [7]
مَبروك			(pass. p.)	congratulations [4]
مَبْلَغ	ج	مَبالَغ	(n., m.)	amount of money [11]

built, constructed [6]	(pass. p.)			مَبْنِيٌّ
moving, movable, mobile [14]	(n., m.)			مُتَحَرِّك
backward, retarded, falling behind [16]	(act. p.)	مُتَخَلِّفون	ج	مُتَخَلِّف
meter (measurement of length) [4]	(n., m.)	أمتار	ج	مِتر
broken, out of order [11]	(act. p.)			مُتَعَطِّل
average, medium, intermediate [11]	(act. p.)			مُتَوَسِّط
proverb [19]	(n., m.)	أمْثال	ج	مَثَل
similar, like, equal, analogous [14]	(n., m.)	أمْثال	ج	مِثْل
to represent, to exemplify, to act [9]	(v.)	تَمْثيل	(يُمَثِّلُ)	مَثَّلَ
chilled food products; ice cream [5]	(act. p.)	مُثَلَّجات	ج	مُثَلَّج
abode, dwelling [20]	(n., m.)	مَثاوٍ	ج	مُثوى
like, similar, equal [15]	(n., m.)	مُثُل	ج	مَثيل
field, area of specialization [5]	(n., m.)	مَجالات	ج	مَجال
adjacent, neighboring [5]	(act. p.)			مُجاوِر
society, community [16]	(pass. p.)	مُجْتَمَعات	ج	مُجْتَمَع
council, assembly [6]	(n., m.)	مَجالِسُ	ج	مَجْلِسٌ
group; set [11]	(pass. p.)	مَجموعات	ج	مَجموعة
responder [12]	(n., m.)	مُجيبون	ج	مُجيب
needy, poor, destitute, wanting [16]	(pass. p.)	مُحْتاجون	ج	مُحْتاج
imminent, encircling, surrounding [17]	(act. p.)			مُحْدِق

engine, motor [12]	(n., m.)	مُحَرِّكات	ج	مُحَرِّك
crop, yield [20]	(pass. p.)			مَحْصول
motivator, stimulator, incentive [16]	(act. p.)	مُحَفِّزون	ج	مُحَفِّز
toasted [7]	(pass. p.)			مُحَمَّص
axis, axle, pivot [14]	(n., m.)	مَحاوِر	ج	مِحْوَر
contradictory, conflicting, divergent [18]	(act. p.)	مُخالِفون	ج	مُخالِف
summed up, abbreviated, summarized [19]	(pass. p.)			مُختَصر
bed chamber [20]	(n., m.)	مَخادِع	ج	مَخدَع
frightening, intimidating [12]	(adj.)			مُخيف
camp [6]	(n., m.)	مُخَيَّماتٌ	ج	مُخَيَّمٌ
imagination, fantasy [20]	(n., f.)	مُخَيِّلات	ج	مُخَيِّلة
to stretch (out), to reach, to extend [12]	(v.)	مَدّ	(يَمُدُّ)	مَدَّ
extent, range, scope [15]	(n., m.)			مَدى
entrance, foyer, introduction [8]	(n., m.)	مَداخِل	ج	مَدخَل
driven forward, propelled, motivated [16]	(pass. p.)			مَدْفوع
tear duct [20]	(n., m.)	مَدامع	ج	مَدْمَع
doctrine, creed, movement, trend [18]	(n., m.)	مَذاهِب		مَذْهَب
to pass through/by [1]	(v.)	مُرور	(يَمُرُّ)	مَرَّ
correspondent, reporter [5]	(act. p.)	مُراسِلون	ج	مُراسِل
supervisor, observer [13]	(act. p.)	مُراقِبون	ج	مُراقِب

tied, bound, fastened [12]	(pass. p.)			مَربوط
height (e.g., the Golan Heights), hill [2]	(pass. p.)	مُرْتَفَعات	ج	مُرْتَفَع
boiler, caldron [14]	(n., m.)	مَراجِل	ج	مِرْجَل
to rejoice, to be merry [13]	(v.)	مَرَح	(يَمْرَحُ)	مَرِحَ
stage phase [11]	(n., f.)	مَراحِل	ج	مَرْحَلة
nominated; candidate [16]	(pass. p.)			مُرَشَّح
to be ill, to get sick [15]	(v.)	مَرَض	(يَمْرَضُ)	مَرِضَ
to nurse, to tend [16]	(v.)	تَمْريض	(يُمَرِّضُ)	مَرَّضَ
attached, enclosed [17]	(pass. p.)			مُرفَق
center [9]	(n., m.)	مَراكِز	ج	مَركَز
marble [17]	(n., m.)			مَرْمَر
traffic [11]	(n., m.)			مُرور
comfortable (to give comfort) [5]	(act. p.)			مُريح
to joke [7]	(v.)	مَزْح	(يَمزَحُ)	مَزَح
decorated [17]	(pass. p.)			مُزَخْرَف
double, dual [2]	(act. p.)			مُزْدَوِج
chronic, enduring [17]	(act. p.)			مُزمِن
touched (with insanity, madness, mania) [14]	(n., m.)		(مِن الجُنون)	مَسّ
help, assistance, aid [2]	(n., f.)	مُساعَدات	ج	مُساعَدَة
distance [4]	(n., f.)	مَسافات	ج	مَسافة

مَسامّ	ج	مَسامّات	(n., m.)	pores [20]
مُسْتَجِدّ	ج	مُسْتَجِدّون، مُسْتَجِدّات	(act. p.)	new, recent [11]
مُستَجير	ج	مُستَجيرون	(act. p.)	seeker of refuge or asylum [19]
مُسْتَدير			(adj.)	round, circular [14]
مُسْتَشار	ج	مُسْتَشارون	(pass. p.)	consultant, counsel, adviser [19]
مُسْتَشفى	ج	مُستَشفَيات	(n., m.)	hospital [11]
مَسْتَطلِعاً			(act. p.)	inquiring [15]
مُسْتَقِلّ			(act. p.)	independent [17]
مُسْتَمِع			(act. p.)	listener [19]
مُسْتَوى	ج	مُسْتَوَيات	(n., m.)	level, standard [15]
مَسَحَ	(يَمسَحُ)	مَسْح	(v.)	to wipe off, to erase, to clean [8]
مَسْحوق	ج	مَساحيق	(pass. p.)	powder [1]
مُسدَل			(pass. p.)	drawn (a curtain) [12]
مَسْروق			(pass. p.)	stolen [11]
مَسْقيّ			(adj.)	irrigated, supplied with water [9]
مِسَلّة	ج	مِسَلاّت	(n., f.)	obelisk [20]
مَسْموع			(pass. p.)	audible, able to be heard [7]]
مُسِنّ	ج	مُسِنّون	(act. p.)	elderly, old [13]
مَشْتَل	ج	مَشاتِل	(n., m.)	nursery, arboretum [20]
مُشَجِّع	ج	مُشَجِّعون	(act. p.)	fan [1]

a play (theatrical) [2]	(n., f.)	مَسْرَحِيّات	ج	مَسْرَحِيَّة
compassionate [15]	(n., m.)			مُشْفِق
inhabited [6]	(pass. p.)			مَسْكون
common, mutual [2]	(pass. p.)			مُشْتَرَك
baffled, confused, perplexed [17]	(n., m.)	مَشْدوهون	ج	مَشْدوه
bar [7]	(n., m.)	مَشارِب	ج	مَشْرَب
drink, refreshments [7]	(pass. p.)	مَشْروبات	ج	مَشْروب
problem [2]	(act. p.)	مُشْكِلات / مَشاكِل	ج	مُشْكِلة
placenta [20]	(n., f.)	مَشايم	ج	مَشيمة
expenditure, allowance [13]	(pass. p.)	مَصاريف	ج	مَصْروف
worshiper [1]	(act. p.)	مُصَلّون	ج	مُصَلٍّ
classified, sorted [19]	(pass. p.)			مُصَنَّف
misfortune, calamity, disaster [19]	(act. p.)	مَصائِب	ج	مُصيبة
to pass (time), to elapse [7]	(v.)	مُضي	(يَمضي)	مَضى
strait, narrow pass [10]	(n., m.)	مَضائِق	ج	مَضيق
hammer [2]	(n., f.)	مَطارِق	ج	مِطْرَقة
inlaid (with) [20]	(pass. p.)		بِـ	مُطَعَّم
turned off, extinguished [12]	(pass. p.)			مُطفَأ
contemporary [14]	(act. p.)	مُعاصِرون	ج	مُعاصِر

treatment, social intercourse [19]	(n., f.)	مُعامَلات	ج	مُعامَلة
exhibition, fair, show [5]	(n., m.)	مَعارِض	ج	مَعْرِض
knowledge [11]	(n., f.)	مَعارِف	ج	مَعْرِفة
battle [17]	(n., f.)	مَعارِك	ج	مَعْركة
shown, displayed [14]	(pass. p.)			مَعْروض
bit of information [2]	(pass. p.)	مَعْلومات	ج	مَعْلومة
factory, plant [13]	(n., m.)	مَعامِل	ج	مَعْمَل
institution, institute, academy [5]	(n., m.)	مَعاهِد	ج	مَعْهَد
diamond (shape) [3]	(pass. p.)	مُعَيَّنات	ج	مُعَيَّن
glad, delighted	(adj.)	مُغْتَبِطون	ج	مُغْتَبِط
closed [1]	(pass. p.)			مُغْلَق
sudden, unexpected, surprising [13]	(adj.)			مُفاجِئ
open [1]	(pass. p.)			مَفتوح
bedspread, bed cover, tablecloth [15]	(n., m.)	مَفارِش	ج	مَفْرَش
lost [17]	(pass. p.)			مَفْقود
screwdriver [2]	(n., m.)	مِفَكّات	ج	مِفَكّ
thinker [18]	(act. p.)	مُفَكِّرون	ج	مُفَكِّر
warrior, fighter, combatant [17]	(act. p.)	مُقاتِلون	ج	مُقاتِل
article, essay, way of speaking [19]	(n., m.)	مَقالات	ج	مَقال

مَقالة	ج	مَقالات	(n., f.)	essay, article, editorial [8]
مَقام	ج	مَقامات	(n., m.)	standing, rank, position, prestige [19]
مُقْبِل			(act. p.)	next, coming [7]
مِقْدار	ج	مَقادير	(n., m.)	measure, quantity, amount [3]
مَقدِرة	ج	مَقدِرات	(n., f.)	power, strength, capacity [19]
مُقَرَّب	ج	مُقَرَّبون	(pass. p.)	close companion, favorite [18]
مَقصود			(pass. p.)	intended [19]
مَقْعَد	ج	مَقاعِد	(n., m.)	seat [14]
مُقَوِّم	ج	مُقَوِّمات	(n., m.)	components [20]
مَقْهى	ج	مَقاهٍ/ المَقاهي	(n., m.)	café [9]
مُكالَمَة	ج	مُكالَمات	(n., f.)	(telephone) call, conversation, talk [1]
مَكْتوب			(pass. p.)	written [7]]
مَكْشوف			(pass. p.)	uncovered, bare, exposed [14]
مَكَّنَ	(يُمَكِّنُ)	تَمكين	(v.)	to enable, to make possible [11]
مَلأَ	(يَملأُ)	مَلْء	(v.)	to fill, to fill up [12]
مُلائِم			(act. p.)	suitable [18]
مَلَكَ	(يَمْلِكُ)	مُلْك / مَلْك / مِلْك	(v.)	to own, to possess [19]
مَلِكة	ج	مَلِكات	(n., f.)	queen [10]
مَليّ			(n., m.)	a long period of time [15]

enjoyable, pleasant, interesting [5]	(adj.)			مُمْتِع
kingdom [6]	(n., f.)	مَمالِكُ	ج	مَمْلَكةٌ
cursed, damned, evil, wicked [14]	(pass. p.)	مَلاعين	ج	مَلْعون
place of entertainment [7]	(n., m.)	مَلاهٍ	ج	مَلْهى
full [5]	(adj.)			مَمْلوء
possible [5]	(adj.)			مُمْكِن
suitable, appropriate [3]	(act. p.)			مُناسِب
occasion, opportunity [19]	(n., f.)	مُناسَبات	ج	مُناسَبة
discussion [15]	(n., f.)	مُناقَشات	ج	مُناقَشة
team [1]	(pass. p.)	مُنْتَخَبات	ج	مُنْتَخَب
park, recreation ground [13]	(n., m.)	مَنازه	ج	مُتَنَزَّه
victor, conqueror, victorious [16]	(act. p.)	مُنْتَصِرون	ج	مُنْتَصِر
middle, mid- [9]	(pass. p.)			مُنْتَصَف
the extreme, the utmost [12]	(n., m.)			مُنْتَهى
status, rank, position [18]	(n., f.)			مَنزِلة
cheerful, in high spirits [14]	(adj.)		(الصَدْر)	مُنْشَرِح
area, region, zone [6]	(n., f.)	مَناطِق	ج	مِنْطَقةٌ
to prohibit, prevent [1]	(v.)	مَنْع – مَمْنوع	(يَمْنَع)	مَنَعَ
saw [2]	(n., m.)	مَناشير	ج	مِنْشار

slope, incline, descent (of river) [17]	(pass. p.)	مُنْحَدَرات	ج	مُنْحَدَر
unlucky, unfortunate, ill-fated [12]	(pass. p.)	مَناحيس	ج	مَنحوس
logic [18]	(n., m.)			مَنْطِق
organization [16]	(pass. p)	مُنَظَّمات	ج	مُنَظَّمة
reflected [17]	(act. p.)			مُنْعَكِس
alone, solitary, isolated [16]	(act. p.)	مُنْفَرِدون	ج	مُنْفَرِد
s.o. venting [12]	(act. p.)			مُنَفِّس
festival, fair [11]	(n., m.)	مِهْرَجانات	ج	مِهْرَجان
lately [13]	(adv.)			مُؤَخَّراً
well-behaved, well-mannered, polite, courteous [15]	(pass. p.)	مُؤَدَّبون	ج	مُؤَدَّب
author, writer [17]	(n., m.)	مُؤَلِّفون	ج	مُؤَلِّف
straight razor, razor blade [14]	(n., m.)	أمْواس	ج	موسى
music [2]	(n., f.)			موسيقا
fashion (Italian *moda*) [15]	(n., f.)	موضات	ج	موضة
subject, topic, theme, item [15]	(n., m.)	مَواضيع	ج	مَوْضوع
employee, civil servant [3]	(pass. p.)	مَوَظَّفون	ج	مُوَظَّف
master, lord, chief [19]	(n., m.)	مَوالٍ	ج	مَوْلى
talent [20]	(n., m.)	مَواهِب	ج	مَوْهِبة
minaret [20]	(n., f.)	مآذِن	ج	مِئذَنة

مَيَّزَ	(يُمَيِّزُ)	تَمْييز	(v.)	to distinguish [19]
ميزة	ج	ميزات	(n., f.)	distinguishing feature [20]
ميزانيّة	ج	ميزانيّات	(n., f.)	budget [11]

ن

نادى	(يُنادي)	مُناداة	(v.)	to call, to cry out, to shout [5]
نار	ج	نيران	(n., f.)	fire, heat [3]
ناطور	ج	نَواطير	(n., m.)	guard, keeper, warden [20]
نافورة	ج	نَوافير / نافورات	(n., f.)	fountain [17]
ناقة	ج	نوق / ناقات	(n., f.)	she-camel [19]
نال	(يَنالُ)	نَوْل	(v.)	to obtain, to get, to win [15]
ناي	ج	نايات	(n., m.)	lute [2]
نَبَأ	ج	أنباء	(n., m.)	news [11]
نَبَحَ	(يَنبَحُ)	نُباح	(v.)	to bark [12]
نَبْع	ج	يَنابيع	(n., m.)	spring, water source [10]
نَبيّ	ج	أنبياء	(n., m.)	prophet [10]
نَبيل	ج	نُبَلاء	(n., m.)	noble, highborn, magnanimous [19]
نَتَفَ	يَنْتِفُ	نَتْف	(v.)	to pluck out [20]

result, outcome [12]	(n., f.)	نَتائج	ج	نَتيجة
to scatter, to sprinkle [20]	(v.)	نَثْر / نِثار	(يَنْثُرُ)	نَثَرَ
to survive [17]	(v.)	نَجاة	(يَنْجو)	نَجا
carpentry [2]	(n., f.)			نِجارة
to succeed, to pass, to be successful [11]	(v.)	نَجاح	(يَنجَحُ)	نَجَحَ
star [8]	(n., m.)	نُجوم	ج	نَجْم
brass [2]	(n., m.)			نُحاس
about, approximately, toward [4]	(adv.)			نَحوَ
palm, date palm [10]	(n., m.)			نَخيل
companion, confidant [19]	(n., m.)	نُدَماء	ج	نَديم
dispute, controversy [14]	(n., m.)	نِزاعات	ج	نِزاع
picnic, excursion, stroll, promenade [19]	(n., f.)	نُزهات	ج	نُزهة
to lower [1]	(v.)	تَنْزيل	(يُنَزِّل)	نَزَّلَ
relationship [5]	(n., f.)	نِسَب	ج	نِسبة
concerning, with regard to [5]				بالنِسبة لِـ
activity, vigor, liveliness [16]	(n., m.)	أنْشِطة	ج	نَشاط
to break out (war / rebellion) [17]	(v.)			نَشِبَ (يَنشَبُ) نُشوب (الحَرْب/ الثَوْرة)
to spread, to publish [11]	(v.)	نَشر	(يَنشُرُ)	نَشَرَ
to pick up [20]	(v.)	نَشْل	(يَنْشُلُ)	نَشَلَ
passage, text [2]	(n., m.)	نُصوص	ج	نَصٌّ

نَصيب	ج	نُصُب/ أنصِبة	(n., m.)	share, portion, cut [16]
نَصيحة	ج	نَصائح	(n., f.)	advice, counsel [16]
نَضِجَ	(يَنْضَجُ)	نَضْج / نُضْج	(v.)	to become ripe, mature, well-cooked [3]
نَضَح	(يَنْضَحُ)	نَضْح	(v.)	to exude, to ooze, so seep, to leak [19]
نَظَرَ	(يَنْظُر)	نَظَر	(v.)	to look at, regard, see, observe [1]
نَظَريّة	ج	نَظَريّات	(n., f.)	theory [18]
نَظَم	(يَنْظِم)	نَظْم	(v.)	to write or compose poetry [2]
نَظَّمَ	(يُنَظِّمُ)	تَنظيم	(v.)	to organize, to put in order [11]
نُعمى			(n., m.)	happiness [20]
نِعْمة	ج	نِعَم	(n., f.)	easy life, blessing [8]
نَغَم	ج	أنْغام	(n., m.)	note, tune, melody [7]
نَفَخ	(يَنْفُخ)	نَفْخ	(v.)	to blow, to inflate [2]
نَفِدَ	(يَنْفَدُ)	نَفاد	(v.)	to be used up, to be exhausted [15]
نَفَّذَ	(يُنَفِّذُ)	تَنْفيذ	(v.)	to execute, to carry out, to implement [19]
نَفْس	ج	أنْفُس / نُفوس	(n., f.)	soul, spirit, psyche, mind [14]
نَفَّسَ	(يُنَفِّسُ)	تَنفيس	(v.)	to vent (frustrations) [12]
نَفَعَ	(يَنفَعُ)	نَفْع	(v.)	to be useful, to benefit [11]
نَقْد	ج	نُقود	(n., m.)	money, currency [8]
نُقْطة	ج	نُقَط / نِقاط	(n., f.)	point, drop, period [16]
نَقير			(n., m.)	tiny spot on a date pit [19]

to keep moving [15]	(v.)	تَنْقيل	(يُنَقِّلُ)	نَقَّلَ
joke, anecdote [8]	(n., f.)	نُكَت/ نِكات	ج	نُكتة
to forbid, to prohibit, to prevent [19]	(v.)	نَهْي	(يَنْهى)	نَهى
final [1]	(adj.)			نِهائيّ
to reproach, to scold, to chide [15]	(v.)	نَهْر	(يَنْهَرُ)	نَهَرَ
river [20]	(n.)	أَنْهُر	ج	نَهْر
to intend, to determine [2]	(v.)	نِيَّة	(يَنْوي)	نَوى
date pit, nucleus, kernel [19]	(n., f.)	نَوَيات	ج	نَواة
light (not dark) [12]	(n., m.)	أنوار	ج	نور
sea gull [20]	(n., m.)	نَوارِس	ج	نَوْرَس
loom [20]	(n., m.)	أَنْوال	ج	نَوْل
parliamentary, representative [16]	(adj.)			نِيابيّ
medal [20]	(n., m.)	نياشين	ج	نيشان
neon [7]	(n., m.)			نِيون

ه

there it is, there you are, here! [1]	(voc. part.)			ها
notions, misgivings [20]	(n., m.)	هَواجِس	ج	هاجِس
to attack, to assail [18]	(v.)	مُهاجَمة	(يُهاجِمُ)	هاجَمَ
Hashemite (ruling family in Jordan) [6]	(adj.)			هاشِمِيٌّ

to descend, to land, to drop [9]	(v.)	هُبوط	(يَهبُط/يَهبِطُ)	هَبَطَ
to shout, to cry, to yell, to exclaim [15]	(v.)	هُتاف	(يَهتِفُ)	هَتَفَ
to be quiet, be calm [1]	(v.)	هُدوء	(يَهْدَأ)	هَدَأ
to threaten [12]	(v.)	تَهديد	(يُهَدِّدُ)	هَدَّدَ
target, aim, goal [16]	(n., m.)	أهْداف	ج	هَدَف
quietness, peace, truce, armistice [15]	(n., f.)	هُدُنات	ج	هُدْنة
to escape, to flee [19]	(v.)	هُروب	(يَهْرُبُ)	هَرَبَ
to hurry, to hasten, to rush [11]	(v.)	هَرَع	(يُهْرَعُ)	هُرِعَ
dessert made from semolina [3]	(n., f.)			هَريسة
to neutralize, to defeat [20]	(v.)	هَزْم	(يَهْزِمُ)	هَزَمَ
defeat, rout [16]	(n., f.)	هَزائِم	ج	هَزيمة
hill [17]	(n., f.)	هِضاب / هَضَبات	ج	هَضْبة
like this, so, thus [5]	(dem.)			هكَذا (هاكَذا)
hallucination, vision [20]	(n., f.)	هَلْوَسات	ج	هَلْوَسَة
happiness, good health, well being [3]	(n., m.)			هَناء
hobby [2]	(n., f.)	هِوايات	ج	هِواية

و

to face, to encounter, to oppose, to confront [16]	(v.)	مُواجَهة	(يُواجِهُ)	واجَهَ
store window, façade [13]	(n., f.)	واجِهات	ج	واجِهة

to agree, to consent [13]	(v.)	مُوافَقة	(يُوافِقُ)	وافَقَ
located, existing [6]	(act. p.)			واقِع
ruler, governor [9]	(n., m.)	ج وُلاة	(الوالي)	والٍ
string [2]	(n., m.)	أوْتار	ج	وَتَر
loneliness, being alone [12]	(n., f.)			وَحدة
to like, to want [13]	(v.)	وُدّ	(يَوَدُّ)	وَدَّ
to occur, to appear, to be found [19]	(v.)	وُرود	(يَرِدُ)	وَرَدَ
to get s.o. in trouble [8]	(v.)	تَوريط	(يُوَرِّطُ)	وَرَّط
playing cards [2]	(n.)		وَرَق اللَعِب	
(foreign) ministry; state department (US) [2]	(n., f.)	ج وِزارات	(الخارجية)	وِزارة
to distribute, to dispense; to disburse [16]	(v.)	تَوْزيع	(يُوَزِّعُ)	وَزَّعَ
to weigh [8]	(v.)	وَزْن	(يَزِنُ)	وَزَنَ
waist, middle, surroundings [5]	(n., m.)	أوْساط	ج	وَسَط
to describe [19]	(v.)	وَصْف	(يَصِفُ)	وَصَفَ
national [9]	(adj.)		وَطَنيّ	وَطَنيّ
function, task, duty [1]	(n., f.)	وَظائِف	ج	وَظيفة
vessel, container [3]	(n., m.)	أوْعِية	ج	وِعاء
to promise [4]	(v.)	وَعْد	(يَعِدُ)	وَعَدَ
death [5]	(n., f.)	وَفَيات	ج	وَفاة
harmony, concord, conformity [18]	(n., m.)			وِفاق

to stop, halt [1]	(v.)	وُقوف	(يَقِف)	وَقَفَ
fuel [12]	(n., m.)			وَقود
agency (news) [11]	(n., f.)	وَكالات	ج	وَكالة
to wail, to howl, to lament [14]	(v.)	وَلْوَلة	(يُوَلْوِلُ)	وَلْوَلَ
fancy, imagination, misconception [20]	(n., m.)	أوْهام	ج	وَهَم

ي

lottery [13]	(n., m.)	وُدّ		يانَصيب
manual, done by hand [2]	(adj.)			يَدَويّ

أقوال العرب وأمثالهم

أدّى لـِ / إلى (١٩)	*to lead to*
إذ إنّ (١٦)	*for, since* (think of it as an elegant form of لأنّ)
أرَتْني النُجوم في الظُهْر (١٤)	*x caused me to see stars at noon*
اِسْمَحْ لي... (٥)...	*May I . . .; Allow me to . . .*
إلى جانب + اسم (١٦)	*in addition to* or *besides*
إلاّ أنّ (١٦)	*but, however* (think of it as an elegant form of لكنّ)
أَلَيْسَ كَذلِك (٤)	*isn't that right?*
الله يُبارِك فيكَ (٤)	*response to* مَبروك *means God bless you*
الله يَقْطَعُك (١٥)	*May God take you*
بِتَهْذيب (١٤)	*politely*
باحْتِرام (١٤)	*respectfully*
باحتِشام (١٤)	*modestly*
باخْتِصار (١٤)	*in short, briefly*
باعتدال (١٤)	*moderately*
بالأخصّ (٢٠)	*in particular*
بالتَدريج / تَدريجيّاً (١٧)	*gradually*

by the way	بالمُناسَبة (١٢)
recklessly	بِرُعونة (١٤)
quickly	بِسُرعة (١٤)
viciously	بِشَراسة (١٢)
in other words	بِعِبارةٍ أخرى (١٩)
with pleasure	بِكُلِّ سُرور (٥)
regularly	بانتِظام (١٤)
instead of	بَدَلاً مِن (١٣)
by the very nature of the case, as is only natural	بطبيعة الحال (٢٠)
not to be of noble descent	بلا حَسَبٍ ولا نَسَبٍ (٢٠)
because; due to the fact that	بِما أنَّ . . . فَـ (١٦)
including; to include	بِما في ذلِكَ (١٦)
between me and myself	بيني وبَيْنَ نَفْسي (١٣)
at your service	تَحتَ أمْرِكَ. (٥)
imparting s.th. on	تُضْفي + مفعول به + على (١٧)
it is worth mentioning	جَديرٌ بالذِكْر / والجَديرِ بالذِكْرِ (١٥)
throughout the land/country/world	جَميع أنْحاء + مَكان (١٦)

Lady Luck was (not) with me	(لم) يُحالِفني النَجاح / الحَظّ (١٦)
to take the place of	حَلَّ مَحَلَّ (٢٠)
better luck next time, or *how about a raincheck*	خيرُها بِغَيرِها (١٢)
no sooner than; before long	سُرعانَ ما (١٦)
to fall before (at the hands of)	سَقَطَ أمامَ (١٧)
in touch with	على صِلةٍ بِـ (١٨)
at the beginning,/middle/end of; the beginning/ middle/final stages of	في أوائل/ أواسِط/ أواخِر + تَوقيت (٥)
concerning, regarding	في ما يَتَعَلَّقُ بِـ (١٨)
one day	في يَوْمٍ مِنَ الأيّام (١٣)
throughout the land/country/world	كافة أنْحاء + مكان (١٦)
It was and continues to be	كانَ ومازالَ (٢٠)
just as; in addition	كَما أنَّ (١٦)
because so and so is . . . ; due to the fact that . . . because . . .	كَونُك + خَبَر مَنصوب (١٥)
it is necessary	لابُدَّ مِن (١١)
s.th. has nothing to do with the topic at hand	لا دَخْلَ لِـ . . . في (١٥)
unrivaled; incomparable	لا مَثيلَ لَه (١٥)
there was no answer	لا مِن مُجيب (١٢)

لَبّى حاجة (١٦)	*to fulfill the need*
لِحُسْنِ الحَظ (١٢)	*fortunately*
ما دامَ طَويلاً / لَمْ يَدُمْ طَويلاً (١٨)	*did not last long*
ما لَبِثَ أنْ (١٥)	*it wasn't long before; no sooner did . . . than*
مَبروك! (٤)	*congratulations*
مَحْروم مِن (٢٠)	*to be deprived from*
مِن خِلالِ (١٨)	*via, by way of, through, from*
نَتيجَةَ + مُضاف إليه (١٦)	*as a result of . . .*
نسبةً لـ / بالنِسْبَةِ لِـ (١٨)	*with regards to, in respect to*
نَفادُ الصَبْرِ (١٩)	*losing patience*
الواحِدةُ تِلْوَ الأخْرى (١٧)	*one after another*
(وَ)الحَقيقة أنَّ (١٦)	*really, actually*
وَمِنْ ثَمَّة (٢٠)	*hence*
هَل عِندَكَ مانِع أنْ . . . (٥)	*do you have any objection to . . .*

Appendix A

إجابات التمارين

الدرس الأول

تمرين ١

١- مُرور / حافِلة
٢- سيلان / شاي
٣- ماء / شُرْب
٤- اِسْحَب / اِدْفع
٥- مَفْتوح / مُغْلَق
٦- أحمر شفاه / مَسحوق تَجميل
٧- جَوّال / نَقّال
٨- مَصْرِف / فَرْع

تمرين ٢

١- أسبوع
٢- شاشة
٣- مسحوق
٤- مجلة
٥- جَمال
٦- ملابس

تمرين ٣

١- في دبي عنوان المحل التجاري/ عنوان المحل التجاري في دبي.

٢- تكتب كلمة (اسحب) على الأبواب/ كلمة (اسحب) تكتب على الأبواب.

٣- يحمل الهاتف الجوال من مكان إلى مكان/ الهاتف الجوال يحمل من مكان إلى مكان/ من مكان إلى مكان يحمل الهاتف الجوال.

٤- يخلع المصلون أحذيتهم قبل الدخول إلى المسجد/ قبل الدخول إلى المسجد يخلع المصلون أحذيتهم.

تمرين ٤

١- بمناسبة الافتتاح وإدارتها الجديدة.
٢- أزياء نيڤين للعرائس

٣- عنوان المحل: مجمع البواب عمارة رقم ١٩٩ ط ٢ ورقم هاتفه: ٠٧٧٦٦٦٨٠٨٠-٥٦٦٤٤٤٩

تمرين ٥

١- اِسم المصرِف »فرنسبَنك«
٢- عنوان الفرع الجديد: عين المريسة—بناية النورس.
٣- نعم، جامع عين المريسة مقابل المصرِف.
٤- هناك خطان هاتفيان لهذا الفرع.
٥- بدأ المصرِف أعماله ١ تشرين الأول ٢٠١١.

تمرين ٦

١- قِفْ، اتّجاه واحد
٢- اخلع حذاءك قبل الدخول إلى المسجد من فضلك
٣- شاشة عرض
٤- عين المريسة
٥- أزياء للعرائس

تمرين ٨

١- إذا رأيتُ / شاهدتُ الأهرام، فسأكون سعيداً / مسروراً.

٢- إذا درستَ كثيراً فستنجح.

٣- يا أمي، إذا اشتريتِ لي هذا الكتاب، فسأقرؤه .

4. If you graduate from this university, you will find work.
5. If you take this class / course, then you will succeed in your program.
6. If the classroom ambiance is suitable for teaching and learning, then you will learn a lot.

تمرين ١٠

إجابات متنوعة

تمرين ١١

1. You should eat less.
2. What a difference between the Arabic language and English.
3. I have to go to the market / store.
4. Do you have to do your homework?
5. Here is your notebook, professor.

تمرين ١٢

١- عليك بشُرْب الماء.　　٢- شتّانَ ما بين هالة وأختِها.　　٣- إليك قلمك.

٤- أفٍّ من هذا الطقس.　　٥- أيّها السيدات والسادة، إليكم السيّد ناجي الحلبي.

٦- على كلّ الطلاب كتابة صفحة عن رياضتهم المفضّلة.

تمرين ١٤

اسم فاعل	اسم مفعول
مُنْتَخِب	مُنْتَخَب
مُدَخِّن	مُدَخَّن
مُشَجِّع	مُشَجَّع
مُصَمِّم	مُصَمَّم
مُطالِع	مُطالَع

تمرين ١٥

١- تُكْتَبُ العربية من اليمين إلى اليسار.

٢- يقال إن دمشق أقدم مدينة مأهولة في العالم.

٣- تُشتَهر حلب بطعامها اللذيذ.

٤- بُنِيَت الأهرام منذ آلاف السنين.

٥- وُلِدَ جمال عبد الناصر قرب الإسكندرية في مصر.

تمرين ١٦

مَصدَر	فِعْل أمْر	اسم مَفعول	اسم فاعِل	إضافة وإضافة مركبة
دِعاية	اِخلَع	مكتوبة	نقّال	إشارات المرور
إعلان	اِشْرَبوا	مُنتخَب	جوّال	إشارة الوقوف
تصميم	قِفْ	ممنوع	مُشجِّع	أحمر الشفاه
تَنَصُّت	اِستفدْ	مستورَد	صالح	لافتات الدخول والخروج
استِخدام	اِستمتعْ	مأخوذ	لافِتة	قاعة المطالعة
تدخين		مسحوق		
مُرور				
تَحَكُّم				
وُقوف				
سُهولة				

تمرين ١٧

١- يحمي من التنصُّت، تصميم أنيق، شاشة عرض كبيرة.

أ- هاتف نقّال، هاتف جوّال، هاتف خَلَوي

٢- الجمال، الأناقة، التميُّز

٣- تتكلم المقالة عن مؤسسة الإمارات للنقل التي خصصت حافلاتها لنقل أربعين مشجِّعاً إلى مدينة زايد.

تمرين ١٨

أ- ١- عام ٢٠٠٠ ٢- للبنين والبنات ٣- الحرية ٤- شارع عمر المختار

ب- ١- للكيمياء والفيزياء ٢- شَتَويّ ٣- الميدان ٤- لكرة المضرب والسلّة والطائرة

ج- ١- كل ما سبق ٢- شهر آب ٣- ٢٩٧٤٥٦١

الدرس الثاني

تمرين ٢

١- جريدة / صَحيفة
٢- تَخَصُّص / طِبّ
٣- رياضة / كرة القدم
٤- ناي / آلة موسيقية
٥- اِستَلَم / رِسالة
٦- حاسوب / بَرمَجة
٧- نَظَم / شِعر
٨- خَشَب / مِنشار

تمرين ٣

١- طَبلة
٢- تكْلِفة
٣- وَتَر
٤- عِلم الأحياء
٥- لون
٦- شركة

تمرين ٤

١- تراسلت مع طالب من أوستراليا.
٢- سيتابِع سامِر دراسة الطبّ في الخارِج.
٣- هل قرأتَ رِوايةَ "اللص والكلاب" لنَجيب محفوظ؟
٤- حَصَلَتْ رشا على علامةٍ جيّدةٍ في الامتِحان.

تمرين ٥

١- قطّة
٢- سمكة
٣- مِطرقة
٤- طبلة

تمرين ٦

٢ يحمل الرجل لوحاً طويلاً من الخشب.
٣ يصنع الرجل أوانيَ فخّارية تُستعمَل لِزراعة النَباتات.
٤ يُحاوِل الطَبيب البَيطريّ أن يُعالَج الكلب المَريض. هو يسمع نَبَضات قلبه.
١ يَدُقّ الرجل المِسمارَ بالمِطرقة.

تمرين ٨

١- الاسم والعنوان والدراسة والرياضة المفضّلة والهوايات.
٢- المراسلة والرحلات وكرة القدم.
٣- لأن والدها لا يستطيع تحمّل تكاليف الدراسة.
٤- ليخصِّص يوماً بالأسبوع لعلاج الفقراء مجّاناً.
٥- بلا ما بين النهرين.
٦- المِطرقة والمِنشار والكمّاشة والمفكّ.

تمرين ٩

١- لأنهم يرغبون بالتراسل مع القرّاء الآخرين.

٢- لانا خضري

٣- إما في التدريس أو في وزارة الخارجية لأنها لن تتابع دراستها في الخارح.

٤- النجارة وصناعة الفخار والكهرباء والدهان.

٥- العود مصنوع من خشب الورد وله عشرة أوتار أو اثنا عشر وتراً

٦- تسمّى الشدة وأبو الفول والبريبة والباصرة من بعض الألعاب.

تمرين ١٠

١- درس حازم الهندسة في جامعة القاهرة.
ثم تابع دراسته في ولاية أيوا في الولايات المتحدة.
حيث حصل على شهادة الماجستير في الهندسة.
عمل بعد تخرّجه في شركة لإنشاء الطرقات في شيكاغو.
بعد سبع سنوات عاد إلى مصر حيث قابل زوجته.
عادا معاً إلى الولايات المتحدة ليعملا ويسكنا هناك.

تمرين ١٢

١- لو كنتُ غنياً لاشتريتُ بيتاً جديداً.

٢- لولا المطر لحضرتُ الحفلة.

٣- لو تتصل بي أختي أكثر.

٤- لو سافرتُ بالطائرة لما شاهدتُ تلك المدن الجميلة.

٥- لو لا الماء لما كان هناك حياة على وجه الأرض.

٦- لو كان لديّ وقت أكثر!

تمرين ١٣

١- في درس أمس قَرَأَ الطُلاّبُ الشِعرَ واستَمَعوا إلى الأغنية.

٢- الصَديقان تَراسَلا لِمُدّةِ عام.

٣- ظَهَرَت المُغَنيَّةُ على شاشَةِ التِلفاز سعيدة في الليلة الماضية.

٤- تَكتُبُ أخَواتي القِصَّةَ و يَنظِمنَ الشِعر.

تمرين ١٤

١- قابلناهم لدى ذهابهم إلى السينما.

٢- لدى هشام أختان.

٣- المفاتيح لدى المدير.

٤- ألدَيْك قلم؟

٥- لديَّ عنوان جديد الآن.

تمرين ١٥

آ- معلومات شخصية عن سلمى

ب- تدرس سلمى التاريخ الإسلامي، تحبّ السفر، هوايتها التصوير، لونها المفضّل الأخضر، تتمنى لو تتابع دراستها.

ج- إجابات متنوعة

د-

١- خطأ، تدرس التاريخ الإسلامي. ٢- خطأ، تحبّ السفر والتصوير. ٣- صواب

ه-

١- أسرتها وأصدقائها ٢- السفر ٣- الأشجار

الدرس الثالث

تمرين ١

١-تعليم المشاهدات طريقة صُنع حلوى شامية. ٢-طريقة الصُنع، المقادير، الموادّ اللازمة

٣-إجابات متنوعة مثل: تحضير هريسة اللوز، أو حلوى شامية.

تمرين ٢

١-الثامنة ٢- ثلاثة أطفال ٣- ربّات البيوت الموظّفات ٤- هريسة اللوز

٥- السميد ٦- عشرين دقيقة ٧- على وجه كلّ مُعيّن ٨- القَطر

تمرين ٤

١-نار / مَوقِد ٢- زُبدة / لَبَن ٣- موادّ / مَقادير ٤- دقيقة / ساعة

٥- شامي / دِمشقيّ ٦- طِفل / أمّ ٧- صَعْب / سَهْل

تمرين ٥

١- ثلاثاء ٢- شَجَرة ٣- ليمون ٤- صينية ٥- لَوْزة

تمرين ٦

١- ضَعي الصينيّة على الطاولة. / على الطاولة ضعي الصينية.

٢- اِنتظرنا أمام باب المسرح. / أمام باب المسرح انتظرنا.

٣- يغلي الماء عند دَرَجة حرارة مئة./ عند درجة حرارة مئة يغلي الماء.

٤- يجِد بعض الطلاّب صُعوبة في تكلُّم العربية.

٥- حَرِّك الدِهان جَيّداً ثُمَّ ادهن الجِدار بالفُرشاة.

تمرين ٧

١- ضَعِ الحاسوب الجديد على الطاولة

٢- أولاً صِل لوحة المفاتيح بالحاسوب.

٣- ثُمَّ صِلِ الحاسوبَ بالكَهرباء.

٤- انتظر دقيقة أو دقيقتين ليُحمِّلَ الحاسوب برامجه.

٥- اِبْدأ بكتابة رسالتك.

تمرين ٨

إجابات متنوعة

تمرين ٩

١- يجِبُ أن أحضر هذا الكتاب معي إلى المدرسة غداً.

٢- يجِبُ ألا ننسى أصدقاءنا.

٣- يجِبُ أن تكتب اسمك على هذه الورقة.

٤- وجب عليها أن تركب الحافلة إلى عملها.

٥- يجِبُ ألا تكتب على الجدران.

٦- يجِبُ تحريك الخلطة.

تمرين ١٠

١- أتَيْنا بالسيّارة.

٢- صنعَت هذا الطَبَق بِنَفْسِها.

٣- أنظِّف أسناني بالفُرشاة.

٤- عملتُ هذا التمرين بصُعوبة.

٥- حملوا البرّاد بسُهولة.

تمرين ١١

١- أختُها جميلةُ الوجه.

٢- أخي كثير الأولاد.

٣- بعض اللغات سهلة التعلم.

٤- أحمد كبير القدمَيْن.

٥- هذه سيّارة غاليةُ الثَمَن.

تمرين ١٢

أوَّلاً، أحْضِرْ حقيبة كبيرة.

ثانياً، افْتح الحقيبة ونظّفْها من الداخل.

ثالثاً، أحْضِرْ ملابِسك وأمتعتك وضعها في الحقيبة.

رابعاً، أغْلِق الحقيبة واقفلها بالمفتاح.

خامِساً، اِتَّصِلْ بسيارة الأجرة لتأخذَكَ إلى المطار.

سادساً، انْزِلْ إلى الشارع لِتنتظرَ سيارة الأجرة.

تمرين ١٤

١- ها أنا أكتب لك من تونس.

٢- ها هو يقود سيّارته الجديدة.

٣- ها هي أمي تحضِّر حلوى.

٤- ها هم قادمون ليلعبوا كرة السلّة.

تمرين ١٥

١- اِنتظريني أمام موقف الحافلة.

٢- لا تنسوا كتابة أسمائكم على الورقة.

٣- أَحْضرن كتبَكنّ غدا

٤- أَحضر السيارة إلى الباب.

٥- يا أختي، أعطيني الجريدة لو سمحتِ.

تمرين ١٦

أ

١- دراجة ثابتة

٢- لأنها جيّدة لصحتهم.

٣- لا يقوم بأي رياضة الآن لكنه يريد أن يبدأ ممارسة رياضة ما.

٤- إجابات متنوع.

ب-

١- صواب ٢- صواب ٣- خطأ، تعرف كثيراً. ٤- خطأ، ليس لديه دراجة ثابتة.

ج

١-بركوب الدراجة ٢- الشوارع فيها سيّارات كثيرة. ٣- للقلب ٤- خمس مرات أسبوعياً.

الدرس الرابع

تمرين ١

١-عاشَ / سَكَنَ ٢- ألو / مَرحباً ٣- أهل / أسرة ٤- مشى / سارَ

٥-بِطاقة / رِسالة ٦- طَريق / شارِع ٧- بَلَغَ / وَصَلَ ٨- حافلة / مَوْقِف

تمرين ١

١-ساحة ٢- مِصعَد ٣- صَديق ٤- رَحَّبَ

٥- عَمَلٌ ٦- خَريطة ٧- شَوق

تمرين ٢

إجابات متنوعة

تمرين ٤

١- انتقال ميساء من شقّة إلى شقّة أخرى.

٢- لترحِّبَ بها وتدُلّها على شقّتِها.

٣- سبب الانتقال إلى شقّة جديدة ، انتظارها لزيارة صديقتها.

٤- هالة صديقة ميساء، ويوسف ابنها، فيصل زوجها.

٥- في الشهر الماضي.

٦- لأن شقّتها القديمة كانت صغيرة وبعيدة عن دار أهلها.

٧- عنوانها شارع الرازي بناية ١٦٨ شقة .

٨- الطابَق الرابع.

٩- في ساحة الشهداء.

١٠- لأن شقّتها جديدة وقريبة من دار أهلها وقريبة من عمل زوجها.

تمرين ٥

١- بِنايتُنا مؤلَّفة من سِتّة طوابِق. / من ستة طوابق مؤلفة بنايتنا.

٢- نَزلتُ من الحافِلةِ أمام المَصرِف. / أمام المصرف نزلت من الحافلة.

٣- مَحَلّ سامي عِند تقاطُع شارعَيْ السَلام والنيل. / عند تقاطع شارعي السلام والنيل محل سامي.

٤- خُذْ أوَّل شارِع إلى اليمين واتّجه شَمالاً.

تمرين ٦

١- ابن خالي لديه عائلة مؤلّفة من زوجته ووَلَد وبنتَيْن.
يسكُن وأسرته في بِناية من سبعة طوابِق
شقّتُه في الطابَق الرابع لكنَّه لا يستعمِل المِصعَد.
يقول إن صُعود الدَرَج رياضة له.
تريد زوجته الانتقال إلى شقّة أكبر في حي قريب من عَمَلِها.
لكنَّه لا يريد الانتِقال لسَبَبَيْن.
أوّلاً: لأن ذلك الحي مزدحِم
ثانياً: لأن الشقُق هناك أغلى بكثير من شقّتهم.

تمرين ٨

١- رحّبَت بنا ترحيباً حارّاً.

٢- اتّجهنا اتّجاهاً خاطئاً.

٣- عبرنا الشارع عبوراً صحيحاً.

٤- يكتب كتابةً جميلةً.

٥- اِنعطفَت السيّارة اِنعطافاً حادّاً.

٦- صلّحَ البرّاد تصْليحاً جيّداً.

تمرين ٩

١- إن تصِل متأخِّراً فلن تجِدَني.

٢- إن تمارس الرياضة أمارسها معك.

٣- إنْ نامَ مُبَكِّراً فقد يكونُ مريضاً

٤- إنْ تَذهَبْ إلى باريس فرُبَّما ذهبتُ معك.

٥- إنْ انقَطَعَ عنِ الدِراسة فعمله موجود.

٦- إنْ ذهبتَ إلى لندَن فزُرْ حديقةَ الحيوانات.

تمرين ١٠

١- تناولَت هالة عدّة أطباق على العشاء حتّى الحلوى.

٢- لم يقُد والدي سيّارة حتّى صار في الخمسين.

٣- دعَتني إلى الغداء حتّى تتكلّمَ معي.

٤- بقيتُ في الجامِعة حتّى الساعة الخامِسة.

٥- ذهبوا إلى محطة القِطار حتّى يروا الرئيس.

تمرين ١١

١- أخبرَني فريد نفسه أنّ المحلات مغلَقة.

٢- أين ترى نفسك بعد عشر سنوات من الآن؟

٣- طبعَت سامية الرِسالة بنفسِها.

٤- حمل سائق سيارة الأجرة حقيبتي إلى شقتي بنفسه.

تمرين ١٢

عزيزي الرياض

أرجو أن تكون وأسرتك بخير وأن يكون الطقس في عمان جميلاً كما هو في الشام سأكون سعيداً جداً إذا زرتني في دكاني الجديدة حين تأتي إلى دمشق في الشهر القادم. عنوان دكاني ليس صعباً أنت تعرف ذلك الجزء من المدينة خصوصاً وأنك ستنزل في دار ابن عمك هيثم القريبة من شارع العابد

تستطيع أن تأتي إلى دكاني مشياً من موقف الحافلات. إذا كنت عند التقاطع في شارع العابد مع شارع ستة وعشين أيار امشِ نحو الغرب واجتز طريق الصالحية واستمر في المشي في طريق العابد إلى أن تصل إلى شارع الحرية هنا انعطف إلى اليسار وامشِ في هذا الشارع إلى الجنوب بعد قليل ترى فندق أمية على يسارك استمر في المشي وسترى ثانوية ابن الخلدون إلى يسارك

هنا تكون قد وصلت إلى شارع ابن رشد انعطف إلى اليمين وسر نحو الغرب مسافة خمسين متراً ثم انعطف يميناً مرة أخرى في شارع ضيق تقع دكاني في أول هذا الشارع وهي ثاني دكان على اليسار.

أرجو أن يكون عنواني سهلاً أنتظر زيارتك يا أخي بفارغ الصبر وإلى اللقاء سلامي إلى هاني وصفوان.

أخوك المشتاق

ماهر

تمرين ١٣

ب

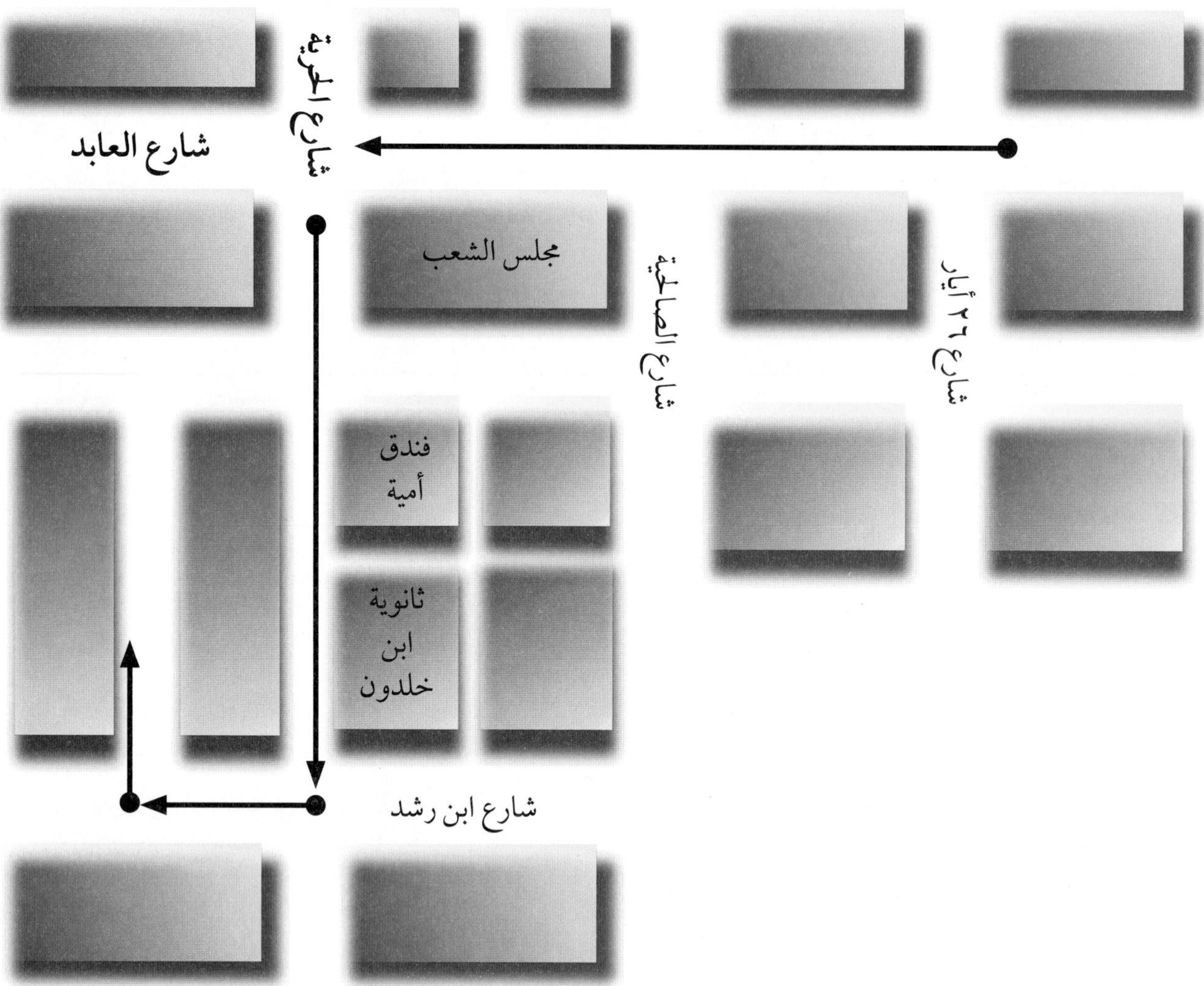
شارع الحرية
شارع العابد
مجلس الشعب
شارع الصالحية
شارع ٢٦ أيار
فندق
أمية
ثانوية
ابن
خلدون
شارع ابن رشد

الدرس الخامِس

تمرين ١

١- لَحظة / ثانية　　٢- اِرتَدى / لَبِسَ　　٣- وَفاة / حياة　　٤- داخِل / خارِج

٥- مَملوء / فارِغ　　٦- مُثَلَّجات / بُوظة　　٧- قابَلَ / اِلتَقى　　٨- صَبيّ / وَلَد

٩- جَوّ / طَقس

تمرين ٢

١- كَريم　　٢- وَطَن　　٣- فِضّة　　٤- مَوت

٥- طَبَق　　٦- مَعهَد　　٧- سائح

تمرين ٣

١- صواب

٢- خطأ، هنّ من دمشق.

٣- خطأ، إحدى الفتيات ترتدي اللباس الإسلامي.

٤- خطأ، وفاته جعلَتْها تترَك الدراسة.

٥- خطأ، يحمِل بِضاعته على ظَهْره.

تمرين ٤

١- المعرِض　　٢- التلفاز　　٣- دول عربية وأجنبية　　٤- بالسيّارة

٥- أنيقة　　٦- المغربي　　٧- الداخلية　　٨- خزّاناً

تمرين ٥

١- مقابلات تجريها مذيعة مع زوّار معرض دمشق.

٢- أسرة من زحلة تزور المعرض ومقابلة مع ثلاث فتيات ومقابلة مع بائع العرقسوس.

٣- معرِض دمشق الدولي أو مقابلات في المعرِض.

٤- في أواسط الصيف من كلّ عام.

٥- أربعة أشخاص.

٦- يملك مطعماً ويعمل فيه.

٧- لأنه كان موظّفاً بسيطاً.

٨- يحمِل إبريق ماء ليغسل به الكؤوس بعد أن يشرب الزبائن.

تمرين ٦

١- جَوّ المَكتبة مُريح لِلدِراسة.

٢- هَنادي فتاة تَرتَدياللِباس الإسلاميّ.

٣- قامَت الفَتاة بعملِها بِكُلِّ سُرور.

٤- لا أشرَب الماء إلاّ مُثَلَّجاً.

٥- نادى الأب إلى ابنِه لِلدُخول.

٦- أجرَت المُذيعةُ مُقابَلَةً مع سائِحٍ فَرَنسيّ.

٧- يَزور المَعرِض سُيّاح من بِلاد عَربيّة وأجنبيّة.

تمرين ٨

إجابات متنوعة

تمرين ٩

١- أخبَرَني صَديقي أن هناك مَعرِضاً لصوَرٍ من البحرين.
وسيُقام هذا المَعرِض في المتحف الوطنيّ بِحَلَب ويبدأ في ١ أيلول.
في الأول من أيلول ذهبت إلى المَعرِض مع صَديقَيَّ حسام وهِشام.
وكان في المَعرِض أكثر من ١٥٠ صورة من تاريخ البحرين القَديم.
بعض الصوَر كانت عن قَرية أثريّة يَبلُغ عُمرُها أكثر من ألفَي (٢٠٠٠) سنة.
أعجبتنا الصوَر كثيراً وتمنّينا لو نذهب إلى البحرين لرؤية تِلكّ القَرية.
يظهَر في تِلكَ الصوَر هندسة البيوت في القَرية.
كما يظهَر في الصوَر أيضاً المكان الذي كان يُخزَّن فيه البَلَح (dates).

تمرين ١٠

إجابات متنوعة

تمرين ١١

١-طبعاً　　٢- شكراً　　٣- العَفو　　٤- لا أبداً

٥- الحَمدُ لله　　٦- إن شاء الله

تمرين ١٤

١- عليَّ أن أذهَبَ إلى الحَمّام.

٢- علَيك تَنظيفُ الشقّة.

٣- عليَّ أن أُكْمِلَ واجِباتي البَيْتية.

٤- كانَ علينا أن ننتظرَهم ساعةً.

تمرين ١٥

١- أتمشي إلى الجامِعة؟

٢- أتأتي متأخراً لحفلة تخرُّجك؟

٣- أذلك أستاذُك؟

٤- ألم يقُل إننا يجب أن نكونَ هناك في الساعة الثالثة؟

٥- أدرسَتْ العُلوم السياسية أم الدراسات الدولية؟

٦- أتشاهد التلفاز في أسبوع الامتحانات؟

تمرين ١٦

١- لا أذهب إلى السينما إلاّ مع أصدقئي.

٢- حضر جميع الطلاّب إلاّ واحداً.

٣- زوجتك إنْ هي إلاّ صديقتك.

٤- ما ذهبنا إلى البحر مرّةً إلاّ وسبحنا.

٥- كلّ السيّدات في الصورة معهنّ كبل إلاّ واحدة.

٦- ما اتصلت بها بالهاتف مرّةً إلاّ أجاب ابنُها.

تمرين ١٧

١-قوبِلَت ٢- أقيمَ ٣- رُؤيَ ٤- أُحْضِروا ٥-أُسْتُعْمِلَ

تمرين ١٨

١- عندي اِمتحان اليومَ.

٢- وصلَتِ الطائرةُ مساءً.

٣- دخلنا المبنى وقتَ خروجِ الموظَّفين.

٤- استمرّ الفيلمُ ساعتين.

٥- بقينا في بيروتَ خمسةَ أيّام.

٦- سكنتُ في شقّةٍ كلّ السنة.

تمرين ١٩

امكن أن تقدمي نفسك؟

اسمي زينا نعمة أنا من عمان في الأردن لي ثلاثة إخوة لكن ليس لي أخت.

ماذا تفعلين هنا في الولايات المتحدة؟

أدرس الموارد البشرية

لماذا اخترت هذا المجال؟

أحب أن أتعامل مع الناس بشكل عام وأساعدهم

ماذا ستفعلين بعد تخرجك؟

أحب أن أعمل في شركة أجنبية في عمان

أأنت وحدك هنا؟

أخي معي وهو يدرس المحاسبة.

أتعجبك الحياة في أمريكا بصورة عامة؟
نعم، كل شيء يبدو سهلاً وأناس يحبون أن يساعدوك.
ما الشيء الذي يعجبك أكثر من سواه؟
النظام واحترام الإنسان وحقوقه.
وما الشيء الذي لا يعجبك؟
عدم الاهتمام بما يجري في العالم والاهتمام فقط بالأمور العادية كالرياضة مثلاً.
ماذا تتمنين في الشهور القليلة المقبلة؟
أتمنى أن أتخرج في الوقت المحدد وأن أبدأ العمل مباشرةً. وأتمنى أيضاً أن أتزوج وأنجب أولاداً كثيرين وأن أتابع دراستي للحصول على شهادة الدكتوراه وأن أزور عدة بلادان.
كيف ينظر الناس إلى المرأة العربية في الغرب؟
يظن كثيرون إنها غير متعلمة وخادعة للزوج ولا تخرج من بيتها. هذه صورة غير صحيحة أبداً هناك الطبيبات والمهندسات والفنانات والأستاذات الجامعيات والقاضيات والسياسيات وهناك نساء في الأعمال التجارية بل إن هناك وزيرات في الحكومة كما في سورية وبعض البلاد العربية الأخرى
وما هي هواياتك؟
القراءة والرياضات ومشاهدة الأفلام السينمائية.
ما لونك المفضل؟
البنفسجي
ما مدينتك المفضلة؟
روما.
هل زرتها ولماذا تفضلينها؟
نعم، زرتها منذ عامين وأحبها لأنها جميلة وملئة بتاريخ وكأنها متحف كبير.
وما طعامك المفضل؟
المثلجات وأحبها كثيراً.
شكراً على المقابلة وأتمنى لك حياة ناجحة سعيدة

ب

١- النِظام　　٢- الموادّ البشريّة　　٣- ربّةُ بيت　　٤- القراءة

ج
إجابات متنوعة

الدرس السادِس

تمرين ١

١-سياحة ٢- هَدوء ٣- حَديث ٤- قيادة ٥- اِستِراحة

تمرين ٢

إجابات متنوعة

تمرين ٣

١-شقّة أخيه ٢- حِمص ٣- الحدود السورية الأردنية ٤- أحمد نحاس

٥- سفح جبل الجوفة ٦- مسكونة ٧- عمّان ٨- ١٩٤٦

تمرين ٤

١- خطأ، رامي طالب ويعمل سائقاً أيضاً. ٢-صواب ٣-خطأ، من حلب إلى عمّان.

٤-صواب ٥-خطأ، كان اسمها فيلادلفيا.

٦-خطأ، جبل التاج هو أعلى جبل. ٧-صواب

تمرين ٥

١-اِشتَغَلَ / عَمِلَ ٢- الأوَّل / الثاني ٣- جِهاز كَهرَبائيّ / بَرّاد

٤- طَريق / شارِع ٥- تجَوَّل / مَشى ٦- مَسرَح / سينما ٧- شاحِنة / سيّارة

ب

١-حَرَمُ / الجامعة ٢- سَفحُ / الجَبَل ٣- شَهادةُ / القيادة ٤- مَجلِسُ / الأمّة

ج

١-أصبَحَ / صارَ ٢- ساقَ / قادَ ٣- رَجَعَ / عادَ ٤- سَنة / عام

٥- بَيْت / دار

تمرين ٦

إجابات متنوعة

تمرين ٧

إجابات متنوعة

تمرين ٨

١- في مادبا

٢- محفورة في الصخر الورديّ اللون وكانت مركزاً مهمّاً للتِجارة والقوافل

٣- تُقام حفلات موسيقية في مسرح جَرَش الروماني ٤- هي ميناء الأردن الوحيد ٥- إجابات متنوعة

تمرين ١١

١- وصل الطلاّب مُتأخّرين إلى غُرفة الصفّ. ٢- تكلّمنا مع المُذيع وَجهاً لِوجه.

٣- رأت سِهام أمَّها ماشيةً في الشارِع. ٤- ركبوا الطائرة مُسافِرين إلى الجزائر.

٥- سمِعتُ أُغنية فَيروز من الإذاعة. ٦-دخل فَريد الغرفة قائلاً: إنه لن يعمل في هذا البلد بعدَ الآن.

ب

١- ماشياً ٢- ضاحِكَين ٣- جالِساً ٤- حامِلاً

ج

١- دخلَت الغرفة راكِضةً. ٢- وَصَلَ متأخّراً ثلاثين دقيقة

٣- وضعتُ درّاجتي بين سيّارتَيْن ٤ - وقفَت أمامنا تقرأ الشِعر.

تمرين ١٢

١- مادُمتُ حياً سأستمرّ في التعلُّم. ٢- لا يزال هاني يدرس الهندسة الكهربائية.

٣- كانَ رجُلاً فقيراً قبل أن يصير غَنياً. ٤- صار البنزين غالياً.

٥- لا تحتاجين إلى سيّارة مادمتِ تسكنين قرب حرم الجامعة.

تمرين ١٣

١-مَسرور ٢- مَسوق ٣- مَمشيّ ٤- مَتْبوع

٥- مُداوىً ٦- مُغادَر ٧- مُهْتَدٍ ٨- مَقود ٩- مَنسيّ

تمرين ١٤

ا

١- زيارة الكاتب ووالدته لأخته في مدينة أخرى.

٢- السفر بالطائرة، الاستقبال في المطار، مباني أبو ظبي وشوارعها.

٣- والدته ٤- بمدينة أبو ظبي في مبنيً عالٍ

٥- عريضة ونظيفة ٦- شاهد أشجاراً على الجانبين ٧- نسرين

ب

١- أبو ظبي ٢- أخته وابنتها ٣- شوارع حديثة

ج

إجابات متنوعة

الدرس السابع

تمرين ١

١-سُرعة / بَرْق ٢- حَلْبة / رَقْص ٣- صَوْت / مَسْموع ٤- مُسامَحة / عُذْر

٥- فِرْقة / موسيقية ٦- ثوب / لِباس ٧- طاوِلة / مائدة ٨- بار / مَشْرَب

٩- بَعَثَ / أرْسَلَ ١٠ - رأى / شاهَدَ

تمرين ٢

١-خافِت / قَويّ ٢- فائِت / مُقبِل ٣- داخِل / خارِج ٤- شابٌ / فتاة

تمرين ٣

١-نَوى ٢- ثَوْب ٣- تأخير ٤- خَرَجَ ٥- عُذْر

تمرين ٤

١-ثَقيلة ٢- شقّة غادة ٣- شباب وفتيات ٤- شباب وفتيات ٥- كولا

٦- صَحْن صغير ٧- مليسا وليندا ٨- دولة الإمارات ٩- الموسيقا الصاخِبة

١٠- تأخير الرد

تمرين ٥

١-تأخير ٢- يجري ٣- مضى ٤- الكحولية

٥- شَوق ٦- دعاني ٧- ألاّ ٨- مائِدة

تمرين ٧

١- زارت غادة الملهى الليلي مساء يوم السبت.

٢- اسم الملهى الليلي ((الفصول الأربعة))

٣- البينيا كولادا مشروب كحولي مكسيكي.

٤- قامت مليسا وليندا إلى الرقص.

٥- تعيش نجوى في دولة الإمارات.

٦- مَروان زوج نجوى.

تمرين ٨

١- زارت غادة ملهىً ليلياً مع ثلاث صديقات.

٢- كان اسم الملهى مكتوباً على لافِتة كبيرة.

٣- كان جَوّ الملهى صاخباً والأضواء خافتةً.

٤- كادت سلوى أنْ تنسى موعد طائرتِها.

٥- رقصنا كثيراً في حفلة زَواج صديقي في الشهر الفائت.

٦- وَقَفَ أيمن وزوجته أمام باب المطعم وتحدثا معنا بضع دقائق.

تمرين ٩

١- خطأ، أتت غادة إلى أمريكا منذ سنة ونصف.

٢- خطأ، غادة لا تجيد الرقص وزارَت الملهى الليلي لأنه قد دعَتها صديقاتها.

٣- خطأ، كانت طاولة غادة وصديقاتها بعيدة عن الفرقة الموسيقية.

٤- خطأ، لم ترقصْ غادة لأنّها لا تجيد الرقص.

٥- خطأ،خطأ، لم يرد في النص أن الفتيات تناولن عشاء لذيذا.

٦- خطأ، لا تعرف غادة نكهة المشروبات الكحولية لأنّها لا تتناول المشروبات الكحولية.

٧- خطأ ، لأن الشاب لم يدعُ غادة إلى الرقص، وإنما دعا ليندا.

٨- خطأ، وصلَت رسالة نجوى في أوائل آذار لكن لا نعرف التاريخ بالتحديد.

تمرين ١٠

١- علِمتُ من صديقي أنّ مطعماً جديداً اسمه "الصحّة" قد فتح أبوابه.
في يوم الخميس الفائت ذهبنا إلى ذلك المطعم الجديد.
وحين وصلنا إليه شاهدنا لافِتة كبيرة كُتِب عليها اسم المطعم بالأضواء.
دخلنا المطعم ووجدنا فيه عدداً كبيراً من الموائد.
قادتنا النادلة إلى مائدة قريبة من الشبّاك.
ثمّ حضر نادِل آخَر وسألنا ماذا نطلب.
طلبتُ كُبّة مع الحمَّص وطلبَت زوجتي دجاجاً مَشوياً.
يجِب أنْ أقول: إنَّ الطعام كان لذيذاً ولم يكُنْ غالياً.

تمرين ١١

في مدينة دمشق القديمة يوجَد عددٌ من المقاهي الشعبيّة. والمقهى هو مكانٌ لِلرجالِ فقط يشربون فيه الشاي والقهوة (ومن هنا تأتي كلمة "مقهى") ويلعبون الورق وطاولة الزهر. يأتي إلى بعض هذه المقاهي عددٌ كبير من الزبائن فيضعون لهم كراسيَ على الرصيف في الشارعِ حيثُ يجلسون ويشربون الشاي والقهوة ويراقبون الناس الّذين يمشون في الشوارع في هذه المقاهي يتكلّم النادِل عادةً مع الزبائن بصوتٍ عالٍ، ويُحضِر لهم ما يطلبون بسُرعة كبيرة. لكن إذا أردت أن تجلِسَ مدّة طويلة في مقهى مثل هذا فيجب أنْ تطلبَ فنجان قهوةٍ أو شاي أو غير ذلك كلّ نِصْفِ ساعة تقريباً أو يجِبُ أنْ تتركَ المقهى.

تمرين ١٢

ا

وصلَت أمّ عدنان على خطوط "يو إس إير" الجوية إلى نيويورك من كلمبس في طريقِ عودتِها إلى سورية. ما سافرَت أمّ عدنان على هذه الطائرة مِن قَبل. نزلَت في فندقٍ قريبٍ من وسط المدينة، كَيْ تَشتريَ (ما) تريد مِن ملابس وهدايا وغيرِها، وترى (ما) يجري في هذه المدينة الكبيرة. ما أعجبتها جميع البضائع في السوق، لكنَّ بعضَها كان (كما) تريد تماماً. في ذلك اليوم تحدَّثَت مع سيِّدة أمريكيّة باللغة الفَرنسيّة، وكانت سعيدة جدّاً بذلك. دعَتها تلك السيِّدة إلى فنجان قَهْوة فقبِلَت. قضَت معها أمّ عدنان أكثر من ساعتين، ثمَّ تركَتها وذهبَت إلى الفندق، وما عَرَفَت (ما) تعمل ولا أين تسكن.

ب

١- ما درس عدنان العربية في جامعة ميشغان.

٢- تريد لينا أن تعرف ما يعمل الرئيس في البيت الأبيض.

٣- ما رقمُ هاتفك يا نجوى؟

٤- ماذا يجري في الطابق الأعلى؟

٥- ما نزلَت فاطمة في فندق هيلتون في مدينة نيويورك.

الدرس الثامِن

تمرين ١

١-مُحضَّر / مطبوخ	٢- رئيس تَحرير / صَحيفة	٣- باوند / رَطل	٤- إرْباً / قِطَعاً
٥- شِحْنة / ميناء	٦- ثَمَن / نُقود	٧- قَذِر / نَظيف	٨- فَرْخ / دَجاجة

تمرين ٢

١-لافِتة ٢- حِذاء ٣- حَساسية ٤- مُدير تَحرير ٥- ديك مَشوي

تمرين ٤

١- الاحتفال بعيد الشكر.

٢- فهم الكاتب من زميله أنه اشترى ديكاً وزنه ١٥ كيلوغراماً، بحث في السوق عن ديك كبير، قطّع الديك حتّى يستطيع إدخاله الفرن، كان الديك مرسلاً خصّيصاً إلى السفارة الأمريكية.

٣- سوء تفاهم

تمرين ٥

١-حية ٢- بالحساسية ٣- بخير ٤- قَذِر

٥- ذهاباً فقط ٦- أبيه ٧- ساعي المكتب ٨- لصداع ومشاكل

٩- يشويه بالفرن ١٠- السفارة الأمريكية

تمرين ٧

١-خطأ، قد يتزوّج ٢- خطأ، ما قاله الطبيب لم ينفع. ٣- صواب

٤- خطأ، الفندق أقذر من الشارع ٥- خطأ، لا يزال ينتظر أن يربح تذكرة إياب. ٦- خطأ، كان في بيروت.

٧- خطأ، يحتفل به الأمريكيون. ٨- خطأ، لم يفهم الكاتب ما قاله مدير التحرير.

تمرين ٨

١- أردتُ وثلاثة من أصدقائي أن نقضيَ إجازة الربيع على الشاطئ.
أولاً اشترينا تذاكر القطار.
في يوم السفر اتّجهنا إلى محطة القطار بسيّارة أم عبد الرحيم.
وصلنا إلى المحطة في الساعة السابعة، أي قبل موعد القطار بنصف ساعة.
كان القطار موجوداً في المحطة وفيه بعض الركّاب.
صعدنا إلى القطار ووضعنا الحقائب في مكانها.
جلستُ إلى جانب الشبّاك وجلس عبد الرحيم مقابلي.
أمّا مروان وسعيد فجلسا إلى يسارنا.
استغرقت الرحلة خمس ساعات إذ وصلنا في الساعة الثانية عشرة والنصف.
ركِبنا سيّارة أجرة من المحطة إلى الفندق.

تمرين ٩

١-خرجتُ من الباب وإذا بها تُمطِر. ٢-دخلَت الأمّ غرفة النوم وإذا بالطفل الصغيرعلى الأرض.

٣-ذهب إلى المصرف لسحبِ بعض النُقود وإذا به مُغلَق. ٤-وصلنا إلى دار السينما وإذا بنادية تنتظرنا.

تمرين ١٠

١- كاد اليوم أن ينتهي. ٢- ما كاد الفيلم أن يبدأ حتّى رنّ جرس الهاتف.

٣- لا أكاد أرى البحر من هذه النافذة. ٤- تكاد طائرة سامي أن تصل.

تمرين ١١

١-قد يتأخّرون قليلاً هذا المساء. ٢-لقد أخذَتْ حبتَي أسبرين ولم تنفعاها.

٣-لو كنتُ مكانك لشاركتُ بالمهرجان المسرحيّ. ٤-كاد يُجَنُّ من الفرح.

تمرين ١٢

ا

١- تواصل غير ناجح

٢- تسكن حنان مع ريم، تركَت أخت ريم رسالة تذكّر أختها بعيد ميلادها، نقلت حنان الرسالة الخطأ.

٣- قرأتْ رسالتَيْن واحدة من ريم والأخرى من أخت ريم.

٤- اِتّصلَت لتخبِرَها بأمر رسالة أختها وأنّها يجب أن تأخذ أباها إلى الحفلة.

٥- سمر أخت ريم، وهديل صديقة ريم، وأُبَيّ ابن سمر.

ب

١- على الأرض ٢- رسالة من ريم ٣- أباها.

ج

إجابات متنوعة

د

١- خطأ، تحت الباب. ٢- خطأ، حضرت لكنها لم تجد أختها فتركَت رسالةً.

٣- خطأ، بسبب كتابة اسم الابن دون تشكيل.

الدرس التاسِع

تمرين ١

١-عَثَر / وَجَد　　٢- حارّة / زُقاق　　٣- شاغِر / فارِغ　　٤- جامِع / مَسجِد

٥- حِكاية / قِصّة　　٦- الآراميّة / السِريانيّة　　٧- حُجْرة / غُرفة

تمرين ٢

١-تأشيرة / دُخول　　٢- جواز / سَفَر　　٣- سيرة / عَنتَرة　　٤- خيال / الظِل

٥- سورة / الفاتِحة　　٦- خُطوط / الطيران　　٧- سيّارة / أُجرة　　٨- مُتحَف / دِمشق

تمرين ٣

١-نَبات　　٢- المعادي　　٣- تأخّر

تمرين ٥

١- زيارة مايكل إلى دمشق مع صديقيه.

٢- نزل مايكل وصديقاه في فندق قريب من سوق الحميدية، تاريخ مختصر لمدينة دمشق، زاروا متاحف دمشق ومعالمها، تناولوا القهوة في فندق الميريديان.

٣- أقدم مدينة

٤- ٢٠ جنيهاً

٥- فيها ثلاثة أسرّة ومغسلة لكن ليس فيها حمّام.

٦- لأن صديقة لهم أعطتهم اسم هذا الفندق.

٧- تُحكى اللغة السريانية في معلولا، وجبعدين، ونجعا

٨- في قصر العظم.

٩- الحياة الدمشقية القديمة.

١٠- رقيماً فخّاريا نُقِشَت عليه أوّل أبجدية في العالم.

تمرين ٦

إجابات متنوعة

تمرين ٧

١-خطأ، لم يكن فيه غرفة شاغرة.　　٢- خطأ، دون حمّام.　　٣- صواب

٤- خطأ، كان والياً منذ حوالي ٢٧٠ سنة.　　٥- خطأ، في متحف التقاليد الشعبية.

٦- خطأ، في متحف دمشق الوطني　　٧- صواب

تمرين ٨

١- مع صديقين ٢- تأشيرة ٣- المسجد ٤- متحف دمشق الوطني

تمرين ٩

١- شاهدنا أدوات التجميل القديمة في المتحف. / في المتحف شاهدنا أدوات التجميل القديمة.

٢- ركبت السيارة إلى الحي الذي أسكن فيه./ إلى الحي الذي أسكن فيه ركبت السيارة.

٣- • اكتشفت أول أبجدية في العالم في رأس الشمرة. / في رأس الشمرة اكتشفت أول أبجدية في العالم.

تمرين ١٠

١- أراد أسامة وزوجته كريمة السفر من القاهرة إلى بيروت من أجل عطلة الصيف.

وصل أسامة وكريمة إلى المطار قبل موعد إقلاع الطائرة بساعتين.

توجّها أوّلاً إلى مكان وزن الحقائب.

كان معهما أربع حقائب.

بعد وزن حقائبهما توجّها إلى مركز الجوازات.

عند انتهائهما من الجوازات جلسا في قاعة الانتظار أمام البوابة رقم ١٨ .

سمعا إعلاناً من السمّاعات عن إقلاع طائرتهما.

قال الإعلان: "الرجاء من حضرات الركّاب التوجّه إلى البوابة رقم ١٨ ".

صعِد الركّاب إلى الطائرة قبل نصف ساعة من موعد إقلاعها.

جلست كريمة في مقعد إلى جانب الشبّاك وجلس نديم إلى يسارها.

تمرين ١١

إجابات متنوعة

تمرين ١٢

١- أدرس الدراسات الإسلامية بما فيها القرآن والحديث.

٢- بما أنّ دمشق من أقدم المدن، فلها آثار من حضارات مختلفة فيها.

٣- بما أنك تسكن بعيدا عن حرم الجامعة فستحتاج إلى سيارة

٤- أحب ما كتبتِ. ٥- هل لاحظتَ ما لاحظتُ؟

تمرين ١٣

ا

١-لِـ ٢- إلى ٣- إلى ٤- (لا شيء أو) بـ ٥- إلى - في

٦- على ٧- لِـ ٨- إلى ٩- على ١٠- مع

ب

١- وصلتُ من لندن يوم السبت.

٢- نزلَت في بيت أمّها.

٣- رأيتُه جالساً إلى تلك الطاولة.

٤- يا هالة، هل تحدّثتِ مع زوجكِ عن شِراء تلك الساعة؟

٥- ماذا قال لك هؤلاء الرجال؟

٦- متى عُدتِ إلى البيت أمس بالليل يا سارة؟

٧- هل دفعتَ للرجل؟

٨- أريد أن أحصل على سيّارةٍ.

تمرين ١٤

١- عليَّ أن أغسل السيّارة يوم الأحد.

٢- اِشترَت هالة كتاباً عن التاريخ الأمريكيّ لِتقرأه.

٣- علينا أن نكون في البيت في الساعة الثامنة كي نشاهد برنامجنا التلفزيونيّ المفضَّل.

٤- مَن عليه الفواكه؟

تمرين ١٥

ا

١- زيارة كارول وأصدقائها للأردنّ وسورية.

٢- السفر بالطائرة إلى الأردن، زيارة عمّان وجَرَش والبتراء، السفر إلى سورية بالحافلة، زيارة حمص وحماة وحلب.

٣- من أمريكا ٤- بالطائرة ٥- في حماة

ب

١- أسبوعاً ٢- الجنوب ٣- سورية ٤- حِمص ٥- الفُندُق

ج

إجابات متنوعة

د

١- خطأ، بالسيّرة

٢- خطأ، في دمشق وفي حلب

٣- خطأ، من سوق الحميدية بدمشق

٤- خطأ، توقّفوا بحمص

الدرس العاشر

تمرين ١

١-الفُرس / إيران ٢- ذَهَبٌ / فِضّة ٣- آثار / تاريخ ٤- ظَنَّ / فَكَّرَ

٥- حِكاية / قِصّة ٦- جَيِّد / حَسَن ٧- قَدْ (يَفْعَل) / رُبَّما

تمرين ٢

١-الجيش ٢- حَرْب ٣- عَثَرَ ٤- نَبيّ ٥- أعمدة عظيمة

تمرين ٣

١-قَلْعة / حلب ٢- مَعبَد / بَعْل ٣- لورَنْس / العرب

٤- فُندُق بارون ٥- بِلاد / الشام ٦- خان / الخليلي

تمرين ٤

١-خطأ، بالحافلة ٢- خطأ، في تدمر ٣- صواب

٤- خطأ، في روما ٥- خطأ، في بارون حيث نزل لورنس ٦- خطأ، في حلب.

تمرين ٦

١- زيارة طلاّب أمريكيين إلى تجمر وحلب.

٢- زيارة تدمر ليوم واحد، معلومات عن تدمر وملكتها المشهورة، النزول في فندق بارون القديم، قصّة حلب الشهباء، أسواق حلب القديمة ٣- رحلة في تاريخ سورية ٤- ٢١٠ كيلومترات

٥- مشوا في شوارع المدينة وتناولوا الكباب الحلبيّ.

٦- لأنه انتصر على الفُرس مرتين وخلّص إمبراطور روما من الأسْر.

٧- استولت على مصر وكلّ سورية وآسيا الصُغرى. ٨- لأن النبيّ إبراهيم حلب بقرته الشهباء فيها.

تمرين ٧

١- بالحافلة ٢- تدمر ٣- بارون ٤- القلعة ٥- رخيصة

تمرين ٨

١- عِلمتُ أن أحمد لن يسافِرَ إلى دُبي. ٢-تتكلّم هالة اللغة الألمانيّة بطلاقة.

٣- كانت زنوبيا زعيمة عظيمة الذكاء. ٤-امتدّت الدولة الإسلاميّة من الصين إلى الأندلس.

٥- كان إله المطر والخِصب يسمّى بَعْل في سورية القديمة

تمرين ٩

١- أردتُ أنا وصديقاتي أن نترك المدينة لبضعة أيّام لنستمتع بجو الريف.
لذلك قرّرنا أن نستأجر حافلة صغيرة مع سائقها تـُقِلـُّنا إلى الكفرون.
والكفرون بلدة صغيرة جملية تقع في الجبال في غرب سورية الأوسط.
غادرنا دمشق في الساعة السابعة صباحاً.
توقّفنا مرّتين في الطريق ووصلنا الكفرون مساء.
استأجرنا داراً كبيرة فيها أربع غرف نوم.
قَضينا أيّامنا هناك في زيارة الأماكن الجميلة والمطاعم في الجبال.
قضينا خمسة أيّام هناك عُدنا بعدها إلى دمشق.
لقد استمتعنا جدّاً بهذه الرحلة، واتّفقنا أن نكرّرها مرّة أخرى.

تمرين ١١

إجابات متنوعة

تمرين ١٢

١- أتمنّى لو كانت المحلات مفتوحة الآن.
٢- حوصِرَت القلعة شهرين.
٣- صار هُمام طبيباً في سن الرابعة والعشرين.
٤- أستاذنا واسِع الثقافة.
٥- تدرس رنا الحقوقَ، مادتَها المفضّلة.
٦- ليست السماء غائمة.

تمرين ١٣

أ-

١-كان ضيوفها قد خرجوا، كسرت قطّتها وعاء فيه شجرة، وضعت الشجرة في وعاء جديد.
٢-مَيْ زيادة. ٣-ضيوفها ٤-سمعَتْ صوت شيء ينكسر.
٥-قطّتها البيضاء ٦-جمعت التراب ووضعته في وعاء جديد ووضعت الشجرة فيه.

ب -

١-فلسطينية ٢- في غرفة الاستقبال ٣- أسبوع ٤- الشمس

ج - إجابات متنوعة

د-

١- صواب ٢- خطأ، بعد أن خرجوا ٣- خطأ، حمدت الله أن الشجرة لم تمت.

الدرس الحادي عشر

تمرين ١

١-نِسبة / مُتَوَسِّط　　٢- تلميذ / طالب　　٣- وزير / دَولة　　٤- أيْ / يعني

٥- مُستجِد / جديد　　٦- تعليم / مدارس　　٧- سرق / لِصّ

تمرين ٢

١-فارق　　٢- عمود　　٣- تخدير　　٤- كهرباء　　٥- إصابة　　٦- مهرجان

تمرين ٣

١- أخبار متنوعة من الصحف

٢- التعليم في الجزائر، علاج اللوزتين بطريقة حديثة، حادث مرور، عملية سطو على منزل، مكتبة نسائية بجدة، معرض الكتاب بدمشق، مهرجان مسرحي بليبيا

٣- تُخدّر اللوزتان ثمّ تُسلّط أشعة الليزر عليهما لمدة دقيقتين وتُعاد هذه العملية من أربع إلى ستّ مرّات.

٤- السرقة لا تنفع.

تمرين ٤

١-٨٥٪　　٢- أقلّ من دقيقتين　　٣- شهرين　　٤- بالسيّارة

٥- شقّة رجل وزوجته　　٦-مكتبة نسائية　　٧- ٤٠ لوحة　　٨- الخط العربيّ

تمرين ٥

١-خطأ، إجباري لمدة ست سنوات.　　٢-صواب　　٣-خطأ، بعض الناس لا تنفعهم هذه العملية.

٤-خطأ، سيّارة الإسعاف　　٥-صواب

تمرين ٦

١- ربع ميزانية الدولة　　٢- ٢٨ مليون　　٣- إجابات متنوعة

٤- أكثر من ٩٩٪　　٥- حملوه خارج السيّارة

٦- جهاز تلفزيون وجهاز راديو ومسجلّة وساّعتين وحلي ومبلغ من المال

تمرين ٨

١- يُعالج الطبيبُ المرضى في عيادتِه.　　٢- يجب ألا تزيد سرعة السيّارات عن ١٠٠ كيلومتر بالساعة.

٣- عفواً يا أخي، هذا الهاتف متعطِّل.　　٤- سمعتُ البابَ يُدَقُّ فهُرِعتُ لأفتحَه.

٥- سقطت الطفلةُ على الأرضِ فأصيبَت وسال الدمُ مِن رِجلها.

تمرين ٩

١- عَلِمَ المُراسلُ الصحفي من الشرطة أن النار قد اشتعلت في شقة.
فركب سيارته وهُرِع إلى العنوان الّذي حصل عليه من الشرطة.
في الطريق إلى الشقة سمع سيارات الإطفاء تتجه إليها.
حين وصل إلى العنوان كانت إحدى سيارات الإطفاء تقف أمام المنزل.
وكان رجال الإطفاء يحاولون إطفاء النار بالماء.
بعد حوالي ربع ساعة نجح رجال الإطفاء في إطفاء النار وغادروا الشقة.
بعد خروج رجال الإطفاء من الشقة، دخلها المراسل فوجد الجدران سوداء اللون.
وكانت مياه سوداء قذرة على الأرض والأثاث.
التقط بعض الصور للشقة من الداخل قبل أن يغادرها.
ثم هُرِع المراسل بعد ذلك عائداً إلى صحيفته كي يكتب الخبر وينشره.

تمرين ١٠

١- قابل سامي صديقاً قديماً وهو في طريقه إلى العمل.
٢- نامت وجهاز التلفاز مفتوح.
٣- رأيتهم وهم يمشون.
٤- مشى إلى المدرسة والطقس بارد.

تمرين ١١

١- لا بد أن تحضّر لرحلتها إلى باريس.
٢- لابد أن يجدوا شقّة جديدة.
٣- لا بدّ أن تحصل على جواز سفر إذا أردتَ السفر إلى الخارج.
٤- لا بدّ من التخدير كي يجري الطبيب العملية.

تمرين ١٢

آ

أُجريَتْ، هُرِع، اعتُقِلَ، أُقيمَ (ماضٍ)، تُسلَّط (مضارع)

ب

١- قد نسافر إلى الأردن لنشاهد فيها الآثار الرومانية القديمة .
٢- لم يعيشوا بالدار البيضاء أكثر من سنتين.
٣- وصلنا إلى المسرح وقد انتهت الحفلة الموسيقية.
٤- هُرِعت البنت الصغيرة لتفتح الباب لأبيها.

تمرين ١٣

آ

١-قطّة على الشجرة / لصّ على السطح ٢-رجال الإطفاء يساعدون سيّدة في إنزال قطّتها من أعلى الشجرة.

٣-أمسك رجال الإطفاء بلص، اتصلوا بالشرطة. ٤-أمسك – to grab, to apprehend

٥-هرب - to flee ٦-سُلَّم- ladder ٧-سَطح- roof

٨-نعم لأنها حصلت على قطّتها واعتُقِل اللصّ.

ب

١-أمام الدار ٢- رجلاً ٣- سُلَّم ٤- الشجرة ٥- الرجل ٦- الليل

ج - إجابات متنوعة

د

١-خطأ، اللصّ كان على السطح. ٢- صواب ٣- خطأ، اتصلت بالإطفاء

٤- صواب ٥- خطأ، أمسك به رجال الإطفاء لكن الشرطة اعتقلته. ٦- خطأ، أنزلها رجل الإطفاء

ه

١-يساعدوا السيّدة في قطّتها. ٢- في أعلى الشجرة ٣- رجال الإطفاء أمسكوا به

٤-المخفر ٥- يأتي الليل

الدرس الثاني عشر

تمرين ١

١-إجازة/ عُطلة ٢- غَضِبَ / حَنِقَ ٣- مَزرعة / ريف

٤- مُغلَق / مُسدَل ٥- بِبطءٍ / بِسرعة ٦- بدأ / شَرَعَ

تمرين ٢

١-عدّاد / المَسافة ٢- مَحطّة / الوقود ٣- مُحرِّك / السيّارة ٤- جَرَس / البيت

تمرين ٣

١- عامِل ٢- سِتارة ٣- نُباح ٤- فَرَح ٥- عُطلة

تمرين ٥

١-دعوة لزيارة مزرعة وقضاء يومين فيها.

٢-زوجة الكاتب وأولاده مسافرون. دعوة لزيارة صديقه في مزرعته، لم يكن الصديق في المزرعة، العودة ليلاً إلى بيته، أخطأ في قراءة موعد الزيارة.

٣-إجازة لم تتحقّق
٤-عبد الرحمن التلمساني
٥-لأن كل شيء لم يجرِ كما يجب.
٦-في الريف

تمرين ٦

١- خطأ، ليقضي يومين عنده.
٢- خطأ، شعر بالوحدة بعد سفر زوجته وأولاده إلى بيروت.
٣- صواب
٤- خطأ، توقّف في محطّة الوقود

تمرين ٧

١- يتّسع خزّان سيّارتي لخمسين ليترا من الوقود.
٢- أشعر بشوق شديد لأمي وأبي وإخوتي.
٣- لمّا اقتربتُ من البيت وجدتُ كلّ النوافذ مفتوحة.
٤- قضى زُهَير إجازة في قرية صغيرة في الريف.

تمرين ٨

١-لأنه يحتاج إلى إجازة
٢- ظهراً
٣- أشجاراً
٤- نسي
٥- كان مربوطاً بجنزير طويل
٦- ينفّس عن غضبه
٧- محطّة وقود

تمرين ١٠

إجابات متنوعة

تمرين ١١

عملتُ ساعاتٍ طويلةً في الأسبوع الماضي وشعرتُ أني أريد أن أنام متأخرة يوم الجمعة. لذلك حين اتّصلَت بي صديقتي نور ودعتني لقضاء يوم الجمعة في مزرعة والدها اعتذرتُ وقلتُ لها آسفة وإني أريد أن أنامَ ولن أستطيعَ الذهابَ معها. في ليلة يوم الخميس أغلقتُ النوافذ في بيتي وأسدلتُ الستائر كي لا أسمع أيَّ صوتٍ من خارج البيت. في الصباح وقبل الساعة السادسة استيقظتُ على صوت جرس الهاتف. رفعتُ السمّاعة وأنا نصف نائمة وكان الرقم خطأ. عدتُ إلى السرير وحاولت أن أنام. لكن بعد دقائق سمعتُ نباح / عواء كلبٍ من الطريق. بقي الكلب تحت نافذتي ينبَحُ أكثر من عشر دقائق وشعرتُ بـخوف شديد. بعد قليل ذهب الكلب وأغمضتُ عينيَّ واسترخيتُ. مضت بضع دقائق وإذا بي أسمع شخصاً يدق بابي بقوة، فهُرِعتُ إلى البابِ لأرى ما يجري، وإذا بشرطي يقف بالباب. سألني إن كنت اتصلت بالشرطة لأشكوَ كلباً. قلت لا، فاعتذر الشرطي وذهب.
في تلك اللحظة ذهب عني النوم تماماً ولم أحبَّ أن أرجعَ إلى السرير. تذكّرتُ دعوة نور، فهُرِعتُ إلى الهاتف واتصلتُ بها راجيةً أنّها ما زالت في البيت. رنّ جرسُ هاتفها عدّة مرّات ولا من مجيب وتبيّن لي أنّها قد ذهبت إلى مزرعة والدها فقلت خَيرُها بـغيرِها.

عدّاد المسافة – odometer
محطّة الوقود – gas station
بِطاقة دعوة – invitation card
محرِّك السيّارة – car engine
جرس البيت – door bell

تمرين ١٢

١-خيرها بغيرها ٢- بالمناسبة ٣- ولا من مجيب ٤- لُحسن الحظ

تمرين ١٤

١- يسكن عمي في قرية بعيدة في الريف ولم أزرْهُ منذ أشهر.
فقرّرتُ أن أزورَه وأقضيَ معه بضعة أيّام في الريف.
لذلك اشتريتُ تذكرة قطار إلى بلدته ذهاباً وإياباً.
في صباح يوم الخميس ذهبتُ إلى مَحطّة القطار.
وصعدتُ إلى إحدى العربات وجلستُ إلى جانب النافذة.
غادر القطار المَحطّة في موعده.
وفي الطريق شاهدتُ مزارعَ كثيرةً من نافذة القطار.
وصل القطار إلى مَحطّة بلدة عمي بعد ثلاث ساعات تقريباً.
نزلتُ من العربة وكان عمي في انتظاري بالمَحطّة مع ابنه.
ركِبنا شاحنة ابن عمي الصغيرة وانطلقنا إلى دار عمي في المزرعة.
قضيتُ في دار عمي خمسة أيّام استمتعتُ بها استمتاعاً عظيماً.

تمرين ١٥

١- عَسى ٢- شَرَعَتْ ٣- عساها ٤- بدأَت ٥- عساني

تمرين ١٦

١-عَسى أن تصل الطائرة بموعدها. ٢-بدأتْ تتكلّم اللغة العربية في سنّ الخامسة عشرة.
٣-عساها تعود في الأسبوع المقبل. ٤-بدأ طلاّب صفّي يتراسلون بالعربية مع طلاّب من الوطن العربيّ.

تمرين ١٧

١-الأخَوان ٢- أبي ٣- فيها ٤- ذا ٥- أخٌ ٦- أفواه

تمرين ١٨

١-هذه الرسالة لأبيك. ٢- عندي أخٌ يسكن في ألاسكا. ٣- أهذان أخَواك؟
٤- كم أخاً لك؟ ٥- هاني رجلٌ ذو مشاكلَ كثيرة.

تمرين ١٩

١-أن تنسى ٢- أنْ تَبني ٣- أنْ تجدَ ٤- نكتبُ

تمرين ٢١

آ

١- الخروج لشراء حاجات من السوق.

٢- الخروج من البيت في طقس سيئ، تقديم الحلوى والشراب للضيوف، أماكن وقوف السيّارات، وقت إغلاق المحلاّت.

٣- المحل مغلق ٤- ماطر وبارد

٥- لأنّ أصدقاءه سيحضرون للزيارة وليس لديه ما يقدمه لهم.

٦- عاد دون حلوى وزجاج شباك سيّارته مكسور وكان يشعر بالغيظ وملابسه مبتلّة وابنه يبكي.

ب

١-لأن أصدقاءه سيحضرون ٢- سنتان ٣- على كرسي

٤- مقابل ٥- السيّارة ٦- الطفل كان في السيّارة

ج

إجابات متنوعة

د

١-صواب ٢- خطأ، ذهب الأب لشراء الحلوى.

٣- خطأ، كسر الشرطي زجاج النافذة لأن الطفل بالسيّارة والمفتح داخلها. ٤- خطأ، اعتذروا عن الحضور.

الدرس الثالث عشر

تمرين ١

١-مُسِنّ / شاب ٢- ذَهاب / إياب ٣- سَعادة / حُزْن

٤- فَقير / غَنيّ ٥- مَريض / صَحيح

تمرين ٢

١-موقِف / حافِلة ٢- أجر / نُقود ٣- حِذاء / جوارِب

٤- مُساعَدة / إعانة ٥- سَحْب / يانصيب ٦- مَريض / دواء

تمرين ٣

١-دواء ٢- معمَل ٣- نَفْس ٤- مَصروف

تمرين ٥

١- الحلم والواقع يختلفان

٢- الإعجاب بالملابس والأحذية العالية، السفر إلى أوروبا علامة الغِنى، مساعدة الناس الآخرين، الفقر والمرض

٣- لأنها تحلم أحلاماً حلوة. ٤- حين تربح الجائزة الكبرى.

٥- ساعدت به أهلها وخالها وجارتها أم خالد.

تمرين ٦

١- خطأ، كانت تحلم بأن يجعها مراقبة. ٢- خطأ، هي جارة سهام الفقيرة.

٣- صواب ٤- خطأ، أرادت أن تزور بلداناً أوروبيةً إذا ربحت الجائزة الكبرى باليانصيب.

٥- خطأ، كانت تحلم أن تشتري أحذية غالية.

تمرين ٧

١-الإعدادي ٢- ولدان وأربع بنات ٣- تساعد أهلها

٤- دكّان أبي خليل ٥- دواء ٦- ٤٨

تمرين ٨

١-إذا ربِحتُ في اليانصيب فسوف أشتري داراً جديدة. ٢-هل يكفيك مبلغ خمسمئة دولار شهرياً مصروفاً ؟

٣-قال ماهر لنفسه يجب أن أتخرّج هذه السنة. ٤-تحتاج الدول الفقيرة إلى مساعدة دول العالم الغنية.

تمرين ٩

١- كان هشام معجباً جداً بفتاة اسمها دانة من أيّام المدرسة وشعر أنه يحبّها وتمنّى أن يتزوّجَها.

لكن المشكلة أنه كان فقيراً ودانة من أسرة غنية فلم يفكّر بخطبتها. (thinking about engaging her)

حين تخرّج من الجامعة حصل على عمل جيّد في مصرف وبسرعة نجح في عمله.

بعد أن نجح بعمله قال لنفسه إنّه يجب أن يطلبها من أسرتها زوجةً له.

لذلك اتّصل بأبيها وشرح له قصّته وقال له إنّه يودّ الزواج من ابنته. (he wanted)

ردّ الأب أنّه يجب أن يسأل ابنته دانة أوّلاً.

لمّا سألها أبوها عن رأيها بهشام قالَت له إنها لا تعرفه جيّداً. (his opinion)
فسألها أبوها إن كانت تحبّ أن تراه حتّى تتعرّف عليه أكثر.
وافقَت دانة أن ترى هشاماً وأن يخرجا معاً لتعرف شعورها نحوه. (she agreed)
فخرجا إلى المُتَنَزّهات معاً وإلى المطاعم وأحياناً إلى دار السينما. (places for picnics)
لكنّ دانة أعجبها هشام بعد التعرّف عليه وشعرَت أنها قد أحبّته.
فلمّا طلبها هشام خطيبةً له وافقَت، ووافقَت أسرتها أيضاً.(she agreed / a fiancee)

تمرين ١١

١- فتحتُ البابَ فإذا بصديقي يقِفُ هناك.
٢- هل تعرفون الأستاذَ الجديدَ الّذي أتانا من تونس.
٣- لا نعرِف مَن جعل أحمد رئيس هذا النادي.
٤- أحبّ أنْ أعملَ في بلدٍ طقسُه مُعتدِل.
٥- لا أكاد أعرِف أحداً في هذا المكان.
٦- أعجبني كلّ ما رأيت في المُتحف.
٧- إذا كتبَتْ لي فسوف أكتب لَها.
٨- لَمْ تَصِلْ سامية إلى عَمَلِها حتّى الآن.
٩- لو عرفتُ أنّ الطقسَ حارّ للَبسْتُ قَميصاً.
١٠- هل تعرِفون مَن يسكن معهم في الشقّة ؟

تمرين ١٣

آ

١- معظم الناس أرادو دخول التلفاز إلى بيوتهم.
٢- رجاء الأولاد لأبيهم ليشتري لهم تلفازاً، علاقة الجيران بعضهم بعض، برامج الأخبار، المسلسلات المعروضة محلية وأجنبية.
٣-١٩٥٩. ٤-الدولة ٥-الأخبار ٦-الأقارب والأصدقاء والجيران.

ب

إجابات متنوعة

ج

١- خطأ، لم يكن عند أحد تلفاز.
٢- خطأ، شاهدوا أخباراً محلية ومن العالم.
٣- خطأ، تعرض البرامج في المساء فقط.
٤- خطأ، خمس ساعات.
٥- خطأ، كانت دهشتهم أعظم.

د

١- التلفاز سوف يدخل إلى البيوت.
٢- يشتري لهم تلفازاً.
٣- إنّ مشاهدة التلفاز مثل مشاهدة الأفلام في السينما.
٤- تموز

الدرس الرابع عشر

تمرين ١

١-وَقود / بَنزين　　٢- سَيْر / مَشي　　٣- مُغْتَبِط / سَعيد

٤- شَجاعة / بَسالة　　٥- مَكان / بُقْعة　　٦- طَريق / شارِع

تمرين ٢

١-نُجوم / الظُهْر　　٢- لَوْح / ثَلْج　　٣- بِئر / ماء

٤- مِحوَر / العَجَلة　　٥- راضي / النفس　　٦- مُنشرِح / الصَدْر

تمرين ٤

١- في مصر.　　٢- اختار مهنة الأدب، وعمل قبل ذلك مدرسا وصحفيا.

٣-اسم كتاب من كتبه.　　٤- البنزين والزيت.

تمرين ٥

١-مُنشرِح　　٢- ثَلْج　　٣- ذخيرة　　٤- نِزاع　　٥- زَبون

تمرين ٦

١-عشرين　　٢- ثلاثينات　　٣- ليملأ خزّان الماء

٤- لا يتوقف عند محطات الوقود　　٥- في الصيف أكثر من الشتاء

تمرين ٧

آ

١- خطأ، خرجت من محورها وهو يسير مغتبطاً.　　٢- صواب

ب

١- مغتبط / راضي النفس / منشرح الصدر　　٢- بنزين، نفط، زيت

٣- بنزين، زيت، عجلة، محوَر، خزّان الماء، علامة الخطر الحمراء، مقعد خلفي، خزّان البنزين

٤- الشتاء، الصيف

تمرين ١٠

١- حبّ الحلاّقين للثرثرة　　٢- إعجاب الناس باليابانيين، حبّ الناس للكلام بالسياسة والأمور الدولية، عدم خروج الرجال إلى الطريق دون غطاء رأس.　　٣- في مصر.　　٤- أخبار الحرب الروسية اليابانية

٥- لأنه رسم أشكالاً هندسيةً على رأسه.　　٦- يركض في الشارع دون غطاء رأس.

تمرين ١١

آ

١-لصديق الكاتب ٢- الحلاّقين ٣- رأس زبونه ٤- لسان الزبون ارتبط

ب

١- خطأ، يغطون رؤوسهم ٢- خطأ، كان يعجبه الجيش الياباني

٣- صواب ٤- خطأ، كان هناك زبائن آخرون. ٥- صواب

تمرين ١٣

١-قامَت الحرب العالمية الثانية عامَ ١٩٣٩. ٢-رسم داڤينشي صورة المسيح مع أصحابه وهو يتناول العشاء.

٣-عمل لِنكَن محامياً قبل أن يكون رئيساً. ٤-عرف الناس النفط في العراق منذ آلاف السنين.

٥-تقص رانية شعرها قصيراً بينما يحبّه زوجها طويلاً.

تمرين ١٤

١- كان عدد من الناس يجلسون في مقهى إلى جانب الطريق.
وكان هناك سيّارات تسير في وسط الشارع أمام المقهى.
فجأةً ظهرَت قطّة أمام إحدى السيّارات فانحرف السائق إلى اليمين.
لكنّ السائق لم يستطع أن يوقف السيّارة فصعِدَت على الرصيف.
استمرَّت السيّارة في السير على الرصيف ودخلَت المقهى.
لحسن الحظّ لم يُصَب أحد من الزبائن.
إلاّ أنّ الواجهة الزجاجية وعدداً من الطاولات والكراسي تحطّمَت.

تمرين ١٥

كانت غرفة نومي حارة جداً فلم أستطع أن أنام. لذلك نهضتُ وذهبتُ إلى النافذة وفتحتُها، لكن صوت الشارع دخل الغرفة ومنعني من النوم. لهذا قرّرتُ أن أقرأ قليلاً فذهبتُ إلى المكتبة وأخذتُ كتاباً وشرعتُ أقرأ حتى نمتُ.

تمرين ١٧

و (لمّا) p، و(صعدوا) t، و(جلسوا) t، ثمّ t، و(عمله) p، و(لم) p، فـ(قال) p، و(طلب) c، فـ(رفض) t، و(قال) c، و(طبل) p، أو c، فـ(اضطُرّ) t، لأنّ c، و(لم) c

تمرين ١٩

١-بيعَتْ ٢- أواسِط ٣- أخذوا ٤- حمراء اللون ٥- لاحظَتْ

تمرين ٢٠

آ

١-أقلّ من ثلاث سنوات ٢- ٦٠٠٠ ٣- تحت سن

ب

١-صواب ٢- خطأ، اسم المديرة بغدادي ٣- خطأ، يسكنون مع أسرهم.

ج

١-تعليمهم ٢- الصحية ٣- ومكاتب الدولة

د

١-توفير مستقبل جيّد للأيتام. ٢- حصلوا على عمل في مكاتب الدولة والشركات التجارية

٣- يعمل وينشئ عائلة

الدرس الخامس عشر

تمرين ١

١-بَلى / نعم ٢- حُجرة / غرفة ٣- دين / إسلام ٤- جائزة / نوبل

٥- سورة / قرآن ٦-جنّة / سماء ٧- نال / حصل على

تمرين ٢

١-نعم / كَلا ٢- مَرِضَ / شُفِيَ ٣- جميل / قَبيح ٤- هُدنة / حَرْب

٥- صَمَتَ / هَتَفَ ٦- مُؤَدَّب / شقيّ ٧- جنّة / نار

تمرين ٣

١- سخرية ٢- يا ٣- مَفرَش ٤- تثاءب

تمرين ٦

١- الفكرة الرئيسة تعايش الأديان ومن الأفكار الثانوية تعليم الدين بالمدرسة وأي الأديان أصحّ وانتماء الإنسان لدين معيّن وتسامح الأطفال الديني ومعنى الله بالنسبة للطفل وأعمال الناس في الدنيا والموت والجنّة والنار.

٢- إجابات متنوعة ٣- تربية حديثة تعطي الطفل فرصة التفكير والتعبير عن نفسه.

٤- حتّى تفهم الفرق بين الأديان. ٥- أراد متابعة سلسلة الأجداد إلى ما لا نهاية.

٦- لا لأنه يعتبرها صغيرة لا تفهم هذه الأمور. ٧- نبي المسلمين

٨- بقدرة خاصة ٩- جعل الناس يعملون أشياء حسنة قبل أن يموتوا.

١٠- لا، لأنها نهرت ابنتها حين سألت عن الموت. ١١- علامات استفهام راسبة في أعماقه.

تمرين ٧

آ

١ -درس الدين ٢- تطَرّز ٣- صديقة البنت ٤- الصلاة والعبادة

٥- في كلّ مكان ٦- ابن خال البنت ٧- الجنّة ٨- طبيعة الله

ب

١ -خطأ، لأن أباها مسيحي. ٢- صواب ٣- خطأ، يتَبِعون آباءهم.

٤- صواب ٥- صواب ٦- خطأ، بعض الأنبياء رأوه كما يقال.

٧- خطأ، في كلّ مكان. ٨- خطأ، توفّي ٩- صواب

ج

إجابات متنوعة

تمرين ٨

١ -حوار ٢- حقيقة ٣- فرق ٤- مَرِض ٥- حيرة

تمرين ٩

١- إذا عمل الإنسان عملاً حسناً ومات ذهب إلى الجنّة.

٢- سورة الفاتحة هي أول سورة في القرآن الكريم.

٣- أنا إنسان حرّ أفعل ما أريد.

٤- تفضّل أمّي أن تأكل الفواكه بعد الطعام.

٥- سأقابله يوم الخميس بالرغم من انشغالي بالدراسة.

تمرين ١٠

١- تثاءبت الطفلة الصغيرة وفتحت عينيها في سريرها صباحاً.
قبل أن تنهض من السرير فكّرت فيما ستفعل ذلك اليوم.
أوّلاً ستلبس ملابسها وتذهب إلى المدرسة.
وفي المدرسة ستدخل غرفةّ الدرس وتتعلّم القراءة وبعض الأغاني.
ثمَّ تخرُج مع صاحباتها إلى الملعب وتلعب معهنّ.
وفي نهاية النهار سوف تعود إلى دارها متعبة.
لم يعجبْها ما ستفعل ذلك اليوم فقررّت أن تبقى في البيت.
لكنّها فكّرت أن أمّها لن تتركها تبقى في البيت دون مدرسة.
لذلك تظاهرت أنّها مريضة ولا قدرة لها على الذهاب إلى المدرسة.

تمرين ١١

١-لِمَ ٢- مِمَّن ٣- عَمّ ٤- عَمَّ

٥- عَمَّن ٦- إلامَ ٧- أَلَم ٨- مِمَّ

تمرين ١٢

آ

١-العلوم والرياضيات ٢- بأن يكون ممثلاً ٣- لأنه قال لها إنه يجب أن يعمل في العيادة مساء وسوف يقابلها في المسرح. ٤- نعم ٥- حُلم تحقّق

ب

١-صواب ٢- خطأ، هي صيدلانية ٣- خطأ، في التاسعة ٤- خطأ، لم تعرف أنه كان سيمثّل.

٥- خطأ، كان يذهب وزوجته مرّة بالأسبوع. ٦- خطأ، لأنها كانت تظنّ أنه سيدخل من الباب.

ج

١-المدرسة ٢- عيادة ٣- ممثّلاً ٤- أصدقائه

٥- على المسرح ٦- في الساعة التاسعة

الدرس السادِس عشر

تمرين ١

١-غَنيّ / فَقير ٢- مَرَض / صَحّة ٣- وفاة / وِلادة ٤- اِستيقظ / نام

٥- أعطى / أَخَذَ ٦- اِعتزّ / ذلَّ ٧- ذَكَرٌ / أُنْثى

تمرين ٢

١-السُلّ / الكوليرا ٢- مُنظَّمة / جمعية ٣- مقالة / صَحيفة ٤- صليب / المسيحية

٥- عثماني / تركيّ ٦- دُهن / زيت ٧- شَهِدَ / رأى ٨- مُنفرِد / وحيد

تمرين ٣

١-متخلّف ٢- نقطة ٣- اِفتتح ٤- عدم

تمرين ٦

١- حين امتدت الدولة العثمانية في القرن السادس عشر وقعت بلاد الشام تحت الحكم العثمانيّ لمدة ٤٠٠ سنة تقريباً

٢- بدأ عام ١٩٢٠ وانتهى عام ١٩٤٤. ٣-نعم

٤- الفكرة الرئيسة حول دور المرأة في المجتمع، ومن الأفكار الثانوية تعليم المرأة والمرض الّذي ازداد أثناء الانتداب الفرنسيّ ونظرة الناس إلى المرأة المتعلمة تعليماً عالياً والصحّة.

٥- تكرّرت حوادث الوفيات بين الأطفال بسبب مرض السلّ والكوليرا وغيرهما.

٦- إجابات متنوعة.

تمرين ٧

آ

١-صيدلياً ٢- علي طه ٣- أحسن ٤- الحكم العثماني ٥- شركة سورية

٦- زوجها ٧- جمعية خيرية ٨- ثلاثة كتب ٩- شُرْب الكثير من الماء

ب

١- خطأ، لم تنجح بحملتها الانتخابية. ٢- خطأ، تأقلم زملاؤها معها بسرعة.

٣- صواب ٤- خطأ، لم ترزق بأطفال. ٥- خطأ، هي جمعية خيرية.

تمرين ٨

١-أستيقظ في الساعة السادسة صباحاً. ٢-أثبت أخي أنه قادر على العمل والدراسة معاً.

٣-انتخبتُ المرشّح المستقِل في الانتخابات الماضية. ٤-حصل فريد على عمل جيّد عوَّضه عن سنوات فَقْره.

٥-استولى المنتصرون في الحرب العالمية الأولى على ممتلكات الدولة العثمانية .

تمرين ٩

١- انتَسَبَت سلمى إلى جمعية خيريّة لتساعد الفقراء.
وكان عملها التعرّف على الأسَر الفقيرة.
وقد تعرّفَت من خلال عملها على عدد من هذه الأسَر المحتاجة.
وشعرَت بأنّها يجب أن تساعد هؤلاء الناس.
فزارَت شركات كبيرة تطلب منهم مالاً لمساعدة هؤلاء الفقراء.
وقد تبرّعَت الشركات بالمال والمنتجات لمساعدتِهم.
بقيَت سلمى عُضوة في الجمعية إلى أن انتقل عمل زوجها إلى مدينة أخرى.
لكنّ سلمى لم تنسَ أنْ ترسل للجمعية مالاً كلّ شهر.

تمرين ١١

آ

١-إلاّ أنّه ٢- بل من الموصل ٣- حيث يسكن أخوها هناك ٤- لأن

٥- كما عمِل ٦- لأنها مريضة ٧- حتّى ٨- إلى جانب أنّها

ب إجابات متنوعة

تمرين ١٢

١-الّتي ٢- الّذين ٣- ما ٤- اللذان

٥- مَنْ ٦- اللاتي ٧- اللتين ٨- الّذي

تمرين ١٣

آ

١- الفكرة الرئيسة سيرة هدى شَعراوي ومن الأفكار الثانوية ثورة مصر على الإنكليز والحجاب والجمعيات الخيرية ودور المرأة والمؤتمرات النسائية.

٢- في جنوب مصر. ٣- كان رئيس أوّل مجلس نيابي في مصر

٤- قامت ثورة مصر على الإنكليز ٥- ٦٨ سنة

ب

١- خطأ، ثلاث لغات. ٢- صواب ٣- صواب

ج

١- يوم يتذكر فيه العرب وفاة هدى شعراوي.

٢- كان والد هدى شعراوي أوّل رئيس مجلس نيابي مصري وكان زوجها عضو الجمعية التشريعية. أسّست هدى جمعيات خيرية ونسائية وقادت المظاهرات ضد الإنكليز وكانت أوّل مسلمة تخرج سافرة في مصر.

٣- تحرّر المرأة المصرية / دور أكبر للمرأة العربية.

د

١-الإنكليز ٢- سافرة ٣- الاتحاد النسائي ٤- المصرية

ه

إجابات متنوعة

الدرس السابِع عشر

تمرين ١

١- جيش / عسكريّ ٢- قصر / قلعة ٣- موسيقا / فنّ ٤- معركة / حَرب

٥- خليفة / ملك ٦- سور / جدار ٧- نافورة / ماء ٨- أسَد / حيوان

٩- طول / عرْض

تمرين ٢

١-سفح ٢- ضَعف ٣- دولة ٤- سقوط

تمرين ٦

١- فتح الأندلس وتاريخها

٢- استطلاع موسى بن نصير أحوال إسبانيا، إرسال طارق بن زياد لفتحها عام ٧١٢، جعل إشبيلية أوّل عاصمة للأندلس، تأسيس دولة أموية جديدة بعد سقوطها بدمشق، إعلان الخلافة عام ٩٢٩، ضعف الأندلس بعد سقوط الخلافة عام ١٠٣١، سقوط غرناطة.

٣- موسى بن نصير ٤-عام ٧١١ لاستطلاع أحوال إسبانيا

٥- إشبيلية، وقد كانت الأندلس تابعة للدولة الأموية بدمشق ٦-أيام الخلافة الأموية

٧- نشوب الثورات سقوط الخلافة ، ظهور دويلات الطوائف، تعاون الطوائف مع أعدائهم ضد بعضهم لبعض.

٨- عام ١٤٩٢ ٩- الاتحاد في دولة واحدة يجعلهم أقوى ١٠- إجابات مختلفة

تمرين ٧

١-سرّاً ٢- إشبيلية ٣- ١٠٣١ ٤- دويلات صغيرة ٥- غرناطة

تمرين ٨

آ

١- قصر الحمراء أجمل قصر في الأندلس

٢- يحوي القصر أبهاء وقاعات، هناك أقواس عديدة على أعمدة، الماء والنافورات تضفي جمالاً على القصر

٣- سامي الكيالي، ممثل سورية في اليونيسكو

٤- ربّما بسبب لون أسواره وجدرانه

٥- بهو السباع

ب

١- خطأ، أرسل طارق بن زياد على رأس جيش. ٢- خطأ، الأمويون ٣- صواب

٤- خطأ، انتصر المسيحيون على المسلمين ٥- صواب

تمرين ٩

آ

١-البحرات والنوافير ٢- هضبات عالية ٣- بهو البركة ٤- العدل ٥- أسداً

ب

١- خطأ، في القرن ١٤ ٢- خطأ، ممثل سورية باليونيسكو

٣- خطأ، بنيت واجهة قصر العدل على شكل حدوة فرس ٤- صواب

٥- خطأ، يتكوّن مدخل القصر من أربعة أبراج

تمرين ١٠

١- خرج والي البلاد على رأسِ جيشٍ من ألفي مقاتل.

٢- ازدهرت العلوم والفنّون والآداب بعد انتهاء الحرب لكن لم يتحسّن الاقتصاد

٣- تتكوّن المدينة من ستّة أحياء رئيسة بالإضافة إلى السوق التجارية.

٤- نظم الوزير لسان الدين بن الخطيب أجمل القصائد الشِعرية الأندلسية.

تمرين ١١

١- صار مُعاوية بن أبي سُفيان والي الشام في عهد الخليفة الثاني عمر بن الخطاب.

٢- وقد استطاع مُعاوية الاستيلاء على الحكم في عهد عليّ بن أبي طالب الخليفة الرابع.

٣- وفي عام ٦٦١ تمكّن مُعاوية من تأسيس الدولة الأمويّة ونقل العاصمة إلى دمشق.

٤- وكان الأمويّون يفضّلون العرب على غيرهم من المسلمين.

٥- لذلك ظهرت معارضة شديدة ضدّ الأمويّين خصوصاً بين غير العرب في الجزيرة والعراق وفارس.

٦- وتحالَف العبّاسيّون أعداءُ الأمويّين مع الفرس وثاروا عليهم.

٧- قاوم الخليفة مروان الثاني الثورة على دولته طوال أيّام حكمه (من ٧٤٤ إلى ٧٥٠) لكنّ الثورة العبّاسيّة كانت أقوى منه.

٨- وهكذا سقطت الدولة الأمويّة عام ٧٥٠ وانتقلت العاصمة إلى بغداد وقُتِلَ معظم الأمويّين.

٩- لكنّ أحد أفراد الأسرة الأمويّة (عبد الرحمن بن مُعاوية) نجا من الموت وفرّ إلى الأندلس حيث أسّس دولة أمويّة هناك عام ٧٥٦.

تمرين ١٢

١-تدفّق / النهر	٢- عَصَفَت / الريح	٣- نظم / الشِعر	٤- لحّن / أغنيّة
٥- أطلَق / اسماً	٦- نَشِبَت / الحرب	٧- فتح / بلداً	٨- هزم العدّو

تمرين ١٣

١- مُؤلِّف	كاتب	٢- أتى	جاء
٣- عادَ	رجع	٤- بَعَثَ	أرسل
٥- تِلْوَ	بعد	٦- فَرْد	شَخْص
٧- مَسْجد	جامع	٨- رُخام	مَرمَر
٩- عَقْد	قَوْس	١٠- جَمال	رَوْعة
١١- استمرّ	طلّ	١٢- سنة	عام

تمرين ١٤

١- قصر، قلعة ، بنى، قاعة، بهو، حمّام، مسجد، قوس، عمود، رُخام، بحرة، نافورة، سور، جدار، حديقة، مدخل، برج، قبّة، رواق، عقد

٢- والٍ، قائد، خليفة، خِلافة، دولة، حاكم، دويلة، مملكة، ملِك

٣- جيش، مقاتل، ثورة، سَقَطَ، فَتَحَ، عدو، معركة، انسحب، تساقط

٤- الخلافة الأموية، ملوك الطوائف، ممالك، المرابطون، الموحدون

٥- شِعر، موشّح، أديب، قصيدة، بَيت شِعر، مغنٍّ تَلحين

تمرين ١٥

التفضيل: أفضل، أولى، أكثر، آخِر، أهم، أعظم، أظهر، أكبر، أحسن

المجهول: قُتِل، سُمّيَت، هُزِموا، يُقصَد، بُنِيَ، بُدِئَ، حُصِّن، غُطِّيَت، بُنِيت، نُظِم، تُهجَري، أُجَنّ

تمرين ١٦

أ

١- الفكرة الرئيسة مساعدة الخليفة الأموي بدمشق لأميرة إسبانية في استعادة أملاكها من أعمامها، ومن الأفكار الثانوية سفر سارة من إسبانيا إلى دمشق، استيلاء أعمام سارة على أملاكها، زواج سارة من أحد رجال هشام بن عبد الملك، تأسيس عبد الرحمن بن معاوية بن هشام بن عبد الملك الدولة الأموية بالأندلس.

٢- إجابات متنوعة ٣- إلى ميناء عسقلان. ٤- عبد الرحمن الداخل

ب

١-خطأ، استولى أبناؤه على أملاك سارة، ٢- صواب ٣- صواب

٤- خطأ، جعل العاصمة قرطبة ٥- خطأ، تزوجا وعاشا في إشبيلية

ج

إجابات متنوعة

د

١- ثلاثة أعمام ٢- لتطلب المساعدة ٣- ولدان ٤- عيسى بن مُزاحِم ٥- إشبيلية

الدرس الثامِن عشر

تمرين ١

١-توفّي / دُفِنَ ٢- قانون / شَرْع ٣- حَقّ / صَدَّق ٤- قصر / بَلاط

٥- شرح / تفسير ٦- كَوْن / عالَم ٧- دام / استمرّ ٨- سورة / أية

تمرين ٢

١-اتّهم / عفا (عن) ٢- رَضِيَ / غَضِب ٣- حُبّ / كُره ٤- مخالِف / ملائم

٥- كُفْر / إيمان ٦- ظاهِر / باطِن ٧- غِذاء / سُمّ ٨- هاجم / أيّد

تمرين ٣

١-مدفَن ٢- صِراع ٣- دَفَن ٤- تهافُت ٥- لخَّص ٦- مَنَعَ

تمرين ٦

١- إجابات متنوعة، مثلاً خالف ببعض آرائه العقيدة الإسلامية، شرح أعمال أرسكو)

٢- إجابات مختلفة (مثلاً: تعرّفه إلى ابن طُفَيل والخليفة، واتّهامه بالكفر)

٣- الكليّات، فصل المقال، تهافت التهافت

٤- عرّف الغرب بأرِسطو وقام بشرح أعماله

٥- اتُّهِم بالكُفر

تمرين ٧

آ

١-٧٢ عاماً ٢- كفيلسوف وطبيب ٣- الرأي العام ٤- تهافت التهافت ٥- مذهب

٦- الوفاق ٧- البعث ٨- الأعراف ٩- حقّ

ب

١-صواب ٢- خطأ، أخذه عن أبي مروان البلنسي وأبي جعفر هارون ٣- خطأ، كُرْه أعدائه له

٤- خطأ، توفّي في مرّاكش ودُفن في قرطبة ٥- صواب ٦- صواب ٧- خطأ، الفلاسفة فقط

تمرين ٨

١- الأدب، اللغة، الطبّ، الفقه، الفلسفة، المنطق، علم النفس، العقل، الفلك، الحكمة، الجدل، علم الكلام

٢- ابن، أب، جد ٣- قاضٍ، قاضي القضاة، ملك، خليفة، أسقف

٤- أمّا، فـ، لأن، و، إلا أن، ك، إذا، أي، إنّما

تمرين ٩

١- وُلِد ابنُ خَلِّكان في عام ١٢١١ م بالعراق من أسرة البرامِكة المشهورة.
٢- وهي الأسرة الّتي كان منها وُزَراء هارون الرشيد.
٣- درس علوم الدين في حلب ودمشق والقاهرة.
٤- عيَّنه السلطان بيبَرس قاضيَ القُضاة في دمشق بعد أن صار عالِماً معروفاً.
٥- ألَّف ابن خَلِّكان "كتاب وَفَيات الأعيان".
٦- وهذا الكتاب يحوي سيَرَ أكثر من ٨٠٠ رجل مشهور.
٧- ويُعتبَر كتابه هذا مرجعاً هامّاً في تاريخ الشخصيّات العربيّة والإسلاميّة.
٨- ولا يوجَد إلاّ كتاب الواقِدي بهذه الأهميّة.

تمرين ١٠

١-لم أفهم نظرية النسبية لأينشاتاين فشرحها لي أستاذي. ٢-وُلِد ابن طُفَيْل ببلدة آش في الأندلس ونشأ بغرناطة.
٣-تعرّفنا على جارنا أبي عِماد مِن خِلال ابنتِه رَنا. ٤-حاولَت لَمى أن توافق بين عملها ودراستها فلم تنجح.
٥-تُرجِم عدد كبير من مؤلّفات نجيب محفوظ إلى اللغة الأجنبية.

تمرين ١١

١- طلبتُ كتابَه فأعطاني إيّاه.
٢- قَطَّعَت التفاحةَ وأطعمتهم إيّاها.
٣- سألناه عن الصور من رحلتِه فأرانا إيّاها.

تمرين ١٢

آ

١-سيرة ابن القفّع ٢- ترجمته لقصص هندية وقتل الخليفة له
٣- ربّما لأنه اتُّهِم باعتِناق العقيدة المانوية. ٤- كليلة ودمنة

ب

١-صواب ٢- خطأ، عمل كاتباً بالدولة ٣- خطأ، بسبب اتّهامه باعتناق المانوية ٤- صواب

ج

إجابات متنوعة

د

١-إسلامي ٢- الفهلوية ٣- سياسية ٤- خليفة

الدرس التاسِع عشر

تمرين ١

١- حِلم / غَضَب ٢- طارَ / وَقَعَ ٣- شَبّ / شابَ ٤- حَرب / سلام

٥- عَدوّ / صَديق ٦- عاميّ / فَصيح ٧- جاهِل / عاقِل ٨- ضَجيج / هُدوء

تمرين ٢

١- حِكمة / مَثَل ٢- اختار / أخذ ٣- أسد / شِبْل ٤- ناقة / جَمَل

٥- مَولاي / سَيِّدتي ٦- عير / حَمير ٧- خَيْر / أفضل ٨- شَرْوى / مِثل

تمرين ٣

١- ناقة ٢- فائدة ٣- رَذاذ ٤- رحى ٥- خُدعة

تمرين ٥

١- ١٩ ٢- ٨ ٣- ٤١ ٤- ٤ ٥- ١٢

٦- ١٧ ٧- ٤٢ ٨- ٣ ٩- ١١ ١٠- ٣٤

تمرين ٦

١- ٧ ٢- ٤٠ ٣- ٣٠ ٤- ٢ ٥- ٤

٦- ٢٥ ٧- ٥ ٨- ١٠ ٩- ٣٩

تمرين ٧

١- مطر ٢- صار ٣- نضح ٤- توضيح، إظهار

٥- هزم ٦- عاشَرَ ٧- صمت

تمرين ٨

١- ٢٩ في الدرس يشبه ٢ في الاستماع.

a.	Speech is silver, but silence is golden.	6
b.	A bird in the hand is worth two in the bush.	8
c.	Actions speak louder than words.	5
d.	Prevention is better than cure.	4
e.	Cleanliness is next to godliness.	11
f.	Let bygones be bygones.	12
g.	Out of sight, out of mind.	7
h.	A tempest in a teapot.	14

3. *Never put off till tomorrow what can be done today.*

٤- ٩

الدرس العشرون

تمرين ١

١-لاقَ / ناسَبَ　　٢- مُخَيِّلة / تَصَوَّرات　　٣- سَعى (إلى) / حاوَلَ

٤- هَزَمَ / تَغَلَّبَ (على)　　٥- خاطِر / بال　　٦- مَنْزِلة / مكانة

تمرين ٢

١-كانَ / وَمازالَ　　٢- بِطَبيعة / الحال　　٣- حَلَّ / مَحَلّ

٤- وَمِن / ثَمّة　　٥- بِلا حَسَب / ولا نَسَبٍ

تمرين ٤

١-فسيفساء　　٢- مُحاصَرة　　٣- سَلَبَ　　٤- سَعى　　٥- مَثْوى

تمرين ٥

١-نظم الشعر　　٢- الحفظ　　٣- متسللةً　　٤- مدمّرة　　٥- أقواله ونشاطاته

تمرين ٦

١- أمّ	٥- خالدة	٩- كلام
٢- نوافذ	٦- حوّلوه	١٠- غيمة
٣- أصدقاء	٧- مائدة	١١- قاعدة
٤- زائدة	٨- أعيد	١٢- الوطن

تمرين ٧

١- إجابات متنوعة (مثلاً يرمز السِجن إلى الحياة في الغربة والنوارس قد ترمز إلى الطيور التي رآها محمود والعشبة ترمز إلى البيت إلى الوطن إلى مسقط رأسه والقمر رمز لشيء مشترك بين فلسطين والحياة في الغربة، أو قد تشير الطيور إلى الصهاينة الذين سرقوا أرضه وسرقوا خيراتها لأن النورس يطلق عليه (قرصان البحر) لأنه يقوم بسرقة بيض الطيور الأخرى، فيتغذى عليها وعلى فراخها.)

٢- إجابات متنوعة (مثلاً إعادة الأراضي الفلسطينية المحتلة إلى الفلسطينيين.

٣- إجابات متنوعة (مثلاً الرؤية الواضحة في القصيدة تتلخص بمبدأ عدم التنازل عن الأرض، فمهما ابتعد الفلسطيني أو اغترب أو نُفِيَ ستبقى فلسطين بداخله أبد الآبدين.)

تمرين ٨

١- تتغلّب على الموت الفنون والأغاني والآثار الفرعونية والنقوش في الصخور.

٢- إنّ الفكرة الأساسية التي يركز درويش عليها هي أنّ الإنسان يفنى لكن أثره يبقى مخلداً، وهذا بحد ذاته انتصار على الموت والفناء. وأمام هذه الرؤية يستحضر درويش آثاراً فنية وأدبية قديمة ما زالت خالدة على الرغم من فناء أجساد أصحابها (مسلّة المصري، مقبرة الفراعنة، الأغاني، النقوش على حجارة معبد).

٣- في المقطع بُعْد فلسفي وفكري يؤكد فيه الشاعر أنّ الموت يُفني الجسد وينال منه فقط، لكنه غير قادر على إفناء الأثر الأدبي أو الفنون عامة.

٤- إجابات متنوعة

تمرين ٩

١- قال الشهيدُ لمستمعيه: أَعِدْ للقواميس كُلَّ الكلام الذي كُنْتَ أَهْدَيْتَنِيه، وخفِّفْ عن النائمين طنين الصدى لا تَسِرْ في الجنازة: لا تُصَدِّقْ زغاريدهُنَّ. وصدّق أَبي حين ينظر في صورتي باكياً.

٢- إنّ أهم الأسباب التي دفعت الشهيد لان يضحي بنفسه هو العجز عن تحقيق الحياة الطبيعية واليومية.

٣- إلى ماذا يفتقر الشهيد في حياته وبمَ يتمتع؟ فالشهيد بنظر درويش هو الإنسان المحروم من الحياة الطبيعية. في ضوء هذه الرؤية يتجلى الشهيد عند محمود درويش محباً للحياة على الأرض، لكنها لم تتحقق له، ففتّش عنها في مكان آخر. والشاعر -هنا- يطرح قضية الشهيد ليس بثوب الأيدولوجيات الدينية التي تقدّس الشهادة وتركّز على ثواب الآخرة للشهيد، وإنّما يطرح قضية الشهيد من خلال رؤية إنسانية حضارية تركز على معاناة الشهيد الذي لم يستطع تحقيق حقه بالحلم، والوطن، وبالحياة الطبيعية التي كان يتمناها على أرضه.

٤- يصوّر الشاعر صورة واضحة بشأن وضع العائلة بعد الاستشهاد والمعاناة التي عاشتها.

٥- إجابات متنوعة

تمرين ١٠

١- المتكلّم سجين يخاطب شرطياً إسرائيلياً

٢- في القصيدة أبعاد ثقافية واجتماعية كثيرة فمن حيث الثقافية تبدو من خلال حديثه عن الهوية، وعن اغتصاب الأرض، وعن مخططات العدو، أما الاجتماعية فتبدو من خلال حديثه عن اللباس الفلسطيني، وعن حالة القرى الفلسطينية، ووضعها الاجتماعي السيئ.

٣- تحمل مقومات الهوية العربية العامة والفلسطينية خاصة التي تتجلى في (اللغة ، العادات والتقاليد، حب الوطن، شموخ النفس، الإباء وعدم الاستسلام، التمسك بالتاريخ والأصول والمنابت، وعدم التنازل عن الأرض للمُغْتصبين).

تمرين ١١

أسلّ: to remove s.th. gently — محجر – quarry — الصدقات – alms

أصْغُر – to be submissive — رَسَت – to be stable — كوخ - cabin — ناطور بالعامية – حارس

تمرين ١٣

١- الولد – المقصود به الشاعر نفسه / الرحلة – عبارة عن سفره وابتعاده عن الوطن / الأمّ – الوالدة والوطن / شجرة الفل – ذكر الشاعر لـ (شجرة الفل) يوحي ويرمز إلى ارتباط الشاعر الوثيق بداره وأبيه وعائلته وموطنه دمشق.

٢- أهميتها تبرز في شدة إلتصاق الشاعر بوطنه، وكأنه لا يريد أن يفارقه، فأخذ معه كل معالمه البارزة

٣- إجابات متنوعة (مثلاً: تشبيه الأحزان بالعصافير التي تتواجد في كل مكان أينما ذهب و أن العلاقة بينهما هي الكثرة أي كثرة أحزانه)

٤- ما حدث للولد أنه خاض معترك الحياة صغيرا، ثم كبر وأصبح أبا، حدث كل ذلك بسرعة، إلا أنه ما زالت أحلامه أحلام الصغار.

٥- إجابات متنوعة (مثلاً الأم ودمشق رمز مشترك يدل على ابتعاده عن أحضانهما لأن ابتعاده لم يحدث حقيقة لوجود الوطن معه بكل تفاصيله ، وحب الأم باق بداخله والوطن كذلك.

٦- إجابات متنوعة (مثلاً: المقصود هو أن شدة الحب قد يؤدي إلى إيذاء المحبوب وكأن الشاعر أخذ هذا المعنى من القول الدارج: (ومن الحب ما قتل)

تمرين ١٤

١- لا يستطيع الشاعر نطق اسم دمشق إلا إذا أحسّ بوجودها في فؤاده.

٢- يقول نزار إن حبل مشيمته لم ينقطع وأنه لايزال مشدوداً إلى رحم دمشق وإن دلت هذه الاستعارة على شيء تدل على كثرة محبته لها وقرابته إليها رغم عيش حياته في الغربة سنوات طويلة.

٣- قال الشاعر إن دمشق ليست تشبيهاً لهذه الأمور أي الجنّة والقصيدة والعروبة بل تتكون وتتشكل دمشق فعلاً من هذه المقومات.

٤- تشمل بساتين الغوطة ذكريات طفولة نزار.

٥- لو فتحت ثقبا في أبجدية اللغة العربية لوجدت جمال الغوطة قد تمثّلت فيها

٦- يفتقر حائط الصين العظيم المكونات الدمشقية التي يشتاق إليها الشاعر حين يبتعد عن وطنه الحبيب.

٧- من هلوساته أنه يظن نفسه سفرجلة أو رغيف خبز أو سطل عرقسوس أو كوم صبارة أو عنقود عنب أو ركوة قهوة أو سرب سنونو أو قطة شامية أو نافورة ماء. يشبه نفسه بهذه الأشياء لأنه يعتبرها جزءا من حياته، بل هي مكونة لذاته

٨- صار نزار قطعة فسيفساء دمشق عندما صدر كتابه الذي يحمل عنوان: "دمشق...نزار قباني"
٩- يتمنى أن يصبح جزءا من تاريخ دمشق. ترمز هذه الأشياء إلى معالم دمشق وإلى ذكريات طفولته

تمرين ١٥

I am a ring from the Jeweler of Damascus.
A linguistic fabric from the looms of its tailor.
A poetic voice emanating from its throat.
A love letter written by its hand.
A cloud of cinnamon and anise wandering in its markets.
A Jasmine tree my mother left at my window.
Whose white flowers blossom . . . every year.

ب – إجابات متنوعة

تمرين ١٦

أ

١- هوية ٢- لُغاتٍ ٣- قِيَم المدينة والحياة المدنية

ب

١- صواب ٢- خطأ، تتجاوز شهرته حدود منطقة الشرق الأوسط
٣- خطأ، ترعرع أدونيس في ظروف صعبة

ج

١- مجلتا شعر والمواقف ٢- رؤية شاملة للإنسان والحياة. ٣- الحداثة

د

١- دخل المدرسة في الثالثة عشرة من عمره.
٢- المشكلة ليست شعرية إنما اجتماعية وما لم يدخل المجتمع العربي تجربة الحداثة فمن الصعب أن يتأسس شعر حديث.
٣- بسبب المؤسسة الدينية ثابتة متخلفة حسب رأي أدونيس الأمر الذي أدى إلى شق كبير بين الفرد العربي والمؤسسة وأيضاً ليس ثمة تغيرات في المجتمع.

مراجعةُ القواعد

تمرين ١

فعل: سافر، تقع، وصلا، نزلا، كان، وضع، ذهبا، طلبتْ، طلب، أحضر، شرب، يظنّان

فاعل: سامي وزوجتُه، (هي ضمير مستتر)، ألف نزلا، الزوجان، حنينُ، النادل،

مفعول به: المدينةَ، حقائبَها، سمكاً، كبّةً، قهوةً، الضمير (ها) في كلمة (شرباها)

مبتدأ: اللاذقيةُ، الطقسُ (اسم كان)، سامي، الطعامَ (اسم أنَّ)، طعامَ (اسم أنَّ)

خبر: ميناءٌ، جميلاً (خبر كان)، جيّدٌ (خبر أنَّ)، فطلب، يظنان

تمرين ٢

١- يعملان: مرفوع بثبوت النون لأنه من الأفعال الخمسة.

٢- الجامعة: مرفوعة لأنها مبتدأ.

٣- طبيبٌ: مرفوع لأنه خبر.

٤- حاسوباً: منصوب لأنه مفعول به.

٥- الأستاذُ: مرفوع لأنه اسم كان.

٦- متأخراً: منصوب لأنه خبر كان.

٧- هالةُ: مرفوعة لأنها اسم تكون.

٨- السماءَ: منصوبة لأنها اسم إنّ.

٩- طبيباً: منصوب لأنه خبر صار.

١٠- زوجُها: مرفوع لأنه فاعل.

١١- شقةً: منصوبة لأنها مفعول به.

١٢- موقفٍ: مجرور لأنه مسبوق بحرف جر.

تمرين ٣

١- زميلُ ٢- أحمدَ ٣- ميناء ٤- كتابَ

٥- زوجةُ ٦- أوّلِ ٧- مركزَ

تمرين ٤

١- مَشَيْنا عَلى شاطِئِ البَحْرِ.

٢- هذا فُندُقٌ ينامُ فيهِ سائقو الشاحِنات.

٣- وَصَلَتْ طائِرةُ رئيسِ الجُمْهوريةِ مَساءً.

٤- تاريخُ مَدينةِ دِمَشقَ قديم جِدّاً.

٥- اِنْتَظَرْتُ أمامَ غُرْفةِ أستاذِ العربيّةِ.

٦- هذا بَيْتُ أستاذِنا.

٧- إنَّها طالبةُ جامعةٍ.

تمرين ٥

١- أخَذَني صَديقي عادِلٌ لِزيارةِ مَصانِعِ السَيّاراتِ في مِصْر.
٢- سافَرَتْ لَيْلى مَعَ ميخائيلَ إلى صَوْفَرَ في لُبْنان.
٣- قَدَّمَتِ الفتاةُ الطَعام إلى رَجُلٍ جَوْعانَ.
٤- دَرَسْتُ في المَدارِسِ الحُكوميّةِ.
٥- اِلْتَقطنا هذِهِ الصورة في صَحْراءِ الأردُنِّ.
٦- كَتَبْتُ إلى عَدْنانَ رِسالة طَويلة.
٧- مَرَرْنا بِحِمْصَ بَعدَ الظُهْر.
٨- هَل أنتَ صَديقُ عَدنانَ؟
٩- دَرَسَتْ سَميحَةُ في مَدارِسَ خاصَّةٍ.

تمرين ٦

١-أجملُ طقسٍ ٢- أغلى مِن ٣- أكثرُ خضرةً من ٤- ألذُّ
٥- أكثرُ تأخُّرا من ٦- أقلُّ من ٧- أكبرُ ٨- أصغرُ من

تمرين ٧

١-ألفٍ وتسعمِئةٍ وثلاثةٍ وأربعين ٢- ثلاثُ ٣- عشرين ٤- اثنَتا عَشْرَةَ
٥- بألفي ليرة ٦- غرفتا ٧- خمسةَ عَشَرَ ٨- بأحدَ عَشَرَ ٩- ابنٌ واحدٌ

تمرين ٨

١- مساءً ٢- قربَ ٣- ضاحكاً

تمرين ٩

١-الّذي ٢- الّتي ٣- اللتان ٤- مَن ٥- الّذين ٦- ما

تمرين ١٠

١-تصلون ٢- بُنيت ٣- اجلِسوا ٤- ادْخُل ٥- صُنِعَتْ

تمرين ١١

١-تحسّن ٢- استفهم ٣- لاعب ٤- انكسر ٥- اصفَرَّتْ
٦- ارتفعَتْ ٧- تكاتَب ٨- أجلَسَ ٩- حَمّلَ

تمرين ١٢

الاسمُ المُشتَق	المثل من النص	الجذر
اِسمُ الفاعِل	حافلة	حفل
	عامل	عمل
	صاحب	صحب
اِسمُ المَفعول	معروك	عرك
	مصنوع	صنع
	مُفـَضَّل	فضل
	مزروع	زرع
	مطحون	طحن
اِسمُ المَكان	مخبَز	خبز
	مَوقِف	وقف
	مشرِق	شرق
	محلّ	حلّ
	موقِد	وقد
أِسمُ الزَمان	قبلَ	قبل
	يوماً	يوم
	صباحاً	صبح
الصفة المشبّهة	قديم	قدم
	صُلـْب	صلب
	كبير	كبر
	كثير	كثر

اِسمُ التَفْضيل	أقرب	قرب
	أقدم	قدم
	أحسن	حسن
اِسمُ الآلة	عجّانة	عجن

مرين ١٣

١-لن أسكنَ
٢- لم نزُرْ / ما زُرنا
٣- لا تحضِر
٤- لا تعيشُ
٥- أريد غيرَ
٦- ليس بعيداً
٧- لن يسافرَ
٨- ليست
٩- لم أرَ / ما رأيتُ
١٠- ليس
١١- في غيرِ
١٢- لن تعملَ

Appendix B

Representative samples of verb conjugation paradigms are presented in this appendix. The conjugations are separated into three tables, the first of which presents the verb followed by the verbal noun, the active participles and the passive participle. The second table lists in its header the thirteen independent pronouns. Down the side of the table the past tense if followed by the present indicative, subjunctive, and jussive moods. The final category illustrates the imperative. The last chart in this series presents the verb in its various forms.

الفِعْل	المَصْدَر	اِسمُ الفاعِل	اِسمُ المَفْعول
أكَلَ	أكْلٌ	آكِلٌ	ماكولٌ

الضمير	أنا	نَحْنُ	أنتَ	أنتِ	أنتُما	أنتُم	أنتُنَّ	هُوَ	هِيَ	هُما	هُما	هُم	هُنَّ
الماضي	أكَلْتُ	أكَلْنا	أكَلْتَ	أكَلْتِ	أكَلْتُما	أكَلْتُم	أكَلْتُنَّ	أكَلَ	أكَلَتْ	أكَلا	أكَلْتا	أكَلو	أكَلْنَ
المُضارِع المَرْفوع	أكَلْتُ	نأكُلُ	تأكُلُ	تأكُلينَ	تأكُلانِ	تأكُلونَ	تأكُلْنَ	يأكُلُ	تأكُلُ	يأكُلانِ	تأكُلانِ	يأكُلونَ	يأكُلْنَ
المُضارِع المَنْصوب	آكُلَ	نأكُلَ	تأكُلَ	تأكُلي	تأكُلا	تأكُلوا	تأكُلْنَ	يأكُلَ	تأكُلَ	يأكُلا	تأكُلا	يأكُلوا	يأكُلْنَ
المُضارِع المَجْزوم	آكُلْ	نأكُلْ	تأكُلْ	تأكُلي	تأكُلا	تأكُلوا	تأكُلْنَ	يأكُلْ	تأكُلْ	يأكُلا	تأكُلا	يأكُلوا	يأكُلْنَ
الأمر			كُلْ	كُلي	كُلا	كُلوا	كُلْنَ						

This verb exists in the following measures:

	I	II	III	IV	V	VI	VII	VIII	XI	X	
	أكَلَ	أكَّلَ	آكَلَ		تَأكَّلَ	تَآكَلَ	اِنأكَلَ	----	----	اِسْتَأكَلَ	

الفِعْل				المَصْدَر			اِسمُ الفاعِل			اِسمُ المَفْعول			
سَأَلَ				سُؤالٌ / مَسْأَلةٌ			سائِلٌ			مَسْؤولٌ			
الضمير	أنا	نَحْنُ	أنتَ	أنتِ	أنتُما	أنْتُم	أنْتُنَّ	هُوَ	هِيَ	هُما	هُما	هُم	هُنَّ
الماضي	سَأَلْتُ	سَأَلْنا	سَأَلْتَ	سألْتِ	سألْتُما	سألتُم	سألْتُنَّ	سألَ	سألَتْ	سألا	سألَتا	سألوا	سألْنَ
المُضارِع المَرْفوع	أسْألُ	نَسْألُ	تَسْألُ	تَسْألينَ	تَسْألانِ	تَسْألونَ	تَسْألْنَ	يَسْألُ	تَسْألُ	يَسْألانِ	تَسْألانِ	يَسْألونَ	يَسْألْنَ
المُضارِع المَنْصوب	أسْألَ	نَسْألَ	تَسْألَ	تَسْألي	تَسْألا	تَسْألوا	تَسْألْنَ	يَسْألَ	تَسْألَ	يَسْألا	تَسْألا	يَسْألوا	يَسْألْنَ
المُضارِع المَجْزوم	أسْألْ	نَسْألْ	تَسْألْ	تَسْألي	تَسْألا	تَسْألوا	تَسْألْنَ	يَسْألْ	تَسْألْ	يَسْألا	تَسْألا	يَسْألوا	يأسْألْنَ
الأمر			إسْألْ	إسْألي	إسْألا	إسْألوا	إسْألْنَ						

This verb exists in the following measures:

	I	II	III	IV	V	VI	VII	VIII	XI	X	
	سَألَ	----	ساءَلَ	----	----	تَساءَلَ	اِنْسَألَ	----	----	----	

الفِعْل				المَصْدَر			اِسمُ الفاعِل			اِسمُ المَفْعول			
قَرَأ				قِراءةٌ			قارِئٌ			مَقروءٌ			
الضمير	أنا	نَحْنُ	أنتَ	أنتِ	أنتُما	أنْتُم	أنْتُنَّ	هُوَ	هِيَ	هُما	هُما	هُم	هُنَّ
الماضي	قَرَأتُ	قَرَأنا	قَرَأتَ	قَرَأتِ	قَرَأْتُما	قَرَأْتُم	قَرَأْتُنَّ	قَرَأَ	قَرَأَتْ	قَرَأا	قَرَأتا	قَرَأوا	قَرَأْنَ
المُضارِع المَرْفوع	أقْرَأُ	نَقْرَأُ	تَقْرَأُ	تَقْرَأينَ	تَقْرَأانِ	تَقْرَأونَ	تَقْرَأْنَ	يَقْرَأُ	تَقْرَأُ	يَقْرَأانِ	تضقْرَأانِ	يَقْرَأونَ	يَقْرَأْنَ
المُضارِع المَنْصوب	أقْرَأَ	نَقْرَأَ	تَقْرَأَ	تَقْرَأي	تَقْرَأا	تَقْرَأوا	تَقْرَأْنَ	يَقْرَأَ	تَقْرَأَ	يَقْرَأا	تَقْرَأا	يَقْرَأوا	يَقْرَأْنَ
المُضارِع المَجْزوم	أقْرَأْ	نَقْرَأْ	تَقْرَأْ	تَقْرَأي	تَقْرَأا	تَقْرَأوا	تَقْرَأْنَ	يَقْرَأْ	تَقْرَأْ	يَقْرَأا	تَقْرَأا	يَقْرَأوا	يَقْرَأْنَ
الأمر			إقْرَأْ	إقْرَأي	إقْرَأا	إقْرَأوا	إقْرَأْنَ						

This verb exists in the following measures:

	I	II	III	IV	V	VI	VII	VIII	XI	X	
	قَرَأَ	----	----	أقْرَأَ	----	----	اِنْقَرَأَ	----	----	اِسْتَقْرَأَ	

الفِعْل				المَصْدَر			اِسمُ الفاعِل			اِسمُ المَفْعول			
نَفى				نَفْيٌ			نافٍ			مَنْفيٌّ			
الضمير	أنا	نَحْنُ	أنتَ	أنتِ	أنتُما	أنتُم	أنْتُنَّ	هُوَ	هِيَ	هُما	هُما	هُم	هُنَّ
الماضي	نَفيْتُ	نَفَيْنا	نَفَيْتَ	نَفَيْتِ	نَفَيْتُما	نَفَيْتُم	نَفَيْتُنَّ	نَفى	نَفَتْ	نَفَيا	نَفَتا	نَفوا	نَفَيْنَ
المُضارِع المَرْفوع	أنْفي	نَنْفي	تَنْفي	تَنْفينَ	تَنْفيانِ	تَنْفونَ	تَنْفينَ	يَنْفي	تَنْفي	يَنْفيانِ	تَنْفيانِ	يَنْفونَ	يَنْفينَ
المُضارِع المَنْصوب	أنْفيَ	نَنْفيَ	تَنْفيَ	تَنْفي	تَنْفيا	تَنْفوا	تَنْفينَ	يَنْفيَ	تَنْفيَ	يَنْفيا	تَنْفيا	يَنْفوا	يَنْفينَ
المُضارِع المَجْزوم	أنْفِ	نَنْفِ	تَنْفِ	تَنْفِ	تَنْفيا	تَنْفوا	تَنْفينَ	يَنْفِ	تَنْفِ	يَنْفيا	تَنْفيا	يَنْفوا	يَنْفينَ
الأمر			إنْفِ	إنْفي	إنْفيا	إنْفوا	إنْفينَ						

This verb exists in the following measures:

I	II	III	IV	V	VI	VII	VIII	XI	X
نَفى	----	----	----	----	تَنافى	----	اِنْتَفى	----	----

الفِعْل				المَصْدَر			اِسمُ الفاعِل			اِسمُ المَفْعول			
نَسيَ				نَسيٌ / نِسْيانٌ			ناسٍ			مَنْسيٌّ			
الضمير	أنا	نَحْنُ	أنتَ	أنتِ	أنتُما	أنتُم	أنْتُنَّ	هُوَ	هِيَ	هُما	هُما	هُم	هُنَّ
الماضي	نَسيتُ	نَسينا	نَسيتَ	نَسيتِ	نَسيتُما	نَسيتُم	نَسيتُنَّ	نَسيَ	نَسيَتْ	نَسِيا	نَسِيَتا	نَسوا	نَسينَ
المُضارِع المَرْفوع	أنْسى	نَنْسى	تَنْسى	تَنْسينَ	تَنْسَيانِ	تَنْسونَ	تَنْسينَ	يَنْسى	تَنْسى	يَنْسَيانِ	تَنْسَيانِ	يَنْسونَ	يَنْسينَ
المُضارِع المَنْصوب	أنْسى	نَنْسى	تَنْسى	تَنْسي	تَنْسَيا	تَنْسوا	تَنْسينَ	يَنْسى	تَنْسى	يَنْسَيا	تَنْسَيا	يَنْسوا	يَنْسينَ
المُضارِع المَجْزوم	أنْسَ	نَنْسَ	تَنْسَ	تَنْسِ	تَنْسَيا	تَنْسوا	تَنْسينَ	يَنْسَ	تَنْسَ	يَنْسَيا	تَنْسَيا	يَنْسوا	يَنْسينَ
الأمر			إنْسَ	إنْسِ	إنْسَيا	إنْسوا	إنْسينَ						

This verb exists in the following measures:

I	II	III	IV	V	VI	VII	VIII	XI	X
نَسّى	----	----	أنْسى	----	تَناسى	----	اِنْتَسى	----	----

الفِعْل				المَصْدَر			اِسمُ الفاعِل			اِسمُ المَفْعول			
وَجَدَ				وُجود			واجِد			مَوْجود			
الضمير	أنا	نَحْنُ	أنتَ	أنتِ	أنتُما	أنْتُم	أنْتُنَّ	هُوَ	هِيَ	هُما	هُما	هُم	هُنَّ
الماضي	وَجَدْتُ	وَجَدْنا	وَجَدْتَ	وَجَدْتِ	وَجَدْتما	وَجَدْتُم	وَجَدْتُنَّ	وَجَدَ	وَجَدَتْ	وَجَدا	وَجَدَتا	وَجَدوا	وَجَدْنَ
المُضارِع المَرْفوع	أَجِدُ	نَجِدُ	تَجِدُ	تَجِدينَ	تَجِدانِ	تَجِدونَ	تَجِدْنَ	يَجِدُ	تَجِدُ	يَجِدانِ	تَجِدانِ	يَجِدونَ	يَجِدْنَ
المُضارِع المَنْصوب	أَجِدَ	نَجِدَ	تَجِدَ	تَجِدي	تَجِدا	تَجِدوا	تَجِدْنَ	يَجِدَ	تَجِدَ	يَجِدا	تَجِدا	يَجِدوا	يَجِدْنَ
المُضارِع المَجْزوم	أَجِدْ	نَجِدْ	تَجِدْ	تَجِدي	تَجِدا	تَجِدوا	تَجِدْنَ	يَجِدْ	تَجِدْ	يَجِدا	تَجِدا	يَجِدوا	يَجِدْنَ
الأمر			جِدْ	جِدي	جِدا	جِدوا	جِدْنَ						

This verb exists in the following measures:

	I	II	III	IV	V	VI	VII	VIII	XI	X	
	وَجَدَ	----	----	أَوْجَدَ	تَوَجَّدَ	تَواجَدَ	اِنْوَجَدَ	----	----	----	

الفِعْل				المَصْدَر			اِسمُ الفاعِل			اِسمُ المَفْعول			
سَرَّ				سُرورٌ / مَسَرّةٌ			سارٌّ			مَسْرورٌ			
الضمير	أنا	نَحْنُ	أنتَ	أنتِ	أنتُما	أنْتُم	أنْتُنَّ	هُوَ	هِيَ	هُما	هُما	هُم	هُنَّ
الماضي	سَرَرْتُ	سَرَرْنا	سَرَرْتَ	سَرَرْتِ	سَرَرْتُما	سَرَرْتُم	سَرَرْتُنَّ	سَرَّ	سَرَّتْ	سَرّا	سَرّتا	سَرّوا	سَرَرْنَ
المُضارِع المَرْفوع	أَسُرُّ	نَسُرُّ	تَسُرُّ	تَسُرّينَ	تَسُرّانِ	تَسُرّونَ	تَسْرُرْنَ	يَسُرُّ	تَسُرُّ	يَسُرّانِ	تَسُرّانِ	يَسُرّونَ	يَسْرُرْنَ
المُضارِع المَنْصوب	أَسُرَّ	تَسُرَّ	تَسُرَّ	تَسُرّي	تَسُرّا	تَسُرّوا	تَسْرُرْنَ	يَسُرَّ	تَسُرَّ	يَسُرّا	تَسُرّا	يَسُرّوا	يَسْرُرْنَ
المُضارِع المَجْزوم	أَسُرَّ	نَسُرَّ	تَسُرَّ	تَسُرّي	تَسُرّا	تَسُرّوا	تَسْرُرْنَ	يَسُرَّ	تَسُرَّ	يَسُرّا	تَسُرّا	يَسُرّوا	يَسْرُرْنَ
الأمر			سُرْ	سُرّي	سُرّا	سُرّوا	اِسْرُرْنَ						

This verb exists in the following measures:

	I	II	III	IV	V	VI	VII	VIII	XI	X	
	سَرَّ	سَرَّرَ	سارَّ	أَسَرَّ	تَسَرّى	----	اِنْسَرَّ	----	----	اِسْتَسْرى	

الفِعْل				المَصْدَر			اِسمُ الفاعِل			اِسمُ المَفْعول			
رأى				رُؤيةٌ			رأءٍ			مَرْئيٌّ			
الضمير	أنا	نَحنُ	أنتَ	أنتِ	أنتُما	أنتُم	أنتُنَّ	هُوَ	هِيَ	هُما	هُما	هُم	هُنَّ
الماضي	رَأيْتُ	رَأينا	رَأيْتَ	رَأيْتِ	رَأيْتُما	رَأيْتُم	رَأيْتُنَّ	رأى	رَأتْ	رَأيا	رَأتا	رَأوا	رَأيْنَ
المُضارِع المَرْفوع	أرى	نرى	ترى	تَرَيْنَ	تَريانِ	تَرَوْنَ	تَرَيْنَ	يرى	ترى	يَريانِ	تَريانِ	يَرَوْنَ	يَرَيْنَ
المُضارِع المَنْصوب	أرى	نرى	ترى	تري	تَرَيا	تروا	تَرَيْنَ	يرى	ترى	يَرَيا	تَرَيا	يروا	يَرَيْنَ
المُضارِع المَجْزوم	أرَ	نَرَ	تَرَ	تَرِ	تَرَيا	تروا	تَرَيْنَ	يَرَ	تَرَ	يَرَيا	تَرَيا	يروا	يَرَيْنَ

الوزن المعنى	الماضي	الماضي المُضارِع	المُضارِع المَنصوب	المُضارِع المَجزوم	المَصْدَر	اِسمُ الفاعِل	اِسمُ المَفْعول
Form	Perfect				Verbal noun	Active part.	Passive part.
I	فَعَلَ	يَفْعَلُ	يَفْعَلَ	يَفْعَلْ	فِعْل، فِعالة	فاعِل	مَفْعول
	كَتَبَ	يَكْتُبُ	يَكْتُبَ	يَكْتُبْ	كِتابة	كاتِب	مَكْتوب
II	فَعَّلَ	يُفَعِّلُ	يُفَعِّلَ	يُفَعِّلْ	تَفْعيل، تَفْعِلة	مُفَعِّل	مُفَعَّل
	كَرَّمَ	يُكَرِّمُ	يُكَرِّمَ	يُكَرِّمْ	تكْريم	مَكَرِّم	مُكَرَّم
	كَسَّرَ	يُكَسِّرُ	يُكَسِّرَ	يُكَسِّرْ	تكْسير	مَكَسر	مُكَسر
III	فاعَلَ	يُفاعِلُ	يُفاعِلَ	يُفاعِلْ	مُفاعَلة، فِعال	مُفاعِل	مُفاعَل
	هاجَمَ	يُهاجِمُ	يُهاجِمَ	يُهاجِمْ	مُهاجَمة	مُهاجِم	مُهاجَم
	قاتَلَ	يُقاتِلُ	يُقاتِلَ	يُقاتِلْ	مُقاتَلة / قِتال	مُقاتِل	مُقاتَل
IV	أفْعَلَ	يُفْعِلُ	يُفْعِلَ	يُفْعِلْ	إفْعال	مُفْعِل	مُفْعَل
	أخْبَرَ	يُخْبِرُ	يُخْبِرَ	يُخْبِرْ	إخْبار	مُخْبِر	مُخْبَر
V	تَفَعَّلَ	يَتَفَعَّلُ	يَتَفَعَّلَ	يَتَفَعَّلْ	تَفَعُّل	مُتَفَعِّل	مُتَفَعَّل
	تَعَلَّمَ	يَتَعَلَّمُ	يَتَعَلَّمَ	يَتَعَلَّمْ	تَعَلُّم	مُتَعَلِّم	مُتَعَمَّم

الوزن المعنى	الماضي	الماضي المُضارِع	المُضارِع المَنصوب	المُضارِع المَجزوم	المَصْدَر	اِسمُ الفاعِل	اِسمُ المَفْعول
VI	تَفاعَلَ	يَتَفاعَلُ	يَتَفاعَلَ	يَتَفاعَلْ	تَفاعُل	مُتَفاعِل	مُتَفاعَل
	تَنازَعَ	يَتَنازَعُ	يَتَنازَعَ	يَتَنازَعْ	تَنازُع	مُتَنازِع	مُتَنازَع
VII	اِنْفَعَلَ	يَنْفَعِلُ	يَنْفَعِلَ	يَنْفَعِلْ	اِنْفِعال	مُنْفَعِل	مُنْفَعَل
	اِنْكَسَرَ	يَنْكَسِرُ	يَنْكَسِرَ	يَنْكَسِرْ	اِنْكِسار	مُنْكَسِر	مُنْكَسَر
VIII	اِفْتَعَلَ	يَفْتَعِلُ	يَفْتَعِلَ	يَفْتَعِلْ	اِفْتِعال	مُفْتَعِل	مُفْتَعَل
	اِكْتَسَبَ	يَكْتَسِبُ	يَكْتَسِبَ	يَكْتَسِبْ	اِكْتِساب	مُكْتَسِب	مُكْتَسَب
IX	اِفْعَلَّ	يَفْعَلُّ	يَفْعَلَّ	يَفْعَلّ	اِفْعِلال	مُفْعَلّ	
	اِحْمَرَّ	يَحْمَرُّ	يَحْمَرَّ	يَحْمَرّ	اِحْمِرار	مُحْمَرّ	
X	اِسْتَفْعَلَ	يَسْتَفْعِلُ	يَسْتَفْعِلَ	يَسْتَفْعِلْ	اِسْتِفْعال	مُسْتَفْعِل	مُسْتَفْعَل
	اِسْتَعْمَلَ	يَسْتَعْمِلُ	يَسْتَعْمِلَ	يَسْتَعْمِلْ	اِسْتِعْمال	مُسْتَعْمِل	مُسْتَعْمَل

فِهْرِس

ب

ت

ن

ه

و

ي

Index

A

B

C

Illustration Credits

Rabat sign 2 © iStockphoto/Thinkstock; Ramsis Sq. sign 2 © iStockphoto/Thinkstock; Perfume bottles 4 © iStockphoto/Thinkstock; Open door 4 © iStockphoto/Thinkstock; Closed door 4 © iStockphoto/Thinkstock; Stop sign 4 © iStockphoto/ © Jesse Karjalainen; Man smoking 4 © iStockphoto/Thinkstock; Soccer fans 4 © Brian Clark/Saudi Aramco World/SAWDIA; Man on phone 4 © Kevin Bubriski/Saudi Aramco World/SAWDIA; King Tut sign 5 © iStockphoto/ © essxboy; Sign over trash can 5 © iStockphoto/ © SisterSarah; Sign in airport 6 © iStockphoto/Thinkstock; Street sign with minaret 6 © iStockphoto/Thinkstock; Mosque interior 7 © Nik Wheeler/Saudi Aramco World/SAWDIA; Perfume bottle 8 © iStockphoto/Thinkstock; Lipstick 8 © iStockphoto/ © daneger; Makeup kit 8 © iStockphoto/Thinkstock; Cell phone 8 © iStockphoto/Thinkstock; Watch 8 © iStockphoto/ © Vasiliki Varvaki; Restaurant sign 21 © Peter Harrigan/Saudi Aramco World/SAWDIA; Drawing on tiled wall 25 © Bill Lyons/Saudi Aramco World/SAWDIA; Two female friends 26 © iStockphoto/Thinkstock; Woman wearing headscarf 28 © iStockphoto/ © Karina Tischlinger; Man holding book 28 © iStockphoto/Thinkstock; Woman's face 29 © Katrina Thomas and Robert Azzi/Saudi Aramco World/SAWDIA; Man 29 © Torsten Kjellstrand/Saudi Aramco World/SAWDIA; Map of Yemen 30; © Saudi Aramco/Saudi Aramco World/SAWDIA; Sheep with dog 30 © iStockphoto/Thinkstock; Kitten 31 © iStockphoto/Thinkstock; Lute being played 33 © photos.com; Drums 33 © Moeed Hussain/photos.com; Men playing nays 33 © Robert Azzi/Saudi Aramco World/SAWDIA; Tambourine 33 © iStockphoto/Thinkstock; Man playing mijwiz 33 © Chad Evans Wyatt/Saudi Aramco World/SAWDIA; Pliers 34 © iStockphoto/ © ranplett; Hammer 34 © iStockphoto/ © Michal Kolosowski; Hand saw 34 © iStockphoto/ © Rouzes; Screwdriver 34 © iStockphoto/ © LongHa2006; Nails 34 © iStockphoto/Thinkstock; Playing cards 34 © iStockphoto/ © Stefan Witas; Cat 36 © iStockphoto/Thinkstock; Fish 36 © Gunnar Bemert/Saudi Aramco World/SAWDIA; Man hammering 37 © iStockphoto/Thinkstock; Man carrying board 37 © iStockphoto/ © Jim Jurica; Pottery being made 37 © iStockphoto/ © Henry Chaplin; Veterinarian with dog 37 © iStockphoto/ © Monika Wisniewska; Collection of stringed instruments 47 © Peter Keen/Saudi Aramco World/SAWDIA; Muscial score 47 © Thorne Anderson/Saudi Aramco World/SAWDIA; Rabab 47 © Thorne Anderson/Saudi Aramco World/SAWDIA; Lute 48 © Chad Evans Wyatt/Saudi Aramco World/SAWDIA; Artisan crafting instrument 53 © Thorne Anderson/Saudi Aramco World/SAWDIA; Vegetables being cut 54 © iStockphoto/ © Liv Friis-Larsen; Woman preparing food 56 © iStockphoto/ © JazzIRT; Harisa 56 © Politikaner / CC-BY-SA, Wikimedia Commons; Butter 56 © iStockphoto/Thinkstock; Silver tray 56 © iStockphoto/ © Angelo Gilardelli; Semolina 57 © iStockphoto/ © FotografiaBasica; Coconut tree 57 © iStockphoto/ © Lisa Fletcher; Glass with ice water 57 © iStockphoto/ © Stian Magnus Hatling; Saucepan 57 © iStockphoto/ © frytka; Place setting 58 © iStockphoto/Thinkstock; Spices 61 © Brynn Bruijn/Saudi Aramco World/SAWDIA; Food in glass jars 73 © Brynn Bruijn/Saudi Aramco World/SAWDIA; Compass 74 © iStockphoto/Thinkstock; Hand holding note 76 © iStockphoto/Thinkstock; Woman on telephone 78 © iStockphoto/ © airportrait; Sign post 78 © iStockphoto/ © Anton Seleznev; Compass 80 © Robert Azzi/Saudi Aramco World/SAWDIA; Damascus street 84 © Kay Brennan/Saudi Aramco World/SAWDIA; Lamp post 97 © Kay Brennan/Saudi Aramco World/SAWDIA; Reporter 98 © iStockphoto/ © Jose Girarte; Map of Lebanon 101 © NordNordWest/ CC-BY-SA, Wikimedia Commons; Arab family 102 © iStockphoto/ © tunart; Reporter holding microphone 102 © iStockphoto/ © JoseGirarte; Lebanese flag 102 © iStockphoto/ © FotografiaBasica; Woman wearing sunglasses 103 © iStockphoto/ © Joel Carillet; Woman with bag on shoulder 103 © iStockphoto/Thinkstock; Profile of woman's head 103 © iStockphoto/ © Billie Muller; Tourist 104 © iStockphoto/ © Joel Carillet; Blue calligraphy 129 © By Kamal Boullata/Saudi Aramco World/SAWDIA; Petra 130 © iStockphoto/Thinkstock; Scuba diver 132 © Eric Hanauer/Saudi Aramco World/SAWDIA; Driver 132 © Tor Eigeland/Saudi Aramco World/SAWDIA; Skier 132 © iStockphoto/Thinkstock; Mountain peak 132 © iStockphoto/ © fotoVoyager; Castle 132 © Abdullah Y. Al-Dobais/Saudi Aramco World/SAWDIA; Rock climber 132 © iStockphoto/ © Scott Hailstone; Man reading 133 © Torsten Kjellstrand/Saudi Aramco World/SAWDIA; Truck 133 © S. M. Amin/Saudi Aramco World/SAWDIA;

Ancient theater 133 © iStockphoto/Thinkstock; View of Amman (top) 134 © iStockphoto/ © Jamil Nasir; View of Amman (bottom) 134 © iStockphoto/Thinkstock; ID photo 135 © iStockphoto/ © biffspandex; Ruins in Palmyra 136 © Katrina Thomas/Saudi Aramco World/SAWDIA; Map of Jordan 138 © sfari.com; Roman amphitheater in Jarash 139 © iStockphoto/ © syolacan; Mosaic in Madaba 139 © iStockphoto/ © Witold Ryka; Petra 139 © iStockphoto/Thinkstock; Aqaba 140 © iStockphoto/Thinkstock; Aerial view of Palmyra 152 © Katrina Thomas/Saudi Aramco World/SAWDIA; Palmyra, arch and pillars 155 © Katrina Thomas/Saudi Aramco World/SAWDIA; Dancing in night club 156 © iStockphoto/Thinkstock; Night club scene (top) 159 © iStockphoto/Thinkstock; Night club scene (bottom) 159 © iStockphoto/ © vm; Bowl of peanuts 160 © iStockphoto/ © Daniel Loiselle; Friends at bar 160 © iStockphoto/ © kali9; Tiles 169 © Photo Garo/Saudi Aramco World/SAWDIA; Man drawing calligraphy 173 © Robert Azzi/Saudi Aramco World/SAWDIA; Three women 174 © iStockphoto/ © Mash Audio Visuals Pvt. Ltd. Agency; Man laughing 177 © iStockphoto/ © JJRD; Man with woman 177 © iStockphoto/Thinkstock; Doctor and patient 177 © iStockphoto/ © George Cairns; Thief with stolen goods 178 © iStockphoto/Thinkstock; Picture frame 178 © photos.com; Man leaning against wall 178 © iStockphoto/ © Kemter; Man smiling 179 © iStockphoto/ © Nicole S. Young; Turkey with pilgrim hat 179 © iStockphoto/ © nokee; Pilgrim 180 © iStockphoto/ © Joe Cicak; Chick in eggshell 180 © iStockphoto/Thinkstock; Cooked turkey 180 © iStockphoto/ © Liza McCorkle; Distraught man 180 © iStockphoto/ © Kemter; Wood carving 183 © Gian Luigi Scarfiotti/Saudi Aramco World/SAWDIA; Squares pattern 184 © By Kamal Boullata/Saudi Aramco World/SAWDIA; Arches 185 © Dick Doughty/Saudi Aramco World/SAWDIA; Purple and orange design 191 © By Kamal Boullata/Saudi Aramco World/SAWDIA; Room with intricate designs 195 © Bill Lyons/Saudi Aramco World/SAWDIA; Map of Syria 196 © iStockphoto/ © Frank Ramspott; Map of Middle East 199 © iStockphoto/ © Frank Ramspott; Syrian street 200 © Kay Brennan/Saudi Aramco World/SAWDIA; Umayyad Mosque (top) 201 © iStockphoto/ © Anthon Jackson; Azam Palace (middle) 201 © iStockphoto/ © Witold Ryka; Syrian Lira 202 © By Kamal Boullata/Saudi Aramco World/SAWDIA; Alphabet carved in stone 202 © iStockphoto/ © Frank Ramspott;

Ghassan Kanafani 202 © Kimdime/ CC-BY-SA, Wikimedia Commons; Fishawy Café sign 211 © Lorraine Chittock/Saudi Aramco World/SAWDIA; Café in Cairo 211 © Lorraine Chittock/Saudi Aramco World/SAWDIA; Storyteller 211 © George Baramki Azar/Saudi Aramco World/SAWDIA; Storyteller's book 211 © George Baramki Azar/Saudi Aramco World/SAWDIA; Colorful design 212 © By Kamal Boullata/Saudi Aramco World/SAWDIA; Shadow puppets 213 © John Feeney/Saudi Aramco World/SAWDIA; Shadow puppeteers 213 © John Feeney/Saudi Aramco World/SAWDIA; Ahmed El-Khoumy 213 © John Feeney/Saudi Aramco World/SAWDIA; Antara 215 © Saudi Aramco/Saudi Aramco World/SAWDIA; Prince Antar 221 © George Baramki Azar/Saudi Aramco World/SAWDIA; Palmyra ruins 222 © iStockphoto/Thinkstock; Palmyra ruins 224 © Katrina Thomas/Saudi Aramco World/SAWDIA; Palmyra ruins 225 © Katrina Thomas/Saudi Aramco World/SAWDIA; Stamp 225 © iStockphoto/Thinkstock; Coin 225 © Classical Numismatic Group, Inc. / CC-BY-SA, Wikimedia Commons; Palmyra ruins at sunset 226 © Jamie Simpson/Saudi Aramco World/SAWDIA; Lawrence of Arabia 226 © Saudi Aramco/Saudi Aramco World/SAWDIA; Aleppo citadel 226 © Ihsan Sheet/Saudi Aramco World/SAWDIA; Cart in Aleppo market 227 © Ihsan Sheet/Saudi Aramco World/SAWDIA; Sunbeams in Aleppo market 227 © Lynn Simarski/Saudi Aramco World/SAWDIA; Craftsman in Aleppo market 227 © Katrina Thomas/Saudi Aramco World/SAWDIA; Aleppo, panoramic photo 228 © Ihsan Sheet/Saudi Aramco World/SAWDIA; Palmyra, aerial view 235 © Katrina Thomas/Saudi Aramco World/SAWDIA; Shopkeeper in Aleppo market 237 © Ihsan Sheet/Saudi Aramco World/SAWDIA; Arabic newspapers 238 © John Wreford; Classroom 241 © Katrina Thomas/Saudi Aramco World/SAWDIA; Woman with throat pain 242 © iStockphoto/Thinkstock; Man on phone next to ambulance 242 © Samia El-Moslimany/Saudi Aramco World/SAWDIA; Car damaged in accident 242 © iStockphoto/Thinkstock; Jewelry 243 © iStockphoto/ © Liv Friis-Larsen; Thief opening door 243 © iStockphoto/Thinkstock; Book fair 243 © Thomas Hartwell/Saudi Aramco World/SAWDIA; Calligraphy 244 © iStockphoto/ © largeformat4x5; Dancers 244 © iStockphoto/ © Daniel Halvorson; Wood design 245 © Bill Lyons/Saudi Aramco World/SAWDIA; Door 254 © Bill Lyons/Saudi Aramco World/SAWDIA; Cartoon boat in waves 258 © iStockphoto/ © Matias Rafael Mendiola;

Design 260 © Kay Brennan/Saudi Aramco World/SAWDIA; Farm 261 © Nik Wheeler/Saudi Aramco World/SAWDIA; Tractor 261 © iStockphoto/ © Robert Churchill; Barking dog 262 © iStockphoto/ © Brian Asmussen; Ringing doorbell 262 © iStockphoto/ © slobo; Design 268 © Dick Doughty/Saudi Aramco World/SAWDIA; Mosque ceiling and arches 284 © Pat McDonnell/Saudi Aramco World/SAWDIA; Billboard 290 © Saudi Aramco/Saudi Aramco World/SAWDIA; Design 292 © Dick Doughty/Saudi Aramco World/SAWDIA; Bus rider 293 © iStockphoto/ © Ian McDonnell; Woman with money 293 © iStockphoto/ © by_nicholas; Two women shopping 294 © Catherine Yeulet/Photos.com; Jewelry 294 © iStockphoto/ Thinkstock; Books 306 © Dick Doughty/Saudi Aramco World/SAWDIA; Open book 309 © Kevin Bubriski/Saudi Aramco World/SAWDIA; Abd al-Qader al-Mazini 310 © Saudi Aramco/Saudi Aramco World/SAWDIA; Mustafa Lutfi al-Manfaluti 310 © Saudi Aramco/Saudi Aramco World/SAWDIA; Design 312 © Saudi Aramco/Saudi Aramco World/SAWDIA; Oil pumps 313 © iStockphoto/ © David Jones; Map of Iraq 313 © Dick Doughty/Saudi Aramco World/SAWDIA; Model A Ford 314 © iStockphoto/ © Timothy Hughes; Temperature gauge 314 © iStockphoto/ © Massimo Merlini; Man getting haircut 316 © iStockphoto/ © Kevin Russ; Russo-Japanese War 317 © Saudi Aramco/Saudi Aramco World/SAWDIA; Russian cruiser 317 © Saudi Aramco/Saudi Aramco World/SAWDIA; Design 320 © Tor Eigeland/Saudi Aramco World/SAWDIA; Books 335 © Dick Doughty/Saudi Aramco World/SAWDIA; 336 Naguib Mahfouz © Lauren Uram/Saudi Aramco World/SAWDIA; Father and daughter 340 © iStockphoto/ © Tiburon Studios; Girls at school 340 © Katrina Thomas/Saudi Aramco World/SAWDIA; Mosque and church 340 © iStockphoto/ © James Margolis; Cross and minaret 341 © iStockphoto/ © Karen Moller; View from church window 341 © iStockphoto/ © Amit Erez; Interior of Hagia Sophia in Istanbul 342 © iStockphoto/ © airportrait; The Qur'an 342 © Dick Doughty/Saudi Aramco World/SAWDIA; Child's drawing of mosque 343 © Saudi Aramco/Saudi Aramco World/SAWDIA; Mount Hira 343 © Norman MacDonald/Saudi Aramco World/SAWDIA; Crucifixion 344 © iStockphoto/ © Joshua Blake; Qur'an page 344 © Calligraphy By Aftab Ahmad/Saudi Aramco World/SAWDIA; Calligraphy 345 © iStockphoto/ © Yusuf Anil Akduygu; Heaven 345 © iStockphoto/Thinkstock; Path 346 © iStockphoto/ © Josh Scott; Cairo skyline 354 © John Feeney/Saudi Aramco World/SAWDIA; Skyline 361 © Kevin Bubriski/Saudi Aramco World/SAWDIA; Loris Mahir: with other doctors 362, portrait 365, with family 366, graduation 366, playing piano 367 © Saudi Aramco/Saudi Aramco World/SAWDIA; Ottoman art 379 © Ilene Perlman/Saudi Aramco World/SAWDIA; Map of Andalusia 384 © Saudi Aramco/Saudi Aramco World/SAWDIA; Map of Andalusia and North Africa 387 © Saudi Aramco/Saudi Aramco World/SAWDIA; Statue of Ibn Muawiyah 387 © Bonas/ CC-BY-SA, Wikimedia Commons; Mosque in Cordoba 388 © Mats Hilden/CC-BY-SA, Wikimedia Commons; Granada 388 © iStockphoto/ © Thomas Saupe; Alhambra 390 © iStockphoto/ © Adivin; Court of the Lions 390 © iStockphoto/ © Michał Krakowiak; Fountain in the Court of the Lions 391 © Tor Eigeland/Saudi Aramco World/SAWDIA; Alhambra 391 © iStockphoto/ Thinkstock; Design 394 © Bill Lyons/Saudi Aramco World/SAWDIA; Statue of Averroes 413 © Tor Eigeland/Saudi Aramco World/SAWDIA; Qur'an 415 © iStockphoto/ © Retrovizor; Philosophers 416 © iStockphoto/ © ZU_09; Stone arches 417 © Tor Eigeland/Saudi Aramco World/SAWDIA; Man at desk 422 © Susan T. Rivers/Saudi Aramco World/SAWDIA; Page from illustrated book 434 © Kevin Bubriski/Saudi Aramco World/SAWDIA; Design 435 © Tor Eigeland/Saudi Aramco World/SAWDIA; Tiles 445 © Tor Eigeland/Saudi Aramco World/SAWDIA; Mahmoud Darwish 446 © Saudi Aramco/Saudi Aramco World/SAWDIA; Nizar Qabbani 446 © Saudi Aramco/Saudi Aramco World/SAWDIA; Pen and paper 449 © Stockbyte/Photos.com; Mahmoud Darwish 449 © Saudi Aramco/Saudi Aramco World/SAWDIA; Arches 450 © William Tracy/Saudi Aramco World/SAWDIA; Tent 456 © Burnett H. Moody/Saudi Aramco World/SAWDIA; Nizar Qabbani 457 © Saudi Aramco/Saudi Aramco World/SAWDIA; Book page 457 © Dick Doughty/Saudi Aramco World/SAWDIA; Poet 463 © Norman MacDonald/Saudi Aramco World/SAWDIA; Poem by Nizar Qabbani 463-467 © Nizar Qabbani; Page from ancient manuscript 477 © Lorraine Chittock/Saudi Aramco World/SAWDIA; Calligraphy 478 © iStockphoto/ © Ferran Traite Soler; Books 511 © Dick Doughty/Saudi Aramco World/SAWDIA; Book corner 523 © Dick Doughty/Saudi Aramco World/SAWDIA; Grammar manuscript 524 © Dick Doughty/Saudi Aramco World/SAWDIA; Books 529 © Dick Doughty/Saudi Aramco World/SAWDIA.